THE JERUSALEM TALMUD
FIRST ORDER: ZERAÏM
TRACTATES *TERUMOT* AND *MA'SEROT*

W DE G

STUDIA JUDAICA

FORSCHUNGEN ZUR WISSENSCHAFT
DES JUDENTUMS

HERAUSGEGEBEN VON
E. L. EHRLICH

BAND XXI

WALTER DE GRUYTER · BERLIN · NEW YORK
2002

THE JERUSALEM TALMUD
תלמוד ירושלמי

FIRST ORDER: ZERAÏM
סדר זרעים
TRACTATES *TERUMOT* AND *MA'SEROT*
מסכות תרומות ומעשרות

EDITION, TRANSLATION, AND COMMENTARY

BY

HEINRICH W. GUGGENHEIMER

WALTER DE GRUYTER · BERLIN · NEW YORK

2002

ISBN 978-3-11-068128-4
e-ISBN (PDF) 978-3-11-090846-6

This volume is text- and page-identical with the hardback published in 2002.

Library of Congress Control Number: 2020942816

Bibliographic information published by the Deutsche Nationalbibliothek
The Deutsche Nationalbibliothek lists this publication in the
Deutsche Nationalbibliografie;
detailed bibliographic data are available on the Internet at http://dnb.dnb.de.

Printing and binding: CPI books GmbH, Leck

www.degruyter.com

Preface

The present volume is the fourth in a series of five volumes covering the first order of the Jerusalem Talmud. The principles of the edition regarding text, vocalization and Commentary have been spelled out in detail in the Introduction to the first volume. The text is based on the *editio princeps* and, where that text is manifestly corrupt, on manuscript readings. There are no emendations.

The extensive commentary is not based on emendations. Biographical notes have been attached to the names of those personalities not already mentioned in the previous volumes.

Again I wish to thank my wife, Dr. Eva Guggenheimer, who acted as critic, style editor, proof reader, and expert on the Latin and Greek vocabulary. Her own notes on some possible Latin and Greek etymologies are identified by (E. G.).

For ease of study, the text in the present edition has been subdivided into paragraphs and vocalized following the rules of Sephardic rabbinic Hebrew. This is intended as a help for reading and understanding the text, not as a reconstruction of the unrecoverable rabbinic pronunciation at the time of the composition of the Yerushalmi. Genizah fragments show that the text of the existing manuscripts has been partially adapted to Babylonian patterns. The vocalization of the Mishnah, which represents a different and better known development of the Hebrew language, in general follows the text of Ḥ. Yallon. As noted before, the main Amoraic language of the Yerushalmi is Aramaized Hebrew. While Y. Kutscher has traced the disappearance of the gutturals back to Hasmonean times, it is known that in the academy of Rebbi, the center responsible for the edition of the Mishnah, one insisted on a clear distinction between gutturals (Babli *Megillah* 24b). The total disappearance of the gutturals, where there is no difference in sound between חמר (wine), חמור (donkey), עמר (wool), and אמר (lamb), is given as characteristic of uneducated Galileans in Babli *Erubin* 53b and confirmed by the Yerushalmi source *Šir rabba* on *Cant.* 2:4, which notes that for the uneducated, אהבה (love) and איבה (jealousy) sound the same. The Babli (*Sanhedrin* 27b) declares the Samaritans to be uneducated; the particular example is confirmed by Z. Ben Ḥayyim[1]. Since the elimination of gutturals was explicitly rejected by the Amoraim, it must be assumed that their speech, while based on rudimentary grammar, rejected the substandard pronunciation recoverable from contemporary Greek and Latin transcriptions of biblical texts.

---

1 Z. Ben-Ḥayyim, The literary and oral traditions of Hebrew and Aramaic amongst the Samaritans. Vol. III/1, Recitation of the Law, Jerusalem 1961. See on *Deut.* 6:5.

Contents

Introduction to Tractate Terumot 1

Terumot Chapter 1, חמשה לא יתרומו
- Halakhah 1 5
- Halakhah 2 27
- Halakhah 3 30
- Halakhah 4 38
- Halahkah 5 43
- Halakhah 6 46
- Halakhah 7 48
- Halakhah 8 50
- Halakhah 9 56

Terumot Chapter 2, אין תורמין
- Halakhah 1 61
- Halakhah 2 75
- Halakhah 3 77
- Halakhah 4 85
- Halakhah 5 91

Terumot Chapter 3, התורם קישות
- Halakhah 1 96

Halakhah 2 102
Halakhah 3 103
Halakhah 4 105
Halakhah 5 110
Halakhah 7 115
Halakhah 8 119
Halakhah 9 122

Terumot Chapter 4, המפריש
Halakhah 1 126
Halakhah 2 130
Halakhah 3 132
Halakhah 4 139
Halakhah 5 142
Halakhah 6 145
Halakhah 7 147
Halakhah 8 147
Halakhah 9 154
Halakhah 10 155
Halakhah 11 158
Halakhah 12 160
Halakhah 13 164

Terumot Chapter 5, סאה תרומה
Halakhah 1 166
Halakhah 2 171
Halakhah 3 175
Halakhah 4 181
Halakhah 5 183
Halakhah 6 186
Halakhah 7 187
Halakhah 8 189
Halakhah 9 191

Terumot Chapter 6, האוכל תרומה שוגג

Halakhah 1 196
Halakhah 2 209
Halakhah 3 210
Halakhah 4 212
Halakhah 5 214
Halakhah 6 216

Terumot Chapter 7, האוכל תרומה מזיד

Halakhah 1 219
Halakhah 2 237
Halakhah 3 240
Halakhah 4 243
Halakhah 5 243
Halakhah 6 245
Halakhah 7 248

Terumot Chapter 8, האשה

Halakhah 1 250
Halakhah 2 256
Halakhah 3 262
Halakhah 4 268
Halakhah 5 270
Halakhah 6 289
Halakhah 7 291
Halakhah 8 296
Halakhah 9 298
Halakhah 10 311

Terumot Chapter 9, הזורע

Halakhah 1 318
Halakhah 2 320

Halakhah 3 322
Halakhah 4 322
Halakhah 5 328
Halakhah 6 330
Halakhah 7 332
Halakhah 8 334

Terumot Chapter 10, בצל
Halakhah 1 339
Halakhah 2 342
Halakhah 3 344
Halakhah 4 348
Halakhah 5 350
Halakhah 6 352
Halakhah 7 354
Halakhah 8 360
Halakhah 9 363
Halakhah 10 363

Terumot Chapter 11, אין נותנין
Halakhah 1 370
Halakhah 2 374
Halakhah 3 382
Halakhah 4 386
Halakhah 5 389
Halakhah 6 396
Halakhah 7 397

Introduction to Tractate Ma'serot 407

Ma'serot Chapter 1, כלל אמרו
Halakhah 1 409

Halakhah 2 419
Halakhah 3 425
Halakhah 4 429
Halakhah 5 434
Halakhah 6 438
Halakhah 7 449

Ma'serot Chapter 2, היה עובר
Halakhah 1 455
Halakhah 2 464
Halakhah 3 465
Halakhah 4 469
Halakhah 5 473
Halakhah 6 476
Halakhah 7 484

Ma'serot Chapter 3, המעביר
Halakhah 1 491
Halakhah 2 498
Halakhah 3 499
Halakhah 4 508
Halakhah 5 509
Halakhah 6 511
Halakhah 7 514
Halakhah 8 517
Halakhah 9 522
Halakhah 10 523
Halakhah 11 527

Ma'serot Chapter 4, הכובש
Halakhah 1 530
Halakhah 2 535

Halakhah 3 539
Halakhah 4 542
Halakhah 5 544
Halakhah 6 546

Ma'serot Chapter 5, העוקר
Halakhah 1 550
Halakhah 2 553
Halakhah 3 559
Halakhah 4 561
Halakhah 5 568
Halakhah 6 570
Halakhah 7 574

Indices
Index of Biographical Notes 581
Index of Biblical Quotations 581
Index of Greek and Latin Words 582
Index of Hebrew and Arabic words 584
General Index 583

Introduction to Tractate Terumot

The Tractate deals with the rules of Great Heave and heave of the tithe, as given in *Num.* 18:8-32. Great Heave is the gift of the farmer to the Cohen at the time the produce is ready for storage; this heave has no minimum prescribed by biblical law. Heave of the tithe is given to the Cohen by the Levite from his tithe; it must be exactly ten percent. The rules of the heaves are complicated since heaves are sacred food available to any Cohen anywhere and, therefore, in danger of being mixed up with profane or impure food.

Heave, as a gift to the Cohen, must be designated as such. Chapter One, dealing with the rules of designation, contains a discussion of the definitions and legal status of persons incompetent to designate: minors, deaf-mutes who cannot communicate, and the insane.

Chapter Two discusses the groupings of food which can substitute for one another in the designation of heave. Chapter Three gives detailed rules in many special cases. Chapter Four deals with minimal and maximal amounts to be given as heave by rabbinic decree and with the heave obligations of partnerships. Since heave, as sacred food, must be eaten in ritual purity, the rabbinic amounts as well as the rules dealing with pure heave became obsolete when it was no longer possible to observe the rules of purity (cf. *Berakhot* Chapter 1, Note 3). Chapter Five deals with the case that pure and impure heave became mixed; how to save a maximum amount of pure heave. Chapter Six gives the rules for a non-Cohen who ate heave in error; Chapter Seven deals with the non-Cohen who ate heave intentionally, with the rules of competition of penalties, and with cases of doubt about the status of food. Chapter Nine spells out the rules of heave mixed with profane food, as well as heave used as seeds for a new crop. Chapter Eleven finally gives the rules of permitted use of heave, mainly the uses of impure heave available to non-Cohanim.

Two chapters deal with subjects of general interest not otherwise discussed in the Yerushalmi in great detail: Chapter Eight, starting out with rules for dealing with worms in food, is devoted in the main to health regulations and, in the last Halakhah, to the rules of Jewish solidarity. Chapter Ten deals with the rules under which forbidden admixtures in otherwise permitted food may be disregarded. The discussion is important because it shows the development of the rules adopted by the Babli without discussion.

For the interpretation, as always the main guides are Maimonides and R. Simson of Sens. Of the Eighteenth Century commentators, the most useful is R. Eliahu Fulda; the least useful are R. Moses Margalit (פני משה), R. Eliahu Wilna and, from the Twentieth Century, R. H. Kanievski, all of whom tend to emend away the difficult portions and the disagreements with Babylonian tradition. Similarly, the preliminary translation and explanation by Alan J. Avery-Peck and Martin S. Jaffee (Chicago, 1988) heavily depends on the emended Wilna text and a presumed but untenable identification of the Tosephta underlying the Yerushalmi with the Tosephta in our hands. The manuscript evidence, while meager, definitely excludes most emendations. Of modern commentaries, that by R. Saul Lieberman (*Tosefta ki-fshutah,* New York, 1955) and R. Y. Qafeḥ's commented edition and translation of Maimonides's Commentary are most useful. Other sources are quoted by name when used.

חמשה לא יתרומו פרק ראשון

(fol. 40a) **משנה א:** חֲמִשָּׁה לֹא יִתְרוֹמוּ וְאִם תָּרְמוּ אֵין תְּרוּמָתָן תְּרוּמָה. הַחֵרֵשׁ וְהַשּׁוֹטֶה וְהַקָּטָן וְהַתּוֹרֵם אֶת שֶׁאֵינוֹ שֶׁלּוֹ. נָכְרִי שֶׁתָּרַם אֶת שֶׁל יִשְׂרָאֵל אֲפִילוּ בִרְשׁוּתוֹ אֵין תְּרוּמָתָן תְּרוּמָה.

Mishnah 1: Five [persons] cannot give heave and if they gave it is not heave: the deaf and dumb[1], the insane, the minor, and one who gives heave from what is not his. The Gentile who gave heave for a Jew's property, even with the latter's authorization his heave is not heave[2].

1 He is excluded only if he has no way of communicating with others.

2 But a Gentile may voluntarily donate heave from his own produce.

הלכה א: חֲמִשָּׁה לֹא יִתְרוֹמוּ כו'. רִבִּי שְׁמוּאֵל בַּר נַחְמָן שָׁמַע לְכוּלְהוֹן מִן הָכָא דַּבֵּר אֶל בְּנֵי יִשְׂרָאֵל וְיִקְחוּ לִי תְּרוּמָה. פְּרָט לְגוֹי. מֵאֵת כָּל־אִישׁ פְּרָט לְקָטָן. אֲשֶׁר יִדְּבֶנּוּ לִבּוֹ פְּרָט לְחֵרֵשׁ וּלְשׁוֹטֶה. וְזֹאת הַתְּרוּמָה אֲשֶׁר תִּקְחוּ מֵאִתָּם פְּרָט לְתוֹרֵם אֶת שֶׁאֵינוֹ שֶׁלּוֹ.

Halakhah 1: "Five [persons] cannot give heave," etc. Rebbi Samuel bar Naḥman understood all of these from here (*Ex.* 25:2-3)[3]: "Speak to the Children of Israel that *they* should give heave for Me", excluding the Gentile, "from every man", excluding the minor, "whose intention is to volunteer", excluding the deaf-mute and the insane. "The following is the heave you shall accept from *them*", except from one who gives heave for what is not his.

3 While the verses deal with the voluntary heave for the Tabernacle, it is assumed that the word "heave" always has the same meaning (cf. *Berakhot*, Chapter 1, Note 70) and, therefore, is under the same restrictions.

וְיוֹכִיחַ מַעֲשֶׂה שֶׁלָּהֶן עַל מַחֲשַׁבְתָּן דְּתַנִּינָן תַּמָּן הֶעֱלוּ חֵרֵשׁ שׁוֹטֶה וְקָטָן אַף עַל פִּי שֶׁחִישֵּׁב שֶׁיֵּרֵד עֲלֵיהֶן טַל אֵינָן בְּכִי יוּתַּן מִפְּנֵי שֶׁיֵּשׁ לָהֶם[4] מַעֲשֶׂה וְאֵין לָהֶם[4] מַחֲשָׁבָה. וְאֵי זֶהוּ מַעֲשֶׂה שֶׁלָּהֶן. רִבִּי חוּנָא אָמַר בְּתָפוּשׂ בָּהֶן בַּטַּל. וְתַנִּינָן תַּמָּן הוֹרִידָהּ חֵרֵשׁ שׁוֹטֶה וְקָטָן אַף עַל פִּי שֶׁחִישֵּׁב שֶׁיּוּדְחוּ רַגְלֶיהָ אֵין בְּכִי יוּתַּן מִפְּנֵי שֶׁיֵּשׁ לָהֶן מַעֲשֶׂה וְאֵין בָּהֶן מַחֲשָׁבָה. וְאֵי זֶהוּ מַעֲשֶׂה שֶׁלָּהֶן. אָמַר רִבִּי חוּנָא בִּמְשַׁפְשֵׁף בָּהֶן בַּמַּיִם. וְאָמַר אַף הָכָא וְיוֹכִיחַ מַעֲשֶׂה שֶׁלָּהֶן עַל מַחֲשַׁבְתָּם. רִבִּי שְׁמוּאֵל רִבִּי אַבָּהוּ בְּשֵׁם רִבִּי יוֹחָנָן. רִבִּי זְעִירָא בְּשֵׁם רַבָּנִין וְנֶחְשַׁב לָכֶם תְּרוּמַתְכֶם. אֶת שֶׁכָּתוּב בּוֹ מַחֲשָׁבָה אֵין מַעֲשֶׂה שֶׁלּוֹ מוֹכִיחַ עַל מַחֲשַׁבְתּוֹ. וְאֶת שֶׁאֵין כָּתוּב בּוֹ מַחֲשָׁבָה מַעֲשֶׂה שֶׁלּוֹ מוֹכִיחַ עַל מַחֲשַׁבְתּוֹ. וְכָאן הוֹאִיל וְכָתוּב בּוֹ מַחֲשָׁבָה. אֵין מַעֲשֶׂה שֶׁלּוֹ מוֹכִיחַ עַל מַחֲשַׁבְתּוֹ.

Should not their[5] action be proof of their intentions[6]? As we have stated there[7]: "If a deaf-mute, insane, or minor person brought them up, they are not under the category of 'when given' because they have action but no intention." What is their action? Rebbi Ḥuna said, when he grabs it while full of dew[8]. We also have stated there[9]: "If a deaf-mute, insane, or minor person brought them down, even if he thought that [his animals'] feet should be doused, it is not under the category of 'when given' because they have action but no intention." What is their action? Rebbi Ḥuna said, when he rubs them with water. We should also say here, let their action be proof of their intentions! Rebbi Samuel, Rebbi Abbahu, in the name of Rebbi Joḥanan; Rebbi Zeïra in the name of the rabbis (*Num.* 18:27): "Your heave will be credited to you." When thought is mentioned in the verse[10], his action cannot prove his intentions; when thought is not mentioned in the verse, his action can prove his intentions. Since here thought is mentioned in the verse, his action cannot prove his intentions.

4 Reading of Rome ms. Leyden and Venice: בחן.

5 Speaking of deaf-mute, insane, and minor.

6 One should allow non-verbal communication of "intention to volunteer".

7 Mishnah *Makhširin* 6:1: "If somebody brings his produce up to his roof because of worms and dew descended on it, it is not under the category of 'when given' but if he intended this {that the produce should be wetted by dew}, it is under the category of 'when given'. If a deaf-mute, insane, or minor person brought them up, . . .". As explained in *Demay*, Chapter 2, Note 141, produce is not susceptible to impurity unless it came into contact with water (or any other fluid causing impurity, cf. *Demay*, Chapter 2, Note 136) and that contact was desired, since the verse *Lev.* 11:38: "If produce got wetted by water . . . it will be impure" can also be read as: "If water was given on produce . . .". It is inferred that the wetting, even if happening by a passive process, must have an active ingredient, *viz.*, that the moistening of the produce must be agreeable to the owner.

8 In the Babli, *Ḥulin* 13a, R. Johanan explains that he turns the produce over in order to distribute the moisture evenly. This is professional action. R. Simson conjectures that the action envisaged by R. Ḥuna is the same as explained by R. Johanan.

9 Mishnah *Makhširin* 3:8. It is explained in that Chapter that water drawn intentionally will make produce susceptible to impurity even if the contact of the produce with it was unintentional. The example described in Mishnah 8 is that of cattle whose feet have to be washed, either because the animal was used for threshing and now is all dusty, or because of some medical condition. Then the water drops clinging to the animal after it was washed in the river will make produce susceptible to impurity unless the animal was driven to the river by "a deaf-mute, insane, or minor person." Here again, if the cattle are not only driven to the river but actively washed,

intention is clearly shown.

10 The root both of "thought", מחשבה, and "being accounted for", נחשב, is חשב.

אָמַר רִבִּי יוֹסֵי קַשִּׁייָתָהּ קוֹמֵי שְׁמוּאֵל הֲרֵי גִיטִּין הֲרֵי אֵין כָּתוּב בָּהֶן מַחֲשָׁבָה. וְאֵין מַעֲשֶׂה שֶׁלּוֹ מוֹכִיחַ עַל מַחֲשַׁבְתּוֹ. דְּתַנִּינָן הַכֹּל כְּשֵׁרִין לִכְתּוֹב אֶת הַגֵּט אֲפִילוּ[11] שׁוֹטֶה חֵרֵשׁ וְקָטָן. אָמַר רַב[12] הוּנָא וְהוּא שֶׁיְּהֵא פִּיקֵּחַ עוֹמֵד עַל גַּבָּיו. רִבִּי יוֹחָנָן בָּעֵי וְהַיְינוּ וְכָתַב לָהּ לִשְׁמָהּ. חָזַר רִבִּי יוֹסֵי וְאָמַר תַּמָּן זֶה כוֹתֵב וְזֶה מְגָרֵשׁ. בְּרַם הָכָא הוּא חוֹשֵׁב וְהוּא תוֹרֵם. רִבִּי יַעֲקֹב בַּר אָחָא אָמַר הָא אִילּוּ כָּתַב הוּא וְגֵירֵשׁ הוּא גֵּט הוּא. בְּרַם הָכָא הוּא חוֹשֵׁב וְהוּא תוֹרֵם.

Rebbi Yose said, I questioned before Samuel: But with bills of divorce, thought is not written and his action cannot prove his intention! As we have stated[13]: "Everybody is permitted to write a bill of divorce, even an insane person, a deaf-mute, and a minor." Rebbi Huna said, if a sane person directs him. Rebbi Johanan asked, is that (*Deut.* 24:1,3): "he writes for her", for her personally[14]? Rebbi Yose came back and said, there one person writes[15] and another person divorces. But here, the same person thinks and takes heave. Rebbi Jacob bar Aḥa said, there, if he[16] would write himself and divorce, would that not be a divorce? But here, he thinks and takes heave.

11 Reading of the Rome ms. and all Mishnah mss. Leyden and Venice: חוץ מ "except."

12 Reading of the parallel in *Giṭṭin* 2:5 and Babli *Giṭṭin* 22b-23a. Here the reading is א"ר which usually means אמר רבי.

13 Mishnah *Giṭṭin* 2:5.

14 This is an echo of the very short discussion in *Giṭṭin* 2:5. Rebbi Johanan points out that the divorce document must be written specifically for the woman in question. If two men with identical names are married to two women who have the same name, and both want to divorce them on the same day, the two divorce documents will have identical wording. Nevertheless,

if the husbands switch the documents before they are handed to the respective wives, both divorces will be invalid. In both Talmudim, Samuel narrows down the meaning of the Mishnah in that he allows the incompetent only to write the formulaic portion under the direction of a competent person; but the data which make the document valid, date and names of the two persons involved, must be written by a competent person as agent of the husband. The argument here does not consider this restriction, except that R. Yose (Rav Assi of the first generation Amoraïm in Babylonia) is of the opinion that, since a document containing only date and names cannot be signed by witnesses and is not a divorce document, the writing of the incompetent is necessary for the validity of the document and one has to wonder why this is accepted.

15 Writing a valid divorce document and using it for the divorce are two distinct actions; one may be valid without the other. But taking heave is valid only if the taking is intended for heave; the action itself needs thinking; this parallels the action of divorce, not the writing of part of the document.

16 A competent person. Even if he writes all by himself there are two actions. This argument is valid only for R. Eleazar (ben Shamua, the Tanna) who holds that a divorce is validated by handing over the document before two witnesses. But according to R. Meïr who holds that a document is invalid if it has not been signed by two trustworthy witnesses, the writing of the document is not important, only the signing is, and this must be done by two competent persons unrelated to the husband.

רִבִּי יַעֲקֹב בַּר אָחָא רִבִּי חִייָא בְשֵׁם רִבִּי יוֹחָנָן חֲלוּקִין עַל הַשּׁוֹנֶה הַזֶּה. מַהוּ כְדוֹן אֲתִי דְרִבִּי יוֹחָנָן דִּתְרוּמוֹת כְּרִבִּי יִשְׁמָעֵאל בְּנוֹ שֶׁל רִבִּי יוֹחָנָן בֶּן בְּרוֹקָה דְקִידּוּשִׁין. וּדְרִבִּי יוֹחָנָן בְּגִיטִּין כְּרַבָּנִין דְּקִידּוּשִׁין. דִּתְנָן חֵרֵשׁ שׁוֹטֶה וְקָטָן שֶׁקִּידְּשׁוּ אֵין קִידּוּשֵׁיהֶן קִידּוּשִׁין. רִבִּי יִשְׁמָעֵאל בְּנוֹ שֶׁל רִבִּי יוֹחָנָן בֶּן בְּרוֹקָה (fol. 40b) אוֹמֵר בֵּינָן לְבֵין עַצְמָן אֵין קִידּוּשֵׁיהֶן קִידּוּשִׁין. בֵּינָן לְבֵין אֲחֵרִים קִידּוּשֵׁיהֶן קִידּוּשִׁין.

Rebbi Jacob bar Aḥa, Rebbi Ḥiyya, in the name of Rebbi Joḥanan: One disagrees with this Mishnah teacher[17]. How is that? It turns out that Rebbi Joḥanan concerning heaves parallels Rebbi Ismael, the son of Rebbi Joḥanan ben Beroqa concerning sanctification, and Rebbi Joḥanan concerning divorces parallels the rabbis concerning sanctification, as we have stated[18]: "The sanctifications of a deaf-mute person, an insane, and a minor who sanctified are no sanctifications. Rebbi Ismael, the son of Rebbi Joḥanan ben Beroqa says, if they are alone, their sanctifications are no sanctifications. Together with others, their sanctifications are sanctifications."

17 He holds that incompetents may separate heave under the direction of a competent person.

18 Tosephta *Parah* 5:7 reads: "Everybody is able to sanctify except the deaf-mute, the insane, and the minor; but R. Jehudah approves of the minor. R. Ismael, the son of R. Joḥanan ben Beroqa says that the sanctifications of a deaf-mute person, an insane, and a minor, who sanctified in the presence of others, are valid. The sanctification by a sexless person is invalid, for he is possibly uncircumcised, and an uncircumcized person cannot sanctify. The sanctification by a hermaphrodite is valid but R. Jehudah declares it invalid since he possibly is a woman and a woman does not qualify for holy matters."

All this refers to the purification from the impurity of the dead, which needs sprinkling with fresh water to which a minute amount of the ashes of the red heifer must be added. The act of taking the ashes and putting them into a vessel filled with fresh water is called "sanctification." It is a sacral act (*Num.* 19:17) and as such needs the intent of the person executing it. R. Ismael, the son of R. Joḥanan ben Beroqa, applies the principle that for obligations for which "thought" is implied by the verse but not spelled out explicitly, actions may prove intent.

{A sexless person is one without testicles or female sex characteristics. He might be a male with undescended testicles. The hermaphrodite has a penis and testicles as well as female breasts and a vagina; he must be circumcised. The exclusion of women by R. Jehudah is rejected by the rabbis; women nevertheless may not sprinkle since the verse (*Lev.* 19:18) requires this to be done by "a pure male."}

The seeming inconsistency in the positions of R. Johanan is not resolved. {If one assumes that R. Johanan agrees with the position of Samuel (Note 14) there is no inconsistency since he will agree that the incompetent may write only the inconsequential parts of the divorce document.}

תַּנֵּי חֵרֵשׁ שֶׁתָּרַם אֵין תְּרוּמָתוֹ תְרוּמָה. אָמַר רַבָּן שִׁמְעוֹן בֶּן גַּמְלִיאֵל בְּמָה דְבָרִים אֲמוּרִים בְּשֶׁהָיָה חֵרֵשׁ מִתְּחִילָּתוֹ. אֲבָל אִם הָיָה פִּיקֵחַ וְנִתְחָרֵשׁ כּוֹתֵב וַאֲחֵרִים מְקַיְּימִין כְּתַב יָדוֹ. שׁוֹמֵעַ וְאֵינוֹ מְדַבֵּר הֲרֵי הוּא כְפִיקֵּחַ.

It was stated[19]: "If a deaf-mute person gave heave, it is not heave. Rabban Simeon ben Gamliel said, when was this said? If he was born deaf-mute. But if he was normal and became deaf and dumb, he writes and others confirm his signature. [20]If he hears but cannot speak, he is like a normal person."

19 A similar statement is in Tosephta *Terumot* 1:1, quoted in Babli *Giṭṭin* 71a. This and the following paragraphs are also in *Giṭṭin* 7:1 (fol. 48c). Cf. also Mishnah and Halakhah 2.

20 In the Tosephta (1:2) and the Babli, the formulation is: "If he hears but does not speak, he is mute; if he speaks but cannot hear, he is deaf; both have the status of normal persons." The sentence is missing in the Rome ms.

רִבִּי יַעֲקֹב בַּר אָחָא רִבִּי חִייָה בְּשֵׁם רִבִּי יוֹחָנָן חֲלוּקִין עַל הַשּׁוֹנֶה הַזֶּה. אָמְרִין וְהָא מַתְנִיתִין פְּלִיגָא נִתְחָרֵשׁ הוּא אוֹ נִשְׁטָה אֵינוֹ מוֹצִיא עוֹלָמִית. וְיִכְתּוֹב וִיקַיְּימוּ אֲחֵרִים כְּתַב יָדָיו. קַיְּימוּנָהּ בְּשֶׁאֵינוֹ יוֹדֵעַ לִכְתּוֹב. מוֹתִיב רִבִּי בָּא בַּר מָמָל וְהָא מַתְנִיתָא פְלִיגָא וַהֲרֵי שֶׁכָּתַב כְּתַב יָדָיו אוֹ שֶׁאוֹמֵר לַסּוֹפֵר כְּתוֹב וְלָעֵדִים חֲתוֹמוּ אַף עַל פִּי שֶׁכְּתָבוּ וַחֲתָמוּ וְנָתְנוּ לוֹ וְחָזַר וּנְתָנוֹ לָהּ אֵינוֹ גֵט.

אָמַר רִבִּי יָסָה אֱמוֹר סוֹפָהּ וְלֵית הִיא פְלִיגָא אֵינוֹ גֵט עַד שֶׁיִּשְׁמְעוּ אֶת קוֹלוֹ. שֶׁאָמַר לַסּוֹפֵר כְּתוֹב וְלָעֵדִים חֲתוֹמוּ לֹא סוֹף דָּבָר עַד שֶׁיִּשְׁמְעוּ אֶת קוֹלוֹ. אֶלָּא אֲפִילוּ הִרְכִּין בְּרֹאשׁוֹ אַתְּ אָמַר לֵית כָּאן וְאַף הָכָא לֵית כָּאן. אָמַר רִבִּי מָנָא אִית כָּאן הִיא שְׁמִיעַת הַקּוֹל הִיא הַרְכָּנַת רֹאשׁ.

Rebbi Jacob bar Aḥa, Rebbi Ḥiyya, in the name of Rebbi Joḥanan: One disagrees with this Tanna[21]. They say, does not a Mishnah disagree[22]: "If he became deaf-mute or insane, he may never divorce." Why can he not write and have others fulfill his written instructions[23]? They upheld it, if he is illiterate. Rebbi Abba bar Mamal objected, does not a *baraita* disagree[24]: "If he wrote himself, or he told the scribe to write and the witnesses to sign, even though the scribe wrote, the witnesses signed, they gave him [the document] and he in turn gave it to her, it is no divorce." Rebbi Assi said, complete the sentence and there is no disgreement: "it is no divorce unless they hear his voice." But even if he gave a sign with his head you say it is invalid[25], here also it is invalid. Rebbi Mana said, it is valid: hearing the voice has the same status as seeing him nod his head[26]!

21 Rabban Simeon ben Gamliel.

22 Yebamot 14:1: "If a normal man married a normal woman and she became deaf-mute he may divorce her or keep her, but if she became insane he may not divorce her; if he became deaf-mute or insane he may never divorce."

23 According to Rabban Simeon, even if he became deaf-mute it should not make any difference since he may give written instructions.

24 Tosephta *Giṭṭin* 2:8. The text there ends: "it is no divorce unless they hear his voice say to the scribe 'write!', and to the witnesses 'sign!'" That Tosephta clearly disagrees with Rabban Simeon and disqualifies handwriting by a mute.

25 This refers to Mishnah *Giṭṭin* 7:1: "If somebody lost his speech and they said to him, shall we write a divorce document for your wife? if he gave a sign with his head one checks

him out three times; if he indicated 'yes' when it was expected, and 'no' when it was expected, they should write and hand it over." The Tosephta also seems to contradict this Mishnah.

26 The Tosephta contradicts Rabban Simeon ben Gamliel but not the Mishnah. A written authorization is invalid but a direct authorization by the husband to scribe and witnesses, by speech for a normal person and sign language for a mute, is valid. In the Babli (*Giṭṭin* 71a), Rav Cahana in the name of Rav accepts the position of Rabban Simeon, against the Tosephta.

רִבִּי עֶזְרָא בְּעָא קוֹמֵי רִבִּי מָנָא כְּמָה דְּתֵימַר עַד שֶׁיְּהֵרְכִין בְּרֹאשׁוֹ שְׁלֹשָׁה פְּעָמִים וְדִכְוָותָהּ עַד שֶׁיִּשְׁמְעוּ קוֹלוֹ שְׁלֹשָׁה פְּעָמִים. אָמַר לֵיהּ לִשְׁמִיעַת הַקּוֹל פַּעַם אַחַת. לְהַרְכָּנַת הָרֹאשׁ שְׁלֹשָׁה פְּעָמִים.

Rebbi Ezra[27] asked before Rebbi Mana: Just as you say that three times he must give a sign with his head, must one equally hear his voice three times? He said to him, hearing his voice once, giving a sign with his head three times.

27 He is Rebbi Azariah, a student of R. Mana (cf. *Berakhot*, Chapter 1, Note 90).

אָמַר רִבִּי יוּדָן תַּמָּן בְּאוֹמֵר כָּךְ וְכָךְ עָשִׂיתִי הָכָא בְּאוֹמֵר כָּךְ וְכָךְ עֲשׂוּ. רִבִּי בִנְיָמִין בֶּן לֵוִי בָּעֵי אִם יֵשׁ בּוֹ דַעַת לְשֶׁעָבַר יֵשׁ בּוֹ דַעַת לְהַבָּא אִם אֵין בּוֹ דַעַת לְשֶׁעָבַר אֵין בּוֹ דַעַת לְהַבָּא. אָמַר רִבִּי אֲבוּדִימִי בְּחֵרֵשׁ אֲנָן קַיָּימִין וְאֵין שְׁלִיחוּת לְחֵרֵשׁ. אָמַר רִבִּי יוֹסֵי בֵּי רִבִּי בּוּן בְּבָרִיא אֲנָן קַיָּימִין. וְלָמָּה אֵינוֹ גֵט אֲנִי אוֹמֵר מִתְעַסֵּק הָיָה בִשְׁטָרוֹתָיו. וְתַנֵּי כֵן בַּמֶּה דְבָרִים אֲמוּרִים בִּזְמַן שֶׁפֵּירֵשׁ מִתּוֹךְ בּוּרְייו. אֲבָל אִם נִשְׁתַּתֵּק מֵחֲמַת חוֹלְייוֹ דַּייוֹ פַּעַם אַחַת.

Rebbi Yudan said, there, if he said I did such and such, here, if he says do such and such[28]. Rebbi Benjamin ben Levi inquired: If he has understanding for the past, he should have understanding for the future; if he has no understanding for the past, he would not have understanding for the future[29]! Rebbi Eudaimon said, here we deal with a mute; there is no agency for a mute[30]. Rebbi Yose ben Rebbi Abun said, we deal with a sane person[31]. Why is there no divorce? Because I say, he was occupied with his documents. We also stated so: "When was this said? When he explained it in his regular state. But if he was paralyzed by sickness, once is enough[32]."

28 "There" refers to the statement of Rabban Simeon ben Gamliel that written testimony of a deaf-mute is valid, "here" refers to the Tosephta that a written command by a deaf-mute is invalid for a divorce.

29 The argument of R. Yudan makes no sense; R. Benjamin supports R. Joḥanan (Note 21 ff.)

30 He rejects the statement of Rabban Simeon and implies that the Mishnah in *Terumot* also applies to any deaf-mute, whether his disability be congenital or acquired. Since the heave of a deaf-mute is no heave even if the deaf-mute acts for a sane person, it follows that a deaf-mute cannot be an agent and, therefore, cannot appoint an agent. A divorce document must be written by an agent of the husband's since the verse (*Deut. 24:1,3*) requires that "he writes her a scroll of divorce". If nobody can be an agent of the deaf-mute, he cannot divorce since even if he himself writes the document he cannot ask the witnesses to sign.

31 He accepts the statement of Rabban Simeon and shows that R. Joḥanan is wrong; there is no disagreement between Rabban Simeon and the Mishnah in *Giṭṭin*. A congenital deaf-mute cannot marry or divorce, while a hearing person who is mute is considered normal and can divorce by giving written directions, following Rabban Simeon and R. Mana. The only reason we require a triple confirmation of the will to divorce is to ascertain that the husband really wants the divorce, not that he wants to have a document ready should he want to divorce.

32 Sick persons have to be treated with consideration and only the necessary legal forms have to be observed, not formalities that are not

stricly necessary. This is true certainly for critically ill persons, in particular for a childless husband who wants to spare his wife the trouble of freeing herself from an unwelcome brother-in-law (or maybe forbid her to a desirable brother-in-law.)

מָאן תַּנָּא חֵרֵשׁ דְּלָא כְּרִבִּי יוּדָה דְּתַנֵּי אָמַר רִבִּי יוּדָה מַעֲשֶׂה בְּבָנָיו שֶׁל רִבִּי יוֹחָנָן בֶּן גּוּדְגְּדָא שֶׁהָיוּ כוּלּוֹ חֵרְשִׁים וְהָיוּ כָּל־הַטָּהֳרוֹת בִּירוּשָׁלֵם נַעֲשִׂין עַל גַּבֵּיהֶן. אָמְרוּ לוֹ מִפְּנֵי שֶׁהַטָּהֳרוֹת אֵינָן צְרִיכוֹת מַחֲשָׁבָה וְנַעֲשׂוֹת עַל גַּבֵּי חֵרֵשׁ שׁוֹטֶה וְקָטָן. אֲבָל תְּרוּמוֹת וּמַעְשְׂרוֹת צְרִיכוֹת מַחֲשָׁבָה וְאֵינָן נִפְסָלוֹת בְּהֶסֵּח הַדַּעַת. רִבִּי יוֹסֵי בְשֵׁם רִבִּי לָא אֵין כָּתוּב בָּהֶן מַחֲשָׁבָה שְׁמִירָה כָּתוּב בָּהֶן.

Who states "the deaf-mute?" Not Rebbi Jehudah, since it was stated[33]: "Rebbi Jehudah said, it happened that the sons of Rebbi Joḥanan ben Gudgada[34] were all deaf-mutes and all purities[35] in Jerusalem were handled by them. They said to him, because purities do not need thought and may be produced by a deaf-mute, an insane, and a minor[36]. But heaves and tithes need thought and do not become invalidated by absent-mindedness." Rebbi Yose in the name of Rebbi La: Thought is not written in regard to them, only watching[37].

33 Tosephta 1:1; the remark about abent-mindedness is missing there.

34 A Tanna of the first generation. A Levite who in the Temple was a guardian of the gates. In the Babli (*Ḥagigah* 3a) it is reported that his grandsons, the sons of his normal daughter, were ostensibly deaf-mutes. They went to the lectures of Rebbi and when Rebbi prayed that they should be healed, it turned out that they had learned the entire Mishnah and halakhic Midrashim from his lectures. R. Joḥanan all his life ate only food prepared by the standard of purity of sacrifices.

35 "Purities" is food prepared in purity, usually by the standards of purity of heave.

36 If they are continually supervised by a normal adult.

37 In the section dealing with

impurity of sacred food, it is said (*Lev.* 22:9): "They have to keep My watch." Pure food remains in its state only if it is permanently guarded against impurity from the moment it is prepared for impurity (cf. Note 7). A properly instructed deaf-mute may act as a guard.

סִימָנֵי שׁוֹטֶה הַיּוֹצֵא בַלָּיְלָה וְהַלָּן בְּבֵית הַקְּבָרוֹת וְהַמְקָרֵעַ אֶת כְּסוּתוֹ וְהַמְאַבֵּד מַה שֶׁנּוֹתְנִין לוֹ. אָמַר רִבִּי הוּנָא וְהוּא שֶׁיְּהֵא כוּלְּהֶן בּוֹ דְּלָא כֵן אֲנִי אוֹמֵר הַיּוֹצֵא בַלָּיְלָה קֻנִיטְרוֹפּוֹס[38]. הַלָּן בְּבֵית הַקְּבָרוֹת מַקְטִיר לַשֵּׁדִים. הַמְקָרֵעַ אֶת כְּסוּתוֹ כּוֹלִיקוֹס. וְהַמְאַבֵּד מַה שֶׁנּוֹתְנִין לוֹ קִינִיקוֹס.[39] רִבִּי יוֹחָנָן אָמַר אֲפִילוּ אַחַת מֵהֶן. אָמַר רִבִּי בּוּן מִסְתַּבְּרָה מַה דְּאָמַר רִבִּי יוֹחָנָן אֲפִילוּ אַחַת מֵהֶן בִּלְבַד בִּמְאַבֵּד מַה שֶׁנּוֹתְנִין לוֹ אֲפִילוּ שׁוֹטֶה שֶׁבְּשׁוֹטִים אֵין מְאַבֵּד כָּל־מַה שֶׁנּוֹתֵן לוֹ. קוֹרְדְיַיקוֹס[40] אֵין בּוֹ אַחַת מִכָּל אֵילּוּ. מָהוּ קוֹרְדְיַיקוֹס אָמַר רִבִּי יוֹסֵי הַמִּים. אָתָא עוּבְדָא קוֹמֵי רִבִּי יוֹסֵי בְּחַד טַרְסִיי דַּהֲווֹן יְהָבִין לֵיהּ סִימוּק גַּו אָכִים[41] וְהוּא לָעֵי. אָכִים[41] גַּו סִימוּק וְהוּא לָעֵי. אֲמַר דּוֹ הוּא קוֹרְדְיַיקוֹס שֶׁאָמְרוּ חֲכָמִים.

[42]The signs of an insane: One who goes out in the night, stays overnight in a graveyard, tears his clothing, and destroys what one gives to him. Rebbi Huna[43] said, only if all of that is in him since otherwise I say that one who goes out in the night is a man-dog[44]; he who stays overnight in a graveyard burns incense to spirits, he who tears up his clothing is a choleric person[45], and he who destroys what one gives to him is a cynic[46]. Rebbi Joḥanan said, even only one of these is proof. Rebbi Abun said, what Rebbi Joḥanan said, even only one of these is reasonable only for him who destroys what one gives to him; even the greatest idiot does not destroy all one gives to him[47]. The mad dancer[48] does not exhibit any of these signs. What is a mad dancer? Rebbi Yose said, a decrepit one[49]. There came a case before Rebbi Yose of a weaver who,

when one gave him red on black he was exerting himself[50], black on red he was exerting himself. He said, this is the mad dancer described by the Sages.

38 Reading of the text in Giṭṭin 7:1 (fol. 48c) and the Rome ms. here. Leyden: קנוטרוכוס.

39 Reading of the text in *Giṭṭin* 7:1 (fol. 48c) and the Rome ms. here. Leyden: קודייקוס.

40 Reading of the text in *Giṭṭin* 7:1 (fol. 48c) and the Rome ms. here. Leyden: קונדיקוס קודייקוס.

41 Reading of the text in *Giṭṭin* 7:1 (fol. 48c). Mss. and print here: אבוס ""to feed forcibly".

42 Tosephta 1:3, discussed also in Babli *Ḥagigah* 3b.

43 Since he precedes Samuel, the author must be the Babylonian Rav Huna, as given in the Babli.

44 Greek κυ(ν)άνθρωπος (νόσος) "dog-man (malady)"; cf. E. and H. Guggenheimer, *Talmudic Evidence of Greek Spelling*, in: Studi Classici in onore di Quintino Cataudella, vol. 4, pp. 71-72, Catania 1972; *Notes on the Talmudic Dictionary: Gandropos - Qantropos*, Lešōnēnu 35 (1971) 207-210.

45 Greek χολικός "bilious".

46 Greek κυνικός "dog-like", a philosopher who has no use for industrial products.

47 In the Babli, Rav Papa declares this criterion to be the only one to stand alone, all others needing multiple confirmation following Rav Huna.

48 Cf. Greek κόρδαξ, Latin *cordax*, "mad dance", perhaps chorea. This and the following sentences refer to Mishnah *Giṭṭin* 7:1 which states that a mad dancer cannot divorce his wife during an attack of his malady.

49 Arabic הִם "decrepit, senile person".

50 It is not at all clear what his symptoms were. Since the profession of the sick person is mentioned, it seems that he was unable to fit two different strands of thread together on his loom; perhaps the description is of Huntington's chorea or Parkinson's disease.

פְּעָמִים שׁוֹטֶה [פְּעָמִים חָלוּם הֲרֵי הוּא כְּפִיקֵּחַ לְכָל־דָּבָר][51] בְּשָׁעָה שֶׁהוּא שׁוֹטֶה הֲרֵי הוּא כְּשׁוֹטֶה לְכָל־דְּבָרָיו. וּבְשָׁעָה שֶׁהוּא חָלוּם הֲרֵי הוּא כְּפִיקֵּחַ לְכָל־דָּבָר.

אָתָא עוּבְדָא קוֹמֵי שְׁמוּאֵל אָמַר כַּד דּוּ חָלוּם יִתֵּן גֵּט. וְיִשְׁאוֹל כְּרִבִּי שִׁמְעוֹן בֶּן לָקִישׁ. דְּרִבִּי שִׁמְעוֹן בֶּן לָקִישׁ אָמַר לִכְשֶׁיִּשְׁתַּפֶּה דּוּ בָהּ דִּשְׁמוּאֵל. מִן דְּרִבִּי שִׁמְעוֹן בֶּן לָקִישׁ דּוּ אָמַר כַּד דּוּ חָלוּם יִתֵּן גֵּט וְתַחֲלִימֵנִי וְהַחֲיֵינִי.

[52]"If sometimes he is insane [when he is sometimes healthy he is normal in all regards], when he is insane he is insane in all regards, when healthy he is normal in all regards.[53]" A case came before Samuel who said, when he is of sound mind he should deliver the divorce document[54]; one must investigate[55] following Rebbi Simeon ben Laqish; as Rebbi Simeon ben Laqish said, when he is of even mind; that is as Samuel [acted]. Following Rebbi Simeon ben Laqish who said, only if he is of sound mind he may deliver the divorce document; (*Is.* 38:16) "make me healthy and let me live!"

51 Missing in *Giṭṭin* and in the Tosephta.

52 A similar text in Tosephta 1:3.

53 He is a responsible and competent person in all legal respects.

54 It is not enough that he be sane when telling the scribe to write and the witnesses to sign; he must also be sane when he delivers the document. Whether a document can be held over a spell of insanity is a matter of dispute between R. Simeon ben Laqish and R. Joḥanan in *Giṭṭin* 7:1.

55 The text in *Giṭṭin* is slightly different: "Samuel holds with R. Simeon ben Laqish."

מָאן תָּאנֵי קָטָן דְּלֹא כְרִבִּי יוּדָה דִּתְנָן קָטָן שֶׁהִנִּיחוֹ אָבִיו בְּמִקְשָׁה וְהָיָה תוֹרֵם וְאָבִיו מוֹכֵר עַל יָדָיו תְּרוּמָתוֹ תְרוּמָה. לֹא הוּא שֶׁתּוֹרֵם אֶלָּא אָבִיו הוּא שֶׁאִימֵּן עַל יָדוֹ. בָּא אָבִיו וְאִמֵּן עַל יָדוֹ לְמַפְרֵעַ נַעֲשֵׂית תְּרוּמָה. אוֹ מִכָּן וְלָבֹא. אָמַר רִבִּי שַׁמַּי נִישְׁמְעִינָהּ מִן הָדָא. הֲרֵי שֶׁבָּא בַּעַל הַבַּיִת וּמְצָאוֹ עוֹמֵד בְּתוֹךְ שֶׁלּוֹ אוֹמֵר לוֹ לְקוֹט לָךְ מִן הַיָּפִים הָאֵילּוּ אִם הָיוּ יָפִים אֵינוֹ חוֹשֵׁשׁ מִשּׁוּם גֶּזֶל וְאִם לָאו חוֹשֵׁשׁ מִשּׁוּם גֶּזֶל. וְאִם הָיָה לוֹקֵט וְנוֹתֵן לוֹ בֵּין כָּךְ וּבֵין כָּךְ אֵינוֹ חוֹשֵׁשׁ מִשּׁוּם גֶּזֶל. אִית לָךְ מֵימַר לְמַפְרֵעַ נַעֲשֵׂית תְּרוּמָה לֹא מִכָּן וְלָבֹא. וְאוּף הָכָא מִיכָּן וְלָבֹא נַעֲשֵׂית תְּרוּמָה.

Who stated "a minor"? This does not follow Rebbi Jehudah, as we have stated: "A minor whom his father put in a melon field where he was giving heave and his father sold on that basis, his heave is heave. He did not give heave but his father confirmed his action.[56]" When the father came and confirmed his action, is heave made retroactively or for the future[57]? Rebbi Shammai said, let us hear from the following[58]: "When the owner came and found him standing on his property, if he said to him, take from these nice [fruits], if they are nice he does not worry about robbery, otherwise he has to worry. But if he collected and gave to him, in no case does he have to worry about robbery." Can you say it became heave retroactively? No, from now into the future! Here also, it will be made heave from now on into the future[59].

56 This is a shortened version of a text close to Tosephta 1:4: "*Rebbi Jehudah said,* a minor whom his father put in a melon field where he was giving heave and his father sold on that basis, his heave is heave. *They said to him,* he did not give heave but his father confirmed his action." "They" are the Sages of our Mishnah.

57 While produce must be "prepared" for impurity (cf. Note 9), heave is automatically prepared by its holy status and can become impure even if dry. In addition, consumption of heave by a non-Cohen is a deadly sin once heave is sanctified. The question is when the status of holiness is acquired.

58 This also is a shortened *baraita* close to a Tosephta, 1:5: "*How does one give heave from what is not his? If he went to another person's field, collected, and gave heave without permission, if he has to worry that it might be robbery, his heave is not heave; if he does not have to worry then his heave is heave. How does he know whether what he did is robbery or not?* When the owner came and found him standing on his property, if he said to him, take from these nice [fruits], if they are nice he does not worry about robbery, otherwise he has to worry. But if *the owner* collected and *added to his*, in no

case does he have to worry about robbery." The full Tosephta is quoted in the Babli, *Qiddušin* 52b, *Baba Meẓi'a* 21a.

59 The minor (or the stranger in the Tosephta) can do the physical work of separating heave from the rest of the produce but only an adult owner can sanctify it, and only for the future.

אַתֶּם פְּרָט לְשׁוּתָפִין אַתֶּם פְּרָט לְאֶפִּיטְרוֹפִּין אַתֶּם פְּרָט לְתוֹרֵם אֶת שֶׁאֵינוֹ שֶׁלּוֹ. אַתֶּם וְלֹא שׁוּתָפִין. וְהָתְנָן שׁוּתָפִין שֶׁתָּֽרְמוּ זֶה אַחַר זֶה. אֶלָּא כָּאן לִתְרוּמָה גְדוֹלָה כָּאן לִתְרוּמַת מַעֲשֵׂר. כְּלוּם לָֽמְדוּ לִתְרוּמָה גְדוֹלָה אֶלָּא מִתְּרוּמַת מַעֲשֵׂר. אֶלָּא כָּאן לַהֲלָכָה כָּאן לְמַעֲשֶׂה.[60] אַתֶּם וְלֹא אֶפִּיטְרוֹפִּין. וְהָתַנִּינָן יְתוֹמִין שֶׁסָּֽמְכוּ אֵצֶל בַּעַל הַבַּיִת אוֹ שֶׁמִּינָּה לָהֶן אֲבִיהֶן אֶפִּיטְרוֹפִּין חַייָבִין לְעַשֵּׂר פֵּירוֹתֵיהֶן. חֲבֵרַיָּא אָֽמְרִין כָּאן בְּאֶפִּיטְרוֹפּוֹס לְעוֹלָם כָּאן בְּאֶפִּיטְרוֹפּוֹס לְשָׁעָה. רִבִּי יוֹסֵי בָּעֵי אִם בְּאֶפִּיטְרוֹפּוֹס לְעוֹלָם. כְּהָדָא דְתַנֵּי מוֹכֵר מְטַלְטְלִין וְזָנָן אֲבָל לֹא קַרְקָעוֹת. אֶלָּא כָּאן בְּיָתוֹם גָּדוֹל כָּאן בְּיָתוֹם קָטָן.

[61](*Num.* 18:28) "you" excludes partners, "you" excludes guardians, "you" excludes one who gives heave from what is not his[62]. Did we not state (*Terumot* 3:3): "Partners who gave heave one after the other?[63]" But one must be for Great Heave[64], the other for heave of the tithe. Did we not infer the laws of the Great Heave from heave of the tithe[65]? But one is for practice, the other for action[66]. "You" excludes guardians; but did we not state[67]: "Orphans dependent on a home owner, or for whom the father had appointed a guardian, must tithe their produce." The colleagues say, here for a permanent guardian, there for a temporary guardian. Rebbi Yose asked, does that apply to: "he may sell movables to feed them but not real estate[68]?" But here one deals with an adult orphan[69], there with an underage orphan.

60 Reading of the parallel Giṭṭin 5:4. In the mss. and R. Simson here: מעשר "tithes."

61 This paragraph is also in *Giṭṭin* 5:4 (fol. 47a).

62 This *baraita*, not found in *Sifry Num.*, must be from the exegesis of R. Aqiba. It appears, in different form, in Babli *Giṭṭin* 52a.

63 The Sages in that Mishnah declare heave given by one partner without the knowledge of the other as valid.

64 Heave given by the farmer; it is ironically called "Great" because it has no biblical minimum.

65 The verse quoted refers only to the heave of the tithe, the 10% given by the Levites from their tithes.

66 As practice, heave given by guardians is valid; giving tithe by one partner without the knowledge of the other is discouraged.

67 Mishnah *Giṭṭin* 5:4. In the first case, the home owner raises the orphans without being officially appointed guardian, neither by the father nor by the court after the father's death. Nevertheless, the person caring for the orphans becomes de facto guardian.

68 In *Giṭṭin*: "He may sell slaves to feed them but not real estate." All other sources give every guardian the right to sell real estate, under the supervision of the court, for the benefit of his wards.

69 Since they are able to give heave for themselves, they have to do it (if they are competent.)

אַתֶּם פְּרָט לְתוֹרֵם אֶת שֶׁאֵינוֹ שֶׁלּוֹ. מָה אַתְּ עֲבִיד לֵיהּ בְּתוֹרֵם אֶת שֶׁאֵינוֹ שֶׁלּוֹ אוֹ בְּתוֹרֵם אֶת שֶׁל חֲבֵירוֹ. נִישְׁמְעִינָהּ מִן הָדָא הִבְקִיר כְּרִיּוֹ וּמִירְחוֹ וְחָזַר וְזָכָה בוֹ אִין תַּעַבְדִּינֵיהּ כְּתוֹרֵם אֶת שֶׁאֵינוֹ שֶׁלּוֹ אֵין תְּרוּמָתוֹ תְרוּמָה. וְאִין תַּעַבְדִּינֵיהּ כְּתוֹרֵם אֶת שֶׁל חֲבֵירוֹ תְּרוּמָתוֹ תְרוּמָה. נִישְׁמְעִינָהּ מִן הָדָא גָּנַב תְּרוּמַת הֶקְדֵּשׁ וַאֲכָלָהּ שֶׁלּוֹ מְשַׁלֵּם שְׁנֵי חוֹמְשִׁין וְקֶרֶן שֶׁאֵין בְּהֶקְדֵּשׁ תַּשְׁלוּמֵי כֶפֶל. מָנוֹ תוֹרֵם לֹא גִזְבָּר הֲרֵי הוּא תוֹרֵם אֶת שֶׁאֵינוֹ שֶׁלּוֹ וְאַתְּ אָמַר תְּרוּמָתוֹ תְרוּמָה. הֲוֵי לֵית טַעֲמָא דְלֹא כְּתוֹרֵם אֶת שֶׁל חֲבֵירוֹ. אוֹ נֹאמַר מָאן הוּא תוֹרֵם בַּר לֵוִי שֶׁהִקְדִּישׁ תְּרוּמָתוֹ וְהָתַנֵּי רִבִּי הוֹשַׁעְיָא אֶחָד הַמַּקְדִּישׁ טִיבְלוֹ וְאֶחָד הַמַּקְדִּישׁ תְּרוּמָתוֹ. אָמַר רִבִּי אִידִי גִּיזְבָּר כְּמָאן דְּאִינּוּן בַּעֲלִין. וּדְלֹא כְרִבִּי יוֹסֵי. דְּרִבִּי יוֹסֵי אָמַר הוּא גִזְבָּר הוּא אַחֵר.

"'You' excludes one who gives heave from what is not his." What is the interpretation, one who gives heave from what is not his own, or one who gives heave from what is somebody else's? Let us hear the following: If he declared his heap as ownerless and then smoothed it and took possession again, if you refer to one who gives heave from what is not his own, his heave is not heave, if you refer to one who gives heave from what is somebody else's, his heave is heave[70]. Let us hear from the following[71]: "If he stole Temple heave and ate it, he pays two fifths and the principal because there is no double payment for Temple property[72]." Who gave the heave if not the administrator? Is he not giving heave from what is not his[73]? And you say his heave is heave! The reason must be that he does not give heave from another person's property. Or should we say, who gave the heave if not a Levite who dedicated his heave? But did not Rebbi Hoshaia state that there is no difference between him who dedicated his *ṭevel* and him who dedicated his heave? Rebbi Idi said, the administrator is like the owner[74]. This does not follow Rebbi Yose, since Rebbi Yose said the administrator is like any other person[75].

70 Mishnah *Ma'serot* 1:6 states that tithes and heave are due after threshing, when the grain kernels have been assembled into a heap and the heap was smoothed. It is shown in *Ma'serot*, Halakhah 1:1, that property which was ownerless at the moment when heave was due is exempt from heave. This seems to contradict the statement here that if a person declared his grain ownerless before it was smoothed, then gave heave, and only after that again took possession, his heave might be heave. The entire argument is possible only for R. Meïr, since R. Yose holds that property can be abandoned only if another person takes it up (cf. *Peah* 6:1, Note 17). It follows that any heave given in this case is given only because by rabbinic decree this kind of pro forma abandoning was declared invalid; hence,

there is a rabbinic obligation of heave. As the Babli notes (*Nedarim* 44b), any heave given from the repossessed grain must refer to the heap itself; it cannot possibly be given for unabandoned grain which is obligated by biblical decree (if we assume that heave is a biblical obligation after the Babylonian exile, cf. *Ševi'it* Chapter 7, Notes 11 ff.).

71 Mishnah *Terumah* 6:4. Stealing sacred property obligates the thief to pay back the amount taken plus a fine of one fifth (*Lev.* 5:16). The fifth is computed from above (amount stolen = $^4/_5$ amount paid), which is one fourth from below (amount paid = $^5/_4$ amount stolen). Halakhah 6:4 explains that one fifth has to be given to the Temple, restitution of Temple property, and another fifth to a Cohen, as restitution of heave.

72 Double restitution is required only for theft from natural persons: (*Ex.* 22:8) "He shall pay double to his neighbor."

73 If this argument were valid, no corporation would ever be able to be engaged in agriculture in the Holy Land since it never could tithe.

74 Any duly authorized person can give heave for any corporation. The question asked at the start is not answered since we did not find a case in which it would make any difference.

75 This opinion is not supported by any other source in Talmudic literature.

רִבִּי זְעִירָא רִבִּי אָחָא רִבִּי יָסָא רִבִּי יוֹחָנָן בְּשֵׁם רִבִּי יַנַּאי אַתֶּם גַּם אַתֶּם לְרַבּוֹת שְׁלוּחֲכֶם. מָה אַתֶּם בְּנֵי בְרִית אַף שְׁלוּחֲכֶם בְּנֵי בְרִית. אַתֶּם עוֹשִׂין שָׁלִיחַ וְאֵין הַגּוֹי עוֹשֶׂה שָׁלִיחַ. רִבִּי יוֹסֵי סָבַר מֵימַר אֵין גּוֹי עוֹשֶׂה שָׁלִיחַ בְּגוֹי אַחֵר חֲבֵירוֹ הָא בְיִשְׂרָאֵל עוֹשֶׂה. אָמַר לֵיהּ רִבִּי זְעִירָא מִינֵיהּ (fol. 40c) וּמִינֵיהּ אַתֶּם עוֹשִׂין שָׁלִיחַ לֹא בְיִשְׂרָאֵל. וְדִכְוָותָהּ אֵין הַגּוֹי עוֹשֶׂה שָׁלִיחַ וַאֲפִילוּ בְיִשְׂרָאֵל. הָתִיב רִבִּי הוֹשַׁעְיָא וְהָא מַתְנִיתָא מְסַייְעָא לְרִבִּי יוֹחָנָן. אָמַר רַבָּן שִׁמְעוֹן בֶּן גַּמְלִיאֵל וּמָה אִם יִרְצֶה הַגּוֹי הַזֶּה שֶׁלֹּא לִתְרוֹם פֵּירוֹתָיו אֵינוֹ תוֹרֵם. הָא אִם רָצָה תוֹרֵם. רִבִּי אַבָּא אָמַר בְּמַאֲמִין עַל יָדָיו.

[76]Rebbi Zeïra, Rebbi Joḥanan in the name of Rebbi Yannai (*Num.* 18:28): "You, also you," to include your agent. Just as you are in the Covenant, so your agent must be in the Covenant. You appoint an agent,

the Gentile may not. Rebbi Assi wanted to say that the Gentile cannot appoint another Gentile as agent, but he can appoint a Jew. Rebbi Zeïra said, from the *baraita* itself: You appoint an agent: does that not mean Jews? Similarly, the Gentile cannot appoint an agent: not even a Jew. Rav Hoshaia objects: Does the *baraita* support Rebbi Joḥanan? "Rabban Simeon ben Gamliel said: If the Gentile does not wish to give heave from his produce, he cannot give heave." Therefore, if he wants to, he may give heave. Rebbi Abba said, if he confirms it after him.

76 The entire paragraph is from *Demay* 6:1, explained there in Notes 7-10.

רִבִּי יוֹחָנָן בְּשֵׁם רִבִּי יַנַּאי יִשְׂרָאֵל שֶׁאָמַר לְלֵוִי כּוֹר מַעֲשֵׂר יֵשׁ לָךְ בְּיָדִי וְהָלַךְ[77] אוֹתוֹ בֶּן לֵוִי וַעֲשָׂאָן תְּרוּמַת מַעֲשֵׂר עַל מָקוֹם אַחֵר וְהָלַךְ יִשְׂרָאֵל וְנוֹתְנוֹ לְבֶן לֵוִי אַחֵר אֵין לוֹ עָלָיו אֶלָּא תַרְעוֹמֶת. הָדָא דְתֵימַר בְּשֶׁנְּתָנוֹ זֶה עַד שֶׁלֹּא עֲשָׂאוֹ זֶה. אֲבָל אִם עֲשָׂאוֹ זֶה עַד שֶׁלֹּא נְתָנוֹ זֶה לֹא. כְּהָדָא מַתְנִיתָא בִּיטֵּל אִם עַד שֶׁלֹּא תָּרַם בִּיטֵּל אֵין תְּרוּמָתוֹ תְרוּמָה. וְאִם מִשֶּׁתָּרַם בִּיטֵּל תְּרוּמָתוֹ תְרוּמָה וְכוּלָּהּ מִינֵיהּ מִכֵּיוָן שֶׁאָמַר לוֹ כּוֹר מַעֲשֵׂר יֵשׁ לִי בְּיָדָךְ נַעֲשֶׂה שְׁלוּחוֹ נִמְצָא כְּתוֹרֵם בִּרְשׁוּת יִשְׂרָאֵל. פָּתַר לָהּ כְּרִבִּי יוֹסֵי דְּרִבִּי יוֹסֵי אָמַר בַּעַל הַבַּיִת שֶׁתָּרַם אֶת הַמַּעְשְׂרוֹת מַה שֶּׁעָשָׂה עָשׂוּי.

Rebbi Joḥanan in the name of Rebbi Yannai: An Israel who said to a Levite: "You have a *kor* of tithe in my hand", and this Levite went[78] and made it heave of the tithe for other produce but the Israel went and gave it to another Levite, [the first one] has only a complaint on him[79]. That is, if he handed it over[80] before [the first Levite] made it [heave]. But not if this one made it before that one handed it over. Parallel to this Mishnah[81]: "If he terminated: if he terminated before he gave heave, his heave is not heave. But if he terminated after he gave heave, his heave is heave[82]." All this follows: From the moment he said, you have a *kor* of tithe in my hand, he made him his agent and it turns out that he was tithing with the permission of the Israel[83]. One may also explain it following Rebbi Yose, as "Rebbi Yose said: If the owner gave heave from the tithes, what he did is done.[84]"

77 Reading of the Rome ms. Leyden and Venice: הילך, an intrusion from the next paragraph.

78 Without first acquiring the tithe; cf. *Ševi'it* Chap. 8, Notes 13,14.

79 If the Levite ate his other tithe based on the heave of the tithe he thought he had given, he committed an inadvertent sin but has no legal way to ask for damages from the Israel.

80 He actually handed it over to the second Levite. In that case, the tithe was in the possession of a third party and the first Levite was tithing what was not his. The problem is that without an acquisition, the first Levite still seems to be tithing produce over which he has no power and this seems to be forbidden by our Mishnah.

81 Mishnah 3:4. The Mishnah declares that one may appoint an agent for the purpose of giving heave and then proceeds to explain what happens if the agency is terminated by the owner but not in the presence of the appointed agent.

82 Once heave is designated it is irrevocably holy (cf. Note 57).

83 Since the power of an agent cannot be greater than that of the principal and since according to the majority opinion, the only thing the Israel owner may do is separate the tithe of the heave but not declare it as heave of the tithe, the Levite cannot act as an agent but must act as independent principal with the right to give heave; the statements are parallel but the Amoraic statement is not a consequence of the Mishnah.

84 Tosephta 1:9. According to Rebbi Yose, the first Levite becomes the agent of the Israel.

רִבִּי יוֹחָנָן בְּשֵׁם רִבִּי יַנַּיי יִשְׂרָאֵל שֶׁאָמַר לְבֶן לֵוִי כּוֹר מַעֲשֵׂר יֵשׁ לָךְ בְּיָדִי וְהֵילָךְ
אֶת דָּמוֹ חוֹשֵׁשׁ לִתְרוּמַת מַעֲשֵׂר שֶׁבּוֹ. כְּהָדָא אֵילוֹפִיסָה יְהַב לְרִבִּי שִׁמְעוֹן בַּר

אַבָּא מַעֲשֵׂר. אָמַר לֵיהּ מְתוּקָּן הוּא. אָתָא שָׁאַל לְרִבִּי יוֹחָנָן. אָמַר לֵיהּ אֵילוֹפִּיסָה אָחִינוּ נֶאֱמָן הוּא. רִבִּי אִיסָּא בְּעָא קוֹמֵי דְרִבִּי יוֹחָנָן כְּמָה. כְּרִבִּי יוֹסֵי דְּרִבִּי יוֹסֵי אָמַר בַּעַל הַבַּיִת שֶׁתָּרַם אֶת הַמַּעְשְׂרוֹת מַה שֶׁעָשָׂה עָשׂוּי. אָמַר לֵיהּ אִין בבליה קָמַת עֲלֵיהּ.

Rebbi Johanan in the name of Rebbi Yannai: An Israel who told a Levite: "You have a *kor* of tithe in my hand and here is its price[85];" the latter must worry about the heave of the tithe contained in it[86]. For example, Elopisa[87] gave tithes to Rebbi Simeon bar Abba and said, it is in order. He went and asked Rebbi Johanan who said to him, our brother Elopisa is trustworthy. Rebbi Issa[88] asked before Rebbi Johanan, is that following Rebbi Yose, for "Rebbi Yose said: The owner who gave heave from the tithes, what he did is done." He said to him, Babylonian[89], you understood it[90].

85 Tithe of which the heave of the tithe has been separated is totally profane in the hand of the Levite and may be sold by him. If the farmer separated the heave of the tithe, he may contract with the Levite to buy the tithe back from him.

86 Before he can use the money, he must make sure that the tithe would have been profane in his hand. Therefore, he either must ascertain that the farmer separated heave of the tithe or he must give it himself from other tithe that is not yet profane before he can agree to the deal. The Babli, *Giṭṭin* 30b, discusses both versions and finds them in need of emendations.

The Rome ms. has a completely different text: דְּמֵיי כּוֹר מַעֲשֵׂר יֵשׁ לָךְ בְּיָדִי וְהֵא לָךְ אֶת דָּמָיו אֵינוֹ חוֹשֵׁשׁ לִתְרוּמַת מַעֲשֵׂר שֶׁבּוֹ. "The value of a *kor* of tithe you have in my hand and here is its price, he does not have to worry about the heave of the tithe contained in it." According to this version, R. Johanan extends his ruling in the case of R. Simeon ben Abba to all Jews who are tithing.

87 The exact name has not been determined. Levy proposes Εὔελπις, Kohout Ἐλπίας, Krauss Ἀλοπίς. The

Rome ms. reads the name as ליפסה.

88 He probably is Issi bar Hini, a Babylonian who studied with R. Joḥanan and then returned to Babylonia where he founded his own Yeshivah.

89 Reading בבליה for בכליה. Rebbi Joḥanan was known to address his Babylonian students as "Babylonian".

90 For R. Joḥanan, this is practice to be followed. The same conclusion is reached in the Babli; there the statement is attributed not to the late Tanna R. Yose ben Ḥalaphta but to Abba Eleazar ben Gamla (or, ben Gamliel) whose title, Abba, points to the Temple period or the first generation of Jabneh.

(fol. 40a) **משנה ב**: חֵרֵשׁ הַמְדַבֵּר וְאֵינוֹ שׁוֹמֵעַ לֹא יִתְרוֹם וְאִם תָּרַם תְּרוּמָתוֹ תְרוּמָה. חֵרֵשׁ שֶׁדִּבְּרוּ חֲכָמִים בְּכָל־מָקוֹם שֶׁאֵינוֹ לֹא שׁוֹמֵעַ וְלֹא מְדַבֵּר.

Mishnah 2: A deaf person who speaks but cannot hear should not give heave, but if he did, his heave is heave. A "deaf person" mentioned anywhere by the Sages is a deaf-mute.

(fol. 40c) **הלכה ב**: לְמִי נִצְרְכָה לְרִבִּי יוֹסֵי. הַיידֵין רִבִּי יוֹסֵי הַהִיא דְתַנִּינָן תַּמָּן הַקּוֹרֵא אֶת שְׁמַע וְלֹא הִשְׁמִיעַ לְאָזְנוֹ יָצָא. רִבִּי יוֹסֵי אוֹמֵר לֹא יָצָא. אָמַר רַב מַתָּנָה דְּרִבִּי יוֹסֵי הִיא. אָמַר רִבִּי יוֹסֵי הֲוִינָן סָבְרִין מֵימַר מַה פְּלִיגִין רִבִּי יוֹסֵי וְרַבָּנִין בִּשְׁמַע דִּכְתִיב בָּהּ שְׁמַע. הָא שְׁאָר כָּל־הַמִּצְוֹות לֹא. מִן מַה דְּאָמַר רַב מַתָּנָה דְּרִבִּי יוֹסֵי הָדָא אָמְרָה הִיא שְׁמַע הִיא שְׁאָר מִצְוֹות שֶׁבַּתּוֹרָה. מַה טַעֲמָא דְּרִבִּי יוֹסֵי. וְהַאֲזַנְתָּ לְמִצְוֹתָיו וְשָׁמַרְתָּ כָּל־חוּקָּיו. שְׁמַע לְאָזְנֶיךָ מַה שֶׁפִּיךָ מְדַבֵּר.

[91]Who needs this? Rebbi Yose! Which [statement of] Rebbi Yose? What we had stated there: "He who did read the *Shema*ʿ and did not make his ear hear did fulfill his obligation." For whom do we need that? For Rebbi Yose! For which statement of Rebbi Yose? For that which we

have stated: "He who recites the *Shema'* and does not make his ear hear has fulfilled his obligation, Rebbi Yose says that he has not fulfilled his obligation." Rav Mattanah said: That formulation is Rebbi Yose's. Rebbi Yose[91] said: We could be of the opinion that the rabbis and Rebbi Yose disagree only about *Shema'* since there it is written: "hear!", but not about any other obligations. Since Rav Mattanah said "that formulation is Rebbi Yose's", it is the same for all commandments of the Torah. What is the reason of Rebbi Yose? (*Ex.* 15:26) "Bend your ear to His commandments and keep all His basic laws"; your ears should hear what your mouth says.

90 This and the next paragraphs appear also in *Berakhot* 2:4, Notes 159-161.

91 The Amora.

אָמַר רַב חִסְדָּא לֵית כַּאן חֵרֵשׁ. אַשְׁגָּרַת לָשׁוֹן. הֵי מַתְנִיתָא. אָמַר רִבִּי יוֹסֵי מִסְתַּבְּרָא יוֹדֵי רַב חִסְדָּא בִּתְרוּמוֹת דְּהִיא דְרִבִּי יוֹסֵי. אָמַר רִבִּי יוֹסֵי[92] בֵּי רִבִּי בּוּן עַל כּוֹרְחָךְ אִיתְמַר דְּהִיא דְרִבִּי יוֹסֵי דְתַנִּינָן חֲמִישְׁתֵּי קַדְמִיָּתָא וְלֹא תַנִּינָתָא עִמְּהוֹן. וְאִין מִשּׁוּם שֶׁאֵין תְּרוּמָתוֹ תְרוּמָה. וְהָא תַנִּינָן חֲמִישְׁתֵּי אַחֲרָיָיתָא וְלֹא תַנִּינָתָהּ עִמְּהוֹן. הֲרֵי סוֹפָךְ מֵימַר דְּרִבִּי יוֹסֵי הִיא.

Rav Ḥisda said: The deaf-mute person is not mentioned; it is a formula. In which Mishnah? Rebbi Yose said: It is reasonable to think that Rav Ḥisda concedes that the statement from *Terumot* is from Rebbi Yose. Rebbi Yose bar Rebbi Abun said: It must be said that that one is Rebbi Yose's since we have stated the first five cases and did not include it[93], because their *terumah* is not *terumah*. Then we have stated the five later ones and did not include it. So in the end you must say, that one is by Rebbi Yose.

92 The name is missing here; it has been supplied from the parallel in *Berakhot*.

93 The case of the deaf person who is able to speak is not included in Mishnah 1, detailing those whose heave is invalid, nor in Mishnah 6 in the list of people who should not give heave but whose heave is heave. Cf. *Berakhot*, Chapter 2, Notes 162-166.

תַּמָּן תַּנִּינָן הַכֹּל חַייָבִין בִּרְאִייָה חוּץ מֵחֵרֵשׁ שׁוֹטֶה וְקָטָן. חֲבֵרַייָא בְשֵׁם רִבִּי לָעְזָר לְמַעַן יִשְׁמְעוּן וּלְמַעַן יִלְמְדוּן. עַד כְּדוֹן מְדַבֵּר וְאֵינוֹ שׁוֹמֵעַ וְאֵינוֹ מְדַבֵּר. רִבִּי הִילָא בְשֵׁם רִבִּי לָעְזָר לְמַעַן יִלְמְדוּן וּלְמַעַן יְלַמֵּדוּן. אָמַר רִבִּי יוֹנָה הָדָא אָמְרָה דְּלֵית כְּלָלוֹי דְּרִבִּי כְּלָלִין דְּתַנִּינָן חֵרֵשׁ הַמְדַבֵּר וְאֵינוֹ שׁוֹמֵעַ לֹא יִתְרוֹם וְסָבְרִינָן מֵימַר שׁוֹמֵעַ וְאֵינוֹ מְדַבֵּר חֵרֵשׁ. מְדַבֵּר וְאֵינוֹ שׁוֹמֵעַ אֵינוֹ[94] חֵרֵשׁ. הָתַנִּינָן חֵרֵשׁ שֶׁנֶּחֱלַץ[95] וְהַחֵרֶשֶׁת שֶׁחָלְצָה וְהַחוֹלֶצֶת לְקָטָן חֲלִיצָתָהּ פְּסוּלָה. וְאָמַר רִבִּי יוֹחָנָן בְּשֶׁאֵינָן יְכוֹלִין לוֹמַר וְאָמַר וְאָמְרָה וְתַנִּינָן חֵרֵשׁ שֶׁדִּבְּרוּ חֲכָמִים בְּכָל־מָקוֹם שֶׁאֵינוֹ לֹא שׁוֹמֵעַ וְלֹא מְדַבֵּר. הָדָא מְסַייְעָא לְרִבִּי יוֹנָה דְּרִבִּי יוֹנָה אָמַר הָדָא אָמְרָה דְּלֵית כְּלָלוֹי דְּרִבִּי כְּלָלִין.

There[96], we have stated: "Everybody is obligated for appearance except the deaf-mute, the insane, and the minor." The colleagues in the name of Rebbi Eleazar (*Deut*. 31:12): "So they should hear and learn[97]." So far one who speaks but cannot hear; what about one who hears but cannot speak[98]? Rebbi La in the name of Rebbi Eleazar (*Deut*. 31:12): "So they should learn," so they should teach[99]. Rebbi Jonah said, this means that the principles of Rebbi are no principles[100], since we have stated: "A *ḥereš* who speaks but cannot hear should not give heave," and we thought that one who hears but does not speak is *ḥereš*, one who speaks but does not hear is not[94] *ḥereš*[101]. But we have stated[102]: "The *ḥereš* whose shoe was taken off, the female *ḥereš* who took off the shoe, and she who takes off the shoe of a minor, all performed invalid ceremonies." And Rebbi Joḥanan said, because they cannot say (*Deut*. 25:8): "he shall say", (*Deut*.

25:7,9) "she shall say.[103]" We also have stated: "A "deaf person" mentioned anywhere by the Sages is a deaf-mute[104]." This supports Rebbi Jonah, for Rebbi Jonah said, this means that the principles of Rebbi are no principles.

94 Reading of the parallel in *Ḥagigah* 1:1 (fol. 75d).

95 Reading of Mishnah *Yebamot* 12:5, the Rome ms., and the parallels in *Ḥagigah* and *Yebamot* 12:5 (fol. 12d). Leyden and Venice: חלץ.

96 Mishnah *Ḥagigah* 1:1. The "appearance" is the assembly of all of Israel at the feast of Tabernacles during the Sabbatical year (*Deut.* 31:10-13); one derives from this the rules of appearance at all festivals of pilgrimage.

97 The spelling is not masoretical.

98 He should be obligated.

99 The first conjugation verb could also be vocalized as a causative. The same argument is given in the Babli (*Ḥagigah* 3a) where it is noted that the second clause, "and learn", would be superfluous if one excluded only the deaf but not the mute.

100 In the language of the Babli: One does not make inferences from general principles, even when the exceptions are enumerated.

101 Since he is not mentioned in the Mishnah.

102 Mishnah *Yebamot* 12:5, speaking of the ceremony of *ḥaliẓah*, the taking off of one shoe, which frees the widow of a childless man from having to marry her brother-in-law (*Deut.* 25:4-10). The formalized statements by widow and brother-in-law before the court as described in the verses are an integral part of the proceedings.

103 Hence, the person who is deaf but not mute can perform a valid procedure. This is also the position of the Babli, *Yebamot* 104b.

104 This contradicts the formulation of the Mishnah in *Yebamot*.

(fol. 40a) **משנה ג**: קָטָן שֶׁלֹּא הֵבִיא שְׁתֵּי שְׂעָרוֹת. רִבִּי יְהוּדָה אוֹמֵר תְּרוּמָתוֹ תְרוּמָה. רִבִּי יוֹסֵי אוֹמֵר אִם עַד שֶׁלֹּא בָּא לְעוֹנַת נְדָרִים אֵין תְּרוּמָתוֹ תְרוּמָה. וּמִשֶּׁבָּא לְעוֹנַת נְדָרִים תְּרוּמָתוֹ תְרוּמָה.

Mishnah 3: Rebbi Jehudah says, the heave given by a minor who has not yet grown two pubic hairs is heave. Rebbi Yose says, before he came to the time of vows[105], his heave is not heave. After he has reached the time of vows, his heave is heave.

105 Mishnah *Niddah* 5:6: "The vows of a girl 11 years and one day of age are investigated (one inquires whether she understands the notion and severity of vows; if she does, her vows are valid.) If she is 12 years and one day old, her vows are *prima facie* valid but one investigates them during all of her thirteenth year. The vows of a boy 12 years and one day old are investigated; if he is 13 years and one day old, his vows are *prima facie* valid but one investigates them during all of his fourteenth year. Before that time, even if they say we know before Whom we made the vow and to Whom we dedicated a sacrifice, their vows are not vows and their dedications not dedications." According to Rashi, "the time of vows" is when the vows are investigated; according to Maimonides [in his Code (*Nedarim* 11:3) and in the first and third versions of his Mishnah Commentary] it is the time when all vows are automatically valid. {Rashi's opinion and the similar one of Maimonides in the second version of his Commentary are the only ones compatible with the Yerushalmi; Maimonides's other opinion can be justified by the Babli, *Niddah* 46b-47a.}

(fol. 40c) **הלכה ג**: תַּנֵּי בְשֵׁם רִבִּי מֵאִיר לְעוֹלָם אֵין תְּרוּמָתוֹ תְרוּמָה עַד שֶׁיָּבִיא שְׁתֵּי שְׂעָרוֹת. רִבִּי אַבָּא בַּר כַּהֲנָא בְּשֵׁם רַבָּנִין וְנֶחְשַׁב לָכֶם תְּרוּמַתְכֶם אֶת שֶׁכָּתוּב בּוֹ מַחֲשָׁבָה תּוֹרֵם. וְאֶת שֶׁאֵין כָּתוּב בּוֹ מַחֲשָׁבָה אֵינוֹ תוֹרֵם. הָתִיבוֹן הֲרֵי גוֹי שֶׁאֵין כָּתוּב בּוֹ מַחֲשָׁבָה וְתוֹרֵם. רִבִּי יוּדָה בְּשֵׁם רִבִּי הִילָא וְלֹא תִשְׂאוּ עָלָיו חֵטְא אֶת שֶׁהוּא בִנְשִׂיאַת עָוֹן תּוֹרֵם וְאֶת שֶׁאֵינוֹ בִנְשִׂיאַת עָוֹן אֵינוֹ תוֹרֵם. הָתִיבוֹן הֲרֵי גוֹי אֵינוֹ בִנְשִׂיאַת עָוֹן וְתוֹרֵם. וְתַנֵּי רִבִּי הוֹשַׁעְיָה גוֹיִם אֵין לָהֶן מַחֲשָׁבָה. תַּמָּן לְהַכְשִׁיר וְכָאן לִתְרוּמָה.

Halakhah 3: [106]It was stated in the name of Rebbi Meïr: His heave is never heave unless he grew two pubic hairs[107]. Rebbi Abba bar Cahana in the name of the rabbis (*Num*. 18:27): "Your heave will be credited to you.[10]" Anybody for whom "thought" is written may give heave. But anybody for whom "thought" is not written cannot give heave. They objected: But "thought" is not written for a Gentile, and he may give heave[108]! Rebbi Jehudah[109] in the name of Rebbi La (*Num*. 18:32): "You should not carry guilt because of it.[110]" He who may carry guilt can give heave, he who cannot carry guilt cannot give heave. They objected: But a Gentile cannot incur guilt[111], and he may give heave! And did not Rebbi Hoshaia state that Gentiles have no "thought"? That is for preparation, here we talk about heave[112].

106 This and the next paragraph are also in *Yebamot* 13:2 (fol. 13 c/d).

107 As a sign of puberty. Growing pubic hair is the accepted standard of the onset of puberty, the end of childhood, and the start of responsibility to keep all religious obligations (*Bar Mizwah*). In all matters of biblical commandments, this standard cannot be relaxed.

108 Since a Gentile is not bound by the laws of the Torah (except for the commandments given to Noah), no verse requiring intent can apply to a Gentile. On the other hand, Mishnah 3:9 states that voluntary heave given by a Gentile is heave and subject to all its laws and requirements.

109 He is Rebbi Yudan.

110 The verse refers to the heave of the tithe. The Levites will be free of guilt if they give heave of the tithe before eating their part of the tithe. The rule established here is then also transferred to the Great Heave.

111 His heave is purely voluntary; even if he gives heave but mishandles it, he will not incur guilt. This shows that the second argument cannot be true; in this respect, the laws of the Great Heave cannot be derived from those of the heave of the tithe since no Gentile possibly can give heave of the tithe. One is stuck with the first

explanation.

112 Since a Gentile cannot become impure in biblical law, he cannot make anything impure in biblical law, and his intentions are irrelevant and inactive in preparing food for impurity, cf. Notes 7,9. But since heave must be declared, we must hold that the Gentile may validly declare some of his produce to be heave. This proves that the first objection is invalid: Even though the intentions of the Gentile are never required by biblical law, his voluntary intentions are accepted for heave.

רִבִּי אָחָא רִבִּי חִינְנָא בְשֵׁם רַב כַּהֲנָא כְּדִבְרֵי מִי שֶׁהוּא אוֹמֵר אֵינוֹ תוֹרֵם אֵינוֹ מַקְדִּישׁ. וְלָמָּה לֹא אָמַר כְּדִבְרֵי מִי שֶׁהוּא אוֹמֵר תּוֹרֵם מַקְדִּישׁ. בְּגִין דְּרִבִּי יוּדָה דְּרִבִּי יוּדָה אוֹמֵר תּוֹרֵם וְאֵינוֹ מַקְדִּישׁ. וְרִבִּי יוֹחָנָן אָמַר אֲפִילוּ כְּמַה דָּמַר אֵינוֹ תוֹרֵם מַקְדִּישׁ וּמָהוּ מַקְדִּישׁ עוֹלָה וּשְׁלָמִים. לְהָבִיא חַטָּאת חֵלֶב אֵינוֹ יָכוֹל שֶׁאֵין לוֹ חַטָּאת[113] חֵלֶב. חַטָּאת דָּם אֵינוֹ יָכוֹל שֶׁאֵין לוֹ חַטָּאת דָּם. מָהוּא שֶׁיָּבִיא קָרְבַּן זִיבָה וְקָרְבַּן צָרַעַת מֵאַחַר שֶׁהוּא חוֹבָה אֵינוֹ מֵבִיא אוֹ מֵאַחַר שֶׁהוּא מְטַמֵּא בָּהֶן מֵבִיא. פְּשִׁיטָא לָךְ שֶׁהוּא מֵבִיא. מָהוּ שֶׁיֵּעָשֶׂה בָּהֶן שָׁלִיחַ. מֵאַחַר שֶׁהוּא מְטַמֵּא בָּהֶן הוּא נַעֲשֶׂה בָּהֶן שָׁלִיחַ אוֹ מֵאַחַר שֶׁאֵינוֹ נַעֲשֶׂה שָׁלִיחַ לְכָל־הַדְּבָרִים אֵינוֹ נַעֲשֶׂה בָּהֶן שָׁלִיחַ. הָתִיב רִבִּי יוּדָן הֲרֵי יֵשׁ לוֹ טֶבֶל דְּבַר תּוֹרָה אֵינוֹ פוֹטֵר טִבְלוֹ דְּבַר תּוֹרָה. וְכָאן אַף עַל פִּי שֶׁהוּא מְטַמֵּא בָּהֶן אֵינוֹ נַעֲשֶׂה שָׁלִיחַ. מָהוּ שֶׁיָּבִיא בִּיכּוּרִים כְּרִבִּי יוּדָה דּוּ אָמַר הוּקְשׁוּ לְקָדְשֵׁי הַגְּבוּל אֵינוֹ מֵבִיא כְּרַבָּנִין דּוּ אָמְרִין הוּקְשׁוּ לְקָדְשֵׁי מִקְדָּשׁ מֵבִיא. מָהוּ שֶׁיָּבִיא חֲגִיגָה מֵאַחַר שֶׁהוּא חוֹבָה אֵינוֹ מֵבִיא אוֹ מֵאַחַר שֶׁהוּא מְשַׁנֵּיהוּ לְשֵׁם שְׁלָמִים מֵבִיא. מַהוּ לְהָבִיא פֶּסַח. מֵאַחַר שֶׁהוּא חוֹבָה לֹא יָבִיא אוֹ מֵאַחַר דְּאָמַר רִבִּי שִׁמְעוֹן בֶּן לָקִישׁ בְּשֵׁם רִבִּי יוּדָן נְשִׂיָּא מֵבִיא אָדָם פֶּסַח בִּשְׁאָר יְמוֹת הַשָּׁנָה וּמְשַׁנֵּהוּ לְשֵׁם שְׁלָמִים מֵבִיא. מָהוּ שֶׁיָּבִיא מַעֲשֵׂר בְּהֵמָה וְאִין יִסְבּוֹר רִבִּי מֵאִיר מִכֹּל מַעְשְׂרוֹתֵיכֶם הוּקְשׁוּ מַעְשְׂרוֹת זֶה לָזֶה כְּשֵׁם שֶׁאֵינוֹ[114] מֵבִיא מַעֲשֵׂר דָּגָן כָּךְ אֵינוֹ[114] מֵבִיא מַעֲשֵׂר בְּהֵמָה. מָהוּ לַעֲשׂוֹת תְּמוּרָה אִין סָבַר רִבִּי מֵאִיר הוּקְשׁוּ כָּל־הַמַּעְשְׂרוֹת זֶה לָזֶה כְּשֵׁם שֶׁאֵינוֹ[114] מֵבִיא מַעֲשֵׂר דָּגָן כָּךְ אֵינוֹ[114] מֵבִיא מַעֲשֵׂר בְּהֵמָה. כָּךְ אֵינוֹ[114] מֵבִיא מַעֲשֵׂר בְּהֵמָה. כָּךְ אֵינוֹ עוֹשֶׂה תְמוּרָה. וְיִסְבּוֹר כְּרִבִּי

שִׁמְעוֹן דְּרִבִּי שִׁמְעוֹן אָמַר מַעֲשֵׂר בְּהֵמָה לָמֵד עַל כָּל־הַקֳּדָשִׁים לִתְמוּרָה. כְּשֵׁם שֶׁאֵינוֹ[114] מֵבִיא מַעֲשֵׂר דָּגָן כָּךְ אֵינוֹ[114] מֵבִיא מַעֲשֵׂר בְּהֵמָה. כְּשֵׁם שֶׁאֵינוֹ[114] מֵבִיא מַעֲשֵׂר בְּהֵמָה. כָּךְ אֵינוֹ עוֹשֶׂה תְמוּרָה. כְּשֵׁם שֶׁאֵין מֵמִיר בּוֹ כָּךְ אֵינוֹ מֵמִר בְּכָל־הַקֳּדָשִׁים. מָה הוּא שֶׁיְּהוּא חַיָּיבִין עַל קֳדָשָׁיו מִבְּחוּץ כַּהֲנָא אָמַר אֵין חַיָּיבִין עַל קֳדָשָׁיו מִבְּחוּץ. רִבִּי יוֹחָנָן וְרִבִּי שִׁמְעוֹן בֶּן לָקִישׁ אָמַר חַיָּיבִין. וְהָדָא (fol. 40d) דְכַהֲנָא פְלִיגָא. דְּרִבִּי יְהוּדָה פּוֹטֵר טִבְלוֹ דְּבַר תּוֹרָה. וְתֵימַר אָכֵן כְּמָאן דְּאָמַר מֵאֵילֵיהֶן קִבְּלוּ עֲלֵיהֶן אֶת הַמַּעְשְׂרוֹת.

Rebbi Aḥa, Rebbi Ḥinena in the name of Rav Cahana: Following the opinion that someone who cannot give heave cannot dedicate to the Temple[115]. Why did he not say: following the opinion that he can give heave, he can dedicate to the Temple? Because of Rebbi Jehudah, for Rebbi Jehudah says he can give heave but cannot dedicate[116]. But Rebbi Joḥanan says, even following the opinion that he cannot give heave, he can dedicate[117]. What can he dedicate? Holocaust and well-being offerings[118]. He cannot bring a sin sacrifice for fat because he is not obligated to a sin sacrifice for fat. He cannot bring a sin sacrifice for blood because he is not obligated to a sin sacrifice for blood[119]. May he bring a sacrifice relating to gonorrhea and skin disease[120]? Since it is obligatory can't he bring it[121], or since he becomes impure by these can he bring it[122]? If it is obvious for you that he brings, can he become an agent for these[123]? Since he may become impure by these, may he become an agent, or since he cannot become an agent for anything else, can't he become an agent for these? Rebbi Yudan objected: His produce is *ṭevel* from the Torah but he cannot free his *ṭevel* by Torah law[124]! So here, even though he may become impure by them, he cannot become an agent. May he bring First Fruits following Rebbi Jehudah who says that

First Fruits have the status of territorial consecrated things[125]? He may not bring following the rabbis who say they have the status of things consecrated to the Temple. May he bring a sacrifice of pilgrimage[126]? Since it is obligatory can't he bring it, or since he may change its name to well-being offering, may he bring it? May he bring a Passover sacrifice? Since it is obligatory can't he bring it, or since Rebbi Simeon ben Laqish said in the name of Rebbi Yudan the Prince, a person may bring a Passover sacrifice any day of the year when he changes its name to well-being offering[127], may he bring it? May he bring tithes of animals[128]? If Rebbi Meïr is of the opinion (*Num.* 18:28): "From all your tithes," that all tithes were bracketed together[129], then since he cannot bring tithes of grain he cannot bring tithes of animals. May he make substitutions[130]? If Rebbi Meïr is of the opinion that all tithes were bracketed together, then since he cannot bring tithes of grain he cannot bring tithes of animals; since he cannot bring tithes of animals he cannot make substitutions[131]. One may hold with Rebbi Simeon, since Rebbi Simeon says that tithes of animals teach you for all sacrifices about substitutions. That means, since he cannot bring tithes of grain he cannot bring tithes of animals; since he cannot bring tithes of animals he cannot make substitutions; since he cannot make substitutions for these he cannot make substitutions for any sacrifices. Is one guilty sacrificing for him outside the Temple[132]? Cahana said, one cannot be guilty sacrificing for him outside the Temple. Rebbi Joḥanan and Rebbi Simeon ben Laqish say, one is guilty[133]. The statement of Cahana disagrees since Rebbi Jehudah frees his *ṭevel* as biblical law[134]. We can say he [Cahana] is following him who says they accepted tithes voluntarily[135].

113 Text of the parallel in *Yebamot*. The Leyden text has here an inserted word: חטאת אינו חלב.

114 Text of the parallel in *Yebamot*, word missing here but required by the text on substitutions.

115 The entire paragraph deals with the minor who is able to give heave but has not yet grown two pubic hairs, for R. Yose if he is able to make vows and for R. Jehudah even if he is younger.

116 The statement regarding heave is in the Mishnah. The statement about sacrifices must have been in a *baraita* not otherwise transmitted. Since a voluntary sacrifice must be dedicated by a vow, even R. Jehudah must agree that a minor who may not make a vow cannot dedicate a sacrifice.

117 In contrast to heave, where the exclusion of minors is based on a verse mentioning "every man" (cf. Note 3), sacrifices are attributed to "a human" (*Lev*. 1:2), including a minor.

118 These are voluntary offerings that also may be brought by Gentiles. Therefore, persons not under the obligations of biblical commandments may dedicate these sacrifices. {The use of the translation "well-being offering" for שלמים does not imply that this is the correct meaning of the word.}

119 Since a minor is not obligated under the law, he cannot sin and, therefore, can never bring a sin offering. It is forbidden to eat the blood of any animal (*Lev*. 17:10-14); transgression of the prohibition is a sin which heaven will punish with extermination if intentional but which, if committed unintentionally, may be atoned for by a sin sacrifice (or, even if intentional, by repentance and the Day of Atonement). "Sacrifice for blood" is a catchword for "sacrifice to atone for a sin punishable by extermination." It is also forbidden to eat those lumps of fat of cattle, sheep, or goats which would be burned on the altar if the animal were a sacrifice (*Lev*. 7:23). Punishment for this offense, if documented by two witnesses, is whipping. Therefore, "sacrifice for fat" is a catchword for "sacrifice to atone for an unintentional simple sin."

120 These are obligatory sacrifices of purification when the condition is healed, *Lev*. 15:14-15, 14:1-32. Without these sacrifices, the afflicted person cannot touch any dedicated food.

121 A minor cannot be obligated for anything. Since the courtyard of the Temple is reserved for sacrifices, it is forbidden to bring profane animals into it. Therefore, the priests should be

required to refuse entry to such a sacrifice when brought by a minor.

122 If he has parents, the parents will bring the sacrifice for him to make sure the entire family can partake of the family offerings. Here we speak about a minor who is an orphan.

123 To present somebody else's sacrifice for the purification of that person.

124 If the orphan minor owns agricultural land, the harvest before taking heave will become *ṭevel* (cf. *Peah*, Chapter 1, Note 303) and be forbidden for consumption. The prohibition is removed by giving heave. R. Meïr, quoted above, will prevent the minor from putting his own *ṭevel* in order himself.

125 First Fruits are an obligation of the farmer (*Deut.* 26:1-11). In Mishnah *Bikkurim* 2:1 it is stated that First Fruits must be eaten by Cohanim under the rules of heave. In Mishnah 3:10, R. Jehudah states that after presentation in the Temple, First Fruits may be given to any Cohen but the rabbis require that they be eaten by the priests serving in the Temple at the moment of presentation. This means that for R. Jehudah, the status of First Fruits is that of heave which may be eaten in the entire territory of the Holy Land (called "territorial consecrated things") but for the rabbis they are consecrated to the Temple.

126 A pilgrimage to the Temple at one of the festivals of pilgrimage carries with it the obligation of two sacrifices, the sacrifice of appearance, (ראיון, *Deut.* 16:16) which is a holocaust, and a family sacrifice, (חגיגה, *Deut.* 16:11,14; 12:18) which is a well-being offering.

127 If somebody selected an animal as Passover sacrifice but then it disappeared before the holiday and another animal was dedicated, if the originally dedicated animal reappears it is brought as a well-being offering any time after the holiday (Babli *Pesaḥim* 70b).

128 *Lev.* 27:32-33. Every tenth newborn in a herd of cattle or flock of sheep and goats has to be offered as a sacrifice. Tithes of produce are mentioned there in verses 30,31.

129 In *Sifry Deut.* 105, this is derived from another verse as anonymous statement.

130 In *Lev.* 27:10, it is stated that one may not substitute a different animal for an unblemished animal already designated as sacrifice. The act of substitution is not invalid but

sinful and causes both animals to become sacrifices. Since a minor cannot sin, it is questionable whether his act of substitution is valid.

131 The prohibition of substitution is repeated in *Lev.* 27:33, speaking of the tithe of animals. Since the tithe of animals is dedicated as sacrifice, the mention of the prohibition seems to be superfluous; it is taken to indicate that the rules of validity of tithes determine the rules of validity of substitutions.

132 It is sinful to sacrifice an animal outside of the Temple (*Deut.* 12:23). If the minor's dedication of an animal as sacrifice is valid in biblical law, it is sinful to slaughter the animal outside the Temple. But if the dedication is valid only by rabbinic practice, the animal becomes dedicated only by its acceptance by the priests in the Temple and slaughter outside the Temple is not sinful.

133 The disagreement is quoted, in slightly changed form, in Babli *Niddah* 46b. In contrast to the Yerushalmi, the Babli states that RR. Joḥanan and Simeon ben Laqish declare the slaughterer guilty only by rabbinic practice.

134 Since *ṭevel* comes into being by agricultural activity, not by the minor's choice, if R. Jehudah permits the minor to give heave, he lets him remove a biblical prohibition and, therefore, gives the minor's actions validity in biblical law.

135 R. Eleazar in *Ševi'it* 6:1 (Note 11). Since R. Eleazar is mentioned only if R. Joḥanan disagrees, R. Joḥanan here holds that heave today is a biblical commandment, following R. Yose ben Ḥanina [*loc. cit.* Note 8; *Seder Olam* Chapter 30, cf. in the author's edition (Northvale, N.J., 1998), pp. 257-259, x-xi.]

(fol. 40a) **משנה ד**: אֵין תּוֹרְמִין זֵיתִים עַל הַשֶּׁמֶן וְלֹא עֲנָבִים עַל הַיַּיִן וְאִם תָּֽרְמוּ בֵּית שַׁמַּאי אוֹמְרִים תְּרוּמַת עַצְמָן בָּהֶן. וּבֵית הִלֵּל אוֹמְרִים אֵין תְּרוּמָתוֹ תְּרוּמָה.

Mishnah 4: One may not give olives as heave for oil nor grapes for wine. If one did, the House of Shammai say they contain their own heave[136], but the House of Hillel say his heave is not heave.

136 Heave was given only for olives but not for oil. For the House of Hillel, both olives and oil remain *ṭevel*.

(fol. 40d) **הלכה ד**: תַּמָּן תַּנִּינָן אֵין תּוֹרְמִין מִדָּבָר שֶׁנִּגְמְרָה מְלַאכְתּוֹ עַל דָּבָר שֶׁלֹּא נִגְמְרָה מְלַאכְתּוֹ וְכָא אַתְּ אָמַר הָכֵין. רִבִּי אִילָא בְשֵׁם רִבִּי יוֹחָנָן מִפְּנֵי גֶזֶל הַשֵּׁבֶט. מָהוּ מִפְּנֵי גֶזֶל הַשֵּׁבֶט. אָמַר רִבִּי חֲנַנְיָה מִפְּנֵי הַטּוֹרַח. הַגַּע אַצְמָךְ שֶׁהָיְתָה שְׂעוֹרָה שֶׁל אוֹרֶז נַחַת רוּחַ הוּא לְאָדָם לִהְיוֹת כּוֹתֵשׁ כָּל־שֶׁהוּא. הַגַּע אַצְמָךְ שֶׁהָיְתָה שִׁבֳּלִים. עַד כָּאן קַשְׁיָן. רִבִּי חֲנִינָא רִבִּי מָנָא לֹא אָמַר כֵּן אֶלָּא שֶׁהוּא מְבַקֵּשׁ לִתְרוֹם לְפִי שֶׁמֶן וְאֵינוֹ תוֹרֵם אֶלָּא לְפִי זֵתִים. הַגַּע אַצְמָךְ שֶׁתָּרַם לְפִי שֶׁמֶן. כְּדוֹן עֲבַד כֵּן זְמַן חוֹרָן לָא עֲבַד כֵּן. וְלֹא עוֹד אֶלָּא דְחַבְרֵיהּ חָמֵי לֵיהּ וְאוֹמֵר זֶה מִתְכַּוֵין לְרַבּוֹת וַאֲנִי אֵינִי מִתְכַּוֵין לְרַבּוֹת.

Halakhah 4: There, we stated: "One does not give heave from finished for unfinished," and here you say so[136]? Rebbi Illa in the name of Rebbi Joḥanan: Because of robbing the tribe. What means, because of robbing the tribe? Rebbi Ḥanania said, because of the exertion[137]. Think about it, if there was a grain of rice[138]? People willingly will pound something. Think about it, if it were in ears? So far goes our question. Rebbi Ḥanina, Rebbi Mana did not say so but he wanted to give heave proportional to the oil and gave only proportional to olives[139]. Think about it, if he gave proportional to the oil? Now he did so, another time he will not do so[140]. In addition, his neighbor will see him and say, this one wants to give a lot but I do not want to give a lot.

136 Mishnah 1:10: "One does not give heave from finished produce for unfinished, nor from unfinished for finished . . . but if one gave heave, it is heave." Grapes and olives are unfinished produce, wine and oil are finished. Why does the House of Hillel say, there is no heave?

137 The Cohen must himself turn the olives into oil, the grapes into wine, but the verse says that heave is given as (*Num.* 18:27) "grain from the threshing floor and complete produce from the (oil or wine) press."

138 This speaks about grain (mentioned in the verse but not in the Mishnah). One does not give heave from finished produce for unfinished; the rice kernel will not be peeled by threshing the wheat. Hence, even if grain is given as heave after threshing, the Cohen might have some additional work to do. The same argument applies to the next question. Since grain is mentioned, Maimonides (*Terumot* 5:18) decides that cut grain cannot be given as heave for threshed grain. The parallel in *Sifry* (*Num.* 121) mentions only grain and wine.

139 The decree of the House of Hillel is not biblical, not based on the verse, but rabbinic. While heave has no fixed percentage in biblical law, there are rabbinic guidelines on how much to give (Mishnah 4:3). Since olive oil is so much more valuable than raw olives, if the grower gives the required volume of oil as volume of olives, he will have given too little.

140 We have to explain the reason of the Mishnah to the uneducated; therefore, the explanation is in Aramaic.

חִזְקִיָּה אָמַר לֹא אָמְרוּ אֶלָּא זֵיתִים עַל הַשֶּׁמֶן וַעֲנָבִים עַל הַיַּיִן הָא שְׁאָר כָּל־הַדְּבָרִים לֹא. אָמַר רִבִּי יוֹחָנָן לֹא שְׁנִייָא הִיא אֶלָּא זֵיתִים עַל הַשֶּׁמֶן וַעֲנָבִים עַל הַיַּיִן הָא שְׁאָר כָּל־הַדְּבָרִים. חֲבֵרַיָּא בְּשֵׁם רִבִּי יוֹחָנָן וַאֲפִילוּ עַל אָתָר.[141]

Ḥizqiah said, they mentioned only olives for oil and grapes for wine, hence not for any other produce. Rebbi Joḥanan said, not only olives for oil and grapes for wine but also any other produce[142]. The colleagues in the name of Rebbi Joḥanan: Even immediately[143].

141 Reading of Venice text and Rome ms. Leyden: אחד.

142 Ḥizqiah cannot mean that only oil and wine are covered by Mishnah 4, everything else by Mishnah 10, since grain was added to the list both by the Yerushalmi and the *Sifry*. Therefore, one must conclude that here starts the discussion of the condition under which the House of Shammai accepts that at least the fruits themselves have been tithed. According to R. Joḥanan, any produce undergoing a manufacturing process, such as date honey and date beer from dates, is covered by Mishnah 4 for the House of Shammay (explanation of R. J. I. Kanievski).

143 Even if the producer would immediately start converting the olives or grapes into oil and wine and hand the Cohen the finished product, it still is no heave for the House of Hillel (Explanation of R. H. Kanievski).

רִבִּי חֲנַנְיָא רִבִּי אִימִּי בְּשֵׁם רִבִּי יוֹחָנָן דִּבְרֵי בֵית שַׁמַּאי נַעֲשָׂה כְּאוֹמֵר הֲרֵי זֶה תְּרוּמָה עָלֶיהָ וְעַל שֶׁלְּמַטָּן. רִבִּי חֲנַנְיָא סָבַר מֵימַר בְּמִינוֹ. אָמַר לֵיהּ רִבִּי זְעִירָא לֹא תְקַבֵּל עָלֶיךָ כֵן. מִכֵּיוָן שֶׁאָמַר הֲרֵי זוֹ נִפְטַר מַה שֶׁבְּיָדוֹ וְהַשְּׁאָר חוּלִין וְחוּלִין פּוֹטְרִין אֶת הַטֶּבֶל. אָמַר רִבִּי חֲנַנְיָה בְּרֵיהּ דְּרִבִּי הִלֵּל כְּאַחַת מִכֵּיוָן שֶׁאָמַר הֲרֵי זוֹ נִפְטַר מַה שֶׁבְּיָדוֹ וְנִפְטַר מַה שֶׁלְּמַטָּן. אָמַר רִבִּי חֲנִינָה נִרְאִין הַדְּבָרִים בִּתְרוּמָה גְדוֹלָה שֶׁהִיא צְרִיכָה לִתְרוֹם מִן הַמּוּקָף. אֲבָל בִּתְרוּמַת מַעֲשֵׂר צְרִיכָה שֶׁתְּהֵא מְצוּמְצֶמֶת בְּמִידָּה בְּמִשְׁקָל וּבְמִנְיָן.

Rebbi Ḥananiah, Rebbi Immi in the name of Rebbi Joḥanan: The argument of the House of Shammai is that he is like one who says: This shall be heave for itself and what is below it[144]. Rebbi Ḥananiah wanted to say, of its own kind[145]. Rebbi Zeïra said to him, do not accept that. When he said "this shall be[146]", what is in his hand was freed and the rest becomes profane, may profane free *ṭevel*? Rebbi Ḥananiah the son of Rebbi Hillel[147] said, it is simultaneous. When he said "this shall be", what is in his hand was freed together with the rest. Rebbi Ḥanina said, that is convincing for the Great Heave where one must give heave from what is earmarked[148]. But heave of the tithe must be defined by measure, weight, or count.

144 Since the House of Shammai accept that heave given for olives and oil is heave for the olives, they must accept that if one gives heave for two physically separate batches of olives, it must be valid.

145 The argument is valid for one kind, for example olives. But if somebody has olives and grapes, he cannot give heave simultaneously for two batches of each.

146 He really has to say: "This shall be heave." At that moment, the batch from which he took the olives becomes freed from the obligation of heave and the next Mishnah will state that heave may be given only from *ṭevel*, not from profane produce.

147 A fifth generation Galilean Amora, quoted only in the Yerushalmi.

148 Mishnah *Ḥallah* 1:9. Since heave is given by estimate, it must be given from a well-defined lot. But heave of the tithe is exactly ten percent; it may be given anywhere if the volume, weight, or number of the produce to be tithed has been determined beforehand.

תַּנִּינָן תַּמָּן אֵין תּוֹרְמִין מִן הַטָּמֵא עַל הַטָּהוֹר. תַּנֵּי בְּשֵׁם רִבִּי יוֹסֵי וְאִם תּוֹרֵם מִן הַטָּמֵא עַל הַטָּהוֹר בֵּין בְּשׁוֹגֵג בֵּין בְּמֵזִיד מַה שֶּׁעָשָׂה עָשׂוּי. מָה אָמַר רִבִּי יוֹסֵי הָכָא וּמָה אִין תַּמָּן שֶׁכּוּלּוֹ הֶפְסֵד לַכֹּהֲנִים אַתְּ אָמַר מַה שֶּׁעָשָׂה עָשׂוּי הָכָא דְּאֵין כּוּלּוֹ הֶפְסֵד לַכֹּהֲנִים לֹא כָּל־שֶׁכֵּן. אַשְׁכָּח תַּנֵּי בְּשֵׁם רִבִּי יוֹסֵי אֵין תּוֹרְמִין זֵיתִים עַל הַשֶּׁמֶן וְלֹא עֲנָבִים עַל הַיַּיִן וְאִם תָּרַם בֵּית שַׁמַּאי אוֹמְרִים תְּרוּמַת עַצְמָן בָּהֶן. וּבֵית הִלֵּל אוֹמְרִים אֵין תְּרוּמָתָן תְּרוּמָה. מְחְלְפָה דְּרִבִּי יוֹסֵי. תַּמָּן הוּא אוֹמֵר מַה שֶּׁעָשָׂה עָשׂוּי. וְכָא הוּא אָמַר אֵין תְּרוּמָתָן תְּרוּמָה. תַּמָּן טוּמְאָה אֵינָהּ מְצוּיָה וְאֵין בְּנֵי אָדָם טוֹעִין לוֹמַר שֶׁתּוֹרְמִין וּמְעַשְּׂרִין מִזֶּה עַל זֶה. אֲבָל זֵיתִים עַל הַשֶּׁמֶן וַעֲנָבִים עַל הַיַּיִן מְצוּיִין הֵן. וְאִם אָמַר כֵּן אַף הוּא סָבַר מֵימַר שֶׁמּוּתָּר לִתְרוֹם זֵיתִים עַל הַשֶּׁמֶן וַעֲנָבִים עַל הַיַּיִן.

There[149], we have stated: "One may not give heave from impure for pure produce." It was stated in the name of Rebbi Yose[150]: "If he gave heave from impure for pure produce, what he did is done." What does Rebbi Yose say here? If there, where all is lost for the Cohanim[151], he says that what he did is done, here, where not all is lost for the Cohanim[139], so much more? It was found stated in the name of Rebbi Yose: "One may not give olives as heave for oil or grapes for wine. If one did, the House of Shammai say it contains their own heave, but the House of Hillel say his heave is not heave." Rebbi Yose contradicts himself. There he says, what he did is done; here he says, his heave is not heave. There, impurity is infrequent[152] and people will not err to say that one may give heave from the impure on the pure produce. But olives for oil and grapes for wine is frequent; if you say so, one will say that one may give heave of olives for oil and grapes for wine.

149 Mishnah 2:2.

150 Tosephta 3:19.

151 Impure heave must be destroyed, except for impure olive oil which may be used as fuel.

152 For dry produce, even the produce of the vulgar will not be prepared for impurity. For wine and oil, the product in the hand of the vulgar is impure and the question does not arise; in the hand of the fellow it will be shielded from impurity (cf. *Demay*, Introduction).

(fol. 40a) **מִשְׁנָה ה**: אֵין תּוֹרְמִין מִן הַלֶּקֶט וּמִן הַשִּׁכְחָה וּמִן הַפֵּיאָה וּמִן הַהֶבְקֵר וְלֹא מִמַּעֲשֵׂר רִאשׁוֹן שֶׁנִּיטְּלָה תְרוּמָתוֹ וְלֹא מִמַּעֲשֵׂר שֵׁנִי וְהֶקְדֵּשׁ שֶׁנִּיפְדּוּ וְלֹא מִן הַחַיָּיב עַל הַפָּטוּר וְלֹא מִן הַפָּטוּר עַל הַחַיָּיב וְלֹא מִן הַתָּלוּשׁ עַל הַמְּחוּבָּר וְלֹא מִן הַמְּחוּבָּר עַל הַתָּלוּשׁ וְלֹא מִן הֶחָדָשׁ עַל הַיָּשָׁן וְלֹא מִן הַיָּשָׁן עַל הֶחָדָשׁ וְלֹא מִפֵּירוֹת הָאָרֶץ עַל פֵּירוֹת חוּצָה לָאָרֶץ וּמִפֵּירוֹת חוּצָה לָאָרֶץ עַל פֵּירוֹת הָאָרֶץ וְאִם תָּרְמוּ אֵין תְּרוּמָתָן תְּרוּמָה.

Mishnah 5: One may not give heave from gleanings, abandoned sheaves, *peah*, and ownerless property[153]; not from First Tithe of which its heave was taken[154]; not from Second Tithe and dedicated produce[155] which were redeemed; not from what is obligated on what is free from obligation or from what is free on what is obligated; not from harvested produce for what is standing[156] or from what is standing for what was harvested; not from new produce for old or from old for new[157]; not from produce of the Land for that of foreign countries[158] or from foreign countries for produce of the Land. If heave was given, it is not heave.

153 As explained in Tractate *Peah*, all these are exempt from heave and tithes. All examples of this Mishnah are amplifications of the statement that one may not give heave "from what is obligated on what is free from obligation, nor from what is free on what is obligated".

154 While First Tithe is normally taken from produce for which heave was already given, since it is under the obligation of heave of the tithe it still may be used to give the Great Heave as long as heave of the tithe was not given.

According to R. Simson, the Mishnah cannot speak of regular tithe which is totally profane after heave of the tithe is taken but must speak of First Tithe taken before threshing, when there was no obligation of Great Heave, and which is only under the obligation of heave of the tithe and becomes profane without Great Heave (*Ḥallah*, Halakhah 1:4).

Maimonides, in the later versions of his Commentary, reads שלא ניטלה. This text is also confirmed by the Kaufmann and Cambridge mss. of the Mishnah. Since the Halakhah does not discuss the text, the original reading cannot be ascertained.

155 Second tithe and Temple property have only restricted use; once they have been redeemed they are fully profane and free from obligation.

156 Standing produce is not under any obligation of heave.

157 Since it says (*Deut*. 14:22); "You should tithe both tithes of all produce of your land which grows *every year*," it follows that one may not give heave

and tithes from the produce of one year on that of another (*Sifry Deut.* 105).

158 Which are free from any obligation by biblical law.

(fol. 40d) **הלכה ה**: רִבִּי יוֹחָנָן בְּשֵׁם רִבִּי יַנַּאי זֶה אֶחָד מִשְּׁלֹשָׁה מִקְרִיּוֹת מְחוּוָרִין שֶׁבַּתּוֹרָה וּבָא הַלֵּוִי כִּי אֵין לוֹ חֵלֶק וְנַחֲלָה עִמָּךְ. מִמַּה שֶּׁיֵּשׁ לָךְ וְאֵין לוֹ אַתְּ חַיָּב לִיתֵּן לוֹ. יָצָא הֶבְקֵר שֶׁיָּדָךְ וְיָדוֹ שָׁוִין בּוֹ.

Halakhah 5: Rebbi Joḥanan in the name of Rebbi Yannai: This is one of three well-explained verses[159] in the Torah (*Deut.* 14:27): "The Levite shall come, for he has neither part nor inheritance with you." You must give him from what you have while he has not. This excludes ownerless property where your and his hands are equal.

159 The other two verses are *Num.* 18:12 (Halakhah 2:4) and *Deut.* 26:3 (Halakhah 8:1). The argument here is repeated in *Ma'serot* 1:1, *Ḥallah* 1:4, *Nedarim* 4:10. In *Sifry Deut.* 109, a similar statement is attributed to R. Eliezer ben Jacob.

הִיא לֶקֶט הִיא שִׁכְחָה הִיא פֵּיאָה הִיא הֶבְקֵר וְלֹא כְּבָר תַּנֵּיָית הֵן כּוּלְּהוֹן. כֵּן הִיא מַתְנִיתָא וְלֹא מִפֵּירוֹת שֶׁהֵבִיאוּ שְׁלִישׁ עַל פֵּירוֹת שֶׁלֹּא הֵבִיאוּ שְׁלִישׁ וְאִם תָּרַם אֵין[160] תְּרוּמָתוֹ תְּרוּמָה. עַל דַּעְתֵּיהּ דְּחִזְקִיָּה בְּמַחְלוֹקֶת. עַל דַּעְתֵּיהּ דְּרִבִּי יוֹחָנָן דִּבְרֵי הַכֹּל.

Gleanings, forgotten sheaves, *peah*, and ownerless property all have the same rule. Did one not already state everything[161]? Thus you have to understand the Mishnah: [One may] not [give] from produce one third ripe for produce not yet one third ripe, and when he gave heave, it is not heave. For Ḥizqiah it is a point of contention, for Rebbi Joḥanan it is everybody's opinion[162].

160 Reading of the Rome ms., missing in Leyden and Venice texts; cf. *Sefer Nir ad loc.*

161 In the Mishnah, only "from what is obligated on what is free from obligation but not from what is free on what is obligated" would be needed; everything else is just illustration. However, it has just been stated that the first part is necessary to show that "gleanings, forgotten sheaves, *peah*, and ownerless property all have the same rule". Similarly, one may make a point that the last case, concerning produce of the Land and of foreign countries, is necessary since if we hold that heaves now are only a rabbinical obligation, it is difficult to see what should be the difference between the heave of the Land and that of the surrounding countries where heave is rabbinical all the time. The only questionable part therefore remains that about standing and harvested produce which seems totally superfluous since nobody would ever think that standing produce was subject to heave. The answer is that "standing" does not really mean standing, but produce harvested at a time in its development when it is not yet human food and should have remained standing.

162 The disagreement of Ḥizqiah and R. Joḥanan above, Note 142. For one third grown, cf. *Ševi'it* Chapter 5, Notes 20-21, for the rules of gleanings etc., cf. *Kilaim* Chapter 6, Note 24.

(fol. 40a) **משנה ו**: חֲמִשָּׁה לֹא יִתְרוֹמוּ וְאִם תָּֽרְמוּ תְרוּמָתָן תְּרוּמָה. הָאִילֵּם וְהַשִּׁיכּוֹר וְהֶעָרוֹם וְהַסּוֹמֶה וּבַעַל קֶרִי לֹא יִתְרוֹמוּ וְאִם תָּֽרְמוּ תְרוּמָתָן תְּרוּמָה.

Mishnah 6: Five categories of persons should not give heave but if they gave, their heave is heave. The mute, the drunk, the naked person, the blind, and a man who had an emission of semen should not give heave but if they gave, their heave is heave.

(fol. 40d) **הלכה ו**: יֵשׁ מֵהֶן מִפְּנֵי בְרָכָה וְיֵשׁ מֵהֶן מִפְּנֵי שֶׁאֵין יְכוֹלִין לִתְרוֹם מִן הַמּוּבְחָר. הָאִילֵּם וְהֶעָרוֹם וּבַעַל קֶרִי מִפְּנֵי בְרָכָה הַסּוֹמֵא[163] וְהַשִּׁיכּוֹר שֶׁאֵין יְכוֹלִין לִתְרוֹם מִן הַמּוּבְחָר.

Halakhah 6: "Some of these [rules] are because of the benediction, some because the [persons] are unable to give from the best. The mute, the naked person[164], and the man who had an emission[165] because of the benediction, the blind and the drunk because they cannot give from the best."[166]

163 The Leyden and Venice texts add here והשוטה "and the insane", an intrusion from Mishnah 1 absent in the Rome ms.

164 He may not utter the Divine name, cf. *Berakhot* Chapter 3, Note 210.

165 Cf. *Berakhot* Halakhah 3:4 ff.

166 A much shortened version of Tosephta 3:1-2.

אַבָּא בַּר רַב הוּנָא אָמַר שָׁתוּי אַל יִתְפַּלֵּל וְאִם הִתְפַּלֵּל תְּפִילָּתוֹ תַּחֲנוּנִים. שִׁיכּוֹר אַל יִתְפַּלֵּל וְאִם הִתְפַּלֵּל תְּפִילָּתוֹ גִידּוּפִין. אֵי זֶהוּ שָׁתוּי כָּל־שֶׁשָּׁתָה רְבִיעִית שִׁיכּוֹר שֶׁשָּׁתָה יוֹתֵר. תַּמָּן אָמַר כָּל־שֶׁאֵינוֹ יָכוֹל לְדַבֵּר לִפְנֵי הַמֶּלֶךְ. רִבִּי זְעִירָא בְּעָא קוֹמֵי רִבִּי אִיסִּי שִׁיכּוֹר מָהוּ שֶׁיְּבָרֵךְ. אָמַר לֵיהּ וְאָכַלְתָּ וְשָׂבָעְתָּ וּבֵרַכְתָּ וַאֲפִילוּ מְדוּמְדָּם. לֹא צוֹרְכָא דְּלֹא מָהוּ שֶׁיִּקְרָא שְׁמַע אָמַר אַבָּא בַּר אָבִין חַד חָסִיד שָׁאַל לְאֵלִיָּה זָכוּר לַטּוֹב עָרוֹם מָהוּ שֶׁיִּקְרָא שְׁמַע. אָמַר לֵיהּ וְלֹא יֵרָאֶה בְךָ עֶרְוַת דָּבָר עֶרְוַת דִּיבּוּר. תַּנֵּי חִזְקִיָּה בֵּין לִקְרוֹת בֵּין לְבָרֵךְ.

Abba bar Rav Huna said, one who drank [wine] should not pray but if he did pray, his prayer is a supplication. A drunk should not pray but if he did pray, his prayer is blasphemy. What is one who drank [wine]? Someone who drank a *quartarius*[167]; a drunk is one who drank more. There[168], it is said if he cannot speak before a king. Rebbi Zeïra asked before Rebbi Assi: May a drunk recite Grace? He said to him (*Deut.*

11:15): "When you will eat and be satiated, then you must praise", even if you are sleepy. The question is only, may he recite the *Shema'*? Abba bar Avin[169] said, a pious person asked Elijah, may he be remembered for the good, may a naked person recite the *Shema'*? He said to him (*Deut.* 23:15): "He should not see in you a thing of turpitude," a word of turpitude. Ḥizqiah stated: both[170] for reciting [Grace] and reading [the *Shema'*].

167 A quarter of a *log*, cf. *Berakhot*, Chapter 3, Note 227. In the Rome ms: "Even if he drank less than a *quartarius*."

168 In Babylonia.

169 He might be identical with Rebbi Abba bar Avina, a Babylonian of the second generation who immigrated into Galilee and was ordained there.

170 The argument of Elijah applies in both cases.

(fol. 40a) **משנה ז**: אֵין תּוֹרְמִין לֹא בְמִידָּה וְלֹא בְמִשְׁקָל וְלֹא בְמִנְייָן אֲבָל תּוֹרֵם הוּא אֶת הַמָּדוּד וְאֶת הַשָּׁקוּל וְאֶת הַמָּנוּי. אֵין תּוֹרְמִין בְּסַל וּבְקוּפָּה שֶׁהֵן שֶׁל מִידָּה. אֲבָל תּוֹרֵם הוּא בָּהֶן חֶצְייָן אוֹ שְׁלִישָׁן. לֹא יִתְרוֹם בִּסְאָה חֶצְיָיהּ שֶׁחֶצְיָיהּ מִידָּה.

One gives heave neither by measure, nor by weight, nor by count[171]. But one may give heave from what was measured, weighed, or counted. One does not give heave in a measuring basket or box, but one may give in them a half or a third[172]. One should not give half a *seah of* heave[173] in a *seah* vessel because half of it is a [standard] measure.

171 Since no amount is specified for heave in biblical law (cf. *Peah* Chapter 1, Note 9), the verse requires only thought in specifying the heave. "To measure" means to determine the volume.

172 If no marks for $^1/_2$ or $^1/_3$ are on the measuring device.

173 Cf. *Berakhot* Chapter 3, Note 164. Half a *seah*, three *qab*, is a commercial measure (as dry measure *tarqab*, as fluid measure *hin*). Its size can be estimated in a *seah* vessel.

(fol. 40d) **הלכה ז**: תַּמָּן תַּנִּינָן הַמּוֹנֶה מְשׁוּבָּח וְהַמּוֹדֵד מְשׁוּבָּח הֵימֶנּוּ וְהַשּׁוֹקֵל מְשׁוּבָּח מִשְּׁלָשְׁתָּן. וְכָא אַתְּ אָמַר כֵּן. אָמַר רִבִּי יְהוֹשֻׁעַ בֶּן לֵוִי כָּאן בִּתְרוּמָה גְדוֹלָה כָּאן בִּתְרוּמַת מַעֲשֵׂר. וְתַנֵּי כֵן אֱלִיעֶזֶר בֶּן גִּימֶל אוֹמֵר מְנַיִין שֶׁאֵין תּוֹרְמִין לֹא בְמִידָּה וְלֹא בְמִשְׁקָל וְלֹא בְמִנְייָן תַּלְמוּד לוֹמַר וְנֶחְשַׁב לָכֶם תְּרוּמַתְכֶם. בְּמַחֲשָׁבָה אַתְּ תּוֹרֵם וְאֵין אַתְּ תּוֹרֵם בְּמִשְׁקָל וּבְמִידָּה וּבְמִנְייָן. מָה תְרוּמָה גְדוֹלָה בְּמַחֲשָׁבָה אַף תְּרוּמַת מַעֲשֵׂר בְּמַחֲשָׁבָה.

Halakhah 7: There[174], we have stated: "One who counts is praiseworthy, he who measures is better, and he who weighs is the best of the three." And here, you say so? Rebbi Joshua ben Levi said, here for the Great Heave, there for the heave of the tithe[175]. We have stated so[176]: "Eliezer ben Gimel says, from where that one does not give heave by measurement, weight, or count? The verse says (*Num.* 18:27): 'Your heave will be thought of for you'. You give heave by thought, you do not give heave by measurement, weight, or count. Just as this is for the Great Heave, so it is for the heave of the tithe[177]."

174 Mishnah 4:6.

175 Which is called "tithe of the tithe", one tenth of one tenth.

176 Babli *Bezah* 13b ("Abba Eleazar ben Gimel"), *Giṭṭin* 30b ("Abba Eleazar ben Gamla"), *Bekhorot* 58b ("Abba Eleazar ben Gomel"), *Menaḥot* 54b ("Abba Eleazar ben Gomel").

177 The later Sages, Tannaïm and Amoraïm, disagree with this last statement even though it agrees better with the verse.

וְהָתַנִּינָן אֲבָל תּוֹרֵם הוּא אֶת הַמָּדוּד וְאֶת הַשָּׁקוּל וְאֶת הַמָּנוּי. אָמַר רִבִּי לָעְזָר כֵּינִי מַתְנִיתָא מוֹדֵד אָדָם אֶת טִיבְלוֹ וּמַכְנִיסוֹ לְתוֹךְ בֵּיתוֹ וּבִלְבַד שֶׁלֹּא יִתְרוֹם בְּמִידָּה. שׁוֹקֵל אָדָם אֶת טִיבְלוֹ וּמַכְנִיסוֹ לְתוֹךְ בֵּיתוֹ וּבִלְבַד שֶׁלֹּא יִשְׁקְלֶנּוּ בְּמִשְׁקָל. מוֹנֶה הוּא אָדָם אֶת טִיבְלוֹ וּמַכְנִיסוֹ לְתוֹךְ בֵּיתוֹ וּבִלְבַד שֶׁלֹּא יִתְרוֹם בְּמִנְיָין.

Did we not state: "But one may give heave from what was measured, weighed, or counted"? Rebbi Eleazar said, so is the Mishnah: [178]"A person may measure his *ṭevel* and bring it into his house on condition that he not give heave by measure. A person may weigh his *ṭevel* and bring it into his house on condition that he not weigh[179] by weight. A person may count his *ṭevel* and bring it into his house on condition that he not give heave by count."

178 Tosephta 3:4, in the name of R. Jehudah.

179 In the Tosephta, the sentence reads: "A person may weigh his ṭevel and bring it into his house on condition that he not tithe by weight". This seems to be the correct reading, adopted by all commentators.

(fol. 40a) **משנה ח**: אֵין תּוֹרְמִין שֶׁמֶן עַל זֵיתִים הַנִּכְתָּשִׁין וְלֹא יַיִן עַל עֲנָבִים הַנִּדְרָכוֹת. וְאִם תָּרַם תְּרוּמָה וְיַחֲזוֹר וְיִתְרוֹם. הָרִאשׁוֹנָה מְדַמַּעַת בִּפְנֵי עַצְמָהּ וְחַיָּבִין עָלֶיהָ חוֹמֶשׁ אֲבָל לֹא שְׁנִיָּיה.

Mishnah 8: One does not give oil as heave on crushed olives, nor wine on pressed grapes. If one did, it is heave and he has to give another heave[180]. The first one creates *dema'*[181] by itself and one has to pay the fifth[182] but not the second[183].

180 According to R. Simson and R. Isaac Simponti, the second heave has to be given only from the oil produced from the crushed olives after the first heave was given, and so from the future wine from the already pressed grapes. However, by Tosephta 3:15, in that case the second heave is true heave subject to *dema'* and fifth. Therefore, the opinion of Maimonides is preferable, that the second heave has to consist of crushed olives or pressed grapes.

181 Cf. Mishnah 3:2.

182 Cf. Mishnah 6:1.

183 The second heave is profane food that must be eaten by the Cohen in ritual purity; this is a fine for breaking the rules.

(fol. 40d) **הלכה ח**: תַּמָּן תַּנִּינָן אֵין תּוֹרְמִין מִדָּבָר שֶׁנִּגְמְרָה מְלַאכְתּוֹ עַל דָּבָר שֶׁלֹּא נִגְמְרָה מְלַאכְתּוֹ וְהָכָא אַתְּ אָמַר הָכֵן. רִבִּי הִילָא בְּשֵׁם רִבִּי יוֹחָנָן מִפְּנֵי גֶּדֶר מֵי חַטָּאת שֶׁלֹּא יְהוּ מֵי חַטָּאת בְּטֵילִין. מִי חָמוּר גֶּזֶל הַשֵּׁבֶט אוֹ גֶּדֶר מֵי חַטָּאת. נִישְׁמְעִינָהּ מִן הָדָא זֵיתִין עַל הַזֵּיתִין וְהוּא עָתִיד לְכוֹתְשָׁן עֲנָבִים עַל עֲנָבִים וְהוּא עָתִיד לְדוֹרְכָן תְּרוּמָה וְיַחְזוֹר וְיִתְרוֹם. הֲרֵי יֵשׁ כָּאן גֶּזֶל הַשֵּׁבֶט וְגֶדֶר מֵי חַטָּאת. וְתַנֵּי עֲלָהּ תְּרוּמָה וְיִתְרוֹם. הָדָא אָמְרָה שֶׁגֶּדֶר מֵי חַטָּאת חֲמִיר מִגֶּזֶל הַשֵּׁבֶט.

Halakhah 8: There, we have stated[184]: "One does not give heave from incompletely processed produce for completely processed produce," and here you say so? Rebbi Hila in the name of Rebbi Joḥanan: Because of a "fence" for the purification water, lest purification water become useless[185]. What is more serious, robbing the tribe[137] or [breaching] the "fence" for purification water? Let us hear from the following[186]: "[If one gave heave of] olives for olives and in the future he will crush them, grapes for grapes and in the future he will press them, it is heave and he has to give heave a second time." In this case there is both robbing the tribe and the "fence" for the purification water, but we have stated that it is heave and he has to give heave a second time. This proves that the "fence" for the purification water is more serious than robbing the tribe.

184 Mishnah 10, contradicting our Mishnah here since in Mishnah 10 no obligation is stated to give heave a second time.

185 "Purification water" is fresh water with some ashes of the red heifer, used to purify people from the impurity of the dead (*Num.* 19). It is true that heave must be eaten by the Cohen in purity but normally immersion in a ritual bath is enough and sprinkling with purification water is not always necessary. All commentators, from the Gaonim to R. S. Lieberman, explain that "fence for the purification water" simply means that one tries to force the olive or wine grower to produce his oil and wine in ritual purity, for if one would permit giving heave from oil (wine) on oil olives (wine grapes), he either would make only a small amount in purity until he has given heave, or he would buy a small quantity of pure olives (grapes) from a fellow and pay the fellow to give heave in his name from his pure fluids. While this explanation seems pertinent, it does not explain the expression "fence for purification water"; it also contradicts the general tendency, clearly apparent in Tractate *Demay*, not to force the vulgar to conform to standards of observance he could not honestly sustain. But there seems no better explanation.

186 Tosephta 3:14. In the first case, Mishnah 4, his heave was not heave but he has to give heave only once and has no monetary loss.

מָה אָמַר רִבִּי יוֹסֵי הָכָא. וּמָה אִין רִבִּי מֵאִיר דְּמֵיקַל בְּגֶזֶל הַשֵּׁבֶט וּמַחְמִיר בְּגֶדֶר מֵי חַטָּאת. רִבִּי יוֹסֵי דְּמַחְמִיר בְּגֶזֶל הַשֵּׁבֶט לֹא כָּל־שֶׁכֵּן דּוּ מַחְמִיר בְּגֶדֶר מֵי חַטָּאת. אַשְׁכַּח תַּנֵּי בְּשֵׁם רִבִּי יוֹסֵי אֵין תּוֹרְמִין זֵיתִים עַל הַשֶּׁמֶן וְלֹא עֲנָבִים עַל הַיַּיִן וְאִם תָּרַם תְּרוּמָתוֹ תְרוּמָה וְאֵין צָרִיךְ לִתְרוֹם דִּבְרֵי רִבִּי מֵאִיר. רִבִּי יוֹסֵי אוֹמֵר בֵּית שַׁמַּאי אוֹמְרִים תּוֹרְמִין וּבֵית הִלֵּל אוֹמְרִים אֵין תּוֹרְמִין. הַכֹּל מוֹדִין שֶׁאִים תָּרַם שֶׁאֵין צָרִיךְ לִתְרוֹם שְׁנִייָה. הֲוֵי רָעְיוֹן רִבִּי מֵאִיר מֵיקֵל בְּגֶזֶל הַשֵּׁבֶט וּמַחְמִיר בְּגֶדֶר מֵי חַטָּאת. רִבִּי יוֹסֵי מַחְמִיר בְּגֶזֶל הַשֵּׁבֶט וּמֵיקֵל בְּגֶדֶר מֵי חַטָּאת.

What would Rebbi Yose say here? Since Rebbi Meïr takes "robbing the tribe" lightly but takes the "fence" for purification water seriously, Rebbi Yose who takes "robbing the tribe" seriously, certainly must take the "fence" for purification water seriously! It was found stated in the name of Rebbi Yose[187]: "One may not give olives as heave for oil or grapes for wine; if one did, his heave is heave and he does not have to give heave [a second time], the words of Rebbi Meïr. Rebbi Yose says, the House of Shammai say one gives heave but the House of Hillel say one does not give heave. Everybody agrees that if he gave heave, he does not have to give heave a second time." There is proof that Rebbi Meïr takes "robbing the tribe" lightly but the "fence" for purification water seriously[188], Rebbi Yose takes "robbing the tribe" seriously[189] but the "fence" for purification water lightly[190]!

187 A quite different version is in Tosephta 3:14: "One does not give oil as heave on crushed olives, nor wine on pressed grapes. If one gave, it is heave and he has to give another heave. The first one creates *dema'* and is subject to the fifth, but not the second one. From the latter one has to remove the tithes. Rebbi Yose says . . ." This Tosephta cannot be the source of the discussion here (as asserted by R. Eliahu Wilna and R. Moses Margalit) since the implication for R. Yose would be the opposite of what is asserted here and it is seen in the next paragraph that in the opinion of the Yerushalmi, R. Yose considers the second heave conditional and real heave. A Tosephta text closer to the Yerushalmi is reported in מלאכת שלמה (R. Solomon Adani) on the Mishnah.

188 While Mishnah 4 cannot be R. Meïr's, it is assumed that Mishnah 8 is.

189 It is obvious that originally, the Yerushalmi must have read in R. Yose's *baraita*: "he must give heave a second time", but there is no supporting manuscript evidence. Of all the explanations of this confusing paragraph, the best is *Tosefta Ki-fshutah* pp. 332-333.

190 This is established in the next paragraph.

תַּמָּן תַּנִּינָן רִבִּי יוֹסֵי אוֹמֵר שִׁשָּׁה דְבָרִים (fol. 41a) מִקּוּלֵּי בֵית שַׁמַּאי וּמֵחוּמְרֵי בֵית הִלֵּל הָעוֹף עוֹלֶה עַל הַשּׁוּלְחָן עִם הַגְּבִינָה וְאֵינוֹ נֶאֱכַל כְּדִבְרֵי בֵית שַׁמַּאי וּבֵית הִלֵּל אוֹמְרִים לֹא עוֹלֶה וְלֹא נֶאֱכַל. תּוֹרְמִין זֵיתִים עַל הַשֶּׁמֶן וַעֲנָבִים עַל הַיַּיִן כְּדִבְרֵי בֵית שַׁמַּאי וּבֵית הִלֵּל אוֹמְרִים אֵין תּוֹרְמִין. אָמַר רִבִּי מָנָא וְלֵית כָּאן זֵיתִים עַל הַשֶּׁמֶן אֶלָּא שֶׁמֶן עַל זֵיתִים. דְּהִיא דְּרִבִּי יוֹסֵי דְּרִבִּי יוֹסֵי אוֹמֵר תְּרוּמָה וְיַחְזוֹר וְיִתְרוֹם בְּשֶׁאֵין הָרִאשׁוֹנָה קַייֶמֶת אֲבָל אִם הָיְתָה הָרִאשׁוֹנָה קַייֶמֶת קוֹרֵא לָהּ שֵׁם וְדַיּוֹ.

There[191] we have stated: "Rebbi Yose says, in six matters are the House of Shammai lenient and the House of Hillel restrictive: Fowl may be served on the table together with cheese but cannot be eaten together according to the House of Shammai, but the House of Hillel say it may not be served or eaten[192]. One gives heave from olives on oil and from grapes on wine according to the House of Shammai, but the House of Hillel say one may not." Rebbi Mana said, it cannot be "from olives on oil" but "from oil on olives" because this is Rebbi Yose's! For Rebbi Yose says it is heave and he has to give another heave; that is, if the first [heave] does no longer exist but if the first exists he gives it its name and that is enough[193].

191 Mishnah *Idiut* 5:2. The other four examples refer to Mishnaiot in *Kilaim, Ḥallah, Miqwaot, Pesaḥim.*

192 Everybody agrees that fowl meat is not meat in the biblical sense since it says: "You may not cook a kid goat in its mother's milk" and birds have no milk. Nevertheless, as rabbinic "fence", one may not eat birds' meat with any milk product.

193 If the heave given first can be extended to cover the oil produced from the olives after heave was separated, it follows that R. Yose assumes that olives which were started in purity will be kept in purity until the last drop of oil has been extracted and the heave is legitimate as given from "pure on pure." It follows that R. Yose rejects any consideration of a

"fence for purification water"; he requires a genuine second heave only if either the first one was eaten or if the additional oil was made impure; in the latter case one may not use the first heave following Mishnah 2:1.

תַּנֵּי שְׁנִיָּה לֹא תֵאָכֵל עַד שֶׁיּוֹצִיא עָלֶיהָ תְּרוּמוֹת וּמַעְשְׂרוֹת רִאשׁוֹנָה מָה הִיא. מִן מַה דְתַנֵּי חָזַר וְעָשָׂה זֵתִים רִאשׁוֹן שֶׁמֶן וַעֲנָבִים יַיִן קוֹרֵא שֵׁם וְאֵינוֹ צָרִיךְ לִתְרוֹם שְׁנִיָּה הָדָא אָמְרָה שֶׁהוּא צָרִיךְ לִקְרוֹת שֵׁם לְמַעְשְׂרוֹתָיו.

It was stated[194]: "The second [heave] should not be eaten until one takes from it heaves and tithes." What is the status of the first? From what was stated[195]: "If he came back and made the first olives into oil or the grapes into wine, he gives it a name and does not have to give a second heave." That means that he has to give a name to his tithes.

194 This now refers back to the Mishnah, not the *baraitot* discussed in the meantime. A similar text appears in Tosephta 3:14. Since the Great Heave was already taken the first time, "heaves" here must refer to the heave of the tithe.

195 In the same Tosephta, though not the origin of this *baraita*, the full text is: "If one gives heave of olives on olives which will be crushed or from grapes which will be pressed, it is heave and he has to give a second one. The first creates *dema'* but not the second. The first is subject to the fifth but not the second; but one has to give it a name. If he came back and made the first olives into oil or the grapes into wine, he does not have to give a second heave." "To give a name" means to make a declaration that heave or tithes should be valid for such and such produce. Since one really should give heave and tithes from the finished product, if the oil is produced from the olives for which heave (or tithes) were taken, the name may be extended later to the finished oil or wine.

משנה ט: וְתוֹרְמִין שֶׁמֶן עַל זֵיתִים הַנִּכְבָּשִׁין וְיַיִן עַל עֲנָבִים לַעֲשׂוֹתָן(fol. 40a) צִימּוּקִין. מִי שֶׁתָּרַם שֶׁמֶן עַל זֵיתִים לַאֲכִילָה וְזֵיתִים עַל זֵיתִים לַאֲכִילָה וְיַיִן עַל עֲנָבִים לַאֲכִילָה וַעֲנָבִים עַל עֲנָבִים לַאֲכִילָה וְנִמְלַךְ לְדוֹרְכָן אֵינוֹ צָרִיךְ לִתְרוֹם.

Mishnah 9: One may give oil as heave for olives being pickled[196] and wine for grapes to be made into raisins. If one gave oil as heave for table olives, or olives for table olives, or wine for table grapes, or grapes for table grapes, when he changed his mind to press them he does not have to give heave[197].

196 Since for most people, olive oil is more valuable than pickled olives, substitution is permitted. The problem of not completely cured pickles and future raisins will be addressed in the Halakhah.

197 Since the heave was legitimate when given, it cannot become delegitimized later.

(fol. 41a) **הלכה ט**: תַּנִּינָן דְּבַתְרָהּ אֵין תּוֹרְמִין מִדָּבָר שֶׁנִּגְמְרָה מְלַאכְתּוֹ עַל דָּבָר שֶׁלֹּא נִגְמְרָה מְלַאכְתּוֹ. וְהָכָא לְשֶׁעָבַר הָא לְכַתְּחִילָּה לֹא אֲפִילוּ בַתְּחִילָּה. אִין תֵּימַר שַׁנְיָיא הִיא מִדָּבָר שֶׁנִּגְמַר מְלַאכְתּוֹ הָא תַנִּינָן הַפֶּרֶד וְהַצִּימּוּקִים וְהֶחָרוּבִים מִשֶּׁיַּעֲמִר עֲרֵימָה. רִבִּי יוֹסֵי בֶּן יוֹסֵי בְּשֵׁם רִבִּי יִצְחָק בֶּן לָעְזָר אֵין לָךְ אָסוּר מִדָּבָר שֶׁנִּגְמְרָה מְלַאכְתּוֹ עַל דָּבָר שֶׁלֹּא נִגְמְרָה מְלַאכְתּוֹ אֶלָּא גוֹרֶן וְיֶקֶב בִּלְבַד.

Halakhah 9: We have stated after this[198]: "One does not give heave from finished produce for unfinished;" there it is for the past, therefore not to start[199], [and here] even to start? If you say, is this different from when it is finished, did we not state[200]: "Dried pomegranate kernels, raisins, and carob from when he made an orderly heap"? Rebbi Yose ben Yose in the name of Rebbi Isaac ben Eleazar: From finished product on unfinished is only forbidden from threshing floor and wine (or oil) press[201].

198 Mishnah 10.

199 In Mishnah 10, it is stated: "If one gave heave, it is heave", which means that it is legitimized after the fact but cannot be accepted if done in defiance of the law. But in Mishnah 9, the language is positive, that everybody is free to give heave.

200 Mishnah *Ma'serot* 1:6, detailing the exact moments when finished produce is subject to heave and tithes. Therefore, grapes to be used to make raisins are definitely unfinished produce.

201 Grain and wine, mentioned in *Num.* 18:27. Since pickled olives and raisins cannot be turned into wine, they are not covered by Mishnah 10. This author will require that raisin wine be made from tithed raisins.

לְפִי מָה הוּא תוֹרֵם לְפִי שַׁמְנָן אוֹ לְפִי אוֹכְלָן. אָמַר רִבִּי יוֹחָנָן אַיְיתִיתֵיהּ מִדְּחִילְפַיי רִבִּי אוֹמֵר לְפִי אוֹכְלָן. רַבָּן שִׁמְעוֹן בֶּן גַּמְלִיאֵל אוֹמֵר לְפִי שַׁמְנָן אֲבָל לֹא עַל גַּרְעִינֵיהֶן. הַכֹּל מוֹדִין בִּכְלוֹכְסִין שֶׁהֵן תּוֹרְמִין לְפִי אוֹכְלָן אֲבָל לֹא עַל גַּרְעִינֵיהֶן. חֲנַנְיָה בָּעֵי וְאַף לְעִנְיַין שַׁבָּת כֵּן. אַשְׁכַּח תַּנֵּי רִבִּי אוֹמֵר בִּרְבִיעִית. רַבָּן שִׁמְעוֹן בֶּן גַּמְלִיאֵל אוֹמֵר כִּגְרוֹגֶרֶת.

What is the basis of his giving heave[202], on basis of their oil or as solid food? Rebbi Yoḥanan said, this was brought from Ḥilfai[203]: "Rebbi said as food, Rabban Simeon ben Gamliel said on basis of their oil, excluding the pits. Everybody agrees that one gives heave for pickled olives[204] as food but not including their pits. Ḥananiah asked, is this the same for the Sabbath[205]? It was found stated: "Rebbi said, by a *quartarius*; Rabban Simeon ben Gamliel said, by the size of a dried fig."

202 While there is no measure of heave indicated in biblical law, Mishnah 5:3 indicates the rabbinical standard of an estimated 2% of the volume for which heave is to be given. Is the basis the volume of oil that could have been extracted if the olives had not been pickled or is it the volume of pitted finished olives?

203 A similar statement is Tosephta 3:15, but there Rebbi is reported to require heave proportional to oil,

Rabban Simeon proportional to the solid food ("the food exluding the pits").

204 In the Tosephta, the Vienna ms. has קולפסין, the Erfurt ms. קלופסין, the printed editions קלפין. The word is usually identified with Greek κολυμβάς, ἥ, Latin *colymbas, -adis*, f., "pickled olives, olives swimming in brine."

205 If one moves something from private to public domain or more than four cubits in the public domain (cf. *Kilaim* Chapter 1, Note 188), it is a punishable offense only if a minimal amount is carried. The minimal amount is defined as a *quartarius* for drinks and the volume of an average dried fig for solid food. The *baraita* quoted here agrees with the text of the Tosephta, not the Yerushalmi.

אָמַר רִבִּי חֲנַנְיָה בְּשֵׁם רִבִּי הִלֵּל וְאַף אֲנָן תַּנִּינָן הָדָא דְמְסַיֵּיעַ לְהָדָא דְתַנֵּי רִבִּי הוֹשַׁעְיָה. זֵיתִין עַל זֵיתִין וְהוּא עָתִיד לְכוֹתְשָׁן עֲנָבִים עַל עֲנָבִים וְהוּא עָתִיד לְדוֹרְכָן תְּרוּמָה וְיַחְזוֹר וְיִתְרוֹם. וְתַנִּינָן מִי שֶׁתָּרַם שֶׁמֶן עַל זֵיתִים לַאֲכִילָה זֵיתִים עַל זֵיתִים לַאֲכִילָה יַיִן עַל עֲנָבִים לַאֲכִילָה וַעֲנָבִים עַל עֲנָבִים לַאֲכִילָה וְנִמְלַךְ לְדוֹרְכָן אֵינוֹ צָרִיךְ לִתְרוֹם. מִפְּנֵי שֶׁנִּמְלַךְ הָא לֹא נִמְלַךְ תְּרוּמָה וְיַחְזוֹר וְיִתְרוֹם.

Rebbi Ḥananiah said in the name of Rebbi Hillel: We have stated in support of the statement of Rebbi Hoshaiah[186]: "[If one gave heave of] olives for olives and in the future he will crush them, grapes for grapes and in the future he will press them, it is heave and he has to give heave a second time." And we have stated[197]: "If one gave oil as heave for table olives, olives for table olives, wine for table grapes, or grapes for table grapes when he changed his mind to press them he does not have to give heave." Because he changed his mind! Therefore, if he did not change his mind he has to give a second heave.

(fol. 40a) **משנה י**: אֵין תּוֹרְמִין מִדָּבָר שֶׁנִּגְמְרָה מְלַאכְתּוֹ עַל דָּבָר שֶׁלֹּא נִגְמְרָה מְלַאכְתּוֹ וְלֹא מִדָּבָר שֶׁלֹּא נִגְמְרָה מְלַאכְתּוֹ עַל דָּבָר שֶׁנִּגְמְרָה מְלַאכְתּוֹ וְלֹא מִדָּבָר שֶׁלֹּא נִגְמְרָה מְלַאכְתּוֹ עַל דָּבָר שֶׁלֹּא נִגְמְרָה מְלַאכְתּוֹ וְאִם תָּרְמוּ תְּרוּמָתָן תְּרוּמָה.

Mishnah 10: One does not give heave from finished[200,201] produce for unfinished, or from unfinished for finished, or from unfinished for unfinished. If heave was given, it is heave.

(fol. 41a) **הלכה י**: רִבִּי אִימִּי בְּשֵׁם רִבִּי שִׁמְעוֹן בֶּן לָקִישׁ וְנֶחְשַׁב לָכֶם תְּרוּמַתְכֶם כַּדָּגָן מִן הַגּוֹרֶן. מִמַּה שֶׁהוּא מְצַוֶּה אֶת בְּנֵי לֵוִי לִתְרוֹם מִן הַגָּמוּר. הָדָא אָמְרָה שֶׁאָסוּר לִיתֵּן לוֹ שִׁבֳּלִים. חִיָּיה בַּר אָדָא בְּשֵׁם רִבִּי שִׁמְעוֹן בֶּן לָקִישׁ מַעֲשֵׂר רִאשׁוֹן שֶׁהִקְדִּימוֹ בַּשִּׁבֳּלִים אָסוּר לוֹכַל מִמֶּנּוּ עֲרַאי וּמַה טַעַם אֶת קָדְשֵׁי בְּנֵי יִשְׂרָאֵל לֹא תְחַלְּלוּ וְלֹא תָמוּתוּ. מָהוּ שֶׁיִּלְקוּ עַל טִבְלוֹ דְּבַר תּוֹרָה. רִבִּי אַשִּׁיאָן בְּשֵׁם רִבִּי יוֹנָה מַתְנִיתָא אָמְרָה אֵין לוֹקִין עַל טִבְלוֹ דְּבַר תּוֹרָה. דְּתַנִּינָן תַּמָּן תְּרוּמַת מַעֲשֵׂר שָׁוָה לַבִּיכּוּרִים בִּשְׁנֵי דְרָכִים וְלִתְרוּמָה בִּשְׁנֵי דְרָכִים. וְנִיטֶּלֶת מִן הַטָּהוֹר עַל הַטָּמֵא וְשֶׁלֹּא מִן הַמּוּקָּף כְּבִיכּוּרִים. וְאוֹסֶרֶת מִן הַגּוֹרֶן וְיֵשׁ לוֹ שִׁעוּר כִּתְרוּמָה. אִית לָךְ מֵימַר אוֹסֶרֶת מִן הַגּוֹרֶן לֹא לְאַחַר מֵירוּחַ. הָדָא אָמְרָה שֶׁאֵין לוֹקִין עַל טִבְלוֹ דְּבַר תּוֹרָה.

Halakhah 10: Rebbi Immi in the name of Rebbi Simeon ben Laqish (*Num.* 18:27): "Your heave will be counted as if it were grain from the threshing-floor." From what He commanded the Levites to give heave, from the finished product[206]. That means it is forbidden to give him ears. Ḥiyya bar Ada in the name of Rebbi Simeon ben Laqish: If First Tithe was given from grain ears, it is forbidden to eat a snack from it[207]. What is the reason? (*Num.* 18:32): "You should not desecrate the holy things of the Children of Israel lest you die." Will one be whipped for its *ṭevel* as biblical law? Rebbi Ashian[208] in the name of Rebbi Jonah: A Mishnah states that one is not whipped for its *ṭevel* as biblical law, as we have stated there[209]: "Heave of the tithe is like First Fruits in two respects and like tithe in two respects. One may give it from pure for impure or not earmarked produce[148], like First Fruits. It makes forbidden from the threshing floor and has a tariff similar to heave." When can you say "from the threshing floor", does this not mean after smoothing[210]? That implies that one is not whipped for its *ṭevel* as biblical law[211].

206 The verse speaks of heave of the tithe and implies that the merit of heave of the tithe which accrues for the Levite is identical with that of the Israel giving heave from the threshing floor. This implies that the Israel gives only from the threshing floor, when all agricultural work connected with the harvest is complete.

207 While heave and tithes are due only after cleaning up the threshed grain, using unthreshed ears for a regular meal would show that the ears are the finished product and subject to heave and tithes. But untithed ears may be eaten as a snack. Here, it is stated that giving heave and first tithe in any form declares the product as finished. If the tithe is tithe, then it is *ṭevel* for heave of the tithe and may not be eaten unless that heave is taken.

208 A Galilean Amora of the fifth generation, student of R. Jonah, possibly Ἀσίων.

209 Mishnah *Bikkurim* 2:5.

210 The end of threshing, when the threshed grain has been collected and assembled in neat heaps.

211 The ears never were threshed, much less smoothed.

אין תורמין פרק שני

(fol. 41a) **משנה א:** אֵין תּוֹרְמִין מִן הַטָּהוֹר עַל הַטָּמֵא וְאִם תָּרְמוּ תְּרוּמָתָן תְּרוּמָה. בֶּאֱמֶת אָמְרוּ הָעִיגּוּל שֶׁל דְּבֵילָה שֶׁנִּטְמָא מִקְצָתוֹ תּוֹרֵם מִן הַטָּהוֹר שֶׁיֵּשׁ בּוֹ עַל הַטָּמֵא שֶׁיֵּשׁ בּוֹ וְכֵן אֲגוּדָּה שֶׁל יָרָק וְכֵן עֲרֵימָה. הָיוּ שְׁנֵי עִיגּוּלִין שְׁנֵי אֲגוּדּוֹת שְׁתֵּי עֲרֵימוֹת אַחַת טְהוֹרָה וְאַחַת טְמֵאָה לֹא יִתְרוֹם מִזֶּה עַל זֶה. רִבִּי אֱלִיעֶזֶר אוֹמֵר תּוֹרְמִין מִן הַטָּהוֹר עַל הַטָּמֵא.

Mishnah 1: One does not give heave from pure produce for impure, but if heave was given it is heave. In truth, they said if a cake of dried figs[1] became partially impure one may give heave from its pure part for its impure part, and similarly for a bunch of vegetable or a heap [of grain][2]. If there were two cakes, two bundles, two heaps, one pure and one impure, one should not give heave from one for the other[3]. Rebbi Eliezer says, one may give heave from pure produce for impure.

1 Fig cakes are not strings of figs put together when they are completely dry but made of fresh figs formed into cakes and then put out to ferment and dry. The sap of figs is not one of the fluids that make food susceptible to impurity (*Demay* Chapter 5, Note 8); if no water touched the cake before it was dry and the individual figs are still recognizable, then if later it is prepared for impurity and one fig was touched by an impure person, this fig will be impure by one degree more than the person who touched and the figs touching this fig will be impure by still one more degree, and so on, cf. *Demay* Chapter 2, Note 137 (higher degree meaning lesser impurity). Since profane food can acquire only impurity in the first and second degrees, all figs not directly touching the impure fig will remain pure (if the cake is dry).

2 These are much less tightly compressed than figs in a fig cake.

3 Since heave can be given only from produce clearly earmarked, one would have to bring the impure cake close to the pure one so they can be enclosed somewhere together and one is afraid that the impure might touch the pure cake and spread the impurity.

(fol. 41b) **הלכה א**: אֵין תּוֹרְמִין מִן הַטָּהוֹר כו'. רִבִּי יוֹחָנָן בְּשֵׁם רִבִּי יַנַּאי וְנֶחְשַׁב לָכֶם תְּרוּמַתְכֶם כְּדָגָן מִן הַגּוֹרֶן וְכִמְלֵאָה מִן הַיֶּקֶב. מַה גּוֹרֶן וְיֶקֶב אִיפְשָׁר שֶׁיְּהֵא מִקְצָתוֹ טָמֵא וּמִקְצָתוֹ טָהוֹר. וְזֶה אַף עַל פִּי שֶׁאֶיפְשָׁר לְמֵידִין אֶיפְשָׁר מִשֶּׁאֵי אֶיפְשָׁר. מֵעַתָּה לֹא יְהֵא תְרוּמָתוֹ תְּרוּמָה מִמֶּנּוּ כְּתִיב.

"One does not give heave from pure produce", etc. Rebbi Johanan in the name of Rebbi Yannai (*Num.* 18:27): "Your heave will be counted as if it were grain from the threshing-floor and what was drawn off from the wine-press.." Since for threshing-floor and wine-press it is impossible that part of it be impure and part pure[4], even so one infers what is possible from what is impossible[5]. In that case, the heave given should not be heave! It is written: "From itself[6]".

4 For fluids it is obvious that if part of it became impure, all is impure. The case of grain is more complicated but in two cases the assertion is certainly true. If the grain is prepared for impurity (*Demay*, Chapter 2, Note 141) before threshing, then in sweeping the grains together to form an orderly heap, any impurity will be spread through the entire heap. If the grain is not prepared, then any moistening of the heap will make the entire heap prepared.

5 The verse quoted refers to heaves of the tithe for grain and wine. For these, it is impossible to give Great Heave (Chapter 1, Note 64) from pure for impure since Great Heave is given only from earmarked produce; it is inferred that nowhere may one give heave from pure produce on impure.

The statement that abstract principles can be transferred from impossible to possible cases is not found in the Babli but Tosaphot refer to it several times to explain the background of talmudic reasoning (*Bezah* 13b, *s. v.* בשם; *Gittin* 30b, *s. v.* וכי; *Menahot* 54b, *s. v.* בך; *Bekhorot* 59b, *s. v.* אף).

6 "From itself" is repeated in *Num.* 18 several times, verses 26, 28, 29, 30, 32. While it is asserted in the next paragraph that heave of the tithe, the subject of that paragraph, need not be from the particular batch of tithe for which it is given, it is emphasized sufficiently to point out that Great Heave may be given from any part of the batch, even if part of it is pure and the remainder impure.

כָּל־הַדְּבָרִים לְמֵידִין וּמְלַמְּדִין תְּרוּמַת מַעֲשֵׂר הִיא מְלַמֶּדֶת וְאֵינָהּ לְמֵידָה תְּרוּמַת מַעֲשֵׂר לִימְּדָה עַל תְּרוּמָה גְדוֹלָה שֶׁלֹּא תְהֵא נִיטֶּלֶת מִן הַטָּהוֹר עַל הַטָּמֵא וְהִיא נִיטֶּלֶת מִן הַטָּהוֹר עַל הַטָּמֵא. מְנַיִין רִבִּי יוֹסֵי בְּשֵׁם חִזְקִיָּה. רִבִּי יוֹנָה בְּשֵׁם רִבִּי יַנַּאי[7] וּנְתַתֶּם מִמֶּנּוּ אֶת תְּרוּמַת יי לְאַהֲרֹן הַכֹּהֵן עֲשֵׂה שֶׁיִּנָּתְנוּ לְאַהֲרֹן הַכֹּהֵן בִּכְהוּנָּתוֹ. כַּהֲנָא אָמַר מִכָּל־חֶלְבּוֹ אֶת מִקְדְּשׁוֹ מִמֶּנּוּ טוֹל מִן הַמְּקוּדָּשׁ שֶׁבּוֹ. תְּרוּמַת מַעֲשֵׂר לִימְּדָה עַל תְּרוּמָה גְדוֹלָה שֶׁהִיא נִיטֶּלֶת מִן הַמּוּקָּף וְהִיא נִיטֶּלֶת שֶׁלֹּא מִן הַמּוּקָּף. מְנַיִין שֶׁתְּרוּמַת מַעֲשֵׂר נִיטֶּלֶת שֶׁלֹּא מִן הַמּוּקָּף. מִכָּל־מַעְשְׂרוֹתֵיכֶם אֶחַד בִּיהוּדָה וְאֶחַד בְּגָלִיל. תְּרוּמַת מַעֲשֵׂר לִימְּדָה עַל תְּרוּמָה גְדוֹלָה שֶׁלֹּא תְהֵא נִיטֶּלֶת אֶלָּא מִן הַגָּמוּר וְאַף הִיא נִיטֶּלֶת מִן הַגָּמוּר.

Everything teaches for itself and for others[7], the heave of the tithes teaches for others what it does not teach for itself[8]. The heave of the tithe teaches for Great Heave that it should not be taken from pure produce for impure but itself can be taken from pure produce for impure. From where? Rebbi Yose in the name of Ḥizqiah, Rebbi Jonah in the name of Rebbi Yannai (*Num.* 18:28): "You shall give from it the Eternal's heave to Aharon the priest;" it should be given to Aharon in his status as priest[9]. Cahana said (*Num.* 18:29): "From its best, the sanctified part from it;" take from its sanctifiable part. The heave of the tithe teaches for

Great Heave that it should be taken from earmarked produce[6] but itself may be taken from non-earmarked. From where that heave of the tithe may be taken from non-earmarked produce? (*Num*. 18:28) "From *all* of your tithes," one in Judea and one in Galilee. The heave of the tithe teaches for Great Heave that it should be taken only from finished produce, itself also should be taken from finished produce[10].

7 Every verse of the Torah first is needed for its subject but then can be used to deduce rules for other cases by the standard rules of inference, either following R. Ismael or R. Aqiba.

8 While very few verses speak about the obligation of the Great Heave and no details are given, the verses dealing with the heave of the tithe are many and partially contradictory. As explained in the paragraph, the general expressions are taken to refer to the Great Heave and the detailed instructions for the heave of the tithe.

9 Sacral meals, the main duty of a Cohen, must all be eaten in strict purity.

10 Chapter 1, Note 206.

תְּרוּמַת מַעֲשֵׂר נִיטֶּלֶת מִן הַטָּהוֹר עַל הַטָּהוֹר וּמִן הַטָּמֵא עַל הַטָּמֵא מִן הַטָּהוֹר עַל הַטָּמֵא וְאֵינָהּ נִיטֶּלֶת מִן הַטָּמֵא עַל הַטָּהוֹר. רִבִּי נְחֶמְיָה אוֹמֵר כְּשֵׁם שֶׁאֵינָהּ נִיטֶּלֶת מִן הַטָּמֵא עַל הַטָּהוֹר כָּךְ אֵינָהּ נִיטֶּלֶת מִן הַטָּמֵא עַל הַטָּמֵא וּמוֹדֵי רִבִּי נְחֶמְיָה בִּדְמַיָּה. עַד כְּדוֹן בְּשֶׁהָיָה לוֹ מֵאוֹתוֹ הַמִּין לֹא הָיָה לוֹ מֵאוֹתוֹ הַמִּין נִישְׁמְעִינָהּ מִן הָדָא. רִבִּי חֲנִינָא עֲנְתָּנַיָא סְלַק עִם רִבִּי זְעִירָא לְחַמַּת גָּדֵר זְבַן לֵיהּ קְלוֹסְקִין בְּעָא מְתַקְּנֵיהּ מִיּוֹם לְחַבְרֵיהּ אֲמַר לֵיהּ לֵית אֲנָן צְרִיכִין חֲשָׁשִׁין לִיחִידָא אִית לָךְ מֵימַר בְּשֶׁהָיָה לוֹ מֵאוֹתוֹ הַמִּין.

Heave of the tithe is taken from pure produce for pure, from impure for impure, from pure for impure, but not from impure for pure[9]. Rebbi Neḥemiah says, just as it may not be taken from impure for pure, so it may not be taken from impure for impure. Rebbi Neḥemiah agrees in the case of *demay*[11]. That is, if he has from the same kind[12]. If he does not have anything from the same kind, let us hear from the following: Rebbi Ḥanina Eyntanaya went with Rebbi Zeïra to Ḥammat Gader. He bought him a roll[13] and wanted to put it in order from one day to the next[14]. He said to him: We do not have to worry about a single opinion! Can you say that he had from the same kind[15]?

11 In Babylonian sources (*Baba Qama* 115b, Tosephta 3:19) this is formulated as: "R. Neḥemiah says, one gives from impure produce for impure only in the case of *demay*," since then the obligation is not clear-cut.

12 The consensus of the commentators is that this refers to R. Neḥemiah's prohibition of giving heave of the tithe from impure for impure food.

13 Greek, cf. *Berakhot* Chap. 6, Note 103.

14 Since it was baked, one can be sure that the Great Heave had been given. The question is only about the heave of the tithe of *demay* which has to be given for bread from an uncertified baker (*Demay* Halakhah 5:1). Since the roll was for next morning's breakfast, R. Ḥanina was wondering whether R. Neḥemiah would permit giving heave now since a roll handled by the unobservant certainly was impure, having been prepared for impurity by the water needed to make the dough.

15 Since R. Ḥanina is told not to worry, this implies that R. Neḥemiah forbids giving heave of the tithe of impure *demay* if some pure food of the same kind is in his possession. However, the question remains open since the only pure roll R. Ḥanania could possibly have bought the next day would have to be one made with fruit juice (*Demay* Halakhah 5:1, Note 8) and it is most unlikely that such rolls would be available commercially.

בֶּאֱמֶת אָמַר רִבִּי לְעָזָר כָּל־מָקוֹם שֶׁשָּׁנוּ בֶּאֱמֶת הֲלָכָה לְמֹשֶׁה מִסִּינַי.

"In truth;[16]" Rebbi Eleazar said that every place where they stated "in truth," it is practice going back to Moses on Mount Sinai.

16 Quote from the Mishnah. This statement is also in *Kilaim* Chapter 2, cf. Note 36.

וְעִיגּוּל שֶׁל דְּבֵילָה שֶׁנִּיטְמָא מִקְצָתוֹ מְכֵיוָן שֶׁנִּיטְמָא מִקְצָתוֹ אֵין כּוּלּוֹ טָמֵא בִּמְחוּבָּר בְּמֵי פֵּירוֹת הִיא מַתְנִיתָא. וְאֵין סוֹפוֹ לֵיחָלֵק וְלַעֲשׂוֹתוֹ שְׁנַיִם. תִּיפְתַּר שֶׁקָּרָא לָהּ שֵׁם בִּמְחוּבָּר.

"If a cake of dried figs became partially impure one may give heave from its pure part for its impure part;" but if part of it becomes impure is not all of it impure[17]? The Mishnah deals with the case that they are connected only by fruit juice[1]. But will it not be cut into two parts in the end[18]? Explain it if he gave it a name when it still was connected.

17 Since figs usually are washed before drying, they are susceptible for impurity and the water will connect all parts of the cake.

18 Since nobody swallows an entire fig cake whole, could not the cake be put in order once a pure part was cut off? The answer is that this is preferred but one cannot take it for granted.

וְכֵן אֲגוּדָה שֶׁל יָרָק. מַתְנִיתִין שֶׁנִּיטְמָאת וְעוֹדָהּ אֲגוּדָה אֲבָל נִיטְמָאת קְלָחִין וַאֲגָדָן לֹא בְדָא. וְאֵין סוֹפָהּ לֵיחָלֵק וְלֵעָשׂוֹת שְׁתַּיִם. תִּיפְתַּר שֶׁקָּרָא לָהּ שֵׁם בִּמְחוּבָּר. אֶגֶד שֶׁנִּיטְמָא שֶׁהִתִּירוֹ וַאֲגָדוֹ מַהוּ.

"And similarly for a bunch of vegetable." The Mishnah deals with the case that it became impure as a bunch but when the single stalks were impure and he bound them together, this does not apply[19]. But will it not be split and made into two parts in the end[18]? Explain it if he gave it a name when it still was connected. What is the situation if a bundle became impure, he unbound it[20] and bound it again?

19 Since unbound it would be giving pure heave for the impure, a later bunching cannot change the situation.

20 In that stage, it would be giving from impure for impure. The question is not answered.

וְלִיתְנֵי עִיגּוּל וְלָא לִתְנֵי אֲגוּדָה נִיתְנֵי אֲגוּדָה וְלָא לִתְנֵי עֲרֵימָה. אִילּוּ תַנִּינָן עִיגּוּל וְלָא תַנִּינָן אֲגוּדָה הֲוִינָן אָמְרִין עִיגּוּל שֶׁכּוּלּוֹ גוּף אֶחָד תּוֹרֵם. אֲגוּדָה שֶׁאֵין כּוּלּוֹ גוּף אֶחָד אֵינוֹ תוֹרֵם. הֲוֵי צוֹרְכָא מִיתְנֵי אֲגוּדָה. וְאִילּוּ תַנִּינָן אֲגוּדָה וְלָא תַנִּינָן עֲרֵימָה הֲוִינָן אָמְרִין אֲגוּדָה שֶׁכּוּלָּהּ תְּפוּשָׂה אַחַת תּוֹרֵם עֲרֵימָה שֶׁאֵין כּוּלָּהּ תְּפִיסָה אַחַת אֵינוֹ תוֹרֵם. הֲוֵי צוֹרְכָא מִיתְנֵי עִיגּוּל וְצוֹרְכָא מִיתְנֵי אֲגוּדָה וְצוֹרְכָא מִיתְנֵי עֲרֵימָה.

Should we have stated only fig cake and neither bunch nor heap? If we had stated about fig cake and not bunch we would have said he may give heave for the fig cake which is all one body but not for the bunch which is not one body. So it is necessary to state also "bunch". If we had stated bunch not heap, we would have said he may give heave for the bunch because it is all held together but not for the heap which is not held together in one piece. So it is necessary to state fig-cake, necessary to state bunch, and necessary to state heap.

מִכֵּיוָן דְּתַנִּינָן הָיוּ שְׁנֵי עִיגּוּלִין וּשְׁתֵּי אֲגוּדוֹת וּשְׁתֵּי עֲרֵימוֹת. מַה צוֹרְכָא דְהַהוּא דָמַר רִבִּי יוֹחָנָן בְּשֵׁם רִבִּי יַנַּיי וְנֶחְשַׁב לָכֶם תְּרוּמַתְכֶם כְּדָגָן וגו'. אָמַר רִבִּי חִיָּה בַּר אָדָא בַּעֲרֵימָה שֶׁל קִישּׁוּאִין וְדִילּוּעִין הִיא מַתְנִיתָא.

Since we stated: "If there were two fig-cakes, two bunches, and two heaps," why do we need this since Rebbi Joḥanan said in the name of Rebbi Yannai (*Num.* 18:27): "Your heave will be counted as if it were grain[4]," etc.[21]? Rebbi Ḥiyya bar Ada said, the Mishnah speaks about heaps of green melons[22] or squash[23].

21 Either this part of the Mishnah or the statement of R. Joḥanan is superfluous.

22 Cf. *Kilaim* Chapter 1, Note 38.

23 Since these are large individual fruits, the argument of R. Joḥanan is not applicable; neither does R. Joḥanan's statement follow from the Mishnah.

הָיוּ שְׁנֵי עִיגוּלִין אֶחָד מִקְצָתוֹ טָמֵא וְאֶחָד מִקְצָתוֹ טָהוֹר מָהוּ שֶׁיִּתְרוֹם מִזֶּה עַל זֶה. וְיָבִיא בְּחָדָא. הָיוּ לְפָנָיו שְׁנֵי כְּרִיים אֶחָד הִפְרִישׁ מִמֶּנּוּ מִקְצָת תְּרוּמוֹת וּמַעְשְׂרוֹת. וְאֶחָד הִפְרִישׁ מִמֶּנּוּ מִקְצָת[24] תְּרוּמוֹת וּמַעְשְׂרוֹת. מָהוּ שֶׁיִּתְרוֹם מִזֶּה עַל זֶה. תַּלְמִידוֹי דְּרִבִּי חִייָה רוֹבָא שָׁאֲלוֹן לְרִבִּי חִייָא רוֹבָה וְאָמַר לוֹן הַכְּסִיל חוֹבֵק אֶת יָדָיו וְאוֹכֵל אֶת בְּשָׂרוֹ. רִבִּי לָעְזָר בְּשֵׁם רִבִּי חִייָה רֹבָה אֵין תּוֹרְמִין וּמְעַשְּׂרִין מִזֶּה עַל זֶה.

If there were two fig cakes, one partially impure and one partially pure[1], may one give heave from one for the other[25]? If he had two heaps[26], and from both of them he had given part of heaves and tithes[27], may he give heave from one for the other? The students of the elder Rebbi Ḥiyya asked the elder Rebbi Ḥiyya and he said to them (*Eccl.* 4:5): "The fool folds his hands and eats his own flesh.[28]" Rebbi Eleazar in the name of the elder Rebbi Ḥiyya: He may not give heave from one for the other.

24 Missing in Venice print, word is in both mss.

25 Since the Mishnah permits taking pure heave also for the impure parts of the same fig cake, may one put both cakes together on a table where they are earmarked and give one heave for both of them?

26 כרי is a heap of freshly threshed grain, ערימה one of totally dry grain.

27 Mishnah 4:1 states that if only partial heave and tithes were taken from a heap they would have no status as heave and tithes but, even though they would now be separated from the heap, they would still count as one for giving heave from an earmarked heap. May one give one heave for both in

this case? The two cases are treated as similar.

28 The answer, "no", is too simple and a thinking person should not have to ask.

הֲרֵי שֶׁהֵבִיא מִינִין הַרְבֵּה בְקוּפָּה וּכְרוּב מִלְמַעְלָן וּכְרוּב מִלְמַטָּן וְדָבָר אַחֵר בְּאֶמְצַע אֵין תּוֹרְמִין וְלֹא מְעַשְּׂרִין מִזֶּה עַל זֶה. הָדָא דְתֵימָא בְּשֶׁאֵין שָׁם חָלָל. אֲבָל אִם יֵשׁ שָׁם חָלָל תּוֹרְמִין וּמְעַשְּׂרִין מִזֶּה עַל זֶה. כָּל־בֵּית הַגִּיתִּים אֶחָד. כָּל־בֵּית הַגְּרָנוֹת אֶחָד. תַּנֵּי אָמַר רִבִּי יוּדָה וְהוּא שֶׁתְּהֵא תוֹפֶסֶת הַגּוֹרֶן בְּאֶמְצַע, עַד כְּדוֹן חִיטִּין וַאֲפִילוּ קַשׁ וַאֲפִילוּ תֶּבֶן.

[29]"If somebody brought many kinds in a box, cabbage on top and cabbage on the bottom but something else in between, he may not give heave or tithe from one for the other." That means, if there is no empty space. But if there is empty space he may give heave or tithe from one for the other[30]. [31]"The entire house of the wine press is one[32]." The entire threshing house is one. It was stated: Rebbi Jehudah said, only if the main threshing place is in the middle. So far this is for wheat; [it is] the same even for stubbles, even for straw.

29 Tosephta 3:8, cf. *Tosephta ki-fshutah* for the textual variants.

30 If the entire box is filled up, the two layers of cabbage are not ear-marked together. But if there is free space where the walls of the box hold together just the two layers of cabbage, they are earmarked and can be tithed together.

31 Tosephta 3:7, in the name of R. Yose.

32 All wine barrels in the house of the wine press are earmarked together.

רִבִּי חַגּוֹי בְּעָא קוֹמֵי רִבִּי יוֹסֵי הָיָה טָמֵא בְאֶמְצַע אָמַר לֵיהּ וַהֲרֵי נָשׁוּךְ. חֲבֵרַיָּא בָּעוֹן קוֹמֵי רִבִּי יוֹסֵי הָיְתָה מַפָּה בְאֶמְצַע אָמַר לוֹן וְהַיְינוּ חֲמִשָּׁה שַׂקִּין בְּגוֹרֶן דְּתַנֵּי חֲמִשָּׁה שַׂקִּין בְּגוֹרֶן אֵין תּוֹרְמִין וְלֹא מְעַשְּׂרִין מִזֶּה עַל זֶה.

Rebbi Ḥaggai asked before Rebbi Yose: Was impure [produce] between them? He said to him, is that biting[33]? The colleagues asked before Rebbi Yose: If there was a blanket between them? He said to them, that is the case of the five sacks, as it was stated: "Five sacks on the threshing floor, one does not give heave and tithes from one for the other.[34]"

33 If three layers are in the box but the middle layer is impure, bottom and top are not prepared for impurity, and there is no empty space, then top and bottom do not go together because they do not physically touch. For the notion of "biting", cf. *Kilaim* Chapter 9, Note 172, Mishnah *Ḥallah* 2:4.

34 This text contradicts the previous statement that the entire enclosed area of the threshing floor is earmarking for heave. In the parallel text in Tosephta 3:10 and Yerushalmi *Ma'aser Šeni* 3:11, the text reads: "One gives heave and tithes from one for the other." While the reading of the Tosephta does not prove anything for the Yerushalmi, the text in *Ma'aser Šeni* indicates that the text here is corrupt. Maimonides (*Terumot* 3:18) and Roš (*Hilkhot Ḥallah* 4) follow the text in *Ma'aser Šeni*.

תַּנֵּי רִבִּי לַעְאיי אוֹמֵר מִשּׁוּם רִבִּי לִיעֶזֶר תּוֹרְמִין מִן הַטָּהוֹר עַל הַטָּמֵא בְּלַח. כֵּיצַד כָּבַשׁ זֵיתִים בְּטוּמְאָה וְהוּא רוֹצֶה לְתוֹרְמָן בְּטָהֳרָה מֵבִיא מַשְׁפֵּךְ שֶׁאֵין בְּפִיו כְּבֵיצָה וּמְמַלֵּא אוֹתוֹ בֵּיצִים וְנוֹתְנוֹ עַל פִּי חָבִית. וְנִמְצָא תוֹרֵם מִן הַמּוּקָּף. לָמָּה לִי פָּחוֹת מִכְּבֵיצָה. אֲפִילוּ כְבֵיצָה לֹא פֵּירוּרִין אִינּוּן שֶׁלֹּא יְטַמְּאוּ זֵיתִים הַרְבֶּה. אָמְרוּ לוֹ אֵין לְךָ כָּל־לַח קָרוּי לַח אֶלָּא יַיִן וְשֶׁמֶן בִּלְבַד. הֵיךְ עֲבִידָא קוֹרָה אַחַת לִשְׁנֵי בוֹרוֹת. שְׁנֵי קוֹרוֹת לְבוֹר אֶחָד. נִיחָא קוֹרָה אַחַת לִשְׁנֵי בוֹרוֹת. אֶלָּא שְׁנֵי קוֹרוֹת לְבוֹר אֶחָד לֹא מִתּוֹךְ שֶׁנִּיטְמָא מִקְצָתָן נִיטְמְאוּ כוּלָּן. רִבִּי לָא בְשֵׁם רִבִּי לָעְזָר תִּפְתָּר שֶׁהָיָה בְלִיבּוֹ לַעֲשׂוֹת תְּפוּשָׂה אַחַת וְנִמְלַךְ לַעֲשׂוֹתוֹ שְׁתֵּי תְפוּשׂוֹת. אָמַר רִבִּי יוֹסֵי בֵּי רִבִּי בּוּן הָדָא דְתֵימַר בְּשֶׁנִּיטְמָא מִשֶּׁיִּשְׁלֶה וּמִשֶּׁיַּקִּיפֶהָ שֶׁכְּבָר נִרְאוּ לְתוֹרְמָן בְּטָהֳרָה. אֲבָל אִם נִיטְמָא עַד שֶׁלֹּא

שִׁילֶּה וְעַד שֶׁלֹּא קִיפֶּה לֹא בְדָא. רִבִּי טָבִי רִבִּי יֹאשִׁיָּה בֵּי רִבִּי יַנַּאי הֲלָכָה כְרִבִּי לִיעֶזֶר. רִבִּי יִצְחָק בַּר נַחְמָן בְּשֵׁם רִבִּי הוֹשַׁעְיָה הֲלָכָה כְרִבִּי לִיעֶזֶר. רִבִּי הוּנָא רִבִּי חֲנַנְיָה אֵין הֲלָכָה כְרִבִּי לִיעֶזֶר. רִבִּי יוֹסֵי בֵּי רִבִּי בּוּן רַב יְהוּדָה בְשֵׁם שְׁמוּאֵל אֵין הֲלָכָה כְרִבִּי לִיעֶזֶר. אָתָא עוּבְדָא קוֹמֵי רִבִּי אִימִּי וְלֹא הוֹרֵי אָמַר תְּרֵין כָּל־קֳבֵיל תְּרֵין אִינּוּן. אָמְרִין לֵיהּ וְהָא רִבִּי יִצְחָק בַּר נַחְמָן הוֹרֵי. אֲפִילוּ כֵן לֹא הוֹרֵי.

It was stated[35]: "Rebbi Illaï[36] says in the name of Rebbi Eliezer: For food in fluids, one gives heave from pure for impure[37]. How is this? If somebody pickled olives in impurity and wants to give heave in purity, he brings a funnel whose opening is less than [the width of] an egg[38], fills it with eggs[39] and puts it on top of the amphora; it turns out that he gives heave from what is earmarked[40]." Why does it have to be less than [the width of] an egg? Are these not single pieces[41]? It is only that not many olives should become impure. "[35]They said to him, the only food fluid called *fluid* is wine and olive oil[42]." How is that? One beam for two pits or two beams for one pit[43]. One understands one beam for two pits, but two beams for one pit? Is it not that if it is partially impure it is totally impure[37]? Rebbi La in the name of Rebbi Eleazar: Explain it, if he had intended to process it in one batch, and he changed his mind to make it in two batches[44]. Rebbi Yose ben Rebbi Abun said, this applies if it became impure after he syphoned off [the froth] and [the seeds] formed lumps. But if it became impure before he syphoned off and lumps were formed, it does not apply. Rebbi Tabi, Rebbi Joshia the son of Rebbi Yannai: Practice follows Rebbi Eliezer. Rebbi Isaac bar Naḥman in the name of Rebbi Hoshaia: Practice follows Rebbi Eliezer. Rebbi Ḥuna, Rebbi Ḥanania: Practice does not follow Rebbi Eliezer. Rebbi Yose ben Rebbi

Abun in the name of Samuel: Practice does not follow Rebbi Eliezer. There came a case before Rebbi Immi and he did not decide; he said there are two against two. They said to him, but Rebbi Isaac bar Naḥman decided! Nevertheless, he gave no opinion.

35 Tosephta 3:18; in *Ḥallah* 2:8 (fol. 58d) the entire paragraph.

36 The father of Rebbi Jehudah, one of the few known students of R. Eliezer.

37 A fluid becomes impure in its entirety if any drop of it becomes impure.

38 An opening smaller than the diameter of an egg lets impurity enter but not leave. Hence, anything in the funnel may become impure but it cannot transmit impurity to the food in the barrel.

39 In the Tosephta and in *Ḥallah*, "olives". This reading is required since eggs are not subject to heave. Also, the width of an egg is only an upper bound on the diameter of the funnel; since all olives touching the impure olives or their brine will become impure, one certainly is interested in minimizing the number of impure olives generated. In addition, unless the diameter of the funnel is less than the width of an olive, the pure olives filled into the funnel must be completely dry, otherwise they all become impure.

40 The amphora and the funnel touching it form a well-defined domain in space.

41 Cf. Note 1. Since the lowest layer of olives becomes impure, only it and the layer directly above will be impure; all others will be pure and usable for heave.

42 The position of R. Eliezer may be accepted but the interpretation given it by R. Illaï is certainly wrong. One has to consider fluids, not wet solid food.

43 For mechanical pressing, grapes or olives are put into a vat and are covered by a circular cover. On top of it is a beam which is depressed either manually or by a viselike device. If two adjacent vats are pressed simultaneously, this certainly is considered earmarked. The beam itself, wood without cavities, cannot become impure.

44 Two beams for one vat are impractical; that case has to be thrown

out. R. Eliezer permits giving heave from pure for impure if the vintner (or olive grower) originally had the intention of processing his entire harvest in one press. Then they become one batch. If later he decides to process in two different presses and it turns out that one is pure, the other impure, he may give heave for his entire harvest from the pure lot.

(fol. 41a) **משנה ב**: אֵין תּוֹרְמִין מִן הַטָּמֵא עַל הַטָּהוֹר וְאִם תָּרַם שׁוֹגֵג תְּרוּמָתוֹ תְּרוּמָה. מֵזִיד לֹא עָשָׂה וְלֹא כְלוּם. וְכֵן בֶּן לֵוִי שֶׁהָיָה לוֹ מַעֲשֵׂר טֶבֶל הָיָה מַפְרִישׁ עָלָיו וְהוֹלֵךְ. שׁוֹגֵג מַה שֶּׁעָשָׂה עָשׂוּי. מֵזִיד לֹא עָשָׂה כְלוּם. רַבִּי יְהוּדָה אוֹמֵר אִם הָיָה יוֹדֵעַ בּוֹ מִתְּחִילָּה אַף עַל פִּי שֶׁהוּא שׁוֹגֵג לֹא עָשָׂה כְלוּם.

Mishnah 2: One may not give heave from impure produce for pure, but if he gave in error[45], his heave is heave, if intentionally, he did not do anything. Similarly, a Levite who has *ṭevel* tithe which he continually uses to give[46], if he is in error, what he did is done, if intentionally, he did nothing. Rebbi Jehudah says, if he had known of it earlier[47], even if he did it in error, he did not do anything.

45 At the moment of giving heave he did not realize that the lot to be put in order was impure. The Babli (*Pesaḥim* 32a) holds the Mishnah to be a biblical law, applicable only if the impure produce had been pure when it came under the obligation of heave. The Yerushalmi agrees that the prohibition has some biblical basis but it assumes the Mishnah to be applicable without restrictions. {Maimonides translates שוגג by Arabic סאהי "inattentive, absent-minded, distracted"; מזיד by מתעמד "deliberate, premeditated, willful; intentional".}

46 He had tithe of which the heave of the tithe was not given. Since heave of the tithe can be given from one lot on another without restriction, the Levite may use one lot to give heave of the tithe for all other lots, but only after he gave heave for the lot itself.

47 That the produce was impure or, if tithe, that it was *ṭevel*. He holds that then his action cannot be unintentional, only negligent.

(fol. 41c) **הלכה ב**: תַּמָּן תַּנִּינָן הַתּוֹרֵם אֶת הַבּוֹר וְאָמַר הֲרֵי זוֹ תְרוּמָה עַל מְנָת שֶׁתַּעֲלֶה בְשָׁלוֹם שָׁלוֹם מִן הַשֶּׁבֶר שָׁלוֹם מִן הַשְּׁפִיכָה אֲבָל לֹא מִן הַטּוּמְאָה. רִבִּי שִׁמְעוֹן אוֹמֵר אַף מִן הַטּוּמְאָה. אָמַר רִבִּי יוֹסֵי בֶּן חֲנִינָה בְּטוּמְאַת טְבוּלֵי יוֹם הִיא מַתְנִיתָא. אָמַר רִבִּי אִילָא שֶׁכֵּן טְבוּלֵי יוֹם מְצוּיִין בֵּין הַגִּיתּוֹת. אָמַר רִבִּי יוֹסֵי אֵין לִטְבוּל יוֹם מַגַּע אֵצֶל טֶבֶל.

Halakhah 2: There[48], we have stated: "If somebody gives heave from a wine cistern and says: 'This should be heave on condition that it be removed whole', it means whole from breakage and whole from spillage[49] but not from impurity. Rebbi Simeon says, also from impurity." Rebbi Yose ben Ḥanina said, this Mishnah speaks of the impurity of *ṭevul yom*[50]. Rebbi Ila said, since *ṭevulê yom* may be present around wine presses. Rebbi Yose said, a *ṭevul yom* has no touch for *ṭevel*[51].

48 Mishnah *Ṭevul Yom* 4:6.

49 If the amphora containing the heave wine breaks or some of its contents are spilled before the amphora is safely removed from the cistern, the wine that flows back into the cistern is *ṭevel* in breakage and profane in spillage, never heave, and does not make the remaining wine *dema'* (cf. *Demay* Chapter 1, Note 175, Chapter 4, Note 25; *Terumot* Chapter 5). *Dema'* wine is almost worthless.

50 A person freed from impurity by immersion in water who will become pure at sundown. His touch does not make impure but it invalidates heave and sacrifices, cf. *Demay* Chapter 6, Note 136.

51 The touch of a *ṭevul yom* invalidates heave but not *ṭevel* and certainly not profane wine. Therefore, a *ṭevul yom* may work in a winery producing pure wine and R. Simeon is right when he assumes that a reservation concerning the touch of a *ṭevul yom* is in the mind of the person taking heave, even if this is not consciously expressed. Cf. also *Ḥallah* 3:2, Note 43.

תַּנֵּי אָמַר רִבִּי יוּדָן בְּמָה דְבָרִים אֲמוּרִים בִּתְרוּמָה גְדוֹלָה שֶׁהִיא צְרִיכָה לִתְרוֹם מִן הַמּוּקָף. אֲבָל בִּתְרוּמַת מַעֲשֵׂר אֲפִילוּ שְׁאָר כָּל־הַדְּבָרִים שְׁלוֹם הֵם. הָיָה תוֹרֵם תְּרוּמָה וּתְרוּמַת מַעֲשֵׂר כְּאַחַת אֵינוֹ שָׁלוֹם. יְהוּדָה בְּרִבִּי אוֹמֵר לֹא עָלְתָה עַל דַּעְתּוֹ שֶׁל זֶה לַעֲבוֹר עַל דִּבְרֵי תוֹרָה לְהַקְדִּים תְּרוּמַת מַעֲשֵׂר לִתְרוּמָה גְדוֹלָה. מָתִיב רִבִּי בָּא בַר מָמָל וְהָא תַנִּינָן אֵין תּוֹרְמִין מִן הַטָּמֵא עַל הַטָּהוֹר הַגַּע עַצְמָךְ שֶׁתָּרַם וְאָמַר לֹא עָלְתָה עַל דַּעְתּוֹ לַעֲבוֹר עַל דִּבְרֵי תוֹרָה. אָמַר רִבִּי בָּא בַר מָמָל אִם אָמַר אַתְּ כֵּן נִמְצֵאת מַבְרִיחוֹ מִן הַקַּלָּה וּמַכְנִיסוֹ לַחֲמוּרָה. טֶבֶל בַּעֲוֹן מִיתָה. טָמֵא שֶׁאָכַל אֶת הַטָּהוֹר בַּעֲשֵׂה.

It was stated[52]: "Rebbi Jehudah said, about what was this said? About Great Heave which must be given from what is earmarked. But for the heave of the tithe, everything is supposed to be whole. If he gave Great Heave and heave of the tithe together, it is not whole." Jehudah ben Rebbi said, he certainly did not want to overstep the words of the Torah in giving heave of the tithe before the Great Heave[53]. Rebbi Abba bar Mamal objected: Did we not state that "one may not give heave from impure produce for pure"? Think about it, when he did it and said, I did not intend to transgress the words of the Torah[54]! Rebbi Abba bar Mamal said, if you say so, you let him flee from a minor sin to a major one! *Ṭevel* is a deadly sin, but an impure person who ate pure food oversteps a positive commandment[55].

52 Tosephta *Ṭevul Yom* 2:16-17, formulated as anonymous statement. {In the Rome ms., the name of the tradent is R. Yose. This reading is proven false in the next paragraph.} The Tosephta cannot represent the Yerushalmi tradition since for תרומה גדולה it has תרומת ראשית "beginning heave", a reference to *Num.* 18:12.

53 He explains why heave of the tithe is under the rules of Great Heave in case both are taken together. If Great Heave were invalidated but not heave of the tithe, it would turn out

retroactively that heave of the tithe was given before the Great Heave, which not only is forbidden but also is very difficult to rectify. Therefore, we assume that he did not want any complications and, if made aware of this problem, would himself want to nullify the entire transaction.

54 Since one may not give impure heave for pure produce, why do we not stipulate that if the person giving in error would be made aware of what he did, he automatically would want to nullify the transaction. The answer is that in this case, the remedy would be worse than the problem.

55 This is the text in both mss. but it is impossible since the impure Cohen who eats heave transgresses a *karet* prohibition. It must read: "a pure person who ate impure food", cf. *Num.* 18:11: "Every pure person in your house shall eat it," *viz.*, pure heave. The details are given in *Bikkurim* 2:1; there the text is as corrected here.

תַּנֵּי בְּשֵׁם רִבִּי יוֹסֵי אִם תָּרַם מִן הַטָּמֵא עַל הַטָּהוֹר בֵּין בְּשׁוֹגֵג בֵּין בְּמֵזִיד מַה שֶׁעָשָׂה עָשׂוּי. רִבִּי פִּינְחָס בְּעָא קוֹמֵי רִבִּי יָסָא כְּדוֹן כְּסָבוּר בָּהֶן שֶׁהֵן טְהוֹרִין וְהָיָה יוֹדֵעַ שֶׁהֵן טְמֵיאִין וְסָבַר שֶׁמּוּתָּר לִתְרוֹם מִן הַטָּמֵא עַל הַטָּהוֹר. אָמַר לֵיהּ יְאוּת רִבִּי סָבַר כְּרִבִּי יוּדָה בְּרַם כְּרִבִּי יוֹסֵי הִיא הָדָא הִיא הָדָא.

It was stated in the name of Rebbi Yose: "If somebody gave heave from impure for pure produce, whether it was in error or intentionally, what he did is done[56]." Rebbi Phineas asked before Rebbi Assi: There[57], it is when he thought that it was pure when he had known that it was impure, but he was of the opinion that one may give heave from impure for pure produce? He said to him, that is so, Rebbi[58] holds with Rebbi Jehudah. But for Rebbi Yose it would not make any difference.

56 Tosephta 3:19.

57 He asks about the statement of R. Jehudah in the Mishnah that previous knowledge invalidates later acts of absentmindedness. It is agreed that this holds if he forgets facts; what if he is in error about the law? One must assume that sometime in the past,

he had been informed of the correct practice.

58 The editor of the anonymous Mishnah.

(fol. 41a) **משנה ג**: הַמַּטְבִּיל כֵּלִים בַּשַּׁבָּת בְּשׁוֹגֵג יִשְׁתַּמֵּשׁ בָּהֶן וּמֵזִיד לֹא יִשְׁתַּמֵּשׁ בָּהֶן. הַמְעַשֵּׂר וְהַמְבַשֵּׁל בַּשַּׁבָּת שׁוֹגֵג יֵאָכֵל מֵזִיד לֹא יֵאָכֵל. הַנּוֹטֵעַ בַּשַּׁבָּת שׁוֹגֵג יְקַיֵּים מֵזִיד יַעֲקוֹר וּבַשְּׁבִיעִית בֵּין שׁוֹגֵג בֵּין מֵזִיד יַעֲקוֹר.

Mishnah 3: He who immerses vessels[59] on the Sabbath, if unintentionally he may use them, if intentionally he may not use them. He who tithes or cooks on the Sabbath, if in error it may be eaten, if intentionally it may not be eaten[60]. He who plants[61] on the Sabbath, if unintentionally he may keep it, if intentionally it must be uprooted. In the Sabbatical year it must be uprooted, whether in error or intentionally.

59 Impure vessels that only may be purified by immersion in a *miqweh* containing at least 40 *seah* of water. Immersion is a rabbinical prohibition on the Sabbath because it is making an unusable vessel usable, which in the case of visibly unusable vessels would be a biblical prohibition and a deadly sin.

60 Tithing is a rabbinical, cooking a biblical prohibition. In both cases, the cook may not eat of his food until after the end of the Sabbath.

61 Also a biblical prohibition. The restriction concerning the Sabbatical year is purely rabbinical, enacted because people tended not to observe the Sabbatical while everybody observed the Sabbath.

(fol. 41c) **הלכה ג**: מַתְנִיתָא בְּכֵלִים גְּדוֹלִים אֲבָל בְּכֵלִים קְטַנִּים מַעֲרִים עֲלֵיהֶן וּמַטְבִּילָן. וְתַנֵּי רִבִּי הוֹשַׁעְיָה מְמַלֵּא הוּא אָדָם כֵּלִי טָמֵא מִן הַבּוֹר וּמַעֲרִים עָלָיו וּמַטְבִּילוֹ. וְתַנֵּי נָפַל דְּלָייוֹ בְּתוֹךְ הַבּוֹר נָפַל כֵּלָיו לְתוֹךְ הַבּוֹר מַעֲרִים עֲלֵיהֶן

וּמַטְבִּילָן. תְּרֵין אֲמוֹרִין חַד אָמַר בְּכֵלִים שֶׁנִּיטְמְאוּ בְּאַב הַטּוּמְאָה. וְחָרֵינָה אָמַר בְּכֵלִים שֶׁנִּיטְמְאוּ בְּוְולַד הַטּוּמְאָה. מָתִיב מָאן דְּאָמַר בְּוְולַד הַטּוּמְאָה לְמָאן דְּאָמַר בְּאַב הַטּוּמְאָה וַאֲפִילוּ בְחוֹל טָעוּן הָעֶרֶב שֶׁמֶשׁ. אָמַר לֵיהּ בְּרוֹצֶה לְהִשְׁתַּמֵּשׁ בָּהֶן חוּלִין בְּטָהֳרָה.

Halakhah 3: [62]Our Mishnah is about large vessels, but with small vessels one may use a ruse and immerse them, as Rebbi Hoshaia had stated[63]: "A person may fill an impure vessel from the cistern as a ruse and immerse it." Also, we have stated: "If his pail or garment fell into the cistern, one may use this as a ruse and immerse them[64]." Two Amoraïm, one says [one may use a ruse] for vessels impure in original impurity; but the other one says [only] for vessels impure in derivative impurity[65]. The one who said in derivative impurity objected to the one who said in original impurity: Even on weekdays, would it not need sundown[66]? He said to him, if he wants to use them in purity for profane food.

62 This paragraph and the next are also in *Šabbat* 2:7, this paragraph also in *Bezah* 2:1.

63 Tosephta *Šabbat* 16:12, *Bezah* 2:9; a similar *baraita* quoted in Babli *Bezah* 18a. The Tosephta makes the procedure explicit: "Vessels impure in original impurity may not be immersed on a holiday, and certainly not on the Sabbath. But one may fill a cup, or a pail, or a bucket in order to drink *at the same time one thinks about it*" [that it should be a valid immersion.] Impurity can be removed only by conscious immersion.

64 At the moment he goes to pull the things out of the cistern, he may intend to have the immersion count for removal of impurity even though the immersion itself was accidental.

65 For original and derivative impurity, cf *Demay* Chapter 2, Note 137. The language of the Tosephta shows that it was unknown to the editors of the Yerushalmi.

66 The vessels are *Tevulê Yom*. As stated in Note 51, immersion purifies immediately for all profane food and purposes.

רִבִּי יִרְמְיָה רִבִּי זְעִירָא בְּשֵׁם רִבִּי חִיָּיה בַּר אַשִׁי אִישָּׁה פִיקַחַת מְדִיחָה כּוֹס כָּן קְעָרָה כָּן תַּמְחוּי כָּן. נִמְצֵאת מַרְבֶּצֶת בֵּיתָהּ בַּשַּׁבָּת.

Rebbi Jeremiah, Rebbi Zeïra in the name of Rebbi Ḥiyya bar Ashi: An intelligent woman washes a cup here, a bowl there, a dish there; it turns out that her entire house was wetted on the Sabbath[67].

67 The parallel is in *Šabbat* 15:3 (fol. 15b). The house has a dirt floor, and periodic wetting is needed to keep the air dust free. The Babli (*Šabbat* 95a) notes that this trick is superfluous in Babylonian practice. The Babli follows R. Simeon for whom any work is permitted on the Sabbath if its intention is legitimate and permitted, even if some side effect would constitute a forbidden action if done by itself, unless the forbidden action is unavoidable. In our case, wetting the floor to strengthen the ground and the adobe house would be an action derivative of building and forbidden. But wetting the floor lightly to avoid dust is a legitimate action and, since in this case the water will evaporate quickly and any building effect would be temporary, it will be permitted outright. It follows that the Yerushalmi rejects the point of view of Rebbi Simeon.

רִבִּי שְׁמוּאֵל בְּשֵׁם רִבִּי אַבָּהוּ בְּשׁוֹגֵג בְּאִיסּוּר וּבְמֵזִיד בְּאִיסּוּר. אָמַר רִבִּי יוֹסֵי מַתְנִיתָא אָמְרָה כֵּן הַמְעַשֵּׂר וְהַמְבַשֵּׁל בַּשַּׁבָּת שׁוֹגֵג יֵאָכֵל מֵזִיד לֹא יֵאָכֵל. בְּשׁוֹגֵג בְּאִיסּוּר וּבְמֵזִיד בְּאִיסּוּר. תַּנֵּי הַמְבוּשָּׁל בְּשַׁבָּת שׁוֹגֵג יֵאָכֵל מֵזִיד לֹא יֵאָכֵל דִּבְרֵי רִבִּי מֵאִיר. רִבִּי יְהוּדָה אוֹמֵר בְּשׁוֹגֵג יֵאָכֵל לְמוֹצָאֵי שַׁבָּת. בְּמֵזִיד לֹא יֵאָכֵל עוֹלָמִית. רִבִּי יוֹחָנָן הַסַּנְדְּלָר אוֹמֵר בְּשׁוֹגֵג יֵאָכֵל לְמוֹצָאֵי שַׁבָּת לַאֲחֵרִים וְלֹא לוֹ. בְּמֵזִיד לֹא לוֹ וְלֹא לַאֲחֵרִים. שְׁמוּאֵל כְּרִבִּי יוֹחָנָן הַסַּנְדְּלָר. רַב כַּד הֲוֵי מוֹרֵי בַּחֲבוּרָתֵיהּ מוֹרֵי כְּרִבִּי מֵאִיר. בְּצִיבּוּרֵי כְּרִבִּי יוֹחָנָן הַסַּנְדְּלָר. אָמַר רִבִּי שִׁמְעוֹן בַּר כַּרְסָנָא כְּרִבִּי יִשְׁמָעֵאל בְּנוֹ שֶׁל רִבִּי יוֹחָנָן בֶּן בְּרוֹקָה הוֹרֵי לוֹן. דְּתַנֵּי רִבִּי יִשְׁמָעֵאל בְּנוֹ שֶׁל רִבִּי יוֹחָנָן בֶּן בְּרוֹקָה כָּל־דָּבָר שֶׁחַיָּיבִין עַל זְדוֹנוֹ כָּרֵת וְעַל שִׁגְגָתוֹ חַטָּאת וַעֲשָׂאוֹ בַּשַּׁבָּת בֵּין בְּשׁוֹגֵג בֵּין בְּמֵזִיד אָסוּר בֵּין לוֹ בֵּין לַאֲחֵרִים

לֹא יֵאָכֵל וְכָל־דָּבָר שֶׁאֵין חַייָבִין עַל זְדוֹנוֹ כָּרֵת וְעַל שִׁגְגָתוֹ חַטָּאת וַעֲשָׂאוֹ בַּשַּׁבָּת בְּשׁוֹגֵג יֵאָכֵל לְמוֹצָאֵי שַׁבָּת לַאֲחֵרִים וְלֹא לוֹ בְּמֵזִיד לֹא לוֹ וְלֹא לַאֲחֵרִים. בָּעִין קוֹמֵי רִבִּי יוֹחָנָן אַתְּ מַה אַתְּ אָמַר אָמַר לוֹן אֲנִי אֵין לִי אֶלָּא מִשְׁנָה הַמְעַשֵּׂר וְהַמְבַשֵּׁל בַּשַּׁבָּת בְּשׁוֹגֵג יֵאָכֵל בְּמֵזִיד לֹא יֵאָכֵל. שָׁמַע רַב חִסְדָּא וָמַר הוּתְּרוּ שַׁבָּתוֹת לֹא כֵן אָמַר רַב הוּנָא בְּשֵׁם רַב וְתַנֵּי רִבִּי חִייָה כֵן בָּרִאשׁוֹנָה הָיוּ אוֹמְרִים הַשּׁוֹכֵחַ תַּבְשִׁיל עַל גַּבֵּי כִירָתוֹ בַּשַּׁבָּת בְּשׁוֹגֵג יֵאָכֵל בְּמֵזִיד לֹא יֵאָכֵל. נֶחְשְׁדוּ שֶׁהָיוּ מַנִּיחִין מְזִידִין וְאוֹמְרִים שְׁכֵיחִין הָיִינוּ וְאָסְרוּ לָהֶן אֶת הַשּׁוֹכֵחַ. וְאַתְּ אָמַר הָכָא הָכֵין. אָמַר רִבִּי הִילָא נֶחְשְׁדוּ לִהְיוֹת מַנִּיחִין וְלֹא נֶחְשְׁדוּ לִהְיוֹת מְבַשְּׁלִין. קָנְסוּ בְּמַנִּיחַ וְלֹא קָנְסוּ בִּמְבַשֵּׁל.

Rebbi Samuel in the name of Rebbi Abbahu: "Unintentionally", when it is forbidden, "intentionally" when it is forbidden[68]. Rebbi Yose said, the Mishnah states this: "He who tithes or cooks on the Sabbath, if unintentionally it may be eaten, if intentionally it may not be eaten"; "unintentionally", when it is forbidden, "intentionally", when it is [equally] forbidden[69]. It was stated[70]: "What was cooked on the Sabbath, if it was done unintentionally it may be eaten, intentionally it may not be eaten, the words of Rebbi Meïr. Rebbi Jehudah said, unintentionally it may be eaten at the end of the Sabbath, intentionally never. Rebbi Joḥanan the Alexandrian[71] said, unintentionally it may be eaten at the end of the Sabbath by others but not by himself, intentionally neither by him nor by others." Samuel followed Rebbi Joḥanan the Alexandrian. Rav in his own group instructed following Rebbi Meïr[72], in public following Rebbi Joḥanan the Alexandrian. Rebbi Simeon bar Karsana[73] said, he instructed us following Rebbi Ismael, the son of Rebbi Joḥanan ben Beroqa. As it was stated[74]: "Rebbi Joḥanan ben Beroqa said, in any case where an intentional sin is punished by extirpation and an unintentional sin by an expiatory offering[75], if the sin was committed on the Sabbath unintentionally or intentionally, the result is forbidden both for him and for others; it may not be eaten. In any case an intentional sin is not punished by extirpation and for the unintentional sin no expiatory offering is due[76]; if it was done on the Sabbath unintentionally the result may be eaten by others after the end of the Sabbath but not by him, intentionally neither by him nor by others." They asked before Rebbi Johanan: What do you say? He said, I have only the Mishnah: "He who tithes or cooks on the Sabbath, if in error it may be eaten, if intentionally it may not be eaten". Rav Ḥisda heard this and said, the Sabbaths have been permitted! Did not Rav Huna say in the name of Rav and did not Rebbi Ḥiyya state[77]: "In earlier times they said, one who forgets some dish on his stove on the Sabbath, unintentionally it may be eaten, intentionally it may not be eaten. People were suspected that they left it intentionally and said, it was forgotten; they forbade it to them when it was forgotten." And here, you say so? Rebbi Ila said, they were suspected to leave it on, they were not suspected to cook. They imposed a fine for forgetting but not for cooking.

68 The two parts must be parallel, the difference between "intentional" and "unintentional" can be only in the mind of the agent. There are two possibilities, either that he forgot that it was Sabbath or that he was unaware that cooking is forbidden on the Sabbath.

69 Since intentionally he must have known that it was Sabbath, the unintentional case must be the same.

70 Tosephta *Šabbat* 2:15; Babli *Ketubot* 34a, and partially in *Šabbat* 38a, *Beẓah* 17a, *Baba Qama* 71a, *Ḥulin* 15a, *Giṭṭin* 52b. From here to the end of the Halakhah, the text is also in *Šabbat* 3:1, fol. 5d.

71 A student of R. Aqiba, Tanna of the fourth generation. It seems that the name *Sandlar* already then meant

"Alexander's".

72 Rav stated the exact rules to his students as theory. But in public he followed more restrictive rules. In Babli *Ḥulin* 15a, Rav is reported to publicly proclaiming R. Jehudah's rule.

73 A Galilean Amora of the fourth generation, student of R. Aḥa. His appearance as reporting Rav's direct instructions to his students seems anachronistic.

74 Tosephta *Šabbat* 2:16.

75 Cooking on the Sabbath.

78 Tithing on the Sabbath.

77 The first sentence here, without the introductory "in earlier times they said", is the first sentence of Tosephta *Šabbat* 2:14. The remainder of that Tosephta, in the name of R. Jehudah, parallels the tannaitic text in the next paragraph.

חָזְרוּ לוֹמַר תַּבְשִׁיל שֶׁהוּא מִצְטַמֵּק וְיָפֶה לוֹ אָסוּר מִצְטַמֵּק וְרַע לוֹ מוּתָּר. אֵי זֶהוּ תַּבְשִׁיל שֶׁהוּא מִצְטַמֵּק וְיָפֶה לוֹ כְּרוּב וַאֲפוּנִין וּבָשָׂר טָרוּף. אָמַר רִבִּי תַּנְחוּם בַּר עִילָּא אַף רָאשֵׁי לִפְתוֹת וְרָאשֵׁי קֵפַלּוֹטוֹת עָשׂוּ אוֹתָן כְּתַבְשִׁיל שֶׁהוּא מִצְטַמֵּק וְיָפֶה לוֹ. בֵּיצִים מָה הֵן. רִבִּי יוֹסֵי בְּשֵׁם רִבִּי יִשְׁמָעֵאל. רִבִּי יִרְמְיָה רִבִּי חֲנִינָה בְּשֵׁם רִבִּי יִשְׁמָעֵאל בֵּי רִבִּי יוֹסֵי אַבָּא עָלָה לְבֵיתוֹ וּמָצָא שָׁם בֵּיצִים וְאָסַר חַמִּין וְהִתִּיר. רִבִּי שְׁמוּאֵל בַּר נָתָן בְּשֵׁם רִבִּי חָמָא בַּר חֲנִינָה אֲנִי וְאַבָּא עָלִינוּ לְחַמַּת גָּדֵר וְהֵבִיאוּ לְפָנֵינוּ בֵּיצִים קְטָנוֹת כְּחִזְרְרִין וְטַעֲמוֹן יָפֶה כְּפִינְקְרֵסִין.

"[77]They came back to say, a dish which will improve the more it shrinks is forbidden, deteriorate the more it shrinks is permitted. What is a dish better the more it shrinks? Cabbage, peas, and chopped meat." Rebbi Tanḥum bar Illa said, they also considered heads of turnips and leeks as dishes better the more they shrink. What about eggs? Rebbi Yose in the name of Rebbi Ismael: Rebbi Jeremiah, Rebbi Ḥanina in the name of Rebbi Ismael ben Rebbi Yose: My father came home and found eggs and forbade them, hot water and permitted it[78]. Rebbi Samuel bar Natan in the name of Rebbi Ḥama bar Ḥanina: I went with my father to Ḥammat Gader where they brought before us eggs small like *ḥizrar* apples[79] and they tasted delicious like sweet bread[80].

78 In the Tosephta, R. Jehudah permits hot water to stay on an open fire only if it came to a boil before the Sabbath.

79 Cf. Mishnah *Kilaim* 4:1. The eggs must have been boiled a very long time to shrink to this small size. The statement might disagree with the Babli which reports that Samuel used eggs dipped alternatingly into boiling and cold water 1000 times as a diagnostic device for ulcers and intestinal bleeding since they were so hard that they were not digested and could be examined after evacuation but were small enough to be swallowed whole (*Nedarim* 50b).

80 Probably Greek πάγκρεας, -ατος, τό "sweet bread, pancreas" (E. G.).

תַּנֵּי לֹא תְמַלֵּא אִישָּׁה קְדֵירָה עֲסָסִיּוֹת וְתוֹרְמוֹסִין וְתִתְּנֵם לְתוֹךְ הַתַּנּוּר עֶרֶב שַׁבָּת עִם חֲשֵׁיכָה. וְאִים נָתְנָה אֲסוּרִין לְמוֹצָאֵי שַׁבָּת עַד כְּדֵי שֶׁיֵּעָשׂוּ. רִבִּי אָחָא אָמַר בְּמֵזִיד כְּרִבִּי מֵאִיר רִבִּי יוֹסֵי אוֹמֵר בְּשׁוֹגֵג כְּרִבִּי יְהוּדָה. אָמַר רִבִּי מָנָא יָאוּת. אָמַר רִבִּי יוֹסֵי הַנּוֹטֵעַ בְּשׁוֹגֵג בַּשַּׁבָּת יְקַיֵּים בְּמֵזִיד יַעֲקוֹר בַּשְּׁבִיעִית בֵּין בְּשׁוֹגֵג בֵּין בְּמֵזִיד יַעֲקוֹר. רִבִּי יוּדָה אוֹמֵר חִילּוּף הַדְּבָרִים בַּשְּׁבִיעִית בְּשׁוֹגֵג יְקַיֵּים בְּמֵזִיד יַעֲקוֹר בַּשַּׁבָּת בֵּין בְּשׁוֹגֵג בֵּין בְּמֵזִיד יַעֲקוֹר מִפְּנֵי שֶׁהֲנָיַית שַׁבָּת עָלָיו. וְכָאן מִכֵּיוָן שֶׁאַתָּה אוֹמֵר הַמְתֵּן לְמוֹצָאֵי שַׁבָּת עַד כְּדֵי שֶׁיֵּעָשׂוּ כְּמִי שֶׁלֹּא נֶהֱנֶה מֵחְמַת שַׁבָּת כְּלוּם. מַה טַעַם דְּרַבָּנִין נֶחְשַׁד עַל הַשְּׁבִיעִית וְלֹא נֶחְשְׁדוּ עַל הַשַּׁבָּתוֹת. דָּבָר אַחֵר מוֹנִין לַשְּׁבִיעִית וְאֵין מוֹנִין לְשַׁבָּתוֹת. הֵיךְ עֲבִידָא נָטַע פָּחוֹת מִשְּׁלֹשִׁים לִפְנֵי שְׁבִיעִית וְנִכְנְסָה לַשְּׁבִיעִית. אִין תֵּימַר חֲשָׁד אֵין כָּאן חֲשָׁד. אִין תֵּימַר מוֹנִין יֵשׁ כָּאן מוֹנִין. נָטַע פָּחוֹת מִשְּׁלֹשִׁים לִפְנֵי שְׁמִינִית[81] וְנִכְנְסָה שְׁמִינִית אִין תֵּימַר חֲשָׁד יֵשׁ כָּאן חֲשָׁד וְאַתְיָא כְּמָאן דְּאָמַר מִפְּנֵי מוֹנִין בְּרַם כְּמָאן דְּאָמַר מִפְּנֵי חֲשָׁד וְקָנְסוּ שׁוֹגֵג מִפְּנֵי מֵזִיד.

It was stated[82]: "A woman should not fill a pot with *'assasiot* and lupines and put them into the oven at the start of the Sabbath, at nightfall. If she did, they are forbidden after the end of the Sabbath until the time they could have been done." Rebbi Aḥa said: intentionally, following

Rebbi Meïr; Rebbi Yose said: unintentionally, following Rebbi Jehudah. Rebbi Mana said, that is correct, did not Rebbi Yose say, "[83]He who is planting on the Sabbath, if unintentional, he may keep it, if intentional, he must tear it out. In the Sabbatical year, he must tear it out whether [planting was] unintentional or intentional. Rebbi Jehudah says, it is the other way around. In the Sabbatical, if unintentional, he may keep it, if intentional, he must tear it out, on the Sabbath he must tear it out whether [planting was] unintentional or intentional because the profit of the Sabbath [is forbidden] to him." And here, since you say that after the end of the Sabbath he has to wait until the time it could have been done, he did not gain anything from the Sabbath. What is the reason of the rabbis[84]? People are suspected about the Sabbatical but not about the Sabbath. Another explanation: One counts Sabbaticals, one does not count Sabbaths[85]. What is this about? If somebody planted less than thirty days before the Sabbatical and now it is the Sabbatical, if it is because of suspicion, there is no suspicion; if it is for counting, it is counted[86]. Less than thirty days before the eighth year and now it is the eighth year, if it is because of suspicion, there is suspicion; can it be explained for counting[87]? But you have to say because of suspicion; they fined for the unintentional because of the intentional[88].

81 From the text in *Šabbat;* here: שביעית. The emendations of the commentators here are without foundation.

82 Tosephta *Šabbat* 3:1. *'Assasiot* are an undetermined kind of legumes (in the words of the Gaonim: they exist in the Land of Israel but not in Babylonia) which need very long cooking to become edible, similar to lupines. Compare Arabic عسر "to harden".

83 Tosephta *Šabbat* 2:21. Both reasons are given in the Tosephta as basis of the decision of the anonymous majority but R. Jehudah's statement is

left without explanation. The *baraita* in the Babli (*Giṭṭin* 53b) gives no reasons at all.

84 The anonymous opinion in the Tosephta.

85 Since the fruits of trees are forbidden the first three years as *'orlah* and must be redeemed in the fourth year, everybody will realize that the tree was illegally planted in the Sabbatical.

86 The first year of *'orlah* is the Sabbatical, the 30 days are not counted; cf. *Ševi'it* 2:6, Mishnah and Note 45.

87 Since the first year counted is the first year of the Sabbatical cycle, nobody will notice that the tree was planted in the last month of the Sabbatical.

88 A reason usually attributed to R. Meïr, cf. *Orlah* 3:7. The text of the last clause in *Šabbat* is longer but the formulation here seems to be the original one.

(fol. 41a) **משנה ד**: אֵין תּוֹרְמִין מִמִּין עַל שֶׁאֵינוֹ מִינוֹ וְאִם תָּרַם אֵין תְּרוּמָתוֹ תְרוּמָה. כָּל־מִין חִטִּים אֶחָד. כָּל־מִין תְּאֵינִים וּגְרוֹגֶרֶת וּדְבֵילָה אֶחָד וְתוֹרֵם מִזֶּה עַל זֶה. כָּל־מָקוֹם שֶׁיֵּשׁ כֹּהֵן תּוֹרֵם מִן הַיָּפֶה וְכָל־מָקוֹם שֶׁאֵין כֹּהֵן תּוֹרֵם מִן הַמִּתְקַיְּימִים. רִבִּי יְהוּדָה אוֹמֵר לְעוֹלָם הוּא תּוֹרֵם מִן הַיָּפֶה.

Mishnah 4: One does not give heave from one species for another species; if he gave, his heave is no heave. All kinds of wheat are one. All kinds of figs, dried figs, and fig cakes are one; he may give heave from one for the other. At a place where there is a Cohen one gives from the best, but where there is no Cohen he gives from what is durable. Rebbi Jehudah says, one always gives from the best.

(fol. 41c) **הלכה ד**: רִבִּי יוֹחָנָן בְּשֵׁם רִבִּי יַנַּאי זֶה אֶחָד מִשְּׁלֹשָׁה מִדְרָשׁוֹת שֶׁהֵן מְחוּוָרִין בַּתּוֹרָה כֹּל חֵלֶב יִצְהָר וְכָל־חֵלֶב תִּירוֹשׁ וְדָגָן מַה נָן קַייָמִין אִם לְלַמֵּד שֶׁהֵן תּוֹרְמִין מִן הַתִּירוֹשׁ עַל הַדָּגָן וּמִן הַדָּגָן עַל הַתִּירוֹשׁ. הָתֵיבוּן הֲרֵי תִּירוֹשׁ

וְיִצְהָר הֲרֵי שְׁנֵי מִינֵי אִילָן וְאֵין תּוֹרְמִין וְלֹא מְעַשְּׂרִין מִזֶּה עַל זֶה. דּוּ אָמַר מַה תִּירוֹשׁ וְיִצְהָר שֶׁהֵן מְיוּחָדִין שֶׁהֵן שְׁנֵי מִינֵי אִילָן אֵין תּוֹרְמִין (fol. 41d) וְלֹא מְעַשְּׂרִין מִזֶּה עַל זֶה. וְאִם אֲנִי מַרְבֶּה שְׁנֵי מִינִן שֶׁבְּדָגָן שְׁנֵי מִינִין שֶׁבִּתְבוּאָה שֶׁאֵין תּוֹרְמִין וְלֹא מְעַשְּׂרִין מִזֶּה עַל זֶה.

Halakhah 4: Rebbi Yoḥanan in the name of Rebbi Yannai: This is one of three obvious inferences in the Torah. (*Num.* 18:12): "All the best of olive oil, all the best of cider and grain[89]." Where do we hold? Is it to conclude that one may give heave from cider for grain and from grain for cider? One must object that cider and olive oil come from two different species of tree and one may not give heave or tithe from one for the other! This means that cider and olive oil are paradigms for two species of trees, in which case one may not give heave or tithe from one for the other. Then I have to add two species of grain, two kinds of produce of which one may not give heave or tithe from one for the other.

89 This is the description of heave; the description as "best" is the basis of the position of R. Jehudah. In the verse, olive oil is treated separately from cider and grain. Everybody agrees that heave of olive oil must be kept separate from that of cider and grain. The argument, known as בנין אב מכתוב אחד, is that if two different species of trees are treated as distinct then two species belonging to completely different families of plants certainly must be treated as distinct.

כָּל־מִין חִטִּין אֶחָד. לָכֵן צְרִיכָה אֲפִילוּ מֵאַגְדּוֹן עַל שַׁמְתִּית וּמִן שַׁמְתִּית עַל אַגְדּוֹן.

"All kinds of wheat are one." It is needed [since it applies] even from white wheat on brown wheat and vice-versa[90].

90 For the determination of these kinds, cf. *Peah* Chapter 2, Notes 85-86.

כָּל־מִין תְּאֵינִים וּגְרוֹגֶרֶת וּדְבֵילָה אַחַת וְתוֹרְמִין מִזֶּה עַל זֶה. תַּנֵּי תּוֹרְמִין תְּאֵינִים עַל הַגְּרוֹגְרוֹת הַגְּרוֹגְרוֹת בְּמִנְייָן. וּגְרוֹגְרוֹת עַל הַתְּאֵינִים בְּמִידָּה אֲבָל לֹא תְאֵינִים עַל הַגְּרוֹגְרוֹת בְּמִידָּה וְלֹא גְרוֹגְרוֹת עַל הַתְּאֵינִים בְּמִנְייָן. רַבָּן שִׁמְעוֹן בֶּן גַּמְלִיאֵל אוֹמֵר סַלֵּי תְאֵינִים וּגְרוֹגְרוֹת מִין אֶחָד הֵן וְתוֹרְמִין וּמְעַשְּׂרִין מִזֶּה עַל זֶה. אָמַר רִבִּי יִשְׁמָעֵאל בֵּי רִבִּי יוֹסֵי אַבָּא הָיָה נוֹטֵל עֶשֶׂר גְּרֹגְרוֹת מִן הַמּוּקְצֶה עַל תִּשְׁעִים תְּאֵינִים שֶׁבְּכַלְכָּלָה. רִבִּי יִרְמְיָה סָבַר מֵימַר אַתָּה רוֹאֶה אֶת הַצָּמֵק כְּאִילּוּ תָפַח וּנְסַב סַלִּין כְּמַה דְאִינּוּן. רִבִּי יוֹנָה וְרִבִּי יוֹסֵי תְּרֵין אָמְרִין דֶּרֶךְ הַתָּפֵח לִצְמוֹק וְאֵין דֶּרֶךְ הַצָּמֵק לִתְפּוֹחַ. וּנְסַב סַלִּין רַבְרְבִין בִּתְאֵינַיָּא. אָמַר לוֹן רִבִּי אָחָא כֵּן רִבִּי אִילַּי רַבְּכוֹן הֲוֵי בָהּ.

"All kinds of figs, dried figs, and fig cakes are one; he may give heave from one for the other." It was stated[91]: "One gives as heave fresh figs for dried figs; dried figs go by count[92]. Dried figs for fresh figs by volume[93], but fresh figs for dry figs do not go by volume, nor dry figs for fresh figs by count. Rabban Simeon ben Gamliel said, baskets of fresh and dried figs are all one kind and one gives heave and tithes from one for the other[94]. Rebbi Ismael ben Rebbi Yose[95] said, my father used to take ten dried figs from the drying place for ninety fresh figs in the container[96]." Rebbi Jeremiah wanted to say, you consider the shriveled ones as if they had swelled and you take the baskets as they are[97]. Rebbi Jonah and Rebbi Yose both say that swollen shrinks but shrunk does not swell; one would have to take large baskets for fresh figs.[98]. Rebbi Aḥa said to them, that is what your teacher Rebbi Ilai thought about it.

91 Tosephta 4:1-3, but there "count" and "volume" are switched. This Tosephta and the one quoted in the next paragraph are discussed in Babli *Menaḥot* 54b.

92 Since figs shrink considerably in drying, if one would tithe the fresh figs for dried figs by volume, he would give much too little since the number of fresh figs would be too small. The

heave discussed here must be heave of the tithe since the Great Heave is given by estimate and exact measurements are frowned upon in that case.

93 This rule must follow Abba Eleazar ben Gamla (Chapter 1, Note 90).

94 Rabban Simeon disagrees with the anonymous Tanna and allows fresh figs to be given by volume for dried figs and dry figs by count for fresh ones. {There is no evidence that Rabban Simeon speaks about places where there is no Cohen to whom to give heave and he allows both fresh figs, the best, or dried figs, the durable ones, to be given, as asserted by R. S. Lieberman.}

95 The same name is given in the Tosephta; in the Babli it is R. Eleazar ben R. Yose, the second prominent son of R. Yose.

96 He disagrees with the anonymous Tanna and requires counting if dry figs are given for fresh ones; he disagrees with Abba Eleazar ben Gamla.

97 Rabban Simeon does not necessarily disagree with the anonymous Tanna; if one takes a dried fig as stand-in for the fresh fig it once was, one may take a small volume of dried figs as equivalent of a large volume of fresh figs.

98 The argument of R. Jeremiah works only one way, *viz.*, taking fresh figs for dried ones. Since R. Simeon declares taking heave permissible both ways, he must disagree with the anonymous Tanna. In the next paragraph, R. Yose argues similarly that cereal in water only expands but never shrinks.

תַּמָּן תַּנִּינָן כְּבֵיצָה אוֹכְלִין שֶׁהִנִּיחָן בַּחַמָּה וְנִתְמַעֲטוּ כֵּן כְּזַיִת מִן הַנְּבֵילָה וְכַעֲדָשָׁה מִן הַשֶּׁרֶץ כְּזַיִת פִּיגּוּל כְּזַיִת נוֹתָר כְּזַיִת חֵלֶב הֲרֵי אֵילּוּ טְהוֹרִין. דְּרוֹמָאֵי אָמְרֵי וְהוּא שֶׁיְּהֵא כְּזַיִת בְּעִיקָּרוֹ[99]. רִבִּי יוֹחָנָן וְרִבִּי שִׁמְעוֹן בֶּן לָקִישׁ תְּרֵיהוֹן אָמְרִין וְאַף עַל פִּי שֶׁאֵין כְּזַיִת מֵעִיקָּרוֹ. תַּמָּן תַּנִּינָן אָמְרוּ לוֹ אַף הָיְתָה חֲסֵירָה אוֹ יְתֵירָה. מָנִי אָמַר לוֹ רִבִּי מֵאִיר פְּעָמִים שֶׁהַשְּׂעוֹר יָפֶה וְהוּא תָּפוּחַ הָא אִילּוּ סוֹלֶת הָיְתָה צְמוּקָה וְעַכְשָׁיו שֶׁהוּא שְׂעוֹר יָפֶה וְהִיא תָפוּחַ אַתְּ רוֹאֶה אֶת הַתָּפוּחַ כִּילּוּ צָמֵק וְנִרְאֵית חֲסֵירָה. וּפְעָמִים שֶׁהַשְּׂעוֹר רַע וְהוּא צָמֵק הָא אִילּוּ סוֹלֶת הָיְתָה תְפוּחָה וְעַכְשָׁיו שֶׁהַשְּׂעוֹר רַע וְהוּא צָמֵק אַתְּ רוֹאֶה אֶת הַצָּמֵק כִּילּוּ תָּפַח וְנִרְאֵית יְתֵירָה. עַל דַּעְתֵּיהּ דְּרִבִּי יִרְמְיָה דְּרוֹמָיָיה וְרִבִּי יוֹחָנָן וְרִבִּי שִׁמְעוֹן בֶּן

לָקִישׁ שְׁלָשְׁתָּן אָמְרוּ דָבָר אֶחָד בִּיתֵירָה. עַל דַּעְתֵּיהּ דְּרִבִּי יוֹנָה וְרִבִּי יוֹסֵי שְׁלָשְׁתָּן אָמְרוּ דָבָר אֶחָד בַּחֲסֵירָה. אִילֵּין דְּבַר פָּטִי בַּשְּׁלוּן אוֹרֶז אַנְשׁוֹן מְתַקְּנָה יָתֵיהּ. חֲבֵרַיָּא סָבְרִין מֵימַר יִיסַּב חַיֵּי לוֹ לְקָבֵל מְבוּשָּׁל. אָמַר לוֹן רִבִּי יוֹסֵי אוּף אֲנָא אָמַר כֵּן לָמָּה שֶׁדַּרְכּוֹ לִתְפּוֹחַ.

There[100], we have stated: "[Profane] food in the volume of an egg that was left in the sun and shrank, similarly the volume of an olive from a carcass[101], or the volume of a lentil of a crawling thing[102], the volume of an olive rejected or overdue [sacrifice][103], or of fat[104], are pure." The Southerners say, only if it originally was the volume of an olive[105]; Rebbi Joḥanan and Rebbi Simeon ben Laqish both say, even if originally it was less than the volume of an olive. There[106], we have stated: "They said to him, that will make it deficient or redundant." Who said this to him? Rebbi Meïr! Sometimes the sour dough will be of high quality and it rises; if it were fine flour it would have shrunk but now, since the sour dough is of high quality it rose; you have to look at the risen [dough] as if it had shrunk; it looks deficient. Sometimes the sour dough is bad and it shrinks[107]; if it were fine flour it would have risen but now, since the sour dough is bad, it shrinks; you have to look at the shrunken [dough] as if it had risen; it looks redundant. According to Rebbi Jeremiah, the Southerners, Rebbi Joḥanan, and Rebbi Simeon ben Laqish, all three say the same thing in case it is redundant[108]. According to Rebbi Jonah and Rebbi Yose, all three say the same thing in case it is deficient. Those of Bar Patti cooked rice and had forgotten to put it in order[109]. The colleagues wanted to say, he should take raw [rice] corresponding to the cooked. Rebbi Yose said to them, I also am saying so because regularly it increases in volume.

99 Reading of the Rome ms. Venice and Leyden: במי עקרו

100 Mishnah *Ṭahorot* 3:4. The discussion is about the second part of the Mishnah, not quoted in the text: "If they were put into the rain and swelled they are impure . . ." The volumes indicated are the minima that may carry impurity or make their consumption a criminal offense.

101 *Lev.* 11:24-25.

102 *Lev.* 11:31-32.

103 Rejected sacrifice is sacrifice made with the wrong intentions, *Lev.* 19:7; overdue is sacrifice left after the allotted time has expired (one night, day and night, or two days and the night in between, as the case may be; *Lev.* 7:17.)

104 The fat in lumps in the body, *Lev.* 7:22-26.

105 In matters of impurity and dietary laws, it is not the actual volume that counts but the volume at the time the impurity or prohibition first arose. If impurity or prohibition are impossible in the original state, they cannot be acquired by subsequent swelling. Rebbi Joḥanan and Simeon ben Laqish hold that only the actual volume at the moment matters. Everybody agrees that his guidelines carry over to the determination of heave of the tithe.

106 Mishnah *Menaḥot* 5:1: "All flour sacrifices are brought unleavened except the breads for a thanksgiving sacrifice (*Lev.* 7:13) and the Two Breads [for Pentecost (*Lev.* 23:17)] which are leavened. Rebbi Meïr says, the sour dough is made from the dedicated flour. Rebbi Jehudah says, this is not of the best but he brings sour dough, puts it into the measuring vessel and fills the latter [with flour.] *They said to him, that will make it deficient or redundant.*"

The problem is that in each case, the amount of flour necessary is prescribed by biblical law. According to R. Meïr, one takes the exact amount, and then takes from this a small amount which is moistened to make it sour; then the sour dough is returned to the original flour which is moistened and kneaded. R. Jehudah notes that this will make poor bread; he prefers real sour dough to be used in addition to the flour of the offering. He is told that in this case, when the finished product must have specified size, his procedure probably will never be exactly right.

107 It does not actually shrink but will not rise. Since the measure was not full to start out with, in order to

accomodate the rising dough, one now will have invalidated the offering because it is too small.

108 This text, confirmed by the mss., is impossible since the Southerners disagree with Rebbis Joḥanan and Simeon ben Laqish precisely in the case of swelling food. In must read: Rebbi Jeremiah, Rebbis Joḥanan, and Simeon ben Laqish all three say the same. The next sentence must then read: The Southerners, Rebbi Jonah and Yose all three say the same. The first group takes all food as is, the others agree only on shrinking, not on expanding food. The statements of Rebbis Jeremiah, Jonah, and Yose are in the preceding paragraph and deal with heave of the tithe.

109 To tithe or at least give heave of the tithe by the rules of *demay*.

(fol. 41a) **משנה ה**: וְתוֹרְמִין בָּצָל קָטָן שָׁלֵם לֹא חֲצִי בָּצָל גָּדוֹל. רִבִּי יְהוּדָה אוֹמֵר לֹא כִּי אֶלָּא חֲצִי בָּצָל גָּדוֹל. וְכֵן הָיָה רִבִּי יְהוּדָה אוֹמֵר תּוֹרְמִין בְּצָלִים מִבְּנֵי הַמְּדִינָה עַל הַכּוֹפְרִים וְלֹא כוֹפְרִים עַל בְּנֵי הַמְּדִינָה מִפְּנֵי שֶׁהוּא מַאֲכַל פּוֹלִיטִיקִים.

Mishnah 5: One gives a small whole onion[110] as heave but not half a large onion. Rebbi Jehudah says it is not so, one rather gives half a large onion. Similarly, Rebbi Jehudah said one gives onions of town people as heave for rural ones but not rural ones for those of town people because they are city-dwellers'[111] food.

110 The anonymous Tanna considers large onions better than small ones and whole onions more durable than divided ones.

111 Greek πολιτικός (adj.), "fit for, belonging to the city". Onions sold in the city are of uniform quality while rural onions are those that cannot be sold in the city.

משנה ו: וְתוֹרְמִין זֵיתֵי שֶׁמֶן עַל זֵיתֵי כֶבֶשׁ וְלֹא זֵיתֵי כֶבֶשׁ עַל זֵיתֵי שֶׁמֶן. וְיַיִן שֶׁאֵינוֹ מְבוּשָּׁל עַל הַמְבוּשָּׁל וְלֹא מִן הַמְבוּשָּׁל עַל שֶׁאֵינוֹ מְבוּשָּׁל. זֶה הַכְּלָל כָּל־שֶׁהוּא כִלְאַיִם בַּחֲבֵירוֹ לֹא יִתְרוֹם מִזֶּה עַל זֶה אֲפִילוּ מִן הַיָּפֶה עַל הָרַע. וְכָל־שֶׁאֵינוֹ כִלְאַיִם בַּחֲבֵירוֹ תּוֹרֵם מִן הַיָּפֶה עַל הָרַע אֲבָל לֹא מִן הָרַע עַל הַיָּפֶה וְאִם תָּרַם מִן הָרַע עַל הַיָּפֶה תְּרוּמָתוֹ תְרוּמָה חוּץ מִן הַזּוּנִים עַל הַחִיטִּים שֶׁאֵינָן אוֹכֶל. וְהַקִּישׁוּת וְהַמְּלָפְפוֹת מִן אֶחָד. רִבִּי יְהוּדָה אוֹמֵר שְׁנֵי מִינִין.

Mishnah 6: Also, one may give oil olives as heave for pickling olives but not pickling olives for oil olives, uncooked wine for cooked wine but not cooked wine for uncooked wine[112]. This is the rule: All that is *kilaim* with another kind, one may not give as heave one for the other, not even good for bad. But all that is not *kilaim* with another kind, one may give the good as heave for the bad but not the bad for the good; if he gave bad for good, his heave is heave except for *zĕwānîn*[113] for wheat because they are not food. Green melons and sweet melons[114] are one kind; Rebbi Jehudah says two kinds.

112 Olives chosen for pickling are those with too little oil for pressing. Cooked wine has lost its alcohol but became sweet.

113 *Kilaim* Chapter 1, Note 1.

114 *Kilaim* Chapter 1, Notes 38,39. As noted in the Halakhah, the last statement is redundant.

(fol. 41d) **הלכה ה**: אָמַר רִבִּי יוֹחָנָן דְּרִבִּי יוּדָה הִיא רִבִּי[115] יוּדָה מַתִּיר מִפְּנֵי שֶׁהוּא מַשְׁבִּיחָן. וְאָמַר רִבִּי יוֹחָנָן מִחְלְפָה שִׁיטָּתֵיהּ דְּרִבִּי יוּדָה. רִבִּי לָעְזָר אָמַר אֵינָהּ מִחְלְפָה תַּמָּן בְּכֹהֵן וְכָאן בִּבְעָלִים. רִבִּי אֶלְעָזָר וְרִבִּי יוֹחָנָן חַד אָמַר מִפְּנֵי שֶׁמְּמַעֲטוֹ מִשּׁוֹתָיו וְחַד אָמַר מִפְּנֵי שֶׁמְּמַעֲטוֹ מִמִּידָּתוֹ וְלֹא יָדְעִין מָאן אָמַר דָּא וּמָאן אָמַר דָּא. מִן מַה דְּאָמַר רִבִּי יוֹחָנָן מִחְלְפָה שִׁיטָּתֵיהּ דְּרִבִּי יוּדָה וְאָמַר רִבִּי אֶלְעָזָר אֵינָהּ מוּחְלֶפֶת תַּמָּן בְּכֹהֵן וְכָאן בִּבְעָלִים הֲוֵי רִבִּי יוֹחָנָן דְּהוּא אָמַר מִפְּנֵי שֶׁמְּמַעֲטוֹ מִשּׁוֹתָיו. רִבִּי יְהוּדָה בֶּן רִבִּי אִימִּי בְּשֵׁם רֵישׁ לָקִישׁ מִפְּנֵי שֶׁמְּמַעֲטוֹ

מְשׁוֹתָיו. מַתְנִיתָא פְלִיגָא עַל רִבִּי יוֹחָנָן וְאַף מִשֶּׁאֵינוֹ מְבוּשָּׁל עַל הַמְּבוּשָּׁל וְכָל־שֶׁכֵּן מִן הַמְּבוּשָּׁל עַל שֶׁאֵינוֹ מְבוּשָּׁל. אָמַר רִבִּי אִימִּי לֹא תַנֵּי רִבִּי יוֹחָנָן.

Halakhah 5: Rebbi Johanan said, [the Mishnah] is Rebbi Jehudah's. "Rebbi Jehudah permits since he improves it[116]." On this, Rebbi Johanan said, Rebbi Jehudah inverted his reasoning[117]. Rebbi Eleazar said, Rebbi Jehudah did not invert his reasoning, there for the Cohen, here for the owners[118]. Rebbi Eleazar and Rebbi Johanan, one of them said because he reduces the number of drinkers, the other says because he diminishes its volume. We did not know who said what. Since Rebbi Johanan said, Rebbi Jehudah inverted his reasoning but Rebbi Eleazar said, Rebbi Jehudah did not invert his reasoning, there for the Cohen, here for the owners, it follows that Rebbi Johanan said because he reduces the number of drinkers[119]. A *baraita* disagrees with Rebbi Johanan: "Even from uncooked for cooked and certainly from cooked for uncooked[120]." Rebbi Immi said, Rebbi Johanan did not state that.

115 Reading of the Rome ms.; Leyden and Venice: דרבי. The Rome reading is the only logically consistent one, as shown by J. N. Epstein, מבוא לנוסח המשנה 2, Jerusalem 5724, p. 246.

116 Mishnah 11:1: "One may not cook heave wine because he diminishes its volume; Rebbi Jehudah permits since he improves it." Since R. Jehudah is not recorded as protesting the rule that cooked wine may not be given for uncooked, it follows that the first part of the Mishnah must be acceptable to R. Jehudah. In slightly shortened form, this paragraph is also in Halakhah 11:1.

117 R. Salomo ben Adrat (*Responsa*, vol. 1, #24; *Responsa ascribed to Nahmanides*, #190) explains that R. Johanan insists that Mishnah 11:1 must read: "Rebbi Jehudah says, one may not cook heave wine because he diminishes its volume; the Sages permit since he improves it." This is difficult to accept since the Yerushalmi elsewhere (e. g., *Ševi'it* Chapter 8, Note 35) accepts Mishnah 11:1 in its original

form. Therefore, it seems that R. Joḥanan sees a real inconsistency in the positions of R. Jehudah.

118 The Cohen may drink his heave wine in any way he wishes. R. Joḥanan rejects the distinction made by R. Eleazar; Mishnah 11:1 also applies to the vintner and we have to find out why R. Jehudah does not allow him to cook the wine.

119 Since cooked wine is not to everybody's taste, the vintner might have difficulty in finding a Cohen willing to drink his heave and the heave might have to be destroyed. There is no problem for R. Eleazar since according to him, the Cohen cooks his own drink.

120 This *baraita* is not recorded elsewhere; in the Tosephta (4:4) Rabban Simeon ben Gamliel permits cooked to be given for uncooked but only as second choice. R. Joḥanan declares the *baraita* invalid.

אָמַר רִבִּי בּוּן בַּר כַּהֲנָא בְּשֵׁם רִבִּי הִילָא[121] וְלֹא תִשְׂאוּ עָלָיו חֵטְא מִמָּה שֶׁהוּא בְנְשִׂיאַת עָוֹן אַתָּה יוֹדֵעַ מַה שֶּׁעָשָׂה עָשׂוּי.

Rebbi Abun bar Cahana said in the name of Rebbi Hila (*Num.* 18:32): "You should not carry sin because of it." Since he is subject to carrying sin, you know that what he did is valid[122].

121 Reading of Rome ms. Name missing in Venice text.

122 The verse declares irregularities in giving heaves as sinful. If irregularly given heave were invalid, it would not be considered given and its giver could not incur sin. This argument is also accepted in Babli *Baba Batra* 143b.

הָא דָבָר שֶׁהוּא אוֹכֶל מוּתָּר.

Hence, something that is food is permitted[123].

מַתְנִיתִין דְּרִבִּי יִשְׁמָעֵאל בֵּי רִבִּי יוֹסֵי. דְּאָמַר רִבִּי יִשְׁמָעֵאל בֵּי רִבִּי יוֹסֵי מִשּׁוּם אָבִיו תּוֹרְמִין מִן הַיַּיִן עַל הַחוֹמֶץ אֲבָל לֹא מִן הַחוֹמֶץ עַל הַיַּיִן. עָבַר וְתָרַם תְּרוּמָתוֹ תְרוּמָה. רִבִּי אוֹמֵר הַיַּיִן וְהַחוֹמֶץ שְׁנֵי מִינִין אֵין תּוֹרְמִין וְלֹא מְעַשְּׂרִין

מִזֶּה עַל זֶה. אָמַר רִבִּי יְהוֹשֻׁעַ בֶּן לֵוִי מִסְתַּבְּרָה יוֹדֶה רִבִּי לִדְבַר תּוֹרָה. מַה טַעֲמָא דְרִבִּי שֶׁאִם אוֹמֵר אַתְּ כֵּן שֶׁמּוּתָּר לִתְרוֹם מִן הַיַּיִן עַל הַחוֹמֶץ אַף הוּא סָבַר מֵימַר שֶׁמּוּתָּר לִתְרוֹם חוֹמֶץ עַל הַיַּיִן.

Our Mishnah is from Rebbi Ismael ben Rebbi Yose, as it was stated[124]: "Rebbi Ismael ben Rebbi Yose says in the name of his father that one may take heave from wine for vinegar but not from vinegar for wine. If somebody transgressed, his heave is heave. Rebbi says that wine and vinegar are two distinct kinds and one does not give heave nor does one tithe from one for the other." Rebbi Joshua ben Levi said, it seems that Rebbi would agree as to biblical law[125]. What is Rebbi's reason? If you say so, that one may give heave of wine for vinegar, he will think that one is permitted to give vinegar for wine.

123 This refers to the Mishnah, that *zewanin* are unacceptable since they are not human food.

124 The statement of R. Ismael ben R. Yose is in Tosephta 4:6; the statement is quoted in *Kilaim* 1:1, Note 21.

125 That one may give heave from good wine for bad vinegar. He forbids it because giving from vinegar for wine is sinful.

וְהַקִּישׁוּת וְהַמְּלָפְפוֹת מִן אֶחָד. רִבִּי יְהוּדָה אוֹמֵר שְׁנֵי מִינִין. רִבִּי יְהוּדָה כְּדַעְתֵּיהּ וְרַבָּנִין כְּדַעְתֵּין דְּתַנִּינָן הַקִּישׁוּת וְהַמְּלָפְפוֹן אֵינָן כִּלְאַיִם זֶה בְזֶה. רִבִּי יְהוּדָה אוֹמֵר כִּלְאַיִם.

"Green melons and sweet melons[114] are one kind; Rebbi Jehudah says two kinds." Rebbi Jehudah keeps to his opinion, the rabbis keep to their opinion, as we have stated (Mishnah *Kilaim* 1:2): "Green melon and sweet melon are not *kilaim* one with the other. Rebbi Jehudah says, they are *kilaim*."

התורם קישות פרק שלישי

(fol. 41d) **משנה א:** הַתּוֹרֵם קִישׁוּת וְנִמְצָא מָרָה אֲבַטִּיחַ וְנִמְצְאָה סָרוּחַ תְּרוּמָה וְיַחְזוֹר וְיִתְרוֹם. הַתּוֹרֵם חָבִית שֶׁל יַיִן וְנִמְצֵאת שֶׁל חוֹמֶץ אִם יָדוּעַ שֶׁהָיְתָה שֶׁל חוֹמֶץ עַד שֶׁלֹּא תְרָמָהּ אֵינָהּ תְּרוּמָה. וְאִם מִשֶּׁתְּרָמָהּ הֶחֱמִיצָה הֲרֵי זוֹ תְרוּמָה. וְאִם סָפֵק תְּרוּמָה וְיַחְזוֹר וְיִתְרוֹם. הָרִאשׁוֹנָה אֵינָהּ מְדַמַּעַת בִּפְנֵי עַצְמָהּ וְאֵין חַייָבִין עָלֶיהָ חוֹמֶשׁ וְכֵן הַשְּׁנִייָה.

Mishnah 1: If one gives a green melon as heave and it turns out to be bitter, a water melon and it turns out rotten, it is heave and he should give heave a second time. If one gives an amphora of wine as heave and it turns out to be vinegar; if it was known that it turned into vinegar before he gave heave it is not heave[1], but if it turned into vinegar after he had made it heave, it is heave. In case of doubt it is heave and heave should be given a second time. Neither the first nor the second [heaves] do create *dema'*[2] by themselves nor does one have to pay the fifth[3].

1 Even the Sages who declare wine and vinegar to be the same, their status as heave is revoked by rabbinic decree (cf. Chapter 2, Note 125).

2 Cf. Chapter 2, Note 49, and the next Mishnah.

3 Cf. Mishnah 6:4 and Chapter 1, Note 71. In the interpretation of Maimonides (*Terumot* 5:22), the last sentence refers both to wine and to melons.

(fol. 42a) **הלכה א:** הַתּוֹרֵם קִישׁוּת כו'. נִיחָא אֲבַטִּיחַ וְנִמְצָא סָרוּחַ. אֶלָּא קִישׁוּת וְנִמְצֵאת מָרָה לֹא מֵעִיקָּרָא הִיא מָרָה. אָמַר רִבִּי יוֹחָנָן עָשׂוּ אוֹתָן כְּסָפֵק

אוֹכֶל. רִבִּי יוֹנָה בָּעֵי וּלְכָל־הַדְּבָרִים עָשׂוּ אוֹתָן כְּסָפֵק אוֹכֶל. מְטַמֵּא טוּמְאַת אוֹכְלִין וְשׂוֹרְפִין אוֹתָהּ בְּטוּמְאָה וְחַיָּבִין עָלֶיהָ חוֹמֶשׁ וְלוֹקִין עָלֶיהָ חוּץ לַחוֹמָה. עֵירֶב בָּהּ נַעֲשֶׂה חַמָּר גַּמָּל. תַּמָּן אָמַר רִבִּי יוֹחָנָן כִּכָּר שֶׁנִּיטְמָא בְּסָפֵק רְשׁוּת הַיָּחִיד וּמַגָּעוֹ בִּרְשׁוּת הָרַבִּים טָמֵא. וְהָכָא טָהוֹר שֶׁהֵן שְׁנֵי סְפֵיקוֹת.

Halakhah 1: "If one gives a green melon", etc. We understand a water melon and it turned out rotten, but a green melon and it turned out bitter, was it not always bitter[4]? Rebbi Joḥanan said, they made it doubtful whether it is food[5]. Rebbi Jonah inquired: Is it doubtful as food in all respects, to become impure as food, that one burns it if impure[6], one owes a fifth for it[3], and one whips for it outside the walls[7], if one made an *'eruv* with it does he become a donkey-camel driver[8]? There[9], Rebbi Joḥanan said, a loaf which became impure in a domain that possibly is private and was touched in the public domain is impure. But in our case it is pure because there are two doubts[10].

4 The heave should be invalid.

5 The question is not whether it is bad quality for good of food but whether it is food at all. If it is food then the heave is heave, if it is not food then there can be no heave.

6 If it has been made heave and becomes impure, must it be burned as heave?

7 If it is Second Tithe while there is a Temple, it must be brought to Jerusalem and consumed there. Once it has entered the walls of the city of Jerusalem, it may not be taken out again and consumption outside the walls is a criminal offense.

8 On the notion of *eruv*, cf. *Peah* Chapter 8, Note 56. The question follows R. Meïr and R. Jehudah in Mishnah *Erubin* 3:4 who declare that a questionable *eruv* makes its owner a donkey-camel driver. A donkey driver has to walk behind his animal, a camel driver before it. A donkey-camel driver is in a dilemma. Without the *eruv*, he would be permitted to go from his house 2000 cubits in each direction. With the *eruv*, he may go 2000 cubits from the *eruv* in each direction. If the validity of the *eruv* is in question, he

may walk on the Sabbath only in the domain which is the intersection of two circular discs of radius 2000 cubits, one centered at his house and the other at the place of his *eruv*.

9 It is not stated exactly where R. Joḥanan stated this rule but in *Ševuot* 2:1 (fol. 33d) he states that food of doubtful impurity (i. e., when an impure person is in doubt whether or not he touched some pure food) in the public domain is pure. This will imply that in a private domain it would be impure, as stated explicitly in Babli *Avodah Zarah* 37b, *Ḥulin* 9a.

10 It is also a principle accepted in both Talmudim that something which is forbidden (or impure) only if two independent doubts are both resolved to forbid (or declare impure) is permitted (or declared pure) since from biblical law it would be permitted (or declared pure) even in the case of only one doubt. It seems that this leniency was a major point of contention between lenient Pharisees and restrictive Sadducees.

תַּנֵּי בְשֵׁם רִבִּי יוֹסֵי אֵין לָךְ מַר בְּקִישׁוּת אֶלָּא תוֹכוֹ. כֵּיצַד הוּא עוֹשֶׂה מוֹסִיף עַל הַחִיצוֹן שֶׁלָּהּ וְתוֹרֵם. רִבִּי בִּנְיָמִין בַּר לֵוִי בָּעֵי דָּבָר שֶׁאֶיפְשַׁר לָךְ לַעֲמוֹד עָלָיו חֲכָמִים חֲלוּקִין עָלָיו אֶלָּא עַל עִיקַּר בְּדִיקָתָהּ חֲלוּקִין.

It was stated in the name of Rebbi Yose: "Green melon can be bitter only inside. What can he do? He adds to the outer part and gives heave[11]." Rebbi Benjamin ben Levi asked: Do the Sages disagree with him about a subject that can be checked? They disagree about the possibility of checking[12].

11 Tosephta 4:5. R. Yose disagrees with the Mishnah; a bitter melon given as heave is always certain heave since the part close to the skin can always be eaten. If the inner part is bitter, one should add some heave from another melon that is still *ṭevel* to avoid giving bad for good. In his opinion, there is nothing questionable.

12 Even if we check a number of melons and do not find one which is totally bad, this does not prove that the next one would not be totally bad.

תָּרַם חָבִית וְנִמְצֵאת מְגוּלָּה. אֲבַטִּיחַ וְנִמְצֵאת נָקוּר תְּרוּמָה וְיַחְזוֹר וְיִתְרוֹם. רִבִּי יוּדָן בַּר פָּזִי רִבִּי שִׁמְעוֹן בְּשֵׁם רִבִּי יְהוֹשֻׁעַ בֶּן לֵוִי לֹא אָסְרוּ אֶלָּא נָקוּר הָא לְכַתְּחִילָּה אָסוּר לִתְרוֹם. רִבִּי יַעֲקֹב דְּרוֹמָיָיה בְּעָא קוֹמֵי רִבִּי יוֹסֵי לֹא מִסְתַּבְּרָא בְּשֶׁרָאוּ אוֹתוֹ נוֹקֵר. אָמַר לֵיהּ יוֹדֵעַ הוּא אִם הִטִּיל בּוֹ אִירֶס. חֲבֵירַיָּא בָּעוּן קוֹמֵי רִבִּי יוֹסֵי מַה בֵּינָהּ לְטָמֵא אָמַר לוֹן טָמֵא בְּעֵינוֹ הוּא שֶׁגָּרְמָה טוּמְאָה. בְּרַם הָכָא עָפָר הוּא.

"If one gave an amphora[13] as heave and it turned out to be uncovered, or a water melon and it turned out to have holes, it is heave and heave should be given a second time."[14] Rebbi Jehudah ben Pazi, Rebbi Simeon [ben Laqish] in the name of Rebbi Joshua ben Levi: They forbade only when it was found to have a hole; therefore, from the start it is forbidden to give it as heave[15]. Rebbi Jacob the Southerner asked before Rebbi Yose: Is this reasonable only if they saw it[16] making the hole? He said to him: Would one know whether it poured poison into it? The colleagues asked before Rebbi Yose: What is the difference between that and the impure[17]? He said to them: The impure is unchanged, so is that which caused impurity. But here, it is dust.

13 An amphora full of wine given as heave for an entire harvest.

14 Tosephta 4:6. Both Talmudim forbid fluids that have stood uncovered and unsupervised since one is afraid a snake might have drunk from it and poured its poison into the drink. Similarly, if the water melon has two small holes which might come from the bite of a snake, we are afraid that the water melon was poisoned. If we were sure that this happened the wine in the amphora or the water melon would not be human food and could not possibly be heave. In case of doubt, one is in the situation described in the Mishnah.

15 If the holes were there when heave was given, it is not heave.

16 The snake. Since we would not know whether the wine or the water melon was poisoned, the suggestion has to be rejected.

17 This refers to Mishnah 2:2 where it is stated that impure produce, when unintentionally given as heave, is valid heave. Why can one not state that a perforated watermelon, when unintentionally given as heave, is unconditionally valid heave? The answer is that impure food is still food but a perforated watermelon is no longer food.

רִבִּי יַעֲקֹב בַּר אָחָא בְשֵׁם רִבִּי יוֹחָנָן הֲלָכָה כְדִבְרֵי רִבִּי. רִבִּי חִייָה בְשֵׁם דְּרִבִּי יוֹחָנָן דְּרִבִּי הִיא. רִבִּי בָּא בַּר כֹּהֵן בְּעָא קוֹמֵי רִבִּי יוֹסֵי לֹא כֵן אָמַר רִבִּי חִייָה בְשֵׁם רִבִּי יוֹחָנָן רִבִּי וַחֲבֵירָיו הֲלָכָה כְרִבִּי. וְאָמַר רִבִּי יוֹנָה וַאֲפִילוּ אֵצֶל רִבִּי לְעָזָר בֵּי רִבִּי שִׁמְעוֹן. אָמַר לֵיהּ בְּגִין דְּתַנֵּי לָהּ רִבִּי יִשְׁמָעֵאל בֵּי רִבִּי יוֹסֵי בְשֵׁם אָבִיו וְאָמַר רִבִּי יוֹסֵי בְשֵׁם רִבִּי יוֹחָנָן רִבִּי יוֹסֵי וַחֲבֵירָיו הֲלָכָה כְרִבִּי יוֹסֵי מֵחֲבֵירָיו דְּלֹא תִיסְבּוֹר לְמֵימַר אוּף הָכָא כֵן לָכֵן צְרִיכָה מֵימַר הֲלָכָה כְרִבִּי.

Rebbi Jacob bar Aḥa in the name of Rebbi Joḥanan: Practice follows Rebbi[18]. Rebbi Ḥiyya in the name of Rebbi Joḥanan: It[19] follows Rebbi. Rebbi Abba bar Cohen asked before Rebbi Yose: Did not Rebbi Ḥiyya [bar Abba] say in the name of Rebbi Joḥanan, [between] Rebbi and his colleagues, practice follows Rebbi[20], and Rebbi Jonah said, including Rebbi Eleazar ben Rebbi Simeon[21]? He said to him, because Rebbi Ismael ben Rebbi Yose stated in his father's name, and Rebbi Yose[22] said in the name of Rebbi Joḥanan, [between] Rebbi Yose and his colleagues, practice follows Rebbi Yose, not his colleagues[23], so you should not say this applies here also[24]; for this reason he had to say that practice follows Rebbi.

18 This refers to the last part of the Mishnah, about giving vinegar as heave for wine, which is declared impossible by Rebbi but possible by R. Ismael ben R. Yose (Chapter 2, Note 125).

19 The Mishnah, and as anonymous statement it determines practice.

20 In the Babli, *Eruvin* 46b, *Ketubot* 21a, *Baba batra* 124b, in the text of Rashi and the Venice prints (and the Rome ms. of the Yerushalmi)

the rule is accepted only for disagreements between Rebbi and a single opponent, but in the Munich ms. and a reading mentioned by R. Moses from Coucy (*Semag Asê* 74), the rule reads as in the Yerushalmi.

21 He was the greatest authority in the days of the young Rebbi.

22 This is the reading in both mss. but, since it belongs to R. Yose's response to R. Abba bar Cohen, it must read ר' יוסה, R. Assi.

23 Accepted as operative statement in Babli *Eruvin* 46b.

24 The rules apply only to disagreements between Sages of the same generation, not to rulings of later generations. In our case, this has to be spelled out since R. Ismael ben R. Yose was the teacher of Rebbi (cf. *Kilaim* Chapter 9, before Note 88.)

רִבִּי זְעִירָא רִבִּי יַעֲקֹב בַּר אִידִי בְּשֵׁם רִבִּי יוֹחָנָן רִבִּי מֵאִיר וְרִבִּי שִׁמְעוֹן הֲלָכָה כְּרִבִּי שִׁמְעוֹן. רִבִּי שִׁמְעוֹן וְרִבִּי יְהוּדָה הֲלָכָה כְּרִבִּי יְהוּדָה. וְאֵין צָרִיךְ לוֹמַר רִבִּי מֵאִיר וְרִבִּי יְהוּדָה שֶׁהֲלָכָה כְּרִבִּי יְהוּדָה. רִבִּי בָּא בַּר יַעֲקֹב בַּר אִידִי בְּשֵׁם רִבִּי יוֹנָתָן רִבִּי מֵאִיר וְרִבִּי שִׁמְעוֹן הֲלָכָה כְּרִבִּי שִׁמְעוֹן. רִבִּי שִׁמְעוֹן וְרִבִּי יוּדָה הֲלָכָה כְּרִבִּי יוּדָה. וְאֵין צָרִיךְ לוֹמַר רִבִּי מֵאִיר וְרִבִּי יְהוּדָה וְרִבִּי שִׁמְעוֹן הֲלָכָה כְּרִבִּי יְהוּדָה. וּמִינָהּ אַתְּ שְׁמַע רִבִּי יוּדָה וְרִבִּי שִׁמְעוֹן הֲלָכָה כְּרִבִּי יוּדָה.

Rebbi Zeïra, Rebbi Jacob bar Idi in the name of Rebbi Joḥanan: [Between] Rebbi Meïr and Rebbi Simeon, practice follows Rebbi Simeon[25]. [Between] Rebbi Simeon and Rebbi Jehudah, practice follows Rebbi Jehudah, and one does not have to mention that [between] Rebbi Meïr and Rebbi Jehudah, practice follows Rebbi Jehudah[26]. Rebbi Abba bar Jacob bar Idi in the name of Rebbi Jonathan: [Between] Rebbi Meïr and Rebbi Simeon, practice follows Rebbi Simeon. [Between] Rebbi Simeon and Rebbi Jehudah, practice follows Rebbi Jehudah, and one does not have to mention that [between] Rebbi Meïr, Rebbi Jehudah, and Rebbi Simeon practice follows Rebbi Jehudah. From this you infer that [between] Rebbi Simeon and Rebbi Jehudah, practice follows Rebbi Jehudah.

25 Cf. Demay Chapter 5, Note 129; Ševi'it Chapter 8, Note 105, Babli Eruvin 46b.

26 Babli *Eruvin* 46b.

(fol. 41d) **משנה ב**: נָפְלָה אַחַת מֵהֶן לְתוֹךְ הַחוּלִין אֵינָן מְדַמְּעָתָן נָפְלָה שְׁנִייָה לְמָקוֹם אַחֵר אֵינָהּ מְדַמְּעָתָן נָפְלָה שְׁתֵּיהֶן לְמָקוֹם אֶחָד מְדַמְּעוֹת כִּקְטַנָּה שֶׁבִּשְׁתֵּיהֶן.

Mishnah 2: If one of them fell into profane [food] it does not create *dema'*[27]. If the other one fell into another place it does not create *dema'*. If both together fell into one place they create *dema'* relative to the smaller one[28].

27 The mixture of heave and profane food; cf. *Demay* Chapter 1, Note 175. The rules of repairing *dema'* are spelled out in Chapter 5.

The Mishnah details the rules of the two heaves given under the circumstances of Mishnah 1. Since each of them is only heave if the other one is not needed by biblical rules, only both together constitute certain heave.

28 If both heaves are given by the rules, the first one will be 2%, the second one 2% of 98% or 1.96% of the original volume.

(fol. 42a) **הלכה ב**: כֵּיצַד הוּא עוֹשֶׂה נוֹתֵן שְׁתֵּיהֶן לַכֹּהֵן וְהַכֹּהֵן נוֹתֵן לוֹ דְמֵי אַחַת מֵהֶן. אֵי זוֹ מֵהֶן נוֹתֵן לוֹ דְּמֵי גְדוֹלָה אוֹ דְמֵי קְטַנָּה. מִן מַה דְתַנִּינָן מְדַמְּעוֹת כִּקְטַנָּה שֶׁבִּשְׁתֵּיהֶן. הָדָא אָמְרָה דְּמֵי גְדוֹלָה נוֹתֵן לוֹ.

Halakhah 2: How does he handle it[29]? He gives both of them to the Cohen; the Cohen pays for one of them. Which one does he pay for, the larger or the smaller one? Since we have stated: "they create *dema'* relative to the smaller one," this implies that he pays for the larger one.

29 This refers to Mishnah 1. When the two heaves have been given, how are they to be disposed of since they are not certain heave but forbidden to laymen?

(fol. 41d) **משנה ג**: הַשּׁוּתָפִין שֶׁתָּֽרְמוּ זֶה אַחַר זֶה. רִבִּי עֲקִיבָה אוֹמֵר תְּרוּמַת שְׁנֵיהֶן תְּרוּמָה וַחֲכָמִים אוֹמְרִים תְּרוּמַת הָֽרִאשׁוֹן תְּרוּמָה. רִבִּי יוֹסֵה אוֹמֵר אִם תָּרַם הָֽרִאשׁוֹן כַּשִּׁיעוּר אֵין תְּרוּמַת הַשֵּׁנִי תְּרוּמָה וְאִם לֹא תָרַם הָֽרִאשׁוֹן כַּשִּׁיעוּר תְּרוּמַת הַשֵּׁנִי תְּרוּמָה.

Mishnah 3: Partners who gave heave one after the other, Rebbi Aqiba says both of their heaves are heave. But the Sages say, the heave of the first one [only] is heave[30]. Rebbi Yose says, if the first one gave the full measure[31] of heave, then his heave is heave, but if the first one did not give the full measure of heave, then the heave of the second is heave.

30 Since the first heave turned *tevel* into profane food and heave may not be given from profane food.

31 The measure to be applied is discussed in the Halakhah but not determined. Partnership cannot apply to the heave of the tithe since the tithe must be given to an individual Levite.

(fol. 42a) **הלכה ג**: מַה נָן קַיָּמִין אִם בִּמְמַחִין אַף רִבִּי עֲקִיבָה מוֹדֵי וְאִם בְּשֶׁאֵינָן מְמַחִין אוּף רַבָּנִין מוֹדֵיין. אֶלָּא כִּי נָן קַיָּמִין בִּסְתָם. רִבִּי עֲקִיבָה אוֹמֵר סְתָמָן אֵינָן מְמַחִין וְרַבָּנִין אָֽמְרִין סְתָמָן מְמַחִין.

Halakhah 3: Where do we hold? If they assigned[32], even Rebbi Aqiba agrees. If they did not assign, even the rabbis will agree. But we assume they were silent. Rebbi Aqiba says, if they are silent they do not assign, but the rabbis hold that by being silent they will assign.

32 The translation follows Maimonides. R. Simson explains: If they were competent [in the laws to be applied.] It is difficult to accept this interpretation in the Halakhah.

עַל דַּעְתֵּיהּ דְּרִבִּי עֲקִיבָה סְאָה שֶׁל רִאשׁוֹן חֶצְיָיהּ טֶבֶל וְחֶצְיָיהּ תְּרוּמָה טְבוּלָה לְמַעְשְׂרוֹת. סְאָה שֶׁל שֵׁנִי חֶצְיָיהּ תְּרוּמָה וְחֶצְיָיהּ טֶבֶל טְבוּלָה לַכֹּל לֹא צוֹרְכָא דְלֹא. חֲצִי סְאָה שֶׁל שֵׁנִי מַהוּ שֶׁתִּפְטוֹר חֲצִי סְאָה שֶׁל רִאשׁוֹן. נִישְׁמְעִינָהּ מִן הָדָא אֲרִיסְטוֹן אַיְיתֵי פֵּירִין וְשִׁייֵר גּוֹ סַקָּא וְתָרַם. אֲתָא עוּבְדָּא קוֹמֵי רִבִּי יוֹסֵי וְאָמַר חֲזָקָה עַל הַכֹּל תָּרַם.

In the opinion of Rebbi Aqiba, the *seah*[33] of the first one is half *ṭevel* and half heave containing undistributed tithes. The *seah* of the second is half heave and half total *ṭevel*[34]. That does not seem necessary: may the half *seah* of the second free the half *seah* of the first? Let us hear from the following: Ariston brought produce, left some in the sack, and gave heave. The case came before Rebbi Yose; he said it is a standing assumption that he gave heave for everything[35].

33 Assuming that the amount of heave given each time is a *seah*. Since R. Aqiba designates both as heave, neither one can be totally heave. It is argued that the first heave is still subject to the tithes to be given after heave was completed.

34 Since no heave comes after this.

35 Everybody gives heave for everything he has since only in this way can he be sure to have fulfilled his obligations. The interpretation of the opinion of R. Aqiba which splits the heaves is rejected.

מַה כְּשִׁיעוּר תּוֹרָה אוֹ כְשִׁיעוּר חֲבֵירָיו. אִין תַּעַבְדִּינֵיהּ בְּשִׁיעוּר תּוֹרָה לֵית רִבִּי יוֹסֵי כְּרַבָּנִין. אִין תַּעַבְדִּינֵיהּ כְּשִׁיעוּר חֲבֵירָיו רִבִּי יוֹסֵי כְּרַבָּנִין.

Does one understand this according to Biblical rules[36], or according to the rules of his colleagues? If you take it as referring to the biblical measure, Rebbi Yose cannot agree with the rabbis. If you take it as referring to the measure of his colleagues[37], Rebbi Yose agrees with the rabbis[38].

36 One grain is enough for an entire silo, cf. *Peah* Chapter 1, Note 9. In this case, it is impossible that the first heave should not free all of the produce and the second case of R. Yose in the Mishnah cannot happen..

37 As explained in Mishnah 4:3.

38 One may argue that R. Yose simply explains the intent of the Sages in detail.

(fol. 41d) **משנה ד**: בְּמַה דְּבָרִים אֲמוּרִים בְּשֶׁלֹּא דִבֵּר אֲבָל הִרְשָׁה אֶת בֶּן בֵּיתוֹ אוֹ אֶת עַבְדּוֹ אוֹ אֶת שִׁפְחָתוֹ לִתְרוֹם תְּרוּמָתוֹ תְרוּמָה. בִּיטֵּל אִם עַד שֶׁלֹּא תָרַם בִּיטֵּל אֵין תְּרוּמָתוֹ תְרוּמָה. אִם מִשֶּׁתָּרַם בִּיטֵּל תְּרוּמָתוֹ תְרוּמָה. הַפּוֹעֲלִין אֵין לָהֶן רְשׁוּת לִתְרוֹם חוּץ מִן הַדְּרוֹכוֹת שֶׁהֵן מְטַמְּאִין אֶת הַגַּת.

Mishnah 4: Where was this said[39]? When he did not say anything. But if he empowered a member of his family, his slave, or his slave girl, their heave is heave. In case he revoked, if he revoked before heave was given, his heave is not heave. But if he revoked after heave was given, his heave is heave. Workers have no right to give heave except for those who press grapes because they make the wine press impure[40].

39 This refers to the preceding Mishnah of two partners giving heave and confirms Maimonides's interpretation of that Mishnah. It is stated here that for heave the relationship between partners is like that between a person and his family.

40 The winepress cannot become impure since it is built into the earth, but the contents of the vat into which the juice flows will become impure if it is touched by an impure person. It is

assumed that the grapes have not become prepared for impurity by the juice lost from crushed grapes in the transport to the press since that juice is lost, against the will of the vintner. If either one of the workers or the vintner is not a Fellow (as defined in the Introduction to Tractate *Demay*), heave must be given before pressing starts. If the vintner is not present, the workers have implied authorization to give heave.

(fol. 42a) **הלכה ד**: וְלֵית הָדָא פְלִיגָא עַל דְּרֵישׁ לָקִישׁ. דְּרֵישׁ לָקִישׁ אָמַר אֵין אָדָם מְבַטֵּל שְׁלִיחוּתוֹ בִּדְבָרִים. תִּיפְתָּר כְּגוֹן שֶׁאָמַר לוֹ לֵךְ וּקְבַע בַּצָּפוֹן וְהָלַךְ וְקָבַע בְּדָרוֹם.

Halakhah 4: Does this not disagree with Rebbi Simeon ben Laqish? As Rebbi Simeon ben Laqish said, nobody may revoke his agency by words. Explain it that he said, go and fix it to the North and [the agent] went and fixed it to the South[41].

41 The disagreement between R. Simeon ben Laqish and R. Johanan, whether a verbal authorization may be revoked by simple pronouncement, not necessarily in the presence of the agent, is in *Giṭṭin* 4:1-2, fol. 45c, and Babli *Qiddušin* 59a. The Babli explains the problem away; its opinion is that R. Simeon ben Laqish disallows verbal revocation only in matters of marriage and divorce which never can be executed by words alone. The Yerushalmi disagrees and holds that R. Simeon ben Laqish always requires an action (in the case of authorization to proceed with a divorce, a court action) to terminate duly established agency. In our case here, he permits a shortcut for termination only if the agent deviates from his instructions. On the other hand, the Yerushalmi notes that in case of an action of divorce, agency can be terminated only in the presence of the agent or by written document delivered to the other party even for R. Joḥanan since any other course of action would have unforseeable consequences.

אָמַר רִבִּי יוֹחָנָן הַדְּרוֹכוֹת מִכֵּיוָן שֶׁהִלְכוּ בָּהֶן שְׁתִי וָעֵרֶב מְטַמְּאִין אֶת הַבּוֹר מִיַּד. וְהָתַנֵּי הַפּוֹעֲלִין שֶׁתָּרְמוּ אֶת הַבּוֹר אֵין תְּרוּמָתָן תְּרוּמָה. וְאִם הָיָה הַבּוֹר קָטָן אוֹ שֶׁהָיוּ הַבַּעֲלִין אֲחֵרִים מְשַׁכְשְׁכִין בָּהֶן[42] תְּרוּמָתָן תְּרוּמָה מִפְּנֵי שֶׁאֲחֵרִים מְשַׁכְשְׁכִין בָּהֶן. הָא אִם אֵין אֲחֵרִים מְשַׁכְשְׁכִין בָּהֶן אֵין תְּרוּמָתָן תְּרוּמָה. מַה כְדוֹ כָּאן בְּיַיִן וְכָאן בְּשֶׁמֶן. וְלֹא הוּא יַיִן הוּא שֶׁמֶן. יַיִן טוּמְאָתוֹ מְצוּיָה. שֶׁמֶן אֵין טוּמְאָתוֹ מְצוּיָה.

Rebbi Johanan said, one makes the vat impure the moment the press men went over it warp and woof[42]. But have we not stated[43]: "If workers gave heave from a vat, their heave is not heave. But if the vat was small or if the owners or others stir it, their heave is heave." Because others stir it, but if others do not stir it, their heave would not be heave! What is this? One statement for wine, the other for oil. But are not wine and oil the same? Wine is frequently impure[44], oil is not.

42 In both wine and oil presses, the vat is covered by wooden planks; the workers stand on the planks and pound on them walking crosswise over them.

43 Tosephta 1:8: "If workers gave heave from a vat, their heave was not heave. But if the vat was small and others *were using* it, their heave was heave." If the vat has to be emptied because of other uses, then time is of the essence and the workers have implicit authorization for heave.

44 Therefore, the workers are authorized to give heave.

תַּנֵּיי מֵאֵימָתַי תּוֹרְמִין אֶת הָעֲנָבִים מִשֶּׁהִילְכוּ בָּהֶן שְׁתִי וָעֵרֶב. מֵאֵימָתַי מְטַמְּאִין אוֹתָן בֵּית שַׁמַּאי אוֹמְרִים מִשֶּׁיּוֹצִיא אֶת הַשֵּׁנִי. וּבֵית הִלֵּל אוֹמְרִים מִשֶּׁיּוֹצִיא אֶת הָרִאשׁוֹן. אָמַר רִבִּי יוֹסֵי הֲלָכָה כְבֵית שַׁמַּאי וְהָרַבִּים נָהֲגוּ כְבֵית הִלֵּל. אָמַר רִבִּי שִׁמְעוֹן נִרְאִין דִּבְרֵי בֵית שַׁמַּאי בִשְׁעַת הַמִּקְדָּשׁ. וְדִבְרֵי בֵית הִלֵּל בַּזְּמַן הַזֶּה. וַחֲכָמִים אוֹמְרִים לֹא כְדִבְרֵי זֶה וְלֹא כְדִבְרֵי זֶה אֶלָּא מוֹצִיא תְּרוּמָה וּתְרוּמַת מַעֲשֵׂר וּמְטַמְּאִין אֶת הַבּוֹר מִיַּד.

It was stated[45]: "When does one start to give heave from grapes? From the moment one went over it warp and woof. When does one start to make them impure? The House of Shammai say, after one removed second [tithe], the House of Hillel say, after one removed first [tithe]. Rebbi Yose said, practice should follow the House of Shammai but the public follow the House of Hillel. Rebbi Simeon says, the words of the House of Shammai were reasonable in the time of the Temple, the words of the House of Hillel are reasonable in the present time. But the Sages say unlike either of them, but that one removes heave and the heave of the tithe; then one may make it impure immediately."

45 Tosephta 3:12. In the Tosephta, the positions of the Houses of Hillel and Shammai are switched, the statement of R. Yose is in the name of R. Jehudah, the statement of R. Simeon is missing, and the Sages are quoted to require removal of heave and tithes. Except for the switch between R. Yose and R. Jehudah, which is undecidable and may stem from an abbreviation ר״י, the reading of the Yerushalmi is superior in every detail.

The problem discussed here and in the next paragraphs is, when may one give finished wine (or olive oil) which happens to be in the building of the press for wine (or oil) to be made from the grapes (or olives) newly brought into the press. The underlying principle is that the fruits must be crushed with some fluid oozing out, so that the fruit can no longer be used as fruit.

מֵאֵימָתַי תוֹרְמִין אֶת הַזֵּיתִים. אִית תַּנָּאֵי תַּנֵּי מִשֶּׁיִּטָּחֵנוּ. וְאִית תַּנָּאֵי תַּנֵּי מִשֶּׁיִּטְעֲנוּ. נִיחָא לְמָאן דָּמַר מִשֶּׁיִּטְעֲנוּ. לְמָאן דָּמַר מִשֶּׁיִּטָּחֵנוּ לֹא כֵן אָמַר רִבִּי יוֹחָנָן הַדְּרוֹכוֹת מְכֵיוָן שֶׁהִלְכוּ בָּהֶן שְׁתִּי (fol. 62b) וָעֵרֶב מְטַמְּאִין אֶת הַבּוֹר מִיַּד. אֶלָּא כָאן בְּיַיִן כָּאן בְּשֶׁמֶן. וְלֹא הוּא יַיִן הוּא שֶׁמֶן מַה בֵּין יַיִן מַה בֵּין שֶׁמֶן. יַיִן טוּמְאָתוֹ מְצוּיָה. שֶׁמֶן אֵין טוּמְאָתוֹ מְצוּיָה. אָמַר רִבִּי חִיָּיה בַּר אָדָא כָּאן וְכָאן הַטּוּמְאָה מְצוּיָה אֶלָּא שֶׁהַטּוּמְאָה מְצוּיָה בְּיַיִן יוֹתֵר מִבְּשֶׁמֶן.

"When does one start to give heave from olives? Some Tannaïm state, when they have been ground[46], and some Tannaïm state, when they are being weighted[47]. It is clear following him who says when they are being weighted. For him who says when they have been ground, did not Rebbi Joḥanan say, one makes the vat impure the moment the press men went over it warp and woof? This one is for wine, the other one for oil. Is not wine under the same rules as oil? What would be the difference between wine and oil? Wine is frequently impure, oil is not frequently impure. Rebbi Ḥiyya bar Ada said, both are frequently impure but impurity is found with wine more often than with oil.

46 In Tosephta 3:13, this is the opinion of R. Simeon, the opposing opinion that of the anonymous majority. Since the Yerushalmi does not quote names, it abstains from deciding between the opinions.

47 Except for choice olives from which oil can be obtained by squeezing by hand, olives have to be ground before they are put into the vat to be pressed, and the pressing is mechanical weighting down.

תַּנֵּי רִבִּי יוֹסֵי בֵּי רִבִּי יוּדָה אוֹמֵר אִם רָצָה מֵבִיא זֵיתִים וְנוֹתְנָן תַּחַת הַמָּמָל וְהוֹלֵךְ וּבָא עֲלֵיהֶן. אָמְרוּ לוֹ לֹא דוֹמִין זֵיתִים לָעֲנָבִים. עֲנָבִים דִּיהוּת וְנוֹתְקוֹת אֶת הַיַּיִן זֵיתִין קָשִׁין וְאֵינָן נוֹתְקִין אֶת הַשֶּׁמֶן.

"[48]Rebbi Yose ben Rebbi Jehudah said, if he wishes he may bring olives, put them under the pounding stone[49], and tread on it. They said to him, olives cannot be compared to grapes. Grapes are soft[50] and release the wine, olives are hard and do not release the oil[51]."

48 Tosephta 3:13.

49 Explanation of the Babli, *Baba Batra* 67b.

50 In the Tosephta: ריכות

51 Without mechanical pressure greater than that generated by people standing on top of the press.

(fol. 41d) **משנה ה**: הָאוֹמֵר תְּרוּמַת הַכְּרִי הַזֶּה בְּתוֹכוֹ וּמַעְשְׂרוֹתָיו בְּתוֹכוֹ וּתְרוּמַת מַעֲשֵׂר זֶה בְּתוֹכוֹ רִבִּי שִׁמְעוֹן אוֹמֵר קוֹרֵא שֵׁם. וַחֲכָמִים אוֹמְרִים עַד שֶׁאוֹמֵר בִּצְפוֹנוֹ אוֹ בִדְרוֹמוֹ. רִבִּי אֶלְעָזָר חִסְמָא אוֹמֵר הָאוֹמֵר תְּרוּמַת הַכְּרִי מִמֶּנּוּ עָלָיו קוֹרֵא שֵׁם. רִבִּי אֱלִיעֶזֶר בֶּן יַעֲקֹב אוֹמֵר הָאוֹמֵר עִישּׂוּר מַעֲשֵׂר זֶה עָשׂוּי תְּרוּמַת מַעֲשֵׂר עָלָיו קָרָא שֵׁם.

Mishnah 5: He who says the heave of this heap is contained in it, the tithes are contained in it and the heave of this tithe is contained in it, Rebbi Simeon says he gave it a name[52] but the Sages say, only if he said in its Northern or Southern part. Rebbi Eleazar Ḥisma[53] says, he who says, the heave of this heap is from it for itself, gave it a name. Rebbi Eliezer ben Jacob says, he who says, one tenth of this tithe is made heave of the tithe for it, gave it a name[54].

52 In that case, the entire heap becomes *dema'* and can be used only by a Cohen since the heaves are valid but their place is indeterminate. The Sages hold that *dema'* can be created only by heave falling into profane food; heave and *dema'* can never be created simultanously. They hold that designating heave without indicating its place is an invalid action.

53 Tanna of the second generation, student of R. Joshua. He admits even more possibilities than R. Simeon since the latter at least requires a declaration that the heave be "contained in it" whereas R. Eleazar Ḥisma already makes the declaration valid if only "from it" is declared. Since tithes and the heave of the tithe do not have to be earmarked, he will hold that tithes and heave of the tithe can be declared without specifying any place.

54 R. Eliezer ben Jacob holds with the Sages for heave, which must be earmarked, and possibly for the first tithe. But he rejects the restrictions for heave of the tithe which may be given from any place (Chapter 2, Note 6).

(fol. 42b) **הלכה ה**: רִבִּי יוֹסֵי בֵּי רִבִּי בּוּן בְּשֵׁם רִבִּי יוֹחָנָן אַתְיָא דְרִבִּי שִׁמְעוֹן כְּבֵית שַׁמַּאי דְּבֵית שַׁמַּאי אָמְרִין קִדְּשׁוּ מְדוּמָעִין. כֵּן רִבִּי שִׁמְעוֹן אוֹמֵר קִדְּשׁוּ מְדוּמָעִין.

Halakhah 5: Rebbi Yose ben Rebbi Abun in the name of Rebbi Joḥanan: Rebbi Simeon goes with the House of Shammai since the House of Shammai say it is sanctified as *dema'*[55] and so Rebbi Simeon says it is sanctified as *dema'*.

55 While this statement is repeated in Halakhah 4:5, it is difficult to find its origin. The commentaries refer to Mishnah 1:4, which is inapplicable since there no *dema'* is created.

עַד כְּדוֹן בְּאוֹמֵר בְּתוֹכוֹ אָמַר בּוֹ מָה. נִישְׁמְעִינָהּ מִן הָדָא מַעֲשֵׂר שֵׁנִי שֶׁבְּחֵפֶץ זֶה מְחוּלָּל עַל הַמָּעוֹת הַלָּלוּ וְלֹא קָרָא לוֹ שֵׁם. רִבִּי שִׁמְעוֹן אוֹמֵר קוֹרֵא לוֹ שֵׁם וַחֲכָמִים אוֹמְרִים לֹא עָשָׂה כְּלוּם עַד שֶׁיֹּאמַר בִּצְפוֹנוֹ אוֹ בִדְרוֹמוֹ. הָדָא אָמְרָה הִיא תוֹכוֹ הִיא בוֹ.

So far if he says "contained in it". What if he said "in it"? Let us hear from the following[56]: "The second tithe in this property shall be redeemed by those coins" and he did not specify[57], Rebbi Simeon said he gave it its name but the Sages say he did not do anything unless he says, in its Northern part, or in its Southern part." That means there is no difference between "contained in it" and "in it".

56 Tosephta *Ma'aser Šeni* 3:17.

57 In the Tosephta: He did not specify its place. The Tosephta deals with the case that the owner wants to redeem second tithe at the moment he is tithing his produce. While he does not have to separate the tithe, as explained in Tractate *Demay*, he must indicate its place.

דִּבְרֵי חֲכָמִים. רִבִּי זְעִירָא בְּשֵׁם רִבִּי אֲבוּדָמָא דְחֵיפָה בְּשֵׁם רִבִּי שִׁמְעוֹן בֶּן לָקִישׁ וְנֶחְשַׁב לָכֶם תְּרוּמַתְכֶם. וַהֲרֵמוֹתֶם. מַה מַחֲשָׁבָה בִמְסוּיָּים. אַף הַתּוֹרֵם בִּמְסוּיָּים.

The words of the Sages[58]. Rebbi Zeïra in the name of Rebbi Eudaimon from Haifa in the name of Rebbi Simeon ben Laqish (*Num.* 18:27): "Your heave will be thought of;" (*Num.* 18:26) "you shall lift." Just as thought has to be definite, so your giving heave has to be definite[59].

58 This refers to the sentence of the Mishnah starting "but the Sages say."

59 The order of the verses should be reversed: Because your heave is thought of, it must be parallel to what you would do if you lifted the heave out of the produce. Since what you lift is well defined, what you think of also must be well defined.

אָמַר תְּרוּמַת הַכְּרִי הַזֶּה וְזֶה בְזֶה. אָמַר רִבִּי יוֹחָנָן מָקוֹם שֶׁנִּסְתַּיְּימָה תְרוּמָתוֹ שֶׁל רִאשׁוֹן שָׁם שֶׁנִּסְתַּיְּימָה תְרוּמָתוֹ שֶׁל שֵׁינִי. רִבִּי יִצְחָק בַּר לָעְזָר בָּעֵי סְאָה תְּרוּמָה שֶׁנָּפְלָה לְתוֹךְ הַכְּרִי וְאָמַר תְּרוּמַת הַכְּרִי הַזֶּה בְּתוֹכוֹ מָקוֹם שֶׁנָּפְלָה אוֹתָהּ סְאָה שָׁם נִסְתַּיְּימָה תְרוּמָה שֶׁל כְּרִי.

If he said, the heave of this and that heap should be in this one; Rebbi Joḥanan said, the place where the heave of the first ended, there the second also ends[60]. Rebbi Isaac ben Eleazar asked: If a *seah* of heave fell into a heap[61] and he said, the heave of this heap is contained in it[62], does the heave of the heap end at that *seah*?

60 Since this follows the rules of the Sages for whom no *dema'* is created, it is understood that both times he indicated that the heave should be, e. g., in the Northern part of the heap. Then we assume that he intended to lift the two heaves together; the two heaves must be contiguous. The rules of lifting in this case of vague determination are spelled out in the next paragraph.

61 Here it is assumed that the original volume of the heap is at least 100 *seah*. In that case, no *dema'* is created but the original heave or its equivalent may simply be lifted out as explained in Chapter 5. If the argument of R. Joḥanan is correct, here

also the new heave should be adjacent to the heave to be lifted.

62 Assuming that the heave fell into the center of the heap; in that case the declaration is acceptable also to the Sages.

אָמַר תְּרוּמַת הַכְּרִי הַזֶּה בִּצְפוֹנוֹ מֶחֱצְיוֹ וּלְצָפוֹן מְדוּמָּע דִּבְרֵי רִבִּי וְנָסַב פַּלְגָּא. וַחֲכָמִים אוֹמְרִים עוֹשֶׂה אוֹתָהּ כְּמִין כִּי חַד מִן אַרְבָּעָה. רַבָּן שִׁמְעוֹן בֶּן גַּמְלִיאֵל אוֹמֵר נוֹטֵל תְּרוּמָתוֹ מִצְּפוֹן צְפוֹנוֹ חַד מִן תּוֹמַנְיָא.

"[63]If he said, the heave of this heap shall be in its Northern part, the Northern half is *dema'*, the words of Rebbi;" he takes one half. "But the Sages say, like a X[64];" one quarter. "Rabban Simeon ben Gamliel says, he takes its heave from the Northernmost part;" one eighth[65].

63 Tosephta 4:9. Everybody agrees that "the Northern part" is not specific enough to denote the place of heave; the reasonable thing would be to remove the grain for heave first and then give it a name; in that way only 2% has to be given.

64 Capital Greek letter χ.

65 It is assumed that the heap is in the form of a perfect cone with circular base. It is easy to understand the positions of Rebbi and the Sages. Rebbi draws a plane perpendicular to the base plane in East-West direction through the center. Anything in the Northern half of the heap now may be heave; therefore, the entire Northern half is *dema'*. The Sages draw a plane perpendicular to the base plane in North-South direction through the center and then two planes perpendicular to the base plane, making ±45° angles with the North-South plane, cutting the base plane in two lines forming a χ. The volume cut out by the Northern half of these planes is $^1/_4$th of the entire volume.

It is more difficult to reconstruct the Talmud's interpretation of the argument of Rabban Simeon ben Gamliel. If the idea is that in the base plane one draws a chord of the base circle so that it cuts off $^1/_8$th of the area of the circular disk, let 2α be the angle of the circular sector subtended by the segment measured in radians and choose the radius of the circle as unit of measurement. Then the area of the segment is the area of the sector minus the area of the triangle from the center:

$$A = \alpha - \sin\alpha \cos\alpha = \pi/8$$

or $\alpha = .8832$ rad $= 50.63°$. In that case, the height h of the segment is $1 - \cos\alpha = .365$ of the radius of the base circle. However, if the idea is that the volume cut off from the cone by a plane, perpendicular to the base plane, through the chord, should be one eighth of the total volume then the problem is indeterminate since the ratio of radius of the circle to the height of the cone is not given. If this is assumed to be 1, the equation to be solved is

$$(\alpha - \sin\alpha \cos\alpha)(1-\cos\alpha) = 3\pi/8$$

or $\alpha = 1.4526$ rad $= 83.22°$. However, the most likely explanation seems to be that in a heap of base radius r and height H, the total volume is computed as $^1/_3\pi r^2 H$ and one eighth of this is taken from the northernmost part of the heap.

תְּרוּמַת שְׁנֵי כְּרִיִים כְּאַחַת מַהוּ. רִבִּי יוֹחָנָן אָמַר קִדְּשׁוּ מְדוּמָעִין. רִבִּי שִׁמְעוֹן בֶּן לָקִישׁ אָמַר לֹא קִדְּשׁוּ מְדוּמָעִין.

What if the heave of two heaps [was given] together[66]? Rebbi Johanan said, they are both forbidden as *dema'*, but Rebbi Simeon ben Laqish said, they are not forbidden[67].

66 He gave heave for two heaps together which is perfectly legal. But he used the language of the Mishnah, "in the Northern part of one of them" and either he did not specify which of them or he did and forgot what he specified.

67 This sentence is from *Demay* 7:9 and explained there, Note 135.

אָמַר רִבִּי הוֹשַׁעְיָה בַּר שַׁמַּאי הָיוּ לְפָנָיו שְׁתֵּי סָאִין וּכְרִי אֶחָד וְאָמַר אֶחָד מִן הַסָּאוֹת הַלָּלוּ עֲשׂוּיָה תְרוּמָה עַל הַכְּרִי הַזֶּה קִידְּשָׁם וְאֵינוֹ יוֹדֵעַ אֵי זֶהוּ. הָיוּ לְפָנָיו שְׁנֵי כְּרִיִים וּסְאָה אַחַת וְאָמַר הֲרֵי זֶה תְרוּמָה עַל אֶחָד מִן הַכְּרִיִים הַלָּלוּ נִיתְקָן וְאֵין יָדוּעַ אֵי זֶהוּ.

Rebbi Hoshaia bar Shammai said, if he had before him two *seot* and one heap[68] and said, one of the *seot* is heave for this heap, he sanctified them and it is not known which one is sanctified[69]. If he had before him two heaps[70] and one *seah* and said, this is heave for one of the heaps, one is put in order but we do not known which one[71].

68 Assuming that the heap contains 50 *seot*.

69 Hence, both have to be given to the Cohen who may be required to pay for one of them.

70 Of 25 *seah* each.

71 Heave has to be taken a second time from both heaps with a declaration: "If this heap is already put in order I did not do anything and the grain is profane. But when the heap is still *ṭevel* it shall be heave." All three heaves must be given to the Cohen who may be asked to pay for one of them.

(fol. 41d) **משנה ו**: הַמַּקְדִּים תְּרוּמָה לַבִּיכּוּרִים. מַעֲשֵׂר רִאשׁוֹן לַתְּרוּמָה וּמַעֲשֵׂר שֵׁנִי לָרִאשׁוֹן אַף עַל פִּי שֶׁהוּא עוֹבֵר בְּלֹא תַעֲשֶׂה מַה שֶּׁעָשָׂה (fol. 42b) עָשׂוּי שֶׁנֶּאֱמַר מְלֵאָתְךָ וְדִמְעֲךָ לֹא תְאַחֵר.

Mishnah 6: One who gives heave before First Fruits, First Tithe before heave, Second Tithe before First, even though he transgresses a prohibition what he did is done since it is said (*Ex*. 22:28): "Your fullness[72] you should not make follow your *dema*".

משנה ז: וּמְנַיִין שֶׁיִּקְדְּמוּ הַבִּיכּוּרִים לַתְּרוּמָה. זֶה קָרוּי תְּרוּמָה וְרֵאשִׁית וְזֶה קָרוּי תְּרוּמָה וְרֵאשִׁית. אֶלָּא יִקְדְּמוּ הַבִּיכּוּרִים שֶׁהֵן בִּיכּוּרִים לַכֹּל וּתְרוּמָה לָרִאשׁוֹן שֶׁהִיא רִאשׁוֹנָה וּמַעֲשֵׂר רִאשׁוֹן לַשֵּׁנִי שֶׁיֵּשׁ בּוֹ רֵאשִׁית.

Mishnah 7: From where that First Fruits should precede heave since either one is called heave and first. First Fruits should precede since they are due before everything else, heave before First Tithe because it is first, First Tithe before the Second because it contains "first"[73].

72 In Mekhilta *Mišpaṭim* 19, Babli *Temurah* 4a, it is explained that "your fullness" refers to First Fruits because they are taken when the harvest is still full and nothing had been taken yet.

73 Commentary of Maimonides: "The Eternal called heave 'first' when He said (Deut. 18:4): 'The first of your grain, your cider, and your oil.' He called it heave (Num. 18:8): 'Lo, I gave to you the guarding of My heaves.' The Eternal called First Fruits first when He said (Deut. 26:22): 'You shall take from the first of any produce of the Land.' He called it heave (Deut. 12:27): 'You must bring there . . . and your hand's heave.' They said in Sifry (Deut. 62,73): 'Your hand's heave means First Fruits.' This proves that the verse speaks of First Fruits since it deals only with what has to be brought to the Temple and no heave has to be brought to Jerusalem except First Fruits for which there is an explicit verse. They said that First Tithe contains 'first', i. e., the heave of the tithe about which the Eternal said (Num. 18:26): 'You shall lift from it the Eternal's heave,' and heave is called 'first'". [The statement in Sifry is quoted in *Bikkurim* 2:1 (fol. 64c), Babli *Pesaḥim* 36b, *Yebamot* 73b, *Makkot* 17a, *Ḥulin* 120b, *Me'ilah* 15b.]

(fol. 42b) **הלכה ז**: רִבִּי חָמָא בַּר עוּקְבָּה בְּשֵׁם רִבִּי יוֹסֵי בַּר חֲנִינָה מִן מַה שֶׁעוֹבֵר בְּלֹא תַעֲשֶׂה אַתָּה יוֹדֵעַ מַה שֶּׁעָשָׂה עָשׂוּי. רִבִּי חָמָא בַּר עוּקְבָּא בְּשֵׁם רִבִּי יוֹסֵי בֵּי רִבִּי חֲנִינָא אָמַר לוֹקֶה. אָמַר רִבִּי זְעִירָא מֵתִיבִין קוֹמֵי רִבִּי יוֹחָנָן וְשָׁתִיק. מַה עוֹבֵר לוֹקֶה אוֹ אֵינוֹ לוֹקֶה. אָתָא רִבִּי יַעֲקֹב בַּר אָחָא בְּשֵׁם רִבִּי יוֹחָנָן אֵינוֹ לוֹקֶה. מַה קִיֵּם רִבִּי יוֹחָנָן מְלֵאָתְךָ וְדִמְעֲךָ לֹא תְאַחֵר. פָּתַר לָהּ בְּבִעוּר.

Halakhah 7: Rebbi Ḥama bar Uqba in the name of Rebbi Yose bar Ḥanina: Since he transgresses a prohibition it follows that what he did is valid. Rebbi Ḥama bar Uqba said in the name of Rebbi Yose bar Ḥanina: He is whipped[74]. Rebbi Zeïra said, they objected before Rebbi Joḥanan and he remained silent: If he transgresses, is he whipped or not? Rebbi Aḥa bar Jacob in the name of Rebbi Joḥanan: He is not whipped[75]. How does Rebbi Joḥanan explain (*Ex.* 22:28): "Your fullness you should not make follow your *dema*'". He explains it for removal[76].

74 In Babli *Temurah* 4a, the position of the Yerushalmi is rejected and it is proved that R. Yose ben R. Ḥanina holds that the person is not whipped but R. Eleazar says, he is whipped. The argument ascribed to those who hold with the Yerushalmi is that a simple transgression committed by speech only can never be punished by a court (לאו שאין בו מעשה). Since R. Yose ben R. Ḥanina holds here that the fact that he committed a sin proves that the status of the grain has changed from *ṭevel* to heave and tithes, in the interpretation of the Yerushalmi the transgression is one of fact rather than of speech.

75 He disagrees with R. Zeïra and holds that R. Joḥanan articulated his position.

76 He takes דמע to mean "fluid", derived from דמעה "tear" and reads: Your fullness and your fluids you should not keep too long, referring to tithes of grain, wine, and olive oil which have to be removed from his house and delivered to the poor at the end of the third and sixth years of the Sabbatical cycle.

אֵימָתַי הוּא עוֹבֵר. רִבִּי חִייָא בַּר בָּא אוֹמֵר מִתְּחִילָּה. רִבִּי שְׁמוּאֵל בַּר רַב יִצְחָק אָמַר בְּסוֹף. מַה נְפִיק מִבֵּינֵיהוֹן לְסִירוּף הַכְּרִי נְפַק מִבֵּינֵיהוֹן. עַל דַּעְתֵּיהּ דְּרִבִּי חִייָא בַּר וָא עוֹבֵר. עַל דַּעְתֵּיהּ דְּרִבִּי שְׁמוּאֵל בַּר רַב יִצְחָק אֵינוֹ עוֹבֵר.

When does he transgress? Rebbi Ḥiyya bar Abba says, from the start[77]; Rebbi Samuel bar Rav Isaac says, at the end. What difference comes between them? The burning of the heap is between them[78]; for Rebbi Ḥiyya bar Abba he transgressed, for Rebbi Samuel bar Rav Isaac he did not transgress.

77 The moment he separated what should be given second without giving the first he is guilty. For R. Samuel bar Rav Isaac, a formal transgression is caused only if the first also is given later.

78 He gave First Tithe from a heap which burned before he could give heave. For R. S. Lieberman the meaning is that, according to the second opinion, he has to burn the entire heap in order to avoid committing a sin.

רִבִּי שְׁמוּאֵל בַּר אַבָּא בָּעֵי מַעֲשֵׂר רִאשׁוֹן שֶׁהִקְדִּימוֹ שִׁבְּלִין עוֹבֵר אוֹ אֵינוֹ עוֹבֵר אֶלָּא עַל סֵדֶר.

Rebbi Samuel bar Abba asked: First Tithe which he preceded to ears, does he transgress or is he transgressing only the right order[79]?

79 Since the obligation of heave starts only after threshing, First Tithe given from ears of grain is free from the obligation of heave and cannot be said to be given before heave; but giving it certainly does not follow the prescribed order.

תַּנִּיֵין קוֹמֵי דְרִבִּי אַבָּהוּ תְּרוּמָה אֵינָהּ מְעַכֶּבֶת אֶת הַבִּיכּוּרִין. אָמַר לוֹן דְּאַבָּא פַּנִּימוֹן הִיא. רִבִּי יוֹסֵי בָּעֵי הֵיידָא דְּאַבָּא פַּנִּימוֹן. אָמַר לֵיהּ רִבִּי מָנָא שְׁמָעִית אַבָּא תַּנֵּי בִּיכּוּרִים בִּימִינוֹ וּתְרוּמָה בִשְׂמֹאלוֹ. אִית תַּנָּיֵי תַנֵּי עוֹבֵר אִית תַּנָּיֵי תַנֵּי אֵינוֹ עוֹבֵר. מָאן דָּמַר עוֹבֵר רַבָּנִין. מָאן דָּמַר אֵינוֹ עוֹבֵר אַבָּא פַּנִּימוֹן.

They stated before Rebbi Abbahu: "Heave does not interfere with First Fruits.[80]" He said to them, this is from Abba Palaemon[81]. Rebbi Yose asked, which [statement of] Abba Palaemon? Rebbi Mana said to him, I heard my father stating: "First fruits in his right hand, heave in his left hand." Some Tannaïm state, "he transgresses,", some Tannaïm state, "he does not transgress." He who says he transgresses, the rabbis; he who says he does not transgress, Abba Palaemon[82].

80 Tosephta 4:10. Even if heave was taken, First Fruits still may be given from the same crop.

81 A Tanna of the fifth generation; in Babylonian sources he appears as פלימו. In *Soṭa* 1:2 (fol. 16c), corresponding to Babli 4a, his name is Minyamin (a form of Binyamin).

[*Palaemon*, Greek Παλαίμων, name of a sea-god, also epithet of Heracles a. o., also used in Roman times (e. g. *Remmius Palaemon*, Roman grammarian in the time of Tiberius and Claudius.)

Because of the acoustic similarities between *Palaemon* and its counterpart *Binyamin* in the parallel passages, the Greek name might be a כינוי for the Biblical name, which would explain the apparent discrepancy. On the use of specific, traditional substitutes, כינוים, for a person's Hebrew name, see also E. & H. Guggenheimer, *Jewish Family Names and their Origins*, an Etymological Dictionary, Hoboken N.J. 1992, pp. xiv-xv; *Etymologisches Lexikon der jüdischen Familiennamen*, München 1996, p. xv. (E. G.)]

82 This refers to the disagreement between R. Ḥiyya bar Abba and R. Samuel bar Rav Isaac: For Abba Palaemon, a sin can be committed only in changing the prescribed order of heave and tithes, but changing the order between First Fruits and heave means disregarding a positive commandment, not transgressing a prohibition.

(fol. 42a) **משנה ח**: הַמִּתְכַּוֵּין לוֹמַר תְּרוּמָה וְאָמַר מַעֲשֵׂר מַעֲשֵׂר וְאָמַר תְּרוּמָה. עוֹלָה וְאָמַר שְׁלָמִים שְׁלָמִים וְאָמַר עוֹלָה. שֶׁאֵינִי נִכְנַס לַבַּיִת זֶה וְאָמַר לָזֶה. שֶׁאֵינִי נֶהֱנֶה לָזֶה וְאָמַר לָזֶה לֹא אָמַר כְּלוּם עַד שֶׁיְּהֵא פִּיו וְלִבּוֹ שָׁוִין.

Mishnah 8: If somebody intends to say[83] heave but says tithe, tithe but says heave, fire offering but says well-being offering, well-being offering but says fire offering, that I shall not enter this house[84] and he says that one, that I shall have no enjoyment from this one and he says from that one, he did not say anything unless his statement and his intention be equal.

83 As dedication after separation of the amount (or animal) given.

84 This and the next example are instances of "vows of prohibition", whereby a person forbids otherwise permitted enjoyments to himself (*Num.* 30:3).

(fol. 42b) **הלכה ח**: תַּמָּן תַּנִּינָן בֵּית שַׁמַּאי אוֹמְרִים הֶקְדֵּשׁ טָעוּת הֶקְדֵּשׁ. וְאָמַר רִבִּי יִרְמְיָה בָּא לוֹמַר חוּלִין וְאָמַר עוֹלָה קִדְּשָׁהּ. אָמַר רִבִּי יוֹסֵי בְּמִתְכַּוֵּין לְהֶקְדֵּשׁ אֲנָן קַייָמִין. אֶלָּא שֶׁתָּעָה מֵחֲמַת דָּבָר אַחֵר. וְהָדָא מַתְנִיתָא מַה הִיא. עַל דַּעְתֵּיהּ דְּרִבִּי יִרְמְיָה בְּמַחְלוֹקֶת. עַל דַּעְתֵּיהּ דְּרִבִּי יוֹסֵי דִּבְרֵי הַכֹּל.

Halakhah 8: There[85], we have stated: "The House of Shammai say, dedication in error is dedication." Rebbi Jeremiah said, if he intends to say "profane" and he says "fire sacrifice", he dedicated it[86]. Rebbi Yose said, we consider only if he intended to dedicate but he erred because of something else[87]. What is the status of this Mishnah[88]? In the opinion of Rebbi Jeremiah it is in dispute, in the opinion of Rebbi Yose it is everybody's opinion.

85 Mishnah *Nazir* 5:1. The entire Halakhah is copied from *Nazir*, Halakhah 5:1.

86 This is his interpretation of the House of Shammai's position.

87 The full text of Mishnah *Nazir* 5:1 is: "The House of Shammai say, dedication in error is dedication, but the House of Hillel say, it is no dedication. How is that? If he said, the black bull coming out first from my house shall be dedicated [as sacrifice] and a white one came out, the House of Shammai say, it is dedicated, but the House of Hillel say, it is not dedicated." R. Yose restricts the opinion of the house of Shammai to the case when he wanted to dedicate some animal for a certain kind of sacrifice and the only error is in the individual selected.

88 The Mishnah here in *Terumot*. For R. Jeremiah, it only follows the House of Hillel.

תַּנֵּי בִּשְׂפָתַיִם וְלֹא בַּלֵּב יָכוֹל שֶׁאֲנִי מוֹצִיא אֶת הַגּוֹמֵר בַּלֵּב. תַּלְמוּד לוֹמַר לְבַטֵּא. וּשְׁמוּאֵל אָמַר הַגּוֹמֵר בְּלִבּוֹ אֵינוֹ חַייָב עַד שֶׁיּוֹצִיא בִשְׂפָתָיו. וְהָתַנֵּי כֹּל נְדִיב לֵב זֶה הַגּוֹמֵר בַּלֵּב. אַתָּה אוֹמֵר זֶה הַגּוֹמֵר בַּלֵּב אוֹ אֵינוֹ אֶלָּא הַמּוֹצִיא בִשְׂפָתָיו. כְּשֶׁהוּא אוֹמֵר מוֹצָא שְׂפָתֶיךָ תִּשְׁמוֹר הֲרֵי מוֹצִא בִשְׂפָתָיו אָמוּר. הָא מָה אֲנִי מְקַייֵם כֹּל נְדִיב לֵב זֶה הַגּוֹמֵר בַּלֵּב. מַה דְאָמַר שְׁמוּאֵל לְקָרְבָּן.

It was stated[89]: "With his lips but not in his mind." I could think that I exclude him who decides in his mind, the verse says (*Lev.* 5:4): "To articulate[90]". But Samuel said, he who decides in his mind is not obliged until he pronounces with his lips. But did we not state: "(*Ex.* 35:5) Everyone who volunteers in his mind[91]," that is he who decides in his mind. You say, that is he who decides in his mind, but maybe that is he who pronounces with his lips? When he says (*Deut.* 23:24): "What comes out from your lips you have to keep[92]," that speaks about him who pronounces with his lips. Therefore, how can I confirm "every one who volunteers in his mind?" That is he who decides in his mind. What Samuel said refers to a sacrifice.

89 The main tannaïtic source is *Sifra Wayyiqra* דבורא דחובה פרשה ט. The argument is discussed in Babli *Ševu'ot* 26b.

90 The verse reads: "Or a person who might swear to *articulate with his lips* for bad or good, about all a man might *articulate* in an oath, when he forgot and then remembered about any of these." Since *articulate* is used twice in the same verse it is assumed that the second mention is not identical with the first. Since the first mentions lips, the second cannot speak about the same situation. {Biblical dictionaries tend to define בטא as "speaking hastily" on basis of *Prov.* 12:18. However, as Rashi points out, the context requires:
(17) "He who breathes trust will tell the truth
but a false witness trickery.
(18) There is one who articulates like sword thrusts
but the tongue of the Sages is healing."

The chiastic arrangement of the verses shows that they form a unit. Therefore, the rabbinic use of the word as "carefully articulated" is borne out by biblical usage. Cf. also Arabic بطو "to be slow-going.")

91 The verse is quoted incorrectly (it must be לבו not לב). The verse speaks of voluntary gifts for the Tabernacle; explicit pledges are never mentioned there.

92 "What *comes out from your lips* you have to keep as you made a vow of a voluntary gift to the Eternal your God, *as you pronounced with your mouth.*" A voluntary gift here is a sacrifice; the verse insists that such a vow is valid only if pronounced.

(fol. 42a) **משנה ט**: הַנָּכְרִי וְהַכּוּתִי תְּרוּמָתָן תְּרוּמָה וּמַעְשְׂרוֹתָן מַעֲשֵׂר וְהֶקְדֵּישָׁן הֶקְדֵּשׁ. רִבִּי יְהוּדָה אוֹמֵר אֵין לְנָכְרִי כֶּרֶם רְבָעִי. וַחֲכָמִים אוֹמְרִים יֵשׁ לוֹ. תְּרוּמַת הַנָּכְרִי מְדַמַּעַת וְחַייָבִין עָלֶיהָ חוֹמֶשׁ. וְרִבִּי שִׁמְעוֹן פּוֹטֵר.

Mishnah 9: The heave of the Gentile and the Samaritan is heave, their tithes are tithes, and their dedications are dedications[93]. Rebbi Jehudah says, a Gentile cannot have a fourth year vineyard[94] but the Sages say, he may have. The Gentile's heave creates *dema'* and one is obliged to a fifth[3,95] for it, but Rebbi Simeon frees from the obligation.

93 The dedications of Gentiles are valid dedications by biblical decree (*Lev.* 22:25). Heave and tithes of Gentiles are accepted by analogy. The problem of Samaritans is that they are Sadducees and do not follow rabbinic rules; it is decreed that any heave and tithes given by them under their rules are valid.

94 The yield of the fourth year of a newly planted vineyard is holy and must be redeemed before consumption, *Lev.* 19:24. For R. Jehudah, the obligation of the fourth year is tied to the possession of the Land; for the Sages, it is an extension of the duty of *'orlah* which also applies outside the Land.

95 Since *Lev.* 22:25 implies that

dedication by a Gentile is a meritorious action, it follows that all stringencies of dedications have to be applied.

(fol. 42b) **הלכה ט**: הוֹצִיא לָהֶן תְּרוּמָה מִתּוֹךְ בֵּיתוֹ נוֹהֲגִין בָּהּ בְּטֶבֶל וּבִתְרוּמָה גְדוֹלָה דִּבְרֵי רַבִּי. רַבִּי שִׁמְעוֹן בֶּן גַּמְלִיאֵל אוֹמֵר הֲרֵי זוֹ תְרוּמָה וַדַּאי. הוֹצִיא לָהֶן מַעֲשֵׂר רִאשׁוֹן מִתּוֹךְ בֵּיתוֹ נוֹהֲגִין בְּטֶבֶל וּבְמַעֲשֵׂר רִאשׁוֹן דִּבְרֵי רַבִּי. רַבָּן שִׁמְעוֹן בֶּן גַּמְלִיאֵל אוֹמֵר אֵינוֹ צָרִיךְ לְהַפְרִישׁ אֶלָּא מַעֲשֵׂר רִאשׁוֹן בִּלְבַד. הוֹצִיא לָהֶן מַעֲשֵׂר שֵׁנִי מִתּוֹךְ בֵּיתוֹ נוֹהֲגִין בָּהּ בְּטֶבֶל וּבְמַעֲשֵׂר שֵׁנִי דִּבְרֵי רַבִּי. רַבִּי שִׁמְעוֹן בֶּן גַּמְלִיאֵל אוֹמֵר אֵינוֹ צָרִיךְ לְהַפְרִישׁ אֶלָּא מַעֲשֵׂר שֵׁנִי בִּלְבַד. אָמַר רַבִּי יוֹסֵי בֵּי רַבִּי בּוּן רַבִּי חָשַׁשׁ שֶׁמָּא הִפְרִישׁ מִמִּין עַל שֶׁאֵינוֹ מִינוֹ. וְרַבָּן שִׁמְעוֹן בֶּן גַּמְלִיאֵל חָשַׁשׁ שֶׁמָּא הִקְדִּים.

"[96]If he brought heave from his house[97] one treats it as *ṭevel* and Great Heave, the words of Rebbi[98]; Rabban Simeon ben Gamliel says, it is certainly heave. If he brought First Tithe from his house, one treats it as *ṭevel* and First Tithe, the words of Rebbi; Rabban Simeon ben Gamliel says, he needs only to separate First Tithe. If he brought Second Tithe from his house, one treats it as *ṭevel* and Second Tithe, the words of Rebbi; Rabban Simeon ben Gamliel says, he needs only to separate Second Tithe." Rebbi Yose ben Rebbi Abun said, Rebbi worries that maybe he gave from one kind on another[99] but Rabban Simeon ben Gamliel worries thay maybe he inverted the order[100].

96 Tosephta 4:13. The entire Halakhah deals only with Gentiles. For the treatment of Samaritans either as Jews or as Gentiles cf. *Demay* 3:4, p. 467.

97 The preceding Tosephta stated that heave and tithes given by the Gentile from the threshing floor are unquestionably valid since they were given in the open and following the rabbinic rules. The problem is only with gifts given from the barn where we do not know how these were separated.

98 Rebbi requires that the produce be treated as heave, to be consumed only by a Cohen, but also as *ṭevel*, that even the Cohen may use it only if he gave heave for it from another batch of the same produce. Similarly, in the other cases Rebbi requires that heave and tithes be given from the Cohen's own produce.

99 In that case, the heave and tithes would be invalid.

100 He does not have to worry, but if the Gentile might have separated tithe before heave nothing bad has happened since heave and tithes are valid by Mishnah 6 and the Gentile is not subject to the rabbinic prohibitions.

תְּרוּמַת הַנָּכְרִי מְדַמַּעַת וְחַיָּבִין עָלֶיהָ חוֹמֶשׁ. רִבִּי שִׁמְעוֹן פּוֹטֵר. אָמַר רִבִּי זְעִירָא אֲמָרָהּ קוֹמֵי רִבִּי אַבָּהוּ בְּשֵׁם רִבִּי יוֹחָנָן מַה פְלִיגֵי בִּתְרוּמַת גּוֹרְנוֹ. אֲבָל גּוֹי שֶׁלָּקַח מִפֵּירוֹת יִשְׂרָאֵל אַף רִבִּי שִׁמְעוֹן מוֹדֵי אָמַר לִי רִבִּי אַבָּהוּ בְּשֵׁם רִבִּי יוֹחָנָן הִיא מַחְלוֹקֶת. וְקַשְׁיָא עַל דְּרִבִּי שִׁמְעוֹן פּוֹטֵר טִבְלוֹ דְּבַר תּוֹרָה וְאַתְּ אָמַר הָכֵן. וְכִי קֳדָשִׁים אֵינָן תּוֹרָה וְרִבִּי שִׁמְעוֹן פּוֹטֵר. וְתַנִּינָן תַּמָּן קָדְשֵׁי גוֹיִם אֵין חַייָבִין עֲלֵיהֶן מִשּׁוּם פִּיגּוּל וְנוֹתָר וְטָמֵא הַשּׁוֹחְטָן בַּחוּץ פָּטוּר דִּבְרֵי רִבִּי יוֹסֵי. וְרִבִּי שִׁמְעוֹן מְחַייֵב. הֲווֹן בָּעֵיי מֵימַר מַה פְלִיגִין בְּחוֹמֶשׁ הָא בְדִימּוּעַ לֹא. אַשְׁכַּח תַּנֵּי הִיא הָדָא הִיא הָדָא.

"The Gentile's heave creates *dema*' and one is obligated to a fifth[3,95] for it, but Rebbi Simeon frees from the obligation." Rebbi Zeïra said, I said this before Rebbi Abbahu in the name of Rebbi Joḥanan: They disagree only for the heave of his threshing floor. But for a Gentile who bought the produce of a Jew[101], even Rebbi Simeon will agree. Rebbi Abbahu said to me in the name of Rebbi Joḥanan, the disagreement is about the latter case. It is difficult according to Rebbi Simeon, does he free his *ṭevel* from the Torah and you say so[102]? But are sacrifices[103] not from the Torah, and nevertheless Rebbi Simeon frees, as we have stated there[104]: "Sacrifices of Gentiles are not subject to *piggul*[105], left-overs[106], and impurity and one who slaughters them outside[107] is free [from punishment], the words of Rebbi Yose, but Rebbi Simeon declares him guilty." They wanted to say that they disagree only about the fifth but not about *dema'*. They found stated: It is all the same.

101 After it was harvested. R. Simeon teaches that real estate in the Land of Israel held by Gentiles is free from all obligations of the Land, cf. *Peah* Chapter 4, Note 129, *Demay* Chapter 5, Note 102.

102 If the Gentile bought produce after threshing, obligated for heave but before heave was taken, then his heave will free the grain for consumption by Jews. Since his heave has all the force of heave given by a Jew, why should it not be subject to all rules of heave?

103 Sacrifices given to the Temple by Gentiles are accepted by biblical law, cf. Note 93.

104 Mishnah *Zebaḥim* 4:5, and similarly Tosephta *Zebaḥim* 5:6. In all these texts, R. Simeon is quoted as freeing from punishment and R. Yose as declaring guilty. This is also a necessary reading here since the argument is that R. Simeon considers the Gentile's sacrifice to be a genuine sacrifice acceptable to Heaven but not subject to any of the restrictions imposed on Jewish sacrifices; in parallel, the Gentile's heave is heave but subject to its rules. (In some Mishnah mss. and editions, "R. Simeon" is replaced by "R. Meïr.") Maimonides, both in his Commentary and his Code (*Pesule Hammuqdašim* 18:24) follows R. Simeon, against the rule that R. Yose prevails over R. Simeon. As R. Aqiba Eiger points out, the Babli quotes two instances (*Zebaḥim* 116b, *Menaḥot* 109b) of actual sacrifices performed for Gentiles outside the Land. Since the action of a respected authority, in this case Rava, the unquestioned leader of his generation, overrides all decision rules, Maimonides is justified.

105 A sacrifice brought with the intent of eating it at an inappropriate time or inappropriate place, a deadly sin (*Lev.* 7:18, 19:7).

106 Leftovers from sacrificial meat remaining after the allotted time, whose consumption is sinful.

107 Sacrificed outside the Temple, a prohibition restricted to "the Children of Israel", *Lev.* 17:3.

המפריש פרק רביעי

(fol. 42c) **משנה א**: הַמַּפְרִישׁ מִקְצָת תְּרוּמָה וּמַעְשְׂרוֹת מוֹצִיא מִמֶּנּוּ תְּרוּמָה עָלָיו אֲבָל לֹא לְמָקוֹם אַחֵר רִבִּי מֵאִיר אוֹמֵר אַף מוֹצִיא הוּא לְמָקוֹם אַחֵר תְּרוּמָה וּמַעְשְׂרוֹת.

Mishnah 1: If somebody separates parts of heave or tithes, he takes from this its own heave or tithes but not for another place[1]. Rebbi Meïr says, he may even take it for another place.

1 R. Simson explains: If somebody desires to give the full amount of heave (Mishnah 3) but at the moment takes only a smaller amount, or if he does not take the full 10% as tithes, then what he took is heave or tithes but the remainder is profane food and *ṭevel* mixed together and he may take the rest of his obligation from the same heap since, in this case, we say that what he takes out is *ṭevel* and not profane. {For heave he must have the intention to give more since there is no biblical minimum for heave.} But for another heap we do not allow him to take heave or tithes from what is partially profane. R. Meïr's position is that we accept that heave taken in any permissible way retroactively turns its material into *ṭevel*, so that in any case only correct heave or tithes were taken (cf. *Demay* Chapter 5, Notes 45,63.).

Maimonides explains the Mishnah as stating that partial heave or tithes possibly remain *ṭevel* and therefore one must give heave or tithes from the separate produce. It cannot be returned to the original heap because possibly it is heave. R. Meïr considers it certain *ṭevel*. R. Abraham ben David (*Ma'aser* 1:15) declares "I have no idea where he or his teacher could have picked up such an idea," but the correct explanation is that given by R. Simson.

הלכה א: הַמַּפְרִישׁ מִקְצָת תְּרוּמָה וּמַעְשְׂרוֹת כו'. מַתְנִיתִין כְּשֶׁהִפְרִישׁ וּבְדַעְתּוֹ לְהַפְרִישׁ. רִבִּי שְׁמוּאֵל בְּשֵׁם רִבִּי זְעִירָא מַתְנִיתִין בִּסְתָם. אָמַר רִבִּי מָנָא קוֹמֵי רִבִּי יוּדָן מַה וּפְלִיג. אָמַר לֵיהּ סְתָמוֹ בְּשֶׁהִפְרִישׁ כְּדַעְתּוֹ לְהַפְרִישׁ.

Halakhah 1: "If somebody separates parts of heave or tithes," etc. Our Mishnah [is said] in case he separated and it is his intention to separate more. Rebbi Samuel in the name of Rebbi Zeïra, our Mishnah [is said] if he did not say anything. Rebbi Mana said before Rebbi Yudan: Do they disagree? He said to him, if he did not say anything, it is as if it were his intention to separate more[2].

2 The only case where an amount of heave smaller than the rabbinic minimum is accepted as full heave if the person giving heave says so explicitly.

מַה בֵּין מוֹצִיא מִמֶּנּוּ עָלָיו מִמּוֹצִיא מִמֶּנּוּ עַל מָקוֹם אַחֵר. בְּשָׁעָה שֶׁהוּא מִמֶּנּוּ עָלָיו כָּל־הַטֶּבֶל עָלָה בְיָדוֹ. וּבְשָׁעָה שֶׁהוּא מוֹצִיא מִמֶּנּוּ עַל מָקוֹם אַחֵר מִזֶּה וּמִזֶּה עָלָה בְיָדוֹ. וְקַשְׁיָא נָטַל לְהוֹצִיא מִמֶּנּוּ עָלָיו כָּל־הַטֶּבֶל עָלָה בְיָדוֹ וְנִמְלַךְ לְהוֹצִיא מִמֶּנּוּ עַל מָקוֹם אַחֵר מִזֶּה וּמִזֶּה עָלָה בְיָדוֹ. נָטַל לְהוֹצִיא מִמֶּנּוּ עַל מָקוֹם אַחֵר מִזֶּה וּמִזֶּה עָלָה בְיָדוֹ וְנִמְלַךְ לְהוֹצִיא מִמֶּנּוּ עָלָיו כָּל־הַטֶּבֶל עָלָה בְיָדוֹ. פִּיחֵת כָּל־הַטֶּבֶל עָלָה בְיָדוֹ הוֹסִיף מִזֶּה וּמִזֶּה עָלָה בְיָדוֹ.

What is the difference between taking from itself for itself and taking from itself for another place? When it is from itself for itself, what comes into his hand is[3] all *ṭevel*. If he separates from it for another place, both together come into his hand. That is difficult[4]: If he took [produce] with the intention of taking from itself for itself, what comes into his hand is all *ṭevel*. If he changed his mind to use it for another place, both together come into his hand! If he took [produce] with the intention to use for another place, both together come into his hand. If he changed his mind to take from itself for itself, all that came into his hand is *ṭevel*! If he gave too little, all that came into his hand is *ṭevel*[5]. If he added, both together came into his hand[6].

3 Retroactively, it turned out to be heave. But if used for another heap, there is no retroactivity and heave and *ṭevel* are indistinguishable.

4 Clause missing in Rome ms., but quoted by R. Simson.

5 This is the case of our Mishnah. The clause is missing in the Leyden ms.

6 If we speak of heave, what he separated was more than he intended. If we speak of tithe, his produce is in order but his tithe is not, as stated in *Demay* Chapter 5, Note 40.

אַף בְּטוֹעֶה כֵן. הָיָה סָבוּר שֶׁהוּא חַייָב שְׁתֵּי סְאִין וְאֵינוֹ חַייָב אֶלָּא אַחַת רִבִּי אִימִּי בְּשֵׁם רִבִּי שִׁמְעוֹן בֶּן לָקִישׁ אוֹתָהּ הַסְּאָה שֶׁהוּא מַפְרִישׁ עוֹשֶׂה אוֹתָהּ תְּרוּמָה עַל מָקוֹם אַחֵר. וְהָתַנִּינָן אֲבָל לֹא עַל מָקוֹם אַחֵר. תִּפְתָּר בְּמַרְבֶּה בִּתְרוּמָה. נִיחָא בְּמַרְבֶּה בִּתְרוּמָה. וּבְמַעְשְׂרוֹת לֹא תַנֵּי רִבִּי שִׁמְעוֹן בֶּן לָקִישׁ מַעְשְׂרוֹת. אֶלָּא טַעֲמָא דְרִבִּי שִׁמְעוֹן בֶּן לָקִישׁ מִכֵּיוָן דּוּ אָמַר כָּל־הַטֶּבֶל עָלָה בְיָדוֹ מַה בֵּין מוֹצִיא מִמֶּנּוּ עָלָיו מַה בֵּין מוֹצִיא מִמֶּנּוּ עַל מָקוֹם אַחֵר.

Also if he is in error it is so. If he thought that two *se'ot* were due but he owed only one, Rebbi Immi in the name of Rebbi Simeon ben Laqish: That [extra] *seah* which he separated he gives as heave for another place. But did we not state: "but not for another place"? Explain it if he increased the heave[7]. It is acceptable if he increased the heave, but what about tithes? Rebbi Simeon ben Laqish did not state about tithes. But the reason of Rebbi Simeon ben Laqish must be that, since we say that all the *ṭevel* is now in his hands, what is the difference between taking from it its own heave or that for another place[8]?

7 The Mishnah is irrelevant here since it deals with the case that too little heave was given. It is permissible to give too much heave since its amount is not determined in biblical law, in contrast to tithes. Since the extra *seah* was declared as heave, it must remain in the sanctity of heave.

8 If the reason given above, that we declare that all produce in his hand the second time around was genuine *ṭevel*, then this *ṭevel* should be usable for heave in all possible ways. He will restrict the use of the second batch only for freeing its own produce for tithes and heave of the tithe.

מַיי כְּדוֹן בְּשֶׁנִּתְקַן רוּבּוֹ שֶׁל כְּרִי. לֹא נִתְקַן רוּבּוֹ שֶׁל כְּרִי פְּלוּגְתָא דְחִזְקִיָּה וְרִבִּי יוֹחָנָן דְּאָמַר רֵישׁ לָקִישׁ בְּשֵׁם חִזְקִיָּה טֵבֶל בָּטֵל בְּרוֹב. וְרִבִּי יוֹחָנָן אָמַר אֵין הַטֵּבֶל בָּטֵל בְּרוֹב. מִכֵּיוָן שֶׁנָּתַן דַּעְתּוֹ לְהַפְרִישׁ נִסְתַּיְימָה כָּל־חִטָּה וְחִטָּה בִמְקוֹמָהּ. וְאִית דְּבָעֵי מֵימַר כְּהָדָא דְתַנֵּי רִבִּי לִיעֶזֶר בֶּן יַעֲקֹב. דְּתַנֵּי רִבִּי לִיעֶזֶר בֶּן יַעֲקֹב אֵינוֹ מוֹצִיא לֹא עָלָיו וְלֹא עַל מָקוֹם אַחֵר. עַד כְּדוֹן לֹא נִתְקַן רוּבּוֹ שֶׁל כְּרִי. נִתְקַן רוּבּוֹ שֶׁל כְּרִי. וְיָבֹא כְהָדָא הָיוּ לְפָנָיו שְׁנֵי כְרָיִין אֶחָד הִפְרִישׁ מִמֶּנּוּ מִקְצָת תְּרוּמָה וּמַעֲשֵׂר וְאֶחָד הִפְרִישׁ מִמֶּנּוּ מִקְצָת תְּרוּמָה וּמַעֲשֵׂר מָהוּ (fol. 42d) שֶׁיִּתְרוֹם מִזֶּה עַל זֶה. תַּלְמִידוֹי דְרִבִּי חִיָּה רוֹבָא שָׁאֲלִין לְרִבִּי חִיָּה רוֹבָא אָמַר לוֹן הַכְּסִיל חוֹבֵק אֶת יָדָיו וְאוֹכֵל אֶת בְּשָׂרוֹ. רִבִּי לָעְזָר בְּשֵׁם רִבִּי חִיָּה רֹבָה אֵין תּוֹרְמִין וְלֹא מְעַשְּׂרִין מִזֶּה עַל זֶה.

That is[9], if most of the heap was put in order. If most of the heap was not put in order, there is disagreement between Ḥizqiah and Rebbi Joḥanan. As Rebbi Simeon ben Laqish said in the name of Ḥizqiah, *ṭevel* becomes voided by plurality[10], but Rebbi Joḥanan said, *ṭevel* does not become voided by plurality. Since it was his intention to give, each single grain of wheat was labelled at its place[11]. Some want to explain following Rebbi Eliezer ben Jacob, as Rebbi Eliezer ben Jacob stated, that he cannot separate either for itself or for another place[12]. This parallels the following[13]: If there were before him two heaps and from each of them he took part of heave or tithes, may he take heave or tithe from one for the other? The students of the elder Rebbi Ḥiyya asked the elder Rebbi Ḥiyya and he said to them (*Eccl.* 4:5): "The fool folds his hands and eats his own flesh." Rebbi Eleazar in the name of the elder Rebbi Ḥiyya: He may not give heave or tithe from one for the other.

9 If the heave given was more than 50% of what was due, one follows R. Simeon ben Laqish. If less than 50% was given, one follows R. Eliezer ben Jacob in this paragraph. The Mishnah therefore is valid only in case exactly 50% were given.

10 He disagrees with the generally accepted statement that by rabbinic decree, the prohibition of anything that can be put in order is not voided if it becomes an indistinguishable part of other produce or food; cf. *Ševi'it* 6:3, Notes 117-121. It is agreed that in biblical law, the prohibition of any food becomes void by a plurality of permitted matter. Cf. also Halakhah 8, Note 71.

11 As noted before, if it was the farmer's intention to put in order only part of the heap, then the remainder is *ṭevel* and no one knows which grains are profane and which *ṭevel*.

12 If humans cannot distinguish between profane and *ṭevel*, humans cannot use the remainder of the heap for heave or tithes.

13 The following text is from Chapter 2, Notes 26-28.

(fol. 42c) **משנה ב**: מִי שֶׁהָיוּ פֵּירוֹתָיו בִּמְגוּרָה וְנָתַן סְאָה לְבֶן לֵוִי וּסְאָה לְעָנִי מַפְרִישׁ עוֹד שְׁמוֹנֶה סְאִין וְאוֹכְלָן דִּבְרֵי רִבִּי מֵאִיר. וַחֲכָמִים אוֹמְרִים אֵינוֹ מַפְרִישׁ אֶלָּא לְפִי חֶשְׁבּוֹן.

Mishnah 2: If somebody's produce was in a storage bin and he gave a *seah* to a Levite and a *seah* to a poor person, one may separate another eight *se'ot* and eat them, the words of Rebbi Meïr. But the Sages say, he separates only according to the computation[14,15].

14 For this Mishnah, Maimonides gives one but R. Simson and R. Isaac Simponti each give three explanations. Maimonides and R. Simson in his last explanation assume that the Mishnah speaks only of the farmer who is a Fellow. He gave the gifts to the Levite and the poor without saying anything; later he declares them to be tithes. R. Meïr gives him credit for all he gave; the Sages declare that he may use as profane only four times the amount of tithes still in existence at the time of declaration.

15 An explanation suggested by the Halakhah is R. I. Simponti's last: The farmer is a vulgar person (as defined in the Introduction to *Demay*) who may be trusted to have given heave but not tithes. If he was seen giving one *seah* to a Levite and one (or at least $^{9}/_{10}$ of a *seah*) to the poor (in a year when tithe of the poor was due), we may assume that they were given as tithes, or the farmer, when interrogated, may retroactively declare them to be tithes; eight *se'ot* (or exactly $8^{1}/_{10}$) are now in order and any of his workers who is a Fellow (as defined in the Introduction to *Demay*) may eat up to that amount, in the opinion of R. Meïr. But the Sages say, he has to treat any produce of the vulgar farmer according to the rules of *demay*, cf. *Demay* 7:3.

(fol. 42d) **הלכה ב**: רִבִּי לָעְזָר בְּשֵׁם רִבִּי הוֹשַׁעְיָה עָשׂוּ אוֹתָהּ כְּפוֹעֵל שֶׁאֵינוֹ מַאֲמִין לְבַעַל הַבַּיִת.

Halakhah 2: Rebbi Eleazar in the name of Rebbi Hoshaiah: They treated it following the rules of a worker who does not trust his employer[15].

פְּשִׁיטָא הָדָא מִילְּתָא נִשְׂרְפוּ הַפֵּירוֹת הַתְּרוּמָה בְטֵילָה. נִשְׂרְפָה הַתְּרוּמָה לִכְשֶׁיֵּאָכְלוּ הַפֵּירוֹת קָדְשָׁה הַתְּרוּמָה לְמַפְרֵעַ.

The following is obvious: If the produce was burned, the heave becomes invalid[16]. If the heave was burned, when the produce will be consumed, the heave will retroactively have been sanctified[17].

16 Heave was given only for part of the produce, as in Mishnah 1. If the produce then was destroyed, it was never made clear which particular grain was put in order by the heave; the same applies for tithes. Since the heave now does not put anything in order, it is not heave and the Cohen may not consume it before he separates heave and tithes.

17 Following the statement in Halakhah 1, that the selected produce will all be profane.

(fol. 42c) **משנה ג**: שִׁעוּר תְּרוּמָה עַיִן יָפָה אֶחָד מֵאַרְבָּעִים. בֵּית שַׁמַּאי אוֹמְרִים אֶחָד מִשְּׁלֹשִׁים. וְהַבֵּינוֹנִית מֵחֲמִשִּׁים. וְהָרָעָה מִשִּׁשִּׁים. תָּרַם וְעָלָה בְיָדוֹ אֶחָד מִשִּׁשִּׁים תְּרוּמָה וְאֵינוֹ צָרִיךְ לִתְרוֹם חָזַר וְהוֹסִיף חַייָב בְּמַעְשְׂרוֹת. עָלָה בְיָדוֹ מִשִּׁשִּׁים וְאֶחָד תְּרוּמָה וְיַחֲזוֹר וְיִתְרוֹם כְּמוֹת שֶׁהוּא לָמוּד בְּמִידָּה בְּמִשְׁקָל וּבְמִנְייָן. רִבִּי יְהוּדָה אוֹמֵר אַף לֹא מִן הַמּוּקָף.

Mishnah 3: The rate of heave[18]: A generous person one in forty, the House of Shammay say, one in thirty. Average, one in fifty, and stingy, one in sixty. If somebody gave heave and it turned out to be one in sixty, this is heave and he does not have to give more. When he added, [the addition] is subject to tithes[19]. If it turned out to be one in sixty-one, this is heave and he has to add in his usual way, by measure, weight, or count[20]. Rebbi Jehudah says, even from what is not earmarked[21].

18 As rabbinic decrees; without a special declaration heave is not valid unless it complies with these guidelines.

19 Since heave must be given by

estimate, it may be that after the fact it turns out that the heave is less than what the giver intended. As long as a legal amount is given, this is heave and, as such, free from the obligation of tithes. The rest of the produce is now *ṭevel* for tithes. Therefore, if the owner adds to the heave, he adds produce subject to tithing.

20 If one in 61 was taken as heave, the heave is $^1/_{60}$ of the remainder and, therefore, marginally valid even though the a priori standard for the stingy is 1 in 60 from above. One should add to the heave. But since valid heave was given by estimate, the remainder may be measured, following the usual procedures for trading the particular produce.

21 Cf. Chapter 2, Note 6.

(fol. 42d) **הלכה ג**: כְּתִיב שִׁשִּׁית הָאֵיפָה מֵחוֹמֶר הַחִיטִּים וְשִׁשִּׁיתֶם אֶת הָאֵיפָה מֵחוֹמֶר הַשְּׂעוֹרִים. יָכוֹל תּוֹרֵם בַּחִטִּים אֶחָד מִשְּׁלֹשִׁים וּבַשְּׂעוֹרִים אֶחָד מִשִּׁשִּׁים. תַּלְמוּד לוֹמַר וְכָל־תְּרוּמַת שֶׁיְּהוּ כָּל־תְּרוּמוֹת שָׁוֹות. שְׁמוּאֵל אוֹמֵר תֵּן שִׁשִּׁית עַל שִׁשִּׁיתֶם וְנִמְצָא תוֹרֵם אֶחָד מֵאַרְבָּעִים. בֵּינוֹנִית אֶחָד מֵחֲמִשִּׁים. אָמַר רִבִּי לֵוִי כְּתִיב וּמִמַּחֲצִית בְּנֵי יִשְׂרָאֵל תִּקַּח אֶחָד אָחוּז מִן הַחֲמִשִּׁים. כָּל־שֶׁאַתָּה אוֹחֵז מִמָּקוֹם אַחֵר הֲרֵי הוּא כָזֶה. מָה זֶה אֶחָד מֵחֲמִשִּׁים. אַף מַה שֶׁאַתְּ אוֹחֵז מִמָּקוֹם אַחֵר הֲרֵי הוּא כְזֶה. וְהָרָעָה אֶחָד מִשִּׁשִּׁים דִּכְתִיב וְשִׁשִּׁיתֶם אֶת הָאֵיפָה מֵחוֹמֶר הַשְּׂעוֹרִים.

It is written (*Ez.* 45:13): "One sixth of an *ephah* from a *ḥomer* of wheat[22], and you shall take sixths[23] from an *ephah* from a *ḥomer* of barley." I could think he may give heave one thirtieth from wheat but one sixtieth from barley[24]. The verse says (*Ez.* 44:30): "All heave," that all heaves should be equal. Samuel says, add the sixth to the sixths, it turns out that he gives heave one in forty.

"Average, one in fifty." Rebbi Levi said, it is written (*Num.* 31:30): "From the half of the Children of Israel take one part in fifty.[25]" All you take at another place shall be like this; just as this is one in fifty, so what you take at another place shall be like this.

"And stingy, one in sixty," as it is written: "And you shall take a sixth from an *ephah* from a *ḥomer* of barley[26]."

22 An *ephah* is one tenth of a *ḥomer* (Ez. 45:11), a sixth of an *ephah* is one sixtieth of a *ḥomer*. Verse 13 starts: "This is the heave you have to take."

23 A verb formed from "six" whose meaning seems to be: taking parts of one-sixths. It is used in the Halakhah once in the meaning "take one sixth" and once as "take sixths", i. e., "take two sixths;" cf. H. Guggenheimer, *Seder Olam*, (Northvale NJ, 1998), p. 6.

24 This is the reading of both mss.; R. Simson switches the places of "thirty" and "sixty". This is required by the argument but it is not clear whether the change is based on a text or on emendation. If the verse speaks of "sixths" for barley, it would mean that the heave to be given is ${}^{2}/_{60} = {}^{1}/_{30}$. The average of the heaves taken from wheat and barley is then ${}^{1}/_{2}({}^{1}/_{60}+{}^{1}/_{30}) = {}^{1}/_{40}$.

25 In the Tosephta (5:8), this is a statement of R. Yose (the Tanna); probably a Babylonian tradition.

26 Tosephta 5:8, where the entire verse from Ezechiel is quoted; the quote in the Yerushalmi misses a part, probably by scribal error in the *Vorlage* of both mss., induced by the two occurrences of חמר.

בֵּית שַׁמַּאי אוֹמְרִים מִשְׁלֹשִׁים. וְשִׁשִּׁית הָאֵיפָה מֵחוֹמֶר הַשְּׂעוֹרִים. בֵּינוֹנִית מֵאַרְבָּעִים מִן הָדָא דִשְׁמוּאֵל. וְהָרָעָה מִשִּׁשִּׁים מִן הָדָא דְרִבִּי לֵוִי דְּאָמַר רִבִּי לֵוִי בַּר חִינָא כָּל־הַמּוֹצִיא מַעְשְׂרוֹתָיו כְּתִיקְנָן אֵינוֹ מַפְסִיד כְּלוּם. מַה טַעֲמָא וַעֲשִׂירִית הַחוֹמֶר יִהְיֶה הָאֵיפָה מִן הַחוֹמֶר יִהְיֶה מַתְכּוּנְתּוֹ. לֹא צוֹרְכָה דְלֹא כְּמָה דְנָן אָמְרִין תָּרַם וְעָלָה בְיָדוֹ אֶחָד מֵחֲמִשִּׁים תְּרוּמָה וְאֵינוֹ צָרִיךְ לִתְרוֹם כֵּן בֵּית שַׁמַּאי אוֹמְרִים תָּרַם וְעָלָה בְיָדוֹ אֶחָד מֵחֲמִשִּׁים תְּרוּמָה וְאֵינוֹ צָרִיךְ לִתְרוֹם.

"The House of Shammai say, [one] in thirty." "One sixth of an *ephah* from a *ḥomer* of barley[24]." Average, one in forty, following Samuel. Stingy, one in sixty[27] following Rebbi Levi. As[28] Rebbi Levi bar Ḥina[29] said, he who takes out his tithes following the rules does not lose. What is the reason? (*Ez.* 45:11) "The *ephah* shall be one tenth of a *ḥomer*, its measure shall be from the *ḥomer*[30]." For what do you need that? As we say, "if it turned out to be one in fifty[31], this is heave and he does not have to give more;" so the House of Shammai say, if it turned out to be one in fifty, this is heave and he does not have to give more.

27 It must read "one in fifty", as confirmed by Tosephta 5:3 and the text at the end of the paragraph. R. Levi is the one quoted above, for the average giver following the House of Hillel.

28 A scribal error; it should read: Rebbi Levi bar Ḥina said, starting a new topic.

29 It seems that his name should be ר' לוי בר חיתה, an Amora and preacher of the fourth generation, student of R. Abba bar Ḥiyya bar Abba.

30 The verse is misquoted; it should read ועשׂירת החמר האיפה אל החמר יהיה מתכנתה. The plain meaning of the verse is that the *ḥomer* shall be the standard, the *ephah* being derived from it. It is difficult to understand why אל has been changed to מִן; the sermon seems to rely on the original reading of the verse: The *ephah* taken for heave and tithes is *to* the *ḥomer*, additional to the *ḥomer* because God will soon replace it for you.

31 Scribal error; it must be "sixty" as in the Mishnah.

אָמַר רִבִּי חֲנִינָא בַּר אִיסִי לֹא תַנֵּי בַּר קַפָּרָא אֶלָּא תָּרַם וְעָלָה בְיָדוֹ מֵחֲמִשִּׁים וְעַד שִׁשִּׁים תְּרוּמָה וְאֵינוֹ צָרִיךְ לִתְרוֹם.

Rebbi Ḥanina bar Issi[32] said, Bar Qappara did not state so, but "if it turned out to between one in fifty and one in sixty, this is heave and he does not have to give more.[33]"

32 It seems that his name should be R. Ḥanina bar Sisai.

33 He disagrees with the Tanna of the Mishnah and states that heave is legal only if it is > $^1/_{60}$ of the harvest, not ≥ $^1/_{60}$ as stated there.

רִבִּי אִיסִּי בְשֵׁם רִבִּי יוֹחָנָן בְּמִתְכַּוֵּין לִפְטוֹר אֶת כִּירְיוֹ. אֲבָל אִם אֵינוֹ מִתְכַּוֵּין לִפְטוֹר אֶת כִּירְיוֹ אֲפִילוּ אַחַת עַל אַחַת.

Rebbi Assi in the name of Rebbi Joḥanan: If he wanted to free his heap. But if he did not do it in order to free his heap, even one on one[34].

34 This refers to the Mishnah, if the heave was $^{1}/_{60}$ and he added to his heave. If the intention was to give as an obligation, the intention is invalid since heave was already given. But if the intention was simply to give to the Cohen more in the sanctity of heave, this is valid since heave has no upper limit (except that one may not make one's entire crop into heave) and he may even double the original heave.

כַּהֲנָא אָמַר כְּמוֹת שֶׁהוּא לָמוּד. רִבִּי יוֹחָנָן אָמַר אֲפִילוּ אַחַת עַל אַחַת. וְהָתַנִּינָן כְּמוֹת שֶׁהוּא לָמוּד. שֶׁלֹּא לִפְחוֹת. אָמַר רִבִּי לָעְזָר כְּמוֹת שֶׁהוּא לָמוּד בְּמִידָּה אִם נִתְכַּוֵּון לְהוֹסִיף אֲפִילוּ בְּמִידָּה.

Cahana said, "in his usual way[35]." Rebbi Joḥanan said, even one for one. But did we not state, "in his usual way"? That he should not give less. Rebbi Eleazar said, in his usual way of measurement, but if he wants to add, even one for one.

35 Quote from the Mishnah, in case the heave given turns out to be $<^{1}/_{60}$ of the heap. Cahana reads the Mishnah as stating that the difference between the heave and $^{1}/_{60}$ must be exactly measured and exactly given, R. Joḥanan thinks that the difference must be measured and heave given at least in the amount of difference, and R. Eleazar requires that all additional heave be given by measurement but never less than the difference to $^{1}/_{60}$.

רִבִּי יוֹנָה אָמַר רִבִּי שִׁמְעוֹן בֶּן לָקִישׁ בְּעָא קוֹמֵי רִבִּי יוֹחָנָן תּוֹסֶפֶת תְּרוּמָה מַה הִיא. אָמַר לֵיהּ מִשּׁוּם יָחִיד אֲנִי שׁוֹנֶה אוֹתָהּ. מַה לְחִיּוּב. מִזֶּה לִפְטוֹר. אִין תֵּימַר לְחִיּוּב נִיחָא. אִין תֵּימַר לִפְטוֹר וּמַה אִין רִבִּי יוּדָה דְּאִית לֵיהּ שֶׁלֹּא מִן

הַמּוּקָּף פָּטוּר. רַבָּנִין דְּלֵית לְהוֹן שֶׁלֹּא מִן הַמּוּקָּף לֹא כָּל־שֶׁכֵּן. אָתָא רִבִּי יוֹסֵי רִבִּי אִיסִּי בְּשֵׁם רִבִּי שִׁמְעוֹן בֶּן לָקִישׁ תּוֹסֶפֶת תְּרוּמָה חַיֶּיבֶת בְּמַעְשְׂרוֹת. אָמַר רִבִּי יוֹסֵי הַמִּשְׁנָה אָמְרָה כֵן. אָמַר רִבִּי זְעִירָה לְרִבִּי אִיסִּי הֵיידָא מַתְנִיתָא וְלָא אֲגִיבֵיהּ. אָמַר לֵיהּ דְּדִילְמָא הָדָא דְתַנִּינָן תָּרַם וְעָלָה בְיָדוֹ מִשִּׁשִּׁים וְאֶחָד תְּרוּמָה אֵינוֹ צָרִיךְ לִתְרוֹם. וְלֹא תַנֵּי עֲלֵיהּ חָזַר וְהוֹסִיף חַיָּיב בְּמַעְשְׂרוֹת.

Rebbi Jonah said, Rebbi Simeon ben Laqish asked before Rebbi Johanan: What is the status of additional heave[36]? He said to him, I am stating that as an isolated opinion[37]. Do you mean for obligation or for freeing? If you say for obligation, that is understandable[38]. If you say for freeing, if even Rebbi Jehudah, who permits from the non-earmarked[39], frees it, then the rabbis, who do not agree [to take] from the non-earmarked, certainly must so hold. Rebbi Yose, Rebbi Assi in the name of Rebbi Simeon ben Laqish came: The additional heave is subject to tithes. Rebbi Yose[40] said, the Mishnah said so. Rebbi Zeïra said to Rebbi Assi, which Mishnah? He did not answer him. He said to him, maybe that which we stated: "If he gave heave and it turned out to be one in sixty-one[41], this is heave and he does not have to give more." Did we not state on this: "If he added, it is subject to tithes"?

36 If the heave taken was < $^1/_{60}$ and he is obligated to give more heave by rabbinic decree. Since there is no stated minimum for heave in biblical law, do the rabbis have the power to decree that the addition should be heave, free from tithes, or has the addition to be tithed?

37 The statement that additional heave is subject to tithes if the original heave was ≥ $^1/_{60}$ is declared R. Jehudah's.

38 If R. Jehudah requires tithing also if the original heave is < $^1/_{60}$, we can understand it since the original gift was sufficient for biblical heave.

39 Since R. Jehudah permits to give heave from another place, he makes it clear that he does not consider the additional heave genuine. If, never

theless, he frees the gift from tithes he must hold that the rabbis have the power to decree the gift to be heave. The rabbis, who do not permit taking the addition from non-earmarked produce, must consider the gift as genuine heave and the question should not even be asked.

40 In the Rome ms., R. Assi. This might be the better reading.

41 Since R. Yose uses the Hebrew משנה and not the Aramaic מתניתא, he must refer to our Mishnah, not to some *baraita*; cf. Note 20. One has to assume that Bar Qappara also will require tithing the addition if heave turned out to be exactly one in sixty. In this statement, we know only what happened if the original heave was exactly $^{1}/_{60}$; the question of tithes < $^{1}/_{60}$ still remains open.

עַד כַּמָּה אָדָם פּוֹטֵר טִיבְלוֹ דְּבַר תּוֹרָה. הוֹרָה רִבִּי יוֹנָתָן[42] אֶחָד לְמֵאָה כִּתְרוּמַת מַעֲשֵׂר. אָמַר לֵיהּ רִבִּי יוֹחָנָן מִן מָאן שְׁמָעִיתָהּ. אָמַר לֵיהּ מִפִּילְפּוּל חֲבֵרַייָא שְׁמָעִית הָא. דְּרִבִּי יַנַּאי אָמַר אֲפִילוּ אֶחָד מֵאֶלֶף. אָמַר רִבִּי מָנָא לֵית כָּאן שִׁעוּרָא דִּכְתִיב רֵאשִׁית דְּגָנְךָ תִּירוֹשְׁךָ וְיִצְהָרֶיךָ וַאֲפִילוּ כָּל־שֶׁהוּא.

How far does a man free his *ṭevel* by the word of the Torah? Rebbi Jonathan instructed: One in a hundred like heave of the tithe. Rebbi Joḥanan asked him, from whom did you hear this? He said, from arguments of the colleagues I understood this, although Rebbi Yannai said, even one in a thousand. Rebbi Mana said, there is no measure[43] since it is written (*Deut.* 18:4): "The first of your grain, cider, and oil;" any amount.

42 Reading of the Rome ms. Leyden and Venice: ר' יוחנן ; but R. Joḥanan cannot ask himself.

43 This is the Babylonian opinion, articulated by the first generation Amora Samuel: "One grain frees an entire heap" (*Ḥulin* 137b). It follows that in the time of RR. Jonathan and Yannai, heave was still eaten by Cohanim but in the time of R. Mana all heave was impure and had to be burned.

משנה ד: הָאוֹמֵר לִשְׁלוּחוֹ צֵא וּתְרוֹם תּוֹרֵם כְּדַעְתּוֹ שֶׁל בַּעַל הַבַּיִת וְאִם(fol. 42c) אֵינוֹ יוֹדֵעַ דַּעְתּוֹ שֶׁל בַּעַל הַבַּיִת תּוֹרֵם כְּבֵינוֹנִית אֶחָד מֵחֲמִשִּׁים. פָּחַת עֲשָׂרָה אוֹ הוֹסִיף עֲשָׂרָה תְּרוּמָתוֹ תְרוּמָה אִם נִתְכַּוֵּון לְהוֹסִיף אֲפִילוּ אֶחָד אֵין תְּרוּמָתוֹ תְרוּמָה.

Mishnah 4: If somebody said to his agent: go and give heave, he gives heave following the intentions[44] of the owner. If [the agent] does not know the intentions of the owner, he gives average heave, one in fifty. If he diminished by ten or added ten[45], his heave is heave, but if he intended to exceed [the owner's intention] by even one, his heave is not heave.

44 If it is his intention to give one in 40, 50, or 60.

45 If the heave turns out to be between $^1/_{40}$ and $^1/_{60}$. That is, if the agent does not know the intentions of the owner and wants to follow the rules which require heave to be given by estimate. But if he intends to give not $^1/_{50}$ but $^1/_{49}$, he exceeds his authority and hurts the owner; this automatically terminates his agency. He now is an unrelated person and his heave is not heave by Mishnah 1. The underlying problem of agency is not discussed in the Yerushalmi, but appears in the Babli, *Ketubot* 98b-99b.

(fol. 42d) **הלכה ד**: עַד כְּדוֹן כְּשֶׁאָמַר לוֹ צֵא וּתְרוֹם לְדַעְתִּי. הָיָה יוֹדֵעַ דַּעְתּוֹ שֶׁל בַּעַל הַבַּיִת וְלֹא אָמַר לוֹ צֵא וּתְרוֹם לְדַעְתִּי. נִישְׁמְעִינָהּ מִן הָדָא אִם אֵינוֹ יוֹדֵעַ דַּעְתּוֹ שֶׁל בַּעַל הַבַּיִת. מִפְּנֵי שֶׁאֵינוֹ יוֹדֵעַ הָא יוֹדֵעַ אַף עַל פִּי שֶׁלֹּא אָמַר לוֹ כְּמוֹ שֶׁאָמַר לוֹ.

Halakhah 4: So far, if he said to him, go and give heave following my intentions. If he knew the intentions of the owner but [the owner] did not tell him: go and give heave following my intentions? Let us hear from the following: "If [the agent] does not know the intentions of the owner;" therefore, if he knows even if he did not tell him, it is as if he had told him[46].

46 If he intentionally deviates from the owner's standard, his heave is invalid.

אָמַר רִבִּי בּוּן בַּר כַּהֲנָא הַפּוֹחֵת אֶחָד מֵעֲשָׂרָה תְּרוּמָה וְהַמּוֹסִיף אֶחָד מֵעֲשָׂרָה תְּרוּמָה. אֲבָל לֹא לְחוּלִין שֶׁאֵין הַפְּחָת וְהַתּוֹסֶפֶת שָׁוִין. הֵיךְ עֲבִידָא. הֲוָה יְלִיף תְּרִים חַד מִן חַמְשִׁין כַּד הוּא תְּרִים חַד מִן אַרְבָּעִין מַפְסִיד לֵיהּ שִׁיתָא רוֹבְעִין. כַּד הוּא תְּרִים חַד מִן שִׁיתִין מִתְגַּר לֵיהּ אַרְבָּעָה רוֹבְעִין.

Rebbi Abun bar Cahana said: If someone diminished by ten it is heave, and if he added ten it is heave. This does not apply to the profane [produce] since diminution and addition are not equal[47]. How is that? If he used to give heave one in fifty, if he gives heave one in forty he makes him lose six quarters[48]. If he gives heave one in sixty, he earns him four quarters.

47 For the profane remainder, the difference between maximum and minimum heave is from $98\frac{2}{3}\%$ to $97^1/_2\%$, deviating from 98 only by $^1/_3$ or $^1/_2$.

48 The basis of the computation is an average heave of 1 *seah* of 6 *qab* (cf. *Peah* Chapter 3, Note 108.) The quarter is a quarter *qab*. The heap is originally 50 *seah*. Then heave 1 in 40 is 1.25 *seah*, for an addition of 6/4 *qab*. Heave 1 in 60 is 5/6 *seah* or 1 *seah* minus 4/4 *qab*.

הָכָא אַתְּ אָמַר תְּרוּמָתוֹ תְרוּמָה. וְכָא אַתְּ אָמַר אֵין תְּרוּמָתוֹ תְרוּמָה. אָמַר רִבִּי חֲנִינָא בְּרֵיהּ דְּרִבִּי הִלֵּל כָּאן בְּמִתְכַּוֵּין לִפְחוֹת כָּאן בְּמִתְכַּוֵּין לְהוֹסִיף.

Here you say, his heave is heave, but there you say, his heave is not heave[49]! Rebbi Ḥanina ben Rebbi Hillel[50] said, in one case he intended to diminish, in the other to add.

49 The question is formulated comparing the first part of the Mishnah, when deviations are accepted, and the second part, in which a deviation makes heave invalid. The question is really about the second

part, where it is asserted that intention to add invalidates the agency but intention to diminish is not mentioned at all. The answer is that intention to diminish within the legal bounds does not disqualify the agent.

50 He is R. Ḥananiah ben R. Hillel.

רִבִּי חַגַּיי בְּעָא קוֹמֵי רִבִּי יוֹסֵי. תַּנִּינָן תַּמָּן אָמַר לוֹ תֵּן לָהֶן חֲתִיכָה וְהוּא אָמַר טְלוּ שְׁתַּיִם שְׁתַּיִם. וְהֵם נָטְלוּ שָׁלֹשׁ שָׁלֹשׁ כּוּלָּן מָעֲלוּ. וְהָכָא אַתְּ אָמַר הָכֵין. אָמַר לֵיהּ תַּמָּן מֵחֲתִיכָה רִאשׁוֹנָה נִסְתַּיְימָה שְׁלִיחוּתוֹ שֶׁל בַּעַל הַבַּיִת. בְּרַם הָכָא עַל כָּל־חִטָּה וְחִטָּה נִסְתַּיְימָה שְׁלִיחוּתוֹ שֶׁל בַּעַל הַבַּיִת. מַה נְפַק מִבֵּינֵיהוֹן הָיוּ לְפָנָיו שְׁנֵי כְרִייָה אֶחָד נִתְקַן לְדַעְתּוֹ וְאֶחָד נִתְקַן שֶׁלֹּא לְדַעְתּוֹ.

Rebbi Ḥaggai asked before Rebbi Yose: There[51], we have stated: "If he said to him, give them one piece, but he said, take two each, and they took three each, all committed larceny;" but here you say so? He said to him, there the agency of the owner stopped after the first piece[52], but here each single grain of wheat is under the agency of the owner. What is the difference? If there were before him two heaps, one put in order by his intention, the other put in order not by his intention[53].

51 Mishnah *Me'ilah* 6:1, also quoted in Babli *Ketubot* 98b. The case discussed is of a host who invited guests, told his agent to give each guest a piece of meat, the agent told each one to take two pieces, and each guest took three. Then it turned out that the meat was sacrificial meat illegally taken. The problem is, why should the host be liable for the action of an agent who clearly overstepped his authority, when the Mishnah here declares the agency to be null and void. One would infer that the host should not be guilty of larceny. In the Babli, the owner is held liable only if the agent told the guests to take one piece from the host and one from himself. This cannot be the interpretation of the Yerushalmi.

52 But the owner bears the responsibility for the first piece, while in the case of heave for grain the responsibilities cannot be neatly

divided; the agent either acts for the owner or he does not.

53 The heave from the first heap is valid, from the second invalid.

(fol. 42c) **משנה ה**: הַמַּרְבֶּה בִתְרוּמָה רִבִּי לִיעֶזֶר אוֹמֵר אֶחָד מֵעֲשָׂרָה כִתְרוּמַת מַעֲשֵׂר יוֹתֵר מִכֵּן יַעֲשֶׂנָּה תְּרוּמַת מַעֲשֵׂר אֲבָל לֹא לְמָקוֹם אַחֵר. רִבִּי יִשְׁמָעֵאל אוֹמֵר מֶחֱצָה חוּלִין וּמֶחֱצָה תְרוּמָה. רִבִּי טַרְפוֹן וְרִבִּי עֲקִיבָה אוֹמְרִים עַד שֶׁיְּשַׁיֵּיר שָׁם חוּלִין.

Mishnah 5: If somebody increases heave, Rebbi Eliezer says, up to one tenth like the heave of the tithe. The excess he should make heave of the tithe but not[54] for another place. Rebbi Ismael says, half profane and half heave. Rebbi Ṭarphon and Rebbi Aqiba say more, but he must retain some profane produce.

54 This is the reading in the Leyden ms., the Munich ms. of the Babli, the Palestinian Mishnah edited by Low, and the first prints of the Mishnah (Naples, Riva di Trento, Venice). In all other manuscript sources, including the Rome ms., and the Mishnah prints following the edition of Yomtov Lipman Heller Wallerstein, the reading is: "for another place". That reading is quoted in the Halakhah as variant reading, confirming the text here as the authentic Galilean Mishnah.

The background for the disagreement is that heave of the tithe may be taken from one lot for another but heave itself must be earmarked. Since the produce was given as Great Heave, the rules of heave should apply.

The reasons for the three diverging opinions are given in the Halakhah.

(fol. 42d) **הלכה ה**: רִבִּי יִרְמְיָה בְשֵׁם רִבִּי יוֹחָנָן רִבִּי יַעֲקֹב בַּר אָחָא בְשֵׁם רִבִּי שִׁמְעוֹן בֶּן לָקִישׁ. אַתְיָא דְרִבִּי לִיעֶזֶר כְּבֵית שַׁמַּאי כְּמָה דְבֵית שַׁמַּאי אָמְרִין קִדְּשׁוּ מְדוּמָעִין. כֵּן רִבִּי אֱלִעֶזֶר אוֹמֵר קִדְּשׁוּ מְדוּמָעִין.

Halakhah 5: Rebbi Jeremiah in the name of Rebbi Joḥanan, Rebbi Jacob bar Aḥa in the name of Rebbi Simeon ben Laqish: Rebbi Eliezer follows the House of Shammai; just as the House of Shammai say, it is sanctified as *dema'*, so Rebbi Eliezer says it is sanctified as *dema'*[55].

55 For the statement of the House of Shammai, cf. Chapter 3, Note 55. According to R. Eliezer, if more than 11% is given as heave, then 10% are heave, 1% heave of the tithe, and the remainder is *ṭevel* as long as its tithes have not been given. Then one has the disagreement between Ḥizqiah and R. Joḥanan (Chapter 1, Notes 10-12); following Ḥizqiah, a small amount of *ṭevel* can be disregarded, but not following R. Joḥanan.

עַל דַּעְתֵּיהּ דְּרִבִּי יוֹחָנָן נִיחָא. אֶחָד מֵעֲשָׂרָה שֶׁבּוֹ קָדֵשׁ לְשֵׁם תְּרוּמָה וְהַשְּׁאָר אֶחָד מֵעֲשָׂרָה תְרוּמָה וְהַשְּׁאָר טֶבֶל טָבוּל לְמַעְשְׂרוֹת. לְפוּם כֵּן צָרִיךְ מֵימַר יוֹתֵר מִכֵּן יַעֲשֶׂנָּה תְּרוּמַת מַעֲשֵׂר עַל מָקוֹם אַחֵר. עַל דַּעְתֵּיהּ דְּחִזְקִיָּה קַשְׁיָא. אֶחָד מֵעֲשָׂרָה שֶׁבּוֹ קָדֵשׁ לְשֵׁם תְּרוּמָה וְהַשְּׁאָר אֶחָד מֵעֲשָׂרָה תְרוּמָה וְהַשְּׁאָר טֶבֶל טָבוּל לַכֹּל. וְתַנִּינָן יוֹתֵר מִכֵּן יַעֲשֶׂנָּה כִּתְרוּמַת מַעֲשֵׂר יַעֲשֶׂנָּה תְּרוּמַת מַעֲשֵׂר עַל מָקוֹם אַחֵר. סָבַר חִזְקִיָּה כְּהָדָא דְּתַנֵּי רִבִּי חִיָּיא דְּתַנֵּי רִבִּי חִיָּיא יוֹתֵר מִכֵּן יַעֲשֶׂנָּה תְּרוּמַת מַעֲשֵׂר עַל מָקוֹם אַחֵר.

In the opinion of Rebbi Joḥanan, it is simple. One tenth in it is holy as heave, of the remainder one tenth is heave and the rest is *ṭevel* for tithes. Therefore, he must declare: "The excess he should make heave of the tithe for another place[56]." In the opinion of Ḥizqiah, it is difficult. One tenth in it is holy as heave, of the remainder one tenth is heave and the rest is *ṭevel* for everything[57]. But we have stated: "The excess he should treat as heave of the tithe," he should make it heave of the tithe for another place. Hizkiah holds with what Rebbi Ḥiyya stated, as Rebbi Ḥiyya stated: "The excess he should treat as heave of the tithe for another place."

56 The end of the paragraph shows that one must read here: "but not for another place." Since in the opinion of R. Johanan even irregular heave eliminates all *ṭevel*, the excess over 11% can be separated and used for tithes from which heave of the tithe has already been given.

57 According to Ḥizqiah, *ṭevel* disappears in a plurality of other produce. If the amount given as heave is < 20%, then the *ṭevel* part is less than the heave part and all is heave; one cannot give heave of the tithe since there is no more *ṭevel*. If the amount given is > 20%, then the excess over 10%, if separated, remains *ṭevel* since heave was given to put the heap in order, not what was lifted as heave. That means that of the rest one first has to give heave and then he may lift heave of the tithe; this explains the involved statement in the next sentence. Ḥizqiah in Halakhah 1 of this Chapter holds that heave is determined only when it is actually taken; it is not predetermined which grain will be heave. Since everything is given as heave, it turns out that the problem is solved if Ḥizqiah reads the Mishnah in the version of his father R. Ḥiyya, that if the amount taken is > 20% he may use the excess for any heave of any of his produce. Since Great Heave can be given only from earmarked produce, the natural thing to do is to use it for heave of the tithe which can be given from one place for another. (Explanation hinted at in מיכל המים.)

Since R. Ḥiyya was the teacher of Rav, it is indicated here that the version in the Mishnah found in most mss. is the Babylonian Mishnah.

מַה טַעֲמָא דְרִבִּי יִשְׁמָעֵאל רֵאשִׁית דְּגָנְךָ דַּייוֹ לְרֵאשִׁית שֶׁיְּהֵא כְדָגָן. מְנַיִין שֶׁלֹּא עָשָׂה כְלוּם עַד שֶׁיְּשַׁייֵר מִקְצָת. תַּלְמוּד לוֹמַר מֵרֵאשִׁית וְלֹא כָל־רֵאשִׁית.

What is the reason of Rebbi Ismael? (*Deut*. 18:4) "The beginning of your grain," it is sufficient for the beginning to be like the grain[58]. From where that he did not do anything unless he left some remainder? (*Num*. 15:21) "From the beginning", not all the beginning[59].

58 More than 50% cannot be called "beginning".

59 Prefix מ in talmudic interpretation is partitive; *Sifry Num.* 110.

(fol. 42c) **משנה ו**: בִּשְׁלֹשָׁה פְרָקִים מְשַׁעֲרִין אֶת הַכַּלְכָּלָה בְּבִיכּוּרוֹת וּבִסְיָפוֹת וּבְאֶמְצַע הַקַּיִץ. הַמּוֹנֶה מְשׁוּבָּח וְהַמּוֹדֵד מְשׁוּבָּח הֵימֶינּוּ וְהַשּׁוֹקֵל מְשׁוּבָּח מִשְּׁלָשְׁתָּן.

Mishnah 6: For three periods one calibrates the measuring box[60], for early fruits, late fruits, and in the middle of the summer. He who counts is praiseworthy, he who measures is more praiseworthy, and he who weighs is the most praiseworthy of the three.

60 The basket used to collect figs. Since the sizes of the figs vary during the season, it is necessary to determine how many figs fill a standard basket in order to give correct tithes and heave of the tithe. Measuring is not applicable to the Great Heave.

(fol. 42d) **הלכה ו**: מִמִּי הוּא מְשׁוּבָּח. אָמַר רִבִּי הוּנָה מְשׁוּבָּח מִן הַתּוֹרֵם מִן הָעוֹמֵד. אָמַר רִבִּי חֲנִינָה בְּרֵיהּ דְּרִבִּי הִלֵּל מַתְנִיתִין אָמְרָה כֵן וְהַשּׁוֹקֵל מְשׁוּבָּח מִשְּׁלָשְׁתָּן. אָמַר רִבִּי חִינְנָא תִּפְתָּר בִּשְׁלָשְׁתָּן וְלֵית אַתְּ שְׁמַע מִינָּהּ כְּלוּם.

Halakhah 6: He is praiseworthy relative to whom? Rebbi Huna said, praiseworthy relative to one who estimates heave. Rebbi Ḥinena the son of Rebbi Hillel said, does the Mishnah say so? "He who weighs is the most praiseworthy of the three[61]." Rebbi Ḥinena said, explain it "among the three" and it does not imply anything.

61 If it were possible to estimate, it should be "four" instead of "three".

(fol. 42c) **משנה ז**: רִבִּי לִיעֶזֶר אוֹמֵר תְּרוּמָה עוֹלָה בְּאֶחָד וּמֵאָה. רִבִּי יְהוֹשֻׁעַ אוֹמֵר בְּמֵאָה וָעוֹד. וְעוֹד זֶה אֵין לוֹ שִׁעוּר. רִבִּי יוֹסֵי בֶּן מְשׁוּלָּם אוֹמֵר וְעוֹד קַב לְמֵאָה סְאָה שְׁתוּת לִמְדַמֵּעַ.

Mishnah 7: Rebbi Eliezer says, heave is lifted[62] at the rate of one in 101. Rebbi Joshua says by 100 and more. This "and more" has no measure; Rebbi Yose ben Meshullam says "and more" is one *qab* per one hundred *seah*, one sixth of what makes *dema'*[63].

62 If heave falls into profane food it creates *dema'*. If the amount of heave is small, it is possible to remove ("lift") an amount equal to the heave and transfer the holiness to that food; the remainder of the food then returns to profane status. R. Eliezer states that in this respect "small" means at most 1 in 100 (1 part heave in 101 overall). R. Joshua requires that the amount be strictly less than 1 in 99+ε; ε>0 being arbitrarily small. R. Yose ben Meshullam requires that the amount of heave be at most 1 in 99.1666̄; if the amount of heave is one *seah*, the amount of profane grain has to be 99 *seah* plus one sixth of the amount causing the trouble, i. e., $99^1/_6$ *seah*.

63 Since 1 *seah* makes permanent *dema'* in 100 *seot*, one sixth is a *qab*. R. Joseph Caro (*Kesef Mishneh* on Maimonides *Terumot* 13:1) takes R. Yose ben Meshullam as being more restrictive than R. Eliezer; it is difficult to read this into the Mishnah.

(fol. 42d) **הלכה ז**: מְנַיִין שֶׁאֵין עוֹלִין. אָמַר רִבִּי יוֹנָה כְּתִיב מִכָּל־חֶלְבּוֹ אֶת מִקְדְּשׁוֹ מִמֶּנּוּ. דָּבָר שֶׁאַתְּ מֵרִים מִמֶּנּוּ שֶׁאִם יִפּוֹל לְתוֹכוֹ מְקַדְּשׁוֹ. וְכַמָּה הוּא אֶחָד מִמֵּאָה. רִבִּי אֱלְעָזָר אוֹמֵר (fol. 43a) מוֹסִיף סְאָה וּמַעֲלָה. רִבִּי יְהוֹשֻׁעַ אוֹמֵר מוֹסִיף כָּל־שֶׁהוּא וּמַעֲלָה. רִבִּי יוֹסֵי בֶּן מְשׁוּלָּם אוֹמֵר וְעוֹד קַב לְמֵאָה שְׁתוּת לִמְדוּמָּע. וַהֲלָכָה כִדְבָרָיו.

Halakhah 7: From where that they are not lifted? Rebbi Jonah said, it is written (*Num.* 18:29): "From all its best its sanctifying part from it." Something from which you lift it, so that if this falls into anything it sanctifies it[64]. How much is this? One in one hundred[65]. Rebbi Eliezer says, one adds a *seah* and then lifts. Rebbi Joshua says one adds a small amount and lifts. Rebbi Yose ben Meshullam says "and more" is one *qab* per one hundred, one sixth of what makes *dema'*; practice follows him[66].

64 This argument proves only that heave creates *dema'*, not that *dema'* containing a minute amount of heave may be repaired. The same argument is in *Sifry Num.* 121.

65 In Tosephta 5:8, the argument is made that the smallest amount called heave is heave of the tithe which is 10% of 10% or 1%, and that nothing less is called heave. The argument is rejected. Therefore, the determination of these limits is purely rabbinical.

66 Nevertheless, Maimonides (*Terumot* 13:1) decides according to R. Eliezer, probably because Mishnaiot *Ḥallah* 1:9, *Orlah* 2:1 are anonymous and follow R. Eliezer; in addition the Tosephta (5:8) quotes the ruling of R. Eliezer in the name of R. Yose, the most important teacher of the fourth generation, whose word is almost always to be followed.

(fol. 42c) **משנה ח**: רִבִּי יְהוֹשֻׁעַ אוֹמֵר תְּאֵינִים שְׁחוֹרוֹת מַעֲלוֹת אֶת הַלְּבָנוֹת וְהַלְּבָנוֹת מַעֲלוֹת אֶת הַשְּׁחוֹרוֹת. עִיגּוּלֵי דְבֵילָה הַגְּדוֹלִים מַעֲלִין אֶת הַקְּטַנִּים וְהַקְּטַנִּים מַעֲלִין אֶת הַגְּדוֹלִים. הָעִיגּוּלִין מַעֲלִין אֶת הַמַּלְבֵּנִים וְהַמַּלְבֵּנִים מַעֲלִין אֶת הָעִיגּוּלִין וְרִבִּי אֱלִיעֶזֶר אוֹסֵר. וְרִבִּי עֲקִיבָה אוֹמֵר בְּיָדוּעַ מַה נָּפְלָה אֵין מַעֲלוֹת זוֹ אֶת זוֹ. וּכְשֶׁאֵינוֹ יָדוּעַ מַה נָּפְלָה מַעֲלוֹת זוֹ אֶת זוֹ.

Mishnah 8: Rebbi Joshua says, black figs lift the white ones, and white ones the black[67]. Large fig cakes lift small ones and small ones lift the large[68]. Round fig cakes lift brick-shaped fig cakes and brick-shaped cakes lift round cakes. But Rebbi Eliezer forbids. Rebbi Aqiba says, if it is known what fell in, they do not lift one another, but if it is not known what fell in, they do lift one another[67].

67 This is a sequel to the preceding Mishnah. If some white (i. e., green) figs of heave fell into profane figs both white and black and together the profane are at least 100 times the weight of the heave while the white profane figs alone are less that 100 times the weight of the heave, R. Joshua permits to lift white figs in the weight of the heave but R. Eliezer forbids. In his opinion, the white figs are forbidden as *dema'* but the black ones can be eaten since they certainly are not heave. If they are not forbidden then they are not *dema'* and cannot be counted. R. Aqiba follows R. Eliezer if the characteristics of the heave are known and R. Joshua if they are unknown.

68 This will be clarified at the end of the Halakhah.

(fol. 43a) **הלכה ח**: רִבִּי אִיסִּי בְּשֵׁם רִבִּי יוֹחָנָן טַעֲמָא דְרִבִּי אֱלִיעֶזֶר תְּאֵינִים שְׁחוֹרוֹת שֶׁנָּפְלוּ לְתוֹךְ הַלְּבָנוֹת אוֹכֵל אֶת הַלְּבָנוֹת.

Rebbi Assi in the name of Rebbi Johanan: The reason of Rebbi Eliezer [is that] if black figs fell into white ones, one may eat the white ones[67].

וְהַלְּבָנוֹת מַעֲלוֹת אֶת הַשְּׁחוֹרוֹת. אָמַר רִבִּי לָעְזָר כָּךְ הָיָה רִבִּי לִיעֶזֶר מֵשִׁיב אֶת רִבִּי יְהוֹשֻׁעַ וְהַלְּבָנוֹת מַעֲלוֹת אֶת הַשְּׁחוֹרוֹת מִילְתֵיהּ אָמַר בְּיָדוּעַ מַה נָּפְלוּ מַעֲלוֹת זוֹ אֶת זוֹ. כַּהֲנָא אָמַר אֵין מַעֲלוֹת. עַל דַּעְתֵּיהּ דְּכַהֲנָא מַה בֵּין רִבִּי יְהוֹשֻׁעַ לְרִבִּי עֲקִיבָה בְּשֶׁיָּדַע וְשָׁכַח. עַל דַּעְתֵּיהּ דְּרִבִּי יְהוֹשֻׁעַ מַעֲלֶה. עַל דַּעְתֵּיהּ דְּרִבִּי עֲקִיבָה אֵינוֹ מַעֲלֶה. שִׁמְעוֹן בַּר בָּא בְּשֵׁם רִבִּי יוֹחָנָן וְהוּא שֶׁנָּפְלָה שְׁחוֹרָה אַחַת לְתוֹךְ שְׁתַּיִם לְבָנוֹת כְּדֵי שֶׁתִּיבָּטֵל בְּרוֹב. רִבִּי זְעִירָה בְּעָא קוֹמֵי רִבִּי מָנָא לֹא מִסְתַּבְּרָא בְּתוֹךְ שָׁלֹשׁ שֶׁאִם תֹּאבַד אַחַת מֵהֶן יִהְיוּ שָׁם שְׁתַּיִם. אָמַר לֵיהּ אוּף אֲנָא סָבַר כֵּן.

""White ones lift the black." Rebbi Eleazar said, Rebbi Eliezer answered Rebbi Joshua thus: Do white ones lift the black? His words say, when it is known what fell in they lift one another[69]. Cahana said, they do not lift.[70] In the opinion of Cahana, what is the difference between Rebbi Joshua and Rebbi Aqiba? When he had known but forgot. In the opinion of Rebbi Joshua he lifts, in the opinion of Rebbi Aqiba he does not lift. Simeon bar Abba in the name of Rebbi Joḥanan: That is only if one black one fell into two white ones, that it may be disregarded in a plurality[71]. Rebbi Zeïra asked before Rebbi Mana: Would it not be reasonable [to say] into three so that if one of them is lost there still will be two? He said to him, that is also my opinion[72].

69 For R. Eliezer's objection to make any sense, one has to assume that R. Joshua admits lifting even if it was known that the heave that fell into the container consisted of all white figs.

70 If it is known that white figs fell into the container, even R. Joshua will allow to lift the *dema'* only if there are 100 (or 99+ε) times more white figs than the heave.

71 Since in biblical law, 51% of permitted food eliminates the prohibition of the remaining forbidden 49%, we have to assume that R. Joshua under all circumstances will require that the heave be nullified in biblical law, i. e., that of the kind of the heave more than the heave should have been in the container as profane food. In the Babli, *Yebamot* 82a, this is the opinion of R. Simeon ben Laqish.

72 One has to allow for natural spillage and waste so that at no time is the biblical requirement violated.

בַּר פְּדָיָה אָמַר טוֹחֵן וּמַתִּיר. וְאַף עַל גַּב דְּבַר פְּדָיָה אָמַר אֵין בְּלִילָה אֶלָּא לַשֶּׁמֶן וְיַיִן בִּלְבַד. מוֹדֶה הוּא הָכָא שֶׁהֵן נִבְלָלוֹת.

Bar Pedaiah said, he grinds and makes it permitted[73]. Even though Bar Pedaiah said[74] mixing applies only to oil and wine, he agrees here that they may be mixed[75].

73 If the individual figs are no longer recognizable, the difference between white (green) and black figs vanishes.

74 *Demay* 5:5, Notes 83,84. The mss. there read "Rebbi Pedaiah", Bar Pedaiah in *Demay* is the reading of R. Simson.

75 Bar Pedaiah does not allow mixing of different sorts for heave of the tithe as long as the fruits are recognizable; he will be more accomodating to remove the prohibition of *dema'*.

מִילַּתְהוֹן דְּרַבָּנִין פְּלִיגָא. כַּהֲנָא שָׁאַל לִשְׁמוּאֵל לֹא מִסְתַּבְּרָא הָדֵין מְדוּמָּע דְּתַנִּינָן הָכָא שֶׁרוּבָּהּ תְּרוּמָה. אָמַר לֵיהּ וַאֲנָא סָבַר כֵּן אֶלָּא תְּסַלֵּק לְאַרְעָא דְיִשְׂרָאֵל אַתְּ שְׁאִיל לָהּ. כַּד סְלַק שְׁמַע הָדָא דָמַר רִבִּי יוֹסֵי בְּשֵׁם רִבִּי יוֹחָנָן וַאֲפִילוּ סְאָה שֶׁנָּפְלָה לְתוֹךְ תִּשְׁעִים וְתֵשַׁע חוּלִין. אָמַר רִבִּי אַבָּהוּ כָּךְ מֵשִׁיב רִבִּי שִׁמְעוֹן בֶּן לָקִישׁ אֶת רִבִּי יוֹחָנָן וְאוֹתָהּ סְאָה הִיא פּוֹטֶרֶת אֶת הַכֹּל. וְכִי עִיגּוּל בְּעִיגּוּלִין דָּבָר בָּרִיא שֶׁתְּרוּמָה עָלְתָה בְיָדוֹ וְאַתְּ אָמַר קַל הוּא וְאַף הָכָא קַל הוּא. וִיתִיבִינֵיהּ שַׁנְיָיא בְעִיגּוּלִין שֶׁכְּבָר בָּטְלוּ. רִבִּי יוֹנָה וְרִבִּי יוֹסֵי תְּרֵיהוֹן בְּשֵׁם רִבִּי זְעִירָא אֲפִילוּ חִטִּין בְּחִטִּין טוֹחֵן וּמַתִּיר.

The words of the rabbis disagree[76]. Cahana asked Samuel: Is it not reasonable that the *dema'* which we stated here contains mostly heave[77]? He said to him, that is also my opinion, but when you go to the Land of Israel do ask about this. When he went, he heard what Rebbi Yose said in the name of Rebbi Johanan, even one *seah*[78] that fell into 99 [which were] profane. Rebbi Abbahu said, thus did Rebbi Simeon ben Laqish answer Rebbi Johanan: That one *seah* frees everything? Is a fig cake among fig cakes such a sure thing that heave came up in his hand[79]? But you must say it is [to be taken] lightly; here also it is [to be taken] lightly. Could he not have objected: It is different with fig cakes which already are disregarded[80]? Rebbi Jonah and Rebbi Yose, both in the name of Rebbi Zeïra: Even wheat and wheat he may grind and lift[81].

76 This refers to Mishnah *Ḥallah* 1:4; the entire paragraph appears in the corresponding Halakhah.

77 Mishnah *Ḥallah* 1:4 states that dough made from *dema'* is subject to tithes but free from *Ḥallah*.

78 One *seah* of heave; in order that the *dema'* be free of *ḥallah* the amount of profane flour cannot exceed 99-ε *seot*. This *dema'* is rabbinical; the argument is acceptable only if the obligation of *ḥallah* also is considered only as rabbinical, contradicting the statement at the end of Chapter 9 of *Ševi'it*.

79 The entire idea of lifting heave out of *dema'* is a legal fiction; even with a fig cake lost among fig cakes the chances are slim that the correct cake of heave will be lifted out. It follows that the entire argument is possible only if we agree that heave today is only a rabbinic obligation for which all kind of leniencies are permitted which would be impossible for biblical obligations; cf. *Demay* Chapter 3, Note 121, *Ševi'it* Chapter 6, Note 11. This is the position of R. Joḥanan in Babli *Yebamot* 82a.

80 The only heave ever due by biblical decree is from "grain, cider, and oil." The heave from figs never was biblical; therefore one fig cake of heave indistinguishable from two profane cakes may be disregarded since it is disregarded by biblical law.

81 For example, white and brown wheat kernels. It is clear that this is possible only if all heave during the Second Commonwealth was rabbinic in character.

הָיוּ לְפָנָיו עֶשְׂרִים תְּאֵינִים וְנָפְלָה אַחַת לְתוֹכָן וְאָבְדָה אַחַת לְתוֹכָן וְאָבְדָה אַחַת מֵהֶן. רִבִּי שִׁמְעוֹן בֶּן לָקִישׁ אָמַר סְפֵיקוֹ בָטֵל בְּרוֹב. רִבִּי יוֹחָנָן אָמַר כּוּלָּן נַעֲשׂוּ הוֹכִיחַ. מוֹדֵי רִבִּי יוֹחָנָן שֶׁאִם תָּרַם מֵהֶן עַל מָקוֹם אַחֵר אוֹ שֶׁרִיבָה מִמָּקוֹם אַחֵר עֲלֵיהֶן שֶׁסְּפֵיקָן בָּטֵל בְּרוֹב.

If there were 20 figs before him[82] and one [fig] fell into them and was not recognizable among them and then one of them was lost; Rebbi Simeon ben Laqish said, this doubt disappears in the plurality[83]; Rebbi Joḥanan said, all become subject to proof. Rebbi Joḥanan agrees that if he gave heave for them from another place or added to them from another place the doubt would disappear in the plurality.

82 From the last sentence it is clear that the 20 figs are *ṭevel*. It is impossible to give heave from heave; one must give heave from *ṭevel*. R. Simeon ben Laqish thinks that there is a 50% probability that the lost fig was the one of heave; therefore, the remaining 20 contain 20 figs with probability 50% and 19 figs with probability 100%; they all can be used for heave. R. Joḥanan thinks that every single fig may be heave with probability 4.8%; one would have to prove that a fig chosen for heave is actually *ṭevel*. He agrees that if somehow the figs become part of a greater whole or are all given as heave for a greater whole, all 20 figs can be treated as *ṭevel*. In the second paragraph following it is stated that in case of such a doubt there may not be more than one doubtful piece in 51 figs.

83 Similarly, R. Simeon ben Laqish is quoted in the Babli, *Zebaḥim* 74b: "If a [sealed] amphora of heave was mixed with 100 [identical] amphoras and one of them fell into the ocean, all the rest are permitted" since we assume that the heave fell into the ocean. However, in one opinion in the Babli, R. Simeon ben Laqish would exclude figs from this argument.

רִבִּי שִׁמְעוֹן בֶּן לָקִישׁ בְּשֵׁם רִבִּי הוֹשַׁעְיָה הָיוּ לְפָנָיו מֵאָה וַחֲמִשִּׁים חָבִיּוֹת וְנִתְפַּתְּחוּ. מֵאָה מוּתָּרוֹת וַחֲמִשִּׁים אֲסוּרוֹת וְהַשְּׁאָר לִכְשֶׁיִּתְפַּתְּחוּ מוּתָּרוֹת. אָמַר רִבִּי זְעִירָא לֹא אָמַר אֶלָּא לִכְשֶׁיִּתְפַּתְּחוּ הָא לְכַתְּחִילָּה אָסוּר.

Rebbi Simeon ben Laqish in the name of Rebbi Hoshaia[83]: If there were before him 150 amphoras which were opened: One hundred are permitted, fifty are forbidden, and the remainder will be permitted if they were opened. Rebbi Zeïra said, he said only "*if* they were opened;" therefore at the start it is forbidden.

83 The statement is shortened and has become unintelligible. The full text must have been similar to the parallel in the Babli, *Zebaḥim* 74b: "Rebbi Hoshaia said, if a [sealed] amphora of heave was mixed with 150 [identical] amphoras and 100 of them were opened; he takes from them corresponding to the *dema'* and drinks; the remainder are forbidden until they

will be opened." This statement can only be used to describe the situation here, that in addition to the 150 amphoras of profane wine there now is one unrecognizable one of heave. In the situation of the Yerushalmi, one may drink from all of the 100 amphoras and all of any number of unopened additional ones, but 50 amphoras are permanent *dema'*, forbidden for all except a Cohen. The usual rules of disappearance of *dema'* in a plurality do not apply to amphoras since these are counted by the piece, as explained in Mishnah *Orlah* 3:7. For this reason, R. Zeïra permits the use of any of these amphoras only after the fact since, if it were a biblical prohibition, even one amphora in 1000 would make all of them forbidden.

רִבִּי זְעִירָא בְּשֵׁם רִבִּי פְּדָיָה תְּרוּמָה אוֹסֶרֶת בְּוַדָּייָהּ בְּמֵאָה וּסְפֵיקָהּ בַּחֲמִשִּׁים. הָא שִׁשִּׁים לֹא שִׁבְעִים לֹא עַד חֲמִשִּׁים צְרִיכָה רוֹב מִכָּן וְאֵילַךְ אֵינָהּ צְרִיכָה רוֹב.

Rebbi Zeïra in the name of Rebbi Pedaiah: Heave if certain makes forbidden in 100[84], if it is in doubt in 50. Does that mean not in 60 or 70? Up to 50 it needs a plurality, more it does not need a plurality[85].

84 Here one determines that practice follows R. Eliezer, *viz.*, 1 part heave in 100 cannot be lifted, 1 in 101 (1 heave, 100 profane) can be lifted.

85 If there is doubt whether there is any heave at all, as in the case of figs where one fell in and subsequently one was lost, the *dema'* can be lifted if the amount in doubt is less than 2% of the total.

אָמַר רִבִּי חוּנָא כֵּינִי מַתְנִיתָא עִיגּוּלֵי דְבֵילָה הַגְּדוֹלִים מַעֲלִין אֶת הַקְּטַנִּים בְּמִשְׁקָל וּקְטַנִּים מַעֲלִין אֶת הַגְּדוֹלִים בְּמִנְיָין.

Rebbi Ḥuna said, so is the Mishnah: "Large fig cakes lift small ones" by weight, "and small ones lift the large" by count[86].

86 In each case, one computes the 100 times necessary for lifting; if there are more large cakes one goes by weight, if counting small ones will be advantageous, one goes by numbers. The reason for the possibility of such a change is discussed in *Orlah* 3:1, fol. 62d.

(fol. 42c) **משנה ט**: כֵּיצַד חֲמִשִּׁים תְּאֵינִים שְׁחוֹרוֹת וַחֲמִשִּׁים לְבָנוֹת נָפְלָה שְׁחוֹרָה שְׁחוֹרוֹת אֲסוּרוֹת וּלְבָנוֹת מוּתָּרוֹת. נָפְלָה לְבָנָה הַלְּבָנוֹת אֲסוּרוֹת וְהַשְּׁחוֹרוֹת מוּתָּרוֹת. וּבְשֶׁאֵינוֹ יוֹדֵעַ מַה נָּפְלָה מַעֲלוֹת זוֹ אֶת זוֹ. וּבְזוֹ רַבִּי אֱלִיעֶזֶר מַחְמִיר וְרַבִּי יְהוֹשֻׁעַ מֵיקֵל.

Mishnah 9: How is this[87]? If there are 50 black figs and 50 white, if a black one fell, the black are forbidden but the white are permitted; if a white one fell, the white are forbidden but the black are permitted. If he does not know what fell, they lift one another. In the latter case, Rebbi Eliezer is stringent and Rebbi Joshua lenient[88].

87 The following two sentences explain the position of R. Aqiba in the preceding Mishnah.

88 As explained in the preceding Halakhah (following Note 70).

(fol. 43a) **הלכה ט**: הָכָא רַבִּי לִיעֶזֶר מַחְמִיר וְרַבִּי יְהוֹשֻׁעַ מֵיקֵל. אָמַר רַבִּי יוֹחָנָן תַּנָּאִין אִינּוּן. נִמְצֵאת אוֹמֵר בְּיָדוּעַ לֹא תַעֲלֶה. שֶׁאֵינוֹ בְּיָדוּעַ תַּעֲלֶה דִּבְרֵי רַבִּי לִיעֶזֶר. רַבִּי יְהוֹשֻׁעַ אוֹמֵר בֵּין בְּיָדוּעַ בֵּין בְּשֶׁאֵינוֹ יָדוּעַ תַּעֲלֶה דִּבְרֵי רַבִּי מֵאִיר. רַבִּי יְהוּדָה אוֹמֵר בֵּין בְּיָדוּעַ בֵּין בְּשֶׁאֵינוֹ יָדוּעַ לֹא תַעֲלֶה דִּבְרֵי רַבִּי לִיעֶזֶר. רַבִּי יוֹשׁוּעַ אוֹמֵר בֵּין בְּיָדוּעַ בֵּין בְּשֶׁאֵינוֹ יָדוּעַ תַּעֲלֶה. רַבִּי עֲקִיבָה אוֹמֵר בְּיָדוּעַ לֹא תַעֲלֶה בְּשֶׁאֵינוֹ יָדוּעַ תַּעֲלֶה.

Halakhah 9: Is Rebbi Eliezer stringent and Rebbi Joshua lenient in this case[89]? Rebbi Joḥanan said, it is [a disagreement of] Tannaïm[90]: "You must say that if it is known, it cannot be lifted[91], if it is not known it may be lifted, the words of Rebbi Eliezer. Rebbi Joshua says, whether it is known or unknown, it can be lifted, the words of Rebbi Meïr. Rebbi Jehudah says, whether it is known or unknown, it cannot be lifted, the words of Rebbi Eliezer; Rebbi Joshua says, whether it is known or unknown, it can be lifted. Rebbi Aqiba says, if it is known, it cannot be lifted; if it is unknown, it can be lifted."

89 Do R. Eliezer and R. Joshua always disagree here? From Mishnah 8, one would assume that in case the strain of heave fig is unknown, R. Eliezer and R. Joshua do not disagree that heave can be lifted but disagree about the amount needed.

90 Tosephta 5:10. The statement in the Mishnah is R. Jehudah's, not R. Meïr's.

91 Unless there are 100 profane figs for each heave fig of the known strain of the heave fig. According to R. Jehudah, R. Eliezer requires 100 figs from each strain if the strain of the heave is unknown.

(fol. 42c) **משנה י**: וְכֵן רִבִּי אֱלִיעֶזֶר מֵיקֵל וְרִבִּי יְהוֹשֻׁעַ מַחְמִיר בְּדוֹרֵס לִיטְרָא קְצִיעוֹת עַל פִּי הַכַּד[92] וְאֵין יָדוּעַ אֵי זוֹ הִיא רִבִּי אֱלִיעֶזֶר אוֹמֵר רוֹאִין אוֹתָן כְּאִילּוּ הֵן פְּרוּדוֹת וְהַתַּחְתּוֹנוֹת מַעֲלוֹת אֶת הָעֶלְיוֹנוֹת. וְרִבִּי יְהוֹשֻׁעַ אוֹמֵר לֹא תַעֲלֶה עַד שֶׁיְּהֵא שָׁם מֵאָה כַּדִּים.

Mishnah 10: And so Rebbi Eliezer is lenient and Rebbi Joshua stringent in case somebody presses a pound of cut figs[93] into the mouth of a pitcher and does not remember which. Rebbi Eliezer says, one considers it as if they were separate and the lower ones help to lift the upper ones. But Rebbi Joshua says one may not lift unless there are 100 pitchers[94].

92 Reading of the Rome ms. and all Mishnah mss. Leyden and Venice: בדי "olive presses".

93 Of heave. R. Eliezer permits lifting heave to remove *dema'* if in all pitchers together there were 100 pounds of cut figs.

94 He considers the entire pitcher containing the heave as irredeemable *dema'* since small pieces of figs ooze fluid and mix well with what is below.

(fol. 43a) **הלכה י**: לִיטְרָא קְצִיעוֹת שֶׁדְּרָסָהּ עַל פִּי חָבִית וְאֵין יָדוּעַ הֵיכָן דְּרָסָהּ. עַל פִּי כַוֶּורֶת וְאֵין יָדוּעַ אֵיכָן דְּרָסָהּ. רִבִּי לִיעֶזֶר אוֹמֵר אִם יֵשׁ שָׁם מֵאָה לִיטְרִין יַעֲלֶה וְאִם לָאו לֹא תַעֲלֶה. רִבִּי יְהוֹשֻׁעַ אוֹמֵר אִם יֵשׁ שָׁם מֵאָה פוּמִין תַּעֲלֶה. וְאִם לָאו הַפּוּמִין אֲסוּרִין וְהַשּׁוּלַיִם מוּתָּרִין דִּבְרֵי רִבִּי יוּדָה. רִבִּי מֵאִיר אוֹמֵר רִבִּי לִיעֶזֶר אוֹמֵר אִם יֵשׁ שָׁם מֵאָה פוּמִין תַּעֲלֶה וְאִם לָאו הַפּוּמִין אֲסוּרִין וְהַשּׁוּלַיִם מוּתָּרִין. רִבִּי יוֹשֻׁעַ אָמַר אֲפִילוּ יֵשׁ שָׁם שְׁלֹשׁ מֵאוֹת פּוּמִין לֹא תַעֲלֶה. הָדָא אָמְרָה פּוּמִין עָשׂוּ אוֹתָן כְּדָבָר שֶׁדַּרְכּוֹ לְהִימָּנוֹת. הָדָא מְסַייְעָא לְרִבִּי יוֹחָנָן דּוּ אָמַר תַּנָּיִין אִינּוּן. הָדָא מְסַייְעָא לְמָאן דְּאָמַר דִּבְרֵי רִבִּי מֵאִיר כָּל־הַדְּבָרִים מְקַדְּשִׁין. הָדָא מְסַייְעָא לְמָאן דְּאָמַר תַּנָּיִין אִינּוּן. הָדָא אָמְרָה דְּלַעַת אֲפִילוּ אֶחָד מִמֵּאָה בָהּ אוֹסֵר.

Halakhah 10: "[95]A pound of cut figs which somebody pressed into the mouth of an amphora and does not remember where he pressed, into the mouth of a vase[96] and does not remember where he pressed; Rebbi Eliezer says, if there are 100 pounds it may be lifted, otherwise it cannot be lifted; Rebbi Joshua says, if there are 100 mouths[97] there it may be lifted, otherwise the mouths are forbidden and the sides are permitted, the words of Rebbi Jehudah. Rebbi Meïr says, Rebbi Eliezer says, if there are 100 mouths there it may be lifted, otherwise the mouths are forbidden and the sides are permitted; Rebbi Joshua says even if there are 300 mouths it cannot be lifted." This means that they considered mouths as something that usually is counted[98]. This supports Rebbi Johanan who said, it is a disagreement of Tannaïm[90]. This supports him who says, the words of Rebbi Meïr that everything sanctifies[98]. This supports him who says it is a disagreement of Tannaïm[99]. This means that even one hundredth of a pumpkin forbids[100].

95 A similar text, but not the basis of the *baraita* here, appears in Tosephta 5:11. A third version, closer to the Tosephta, is in the Babli, *Beẓah* 3b, *Zebaḥim* 73a.

96 Arabic בוארה, a vase made from sun-dried clay. In any vase or amphora, the mouth is much narrower than the body.

97 Assuming that all vessels have identical size. If the heave percolates downwards, it percolates only in the right circular cylinder defined by the mouth of the vase. Therefore, anything in the body of the vessel outside that cylinder (the "sides") is certainly permitted.

98 This refers to Mishnah *Orlah* 3:6 dealing with fruits sold by the piece ("usually counted" for sale). If the fruit is forbidden for all use ("sanctified", cf. Introduction to *Kilaim*), if it falls into a container of the same fruits and now is no longer identifiable, there are three opinions in the matter. The rabbis have a list of six kinds of fruit that make all fruits in the same container forbidden for all use, even if there are more than 1000 permitted to one forbidden fruit. R. Meïr disagrees but R. Joḥanan and R. Simeon ben Laqish disagree about the meaning of the disagreement. According to one opinion, R. Meïr simply has an extended list of 10 items, but the other opinion is that he extends the sanctification to everything sold by the piece, not only fruits but also containers of processed fruit.

99 The same disagreement noted from Mishnah 9 carries over to Mishnah 10.

100 This refers to Greek gourd, a variety of pumpkin mentioned in Mishnah *Kilaim* 1:5; its exact identity has not been established. Greek gourd is on the list of the six sanctifying fruits, *Orlah* 3:7. While the Mishnah there only speaks of fruits forbidden for all use, this remark extends the principle to *dema'* which is only forbidden for laymen. It is asserted that the principle that heave disappears in 100 does not apply to the fruits on that list, that their *dema'* can never be lifted.

דְּרָסָהּ וְאֵין יָדוּעַ אֵיכָן דְּרָסָהּ דִּבְרֵי הַכֹּל תַּעֲלֶה. אָמַר רִבִּי אָבִין וְצָרִיךְ שֶׁיְּהֵא בְּכָל־אַחַת שְׁנֵי לִיטְרִין וְכָל־שֶׁהוּא כְּדֵי שֶׁתִּיבָּטֵל בְּרוֹב.

"If he pressed it but it is not known where he pressed it, everybody agrees that it may be lifted.[101]" Rebbi Abin said, but each individual [amphora] must contain somewhat more than two pounds so it should have disappeared in a plurality.

101 The Tosephta quoted (5:11) also considers the case of one pound of cut heave figs pressed into one of 100 fig cakes and states that both RR. Eliezer and Joshua agree, in the opinion of RR. Jehudah and Meïr, that *dema'* can be lifted. Since fig cakes usually are sold by the piece, R. Abin clarifies that this can apply only to the case when the institution of heave already has disappeared as a matter of biblical law.

(fol. 42c) **משנה יא**: סְאָה תְרוּמָה שֶׁנָּפְלָה עַל פִּי מְגוּרָה וּקְפָאָהּ רִבִּי אֱלִיעֶזֶר אוֹמֵר אִם יֵשׁ בְּקִפּוּי מֵאָה סְאָה תַּעֲלֶה בְאֶחָד וּמֵאָה וְרִבִּי יְהוֹשֻׁעַ אוֹמֵר לֹא תַעֲלֶה. סְאָה תְרוּמָה שֶׁנָּפְלָה עַל פִּי מְגוּרָה יִיקַפְּינָּהּ וְאִם כֵּן לָמָּה אָמְרוּ תְּרוּמָה עוֹלָה בְאֶחָד וּמֵאָה בְּשֶׁאֵינוֹ יוֹדֵעַ אִם בְּלוּלוֹת הֵן אִם לְאַיִין נָפְלָה.

Mishnah 11: One *seah* of heave which fell into the opening of a storage bin and congealed[102], Rebbi Eliezer says if the congealed part contains 100 *seah* it may be lifted by 101; Rebbi Joshua says, it should not be lifted [but] a *seah* of heave which fell into the opening of a storage bin one should compress[103]. If this is so, why did they say, heave may be lifted in 101? If one does not know whether it was mixed in[104] or where it fell.

102 The upper part of the grain compressed by the impact of the *seah* that fell in and now clearly separated from the loose grain below. In this case, R. Eliezer will not consider the loose grain below to be of help for the

compacted grain above.

103 One should press the heave together; if it can be taken out as a block, no *dema'* was created. In the Tosephta (5:13), the reading is: יקלפנה "he should skim it off". The interpretation of R. Assi in the Halakhah seems to be based on that interpretation.

104 If the boundary between the new and the old is not visible.

(fol. 43a) **הלכה יא**: מְחְלְפָה שִׁיטָּתֵיהּ דְּרִבִּי אֱלִיעֶזֶר. תַּמָּן הוּא אָמַר הַתַּחְתּוֹנוֹת מַעֲלוֹת אֶת הָעֶלְיוֹנוֹת הָכָא הוּא אָמַר אִם יֵשׁ בְּקִפּוּי הָא אַרְעִייָתָא לֹא. רִבִּי יִרְמְיָה רִבִּי חִייָא בְּשֵׁם רִבִּי יוֹחָנָן שִׁמְעוֹן בַּר בָּא בְּשֵׁם כַּהֲנָא דִּבְרֵי רִבִּי לִיעֶזֶר עָשׂוּ אוֹתָהּ כִּמְרַבֶּה מֵזִיד. רִבִּי אִילָא רִבִּי אַסִּי בְּשֵׁם רִבִּי יוֹחָנָן דִּבְרֵי רִבִּי לִיעֶזֶר עָשׂוּ אוֹתָהּ כִּסְאָה עוֹלָה מִתּוֹךְ מֵאָה. עַל דַּעְתֵּיהּ דְּרִבִּי אַסִּי מוּתָּר לְרַבּוֹת. עַל דַּעְתֵּיהּ דְּכַהֲנָא אָסוּר לְרַבּוֹת. קָפָה וְחָזַר וְקָפָה עַל דַּעְתֵּיהּ דְּרִבִּי אִיסִּי מוּתָּר. עַל דַּעְתֵּיהּ דְּכַהֲנָא אָסוּר. עַל דַּעְתֵּיהּ דְּרִבִּי אִיסִּי אַף עַל פִּי שֶׁלֹּא שִׁיֵּר. עַל דַּעְתֵּיהּ דְּכַהֲנָא וְהוּא שֶׁשִּׁיֵּר.

Halakhah 11: The reasoning of Rebbi Eliezer is inverted: There[105], he says that the lower ones help to lift the upper, and here he says "if the congealed contains", therefore not the bottom ones. Rebbi Jeremiah, Rebbi Ḥiyya in the name of Rebbi Joḥanan, Simeon bar Abba in the name of Cahana: The words of Rebbi Eliezer [imply] that they consider this as if he had added intentionally[106]. Rebbi Hila, Rebbi Assi in the name of Rebbi Joḥanan: The words of Rebbi Eliezer [imply] that they consider it as a *seah* lifted from 100[107]. In the opinion of Rebbi Assi, one is permitted to add[108], in the opinion of Cahana it is forbidden. If it congealed and then congealed a second time, in the opinion of Rebbi Assi it is permitted, in the opinion of Cahana it is forbidden[109]. In the opinion of Rebbi Assi, even if there is no remainder, in the opinion of Cahana only if he left a remainder[110].

105 In Mishnah 10.

106 It is implied by the Mishnaiot of Chapter 5 that profane produce intentionally added to *dema'* is always disregarded. In our case, since he let the heave compact its neighborhood, the loose grain cannot be counted as being the same kind; in the language of the Tosephta (5:13) it is as if the top were wheat and the bottom barley. If then the compacted grain is loosened, it is as if added intentionally.

107 As long as the compacted grain is the same kind as the loose, they still are considered to be one kind and the 1-in-100 rule applies.

108 If one is permitted to undo the compaction, one intentionally adds to the loose grain.

109 For R. Assi, there never was any difference between compacted and non-compacted grain. For Cahana, when the compacted part was forbidden as *dema'*, it cannot become permitted by being loosened.

110 If everything were compacted, it would be as if everything was loose, and the special case of the Mishnah would become meaningless.

(fol. 42c) **משנה יב**: שְׁתֵּי קוּפּוֹת שְׁתֵּי מְגוּרוֹת שֶׁנָּפְלָה סְאָה תְרוּמָה לְתוֹךְ אַחַת מֵהֶן וְאֵין יָדוּעַ לְאֵי זֶה מֵהֶן נָפְלָה מַעֲלוֹת זוֹ אֶת זוֹ. רִבִּי שִׁמְעוֹן אוֹמֵר אֲפִילוּ הֵן בִּשְׁתֵּי עֲיָירוֹת מַעֲלוֹת זוֹ אֶת זוֹ.

Mishnah 12: Two boxes, two storage bins, into one of which a *seah* of heave fell but it is not known into which one it fell, help to lift one another. Rebbi Simeon says, even if they are in two villages they help to lift one another.

(fol. 43a) **הלכה יב**: שְׁתֵּי קוּפּוֹת בִּשְׁתֵּי עֲלִיּוֹת וּשְׁתֵּי מְגוּרוֹת בַּעֲלִיָּה אַחַת. אֲבָל שְׁתֵּי מְגוּרוֹת בִּשְׁתֵּי עֲלִיּוֹת לֹא בְדָא. מַה בֵּין קוּפּוֹת לִמְגוּרוֹת. קוּפּוֹת דַּרְכָּן לְהִתְפַּנּוֹת. מְגוּרוֹת אֵין דַּרְכָּן לְהִתְפַּנּוֹת.

Halakhah 12: "Two boxes in two attics, two storage bins in one attic.[111]" But not two storage bins in two attics. What is the difference between boxes and storage bins? Boxes are usually moved around, storage bins are not.

111 Tosephta 6:12, reading of the Erfurt ms. only.

רִבִּי זְעִירָה רִבִּי חִייָא בְשֵׁם רִבִּי שִׁמְעוֹן הָיוּ לְפָנָיו שְׁתֵּי קוּפּוֹת בְּזוֹ חֲמִשִּׁים סְאָה וּבְזוֹ חֲמִשִּׁים סְאָה וְנָפְלָה סְאָה תְרוּמָה בְּתוֹךְ אַחַת מֵהֶן וְאֵין יָדוּעַ בְּאֵי זֶה מֵהֶן נָפְלָה רָצָה לְהַעֲלוֹת מִזּוֹ מַעֲלֶה מִזּוֹ מַעֲלֶה מֶחֱצָה מִזּוֹ וּמֶחֱצָה מִזּוֹ מַעֲלֶה. וְכֵן שְׁתֵּי מִקְווֹת בְּזֶה עֶשְׂרִים סְאָה וּבְזֶה עֶשְׂרִים סְאָה וְנָפְלוּ שְׁלֹשֶׁת לוֹגִין מַיִים שְׁאוּבִין מִתּוֹךְ אַחַת מֵהֶן וְאֵין יָדוּעַ לְאֵי זֶה מֵהֶן נָפְלוּ רָצָה לְהוֹצִיא קוֹוֶיהָ פְּסוּלָה מִזֶּה מוֹצִיא מֶחֱצָה מִזֶּה וּמֶחֱצָה מִזֶּה מוֹצִיא מַעֲלֶה.

Rebbi Zeïra, Rebbi Ḥiyya in the name of Rebbi Simeon: If two boxes were before him, in each one 50 *seah*, and one *seah* of heave fell into one of them but it is not known into which of them, if he wants to lift from any one of them he may do so, or he may lift half from this one and half from the other[111]. Similarly, if there were two gatherings of water[112], each one containing 20 *seah*, and three *log* of drawn water fell into one of them but it is not known into which of them, if he wants to lift from any one of them its water collection he may do so, or he may lift half from this one and half from the other.

111 Since heave has disappeared by biblical law even at 1 in 50, the two boxes can be taken together to satisfy the rabbinic requirement of 1 in 100.

112 A gathering of water becomes a ritual bath if it contains 40 *seah* of natural water, i. e., water that never was in a vessel which can become impure. If there are less than 40 *seah*, then 3 *log* ($^1/_8$ *seah*) of drawn water by

rabbinic decree makes the entire water unusable. It is stated in Mishnah *Miqwaot* 3:1 that the place of this water can be refilled with natural water for a ritual bath if slightly more than the original content was taken out. This means that, if 20 *seah* were in the *miqweh* and three *log* fell in, then > 20 *seah* has to be taken out. Then in the worst case, if all water drawn out was good water, there are < 3 *log* of disqualified water left and the place may be filled with 40 *seah* of natural water. Maimonides accepts R. Simeon's argument for heave but not for ritual baths.

רִבִּי סִימוֹן בְּשֵׁם בַּר פְּדָיָה הָיוּ לְפָנָיו שְׁתֵּי קוּפּוֹת בְּזוֹ חֲמִשִּׁים סְאָה וּבְזוֹ חֲמִשִּׁים סְאָה וְנָפְלָה סְאָה תְּרוּמָה בְּתוֹךְ אַחַת מֵהֶן וְיָדוּעַ לְאֵי זֶה מֵהֶן נָפְלָה וְאַחַר כָּךְ נָפְלָה בַּשְּׁנִייָה וְאֵין יָדוּעַ לְאֵי זֶה מֵהֶן נָפְלָה אָמַר לַמָּקוֹם שֶׁנָּפְלָה הָרִאשׁוֹנָה נָפְלָה שְׁנִייָה. לָמָּה (fol. 43b) שֶׁתּוֹלִין קַלְקָלָה בִּמְקוּלְקָל. רִיבָּה עַל הַיְּדוּעָה וּבְטָלָהּ שׁוֹגֵג מַעֲלֶה וּמַתִּיר וְהַשְּׁנִייָה חָזְרָה לְהוֹכִיחָהּ. נִמְצְאוּ שְׁתֵּי סְאִין עוֹלוֹת מִן מֵאָה וַחֲמִשִּׁים סְאָה. וּשְׁתֵּי קוּפּוֹת בְּזוֹ חֲמִשִּׁים סְאָה וּבְזוֹ חֲמִשִּׁים סְאָה וְנָפְלָה סְאָה תְּרוּמָה לְתוֹךְ אַחַת מֵהֶן וְאֵין יָדוּעַ לְאֵי זֶה מֵהֶן נָפְלָה וְאַחַר כָּךְ נָפְלָה שְׁנִייָה וְיָדוּעַ לְאֵי זֶה מֵהֶן נָפְלָה אֵין אוֹמֵר לַמָּקוֹם שֶׁנָּפְלָה הַשְּׁנִייָה נָפְלָה הָרִאשׁוֹנָה. רִיבָּה עַל אַחַת מֵהֶן וּבְטָלָהּ שׁוֹגֵג מַעֲלֶה וּמַתִּיר וְהַשְּׁנִייָה אֲסוּרָה עַד שֶׁיַּרְבֶּה לָהּ שׁוֹגֵג.

Rebbi Simon in the name of Bar Pedaiah: "If before him there were two boxes of fifty *seah* each; one *seah* of heave fell into one of them and it is known into which one it fell, then a second [*seah*] fell and it is not known into which it fell, one says that the second fell into the place of the first.[113]" Why? Because one attaches the damage to the damaged. If in error he added to the known one and made [the heave] disappear, he lifts and makes it permitted. The second [*seah*] returns to be proven[114]. It turns out that two *seot* may be lifted from 150 *seah*. "If there were two boxes of fifty *seah* each; one *seah* of heave fell into one of them and it is not known into which one it fell, then a second [*seah*] fell and it is known into which it fell, one does not say that the first fell into the place of the second[115]." If in error he added to one and made [the heave] disappear, he lifts and makes it permitted, but the second one remains forbidden until he would add to it in error.

113 Tosephta 6:13 (both parts); a similar statement also in Tosephta *Miqwaot* 2:3.

114 If the first box contained 101 *seah*, one is lifted as replacement heave. Then the first box contains 100 *seah*, the second 50. The first one is no longer damaged; therefore, it is impossible to say that the second *seah* of heave fell into the first box. But the two boxes together now contain 150 *seah*, and this is more than enough to lift a second *seah* and eliminate *dema'* altogether.

115 The declaration of damage cannot be retroactive.

אָמַר מַה שֶׁלְּמַטָּן תְּרוּמָה מַה שֶׁלְּמַעֲלָן חוּלִּין מַה שֶׁלְּמַטָּן חוּלִּין מַה שֶׁלְּמַעֲלָן תְּרוּמָה. לְדַעְתּוֹ הַדָּבָר תָּלוּי. וְאַף בְּמִקְוֶה כֵן. אָמַר מַה שֶׁלְּמַטָּן קִיוֶיהָ כְּשֵׁירָה. שֶׁלְּמַעֲלָן קִיוֶיהָ פְּסוּלָה. מַה שֶׁלְּמַטָּן קִיוֶיהָ פְּסוּלָה שֶׁלְּמַעֲלָן קִיוֶיהָ כְּשֵׁירָה לְדַעְתּוֹ הַדָּבָר תָּלוּי.

If he said, what is below is heave, above all is profane, or what is below is all profane, above is heave, it depends on his opinion. Also for a *miqweh* it is the same: If he said, all water below is usable, above is unusable, or all water below is unusable, above is usable, it depends on his opinion[116].

116 This refers to the statement of R. Simon, Note 111-112. It is explained that not only may one choose which box (or water pool) to choose to remove heave (or water) from, but he may also choose the place from where to draw.

אַתְּ אָמַר קוּפּוֹת מַעֲלֶה וּמְגוּרוֹת אֵינָן מַעֲלוֹת. הֵיךְ עֲבִידָא שְׁתֵּי מְגוּרוֹת בִּשְׁתֵּי עֲלִיּוֹת וְנָפְלָה סְאָה תְרוּמָה לְתוֹךְ אַחַת מֵהֶן שְׁתֵּיהֶן אֲסוּרוֹת. רִיבָּה עַל אַחַת מֵהֶן וּבִטְּלָהּ שׁוֹגֵג מַעֲלֶה וּמַתִּיר וְהַשְּׁנִייָה לִכְשֶׁיִּרְבֶּה לָהּ שׁוֹגֵג הִיא מוּתֶּרֶת וְאֵינָהּ צְרִיכָה עֲלִייָה שֶׁכְּבָר עָלְתָה תְרוּמָה.

You say, one may lift from boxes but not from storage bins[117]. How is this? Two storage bins in two attics and a *seah* of heave fell into one of them, both are forbidden[118]. If he added to one of them and made [heave] disappear in error, he lifts and makes permitted; the second bin, once he would accidentally add to it, will be permitted and does not need lifting since heave was already lifted.

117 This refers to the statement at the beginning of the Halakhah, Note 111, which refers only to boxes.

118 For the layman.

(fol. 42c) **משנה יג**: אָמַר רִבִּי יוֹסֵי מַעֲשֶׂה בָא לִפְנֵי רִבִּי עֲקִיבָה בַּחֲמִשִּׁים אֲגוּדוֹת שֶׁל יָרָק שֶׁנָּפְלָה אַחַת לְתוֹכָן חֶצְייָהּ תְּרוּמָה וְאָמַרְתִּי לְפָנָיו תַּעֲלֶה לֹא שֶׁהַתְּרוּמָה עוֹלָה בַּחֲמִשִּׁים וְאֶחָד אֶלָּא שֶׁהָיוּ שָׁם מֵאָה וּשְׁנֵי חֲצָיִים.

Mishnah 13: Rebbi Yose said: There came a case before Rebbi Aqiba about 50 bundles of vegetables into which one [bundle] fell half of which was heave, and I said before him that it should be lifted, not that heave might be lifted in 51 but that there were 102 halves.

(fol. 43b) **הלכה יג**: תַּנֵּי בָּלוּל מַעֲלֶה וְשֶׁאֵינוֹ בָלוּל אֵינוֹ מַעֲלֶה. וְהָא תַנִּינָן אָמַר רִבִּי יוֹסֵי מַעֲשֶׂה בָא לִפְנֵי רִבִּי עֲקִיבָה בַּחֲמִשִּׁים אֲגוּדוֹת שֶׁל יָרָק שֶׁנָּפְלָה אַחַת לְתוֹכוֹ וְחֶצְייָהּ תְּרוּמָה וְאָמַרְתִּי לְפָנָיו תַּעֲלֶה הֲרֵי אֵינוֹ בָלוּל וּמַעֲלֶה. הֲוִינָן

בָּעֲייִן לְמֵימַר דָּבָר שֶׁהוּא מַקְפִּיד עַל תַּעֲרוּבָתוֹ אֵינוֹ מַעֲלֶה וּשְׁאֵינוֹ מַקְפִּיד עַל תַּעֲרוּבָתוֹ מַעֲלֶה. הֵיךְ עֲבִידָה. קִישׁוּת טְמֵיאָה שֶׁנָּפְלָה לְתוֹךְ מֵאָה קִישׁוּאִין טְהוֹרִין הוֹאִיל וְאֵינוֹ מַקְפִּיד עַל תַּעֲרוּבָתוֹ מַעֲלֶה. הוּכְשַׁר הוֹאִיל וְהוּא מַקְפִּיד עַל תַּעֲרוּבָתָן אֵינוֹ מַעֲלֶה.

Halakhah 13: It was stated: "If it is mixed, if may be lifted, unmixed it may not be lifted.[119]" But did we not state: "Rebbi Yose said: There came a case before Rebbi Aqiba about 50 bundles of vegetables into which one [bundle] fell half of which was heave, and I said before him that it should be lifted," in that case it is unmixed and may be lifted[120]! We want to say that if he resents the admixture, it cannot be lifted but if he does not resent the admixture, it may be lifted[121]. How is that? An impure green melon which fell into 100 pure ones, since he does not resent the admixture, may be lifted, but in case they were prepared for impurity[122], because then he resents the admixture[123], it may not be lifted.

119 Tosephta 5:13, a statement of R. Yose only, disputed by the other Sages. Since the Mishnah follows R. Yose, it is implied that in the Tosephta also, the opinion of R. Yose is practice to be followed.

120 Presumably, if the farmer bundles his produce he takes pieces as they come and does not mix them up intentionally. R. Yose seems to contradict himself.

121 If the farmer bundled heave with profane produce, obviously it was his intention to give the entire bundle to a Cohen to eat in purity.

122 *Demay*, Chapter 2, Note 141.

123 All his melons will be considered impure since each of them will be in doubt and anything possibly impure is declared impure except on a public road [*Soṭah* 1:2 (fol. 16c), Babli *Soṭah* 28b].

סאה תרומה פרק חמישי

(fol. 43b) **משנה א:** סְאָה תְרוּמָה טְמֵאָה שֶׁנָּפְלָה לְפָחוֹת מִמֵּאָה חוּלִּין אוֹ לְמַעֲשֵׂר רִאשׁוֹן אוֹ לְמַעֲשֵׂר שֵׁנִי אוֹ לְהֶקְדֵּשׁ בֵּין טְהוֹרִין בֵּין טְמֵאִין יֵרָקְבוּ אִם טְהוֹרָה הָיְתָה אוֹתָהּ סְאָה יִמָּכְרוּ לַכֹּהֲנִים בִּדְמֵי תְרוּמָה חוּץ מִדְּמֵי אוֹתָהּ סְאָה. וְאִם לְמַעֲשֵׂר רִאשׁוֹן נָפְלָה יִקְרֵא שֵׁם לִתְרוּמַת מַעֲשֵׂר וְאִם לְמַעֲשֵׂר שֵׁנִי אוֹ לְהֶקְדֵּשׁ נָפְלָה הֲרֵי אֵלּוּ יִפָּדוּ. וְאִם טְמֵאִין הָיוּ הַחוּלִּין יֵאָכְלוּ נִקּוּדִים אוֹ קְלָיוֹת אוֹ יָלוּשׁוּ בְמֵי פֵירוֹת אוֹ יִתְחַלְּקוּ לְעִיסִּיּוֹת כְּדֵי שֶׁלֹּא יְהֵא בְמָקוֹם אֶחָד כַּבֵּיצָה.

Mishnah 1: One *seah* of impure heave that fell into less than 100 [*seah*] of profane produce, or First Tithe, or Second Tithe, or dedicated produce, be it pure or impure, must be left to rot[1]. If that *seah* was pure, all should be sold to Cohanim for the price of *terumah* except for the value of that *seah*[2]. If it fell into First Tithe, heave of the tithe must be given its name[3]; if it fell into Second Tithe or dedicated produce, they should be redeemed[4]. If it was impure and profane[5], it should be eaten as crackers, or dry roasted, or kneaded with fruit juice, or split into pieces of dough so that no volume of an egg should be together.

1 Since impure heave must be destroyed and heave cannot be lifted if it constitutes more than 1% of the whole, all must be destroyed.

2 All is pure *dema'* which may be eaten by the Cohen. The Cohen will pay only little because there are few buyers; the owner is not permitted to charge the regular price to make clear that the Cohen may not give from the produce to lay people. The original heave cannot be charged since it is not the farmer's property.

3 Again, it must be sold to a

Cohen but the Cohen may not eat from it before he declares that 10% of the tithe are to be heave of the tithe. Since First Tithe becomes profane after its heave was removed, if it is still called First Tithe this implies that it still contains heave. Heave of the tithe need not actually be separated; this would be impossible.

4 Since second tithe or food dedicated to the Temple may not contain heave, it has to be redeemed and then consumed as *dema'*.

5 It is assumed that the impure produce is dry and the pure heave has not been prepared for impurity (*Demay* Chapter 2, Note 141). Food in quantities less than the volume of an egg does not accept impurity (Mishnah *Ṭahorot* 1:1); if the heave is of flour, small pieces of half the volume of a hen's egg may be kneaded with water, larger amounts only in fluids which do not prepare (cf. *Demay* 2, Note 136), usually fruit juice other that grape juice or wine.

הלכה א: סְאָה תְרוּמָה טְמֵאָה כו'. תַּנֵּי רִבִּי חִייָה טֶבֶל מַעֲלֶה וּסְפִיחֵי שְׁבִיעִית מַעֲלִין. טֶבֶל מַעֲלֶה שֵׁם לְמַעְשְׂרוֹתָיו. סְפִיחֵי שְׁבִיעִית מַעֲלִין וְיִתְּנוּ לְאוֹכְלֵיהֶן. אָמַר רִבִּי יוֹסֵי מַתְנִיתָא אָמְרָה כֵן סְאָה תְרוּמָה שֶׁנָּפְלָה לְפָחוֹת לְמֵאָה תֵּעָלֶה מִפְּנֵי שֶׁהוּא פָּחוֹת מִמֵּאָה הָא מֵאָה מַעֲלֶה.[6] לֹא טֶבֶל הוּא.

Halakhah 1: "One *seah* of impure heave", etc. Rebbi Ḥiyya stated: "*Ṭevel* lifts, aftergrowth of the Sabbatical lifts.[7]" *Ṭevel*, one lifts and gives a name to his tithes. The aftergrowth of the Sabbatical should be given to those who may eat it. Rebbi Yose said, a *baraita* says so: "A *seah* of heave that fell into less than one hundred may be lifted[7] . . .". Because it is less than 100; hence 100 will lift; is that not from *ṭevel*?

6 Reading of the Rome ms. Leyden and Venice: מעלה תעלה "lifts, may be lifted."

7 Tosephta 6:2: "A *seah* of heave which fell into less than 100 and made it *dema'*, if it was *ṭevel* he uses it as heave and tithes for other produce or he gives a name to the heave of the tithe." 6:3: "A *seah* of heave which fell into 100 of Sabbatical produce shall be lifted, less than that must be left to rot." *Ṭevel* is forbidden to everybody,

including a Cohen, but the Cohen may turn it all into heave and heave of the tithe without actually separating anything.

תַּמָּן תַּנִּינָן מַדְלִיקִין בְּפַת וּבְשֶׁמֶן שֶׁל תְּרוּמָה. חִזְקִיָּה אָמַר לֹא שָׁנוּ אֶלָּא פַּת וְשֶׁמֶן הָא שְׁאָר כָּל־ (fol. 43b) הַדְּבָרִים לֹא. רִבִּי יוֹחָנָן אָמַר לֹא שַׁנְיָיה הִיא פַּת הוּא שֶׁמֶן הוּא שְׁאָר כָּל־הַדְּבָרִים. רִבִּי יוּדָן קַפּוֹדְקִיָּא בָּעֵי חִיטִּין כְּפַת זֵיתִין כְּשֶׁמֶן. רִבִּי שְׁמוּאֵל בַּר נַחְמָן בְּשֵׁם רִבִּי יוֹחָנָן הַמַּדְלִיק בְּפַת וְשֶׁמֶן שֶׁל תְּרוּמָה יִשָּׂרְפוּ עַצְמוֹתָיו. רִבִּי שְׁמוּאֵל בַּר נַחְמָן בָּעֵי קוֹמֵי רִבִּי יוֹחָנָן מָהוּ לְהַדְלִיק. אָמַר לֵיהּ אַדְלִיק וּמַה דִנְפִיל לְשִׁבְטָךְ נְפִיל לָךְ. הַכֹּל מוֹדִין בְּשֶׁמֶן שֶׁהוּא מוּתָּר. דְּאָמַר רִבִּי בָּא בַּר חִיָּיה בְּשֵׁם רִבִּי יוֹחָנָן לְךָ נְתַתִּיו לְמָשְׁחָה. לְמָשְׁחָה לִגְדוּלָּה. לְמָשְׁחָה לְסִיכָה. לְמָשְׁחָה לְהַדְלָקָה.

There[8], we have stated: "One makes a fire with bread and oil of heave." Ḥizqiah said, they taught only bread and oil, therefore nothing else. Rebbi Joḥanan said, there is no difference between bread, oil, and any other thing. Rebbi Yudan from Kappadokia asked, are wheat grains like bread and olives like oil[9]? Rebbi Samuel bar Naḥman said in the name of Rebbi Joḥanan[10], may the bones of him who uses bread and oil of heave to make a fire be burned. Rebbi Samuel bar Naḥman asked before Rebbi Joḥanan: May one make a fire? He said to him, make a fire[11]! Anything given to your tribe was given to you, as Rebbi Abba bar Ḥiyya said in the name of Rebbi Joḥanan (*Num.* 18:8): "For excellence[12]". For excellence for greatness, for excellence for rubbing in, for excellence for lighting.

8 This *baraita* is not found in any collection but it is quoted in Babli *Pesaḥim* 33b, together with the opinions of Ḥizqiah and R. Joḥanan. The heave in this paragraph is impure heave which is forbidden as food.

9 In the Babli, R. Joḥanan explicitly adds wheat grains to bread.

10 The name tradition here is impossible, even though it is supported by both mss. In the next sentence, the same R. Samuel bar Naḥman asks R.

Johanan whether one may use impure heave for lighting. The statement, as noted by R. S. Cirillo, must be in the name of R. Samuel's teacher R. Jonathan; a similar position is taken in the Babli by Rav Ḥisda and his student Rava. They are afraid that storing of impure heave as fuel would lead to people accidentally eating from the forbidden food. (In mss. of the Babli, substitutions of "Johanan" for "Jonathan" and vice-versa are quite frequent.)

11 Of impure heave.

12 "To you (Aaron) I gave it for excellence," referring to all obligatory gifts to the Cohen.

נִיחָא טְהוֹרִין יִרְקָבוּ טְמֵאִין יֵירְקָבוּ. עַל דַּעְתֵּיהּ דְּחִזְקִיָּה נִיחָא. עַל דַּעְתֵּיהּ דְּרִבִּי יוֹחָנָן יִדָּלֵק.[13] סָבַר רִבִּי יוֹחָנָן כְּהָדָא דְרִבִּי יוֹסֵי בֶּן חֲנִינָה שֶׁמָּא יִמָּצֵא בָּהֶן עֲלִיָּיה וּבְדָבָר שֶׁאֵין דַּרְכּוֹ לְהִבָּלֵל.[14] אֲבָל בְּדָבָר שֶׁדַּרְכּוֹ לְהִבָּלֵל שֶׁמָּא יִמָּצֵא בָּהֶן תְּקָלָה.

We understand that when pure it must be left to rot[15], but when impure to rot? In the opinion of Ḥizqiah, this is correct. In the opinion of Rebbi Johanan, should it not be burned? Rebbi Johanan is of the opinion of Rebbi Yose ben Ḥanina, maybe it is possible to find for them something to lift[16]; but only if it is not usually mixed [with other food]. But if it usually is mixed, maybe something untoward will happen[17].

13 Reading of Rome ms. Leyden and Venice: על דעתיה דרבי יוחנן ידליק על דעתיה דחזקיה ניחא יירקבו.

14 Reading of Rome ms. Leyden and Venice: להיכלל "to be included".

15 This is required by the Mishnah.

16 Since rotting takes some time, maybe some more will accidentally fall into the produce which will permit the heave to be lifted.

17 Therefore, it has to be destroyed as quickly as possible, by burning. In the Babli (*loc. cit.* 8), the position of R. Johanan is interpreted that he permits impure heave to be stored as fuel only after it has been denatured.

וְלֹא כֵן סָבְרִינָן מֵימַר אֵין לְהֶקְדֵּשׁ אֶלָּא מְקוֹמוֹ וְשַׁעְתּוֹ. אָמַר רִבִּי חֲנִינָא תִּיפְתָּר שֶׁחָרֵב אוֹתוֹ מָקוֹם וְלֹא מָצָא לְמוֹכְרוֹ[18] אֲפִילוּ בִדְמֵי עֵצִים.

Did we not want to say that dedicated things have only their time and place[19]? Rebbi Ḥanina said, explain it if that place was destroyed and he cannot even sell it for the price of wood.

18 The Leyden ms. and Venice text have here an additional word: אלא.

19 Mishnah *Arakhin* 6:5. If something is donated to the Temple, it has to be sold off at its place at the earliest possible time; one may not transport dedicated articles to a place where they might fetch a better price. If impure heave fell into dedicated produce, why should it rot and not be sold as fuel?

הָדָא אָמְרָה טְהוֹרָה בִטְהוֹרִין אֲבָל טְהוֹרָה בִטְמֵאִין הָדָא הִיא דְתַנִּינָן אִם טְמֵאִין הָיוּ אוֹתָן חוּלִין. עַל דַּעְתֵּיהּ דְּרִבִּי יוֹסֵי נִיחָא דְּאָמַר רִבִּי יוֹסֵי בְשֵׁם חִזְקִיָּה וְרִבִּי יוֹנָה בְשֵׁם רִבִּי יַנַּאי וּנְתַתֶּם מִמֶּנּוּ אֶת תְּרוּמַת יי לְאַהֲרֹן הַכֹּהֵן עֲשֵׂה שֶׁיִּנָּתֵן לְאַהֲרֹן בִּכְהוּנָּתוֹ. עַל דַּעְתֵּיהּ דְּכַהֲנָא דּוּ אָמַר טוֹל מִן הַמְקוּדָּשׁ שֶׁבּוֹ וֶאֱמוֹר אַף הָכָא טוֹל מִן הַמְקוּדָּשׁ שֶׁבּוֹ. וְאַף עַל גַּב דְּכַהֲנָא אָמַר תַּמָּן טוֹל מִן הַמְקוּדָּשׁ שֶׁבּוֹ מוֹדֵי וּבִלְבַד בְּדָבָר שֶׁהוּא זָקוּק לִתְנוֹ לַכֹּהֵן.

This means, pure [fell into] pure, but pure into impure[20]? That is what we have stated: "If it was impure and profane." [21]According to Rebbi Yose, it is appropriate, as Rebbi Yose said in the name of Ḥizqiah, Rebbi Jonah in the name of Rebbi Yannai (*Num.* 18:28): "You shall give from it the Eternal's heave to Aharon the priest;" it should be given to Aharon in his status as priest[22]. In the opinion of Cahana who said, take from its sanctifiable part, also here one should take from the sanctifiable part. Even though Cahana says there, take from its sanctifiable part, he agrees only in what he is required to give to the Cohen[23].

20 This refers to the last part of the Mishnah. Why does the Mishnah give detailed instructions in all possible cases if the produce was pure but for impure produce only if it was profane and not also when it was tithe?

21 The disagreement between R. Yose and Cahana is in Chapter 2, Note 9.

22 Since heave of the tithe makes the tithe *dema'*, everything is forbidden if it is impure and the Mishnah is obvious for R. Yose since impure *dema'* cannot be given to the Cohen.

23 For Cahana, the essence of the obligation is taking heave, not the delivery to the Cohen. But he agrees that one should try to give it to the Cohen in usable form. Therefore, heave of the tithe should be given from another source since this is permitted; then the heave is profane and covered by the Mishnah. For Cahana, there is no question.

וְהָדֵין נִיקּוּדִים כְּהָדָא חַצָּיֵי בֵּיצִים.

Crackers are about the size of halves of eggs.

(fol. 43b) **משנה ב**: סְאָה תְרוּמָה טְמֵאָה שֶׁנָּפְלָה לְמֵאָה חוּלִּין טְהוֹרִין רִבִּי לִיעֶזֶר אוֹמֵר תֵּירוֹם וְתִשָּׂרֵף. שֶׁאֲנִי אוֹמֵר סְאָה שֶׁנָּפְלָה הִיא סְאָה שֶׁעָלְתָה. וַחֲכָמִים אוֹמְרִים תֵּעָלֶה וְתֵאָכֵל נִקּוּדִים אוֹ קְלָיוֹת אוֹ תִילּוֹשׁ בְּמֵי פֵּירוֹת אוֹ תִתְחַלֵּק לְעִיסִּיּוֹת כְּדֵי שֶׁלֹּא יְהֵא בְמָקוֹם אֶחָד כְּבֵיצָה.

Mishnah 2: One *seah* of impure heave that fell into 100 [*seah*] of pure profane produce, Rebbi Eliezer says it should be lifted and burned since I am saying that the *seah* which fell is the *seah* which was lifted. But the Sages say, it should be taken out and eaten[24] as crackers, or dry roasted, or kneaded with fruit juice, or split into pieces of dough so that no volume of an egg should be together[5,6].

24 Rashi in *Bekhorot* 22b explains: "it should disappear (in the profane produce which shall be treated as impure, and the value of one *seah* be

given to a Cohen) or eaten . . ."; cf. also *Bekhorot* 22b *Tosaphot s. v.* תירום, *Šiṭṭah mequbeṣet* Note 32. However, תעלה cannot be translated as "to disappear" since, for that notion, Mishnah 4 uses the expression אבדה במיעוטה "it was lost in its minority."

(fol. 43c) **הלכה ב:** אָמַר רִבִּי סִימוֹן רִבִּי לִיעֶזֶר כְּדַעְתֵּיהּ כְּמָה דוּ אָמַר תַּמָּן כָּל־הַפְּסוּלִין עָלוּ בְיָדוֹ. וְכֵן הוּא אוֹמֵר הָכָא כָּל־הַטְּמֵאִין עָלוּ בְיָדוֹ. רִבִּי זְעִירָא בָּעֵי אוֹ נֹאמַר לֹא אָמַר רִבִּי לִיעֶזֶר אֶלָּה מִפְּנֵי גְדֵירָה. וְלֹא מוֹדֵי רִבִּי לִיעֶזֶר בִּסְאָה שֶׁהֶעֱלָה מִתּוֹךְ טֶבֶל שֶׁהוּא לִקְרָאוֹת שֵׁם לְמַעְשְׂרוֹתֶיהָ. אִין תֵּימַר סְאָה שֶׁנָּֽפְלָה הִיא סְאָה שֶׁעָלְתָה לֹא יְהֵא צָרִיךְ לִקְרוֹת שֵׁם לְמַעְשְׂרוֹתֶיהָ. אָמַר רִבִּי מָנָא יְאוּת אָמַר רִבִּי זְעִירָא דְּתַנֵּינָן דְּבַתְרָהּ סְאָה תְרוּמָה טְהוֹרָה שֶׁנָּֽפְלָה לְמֵאָה חוּלִין טְמֵאִין לֵית רִבִּי אֱלִיעֶזֶר פְּלִיג. אָמְרִין חֲבֵרַיָּא קוֹמֵי רִבִּי יוֹסֵי יְאוּת אָמַר רִבִּי סִימוֹן דִּילֹא כֵן שׂוֹרְפִין אֶת הַתְּרוּמָה מִפְּנֵי גְדֵירָה. אָמַר לוֹן וְכִי שִׁשָּׁה סְפֵיקוֹת דְּתַנֵּינָן לֹא מִפְּנֵי גְדֵירָן אֵין שׂוֹרְפִין וְהָכָא מִפְּנֵי גְדֵירָן אֵין שׂוֹרְפִין אוֹתָן. חֲבֵרַיָּא אָמְרֵי בָּעֵין קוֹמֵי רִבִּי יוֹסֵי מַה נַפְשָׁךְ אִם תְּרוּמָה טְמֵאָה תִישָּׂרֵף אִם חוּלִין הֵן מַה בְּכָךְ שֶׁיִּטַּמְּאוּ אָמַר לוֹן לָאו לְשׁוּם תְּרוּמָה אוֹכְלָהּ. כְּלוּם תְּרוּמָה נֶאֱכֶלֶת אֶלָּא טְהוֹרָה שֶׁמָּא טְמֵאָה. לֹא אֵי אַתֶּם מוֹדִין שֶׁאִים נוֹלָד לָהּ סָפֵק טוּמְאָה בִמְקוֹמָהּ שֶׁאֵינוֹ יָכוֹל לְשׂוֹרְפָהּ. מַה לִי שֶׁנּוֹלָד לָהּ סָפֵק טוּמְאָה בְמָקוֹם אַחֵר מַה לִי שֶׁנּוֹלָד לָהּ סָפֵק טוּמְאָה בִמְקוֹמָהּ. אֶלָּא בְעֵיתוֹן לְמִקְשַׁיָּיה אִיקְשׁוֹן עַל הָדָא דְתַנֵּי רִבִּי הוֹשַׁעְיָה סְאָה תְרוּמָה טְהוֹרָה שֶׁנָּֽפְלָה לְמֵאָה סְאָה תְרוּמָה טְמֵאָה.

Rebbi Simon says, Rebbi Eliezer stays with his opinion. Just as he says there[25], all that is defective was in his hand, so he says here all that is impure is in his hand.

Rebbi Zeïra asked, may we not say that Rebbi Eliezer said it only because of a fence[26]? Does not Rebbi Eliezer agree that for a *seah* lifted from *ṭevel* he must give a name to its tithes[7]? If you say the *seah* which fell is the *seah* which came up, it would not be necessary to give a name to its tithes[27]! Rebbi Mana said, Rebbi Zeïra is correct since we have stated after this[28]: "A *seah* of pure heave which fell into a hundred of impure profane produce," and Rebbi Eliezer does not disagree!

The colleagues argued before Rebbi Yose: Rebbi Simon is correct, because otherwise would one burn heave because of a "fence"? He said to them, are the six doubts which we have stated not because of their "fences"? Do we not also burn here because of its "fence"[29]?

The colleagues said, we asked before Rebbi Yose: In any case, if it is impure heave, it should be burned, if it is profane, why could it not become impure[30]? He said to us, is it not eaten as heave? Heave cannot be eaten except if it is pure, maybe impure? Do you not agree that if a doubt of impurity arose in its place that he cannot burn it[31]? What is the difference whether a doubt of impurity arose at another place or at its place? But if you want to question, then question what Rebbi Hoshaiah stated, since Rebbi Hoshaiah stated: "A *seah* of pure heave that fell into 100 *seah* of impure heave[32]."

25 In Mishnah *Zebaḥim* 8:5, R. Eliezer states that if limbs of valid sacrifices were mixed up with limbs of a sacrifice which had been found defective and one of these had been burned on the altar before the error was detected, then all limbs of the same kind can be brought to the altar. R. Simon interprets this to mean that we say the first limb was from a defective animal and the rest therefore are proper sacrifices.

26 He disagrees with R. Simon; his position is that of R. Eleazar in the Babli (*Zebaḥim* 77b) that R. Eliezer permits the limbs on the altar only if at least two of the same kind are brought simultaneously, so that one of them at least is valid. The "fence" is the fence around the law, a measure of precaution that no biblical law could possibly be violated; cf. *Demay* Chapter 1, Note 89.

27 If it were 100% heave, no tithes would be possible.

28 Mishnah 3. If R. Eliezer would consider all that came into his hand as heave, it would be pure and would not have to be eaten with the precautions indicated in the Mishnah.

29 The reference is to Mishnah *Ṭahorot* 4:5: "For six doubts one burns heave: For the doubt of field of pieces (a field where a grave was ploughed), the doubt of earth from a Gentile country (which is impure by tradition), the doubt of the garments of a vulgar person (who does not observe the rules of purity), the doubt of found vessels, the doubts of spittle and urine (from unknown persons), if one certainly touched them but does not know about their status of purity one burns heave. R. Yose says, even on a doubt whether one touched them in a private domain (cf. Chapter 3, Note 10), but the Sages say, on that doubt in a private domain one suspends and on a public road it is pure." The normal procedure for heave that may be impure is to "suspend", i. e., to leave the heave to rot and then dispose of it if it is no longer food. The questioner assumes that all questionable heave is suspended; R. Yose points out that there are instances in which questionable heave is burned.

30 Why do the Sages have to oppose R. Eliezer; could the lifted *seah* not be burned and all problems would be eliminated?

31 The position of the Sages in Mishnah *Ṭahorot* 4:5: If the heave was of doubtful status before it fell into the 100 other *seah* ("in its place" before it fell), it would have to be suspended, not burned. Why could its replacement be burned now?

32 There is no Tosephta dealing with this case, but everybody agrees that all must be burned; one does not lift one *seah* to let it rot.

וְהָדֵין נִיקוּדִין כְּהָדָא חֲצִי סְאִין.

Crackers are about half of a *seah*.[33].

33 Either this is a scribal error for "half an egg", cf. the end of Mishnah 1, or the translation of ניקודין is not "crackers" but "totally dry" following Rashi (*Bekhorot* 22b) who translates the verse *Jos*. 9:12 הנה יבש והיה נקדים "behold, it is dry and was totally dry" and comments on our Mishnah: "Now, even though there is purity and impurity, the pure part will not become impure without preparation; the impure part becomes voided in the plurality and should be eaten ניקודים."

משנה ג: סְאָה תְרוּמָה טְהוֹרָה שֶׁנָּפְלָה לְמֵאָה חוּלִּין טְמֵאִין תֵּעָלֶה(fol. 43b) וְתֵאָכֵל נִקּוּדִים אוֹ קְלָיוֹת אוֹ תִּילּוֹשׁ בְּמֵי פֵּירוֹת אוֹ תִתְחַלֵּק לְעִיסִּיּוֹת כְּדֵי שֶׁלֹּא יְהֵא בְּמָקוֹם אֶחָד כְּבֵיצָה.

Mishnah 3: One *seah* of pure heave that fell into 100 [*seah*] of impure profane produce should be taken out and eaten as crackers[33], or dry roasted, or kneaded with fruit juice, or split into pieces of dough so that no volume of an egg should be together[5,6].

(fol. 43c) **הלכה ג**: חִזְקִיָּה אָמַר אֲפִילוּ חוּלִין שֶׁשָּׁם לֹא יֵאָכְלוּ אֶלָּא[34] נִיקּוּדִים מִפְּנֵי חַלָּתָן. מִילְּתֵיהּ אָמְרָה אִיסּוּר זָרוּת בָּטֵל וְאִיסּוּר טוּמְאָה לֹא בָטֵל. מִחְלְפָה שִׁיטָּתֵיהּ דְּחִזְקִיָּה תַּמָּן הוּא אָמַר כַּמָּה יְהֵא בְעִיסָּה וִיהֵא יָכוֹל לַעֲשׂוֹתָהּ בְּטָהֳרָה חִזְקִיָּה אָמַר שְׁתוּת אַרְבַּע קַבִּין וְאַרְבָּעַת קַבִּין. וְכָא הוּא אָמַר הָכֵין. אָמַר רִבִּי יוֹסֵי תַּמָּן בְּשֶׁגִּיבֵּל וְאַחַר כָּךְ הִפְרִישׁ. בְּרַם הָכָא בְּשֶׁהִפְרִישׁ וְאַחַר כָּךְ גִּיבֵּל.

Halakhah 3: Ḥizqiah said, even the profane food there should be eaten only as dry crackers because of their *ḥallah*[35]. His word says that the prohibition of the outsider becomes insignificant but the prohibition of impurity does not become insignificant[36]. The arguments of Ḥizqiah seem inverted. There[37], he says: How much can be in a dough that he should be able to make it in purity[38]? Ḥizqiah said one sixth of four *qab* in four *qab*[39]. And here he says so[40]! Rebbi Yose said, there, when he kneaded the dough and then separated, but here when he separated and then kneaded[41].

34 Word missing in Venice print.

35 The heave from the dough which has to be eaten by a Cohen in purity under the rules of heave, *Num.* 15:20.

36 If he is worried about heave, there are two prohibitions to be observed: No outsider (one who is not a Cohen) may eat from it and it may not be eaten in impurity. Since he does not

require that all should be given to the Cohen as *dema'*, it follows that the prohibition of the outsider has disappeared. Since he is worried about impure heave, the prohibition of impurity has not disappeared. The argument cannot refer to the Mishnah here, since everything is impure and any *ḥallah* must be burned. Therefore, Ḥizqiah must refer to Mishnah 2, one *seah* of impure heave which is in 100 *seah* of pure profane grain.

37 This seems to refer to Tosephta *Ḥallah* 2:5: "Impure flour which was mixed with pure flour but the impure is less than its measure (less than the volume of an egg), if he takes [*ḥallah*] he says: This should be *ḥallah* except for the impure part in it." He cannot declare all of it as *ḥallah* since it might contain impure flour and impure *ḥallah* is forbidden as food. But the part of impure flour in the dough is certainly less than the volume of an egg and, therefore, all of it may be eaten by a Cohen. {The explanation of this and the next paragraph follows R. H. Kanievski.}

38 How much impure flour can be in the dough so that pure *ḥallah* can be taken?

39 If will be seen in the next paragraph that $^4/_6$ *qab* is much more than the volume of an egg, Ḥizqiah holds that, in this case, one may separate a small cake for *ḥallah* (whose normal size should be $^1/_{24}$ of the entire dough) to be sure that it does not contain the volume of an egg of impure dough and turn it into *ḥallah*. The remainder may then be worked in impurity. Since *ḥallah* follows the rules of heave, it must be taken from the dough itself. Ḥizqiah must follow R. Eliezer who in Mishnah *Ḥallah* 2:4 permits to give one *ḥallah* for all breads in one large basket. If the bread destined for *ḥallah* is separated from the large impure breads by small loaves of volume less than one egg, no contamination can take place. (The basis of this device is Mishnah *Ḥallah* 2:7).

40 He rejects the trick which he recommends for *ḥallah* and requires that all be consumed either dry or kneaded with pure fruit juice.

41 "There" is here, in *Terumot*, when it is his intention of processing all flour together; "here" is there, in *Ḥallah*, when he is prepared to separate a small cake to be kneaded in purity, the rest in impurity.

אָמַר רִבִּי אַבָּהוּ כָּל־יָמֵינוּ הָיִינוּ טוֹעִין בָּהּ כְּמַקֵּל זֶה שֶׁל סוּמָא עַד שֶׁלְּמַדְנוּהָ מִן חֶשְׁבּוֹן גֵּיֶמֶטְרִיָּה. קַבָּא כַּמָּה עֲבַד עֶשְׂרִין וְאַרְבַּע בֵּיעִין כַּמָּה סְאָה עָבְדָא תִּשְׁעִין

וְשִׁית בֵּיעִין שְׁתוּת דִּידְהוּ שִׁית עֶשְׂרֵה. אִין יְגַבֵּל שִׁית יֵשׁ כָּאן בֵּיצָה טְמֵאָה. וְאִין יְגַבֵּל אַרְבַּע אֵין כָּאן שִׁיּוּר. הָא כֵּיצַד הוּא עוֹשֶׂה מְגַבֵּל[42] חָמֵשׁ וְנוֹטֵל אַרְבַּע.

Rebbi Abbahu said, all our days we were groping about this as with a blind man's stick until we learned it from mathematical computation. How much is in a *qab*? 24 eggs[43]. How much is in a *seah*? 96 eggs[44]. One sixth of it are 16 eggs. If he makes a dough of six, it contains an impure egg[45]. If he makes from four, nothing is left. What does he do? He makes a dough from five and takes four.

42 Reading of the Rome ms. Leyden and Venice: מיגבול, an Aramaic word in a Hebrew text.

43 This is standard; a *qab* is 6 *log* and a *log* 4 eggs. The same division is accepted in the Babli.

44 This is nonstandard; the *seah* in all other places is 6 *qab*, here it is 4. The *seah* here must be the Roman *modius* which is 16 *sextarii*, and the *sextarius* is the *log* since Mishnah *Kelim* 17:11 identifies the רביעית, the fourth part of the *log*, with the Roman *quartarius*, the fourth part of the *sextarius*. {In Babli *Erubin* 83a, a *modius* is estimated as the volume of 217 eggs. Current practice follows the Yerushalmi here.} The amount of pure *ḥallah* to be given from 96 eggs would be the volume of 4 eggs. But since the verse (*Num*. 15:21) reads: "*From* the beginning of your dough you shall give . . . " the dough made for *ḥallah* cannot be exactly the volume of four eggs since something profane must be left over.

45 It is assumed that the flour was thoroughly mixed and homogenized. Since 6 = 96/16, a dough in the volume of 6 eggs contains exactly 1 egg of impure flour and is impure.

מִילְּתֵיהּ דְּחִזְקִיָּה אָמַר בִּלְבַד שֶׁלֹּא תְהֵא כְבֵיצָה טְמֵיאָה נוֹגַעַת בְּגוּמָא. מִילְּתֵיהּ דְּרִבִּי יוֹחָנָן אָמְרָה וּבִלְבַד שֶׁלֹּא תְהֵא כְבֵיצָה טְמֵיאָה נוֹגַעַת בְּעִיסָּה. אָמַר רִבִּי יוֹסֵי לְרִבִּי יִרְמְיָה לֹא מִסְתַּבְּרָא מַה דְּאָמַר חִזְקִיָּה לְשֶׁעָבַר. מַה דְּאָמַר רִבִּי יוֹחָנָן לָבֹא. אָמַר לֵיהּ וְאוּף נָא סָבַר כֵּן. וְאֵי זוֹ הִיא גוּמָא עַל דַּעְתֵּיהּ[46] דְּרִבִּי

יוֹחָנָן. רִבִּי יוֹסֵי בֵּי רִבִּי בּוּן בְּשֵׁם רִבִּי יוֹנָה תִּיפְתָּר שֶׁגִּיבֵּל אַחַת בְּשִׁבַע עֶשְׂרֵה וְאַתְיָא בְּעִיסַּת סְאָתַיִם.[47]

The statement of Ḥizqiah says, on condition that no impurity the volume of an egg touch the indentation[48]. A statement of Rebbi Joḥanan says, on condition that no impurity the volume of an egg touch the dough[49]. Rebbi Yose said to Rebbi Jeremiah: Is it not reasonable that Ḥizqiah spoke to the past and Rebbi Joḥanan spoke to the future[50]? He said, that is my opinion also. What is an indentation in the opinion of Rebbi Joḥanan[51]? Rebbi Yose ben Rebbi Abun in the name of Rebbi Jonah: Explain it that he made a dough with one in seventeen and it came to a dough of two *seah*[52].

46 Reading of the Rome ms., word missing in the other sources.

47 Reading of the Rome ms., Leyden and Venice: מאתים "two hundred".

48 The meaning of this word depends on the interpretation of Mishnah *Ṭahorot* 1:10: "Loaves of sacrificial bread which have water in their גומות, if one of them became impure by a crawling thing, they all are impure; for [loaves of] heave they make impure two stages and disqualify a third. If there is damp fluid between them, even for heave all is impure." According to Maimonides, the indentations are depressions in the bread that still contain fluid. (It seems that for this reason, he wrote in the first version of his Commentary: "Indentations left on top of the bread at the time of cooking", which in the last version he changed into: "at the time of baking.") According to R. Simson, followed by R. Asher ben Ieḥiel, the baking sheet has depressions into which the dough is placed to obtain loaves of uniform size. The explanation of R. Simson seems to be required by the formulation in Tosephta *Ṭahorot* 1:6: "Loaves of sacrificial bread *in their* גומות"

49 The dough for the profane loaves.

50 Ḥizqiah has two restrictions compared to R. Joḥanan. First, all that is in contact with any fluid he declares impure where R. Joḥanan strictly insists that only the volume of at least one egg may induce impurity. Second, in case of doubt he extends impurity

retroactively to all food in contact with the questionable dough; R. Joḥanan rejects retroactivity.

51 Under which circumstances does he admit that the situation envisaged by Ḥizqiah leads to impurity?

52 This criticism is levelled at Ḥizqiah himself and at R. Abbahu's interpretation of his position. The interpretation is rejected because it presupposes that pure and impure flour can be completely mixed, with a constant percentage of impure flour in the pure. Since presumably the two kinds are indistinguishable to the eye, mixing can not be assumed to be perfect. As a rough estimate, R. Joḥanan will admit R. Abbahu's solution if not more than the volume of 17 eggs are mixed with 2 *seah* of pure flour (somewhat below 9%) and thoroughly mixed.

רִבִּי בָּא בַּר מָמָל בָּעֵי וְלֵית הָדָא פְלִיגָא עַל רִבִּי יוֹסֵי בַּר חֲנִינָא. דְּאָמַר רִבִּי יוֹסֵי בַּר חֲנִינָא נְבֵילָה בְטֵילָה בִּשְׁחִיטָה בָּטֵל מַגָּעָהּ וְהֶסֵּיטָהּ לֹא בָטֵל לְפִי שֶׁאֵיפְשַׁר לִשְׁחוּטָה שֶׁתֵּיעָשֶׂה נְבֵילָה. אָמַר רִבִּי יוֹסֵי תַּמָּן אֵיפְשַׁר לִשְׁחִיטָה שֶׁתֵּיעָשֶׂה נְבֵילָה בְּרַם הָכָא אֶיפְשַׁר לְחוּלִין לֵעָשׂוֹת תְּרוּמָה. אָמַר רִבִּי חִזְקִיָּה רִבִּי סִימוֹן קְשִׁיָיתָהּ וְרִבִּי בָּא בַּר מָמָל קִייְמָהּ.

Rebbi Abba bar Mamal asked: Does this not contradict Rebbi Yose bar Ḥanina? As Rebbi Yose bar Ḥanina said, a carcass[54] can become insignificant in slaughtered[55] [meat]; it becomes insignificant for touch, but for motion it cannot become insignificant[56] for slaughtered [meat] can never become carcass [meat][57]. Rebbi Yose said, there it is impossible for slaughtered [meat] to become carcass [meat], but here profane produce may become heave[58]. Rebbi Ḥizqiah said, Rebbi Simon raised the question and Rebbi Abba bar Mamal explained it.

54 A dead animal not ritually slaughtered.

55 Slaughtered by cutting its throat; cf. Arabic سحط "to cut somebody's throat." The biblical Hebrew שחט has exactly the same meaning.

56 Carcasses transmit impurity in the first degree by touch (*Lev.* 11:27), and original impurity if they are carried (*Lev.* 11:28) even if never

touched. If a piece of carcass meat is mixed up with pieces of slaughtered meat, probably it touched a piece belonging to the pure majority, but when all are carried, certainly the carcass piece also was carried. Since the impurity by touch is only probable, it can be disregarded under certain conditions. The impurity by carrying is certain and can never be disregarded.

57 This argument is ascribed to Rav Ḥisda in the Babli (*Bezah* 38b, *Menaḥot* 23a, *Bekhorot* 23a), as a general principle to R. Ḥanina, the father of R. Yose ben R. Ḥanina. The Babli concludes that slaughtered meat cannot become insignificant in carcass meat because it is possible for carcass meat to acquire the purity of slaughtered meat by rotting and becoming unusable as food while it is impossible for slaughtered meat to acquire the impurity of carcass meat.

58 While profane produce may never be used to give heave, if a layman ate heave, he has to replace it by an equal amount of profane food (plus a 25% fine) which acquires the sanctity of heave, cf. Mishnah 6:1.

תַּנֵּי סְאָה תְרוּמָה שֶׁנָּפְלָה לְפָחוֹת מִמֵּאָה הֲרֵי אֵלּוּ מְדוּמָּעִין וְאֵין מְשַׁלְּמִין לָהּ קֶרֶן וְחוֹמֶשׁ עַל מָקוֹם אַחֵר. וְלֹא מִמָּקוֹם אַחֵר עֲלֵיהֶן אֶלָּא לְפִי חֶשְׁבּוֹן. וּבְדָבָר שֶׁאֵין דַּרְכּוֹ לְהִיבָּלֵל אֲבָל בְּדָבָר שֶׁדַּרְכּוֹ לְהִיבָּלֵל הוֹלְכִין אַחַר הָרוֹב אִם רוֹב תְּרוּמָה תְרוּמָה וְאִם רוֹב חוּלִין חוּלִין.

It was stated[59]: "A *seah* of heave that fell into less than a hundred makes it *dema'*. One does not pay for it the amount and a fifth for another place nor from another place for this except by computation[60]." This is for substances which cannot be mixed. But for substances which can be mixed one goes after the plurality. If most of it is heave, it is heave, if most is profane, it is profane[61].

59 Tosephta 6:1.

60 If heave was eaten by a layman, the amount and the fine have to be paid to a Cohen in profane food, Mishnah 6:1. Since *dema'* may be eaten by the Cohen, *dema'* may be given in payment but it may count only for the amount of profane food, not for the heave part in it.

61 As far as payment goes; the argument does not apply to fixing the *dema'*.

(fol. 43b) **משנה ד**: סְאָה תְרוּמָה טְמֵאָה שֶׁנָּפְלָה לְמֵאָה סְאָה טְהוֹרָה בֵּית שַׁמַּאי אוֹסְרִין וּבֵית הִלֵּל מַתִּירִין. אָמְרוּ בֵית הִלֵּל לְבֵית שַׁמַּאי הוֹאִיל וּטְהוֹרָה אֲסוּרָה לְזָרִים וּטְמֵאָה אֲסוּרָה לְכֹהֲנִים מַה טְהוֹרָה עוֹלָה אַף טְמֵאָה תַּעֲלֶה. אָמְרוּ לָהֶן בֵּית שַׁמַּאי לֹא אִם הֶעֱלוּ הַחוּלִין הַקַּלִּין הַמּוּתָּרִין לְזָרִים אֶת הַטְּהוֹרָה תַּעֲלֶה תְּרוּמָה הַחֲמוּרָה הָאֲסוּרָה לְזָרִים אֶת הַטְּמֵאָה. לְאַחַר שֶׁהוֹדוּ רִבִּי לִיעֶזֶר אוֹמֵר תּוּרַם וְתִשָּׂרֵף. וַחֲכָמִים אוֹמְרִים אָבְדָה בְמִיעוּטָהּ.

Mishnah 4: One *seah* of impure heave which fell into 100 *seah* of pure heave, the House of Shammai forbid[62] and the House of Hillel permit. The House of Hillel said to the House of Shammai: Since pure it is forbidden to outsiders and impure is forbidden to priests[63]; just as pure [heave] can be lifted, so impure should be lifted. The House of Shammai answered them no, if simple profane produce which is permitted to outsiders lets pure [heave] be lifted, can one infer that heave, operating under stringent rules, may let the impure be lifted? After they conceded, Rebbi Eliezer said it should be lifted and burned but the Sages say, it was lost in its minority[64].

62 They forbid the entire heave as impure (even if completely dry).

63 Outsiders and Cohanim.

64 Since everything is heave, all the 101 *seah* may be eaten by a Cohen as pure heave.

(fol. 43c) **הלכה ד**: רִבִּי יוּדָן בַּר פָּזִי וְרִבִּי אַייְבוֹ בַּר נַגָּרִי הֲווֹן יָתְבִין אָמְרִין תַּנִּינָן אַחַר שֶׁהוֹדוּ. מִי הוֹדָה לְמִי. בֵּית שַׁמַּאי לְבֵית הִלֵּל. אוֹ בֵּית הִלֵּל לְבֵית שַׁמַּאי. אָמְרִין נֵיצֵא לְחוּץ וְנִלְמַד. נָפְקִין וְשָׁמְעוּן. רִבִּי חִזְקִיָּה רִבִּי אָחָא בְשֵׁם רִבִּי יְהוּדָה בַּר חֲנִינָה לֹא מָצִינוּ שֶׁהוֹדוּ בֵּית שַׁמַּאי לְבֵית הִלֵּל אֶלָּא בְדָבָר זֶה בִּלְבַד. רִבִּי יוֹנָה בְשֵׁם רִבִּי אַבַּיי שָׁמַע לָהּ מִן הָדָא. הַמְּעָרָה מִכְּלִי לִכְלִי וְנָגַע טְבוּל יוֹם בְּקִילוּחַ יַעֲלֶה בְּאֶחָד וּמֵאָה. וְאִם תֹּאמַר בֵּית הִלֵּל יוֹדוּ לְבֵית שַׁמַּאי שֶׁלֹּא תַעֲלֶה. מָאן תַּנָּא הָכָא תַעֲלֶה לֹא בֵּית שַׁמַּאי לֹא[65] בֵּית הִלֵּל. אָמַר רִבִּי חֲנִינָא בְּרֵיהּ דְּרִבִּי הִלֵּל נֹאמַר בֵּית הִלֵּל שָׁנוּ אוֹתָהּ קוֹדֶם שֶׁיּוֹדוּ לָהֶן בֵּית שַׁמַּאי.

אָמַר רִבִּי יוֹסֵי מַתְנִיתָא אָמְרָה כֵן אַחַר שֶׁהוֹדוּ רִבִּי לִיעֶזֶר אוֹמֵר תֵּירוֹם וְתִשָּׂרֵף. וְרִבִּי לִיעֶזֶר לָאו שַׁמּוּתִּי הוּא. אָמַר רִבִּי חִינְנָא מַתְנִיתָא אָמְרָה כֵן אַחַר שֶׁהוֹדוּ אֵילּוּ לָאֵילּוּ (fol. 43d) תַּעֲלֶה בֵּית שַׁמַּאי מְסַלְּקִין לוֹן וְאִינּוּן מוֹדֵיי לוֹן. אָמַר רִבִּי אָבִין יֵשׁ כָּאן תְּשׁוּבָה אַחֶרֶת. כְּהָדָא דְתַנֵּי רִבִּי הוֹשַׁעְיָה וּמַה טְהוֹרָה שֶׁהִיא בְּעָוֹן מִיתָה אֵצֶל הַזָּרִים עוֹלָה. טְמֵאָה שֶׁהִיא בַּעֲשֵׂה אֵצֶל כּוֹהֲנִים לֹא כָּל־שֶׁכֵּן.

Halakhah 4: Rebbi Yudan bar Pazi and Rebbi Ayvo bar Naggari[66] were sitting and saying: We did state "after they conceded"; who conceded to whom? The House of Shammai to the House of Hillel or the House of Hillel to the House of Shammai? They said, let us go out and study. The went out and heard Rebbi Ḥizqiah, Rebbi Aḥa in the name of Rebbi Jehudah bar Ḥanina: We never find the House of Shammai conceding to the House of Hillel except in this matter. Rebbi Jonah in the name of Rebbi Abbai[67] understood it from the following[68]: "If someone pours from vessel to vessel and a *ṭevul yom* touches it, it should be lifted by 101." If you say that the House of Hillel conceded to the House of Shammai that it cannot be lifted, who is the Tanna here, neither the House of Shammai nor the House of Hillel! Rebbi Ḥanina the son of Rebbi Hillel said, we might say that the House of Hillel stated that before they conceded. Rebbi Yose said, the Mishnah said so: "After they conceded, Rebbi Eliezer said it should be lifted and burned", and is Rebbi Eliezer not a follower of Shammai? Rebbi Ḥinena said, the Mishnah said so, after they conceded one to another, the House of Shammai recused themselves and the others[69] teach us. Rebbi Abin says, there is another answer[70], following what Rebbi Hoshaia stated: Since pure [heave], which for outsiders is forbidden as deadly sin, can be lifted, certainly also impure [heave] which is [prohibited] as positive commandment[71] for Cohanim.

65 Reading of the Rome ms. Leyden and Venice: לבית הלל.

66 Galilean Amora of the early fourth generation, student of R. Ḥiyya bar Abba and R. La.

67 His name appears only here, and nothing more is known about him.

68 Mishnah *Ṭevul Yom* 2:7. For most severe impurities it is not enough that the impure person immerse himself in water; after the immersion, as *ṭevul yom* "immersed during the day", he is pure only for profane food. For heave, and certainly for sacrifices, he becomes pure only at sundown. If in the period between his immersion and sundown he touches heave, it becomes unusable; this is classified as "impure in the third degree". If the *ṭevul yom* touches a stream of heave fluid (wine or oil) poured from one vessel to the other, in the opinion of the Sadducees the entire fluid in both vessels becomes unusable (MMT lines 55-58). In rabbinic tradition, only the part touched by the *ṭevul yom* becomes unusable; the fluid cannot be used because unusable heave is contained in it, but it can be repaired by the usual lifting of one out of 101.

69 The Sages, who always represent the tradition of the House of Hillel.

70 Which the House of Hillel could have given to the House of Shammai, in addition to the argument presented in the Mishnah.

71 Which is classified as a misdemeanor, rather than a felony.

(fol. 43b) **משנה ה**: סְאָה תְרוּמָה שֶׁנָּפְלָה לְמֵאָה הִגְבִּיהָהּ וְנָפְלָה לְמָקוֹם אַחֵר רִבִּי לִיעֶזֶר אוֹמֵר מְדַמַּעַת כִּתְרוּמָה וַדַּאי. וַחֲכָמִים אוֹמְרִים אֵינָהּ מְדַמַּעַת אֶלָּא לְפִי חֶשְׁבּוֹן.

Mishnah 5: One *seah* of heave which fell into one hundred[72], was taken out, and fell into another place: Rebbi Eliezer says it creates *dema'* like certain heave but the Sages say, it creates heave only in proportion[73].

72 100 *seah* of profane produce.

73 The amount of certain heave in what was lifted is only $^1/_{101}$ of the lifted produce; in order to remove *dema'* one needs only 1 *seah* of profane produce.

משנה ו: סְאָה תְרוּמָה שֶׁנָּפְלָה לְפָחוֹת מִמֵּאָה וְנִדְמְעוּ וְנָפַל מִן הַמְּדוּמָּע לְמָקוֹם אַחֵר. רִבִּי לִיעֶזֶר אוֹמֵר מְדַמַּעַת כִּתְרוּמָה וַדַּאי. וַחֲכָמִים אוֹמְרִים אֵין הַמְּדוּמָּע מְדַמֵּעַ אֶלָּא לְפִי חֶשְׁבּוֹן. וְאֵין הַמְּחוּמָּץ מְחַמֵּץ אֶלָּא לְפִי חֶשְׁבּוֹן. וְאֵין הַמַּיִם שְׁאוּבִין פּוֹסְלִין אֶת הַמִּקְוֶה אֶלָּא לְפִי חֶשְׁבּוֹן.

Mishnah 6: One *seah* of heave which fell into less than one hundred and made it *dema'* and from the *dema'* fell into another place; Rebbi Eliezer says it creates *dema'* like certain heave but the Sages say, *dema'* creates heave only in proportion; sour agent makes sour only in proportion[74], and drawn water invalidates a ritual bath only in proportion[75].

74 Sour dough of heave which was added to dough to make it rise turns the entire dough into heave (Mishnah *Orlah* 2:6). If from the dough anything was taken for another batch of dough, the latter becomes heave only if the proportional part of the original souring agent alone would have been enough to make the new dough rise. The three cases "in proportion" mentioned here are repeated in Mishnah *Temurah* 1:4.

75 If a *miqweh* contains a little less than the minimum 40 *seah* and three *log* of water are added from a vessel to bring it over the limit, the entire water becomes unfit for a ritual bath. The Babli (*Temurah* 12a-b) gives two explanations for the Mishnah here; there is no Yerushalmi on this part of the Mishnah. According to the final determination of the Babli, "in proportion" here has a meaning totally different from the two preceding cases, in that water from vessels invalidates only if the vessels are in proportion to the three *log*, i. e., if the water is added from at most three vessels, not from four or more. This is accepted by Maimonides in his Code (*Miqwaot* 5:1) with the concurrence of R. Abraham ben David (*Tosaphot Temurah* 12b, *s. v.* יוסף).

(fol. 43d) **הלכה ה**: אָמַר רִבִּי יוֹחָנָן סְאָה תְרוּמָה שֶׁנָּפְלָה לְמֵאָה חוּלִין כָּל־שֶׁהֵן מְבַטְּלִין אוֹתָהּ. מַתְנִיתִין פְּלִיגָא עַל רִבִּי יוֹחָנָן אֵינָהּ מְדַמַּעַת אֶלָּא לְפִי חֶשְׁבּוֹן. רִבִּי יוֹסֵי בְּשֵׁם רִבִּי יוֹחָנָן לֹא תַנֵּי[76] רִבִּי יוֹחָנָן אֶלָּא אֵינָהּ מְדַמַּעַת כָּל־עִיקָּר.

בְּרַם אָמַר וְהוּא שֶׁרָבָה תְרוּמָה עַל הַחוּלִין וְהוּא שֶׁרָבוּ חוּלִין עַל חֶשְׁבּוֹן תְּרוּמָה כְּדֵי שֶׁתִּיבָּטֵל בְּרוֹב. אָמַר רִבִּי לָעְזָר וְהוּא שֶׁנָּפְלוּ לְתוֹךְ מְדוּמָּע אֶחָד. עַל דַּעְתֵּיהּ דְּרִבִּי לָעְזָר חוּלִין שֶׁלְּמַעְלָן חוּלִין שֶׁלְּמַטָּן מִצְטָרְפִין לַעֲלוֹת. סָבַר רִבִּי לָעְזָר מֵימַר חוּלִין שֶׁלְּמַטָּן נַעֲשׂוּ חֲרֵשִׁין.

Halakhah 5: Rebbi Joḥanan said, a *seah* of heave which fell into 100 of profane produce, anything will make it become insignificant[77]. Our Mishnah disagrees with Rebbi Joḥanan: "It creates heave only in proportion[78]". Rebbi Yose in the name of Rebbi Joḥanan, Rebbi Joḥanan stated only: "It does not create any *dema'*.[79]" But[80] they said only when there was more heave than profane, and he when there was more profane than the proportion of heave so that it should become insignificant in the plurality. Rebbi Eleazar said, only[81] if it fell into a *dema'*. In the opinion of Rebbi Eleazar, are the lower and upper profane produce united to lift? Rebbi Eleazar wants to say that the lower profane produce becomes inert[82].

76 Reading of the Rome ms. Leyden and Venice add: בשם

77 If one *seah* was lifted after a *seah* of heave fell into 100 profane *seah*, the new *seah* is only heave by rabbinic decree superimposed on a rabbinic obligation; it is heave in name only and can be made insignificant in the slightest amount of additional profane produce. Quoted in this sense in Halakhah 9:6.

78 According to the Mishnah, the amount into which if fell must still be $^{100}/_{101}$ times the amount lifted.

79 He had another version of the Mishnah before him.

80 The Sages of the Mishnah speak of the case that the amount lifted was taken from the place the heave fell in, when one may assume that more genuine heave than profane grain was lifted. Rebbi Joḥanan speaks of the case when everything was well mixed; in Halakhah 9:6 this is expressed by: "he mills [the grain] and thereby permits it."

81 The Mishnah which relates the disagreement of R. Eliezer and the Sages. Do the Sages permit the profane part of the *seah* that fell into *dema'* to

be added to the profane part of the *dema'* to provide the necessary 100+1 ratio?

82 The position tentatively ascribed to R. Eleazar in the previous sentence is that of R. Joḥanan. R. Eleazar is restrictive and requires the lifted heave to be neutralized on its own when it fell into *dema'*, irrespective of the amount of profane produce in the *dema'* into which it fell. This is the majority position in Tosephta 6:5, opposed by R. Simeon and his son.

הלכה ו: אָמַר רִבִּי יוֹסֵי בֶּן חֲנִינָה וְהוּא שֶׁנָּפְלוּ לְתוֹךְ חֲמִשָּׁה מְקוֹמוֹת אֲבָל אִם נָפְלוּ כוּלָּן לְמָקוֹם אֶחָד אַף רִבִּי לְעֶזֶר מוֹדֵי. רִבִּי יוֹחָנָן אָמַר אֲפִילוּ נָפְלוּ כוּלָּן לְמָקוֹם אֶחָד הִיא הַמַּחֲלוֹקֶת. חִילְפַּיי אָמַר עַל דְּרִבִּי לִיעֶזֶר חוּלִין שֶׁלְּמַטָּן נַעֲשׂוּ חֵרְשִׁין. וְהָא רִבִּי לָעְזָר אָמַר עַל דְּרַבָּנִין חוּלִין שֶׁלְּמַטָּן נַעֲשׂוּ חֵרְשִׁין. מַה בֵּין רִבִּי לִיעֶזֶר וְרַבָּנִין. חוֹמֶר הוּא בִסְאָה שֶׁעָלַת מִתּוֹךְ מֵאָה אוֹ אֵינוֹ אֶלָּא קַל אָמַר כַּיי דְאָמַר רִבִּי סְאָה שֶׁל תְּרוּמָה שֶׁנָּפְלָה לְמֵאָה חוּלִין כָּל־שֶׁהֵן מְבַטְּלִין אוֹתָהּ.

Halakhah 6: Rebbi Yose ben Ḥanina said, only if it fell into five places, but if it fell into one place, even Rebbi Eliezer agrees. Rebbi Joḥanan said, even if all fell into one place, there is disagreement[83]. Ḥilfai said on that of Rebbi Eliezer, the lower profane produce becomes inert[84]. But Rebbi Eleazar also said, the lower profane produce becomes inert. What is the difference between Rebbi Eliezer and the rabbis[85]? Is one more restrictive with a lifted *seah* out of 100[86] or is one more lenient, following what Rebbi Joḥanan said, if a *seah* of heave fell into 100 of profane produce, anything will make it insignificant[87]?

83 In the opinion of R. Yose ben Ḥanina, R. Eliezer agrees in principle with the Sages that the heave in the lifted grain should be counted only in proportion but he thinks that if heave fell in several separate batches each batch needs separate 100-fold profane grain lifting whereas the Sages think that the heave is to be considered as evenly distributed through the entire *dema'* grain. R. Joḥanan disagrees and holds that *dema'* follows the rules of heave as far as consumption is concerned and, therefore, the lifted grain

should be considered all heave.

84 R. Eliezer agrees in principle with the Sages that the heave in the lifted grain should be counted only in proportion but he holds that the heave part of the lifted grain is genuine heave with all its restrictions; the rest is just ballast and disregarded.

85 If one combines Ḥilfai's interpretation of R. Eliezer and R. Eleazar's interpretation of the Sages, one fails to see the difference between them.

86 R. Eliezer holds that the heave which fell is the heave which was lifted (cf. Note 27); he can state this only if he considers the remainder of the grain as inert.

87 For the Sages, this is also a position accepted by R. Eleazar, cf. Note 82. One sees that there is a big difference between R. Eliezer and the Sages, even if R. Eleazar accepts Ḥilfai's argument.

(fol. 43b) **משנה ז**: סְאָה תְרוּמָה שֶׁנָּפְלָה לְמֵאָה הִגְבִּיהָהּ וְנָפְלָה אַחֶרֶת הֲרֵי זוֹ מוּתֶּרֶת עַד שֶׁתִּרְבֶּה תְרוּמָה לַחוּלִּין.

Mishnah 7: One *seah* of heave which fell into one hundred[72], was taken out, and another one fell in: the latter is permitted until there will be more heave than profane[88].

88 The process of lifting can be repeated until one would have more heave than profane produce if each time only profane matter would have been taken out and all heave stayed in. In that case, the mixture will be forbidden by biblical law as soon as there is not more profane than heave matter. The Tanna of the Mishnah assumes that it is impossible that in all these processes only heave be lifted; even in the worst case some profane grain will be lifted. Therefore, he does not have to say "permitted as long as the volume of heave is less than that of profane grain." The grain is permitted unless the amount of heave which fell in is larger than half the original amount of profane grain. This is the position of R. Simson and R. Abraham ben David.

Maimonides's explanation is difficult to understand. He permits the mixture if at most 100 times 1 *seah* fell into the produce and was lifted. He gives no explanation. R. Joseph Caro explains that in the previous Mishnaiot, when the Sages assert that the heave counted in the remaining produce is computed proportionally, they assume that there was perfect mixing of heave and profane before the excess *seah* was lifted. But in that case, if t_i, h_i are the amounts of heave and profane in the mixture after *i seah* fell in and were lifted,

$$h_i = 100(100/101)^i$$

and $h_i < 50$ for integer $i > 69$. {The solution of $100(100/101)^i = 50$ is $i = 69.66\ldots$} Since, by definition, $t_i + h_i = 100$, by the explanation of R. Joseph Caro, the process can be repeated only 69 times and RR. Simson and Abraham ben David would agree.

(fol. 43d) **הלכה ז**: תַּנֵּי רָבַת הַתְּרוּמָה נַעֲשָׂה כְמַרְבֶּה מֵזִיד. וְהָא תַנִּינָן הָיוּ בוֹ אַרְבָּעִים סְאָה נָתַן סְאָה וְנָטַל סְאָה כָּשֵׁר. עַד הֵיכָן. רִבִּי אִיסִּי בְשֵׁם רִבִּי מָנָא בַּר תַּנְחוּם רִבִּי אַבָּהוּ בְּשֵׁם רִבִּי יוֹחָנָן עַד רוּבּוֹ שֶׁל מִקְוֶה. וְכָא אַתְּ אָמַר הָכֵין. תַּמָּן הָיָה רוֹב וְאַתְּ מַרְבֶּה עָלָיו וְהוּא כָשֵׁר. בְּרַם הָכָא כָּל־סְאָה וּסְאָה צְרִיכָה מֵאָה סְאָה. אָמַר רִבִּי יוֹסֵי זֹאת אוֹמֶרֶת דָּבָר שֶׁהוּא בָטֵל דְּבַר תּוֹרָה מְעוֹרֵר אֶת מִינוֹ לֵיאָסֵר.

Halakha 7: It was stated: If the heave became a plurality it is as if he had added intentionally[89]. But did we not state[90]: "If it contained 40 *seah*, he added a *seah* and removed a *seah*, it is in order." How far? Rebbi Assi in the name of Rebbi Mana bar Tanḥum[91], Rebbi Abbahu in the name of Rebbi Joḥanan, up to the larger part of the *miqweh*[92]. And here you say so? There it was a plurality, you add to it and it is in order. But here, every single *seah* needs 100 *seah*. Rebbi Yose said, this means that anything becoming insignificant by biblical law is activated by its own kind to become forbidden[93].

89 It cannot be lifted even in a very large amount of profane produce, as stated in Mishnah 9. If so much heave can fall into profane food it shows that the negligence borders on intentional misconduct.

90 Mishnah *Miqwaot* 7:2. The expression "he added" shows that a religious bath (*miqweh*) which contains the required amount (40 *seah*) of natural water, additional water may intentionally be added from vessels without impairing the validity of the bath.

91 An Amora in Tyre between the second and third generation of Galilean authorities.

92 In the Babli (*Yebamot* 82b), it is made clear that in a *miqweh* of exactly 40 *seah*, exactly 20 *seah* can be added and removed. This also seems to be the meaning here.

93 Since 40 *seah* in a *miqweh* permit the addition of water from a vessel, once the water enters the *miqweh* its quality as poured from a vessel becomes insignificant and it becomes like natural (spring or rain) water. But if the added and removed quantities become more than 20 *seah*, the *miqweh* becomes forbidden. This proves that the insignificance of the invalid water is conditional. The principle stated here is accepted in both Talmudim.

(fol. 43b) **משנה ח**: סְאָה תְרוּמָה שֶׁנָּפְלָה לְמֵאָה וְלֹא הִסְפִּיק לְהַגְבִּיהָהּ עַד שֶׁנָּפְלָה אַחֶרֶת הֲרֵי זוֹ אֲסוּרָה וְרִבִּי שִׁמְעוֹן מַתִּיר.

Mishnah 8: A *seah* of heave fell into 100 [profane] and before he managed to lift it, another one fell in: that is forbidden but Rebbi Simeon permits it.

(fol. 43d) **הלכה ח**: רִבִּי שִׁמְעוֹן אוֹמֵר יְדִיעָתָהּ מְקַדְּשָׁתָהּ. וְרַבָּנִין אָמְרִין הֲרָמָתָהּ מְקַדְּשָׁתָהּ.

Halakhah 8: Rebbi Simeon says, knowledge of it sanctifies; but the rabbis say, its lifting sanctifies it[93].

93 R. Simeon in general accepts the possibility of an action as substitute for the action. Therefore, the first heave is considered already lifted and the

second one fell into 100 *seah* of profane food. R. Simeon must agree that it is forbidden if the second *seah* of heave fell in before the accident of the first *seah* was known to the owner. A Tosephta explains this in the name of R. Eleazar ben R. Simeon (6:5).

Maimonides and the early German authorities (R. Eliezer ben Natan, R. Eliezer ben Joel) decide that R. Eleazar ben R. Simeon's position is intermediary between his father's and that of the rabbis, in opposition to the Yerushalmi (Maimonides, *Terumot* 13:6). Their basis is the Babli (*Šabbat* 142a) which declares that the reason of R. Simeon is that the first batch became insignificant in 100 times its volume when it fell in, so that the second batch fell into 101 units of profane food. This is in direct opposition to the Yerushalmi (R. S. Adani). Most commentators identify the position of R. Eleazar ben R. Simeon with that of the rabbis, cf. *Tosefta ki-Fshuṭah Zeraïm* p. 384; this does not explain why Maimonides in his Commentary refers to the Tosephta rather than the Talmud.

תַּנֵּי סְאָה תְרוּמָה שֶׁנָּפְלָה לְמֵאָה אוֹמֵר לַכֹּהֵן וְלֹא דְמֵי עֵצִים אֲנִי חַייָב לָךְ טוֹל לָךְ דְּמֵי עֵצֶיךָ. וְהוּא אוֹמֵר לוֹ וְכִי סְאָה תְרוּמָה שֶׁנָּפְלָה לְפָחוֹת מִמֵּאָה שֶׁמָּא אֵינָהּ מְדַמֶּעֶת אֶת הַכְּרִי. וְעֵצִים מְדַמְּעִין אֶת הַכְּרִי. וְלֹא סוֹפָךְ מִיתְנִינֵיהּ לְכֹהֵן חוֹרָן וְהוּא נוֹתֵן לוֹ דְמֵי עֵצִים. מַאי כְדוֹן נוֹתֵן לוֹ דְמֵי עֵצִים וְהַשְּׁאָר יַחֲלוֹקוּ. חַד בַּר נַשׁ אַפִּיל שְׂעוֹרִין גּוֹ חִטִּין. אֲתָא עוּבְדָא קוֹמֵי רִבִּי יוּדָה בַּר שָׁלוֹם וְאָמַר יִתֵּן לוֹ דְמֵי שְׂעוֹרִין. וְהַשְּׁאָר יַחֲלוֹקוּ.

It was stated: One *seah* of heave[94] that fell into one hundred, he says to the Cohen, am I not obligated to you for the value of firewood? Take the value of the firewood[95]! But he answers him, does a *seah* of heave which fell into less than 100 not make the entire heave *dema'*? Does firewood create *dema'*? Does he not in the end have to give it to another Cohen[96] who will pay him for the value of the fuel? How is that? He gives him the value of the fuel and they should split the rest[97]. A person spilled barley into wheat. The case came before Rebbi Jehudah bar Shalom[98] who said, let him pay the price of barley; they should split the rest[99].

94 This must be impure heave, as shown by the sequel.

95 It seems, as noted by R. Moses Margalit, that the impure heave was the property of a Cohen when it accidentally fell into less than 100 units heave. (It cannot be exactly 100 units as in the *baraita*, since then the heave would have to be lifted and eaten dry, as stated before.) Since impure heave is only usable as fuel, it may be sold to a Cohen as fuel.

96 Since nothing else can be done with impure *dema'*.

97 The rest over and above the one *seah*, which the owner may give to any Cohen of his choice for payment of its value as fuel.

98 An Amora of the fifth generation, mostly quoted in aggadic matters.

99 Here the situation is different; this really belongs to tractate *Baba Qamma* since the damage is visible. If A hurts B by pouring some of his barley into B's wheat, A has to pay B the difference between the going rates for wheat and barley for B's grain. If later somehow the rate for barley should rise, the profit has to be split between them since A and B are now joint owners of the grain.

(fol. 43b) **משנה ט**: סְאָה תְרוּמָה שֶׁנָּפְלָה לְמֵאָה וּטְחָנָן וּפָחֲתוּ כְּשֵׁם שֶׁפָּחֲתוּ הַחוּלִין כֵּן פָּחֲתָה הַתְּרוּמָה וּמוּתָּר. סְאָה תְרוּמָה שֶׁנָּפְלָה לְפָחוֹת מִמֵּאָה וּטְחָנָן וְהוֹתִירוּ כְּשֵׁם שֶׁהוֹתִירוּ הַחוּלִין כֵּן הוֹתִירָה הַתְּרוּמָה וְאָסוּר. אִם יָדוּעַ שֶׁחִיטִּין שֶׁל חוּלִין יָפוֹת מִשֶּׁל תְּרוּמָה מוּתָּר. סְאָה תְרוּמָה שֶׁנָּפְלָה לְפָחוֹת מִמֵּאָה וְאַחַר כָּךְ נָפְלוּ שָׁם חוּלִין אִם שׁוֹגֵג מוּתָּר אִם מֵזִיד אָסוּר.

Mishnah 9: A *seah* of heave which fell into 100, if he milled it and it lost volume, in proportion to what the profane lost, the heave lost, and it is permitted[100]. A *seah* of heave which fell into less than 100, if he milled it and it increased in volume, in proportion to the increase of the profane is the increase of heave, and it is forbidden. If it is known that the profane wheat was of better quality[101] than the heave, it might be permitted. If a *seah* of heave fell into less than 100 and more profane fell into it later, if it was in error, it is permitted, if intentional, it is forbidden[102].

100 One *seah* may be lifted and the rest is permitted. In this case, differences in quality between heave and profane grain are disregarded.

101 Yielding more flour and less bran.

102 It is *dema'*.

(fol. 43d) **הלכה ט**: וְלֹא סוֹף דָּבָר שֶׁפָּחֲתָה הַתְּרוּמָה אֶלָּא אֲפִילוּ פָּחֲתוּ חוּלִין וּתְרוּמָה בְעֵינָהּ טוֹחֵן וּמַתִּיר. תַּנֵּי אֵין טִנּוּפֶת שֶׁל תְּרוּמָה מִצְטָרֶפֶת עִם תְּרוּמָה לֶאֱסוֹר עַל הַחוּלִין. אֲבָל טִנּוּפֶת שֶׁל חוּלִין מִצְטָרֶפֶת עִם הַחוּלִין לַעֲלוֹת אֶת הַתְּרוּמָה. רִבִּי בִּיבַי בָּעֵי טִינּוּפֶת שֶׁל תְּרוּמָה מָהוּ שֶׁתִּצְטָרֵף עִם הַחוּלִין לַעֲלוֹת אֶת הַתְּרוּמָה. מִן מַה דְּאָמַר רַב הוּנָא קִילְפֵּי אִיסּוּר מִצְטָרְפִין לְהֵיתֵר. הָדָא אָמְרָה טִינּוּפֶת שֶׁל תְּרוּמָה מִטְצָרֶפֶת עִם הַחוּלִין לְהַעֲלוֹת אֶת הַתְּרוּמָה. רַב הוּנָא אָמַר קִילְפֵּי אִיסּוּר מַעֲלִין אֶת הַהֵיתֵר. סְאָה תְרוּמָה שֶׁנָּפְלָה לְמֵאָה אֵין אַתָּה מוֹצִיא זְוָנִין טִינּוּפֶת שֶׁבָּהּ. לְפָחוֹת מִמֵּאָה אַתָּה מוֹצִיא זְוָנִין שֶׁבָּהּ. וְכֵן לוֹג יַיִן צָלוּל שֶׁנָּפַל לְמֵאָה לוֹג יַיִן עָכוּר אֵין אַתְּ מוֹצִיא שְׁמָרִין שֶׁבָּהּ. לוֹג יַיִן עָכוּר שֶׁנָּפַל לְמֵאָה לוֹג יַיִן צָלוּל אַתְּ מוֹצִיא שְׁמָרִין שֶׁבָּהּ.

[103]Not only if the heave lost volume but even if only the profane grain lost but the heave remains as it was, he mills and permits. It was stated: "The waste of heave does not combine with heave to forbid the profane, but the waste of profane combines with the profane to lift the heave[104]." Rebbi Vivian asked: Does the waste of heave combine with profane to lift the heave? Since Rav Huna said, the husks of what is forbidden combine to permit[105], that means waste of heave combines with profane to lift the heave[106]. Rav Huna said, the shells of what is forbidden lift what is permitted. A *seah* of heave which fell into 100, one does not remove *zewanin*[107] in it, into less than 100, one does remove the *zewanin*

in it. Similarly, if one *log* of clear wine[108] fell into 100 *log* of cloudy wine, one would not remove the latter's dregs; if one *log* of cloudy wine fell into 100 *log* of clear wine, one would remove the former's dregs.

103 The entire paragraph is in *Nazir* 6:10 (fol. 55c), part of it in *Orlah* 1:4 (fol. 61b).

104 If after milling, the heave without its waste would be $^1/_{100}$ of the milled profane grain plus its waste, heave could be lifted.

105 The statement of R. Huna refers to *orlah*, fruits in the first three years of a tree's life, which are forbidden for any use and, if they disappear among other fruits, in general make everything forbidden for any use unless the permitted part are 200 times more than the forbidden. Rab Huna instructs to count in the 200 all husks, both from profane as from *orlah* fruit.

106 If after milling, the heave without its waste would be 1% of the remainder, heave can be lifted.

107 *Kilaim* 1:1, Note 1.

108 Of heave.

תַּנֵּי אַף טוֹחֵן הוּא בַּתְּחִילָּה וּמַתִּיר. מַתְנִיתָא דְּרִבִּי יוֹסֵי דְּרִבִּי יוֹסֵי אָמַר אַף יִתְכַּוֵּין וְיִלְקוֹט וְיַעֲלֶה בְאֶחָד וּמָאתַיִם. אָמַר רִבִּי זְעִירָא שֶׁכֵּן דֶּרֶךְ הַכֹּהֲנִים לִהְיוֹת טוֹחֲנִין מְדוּמָּע בְּבָתֵּיהֶן. מַה נְפַק מִבֵּינֵיהוֹן. כִּלְאֵי הַכֶּרֶם עַל דַּעְתֵּיהּ דְּרִבִּי יוֹסֵי טוֹחֵן וּמַתִּיר. עַל דַּעְתְּהוֹן דְּרַבָּנִין אֵינוֹ טוֹחֵן וּמַתִּיר.

It was stated: "One may mill from the start to permit[109]." The *baraita* is Rebbi Yose's, since "Rebbi Yose said, one may collect to lift one in two hundred"[110]. Rebbi Zeïra said[111], Cohanim are used to mill *dema'* in their houses. What is the difference between them? *Kilaim* in a vineyard. In the opinion of Rebbi Yose, one mills to permit; in the opinion of the rabbis, one may not mill to permit.

109 If one has *dema'* and after milling, following the rule of Note 106, it would be possible to lift the heave, one tells the owner to go ahead and mill even though the Mishnah is formulated only as a statement after the fact, if the owner milled it and now comes to ask a rabbinic authority on how to proceed.

110 Mishnah *Orlah* 1:6. Since this is

a minority opinion, it cannot be practice to be followed.

111 In *Orlah* 1:5, the statement is more complete: "R. Zeïra said, it is the opinion of everybody since Cohanim are used to mill *dema'* in their houses." Since this is a required process, one cannot object to its use.

רִבִּי אַבָּהוּ בְּשֵׁם רִבִּי יוֹחָנָן כָּל־הָאִיסּוּרִין שֶׁרִיבָּה עֲלֵיהֶן בְּשׁוֹגֵג מוּתָּר וּבְמֵזִיד אָסוּר. וְלֹא מַתְנִיתָא הִיא בְּשׁוֹגֵג מוּתָּר וּבְמֵזִיד אָסוּר. מַתְנִיתָא בִּתְרוּמָה אָתָה מֵימַר לָךְ אֲפִילוּ שְׁאָר כָּל־הַדְּבָרִים.

Rebbi Abbahu in the name of Rebbi Johanan: All forbidden things[112], if one added against them in error, it is permitted, intentionally it is forbidden. Is that not the Mishnah: "if it was in error, it is permitted, if intentional, it is forbidden"? The Mishnah is about heave, he comes to tell you about all other things.

112 Which can become insignificant in an appropriate plurality (60, 100, 200 times, as the case may be).

רִבִּי אָחָא בְּשֵׁם רִבִּי יוֹנָתָן כְּשֵׁם שֶׁמִּצְוָה לוֹמַר עַל דָּבָר שֶׁהוּא נַעֲשֶׂה. כָּךְ מִצְוָה שֶׁלֹּא לוֹמַר עַל דָּבָר שֶׁאֵינוֹ נַעֲשֶׂה. אָמַר רִבִּי לָעְזָר כְּשֵׁם שֶׁאָסוּר לְטַהֵר אֶת הַטָּמֵא כָּךְ אָסוּר לְטַמֵּא אֶת הַטָּהוֹר. אָמַר רִבִּי אַבָּא בַּר יַעֲקֹב בְּשֵׁם רִבִּי יוֹחָנָן אִם בָּאַת הֲלָכָה תַחַת יָדְךָ וְאֵי אַתָּה יוֹדֵעַ אִם לִתְלוֹת אִם לִשְׂרוֹף. לְעוֹלָם הֲוֵי רָץ אַחַר הַשְּׂרֵיפָה יוֹתֵר מִן הַתְּלִייָה. שֶׁאֵין לְךָ חָבִיב בַּתּוֹרָה יוֹתֵר מִפָּרִים הַנִּשְׂרָפִים וּשְׂעִירִים הַנִּשְׂרָפִים וְהֵן בִּשְׂרֵיפָה. רִבִּי יוֹסֵי בָּעֵי דָּנִין דָּבָר שֶׁאֵין מִצְוָתוֹ לְכֵן מִדָּבָר שֶׁמִּצְוָתוֹ לְכֵן.

Rebbi Aḥa in the name of Rebbi Jonathan: Just as one has a duty to instruct about actions that should be done, so one has a duty to instruct about actions that should not be done. Rebbi Eleazar said, just as it is forbidden to declare the impure as pure, so it is forbidden to declare the pure as impure. Rebbi Abba bar Jacob said in the name of Rebbi Johanan: If a practical case comes before you and you do not know whether to suspend or to burn[113], always try to burn rather than to suspend since there is nothing in the Torah more distinguished than burned bulls and burned rams, and they are burned[114]. Rebbi Yose wondered, is it possible to infer from something whose commandment is in this for something whose commandment is not so[115]?

113 In order *Ṭahorot*, the rule is that heave impure by biblical standards must be burned but heave only impure by rabbinic standards must be "suspended", *viz*, one must leave it to rot until it is no longer food and, therefore, pure according to all standards.

114 In *Lev*. 10:18 it is established as a general rule that any sacrifice whose blood was brought into the sanctuary, to be sprinkled either on the golden altar or before the ark, must be completely burned.

115 The simile is not convincing; one should not rush to treat rabbinic impurity as biblical.

האוכל תרומה שוגג פרק ששי

(fol. 43d) **משנה א:** הָאוֹכֵל תְּרוּמָה שׁוֹגֵג מְשַׁלֵּם קֶרֶן וְחוֹמֶשׁ אֶחָד הָאוֹכֵל וְאֶחָד הַשּׁוֹתֶה וְאֶחָד הַסָּךְ אֶחָד תְּרוּמָה טְהוֹרָה וְאֶחָד תְּרוּמָה טְמֵאָה מְשַׁלֵּם חוֹמֶשׁ וְחוֹמֶשׁ חוּמְשָׁא אֵינוֹ מְשַׁלֵּם תְּרוּמָה אֶלָּא חוּלִין מְתוּקָּנִין וְהֵן נַעֲשִׂין תְּרוּמָה. וְהַתַּשְׁלוּמִין תְּרוּמָה. אִם רָצָה הַכֹּהֵן לִמְחוֹל אֵינוֹ מוֹחֵל.

Mishnah 1: If somebody eats heave in error, he pays principal and fifth[1]; whether he eats, drinks, or anoints[2], whether the heave be pure or impure, he pays. The fifth and the fifth of the fifths[3] he does not pay in heave but in totally profane food which is turned into heave. All payments become heave. Although the Cohen may want to forgive this, he has no right to forgive.

1 *Lev.* 22:14: "Anybody who ate sanctified food in error must add its fifth to it and give the holy food to the Cohen." In the Yerushalmi (6:1) and the *Sifra* [*Wayyiqra pereq* 20(8); *Emor pereq* 6(4)], *its fifth* is interpreted to mean that the addition must be one fifth of the restitution, or one fourth of the principal. In the Babli (*Baba Meẓi'a* 54a) this is the opinion of R. Oshaia, whereas R. Jonathan refers *its fifth* to the principal. The latter opinion is never found in the Yerushalmi. There will be a discussion in the Halakhah whether the expression "give the holy food to the Cohen" means that the designation as reparation makes holy or only its delivery.

2 Since the food enters his body, whether through the mouth or through the skin.

3 If he dedicated the fifth and then inadvertently ate this fifth, since it had become heave as stated in the next sentence, it is subject to the rule of the fifth and he must restitute both the fifth and an additional fifth ($^1/_{16}$ of the original amount.)

(fol. 44a) **הלכה א**: הָאוֹכֵל תְּרוּמָה שׁוֹגֵג כו'. כְּתִיב וְאִישׁ כִּי יֹאכַל קוֹדֶשׁ בִּשְׁגָגָה וְיָסַף חֲמִישִׁיתוֹ. שֶׁיְּהֵא הוּא וְחוּמְשׁוֹ חֲמִשָּׁה.

Halakhah 1: "If somebody eats heave in error," etc. It is written (*Lev.* 22:14): "Anybody who ate sanctified food in error must add its fifth." That it and its fifth make five[4].

4 Cf. Note 1. It is clear that the main inference is from the word עליו not quoted here.

וְלֹא כֵן אָמַר רִבִּי אַבָּהוּ בְּשֵׁם רִבִּי יוֹחָנָן שׁוֹגֵג בְּחֵלֶב מֵזִיד בְּקָרְבָּן מַתְרִין בּוֹ וְלוֹקֶה וּמֵבִיא קָרְבָּן. וְאֵמוֹר אַף הָכָא מֵזִיד בִּתְרוּמָה וְשׁוֹגֵג בְּחוֹמֶשׁ יַתְרוּ בוֹ וְיִלְקֶה וְיָבִיא חוֹמֶשׁ. אָמַר רִבִּי זְעִירָא גְּזֵירַת הַכָּתוּב הוּא. וְאִישׁ כִּי יֹאכַל קוֹדֶשׁ בִּשְׁגָגָה שֶׁתְּהֵא כָּל־אֲכִילָתוֹ בִשְׁגָגָה. כְּמֵזִיד בִּסְפֵיקוֹ כְּשׁוֹגֵג בְּוַדָּאוֹ. אָמַר רִבִּי יוֹסֵי הָדָא אָמְרָה הַשָּׁב לוֹ מִידִיעָתוֹ. חַיָּב עַל שִׁגְגָתָהּ.

Did not Rabbi Abbahu say in the name of Rebbi Joḥanan[5]: If he is in error about fat but intentional about a sacrifice, he can be warned, is whipped, and brings a sacrifice[6]. Say also here, if he has intention about heave but is inadvertent about the fifth, one should warn him and he should be whipped and bring a fifth[7]. Rebbi Zeïra said, it is a decision of the verse, "if somebody eats heave in error," that all his eating should be in error[8]. If he is intentional in doubt it is as if he is unintentional in his certainty[9]. Rebbi Yose said, this means that if somebody forgot after he knew, he is guilty unintentionally[10].

5 This is the attribution in all parallels in the Yerushalmi: *Šabbat* 11:5 (13b), *Baba Qamma* 7:2 (5d). *Šebuot* 3:1 (34b), *Ketubot* 3:1 (27c), except *Terumot* 7:1 (44c) in the name of R. Simeon ben Laqish, and here in the Rome ms. which reads תני. The parallel discussion in the Babli is *Šabbat* 69a.

6 Unintentional deadly sins are atoned for, in general, by sacrifices or,

as in the case of heave, by specified payments. Intentional sins cannot simply be atoned for; the guilt is eliminated either by punishment through a criminal court or by Divine justice (assuming the intentional sinner does not sincerely repent, otherwise repentance and the Day of Atonement will induce Divine mercy to wipe the slate clean.)

As explained in *Kilaim* Chapter 8, Note 9, a criminal court can impose biblical sanctions only if criminal intent is proven by two witnesses. This means that two witnesses testify that the alleged criminal was warned about the criminality of the act he seems intent to commit. The situation here is that the perpetrator knew that eating fat (those fatty parts of domesticated animals which in a sacrifice have to be burned on the altar) was forbidden but did not know what the punishment would be. In the Babli, R. Joḥanan holds that if he knew that eating fat was forbidden but not that it was a deadly sin he committed an intentional sin but an unintentional deadly sin, just as described here by R. Abbahu. If duly warned, he can be punished for eating fat as a misdemeanor but in addition he has to bring a sacrifice for the aspect of deadly sin of which he was oblivious, as asserted here also. R. Simeon ben Laqish does not permit a sacrifice unless the person was ignorant of the fact that the act was punishable.

7 Why is eating heave by an unauthorized person, which also is a deadly sin, not treated similarly, with the payment of the fifth being the equivalent of a sacrifice?

8 He must not have known at all that his eating was punishable.

9 R. Zeïra admits only two cases, if he intended to eat but was not sure that he ate heave, or if he ate certain heave but was oblivious of this fact all the time he was eating.

10 This is described as the quintessential unintentional sin; *Lev.* 5:4: "Or a person who swears, by expression of his lips, to his advantage or detriment, about anything a person is apt to swear, *then he forgot*, but later remembered that he had incurred guilt about one of these."

אָמַר אֲנִי פוֹרֵשׁ מִכְּזַיִת וְאֵינִי פוֹרֵשׁ מִכַּחֲצִי זַיִת. אָמַר רִבִּי בּוּן בַּר חִייָה נַעֲשֶׂה כְּאוֹכֵל חֲצִי זַיִת בְּשׁוֹגֵג וַחֲצִיי זַיִת בְּמֵזִיד. וְאִין יִסְבּוֹר רִבִּי בּוּן בַּר חִייָה כְּרִבִּי שִׁמְעוֹן בֶּן לָקִישׁ דְּרִבִּי שִׁמְעוֹן בֶּן לָקִישׁ אָמַר אָכַל חֲצִי זַיִת בְּהֶעֱלֵם אֶחָד פָּטוּר.

וְהָכָא אָכַל שְׁנֵי חֲצָאֵי זֵיתִין וְחָסֵר כָּל־שֶׁהוּא פָּטוּר. מוֹדֵי רִבִּי שִׁמְעוֹן בֶּן לָקִישׁ בְּאִסּוּרֵי הֲנָיָה וּמוֹדֵי רִבִּי שִׁמְעוֹן בֶּן לָקִישׁ בְּיוֹם הַכִּפּוּרִים וּמוֹדֵי רִבִּי שִׁמְעוֹן בֶּן לָקִישׁ בְּעָתִיד לְהַשְׁלִים.

If somebody said, I would not touch the volume of an olive, but I will touch half the volume of an olive, Rebbi Abun bar Ḥiyya said, he is like a person who eats half the volume of an olive unintentionally and half the volume of an olive intentionally[11]. Would Rebbi Abun bar Ḥiyya hold with Rebbi Simeon ben Laqish since Rebbi Simeon ben Laqish said, if he ate half the volume of an olive during one forgetting spell[12], he is free from punishment. So here, if he ate two times half the volume of an olive minus something, he is free from punishment. Rebbi Simeon ben Laqish agrees in the case of prohibitions of usufruct[13], Rebbi Simeon ben Laqish agrees in the case of the Day of Atonement[14], Rebbi Simeon ben Laqish agrees in case he would complete it in the future[15].

11 Everybody agrees that for any prohibition regarding solid foods, no punishment by an earthly court can be imposed if the quantity consumed was less than the volume of an olive. In Babli *Yoma* 73b, R. Simeon ben Laqish states that less than the established minimum in any case is not forbidden by the Torah, but R. Joḥanan holds that everything forbidden is forbidden in any quantity; it simply cannot be prosecuted if the quantity is minimal. In *Šabbat* 12:6 (13d), this position is ascribed to Rabban Gamliel and the question about two olive halves is not answered.

12 As far as sacrifices in atonement of unintentional sins are concerned, acts committed during separate forgetting spells cannot be combined if half a measure is not sinful; cf. *Šabbat* 12:6 (13:d), Babli *Šabbat* 105a.

13 If *all* usufruct is forbidden, such as grain growing in a vineyard or food from an idolatrous sacrifice, half a measure must be forbidden because its use would be usufruct.

14 In the Babli, R. Simeon ben Laqish only holds that less than a measure, in that case less than the volume of an average dried fig, is forbidden by rabbinic decree. This con

tradicts the Yerushalmi since a rabbinic prohibition can never lead to an obligatory sacrifice.

15 The forbidden material is activated by its own kind; cf. end of Halakhah 5:7.

רִבִּי אַבָּהוּ בְשֵׁם רִבִּי יוֹחָנָן הַמְגַמֵּעַ חוֹמֶץ שֶׁל תְּרוּמָה לוֹקֶה. רִבִּי אַבָּהוּ בְשֵׁם רִבִּי יוֹחָנָן הַכּוֹסֵס חִיטָּה שֶׁל תְּרוּמָה לוֹקֶה. תַּנֵּי הַכּוֹסֵס אֶת הַחִיטָּה שֶׁל תְּרוּמָה מְשַׁלֵּם אֶת הַקֶּרֶן וְאֵינוֹ מְשַׁלֵּם אֶת הַחוֹמֶשׁ. רִבִּי אוֹמֵר אֲנִי אוֹמֵר שֶׁמְּשַׁלֵּם קֶרֶן וְחוֹמֶשׁ. רִבִּי יִרְמְיָה בְּשֵׁם רִבִּי אִימִּי מוֹדִין חֲכָמִים לְרִבִּי בִּמְגַמֵּעַ חוֹמֶץ שֶׁל תְּרוּמָה אַחַר טִיבְלוֹ שֶׁמְּשַׁלֵּם קֶרֶן וְחוֹמֶשׁ שֶׁהַחוֹמֶץ מְיַשֵּׁב אֶת הַנֶּפֶשׁ.

Rebbi Abbahu in the name of Rebbi Johanan[16]: He who swallows heave vinegar is whipped[17]. Rebbi Abbahu in the name of Rebbi Johanan: He who chews a wheat grain of heave is whipped. It was stated: He who chews a wheat grain of heave pays the principal but not the fifth; Rebbi says, I am saying that he pays principal and fifth[18]. Rebbi Jeremiah in the name of Rebbi Ammi: The Sages agree with Rebbi about him who swallows heave vinegar after such *ṭevel*, that he pays principal and fifth because vinegar refreshes the spirit[19].

16 This paragraph is also in *Šabbat* 14:4 (14d), *Yoma* 8:3 (45a); cf. Babli *Yoma* 80b-81a. In the parallels, the statement about payment of principal only is asserted both for vinegar and a wheat grain.

17 If he did it after due warning by two witnesses. The statement implies that drinking a fluid which most people do not use is still called drinking in the legal sense.

18 In the Babli, a parallel statement by R. Jeremiah in the name of R. Johanan speaks about chewing raw barley grains. This is considered a health hazard and therefore not included in the notion of eating in the sense of *Lev.* 22:14. Therefore, one has to pay for the value of what he took, as anybody must who took another's property illegally, since even his own heave is not his property but a Cohen's. The *baraita* here deals with raw wheat kernels which are not a health hazard; it is simply asserted that the fifth applies only to what is considered

eating by a majority of the population.

19 If the person first drank *ṭevel* vinegar, which also is sinful but not subject to the fifth, and then added some more heave vinegar, that makes vinegar food as a folk medicine.

תַּנֵּי אָכַל תְּרוּמָה טְמֵאָה מְשַׁלֵּם חוּלִין טְהוֹרִין וְאִם שִׁלֵּם חוּלִין טְמֵאִין יָצָא. רִבִּי נָתָן אוֹמֵר סוּמָּכוֹס אוֹמֵר שׁוֹגֵג מַה שֶּׁעָשָׂה עָשׂוּי מֵזִיד לֹא עָשָׂה כְלוּם. תַּמָּן תַּנִּינָן אֵין תּוֹרְמִין מִן הַטָּמֵא עַל הַטָּהוֹר. תַּנֵּי בְשֵׁם רִבִּי יוֹסֵי אִם תָּרַם מִן הַטָּמֵא עַל הַטָּהוֹר בֵּין בְּשׁוֹגֵג בֵּין בְּמֵזִיד מַה שֶּׁעָשָׂה עָשׂוּי. אַתְיָא דִיחִידָאָה דְהָכָא כִּסְתָמָא דְתַמָּן וִיחִידָאָה דְתַמָּן כִּסְתָמָא דְהָכָא.

It was stated[20]: If someone ate impure heave, he has to pay in pure profane food, but if he paid in impure profane, he discharged his obligation. Rebbi Nathan says, Symmachos says, if inadvertently, what he did is done, intentionally, he did not do anything[21]. There, we have stated[22]: "One does not give heave from impure produce for pure." It was stated in the name of Rebbi Yose[23], "if he gave heave from impure produce for pure, whether inadvertently or intentionally, what he did is done." It turns out that the single opinion[24] here is like the anonymous one there, and the single there like the anonymous here.

20 The same statement also in Halakhah 7:1 (44c), *Ketubot* 3:1 (27b). In the Babli (*Yebamot* 90a, *Giṭṭin* 54a) the text is quoted in somewhat enlarged form but rejected (since impure heave is paid for as if it were fuel for principal and fifth, cf. Halakhah 5:8, Tosephta 7:2) and reformulated to speak of pure heave; that changed text is in Tosephta 7:7.

21 All traditions of Symmachos are R. Meïr's. The invalidation of payment with impure produce is a fine imposed by the court. Since the Babli accepts R. Meïr's decrees as a matter of principle, they have to reformulate the *baraita* as speaking of pure heave, inapplicable today. These decrees mostly are rejected as minority opinions in the Yerushalmi; there is no need for reformulation.

22 Mishnah 2:2.

23 Tosephta 3:19.

24 Symmachos (R. Meïr); the single

opinion there is R. Yose. Since the subjects are different, there is no contradiction involved.

הֵיךְ עֲבִידָא רִבִּי זְעִירָא בְשֵׁם רִבִּי חֲנִינָה תַּשְׁלוּמֵי תְרוּמָה הֲרֵי הֵן כִּתְרוּמָה לְכָל־דָּבָר אֶלָּא שֶׁגִּידּוּלֵיהֶן חוּלִין. גִּידּוּלֵי תְרוּמָה הֲרֵי הֵן כְּחוּלִין לְכָל־דָּבָר אֶלָּא שֶׁאֲסוּרִין לְזָרִים. אָמַר רִבִּי יוֹסֵי וַאֲנָן תַּנִּינָן תַּרְתֵּיהוֹן תַּשְׁלוּמִין תְּרוּמָה הֲרֵי הֵן כִּתְרוּמָה לְכָל־דָּבָר דְּתַנִּינָן אֵינוֹ מְשַׁלֵּם תְּרוּמָה אֶלָּא חוּלִין מְתוּקָּנִין וְהֵן נַעֲשִׂין תְּרוּמָה. אֶלָּא שֶׁגִּידּוּלֵיהֶן חוּלִין דְּתַנִּינָן גִּידּוּלֵי תְרוּמָה הָא גִידּוּלֵי תַשְׁלוּמִין חוּלִין גִּידּוּלֵי תְרוּמָה הֲרֵי הֵן כְּחוּלִין לְכָל־דָּבָר. דְּתַנִּינָן וְחַייֶבֶת בְּלֶקֶט וּבְשִׁכְחָה וּבְפֵיאָה וַעֲנִיֵּי יִשְׂרָאֵל וַעֲנִיֵּי כֹהֲנִים מְלַקְּטִין אֶלָּא שֶׁאֲסוּרִין לְזָרִים דְּתַנִּינָן וַעֲנִיֵּי יִשְׂרָאֵל מוֹכְרִין אֶת שֶׁלָּהֶן לַכֹּהֲנִים בִּדְמֵי תְרוּמָה וְהַדָּמִין שֶׁלָּהֶן.

How is this[25]? Rebbi Zeïra in the name of Rebbi Ḥanina: The replacements of heave are like heave in every respect except that what grows from them[26] is profane. The growth from heave is like profane in every respect[27] except that it is forbidden for outsiders. Rebbi Yose said, we have stated all three: The replacements of heave are like heave in every respect as we have stated, "he does not pay in heave but in totally profane food which is turned into heave." Except that what grows from them is profane as we have stated[28], "the growth from heave," which implies that what grows from replacement is profane. The growth from heave is like profane in all respects, as we have stated, "[29]it is subject to gleanings, forgotten sheaves, and *peah*; Israel poor and Cohanim poor collect it," except that it is forbidden to outsiders as we have stated, "Israel poor sell theirs to Cohanim for the price of heave but the money is theirs[30]."

25 Here starts the discussion of the Mishnah, that the replacement for heave and the fifth become subject to the laws of heave.

26 If accidentally or inadvertently used as seeds.

27 It is not subject to any purity requirements.

28 Mishnah 9:4: "The growth from heave is heave, the growth from the growth is profane." It is clear from Mishnah 9:2 quoted next, that in most aspects, the growth from heave is like profane produce; it is like heave in that it is forbidden for non-Cohanim. Replacement for heave is not mentioned in that Mishnah.

29 Mishnah 9:2.

30 In contrast to heave which is not the private property of the owner.

תַּנֵּי תַּשְׁלוּמֵי תְרוּמָה אֵין מְשַׁלְּמִין מֵהֶן קֶרֶן וְחוֹמֶשׁ וְאֵין מְשַׁלְּמִין עֲלֵיהֶן קֶרֶן וְחוֹמֶשׁ וְאֵין חַייָבִין בְּחַלָּה וְאֵין הַיָּדַיִם פּוֹסְלוֹת בִּטְבוּל יוֹם כְּדֶרֶךְ שֶׁפּוֹסְלוֹת בְּחוּלִּין. וְאוּף רִבִּי שִׁמְעוֹן וְרִבִּי יוֹסֵי מוֹדֶה בָהּ.

It was stated: One does not use the complement of heave[31] for payment of principal and fifth and for them one does not pay principal and fifth, it is not subject to *ḥallah,* and hands and the *ṭevul yom* do not make it unusable in the way they do not make profane unusable[32]. Even Rebbi Simeon and Rebbi Yose agree with this[33].

31 As *Sefer Nir* notes, it is impossible that this *baraita* deal with replacement of heave in the sense of this Halakhah, since the Mishnah stated clearly that even "the fifth of the fifth" comes under the rules of heave. One has to assume, with R. M. Margalit, that one deals with the complement of heave, if the heave given turns out to be less than $^1/_{60}$ of the harvest, and the farmer has to add the difference; cf. Tosephta 8:2. Since heave has no biblical minimum, that complement is only rabbinic heave and is not covered by *Lev.* 22:14. But since the name of heave has been pronounced over it, it is not profane to be used for payment and cannot become *ḥallah.*

32 The syntax of this sentence is garbled. The *ṭevul yom* makes heave unusable by his touch (Chapter 5, Note 68), the same is true for unwashed hands which are always considered impure in the second degree. Profane food cannot become impure by touch of impurity of second degree in contrast to heave.

There is one opinion in *Soṭa* 5:2 (fol. 20a; Babli *Pesaḥim* 18a) that R. Aqiba asserts the possibility of third degree impurity for profane food, but it is clearly stated there that this is not acceptable practice.

33 It is not clear what the reference is. In Babli *Niddah* 46b-47a, R. Yose and R. Simeon free from *ḥallah* profane dough made to rise by heave (or *dema'*) sour dough (since the action of the sour dough shows it is not insignificant even if less than 1% in volume). Similarly, in Mishnah *Ṭevul Yom* 3:4, R. Yose and R. Simeon declare that such a dough will become unusable by the touch of a *ṭevul yom* (and presumably also of unwashed hands). In both cases, the anonymous majority declares the dough to be profane.

אִם רָצָא הַכֹּהֵן לִמְחוֹל אֵינוֹ מוֹחֵל. בְּשֶׁלֹּא הִפְרִישׁ. הִפְרִישׁ וְאַחַר כָּךְ אָכַל פְּלוּגְתָא דְּרִבִּי וּדְרִבִּי לָעְזָר בֵּי רִבִּי שִׁמְעוֹן. דְּתַנֵּי וְנָתַן לַכֹּהֵן אֶת הַקּוֹדֶשׁ מַתָּנָתוֹ מְקַדְּשָׁתוֹ מִלּוֹכַל בִּתְרוּמָה. וְאַף הַפְרָשָׁתוֹ מְקַדְּשָׁתוֹ לְחַייֵב עָלָיו חוֹמֶשׁ דִּבְרֵי רִבִּי לָעְזָר בֵּי רִבִּי שִׁמְעוֹן. וְאַף הַפְרָשָׁתוֹ מְקַדְּשָׁתוֹ לְחַייֵב עָלָיו קֶרֶן וְחוֹמֶשׁ מִלּוֹכַל בִּתְרוּמָה.

"Although the Cohen may want to forgive this, he has no right to forgive.[34]" That is, if he did not yet separate. If he separated and after that ate[35], the disagreement of Rebbi and Rebbi Eleazar ben Rebbi Simeon, as it is stated: "(*Lev.* 22:14) 'He shall give the holy food to the Cohen,' his delivery sanctifies it so that he cannot eat it because it is heave. Also the separation sanctifies it so that he should be liable for principal and fifth, the words of Rebbi Eleazar ben Rebbi Simeon. Also the separation sanctifies it so that he should be liable for principal and fifth preventing him from eating it because it is heave.[36]"

34 Quote from the Mishnah.

35 Not from the heave but the replacement of the heave.

36 The text is garbled in both mss.; the position of R. Eleazar is quoted twice, that of Rebbi is missing. It is probable that the original text was similar to *Sifra Emor Pereq* 6(7): "I could think that the separation [taking the payment out of some profane food] sanctifies it so that one would be obligated for principal and fifth; the verse says 'He shall give the holy food to the Cohen,' his delivery sanctifies it

so that one [any non-Cohen] will be liable for principal and fifth, but the separation does not sanctify it so that he should be liable for principal and fifth, the words of Rebbi Meïr. Rebbi Eleazar ben Rebbi Simeon says, also the separation sanctifies it so that he should be liable for principal and fifth."

מָחַל וְאַחַר כָּךְ אָכַל תַּפְלוּגְתָא דְרִבִּי יוֹחָנָן וְרִבִּי שִׁמְעוֹן בֶּן לָקִישׁ. דְּאִיתְפַּלְגוּן גָּזַל תְּרוּמָה מִשֶּׁל אֲבִי אִמּוֹ כֹּהֵן רִבִּי יוֹחָנָן אָמַר מְשַׁלֵּם לְשֵׁבֶט. וְרִבִּי שִׁמְעוֹן בֶּן לָקִישׁ אָמַר מְשַׁלֵּם לְעַצְמוֹ. אָמַר רִבִּי יוֹנָה כָּךְ הָיָה מֵשִׁיב רִבִּי שִׁמְעוֹן בֶּן לָקִישׁ לְרִבִּי יוֹחָנָן עַל דַּעְתָּךְ דְּתֵימַר מְשַׁלֵּם לְשֵׁבֶט. וְהָא תַנִּינָן גָּנַב תְּרוּמַת הֶקְדֵּשׁ וַאֲכָלָהּ מְשַׁלֵּם שְׁנֵי חוֹמְשִׁין וְקֶרֶן. וִישַׁלֵּם שְׁלֹשָׁה. רִבִּי יָסָא בְּשֵׁם רִבִּי יוֹחָנָן הַתּוֹרָה אָמְרָה יָצָא בוֹ יְדֵי גְזֵילָה. אָמַר לֵיהּ רִבִּי זְעִירָא לְרִבִּי אִימִּי תַּרְתֵּין מִילִּין אָמְרִין בְּשֵׁם רִבִּי יוֹחָנָן וְלֵית אַתּוּן אָמְרִין מֶהֶן אָמַר רִבִּי יוֹחָנָן יָצָא יְדֵי גְזֵילוֹ וְלֵית אַתּוּן אָמְרִין מָהוּ כְדוֹן וְנָתַן לַכֹּהֵן אֶת הַקּוֹדֶשׁ. מִכֵּיוָן שֶׁנְּתָנוֹ לוֹ יָצָא יְדֵי גְזֵילוֹ. אַתּוּן אָמְרִין בְּשֵׁם רִבִּי יוֹחָנָן בְּמָקוֹם שְׁחִיטָתָהּ שָׁם תְּהֵא שְׂרֵיפָתָהּ. וְלֵית אַתּוּן מְנַהִין מָהוּ כְדוֹן. רִבִּי לָעְזָר בְּשֵׁם רִבִּי הוֹשַׁעְיָה עַל פִּרְשָׁהּ יִשְׂרוֹף. מַה אַתְּ שְׁמַע מִינָהּ. רִבִּי יִרְמְיָה בְּשֵׁם רִבִּי אִימִּי מְקוֹם פְּרִישְׁתָהּ מְחַיְּיִם שָׁם תְּהֵא שְׂרֵיפָתָהּ.

If he [the Cohen] forgave and after that he [the Israel owner] ate, there is disagreement between Rebbi Joḥanan and Rebbi Simeon ben Laqish since they disagreed: If he robbed heave from his maternal grandfather, a Cohen, Rebbi Joḥanan said, he has to pay to the tribe, but Rebbi Simeon ben Laqish said, he pays to himself[37]. Rebbi Jonah said, Rebbi Simeon ben Laqish answered Rebbi Joḥanan thus: According to you, who says he has to pay to the tribe, did we not state: "If he stole heave of the Sanctuary, he has to pay two fifths and the principal[38]." Should he not pay three[39]? Rebbi Yasa in the name of Rebbi Joḥanan: The Torah said, it takes him out of his robbery. Rebbi Zeïra said to Rebbi Ammi: Two things you say in the name of Rebbi Joḥanan but you do not say why. Rebbi Joḥanan said, it takes him out of his robbery but you do not say why. It is so, "he shall give the holy food to the Cohen;" once he gave it, it stopped being his robbery[40]. You say in the name of Rebbi Joḥanan, at the place of its slaughter should be its burning[41]. You do not say why. Rebbi Eleazar in the name of Rebbi Hoshaia, *Num.* 19:5: "On its excrement shall be its burning." How do you understand this? Rebbi Jeremiah in the name of Rebbi Ammi: At the place of its exit from life shall be its burning[42].

37 The robber has to repay the robbery, not double the value he took as is the rule for the thief. It is assumed that the grandfather died after he forgave the grandson for the robbery and the grandson is the only heir. According to R. Joḥanan, the grandfather could not forgive and the grandson cannot inherit; therefore, the restitution has to be made to a Cohen. According the R. Simeon ben Laqish, the grandfather can forgive and the grandson can pay the principal to himself as heir, then sell the heave to a Cohen and pocket the money.

The statement is also in *Pesaḥim* 2:3 (29a).

38 Mishnah 6:4. Stealing and robbing from the Sanctuary have the same status; there is no double restitution. A fifth is required for illicit use of heave (*Lev.* 22:14) and of property of the Sanctuary (*Lev.* 5:16). The two obligations are independent of one another and computed on the same basis.

39 This is only a potentiality, not a certainty. If he denied stealing under oath, another fifth is due (Lev. 5:16). The heave can become property of the Sanctuary only if the Cohen dedicated it. Therefore, if the Cohen may forgive repayment, the thief cannot be forced to swear and there never can be three fifths. But according to R. Joḥanan, the tribe should be able to force the thief to swear in court and the Tanna should have noticed the possibility of a third fifth.

40 Since robbery and sanctity are incompatible, once it is holy it is not subject to the laws of robbery and the third fifth claimed by R. Simeon ben Laqish is not applicable.

41 The red cow whose ashes cleanse from the impurity of the dead (*Num.* 19) must be slaughtered on the stake; its carcass cannot be moved.

42 The entire statement is R. Hoshaia's in Babli *Zebaḥim* 113, in

opposition to R. Johanan who requires the carcass to be moved in case it was slaughtered at a place from which the Temple doors are not visible; cf. also *Sifry Huqqat* 124.

רִבִּי יוֹחָנָן כְּרִבִּי. רִבִּי שִׁמְעוֹן בֶּן לָקִישׁ כְּרִבִּי לָעְזָר בֵּי רִבִּי שִׁמְעוֹן. אָמַר רִבִּי בּוּן בַּר חִיָּיה וְאִין יִסְבּוֹר רִבִּי שִׁמְעוֹן בֶּן לָקִישׁ כְּרִבִּי וּבִלְבַד בְּדָבָר שֶׁהוּא זָקוּק לִיתְּנוֹ לְכֹהֵן אֲבָל בְּדָבָר שֶׁאֵינוֹ זָקוּק לִיתְּנוֹ (fol. 44b) לְכֹהֵן אוּף רִבִּי מוֹדֵי דְהִיא מַתְנִיתָא הִפְרִישׁ פִּדְיוֹן פֶּטֶר חֲמוֹר וּמֵת רִבִּי אֱלִיעֶזֶר אוֹמֵר חַיָּיבִין בְּאַחֲרָיוּתוֹ כְּחָמֵשׁ סְלָעִים שֶׁל בֵּן. וַחֲכָמִים אוֹמְרִין אֵין חַיָּיבִין בְּאַחֲרָיוּתוֹ אֶלָּא כְפִדְיוֹן מַעֲשֵׂר שֵׁנִי. מוֹדֵי רִבִּי לִיעֶזֶר בְּפִטְרֵי חֲמוֹרוֹת שֶׁנָּפְלוּ לוֹ מִבֵּית אֲבִי אִמּוֹ כֹּהֵן מִכֵּיוָן שֶׁהִפְרִישׁוֹ קִדְּשׁוֹ.

Rebbi Johanan follows Rebbi[43], Rebbi Simeon ben Laqish follows Rebbi Eleazar ben Rebbi Simeon[44]. Rebbi Abun bar Hiyya said, even if Rebbi Simeon ben Laqish would hold with Rebbi, but only for something he is obligated to give to a Cohen; but for something he is not obligated to give to a Cohen[45], even Rebbi will agree since that is a Mishnah[46]: "If he separated the redemption of a first-born donkey and then it died, Rebbi Eliezer says one is responsible for alienation[47] as for the five tetra-drachmas of the [human] first-born; but the Sages say, he is not responsible for alienation, as for Second Tithe.[48]" Rebbi Eliezer will agree about first-born donkeys he inherited from the estate of his maternal grandfather, a Cohen, that he sanctified it when he separated it[49].

43 This refers to the disagreement discussed in the previous paragraph. Since only handing the restitution to the Cohen turns it into heave, the Israel grandson of a Cohen cannot make restitution until he gives it to some Cohen.

44 Since separation already sanctifies, when the restitution was set apart before the death of the grandfather it is now legal heave in the hand of the Israel grandson.

45 In our case, he inherits it legally from his Cohen grandfather.

46 *Bekhorot* 1:6. The Babli (*Bekhorot* 12b) holds that the rules for first-borns depend on special expressions in the appropriate verses and are not derived from general principles, against the Yerushalmi. (*Num.* 18:15) "You should certainly redeem the human firstborn, and the firstborn of the impure animal you shall redeem." For R. Eliezer, "certainly" refers to both cases, for the Sages only to the human firstborn. The redemption for a donkey is a lamb (*Ex.* 13:13), for a human it is 5 *šeqel* (*Num.* 3:47).

47 If the lamb was designated for the redemption and then either stolen or lost, the owner must give another lamb as replacement. If the young donkey dies before the lamb is delivered, it is holy and must be buried but the lamb is not given to the Cohen.

48 If the lamb is lost, the owner has fulfilled his duty and the donkey is his. If the young donkey dies before the lamb is delivered, it is a profane carcass and the lamb must be delivered to the Cohen.

49 Since the Cohen may give the lamb to himself; in that case, separation is all that is needed.

אָכַל תְּרוּמַת חָבֵר מְשַׁלֵּם לְחָבֵר. תְּרוּמַת עַם הָאָרֶץ מְשַׁלֵּם לְעַם הָאָרֶץ. וְלֹא נִמְצָא מוֹסֵר טָהֳרוֹתָיו לְעַם הָאָרֶץ. כֵּיצַד הוּא עוֹשֶׂה נוֹתֵן שְׁתֵּיהֶן לְכֹהֵן חָבֵר וְנוֹטֵל דְּמֵי אַחַת מֵהֶן וְנוֹתֵן לְכֹהֵן עַם הָאָרֶץ. רִבִּי בּוּן בַּר חִיָּיה אָמַר קוֹמֵי רִבִּי שִׁמְעוֹן בֶּן לָקִישׁ אַתְיָא כְּמָאן דְּאָמַר הַפְרָשָׁתוֹ מְקַדְּשָׁתוֹ. בְּרַם כְּמָאן דְּאָמַר מַתְּנָתוֹ מְקַדְּשָׁתוֹ בְּלֹא כֵן אֵינוֹ צָרִיךְ זְכִייָה. אָמַר לָהֶן בִּמְזַכֶּה עַל יְדֵי אַחֵר.

One who ate the heave of a Fellow has to pay the Fellow, one who ate the heave of a vulgar person has to pay the vulgar person[50]. Does he then not deliver his pure food to a vulgar person? How does he do it, he gives both to a Cohen Fellow, takes the price of one of them and gives that to the vulgar Cohen[51]. Rebbi Abun bar Ḥiyya said before Rebbi Simeon ben Laqish, this follows him who says, its separation sanctifies. But for him who says, the delivery sanctifies, does it not need acquisition in any case[52]? He said to them, he operates through the services of a third person[53].

50 The notions of Fellow and vulgar person are explained in the Introduction to Demay. The vulgar person is unable to keep his food in purity; giving him pure food, as required by the Mishnah, would be forbidden waste.

51 The amoraic text here has a parallel in Tosephta 7:5: "He who eats heave of a vulgar [Cohen], pays principal and fifth to a Cohen Fellow; the Fellow takes money and indemnifies the vulgar [Cohen].

52 If there is no sanctification without delivery then there is no repayment without delivery and the Cohen Fellow should not be able to acquire heave that is not due him.

53 The Cohen Fellow does not acquire the heave for himself but for the vulgar Cohen. He can do that since it is for the vulgar's benefit. Then he has to buy the heave for himself from what he had acquired for the third person. Since this is a formal institution, the vulgar's consent is implied.

(fol. 43d) **משנה ב**: בַּת יִשְׂרָאֵל שֶׁאָכְלָה תְרוּמָה וְאַחַר כָּךְ נִשֵּׂאת לְכֹהֵן אִם תְּרוּמָה שֶׁלֹּא זָכָה בָהּ כֹּהֵן אָכְלָה מְשַׁלֶּם קֶרֶן וְחוֹמֶשׁ לְעַצְמָהּ. וְאִם תְּרוּמָה שֶׁזָּכָה בָהּ כֹּהֵן אָכְלָה מְשַׁלֵּם קֶרֶן לִבְעָלִים וְחוֹמֶשׁ לְעַצְמָהּ מִפְּנֵי שֶׁאָמְרוּ הָאוֹכֵל תְּרוּמָה שׁוֹגֵג מְשַׁלֵּם קֶרֶן לִבְעָלִים וְחוֹמֶשׁ לְמִי שֶׁיִּרְצֶה.

Mishnah 2: If an Israel woman ate heave and then was married to a Cohen, ate the heave before a Cohen had acquired it, she pays principal and fifth to herself[54], but if she ate heave which a Cohen had acquired, she pays principal to its owner and the fifth to herself since they said, he who eats heave in error pays the principal to its owner and the fifth to a person of his choice.

54 Heave is eaten not only by a Cohen but also by his family (wife, children, slaves.)

(fol. 44b) **הלכה ב**: לֹא הִסְפִּיקָה לְשַׁלֵּם עַד שֶׁנִּתְגָּרְשָׁה. אִיתָא חֲמִי אִילּוּ הָיָה לָהּ כַּמָּה מַעְשְׂרוֹת שֶׁמָּא אֵינָן שֶׁלָּהּ. תַּמָּן מַעְשְׂרוֹת מְסוּיָּמִין בְּרַם הָכָא תְּרוּמָה אֵינָהּ מְסוּיֶּמֶת. מַה דָּמֵי לָהּ פִּיטְרֵי חֲמוֹרוֹת.

Halakhah 2: If she did not manage to pay before she was divorced[55]? Come and see, if she had so many tithes, would they not be hers[56]? There tithes are defined but here the heave is still undefined[57]. What compares to this? First-born of donkeys[58].

55 If she has no children, she reverted to the status of Israel and is forbidden to eat heave.

56 If she got heave or Heave of the Tithe as a Cohen's wife, it remains her property even if she cannot eat it now but must sell it to somebody who can.

57 Since she did not pay, the heave is not designated yet and undetermined things cannot be acquired.

58 It is difficult to know what is meant since there is no Yerushalmi to *Bekhorot*. It seems that one refers to the opinion of the Sages (Note 48) that the lamb is the Cohen's property upon designation, before delivery. In this case, the heave would remain hers if designated before the divorce.

(fol. 43d) **משנה ג**: הַמַּאֲכִיל אֶת פּוֹעֲלָיו וְאֶת אוֹרְחָיו תְּרוּמָה הוּא מְשַׁלֵּם אֶת הַקֶּרֶן וְהֵן מְשַׁלְּמִין אֶת הַחוֹמֶשׁ דִּבְרֵי רִבִּי מֵאִיר. וַחֲכָמִים אוֹמְרִים הֵן מְשַׁלְּמִין קֶרֶן וְחוֹמֶשׁ וְהוּא מְשַׁלֵּם לָהֶן דְּמֵי סְעוּדָתָן.

Mishnah 3: If one serves heave to his workers or his guests, he pays the principal and they pay the fifth[59], the word of Rebbi Meïr. But the Sages say, they pay principal and fifth and he pays them the price of their meal[60].

59 He pays the principal since he robbed the Cohen of his heave. They pay the fifth since they ate heave inadvertently and the fine of eating

heave inadvertently is the payment of the fifth.

60 The Sages hold that the person who eats heave inadvertently has to pay principal and fifth. The host, in addition to the grave sin he incurred by leading innocent people into sin, is fined by having to pay his workers the price of their meal as if it had been profane food, while they pay only $^5/_4$ of the price of heave, which probably is much less.

(fol. 44b) **הלכה ג**: הָא רִבִּי מֵאִיר אָמַר מְשַׁלְּמִין וְרַבָּנִין אָמְרִין מְשַׁלְּמִין. מַה בֵּינֵיהוֹן. אָמַר רִבִּי יוֹחָנָן עִיקַּר סְעוּדָה בֵּינֵיהוֹן. רִבִּי מֵאִיר אָמַר עִיקַּר סְעוּדָה לְבַעַל הַבַּיִת. וְרַבָּנִין אָמְרִין עִיקַּר סְעוּדָה לְפוֹעֲלִין. רִבִּי שִׁמְעוֹן בֶּן לָקִישׁ אָמַר טְפֵילָה בֵּינֵיהוֹן. רִבִּי מֵאִיר אָמַר טְפֵילָה לְבַעַל הַבַּיִת. וְרַבָּנִין אָמְרִין טְפֵילָה לְפוֹעֲלִין. רִבִּי אַבָּהוּ בְשֵׁם רִבִּי שִׁמְעוֹן בֶּן לָקִישׁ הָא לְמָה זֶה דוֹמֶה לְמוֹכֵר חֵפֶץ לַחֲבֵירוֹ וְנִמְצָא שֶׁאֵינוֹ שֶׁלּוֹ שֶׁהוּא חַייָב לְהַעֲמִיד לוֹ מִקְחוֹ. אִילּוּ כְּרִבִּי שִׁמְעוֹן בֶּן לָקִישׁ אִית אֲמְרַת נִיחָא. וְאִין כְּרִבִּי יוֹחָנָן אָמַר עִיקַּר סְעוּדָה בֵּינֵיהוֹן וְאַתְּ אָמַר הָכֵין. כְּרִבִּי מֵאִיר אַתְּ אָמַר. רִבִּי אַבָּהוּ בְשֵׁם רִבִּי יוֹסֵי בֶּן חֲנִינָא שֶׁבַח סְעוּדָה בֵּינֵיהוֹן בְּשֶׁפָּסַק עִמָּהֶן לְהַאֲכִילָן דּוּבְשְׁנֵי חוּלִין וְהֶאֱכִילָן דּוּבְשְׁנֵי תְרוּמָה. וְלֹא כְּבָר אָכְלוּ. כְּמָאן דְּאָמַר טְבָלִים נַפְשׁוֹ שֶׁל אָדָם חָתָה מֵהֶן.

Halakhah 3: Now Rebbi Meïr says, they pay, and the Sages say, they pay, what is between them? Rebbi Joḥanan said, the meal itself is between them. Rebbi Meïr said, the meal is the resposibility of the employer, but the rabbis say, the meal is the resposibility of the workers[61]. Rebbi Simeon ben Laqish said, the exertion is between them. Rebbi Meïr said, the exertion is the resposibility of the employer, but the rabbis say, the exertion is the resposibility of the workers[62]. Rebbi Abbahu in the name of Rebbi Simeon ben Laqish: To what can this be compared, to one who sells something to another person, but it turns out that it was not his [to sell]. Does he not have to replace his buy? If you hold with Rebbi Simeon ben Laqish, this is fine. But if you hold with Rebbi Joḥanan, who said, the meal itself is between them, and you say so? He said following

Rebbi Meïr. Rebbi Abbahu in the name of Rebbi Yose ben Ḥanina: The value of the meal is between them. If he promised them to feed them profane honey-cakes but he fed them heave honey-cakes. Did they not eat already? This follows him who says, a person's soul is afraid of *ṭevel*[63].

61 The responsibility vis-à-vis the Cohen is either on the person who actually ate the Cohen's property or on the person who caused the trouble.

62 Since the Cohen is not compensated by money but by fully profane food, whose resposibility is it to procure the fully profane food in the correct amount?

63 The workers are overcompensated to account for the mental anguish caused them by their employer.

(fol. 43d) **משנה ד**: הַגּוֹנֵב תְּרוּמָה (fol. 44b) וְלֹא אֲכָלָהּ מְשַׁלֵּם תַּשְׁלוּמֵי כֶפֶל דְּמֵי תְרוּמָה. אֲכָלָהּ מְשַׁלֵּם שְׁנֵי קַרְנַיִם וְחוֹמֶשׁ. קֶרֶן וְחוֹמֶשׁ מִן הַחוּלִין וְקֶרֶן דְּמֵי תְרוּמָה. גָּנַב תְּרוּמַת הֶקְדֵּשׁ וַאֲכָלָהּ מְשַׁלֵּם שְׁנֵי חוֹמְשִׁין וְקֶרֶן שֶׁאֵין בְּהֶקְדֵּשׁ תַּשְׁלוּמֵי כֶפֶל.

Mishnah 4: He who steals heave but does not eat it pays double restitution for the value of heave[64]. If he ate it, he pays twice the principal and a fifth. The principal and the fifth from profane food[65] and a principal the value of heave. If he stole heave of the Sanctuary and ate it, he pays two fifths and the principal[38] since double restitution does not apply to the Sanctuary[66].

64 Since this is what he stole.

65 Restitution for the heave, following Mishnah 1.

66 The reason is given at the end of the Halakhah.

(fol. 44b) **הלכה ד**: אָמַר רִבִּי יַנַּאי לִצְדָדִין הִיא מַתְנִיתָא יֵשׁ בּוֹ כְזַיִת וְאֵין בּוֹ שָׁוֶה פְרוּטָה מְשַׁלֵּם לְקֹדֶשׁ. יֵשׁ בּוֹ שָׁוֶה פְרוּטָה וְאֵין בּוֹ כְזַיִת מְשַׁלֵּם לְשֵׁבֶט. יֵשׁ בּוֹ כְזַיִת וְיֵשׁ בּוֹ שָׁוֶה פְרוּטָה. שִׁמְעוֹן בַּר וָוא בְשֵׁם רִבִּי יוֹחָנָן מְשַׁלֵּם לְקֹדֶשׁ. רִבִּי יוֹחָנָן אָמַר מְשַׁלֵּם לְשֵׁבֶט. אָמַר רִבִּי זְעִירָא גְּזֵירַת הַכָּתוּב הִיא וְאִישׁ כִּי יֹאכַל קוֹדֶשׁ בִּשְׁגָגָה לְמָקוֹם שֶׁהַקֶּרֶן מְהַלֵּךְ שָׁם הַחוֹמֶשׁ מְהַלֵּךְ. כַּהֲנָא אָמַר מְשַׁלֵּם שְׁנֵי חוֹמְשִׁין חוֹמֶשׁ לְשֵׁבֶט וְחוֹמֶשׁ לְהֶקְדֵּשׁ.

Halakhah 4: Rebbi Yannai said, the Mishnah is split[67]. If there is the size of an olive but it is not worth a *peruṭah*[68], he pays to the Sanctuary. If it is worth a *peruṭah* but is not the size of an olive, he pays to the tribe. If it is the size of an olive and is worth a *peruṭah*, Simeon bar Abba in the name of Rebbi Johanan, he pays to the Sanctuary[69]. Rebbi Johanan said, he pays to the tribe[70]. Rebbi Zeïra said, it is a decision of the verse (*Lev*. 22:14): "If somebody should eat consecrated food in error," where the principal goes, there the fifth has to go. Cahana said, he pays two fifths, one to the tribe[71] and one to the Sanctuary.

67 The entire argument refers only to the last case, heave stolen from the sanctuary.

68 A *peruṭah*, a small Hasmonean coin, $^1/_6$ or $^1/_8$ of an as. Theft of less than a *peruṭah* is not prosecutable and does not entitle the injured person to ask for restitution. In the case under consideration, there was sin but no monetary restitution is possible; there is no principal but the fifth has to be paid. But Lev. 22:14 ends: He hands over the consecrated food to the Cohen. Since "handing over" implies something substantial, it must be the value of at least a *peruṭah*. This means that in this case, restitution to the Cohen is excluded; the recipient must be the Sanctuary even though legally no larceny has occured.

69 Both the principal and the fifth.

70 For use of heave. The other fifth, for use of consecrated things, must go to the Sanctuary. R. Zeïra disagrees since the argument from the verse applies only to the payment of the fine for heave.

71 Since the principal and the fifth for heave has to be profane food. The question of the second fifth, fine for illicit use of consecrated food, is not addressed here.

שֶׁאֵין בְּהֶקְדֵּשׁ תַּשְׁלוּמֵי כֶפֶל. שֶׁנֶּאֱמַר יְשַׁלֵּם שְׁנַיִם לְרֵעֵהוּ וְלֹא לְהֶקְדֵּשׁ.

"Since double restitution does not apply to the Sanctuary". For it was said (*Ex.* 22:8): "He should restitute double *to his neighbor*," but not to the Sanctuary.

(fol. 44a) **משנה ה**: אֵין מְשַׁלְּמִין מִן הַלֶּקֶט וּמִן הַשִּׁכְחָה וּמִן הַפֵּיאָה וּמִן הַהֶבְקֵר וְלֹא מִמַּעֲשֵׂר רִאשׁוֹן שֶׁנִּיטְּלָה תְּרוּמָתוֹ וְלֹא מִמַּעֲשֵׂר שֵׁנִי וְהֶקְדֵּשׁ שֶׁנִּפְדּוּ שֶׁאֵין הֶקְדֵּשׁ פּוֹדֶה אֶת הַהֶקְדֵּשׁ דִּבְרֵי רִבִּי מֵאִיר. וַחֲכָמִים מַתִּירִין בְּאֵלּוּ.

Mishnah 5: One does not pay with gleanings, forgotten sheaves, *peah*, and abandoned property[72], nor with First Tithe whose heave was taken, nor with Second Tithe[73], nor with dedicated food that was redeemed, for dedicated food cannot redeem dedicated food, the words of Rebbi Meïr. But the Sages permit the latter.

72 All these are exempt from heave; while they are permitted for profane use they are not profane since they are God's gift to the poor.

73 R. Meïr holds that Second Heave is Heaven's property given to the farmer. Since it can never become heave, it is excluded as payment. The Sages consider Second Tithe and dedicated property after redemption, and First Tithe whose heave was taken, as totally profane since their sanctity has been transferred to the money of redemption.

(fol. 44b) **הלכה ה**: רִבִּי שִׁמְעוֹן בֶּן לָקִישׁ אָמַר לָהֶן עַל תַּרְתֵּין אַחֲרַיְיָתָא לָמָּה מִפְּנֵי שֶׁיֵּשׁ בָּהֶן זִיקַת תְּרוּמָה וּמַעְשְׂרוֹת. וְלֶקֶט וְשִׁכְחָה אֵין בָּהֶן זִיקַת תְּרוּמָה וּמַעְשְׂרוֹת. אֶלָּא בְּנְשִׂיאַת פֵּיאָה וּבְקָמַת פֵּיאָה אֲנָן קַיְימִין. לֵית הָדָא פְּשָׁטָה שְׁאִילְתֵּיהּ דְּחִילְפַיי דְּחִילְפַיי שְׁאַל לֶקֶט בְּנְשִׁירָה מַהוּ שֶׁיִּקַדֵּשׁ. רִבִּי יוֹחָנָן אָמַר לֵיהּ וְהָא תַנִּינָן לֶקֶט. אִית לָךְ מֵימַר פֵּיאָה בְּלֶקֶט. רִבִּי יוֹחָנָן אָמַר לֵיהּ עַל כּוּלְּהוֹן.

Rebbi Simeon ben Laqish said, it refers to the last two[74]. Why? Because these have affinity to heave and tithes. Do gleanings and forgotten sheaves never have affinity to heave and tithes[75]? But we deal with growth of[76] *peah* and standing *peah*. Does this not simply answer Hilfai's question, since Hilfai asked: Do gleanings become sanctified in the act of falling down[77]? Rebbi Johanan said to him, but did we not state "gleanings"[78]? How can you have *peah* from gleanings? Rebbi Johanan said to him, about everything[79].

74 The two items the Sages discuss are First Tithe and {Second Tithe or consecrated food}. The second set is taken as a unit because its items can become profane by redemption and they are taken from produce for which heave had been taken.

75 While the obligation of heave starts only with the collection of the grain kernels after threshing, it is possible to give heave from cut grain on the field. The only gift to the poor from grain never potentially heave is *peah*, which should be given as standing grain. But since the obligation of *peah* remains on the cut grain if *peah* was not left standing at harvest time (cf. *Peah*, Chapter 1, Note 275), even *peah* cannot be excluded from any possibility of heave. One has to assume that the addition of "and tithes" is a mnemonic device.

76 The text given is the reading of the Leyden ms.; it is interpreted from Arabic נשא "to rise, to grow", as a synonym for the second term, "standing *peah*". The reading of the Venice print, נשיכת פיאה "the biting of *peah*", is difficult to accept (for the meaning of "biting" cf. *Demay* 6:6, Note 140); that of the Rome ms., משכחת פיאה "finding (Babylonian Aramaic) *peah*", is certainly a scribal error. R. E. Fulda's emendation נשירת פיאה "what falls down from *peah*" is unsupported and irrelevant.

77 Explained in *Peah* 7:3, Note 52. The idea is that if gleanings may be subject to heave, a stalk cannot become gleanings automatically by falling down.

78 The Mishnah expicitly excludes the restriction to *peah* postulated by R. Simeon ben Laqish.

79 In this case, it is difficult to understand the addition of "the latter" to the statement of the Sages. The statement at its face value also would

imply that R. Joḥanan rejects any connection between the possibility of heave and the availability for restitution of heave. If R. Joḥanan accepts such a connection, he can include *peah* only if given from sheaves or stacks, rather than standing grain. In this case, a qualifying "the latter" is acceptable.

(fol. 44a) **משנה ו**: רִבִּי אֱלִיעֶזֶר אוֹמֵר מְשַׁלְּמִין מִמִּין עַל מִין שֶׁאֵינוֹ מִינוֹ בִּלְבַד שֶׁיְּשַׁלֵּם מִן הַיָּפֶה עַל הָרַע וְרִבִּי עֲקִיבָה אוֹמֵר אֵין מְשַׁלְּמִין אֶלָּא מִמִּין עַל מִינוֹ.
משנה ז: לְפִיכָךְ אִם אָכַל קִשּׁוּאִין שֶׁל עֶרֶב שְׁבִיעִית יַמְתִּין לְקִשּׁוּאִין שֶׁל מוֹצָאֵי שְׁבִיעִית וִישַׁלֵּם מֵהֶן. מִמָּקוֹם שֶׁרִבִּי אֱלִיעֶזֶר מֵיקֵל מִשָּׁם רִבִּי עֲקִיבָה מַחְמִיר שֶׁנֶּאֱמַר וְנָתַן לַכֹּהֵן אֶת הַקּוֹדֶשׁ כָּל־שֶׁהוּא רָאוּי לַעֲשׂוֹת קוֹדֶשׁ דִּבְרֵי רִבִּי אֱלִיעֶזֶר וְרִבִּי עֲקִיבָה אוֹמֵר וְנָתַן לַכֹּהֵן אֶת הַקּוֹדֶשׁ קוֹדֶשׁ שֶׁאָכַל.

Mishnah 6: Rebbi Eliezer says, one repays from one kind for another kind which is not the same, on condition that he repay with better quality for worse, but Rebbi Aqiba says, one only repays from one kind for its own.

Mishnah 7: Therefore, if one ate green melon of the year before the Sabbatical, he should wait for green melons of the year following the Sabbatical and repay from them[80]. From the verse which Rebbi Eliezer reads to be lenient, from there Rebbi Aqiba is restrictive, since it is said (*Lev*. 22:14): "He hands over the consecrated food to the Cohen," anything that may be consecrated, the words of Rebbi Eliezer. But Rebbi Aqiba says, "he hands over the consecrated food to the Cohen," the consecrated food he himself ate.

80 Sabbatical produce is all consecrated and cannot be used, even for those kinds that legally can be tended on private plots, or spontaneous growth which is forbidden by rabbinic decree.

(fol. 44b) **הלכה ו**: הָא כֵּיצַד אָכַל יָרָק וְשִׁלֵּם גְּרוֹגֶרֶת. גְּרוֹגֶרֶת וְשִׁלֵּם תְּמָרִים תָּבוֹא לוֹ בְּרָכָה. אָכַל בִּיכּוּרִים מָהוּ מְשַׁלֵּם. אָכַל עֲנָבִים מְשַׁלֵּם יַיִן זֵיתִים מְשַׁלֵּם שֶׁמֶן. אָכַל חַלָּה מָהוּ שֶׁיְּשַׁלֵּם מִפֵּירוֹת שֶׁלֹּא הֵבִיאוּ שְׁלִישׁ שֶׁכֵּן פֵּירוֹת שֶׁלֹּא הֵבִיאוּ שְׁלִישׁ חַייָבִין בְּחַלָּה. אָכַל בִּיכּוּרִים מָהוּ שֶׁיְּשַׁלֵּם בִּמְחוּבָּר לְקַרְקַע שֶׁכֵּן הַבִּיכּוּרִים נִקְנִין בִּמְחוּבָּר לְקַרְקַע.

Halakhah 6: How is this? If he ate vegetable and repaid a dried fig, a dried fig and repaid dates, a blessing should come to him[81]. If he ate first fruits[82], what can he repay? If he ate grapes, he repays wine, olives he repays oil. If he ate *ḥallah*, may he repay with produce not yet one-third ripe since produce not yet one-third ripe is subject to *ḥallah*[83]? If he ate first fruits, may he repay with what is still connected to the ground since first fruits acquire their status while connected to the ground?

81 This follows R. Eliezer as is clear from *Sifra Emor Pereq* 6(6): "From where that one only repays from one kind for its own? The verse says 'he hands over the consecrated food to the Cohen,' therefore, if one ate green melon of the year before the Sabbatical, he should wait for green melons of the year following the Sabbatical and repay from them, the words of R. Aqiba. Rebbi Eliezer says, one repays from one kind for another kind which is not the same, on condition that he repay with better quality for worse. How is this? If he ate a dried fig and repaid dates, a blessing should come to him." This is partially quoted in Babli *Eruvin* 29b, *Pesaḥim* 32a, in a discussion about whether heave has to be repaid by value or by volume.

82 They are subject to the rules of repayment of heave, Mishnah *Bikkurim* 2:1.

83 This question follows R. Aqiba since in the Mishnah (*Ḥallah* 1:3) which states that flour made from unripe grain is free from tithes but subject to *ḥallah*; R. Eliezer dissents and frees it from *ḥallah*. In matters of repayment, *ḥallah* follows the rules of heave (Mishnah *Ḥallah* 1:9).

רִבִּי אָבִין בְּשֵׁם רַבָּנִין דְּתַמָּן זֹאת אוֹמֶרֶת שֶׁאֵין מְשַׁלְּמִין מִפֵּירוֹת חוּצָה לָאָרֶץ וַאֲפִילוּ תֵּימַר מְשַׁלְּמִין מַתְנִיתָן עַד שֶׁלֹּא הִתִּיר רִבִּי לְהָבִיא יָרָק מֵחוּצָה לָאָרֶץ. לֹא אָמַר אֶלָּא קִישּׁוּאִין שֶׁהֵן פֵּירוֹת אִיסּוּר. אֲבָל דָּבָר שֶׁהוּא פֵּירוֹת הֵיתֵר לֹא שֶׁאִם אָמַר אַתְּ כֵּן לֹא נִמְצָא לוֹקֵחַ לוֹ קוֹרְדּוֹם מִדְּמֵי שְׁבִיעִית.

[84]Rabbi Abin in the name of the rabbis from there: This means that one may not repay with produce from outside the Land[85]. Even if you say one may repay, our Mishnah is from before Rebbi permitted the import of vegetables from outside the Land[86]. He mentioned only green melons which are forbidden produce. But not permitted produce[87], because if you say so, does it not turn out that he buys himself an axe from Sabbatical money[88]?

84 Here starts the discussion of Mishnah 7.

85 If one cannot repay during the Sabbatical, this means that no non-Sabbatical fruit is available. Since the only permitted use of Sabbatical produce is consumption, one may not pay his debts with Sabbatical fruit.

86 Mishnah *Ševi'it* 6:4.

87 For example fruits from trees which do not require yearly trimming and fertilizing.

88 By liquidating his debts with Sabbatical produce.

האוכל תרומה מזיד פרק שביעי

(fol. 44b) **משנה א:** הָאוֹכֵל תְּרוּמָה מֵזִיד מְשַׁלֵּם אֶת הַקֶּרֶן וְאֵינוֹ מְשַׁלֵּם אֶת הַחוֹמֶשׁ. הַתַּשְׁלוּמִין חוּלִין. וְאִם רָצָה הַכֹּהֵן לִמְחוֹל מוֹחֵל.

Mishnah 1: If somebody[1] eats heave intentionally, he pays the principal but not the fifth. His payment is profane and if the Cohen wants to forgive this, he may forgive[2].

1 Not a Cohen.

2 *Lev*. 22:14: "Anybody who ate sanctified food *in error* must add its fifth to it and give the consecrated food to the Cohen." The verse explicitly restricts the duty of adding a fifth to the case when heave is eaten in error. Also, the restitution is called holy only in that case. Since the money for restitution is not holy, the Cohen may give it to the offender, i. e., refrain from accepting it. The sin of eating heave intentionally is too great to be forgiven for just a monetary fine. The Mishnah applies only to the case in which the offender was not warned by two witnesses not to sin; in the latter case, he will be whipped by order of the court. Whether he then has to pay is discussed in the Halakhah.

(fol. 44c) **הלכה א:** הָאוֹכֵל תְּרוּמָה מֵזִיד כו'. תַּמָּן תַּנִּינָן אֵלּוּ הַלּוֹקִין וְהָתַנִּינָן אֵלּוּ נְעָרוֹת. הָכָא אַתְּ אָמַר לוֹקֶה. וְהָכָא אַתְּ אָמַר מְשַׁלֵּם. אָמַר רִבִּי יוֹחָנָן לִצְדָדִין הִיא מַתְנִיתִין אִם הִתְרוּ בוֹ לוֹקֶה. אִם לֹא הִתְרוּ בוֹ מְשַׁלֵּם. סָבַר רִבִּי יוֹחָנָן מֵימַר בִּמְקוֹם מַכּוֹת וְתַשְׁלוּמִין מְשַׁלֵּם וְאֵינוֹ לוֹקֶה. וְיִלְקֶה וִישַׁלֵּם. רִשְׁעָתוֹ. רִשְׁעָה אַחַת אַתָּה מְחַייְבוֹ. וְאֵי אַתָּה מְחַייְבוֹ שְׁתֵּי רִשְׁעָיוֹת. וִישַׁלֵּם וְלֹא יִלְקֶה. בִּמְחַייְבֵי שְׁתֵּי רְשָׁעוֹת הַכָּתוּב מְדַבֵּר וְהִפִּילוֹ הַשּׁוֹפֵט וְהִכָּהוּ לְפָנָיו כְּדֵי רִשְׁעָתוֹ בְּמִסְפָּר.

Halakhah 1: "If somebody eats heave intentionally," etc. [2]There, we have stated[3]: "The following are flogged," and we have stated[4]: "These are the girls." Here you say, he is flogged, and there you say, he pays. Rebbi Joḥanan said, the Mishnah is two-sided: If he was cautioned[5], he is flogged; if he was not cautioned, he pays. Rebbi Joḥanan is of the opinion that in a case where there is flogging or restitution, when he pays he is not flogged. Why should he not be flogged and have to pay? (*Deut*. 25:2) "His guilt." You sentence him for one guilt but you may not sentence him for two guilts[6]. The verse speaks of one who may incur two punishments (*Deut*. 25:2): "The judge shall have him laid down and flogged in his presence, a number [of times] because of his guilt."

2 The parallel to the entire Halakhah is in *Ketubot* 3:1 (fol. 27b), shortened also *Baba Qama* 7:2 (fol. 5d), *Makkot* 1:1 (fol. 31a); Babli *Ketubot* 32b, *Baba Qama* 36a, *Makkot* 7b, 13b.

3 Mishnah *Makkot* 3:1-5 gives a list of all transgressions punishable by flogging. The list starts with "him who sleeps with his sister", and later mentions "him who eats *ṭevel* and First Heave of which no heave was taken," where he is punished for eating the heave contained in the produce; hence, eating heave is punished by flogging.

4 Mishnah *Ketubot* 3:1: "These are the girls for which one incurs a fine, . . he who sleeps with his sister, . . ." The fines are incurred either for the rape (*Deut*. 22:19) or the seduction (*Ex*. *22:16)* of a minor girl; cf. Note 26. The Mishnaiot seem to imply that raping one's minor sister (and a non-Cohen's eating heave) is punished by flogging and a fine.

5 In addition, there must be two eye witnesses who saw the transgression; cf. *Kilaim*, Chapter 8, Note 9.

6 "Guilt" (in the singular) here is taken to mean "atonement for his guilt", that for one transgression there can be only one punishment. It is quite possible that with one act one commits a multiple sin; then each sin separately can be punished but no one sin can incur more than one punishment (*Sifry Deut*. 286).

רִבִּי שִׁמְעוֹן בֶּן לָקִישׁ אָמַר אֲפִילוּ לֹא הִתְרוּ בוֹ אֵינוֹ מְשַׁלֵּם מֵאַחַר שֶׁאִילּוּ הִתְרוּ בוֹ הָיָה לוֹקֶה. מַתְנִיתָא פְלִיגָא עַל רִבִּי שִׁמְעוֹן בֶּן לָקִישׁ אֵלּוּ נְעָרוֹת שֶׁיֵּשׁ לָהֶן קְנָס וְאִלּוּ הִתְרוּ בוֹ אֵינוֹ לוֹקֶה. סָבַר רִבִּי שִׁמְעוֹן בֶּן לָקִישׁ כְּרִבִּי מֵאִיר דּוּ רִבִּי מֵאִיר אָמַר לוֹקֶה וּמְשַׁלֵּם. רִבִּי אַבָּהוּ בְשֵׁם רִבִּי שִׁמְעוֹן בֶּן לָקִישׁ מִן הַמּוֹצִיא שֵׁם רָע לָמַד רִבִּי מֵאִיר. וְעָנְשׁוּ אוֹתוֹ מָמוֹן וְיִסְּרוּ אוֹתוֹ מַלְקוּת. וְרַבָּנִין אָמְרִין לְחִידּוּשׁוֹ יָצָא הַמּוֹצִיא שֵׁם רָע דָּבָר שֶׁהוּא יוֹצֵא בְחִידּוּשׁוֹ אֵין לְמֵידִין מִמֶּנּוּ. לְפִי שֶׁבְּכָל־מָקוֹם אֵין אָדָם מִתְחַייֵב בְּדִיבּוּרוֹ. וְכָאן אָדָם מִתְחַייֵב בְּדִיבּוּרוֹ. וּכְשֵׁם שֶׁאֵין לְמֵידִין מִמֶּנּוּ לְדָבָר אַחֵר כָּךְ אֵין לְמֵידִין מִמֶּנּוּ לֹא לְעוֹנְשִׁין וְלֹא לְמַכּוֹת. לֹא כֵן אָמַר רִבִּי אַבָּהוּ בְשֵׁם רִבִּי שִׁמְעוֹן בֶּן לָקִישׁ בְּמֵזִיד בְּחֵלֶב וּבְשׁוֹגֵג בְּקָרְבָּן מַתְרִין בּוֹ וְלוֹקֶה וּמֵבִיא קָרְבָּן. וְהָכָא יִלְקֶה וִישַׁלֵּם. רִבִּי בּוּן בַּר חִייָה בְּשֵׁם רִבִּי שְׁמוּאֵל בַּר רַב יִצְחָק [אָמַר כְּדֵי רִשְׁעָתוֹ.][13] שְׁנֵי דְבָרִים מְסוּרִין לְבֵית דִּין אַתְּ תּוֹפֵס אֶחָד מֵהֶן. יָצָא דָבָר שֶׁהוּא מָסוּר לַשָּׁמַיִם.

Rebbi Simeon ben Laqish said, even if he was not cautioned should he not pay since when cautioned he would be flogged[7]? A Mishnah disagrees with Rebbi Simeon ben Laqish: "These are the girls for which one incurs a fine," but if he was cautioned, will he not be flogged[8]? Rebbi Simeon ben Laqish holds with Rebbi Meïr since Rebbi Meïr said, he is flogged and pays. Rebbi Abbahu in the name of Rebbi Simeon ben Laqish[9]: Rebbi Meïr learned from the calumniator[10]. (*Deut.* 22:19) "And they shall fine him", money; (*Deut.* 22:18) "they shall punish him," flogging. But the rabbis say, [the law of] the calumniator is separate because of its novelty; one cannot learn from a novelty! Because nowhere else will a person become guilty by speech, but here he becomes guilty by speech[11]. Since one cannot transfer this feature, one cannot transfer the rules of either payment or flogging. Did not Rebbi Abbahu say in the name of Rebbi Simeon ben Laqish: If he [eats] fat intentionally but is in error about the sacrifice, if he was cautioned he will be flogged and has to bring a sacrifice[12]! Rebbi Abun bar Ḥiyya in the name of Rebbi Samuel bar Rav

Isaac said, (*Deut.* 25:2) "Because of his guilt." If two possibilities are given to the court, one chooses one of them. This excludes matters in the power of Heaven[14].

7 A similar text is in *Ketubot* 3:1 (fol. 27b), but there the Mishnah here is quoted as proof. In *Ševu'ot* 4:9 (fol. 35d), R. Simeon ben Laqish is quoted as disagreeing with R. Meïr. In the Babli, *Ketubot* 33b, R. Simeon ben Laqish is quoted only as noting that Mishnah 3:1 gives the opinion of R. Meïr without endorsing it.

8 Since Mishnaiot *Ketubot* 3:1 and *Terumot* 7:1 are formulated unconditionally, they should be interpreted as applying any time there are two witnesses to the transgression, independent of witnesses regarding cautioning.

9 In the Babli, *Makkot* 4b, the author is Ulla (R. La).

10 The man who publicly accuses his wife whom he married as a supposed virgin when she was almost an adult (between 12 and $12^1/_2$ years of age), not to have been virginal. If he cannot produce two witnesses who prove the adultery of the wife between the preliminary and the actual marriage, he is fined, whipped, and prohibited to ever divorce his wife.

11 The Halakhah later will discuss the case of perjured witnesses. These, according to the Yerushalmi, in a civil case will pay but not be flogged and, according to the Babli (*Makkot* 4b), in a criminal case will be flogged without prior cautioning. In no case can perjury parallel calumny.

12 Cf. Chapter 6, Notes 5,6.

13 From the text in *Ketubot*, missing here.

14 Since sacrifices are between the individual and Heaven, the procedural rules of the court are inapplicable to the case and nothing can be inferred from rules of sacrifices for court procedures.

הַכֹּל מוֹדִין שֶׁאֵין מָמוֹן אֶצֶל מִיתָה דִּכְתִיב וּמַכֵּה (נֶפֶשׁ) בְּהֵמָה יְשַׁלְּמֶנָּה וּמַכֵּה אָדָם יוּמָת. מַה מַכֵּה בְהֵמָה לֹא חִלַּקְתָּה בָהּ בֵּין שׁוֹגֵג בֵּין מֵזִיד <לִפְטוֹר> [לְחַיְּיבוֹ][15] מָמוֹן אַף מַכֵּה אָדָם לֹא תַחֲלוֹק בּוֹ בֵּין שׁוֹגֵג בֵּין מֵזִיד לִפְטוֹר. בְּמַה פְּלִיגִין. בְּמָמוֹן אֶצֶל מַכּוֹת. רִבִּי יוֹחָנָן אָמַר אֵין מָמוֹן אֶצֶל מִיתָה וְיֵשׁ מָמוֹן אֶצֶל מַכּוֹת. וְרִבִּי שִׁמְעוֹן בֶּן לָקִישׁ אָמַר כְּשֵׁם שֶׁאֵין מָמוֹן אֶצֶל מִיתָה כָּךְ אֵין מָמוֹן אֶצֶל מַכּוֹת.

Everybody agrees that there is no money payment in capital cases[16], as it is written (*Lev.* 24:21): "The slayer of a living[17] animal must pay for it[18] but the slayer of a human shall be put to death." Just as you did not make a difference between unintentional and intentional action of a slayer of an animal to force him to pay money, so you should not make a difference between unintentional and intentional action of a slayer of a human to free him [from paying]. Where do they differ? About money in a flogging case. Rebbi Joḥanan said, there is no money in a capital case but there is money in a flogging case[19], but Rebbi Simeon ben Laqish said, just as there is no money in a capital case so there is no money in a flogging case[20].

15 The text in brackets is the *Ketubot* text, the one in braces is from *Terumot*.

16 In any case where capital punishment is a possibility, payment of money is excluded even if the elements necessary for conviction (two witnesses each for caution and the criminal act) are missing. The argument is quoted in the Babli (*Ketubot* 35a) in the name of the school of Ḥizqiah; it is not found in tannaïtic sources.

17 This word is missing in the Biblical text and in *Ketubot*.

18 Slaying another person's animal is always a civil case, never a criminal one. Therefore, the distinctions basic for criminal cases do not apply.

19 The fine is a punishment which automatically kicks in if the formal requirements for a sentence of flogging are missing (cf. Babli *Ketubot* 34b).

20 Once the possibility of a sentence of flogging is there if one would find the necessary eye witnesses, there is no possibility for the imposition of a fine.

רִבִּי אִימִּי בְּבַלַיָיא בְּשֵׁם רַבָּנִין דְּתַמָּן טַעֲמָא דְרִבִּי שִׁמְעוֹן בֶּן לָקִישׁ רָשָׁע רָשָׁע. נֶאֱמַר רָשָׁע בִּמְחוּיְיבֵי מִיתוֹת. וְנֶאֱמַר רָשָׁע בִּמְחוּיְיבֵי מַכּוֹת. מַה רָשָׁע שֶׁנֶּאֱמַר בִּמְחוּיְיבֵי מִיתוֹת אֵין מָמוֹן אֶצֶל מִיתָה. אוּף רָשָׁע שֶׁנֶּאֱמַר בִּמְחוּיְיבֵי מַכּוֹת אֵין מָמוֹן אֶצֶל מַכּוֹת.

Rebbi Immi the Babylonian[21] in the name of the rabbis from there: The reason of Rebbi Simeon ben Laqish is "criminal, criminal." "Criminal" is mentioned in capital cases[22], "criminal" is mentioned in cases of flogging[23]. Just as for the criminal in capital cases there is no monetary fine, so for the criminal mentioned in flogging cases there is no monetary fine.

21 He is R. Immi (Ammi), the head of the Tiberian academy after R. Joḥanan. His statement is quoted in the Babli (*Ketubot* 35a) by Abbai, one generation after R. Immi.

22 *Num.* 35:31: "Do not take weregild for the life of a human who is a *criminal* condemned to death."

23 *Deut.* 25:2: "If the *criminal* is condemned to flogging, . . ."

נָתָן בַּר הוֹשַׁעְיָה אָמַר כָּאן בְּנַעֲרָה כָּאן בְּבוֹגֶרֶת. נַעֲרָה יֵשׁ לָהּ קְנָס וְאֵין לָהּ מֶכֶר. בּוֹגֶרֶת אֵין לָהּ לֹא מֶכֶר וְלֹא קְנָס וְאֵין לָהּ בּוֹשֶׁת וּפְגָם. רַבָּנִין דְּקֵיסָרִין אָמְרִין תִּיפְתָּר שֶׁפִּיתְּתוֹ אוֹ שֶׁמָּחֲלָה לוֹ. סָבַר נָתָן בַּר הוֹשַׁעְיָה לְמָקוֹם מַכּוֹת וְתַשְׁלוּמִין מְשַׁלֵּם וְאֵינוֹ לוֹקֶה. וְיִלְקֶה וִישַׁלֵּם. כְּדֵי רִשְׁעָתוֹ. רִשְׁעָה אַחַת אַתָּה מְחַייְבוֹ. וְאֵי אַתָּה מְחַייְבוֹ שְׁתֵּי רִשְׁעָיוֹת. מִן עֵדִים זוֹמְמִין. מַה עֵדִים זוֹמְמִין מְשַׁלְּמִין וְאֵינָן לוֹקִין. אַף הָכָא מְשַׁלֵּם וְאֵינוֹ לוֹקֶה. אָמַר רִבִּי יוֹנָה[24] טַעֲמָא דְנָתָן בַּר הוֹשַׁעְיָה וְהִפִּילוֹ הַשּׁוֹפֵט וְהִכָּהוּ לְפָנָיו אֶת שֶׁמַּכּוֹתָיו יוֹצְאוֹת בּוֹ יְדֵי רִשְׁעוֹ יָצָא זֶה שֶׁאָמַר לוֹ עֲמוֹד וְשַׁלֵּם.

Nathan bar Hoshiah[25] said, one speaks about a girl[26], the other about an adult woman. The girl has a fine but cannot be sold, the adult has no fine, she cannot be sold; has she no claim for shame and blemish[27]? The rabbis of Caesarea said, explain it that she seduced him or forgave him[28]. Nathan bar Hoshaiah thinks that in a case of flogging and payment he pays and is not flogged. Why should he not be flogged and have to pay? (*Deut.* 25:2) "Because of his guilt." You sentence him for one guilt but you may not sentence him for two guilts[6]. From perjured witnesses. Just as perjured witnesses pay and are not flogged[29], here also he pays and is not flogged. Rebbi Jonah said, the reason of Nathan bar Hoshaiah: (*Deut.* 25:2): "The judge shall have him laid down and flogged in his presence." It refers to one whose flogging frees him from his guilt, excluding one who is told: get up and pay.

24 Reading of the Rome ms. and the text in *Ketubot*. Leyden and Venice: ר' נתן, an impossible text for chronological reasons.

25 A Babylonian (in the Babli, Rav Nathan bar Hoshaiah) who immigrated into Galilee and became a member of R. Joḥanan's academy.

26 In the technical sense, נערה is a girl who no longer is a minor (so she cannot be sold in marriage, *Ex.* 21:7-11) but is not yet an adult who can marry on her own. Practically, a girl is a minor if she is less than 12 years old and becomes an adult at 12 years 6 months. The father has the right to marry her off as נערה and he collects the fine if she is raped before she is married. The Mishnah in *Ketubot* refers only to נערה since the verse determining the fine uses that expression.

27 Anybody injured by another person has a claim for pain, shame, and diminished standing. Hence, even if the fine is excluded the adult woman has a monetary claim and Nathan bar Hoshaiah cannot assume that the Mishnah in *Makkot* refers to an adult.

28 In the Babli, if she became an adult and forgave him. Since she is an adult, she may waive the monetary claim. In that case, because the rapist does not have to pay, he is whipped. {The נערה cannot waive the claim since the claim is her father's.}

29 Perjury is definitely sinful; it should be punished by flogging. But the verse decrees (*Deut.* 19:19): "Do to him what he intended to do to his brother". If the perjury was in a civil case, the perjurer has to pay to the injured party the amount the latter would have had to pay if the testimony had stood. Since this is the only punishment decreed by the verse, the perjurer cannot be flogged. {In criminal cases, the perjurer is flogged or executed, as the case may be.}

מַתְנִיתִין פְלִיגָא עַל רִבִּי שִׁמְעוֹן בֶּן לָקִישׁ. וְהָא תַנִּינָן הָאוֹכֵל תְּרוּמָה שׁוֹגֵג. פָּתַר לָהּ כְּרִבִּי מֵאִיר דְּרִבִּי מֵאִיר אָמַר לוֹקֶה וּמְשַׁלֵּם. וְהָא תַנִּינָן הָאוֹכֵל תְּרוּמָה מֵזִיד. עַל דַּעְתֵּיהּ דְּנָתָן בַּר הוֹשַׁעְיָה דּוּ אָמַר מְשַׁלֵּם וְאֵינוֹ לוֹקֶה נִיחָא. עַל דַּעְתֵּיהּ דְּרִבִּי יוֹחָנָן דּוּ אָמַר אִם הִתְרוּ בוֹ לוֹקֶה וְאִם לֹא הִתְרוּ בוֹ מְשַׁלֵּם. פָּתַר לָהּ מֵזִיד בְּלֹא הַתְרָיָיה. עַל דַּעְתֵּיהּ דְּרִבִּי שִׁמְעוֹן בֶּן לָקִישׁ לֹא שַׁנְיָיא הִיא מֵזִיד הִיא שׁוֹגֵג. הִיא הִתְרוּ בוֹ הִיא לֹא הִתְרוּ בוֹ. סָבַר רִבִּי שִׁמְעוֹן בֶּן לָקִישׁ כְּרִבִּי מֵאִיר דּוּ אָמַר רִבִּי מֵאִיר לוֹקֶה וּמְשַׁלֵּם.

Our Mishnah disagrees with Rebbi Simeon ben Laqish! Did we not state "If somebody eats heave in error"[30]? He explains it following Rebbi Meïr, since Rebbi Meïr said, he is whipped and pays. But did we not state: "If somebody eats heave intentionally"? In the opinion of Nathan bar Hoshaiah who said, when he pays he is not flogged, it is understandable. In the opinion of Rebbi Joḥanan who said, if he was cautioned he is flogged, but if he was not cautioned he pays, he explains it as intentional without cautioning. In the opinion of Rebbi Simeon ben Laqish there is no difference between intentional and unintentional, between cautioned or not cautioned. Rebbi Simeon ben Laqish holds with Rebbi Meïr since Rebbi Meïr says, he is flogged and he pays.

30 For him, there should be no difference between error and intentional transgression. The answer is that there is a difference, only for the linkage between payment and flogging there is no difference: Either flogging and paying in all cases go together or in no case is there flogging and a fine. Since the Mishnah clearly states that there is a fine, R. Simeon must hold with R. Meïr.

אָמַר רִבִּי חִינְנָא קוֹמֵי רִבִּי מָנָא וְאִין יִסְבּוֹר רִבִּי שִׁמְעוֹן בֶּן לָקִישׁ כָּל־מַתְנִיתִין דְּרִבִּי מֵאִיר קְרִייָא דִּבְרֵי מֵאִיר. וְהָא כְתִיב וְאִישׁ כִּי יֹאכַל קוֹדֶשׁ בִּשְׁגָגָה וגו'. אֶלָּא מִיסְבַּר סָבַר רִבִּי שִׁמְעוֹן בֶּן לָקִישׁ שֶׁהַחוֹמֶשׁ קָרְבָּן. וַאֲפִילוּ יִסְבּוֹר חוֹמֶשׁ

קָרְבָּן קֶרֶן קָרְבָּן. אָמַר רִבִּי יוּדָן בַּר שָׁלוֹם מַתְנִיתִין אָמְרָה שֶׁהַקֶּרֶן קְנָס דְּתַנִּינָן אֵינוֹ מְשַׁלֵּם תְּרוּמָה אֶלָּא חוּלִין מְתוּקָּנִין וְהֵן נַעֲשִׂין תְּרוּמָה. אִלּוּ מִמַּה שֶׁאָכַל הָיָה מְשַׁלֵּם יָאוּת. וְתַנֵּי כֵן אָכַל תְּרוּמָה טְמֵאָה מְשַׁלֵּם חוּלִין טְהוֹרִין וְאִם שִׁלֵּם חוּלִין טְמֵאִין יָצָא. וְלֹא דְמֵי עֵצִים הוּא חַיָּב לוֹ. הָדָא אָמְרָה שֶׁהַקֶּרֶן קְנָס. וּכְמָה דְתֵימַר קֶרֶן קְנָס וְדִכְוָותָהּ חוֹמֶשׁ קְנָס. אֶלָּא אָמַר רִבִּי שִׁמְעוֹן בֶּן לָקִישׁ כְּדַעְתֵּיהּ. כְּמָה דוּ רִבִּי שִׁמְעוֹן בֶּן לָקִישׁ אָמַר תַּמָּן הַכֹּל הָיוּ בִכְלָל לֹא תַעֲנֶה בְרֵעֲךָ עֵד שָׁקֶר. יָצָא זֶה וַעֲשִׂיתֶם לוֹ כַּאֲשֶׁר זָמַם לַעֲשׂוֹת לְאָחִיו לְחַיְּיבוֹ מָמוֹן. וְהָכָא הַכֹּל הָיוּ בִכְלָל וְכָל־זָר לֹא יֹאכַל קוֹדֶשׁ. יָצָא וְאִישׁ כִּי יֹאכַל קוֹדֶשׁ בִּשְׁגָגָה לְחַיְּיבוֹ מָמוֹן.

Rebbi Ḥinena said before Rebbi Mana: If Rebbi Simeon ben Laqish thought the entire Mishnaiot were Rebbi Meïr's, he would call them "the words of Meïr." But is it not written (*Lev.* 22:14): "If a person ate consecrated food in error, etc."? But Rebbi Simeon ben Laqish must hold that the fifth is a sacrifice[31]. But even if he holds that the fifth is a sacrifice, can the principal be a sacrifice? Rebbi Yudan bar Shalom said, the Mishnah declares that the principal is a fine, as we have stated[32]: "He does not pay in heave but in totally profane food which is turned into heave." If he had to pay from what he ate, it would be fine. And it was stated[33]: "If he ate impure heave, he has to pay in pure profane food, but if he paid in impure profane, he discharged his obligation." Does he not owe him the price of wood? That shows that the principal is a fine and since the principal is a fine, the fifth also is a fine. But Rebbi Simeon ben Laqish follows his own opinion. Just as Rebbi Simeon ben Laqish said, there, everybody was under the obligation of (*Ex.* 20:16) "Do not become a false witness against your neighbor", but this one was treated separately, (*Deut.* 19:19) "do to him what he intended to do to his brother", to force him to pay[34]; also here, everybody was under the obligation of (*Lev.* 22:10) "no outsider shall eat holy [food]," but this one was treated separately, (*Lev*. 22:14) "if somebody should eat holy [food] in error," to force him to pay[35].

31 Since every deadly sin committed in error needs a sacrifice for atonement.

32 Mishnah 6:1.

33 Halakhah 6:1, Note 20. Since the restitution must be more valuable than the food taken, the difference in value has the status of a fine.

34 In Tannaitic sources, the two verses are taken together following the principle that every prohibition has to be written twice in the Torah, first to define the prohibition and second to indicate the punishment for violating the prohibition (*Mekhilta deR. Ismael* Yitro 8, p. 233; *Mekhilta deR. Simeon bar Iohai* Yitro p. 152; *Sifry Deut.* 190(19)).

35 Again, the prohibition is defined in v. 10 and the punishment in v. 14; since this is a self-contained unit, no outside principles should be invoked.

וְהָתַנֵּי מוֹדִין חֲכָמִים לְרִבִּי מֵאִיר בְּגוֹנֵב חֶלְבּוֹ שֶׁל חֲבֵירוֹ שֶׁהוּא לוֹקֶה וּמְשַׁלֵּם שֶׁכֵּן הָאוֹכֵל חֵלֶב לוֹקֶה. וְהָתַנֵּי מוֹדִין חֲכָמִים לְרִבִּי מֵאִיר בְּגוֹנֵב תְּרוּמַת חֲבֵירוֹ שֶׁהוּא לוֹקֶה וּמְשַׁלֵּם שֶׁכֵּן הָאוֹכֵל תְּרוּמָתוֹ לוֹקֶה. וְהָתַנֵּי מוֹדִין חֲכָמִים לְרִבִּי מֵאִיר בְּחוֹסֵם פָּרָתוֹ שֶׁל חֲבֵירוֹ שֶׁהוּא לוֹקֶה וּמְשַׁלֵּם שֵׁשֶׁת קַבִּין לְפָרָה וְאַרְבַּעַת קַבִּין לַחֲמוֹר שֶׁכֵּן הַחוֹסֵם פָּרָתוֹ לוֹקֶה. אָמַר רִבִּי יוֹסֵי שֶׁכֵּן בִּמְחוּייָבֵי מִיתוֹת. גָּנַב תְּרוּמַת הֶקְדֵּשׁ וַאֲכָלָהּ לוֹקֶה וּמְשַׁלֵּם מִכָּל־מָקוֹם הִפְסִיד מָמוֹן.

Did we not state:[36] The Sages admit to Rebbi Meïr that one who stole his neighbor's fat is flogged and has to pay since he who eats fat is flogged. Did we not state: The Sages admit to Rebbi Meïr that one who stole his neighbor's heave is flogged and has to pay since he who eats his own heave is flogged[36]. Did we not state: The Sages admit to Rebbi Meïr that one who muzzled his neighbor's cow is flogged and has to pay six *qab* per cow and four *qab* for a donkey since he who muzzles his cow is flogged[37]. Rebbi Yose said, the same holds if death is the penalty. If he stole Temple heave and ate it, he is whipped and has to pay since in any case he caused monetary loss.

36 The first two statements are not in any source except here and in *Ketubot*. One can transgress several commandments in one action, e. g., if the thief immediately upon taking the fat puts it into his mouth. Then the thief acquires the fat (and at the same time makes himself liable for restitution) in the same moment he incurs guilt for eating fat. For each obligation or guilt incurred there is one and only one punishment.

37 Babli *Baba Mezia* 91a, in the interpretation of Rav Papa, against Abbaye who sees in the rule only the opinion of R. Meïr. According to Rav Papa, the thief is obliged to feed the animals from the moment of the theft but is flogged only after he muzzled them for threshing (*Deut.* 25:4).

אָמַר רִבִּי מָנָא קוֹמֵי רִבִּי יוֹסֵי מֵעַתָּה הַבָּא עַל אֲחוֹתוֹ קְטַנָּה[38] יִלְקֶה וִישַׁלֵּם. שֶׁכֵּן הַבָּא עַל אֲחוֹתוֹ בוֹגֶרֶת לוֹקֶה. חָזַר רִבִּי מָנָא וְאָמַר תַּמָּן חָל עָלָיו (fol. 44d) מִיתָה וְתַשְׁלוּמִין כְּאַחַת. בְּרַם הָכָא מֵהַחֲסִימָה הָרִאשׁוֹנָה נִתְחַייֵב מַלְקוּת וּמִכָּן וָאֵילַךְ לְתַשְׁלוּמִין. הָתִיב רִבִּי עֶזְרָא קוֹמֵי רִבִּי מָנָא הַמֵּצִית גְּדִישׁוֹ שֶׁל חֲבֵירוֹ בְּשַׁבָּת מִשִּׁיבּוֹלֶת הָרִאשׁוֹנָה נִתְחַייֵב מִיתָה מִכָּן וְאֵילַךְ לְתַשְׁלוּמִין. וְלֵית אַתְּ אָמַר הָכֵין אֶלָּא עַל כָּל־שִׁיבּוֹלֶת וְשִׁיבּוֹלֶת יֵשׁ בָּהּ הַתְרָייַת מִיתָה.[39] וְאוּף הָכָא עַל כָּל־חֲסִימָה יֵשׁ בָּהּ הַתְרָייַת מַכּוֹת (וְהַתְרָייַת תַּשְׁלוּמִין).[40] אָמַר רִבִּי יוֹסֵי בֵּי רִבִּי בּוּן תְּרֵין אֲמוֹרִין חַד אָמַר בְּחוֹסֵם בִּתְרוּמָה בְּמוּקְדּוּשִׁין. וְחָרָנָה אָמַר בְּחוֹסֵם עַל יְדֵי שָׁלִיחַ. שָׁלִיחַ לוֹקֶה וְהוּא פָּטוּר. דָּם יֵחָשֵׁב לָאִישׁ הַהוּא וְלֹא לִשְׁלוּחָיו.

Rebbi Mana said before Rebbi Yose: If it is so, he who sleeps with his minor sister should be flogged and have to pay since if he sleeps with his adult sister he is flogged[41]. Rebbi Mana reversed himself and said, there death and payment fall on him simultaneously[42]. But here, from the first muzzling he is subject to flogging but only later for payment[43]. Rebbi Ezra[44] objected before Rebbi Mana: He who sets fire to his neighbor's grain stack on the Sabbath is subject to capital punishment from the first ear but only later for payment! One cannot say so, for every single ear there is cautioning for the death penalty. Here also, for every moment of muzzling there is cautioning for flogging (and cautioning for payment). Rebbi Yose bar Abun said, two Amoraïm. One said, if he muzzled for heave which is Temple property[45]. The other one said, if he muzzled through an agent. Then the agent is flogged and he is free (*Lev.* 17:4): "As a blood guilt it will be charged on *this* man," not on his employers[46].

38 Reading of the text in *Ketubot*. In *Terumot*, the words קטנה and בוגרת are switched in the print and Leyden ms. Rome: הַבָּא עַל אֲחוֹתוֹ בוֹגֶרֶת יִלְקֶה וִישַׁלֵּם. שֶׁכֵּן הַבָּא עַל אֲחוֹתוֹ דְּאֵינוֹ לוֹקֶה.

39 Reading of the text in *Ketubot*. In *Terumot* מַכּוֹת וְהַתְרָיַית תַּשְׁלוּמִין.

40 The words in parentheses are not in *Ketubot* and are not relevant since monetary claims do not need cautioning.

41 As stated earlier (Notes 26, 28), the adult sister cannot claim money from the rapist brother who therefore is subject to flogging according to everybody. If the arguments of the previous paragraph are correct, the rapist of his minor sister should be flogged and have to pay.

42 It would be double punishment for one and the same transgression.

43 Any muzzling of a threshing animal is forbidden; the monetary obligation starts only when the threshing ox would have eaten a *peruṭa*'s worth had he not been muzzled. The two obligations are not simultaneous even though they come from transgressing one and the same prohibition.

44 He is R. Azariah (cf. *Berakhot*, Chapter 1, Note 90). The Rome ms. and the *Ketubot* text have ר' זעירא ; that reading is impossible for chronological reasons.

45 Then in one act he transgresses two prohibitions; for heave he is flogged and for larceny of sacred food he must pay. This is not double punishment for the same transgression.

46 In the words of the Babli, "there is no agency for crimes." If the agent is adult and of sane mind, he has to know himself that he is committing a crime and cannot unload the criminal responsibility on his employer. (This principle does not apply to civil claims.) The second explanation is rejected.

שׁוֹגֵג בִּתְרוּמָה וְמֵזִיד בְּחָמֵץ. שׁוֹגֵג בִּתְרוּמָה וּמֵזִיד בְּנָזִיר. שׁוֹגֵג בִּתְרוּמָה וְמֵזִיד בְּיוֹם הַכִּיפּוּרִים[47]. אִין נִפְתְּרִינָהּ בִּשְׁנֵי דְבָרִים נִיחָא. אִין נִפְתְּרִינָהּ בְּדָבָר אֶחָד מַחְלוֹקֶת רִבִּי יוֹחָנָן וְרִבִּי שִׁמְעוֹן בֶּן לָקִישׁ.

In error for heave and intentional for leavened[48], in error for heave and intentional for *nazir*[49], in error for heave and intentional for the Day of Atonement[50]. If one explains it with two things, it is fine[51]. If one explains it for one, this is the disagreement of Rebbi Joḥanan and Rebbi Simeon ben Laqish.

47 Text from *Ketubot* and a parallel *Pesaḥim* 2:3 (fol. 29a/b). Text of *Terumot*: בְּמֵזִיד בִּתְרוּמָה בְּשׁוֹגֵג בְּחוֹמֶשׁ מֵזִיד בִּתְרוּמָה וְשׁוֹגֵג בְּנָזִיר מֵזִיד בִּתְרוּמָה וְשׁוֹגֵג בְּיוֹם הַכִּיפּוּרִים.

48 If during Passover he intentionally ate leavened food (a deadly sin) but unintentionally took heave.

49 If somebody made a *nazir* vow (*Num.* 6) and he intentionally breaks his vow and eats grapes or drinks wine but unintentionally took heave.

50 If during the fast of the Day of Atonement he intentionally ate but unintentionally took heave.

51 If one holds that with one action two different laws have been broken, each infraction is punished according to its separate rules and everybody agrees that for heave he has to pay. But if one holds that for one action there can be only one punishment, he has to pay only according to R. Joḥanan.

תַּמָּן תַּנִּינָן אֵין בֵּין שַׁבָּת לְיוֹם הַכִּיפּוּרִים אֶלָּא שֶׁזֶּה זְדוֹנוֹ בִּידֵי אָדָם וְזֶה זְדוֹנוֹ בְּהִיכָּרֵת. הָא בְתַשְׁלוּמִין זֶה וְזֶה שָׁוִין. מַתְנִיתָא דְרִבִּי נְחוֹנְיָה בֶּן הַקָּנָה דְּתַנֵּי רִבִּי נְחוֹנְיָה בֶּן הַקָּנָה אוֹמֵר יוֹם הַכִּיפּוּרִים כְּשַׁבָּת לְתַשְׁלוּמִין. וְרִבִּי שִׁמְעוֹן בֶּן מְנַסְיָא אוֹמֵר כִּמְחוּייָבֵי כְרִיתוּת כָּךְ חַיְיבֵי מִיתוֹת בֵּית דִּין. מַה בֵּינֵיהוֹן. רִבִּי אָחָא בְשֵׁם רִבִּי אֲבִינָא אָמַר נַעֲרָה נִדָּה בֵּינֵיהוֹן. אָמַר רִבִּי מָנָא אוּף אָחוֹת אִשְׁתּוֹ בֵּינֵיהוֹן. עַל דַּעְתֵּיהּ דְּרִבִּי נְחוֹנְיָה בֶּן הַקָּנָה מַה שַׁבָּת אֵין לָהּ הֵיתֵר אַחַר אִיסוּרָהּ וְיוֹם הַכִּיפּוּרִים אֵין לוֹ הֵיתֵר אַחַר אִיסּוּרוֹ. וְזוֹ הוֹאִיל וְיֵשׁ לָהּ הֵיתֵר אַחַר אִיסּוּרָהּ מְשַׁלֵּם. וְרִבִּי שִׁמְעוֹן בֶּן מְנַסְיָא אוֹמֵר שַׁבָּת יֵשׁ בָּהּ כָּרֵת וְיוֹם הַכִּיפּוּרִים יֵשׁ בּוֹ כָּרֵת וְזוֹ הוֹאִיל וְיֵשׁ בּוֹ כָּרֵת אֵינוֹ מְשַׁלֵּם.

There[52], we have stated: "The only difference between the Sabbath and the Day of Atonement is that intentional infraction of the former is punished by the hands of man, but intentional infraction of the latter is punished by extirpation." Therefore, for payment both follow the same rules. The Mishnah is by Rebbi Neḥoniah ben Haqanah since they stated: "Neḥoniah ben Haqanah says, the Day of Atonement follows the rules of Sabbath for payment. But Rebbi Simeon ben Menassiah says those subject to extirpation equal those subject to capital punishment." What is between them? Rebbi Aḥa in the name of Rebbi Avina said, a menstruating girl is between them[53]. Rebbi Mana said, also his wife's sister is between them[54]. In the opinion of Rebbi Neḥoniah ben Haqanah, just as the Sabbath does not become permitted after its prohibition started[55], so the Day of Atonement does not become permitted after its prohibition started. However, this one will become permitted after her prohibition started, he has to pay. But Rebbi Simeon ben Menassiah said, extirpation applies to Sabbath[56] and the day of Atonement; extirpation applies also to this one, he does not have to pay.

52 Mishnah *Megillah* 1:5. The statement means that everything forbidden on the Sabbath is forbidden on the Day of Atonement, but not vice-versa. Infraction of the laws of the Sabbath is a capital crime but punishment for infraction of the laws of the Day of Atonement is in the hands of Heaven. The question is, how far do we equate the possibility of a death sentence by an earthly court with one by the Heavenly court.

53 If the seduced or raped almost adult girl was impure because of her period, the rapist or seducer is subject to extirpation, *Lev.* 20:18.

54 While punishment for sexual relations with the wife's sister during the lifetime of the wife is not spelled out in the verse, *Lev.* 18:18, all incest prohibitions enumerated in *Lev.* 18 are subject to *Lev.* 18:29: "For anybody who will commit any of these abominations, persons acting thus will be

exterminated from the midst of their people." (Rashi on Mishnah *Keritut* 1:1.)

55 While everything will become permitted again after the end of the Sabbath, nothing will be permitted as long as the Sabbath lasts. But the menstruating almost adult will become permitted again when cleansed from her impurity, in most cases while she still is an almost adult girl.

56 While desecration of the Sabbath is a capital crime, if prosecution is impossible for lack of cautioning or of eye witnesses it is a case for extirpation by Heaven, (*Ex.* 31:14): "Keep the Sabbath because it is holy for you; its desecrator shall be put to death. Anybody doing work on it shall be extirpated from the midst of his people."

רִבִּי יוּדָה בַּר פָּזִי בָּעֵי לָווִין וּכְרִיתוּת מַה אָמְרִין בָּהּ אִילֵּין תַּנָּיֵי. אָמַר רִבִּי יוֹסֵי צְרִיכָה לְרַבָּנִין. אָמַר רִבִּי יוֹנָה וְלָמָּה לֹא שָׁמַע לֵיהּ מִן הָדָא דְּתַנֵּי רִבִּי שִׁמְעוֹן בֶּן יוֹחַי. דְּתַנֵּי רִבִּי שִׁמְעוֹן בֶּן יוֹחַי רִבִּי טַרְפוֹן אוֹמֵר נֶאֱמַר כָּרֵת בְּשַׁבָּת וְנֶאֱמַר כָּרֵת בְּיוֹם הַכִּיפּוּרִים. מַה כָּרֵת הָאָמוּר בְּשַׁבָּת אֵין מָמוֹן אֶצֶל מִיתָה.[57] אַף כָּרֵת הָאָמוּר בְּיוֹם הַכִּיפּוּרִים אֵין מָמוֹן[58] אֶצֶל כָּרֵת. אָמַר רִבִּי מָנָא קוֹמֵי רִבִּי יוֹסֵי מַה צְרִיכִין לֵיהּ כְּרִבִּי שִׁמְעוֹן בֶּן לָקִישׁ בְּרַם כְּרִבִּי יוֹחָנָן אִם מַכּוֹת אֶצֶל מִיתָה יֵשׁ לוֹ לֹא כָּל־שֶׁכֵּן מָמוֹן אֶצֶל מַכּוֹת.[59] אָמַר לֵיהּ וְאַף כְּרִבִּי יוֹחָנָן צְרִיכָה לֵיהּ. אִיתְפַּלְגוּן הַשּׁוֹחֵט אוֹתוֹ וְאֶת בְּנוֹ לְשׁוּם עֲבוֹדָה זָרָה. רִבִּי יוֹחָנָן אָמַר אִם הִתְרוּ בוֹ לְשׁוּם אוֹתוֹ וְאֶת בְּנוֹ לוֹקֶה. לְשֵׁם עֲבוֹדָה זָרָה הָיָה נִסְקָל. רִבִּי שִׁמְעוֹן בֶּן לָקִישׁ אָמַר וַאֲפִילוּ הִתְרוּ בוֹ לְשׁוּם אוֹתוֹ וְאֶת בְּנוֹ אֵינוֹ לוֹקֶה. מֵאַחַר שֶׁאִילּוּ הִתְרוּ בוֹ לְשֵׁם עֲבוֹדָה זָרָה הָיָה נִסְקָל. הָכָא שְׁנֵי דְבָרִים. וְהָכָא דָּבָר אֶחָד.

[60]Rebbi Judah bar Pazi asked: What say these Tannaïm about prohibitions and extirpation[61]? Rebbi Yose said, that is a problem for the rabbis. Rebbi Jonah said, why can we not understand it from what Rebbi Simeon ben Ioḥai stated? As Rebbi Simeon ben Ioḥai stated: "Rebbi Ṭarphon says, extirpation was mentioned for the Sabbath and the Day of Atonement. Since for extirpation mentioned for the Sabbath there is no payment in a case involving the death penalty[61], so for extirpation

mentioned for the Day of Atonement there is no payment in a case involving extirpation[62]." Rebbi Mana said before Rebbi Yose: When do we need this? For Rebbi Simeon ben Laqish! But for Rebbi Johanan, if he admits flogging in death penalty cases, certainly payment in extirpation cases[63]. He said to him, we need it even for Rebbi Johanan! They disagreed: If somebody slaughters [an animal] and its young[64] for idolatrous purposes. Rebbi Johanan says, if he was cautioned about an animal and its young, he is flogged, about idolatry, he is stoned to death. Rebbi Simeon ben Laqish said, even if he was cautioned about an animal and its young, he is not flogged since he would be stoned to death had he been cautioned about idolatry. Here are two cases[65], there it is one case[66].

57 Reading of the text in *Ketubot*: אֵין מַכּוֹת אֵצֶל מִיתָה "there is no flogging in death penalty cases."

58 Reading of the text in *Ketubot*: אֵין מַכּוֹת אֵצֶל כָּרֵת "there is no flogging in extirpation cases."

59 Reading of the text in *Ketubot*: מַכּוֹת אֵצֶל כָּרֵת "there is flogging in extirpation cases."

60 The commentators declare the text in *Ketubot* as original and the one here corrupt. However, the Babli in *Ketubot* 33a-36a seems more to refer to a text like the one in *Terumot* which is preferable as *lectio difficilior*. On the other hand, the last paragraph of the Halakhah shows that the text here is copied from *Ketubot*. Therefore, both versions have to be explained.

61 The text here is based on the earlier text excluding payment in death penalty cases, Note 19. In the Babli, *Ketubot* 34b/35a, this is deduced as above and in addition from *Ex*. 21:22-23, where payment is due if a pregnant woman is injured and an abortion is caused, but no payment is due if the woman is murdered.

62 In the Babli, *Ketubot* 35a, only R. Simeon ben Laqish accepts this reasoning; R. Johanan admits payment concurrent with extirpation.

The text in *Ketubot* deals with the situation in which a simple transgression for which the punishment is flogging is combined with a transgression punishable by extirpation and there was cautioning for the first but not for the second; can the flogging be executed? There is no question that flogging is the earthly punishment for most extirpation transgressions, as stated in Mishnah *Makkot* 3:16: "All those subject to extirpation who were flogged became free from extirpation, as it is written (*Deut*. 25:3): 'that your brother should not be degraded in your eyes;' after he was flogged he is your brother."

63 In the Babli, *Ketubot* 35b, this is deduced from the Mishnah which assigns a fine to a brother who seduced his sister which, in absence of witnesses, is an extirpation case.

For the *Ketubot* text it is obvious that a capital crime can never lead to a sentence of flogging since no sentence can be delivered without the testimony of two witnesses. If there were witnesses it would be a case for the death penalty; without witnesses it is a case for the Heavenly court.

64 Slaughtering an animal and its young on the same day is a simple transgression, *Lev*. 22:28. Idolatrous sacrifices are capital crimes.

65 The prohibition of slaughtering an animal and its young on the same day also applies to profane slaughter; it is unrelated to the prohibition of idolatry. The parallel discussion in the Babli is *Ḥulin* 81b, where it is pointed out that the case discussed must be that the first animal was slaughtered for food but the second for idolatry; only in that case does one act result in two transgressions.

66 The disagreement between R. Joḥanan and R. Simeon ben Laqish is the case that there is only one transgression which, however, cannot be prosecuted in criminal court for lack of eye witnesses.

עַל דַּעְתֵּיהּ דְּרִבִּי שִׁמְעוֹן בֶּן לָקִישׁ מַה בֵּין אִילֵּין תַּנָּיֵי לְאִילֵּין רַבָּנִין לְלָאוִין לֹא לִכְרִיתוּת. אָמַר רִבִּי יוּדָן רִבִּי שִׁמְעוֹן בֶּן לָקִישׁ דּוּ אָמַר כְּרִבִּי מֵאִיר דּוּ אָמַר לוֹקֶה וּמְשַׁלֵּם. אָמַר רִבִּי חֲנַנְיָה הַמֵּצִית גְּדִישׁוֹ שֶׁל חֲבֵירוֹ בְּיוֹם טוֹב בֵּינֵיהוֹן. אִילֵּין תַּנָּיֵי סָבְרִין מֵימַר הוֹאִיל וְאֵין בָּהֶן כָּרֵת מְשַׁלֵּם. וְאִילֵּין רַבָּנִין סָבְרִין מֵימַר הוֹאִיל וְיֵשׁ מַכּוֹת אֵינוֹ מְשַׁלֵּם. מֵעַתָּה אִילּוּ נְעָרוֹת דְּלָא כְּרַבָּנִין. אָמַר רִבִּי מַתַּנְיָה בְּבָא עַל הַמַּמְזֶרֶת בֵּינֵיהוֹן.

According to Rebbi Simeon ben Laqish, what is between these Tannaïm[67] and those rabbis[68]? Rebbi Judan said, Rebbi Simeon ben Laqish [is the one] who said following Rebbi Meïr, who said he is flogged and pays[69]. Rebbi Ḥananiah said, he who puts fire to the grain stack of his neighbor on a holiday[70] is between them. These Tannaïm think, since there is no extirpation, he pays. Those rabbis think, since there is flogging he does not pay. But then "these are the girls" cannot follow the rabbis[71]! Rebbi Mattaniah said, he who sleeps with a bastard girl is between them[72].

67 Rebbis Neḥoniah ben Haqanah and Simeon ben Menassiah who imply that only capital cases and those of extirpation free from payment.

68 The rabbis, also Tannaïm, who disagree with R. Meïr and hold that flogging frees from payment.

69 He disagrees with the rabbis and does not have to try to explain the rabbis.

70 Desecration of a holiday (other than the Day of Atonement) is a simple infraction, not subject to extirpation.

71 The list of *Ketubot* 3:1 notes only those cases in which the rapist could not marry his victim as required by *Deut.* 22:29, either because of an incest prohibition or other biblical restriction on permitted sexual relations. Then the rapist is subject to flogging; according to R. Simeon ben Laqish he never would have to pay. Since this invalidates an entire Mishnah, it is an impossible stance.

72 A bastard is a child born from a sexual union subject to the death penalty or extirpation. The *Ketubot* text reads: "A bastard who sleeps with a bastard girl is between them." It seems that the difference between the two texts is based on a difference in the interpretation of the relevant verse *Deut.* 23:3. The reading here supports Maimonides (*Issure Bi'ah* 15:2) that sexual relations with a bastard (male or female) are only punishable by flogging after marriage; then a fine is due without question. The reading in *Ketubot* supports R. Abraham ben David (*ad loc.*) and Nachmanides (in his *Novellae* to *Ketubot*) that the verse forbids all sexual relations with a bastard since the expression used, "to come", in rabbinic Hebrew means "to sleep with." According to everybody, a male bastard may marry a female bastard.

וְאֵשֶׁת אָחִיו לָאו יְבִימְתּוֹ הִיא. תִּפָּתֵר שֶׁמֵּת אָחִיו וְהָיוּ לוֹ בָנִים וְאֵירֵשׁ אִשָּׁה וּמֵת וּבָא אָחִיו וַאֲנָסָהּ.

But is his brother's wife not his sister-in-law[73]? Explain it that the man's brother died when he had children and had performed the preliminary wedding with a woman when he died and [the surviving] brother came and raped her.

73 This question has no relation to the topics discussed here; it belongs to the discussion of Mishnah *Ketubot* 3:1 and shows that the text there is original. The Mishnah mentions the brother's wife as one of the categories of girls for whom the rapist has to pay the fine of 50 *šeqel*. Now this fine is due only for the rape of a virgin. The only case where the brother's wife still could be a virgin is that the brother died between the preliminary wedding (cf. *Peah* Chapter 6, Note 46; *Demay* Chapter 4, Note 19) and the actual wedding. If the brother died childless, his widow should be married by his brother and she can be married only by the sex act (*Deut.* 25:5, Mishnah *Yebamot* 6:1) and no rape is legally possible. If the brother did have children, his widow is forbidden to the brother under penalty of extirpation. One possible scenario for inclusion of the brother's wife in the list is the one given in the text, when there are no eye witnesses. Another (cf. Rashi *ad loc.*, Tosafot *Ketubot* 29a, *s. v.* והבא) is that the brother is still alive but the girl was divorced after the preliminary ceremony, before the actual marriage, when she is still a virgin but permanently forbidden to her brother-in-law.

(fol. 44b) **משנה ב**: בַּת כֹּהֵן שֶׁנִּישֵּׂאת לְיִשְׂרָאֵל וְאַחַר כָּךְ אָכְלָה תְרוּמָה מְשַׁלֶּמֶת אֶת הַקֶּרֶן וְאֵינָהּ מְשַׁלֶּמֶת אֶת הַחוֹמֶשׁ. וּמִיתָתָהּ בִּשְׂרֵיפָה. נִישֵּׂאת לְאֶחָד מִכָּל־הַפְּסוּלִין מְשַׁלֶּמֶת קֶרֶן וְחוֹמֶשׁ וּמִיתָתָהּ בְּחֶנֶק דִּבְרֵי רִבִּי מֵאִיר. וַחֲכָמִים אוֹמְרִים זוֹ וְזוֹ מְשַׁלְּמוֹת אֶת הַקֶּרֶן וְאֵין מְשַׁלְּמוֹת אֶת הַחוֹמֶשׁ. וּמִיתָתָן בִּשְׂרֵיפָה.

Mishnah 2: The daughter of a Cohen married to an Israel[74] who afterwards ate heave pays the principal but does not pay the fifth; her death is by burning[75]. If she married one of the ineligible[76], she pays principal and fifth and her death is by strangulation[77], the words of Rebbi Meïr. But the Sages say[78], both pay principal but not the fifth and their deaths are by burning.

74 She used to eat heave when unmarried. Once she is married outside the tribe, heave is forbidden to her (*Lev.* 22:12). However, if the marriage is dissolved without issue, she returns to eat heave (v. 13). This implies that even in her marriage she is not a stranger in the sense of v. 13; the obligation of payment of a fifth (v. 14) cannot apply to her. It is clear that one has returned to the case of eating heave in error, not intentionally.

75 If she commits adultery, *Lev.* 21:9.

76 A castrate, bastard, Ammonite or Moabite (*Deut.* 23:2-4), or a Cohen after she had been divorced (*Lev.* 21:7). In these cases, even if her marriage is dissolved, she may never return to eating heave since she is desecrated. R. Meïr holds that she is now a stranger to her former tribe.

77 The normal penalty for adultery, which applies to the adulterer in all cases.

78 Since in *Lev.* 21:9 she is characterized as "daughter of a Cohen man," and this she remains [*Sifra Emor Parašah* 5(7), Babli *Sanhedrin* 51a]. The involved formulation is taken to include also illegitimate offspring of a Cohen [*Sifra Emor Pereq* 1(16)]. In Babli *Keritut* 6a, the opinion of the Sages is traced to R. Jehudah.

(fol. 44d) **הלכה ב:** כָּךְ הִיא מַתְנִיתָא זִינְתָה מִיתָתָהּ בִּשְׂרֵיפָה.

Halakhah 2: So is the Mishnah: If she commits adultery, her death is by burning[79].

79 Only for adultery, not for any other capital crime [*Sifra Emor Pereq* 1(14)].

מַה טַעֲמָא דְרִבִּי מֵאִיר כִּי תֵחֵל לִזְנוֹת בֵּית אָבִיהָ. אֶת שֶׁאֵינָהּ רְאוּיָה לַחֲזוֹר לְבֵית אָבִיהָ. יָצָאת זוֹ שֶׁהִיא רְאוּיָה לַחֲזוֹר לְבֵית אָבִיהָ. נִישְּׂאֵת לְכָשֵׁר וְזִינָת הֲרֵי הִיא רְאוּיָה לַחֲזוֹר לְבֵית אָבִיהָ. מַיי כְדוֹן כִּי תֵחֵל לִזְנוֹת אֶת שֶׁחִילּוּלָהּ

מַחְמַת הַזְּנוּת וְלֹא חִילּוּלָהּ מַחְמַת נִישּׂוּאִין. מַה טַעֲמָא דְרַבָּנִין וּבַת אִישׁ כֹּהֵן מִכָּל־מָקוֹם. מֵעַתָּה אֲפִילוּ חֲלָלָה מִבְּנָהּ. תַּנָּא רִבִּי חִינְנָא בַּר פַּפָּא קוֹמֵי רִבִּי זְעִירָא דְּרִבִּי יִשְׁמָעֵאל אֶת אָבִיהָ הִיא מְחַלֶּלֶת. אֶת שֶׁחִילּוּלָהּ מַחְמַת עַצְמָהּ. וְלֹא שֶׁחִילּוּלָהּ מַחְמַת אָבִיהָ. אָמַר רִבִּי חֲנִינָה שׁוֹנֶה אֲנִי עַל דְּרִבִּי יִשְׁמָעֵאל וַאֲפִילוּ חֲלָלָה מִבְּנָהּ.

What is the reason of Rebbi Meïr? (*Lev*. 21:9) "If she desecrates her father's house by whoring[80]," one who may not return to her father's house; this excludes one who may return to her father's house[81]. If she married acceptably but committed adultery, may she return to her father's house[82]? How is this? "If she desecrates by whoring;" the one whose desecration is by whoring, not the one whose desecration is by marriage[83]. What is the reason of the rabbis? (*Lev*. 21:9) "A Cohen man's daughter," under all circumstances. Then also if her desecration is by her son[84]? Rebbi Ḥinena par Papa stated before Rebbi Zeïra following Rebbi Ismael: (*Lev*. 21:9) "She desecrates her father." One whose desecration is caused by herself, not one whose desecration is because of her father. Rebbi Ḥanina said, I learn from the words of Rebbi Ismael, even if her desecration is by her son[85].

80 "A Cohen man's daughter, if she desecrates her father's house by whoring, she desecrates her father; she shall be burned by fire." The status of an adulterous daughter of a Cohen also determines her status for restitution of heave.

81 The language is difficult. In the Rome ms., "this excludes one who may leave her father's house." The commentators switch the places of "may" and "may not", but the manuscript evidence forbids this emendation. One has to say that the one who may not return is one living (or who lived previously) in a prohibited marriage; the one who may return is the one living in an acceptable marriage who will be able to resume eating heave as a childless widow or divorcee.

82 The previous argument is patently false; a Cohen's daughter

acceptably married by her adultery becomes a permanently disqualified whore.

83 The woman living in a forbidden marriage is disqualified already before her adultery; the special rules for daughters of Cohanim cannot apply to her. The woman married acceptably falls under the rules for Cohanim and their descendants.

84 If the Cohen's daughter sleeps with her own son, the punishment should be death by stoning which is considered a harsher punishment than death by burning.

85 The Babli, *Sanhedrin* 51a, disagrees and in all cases requires the harsher punishment.

וְהָתַנִּינָן רִבִּי לִיעֶזֶר מְחַייֵב קֶרֶן וְחוֹמֶשׁ. וְרִבִּי יוֹשׁוּעַ פּוֹטֵר. הֲווֹן בָּעֵיי מֵימַר מַה פְלִיגִין בְּחוֹמֶשׁ אֲבָל בְּקֶרֶן אֲפִילוּ רִבִּי יוֹשׁוּעַ מוֹדֵי. מַה פְלִיגִין לְשֶׁעָבַר אֲבָל לָבֹא אֲפִילוּ רִבִּי יוֹשׁוּעַ מוֹדֵי.

Did we not state[86]: "Rebbi Eliezer holds him responsible for principal and fifth, but Rebbi Joshua frees." They wanted to say, they disagree about the fifth, but for the principal even Rebbi Joshua agrees[87]. They disagree for the past, but for the future even Rebbi Joshua agrees.

86 Mishnah 8:1, dealing with a man who is informed that he falsely was held to be a Cohen. He should not be treated differently from a woman falsely continuing her lost Cohen status.

87 Since in our Mishnah there is no doubt that restitution of the principal is required.

(fol. 44b) **משנה ג**: הַמַּאֲכִיל אֶת בָּנָיו קְטַנִּים וְאֶת עֲבָדָיו בֵּין גְּדוֹלִים בֵּין קְטַנִּים הָאוֹכֵל תְּרוּמַת חוּצָה לָאָרֶץ וְהָאוֹכֵל פָּחוֹת מִכְּזַיִת תְּרוּמָה מְשַׁלֵּם אֶת הַקֶּרֶן וְאֵינוֹ מְשַׁלֵּם אֶת הַחוֹמֶשׁ וְהַתַּשְׁלוּמִין חוּלִין. אִם רָצָה הַכֹּהֵן לִמְחוֹל לוֹ מוֹחֵל.

Mishnah 3: He who feeds his minor children or his slaves, adult or minor, he who eats heave from outside the Land, and he who eats less than the volume of an olive of heave pays the principal but not the fifth[88]. The payment is profane and if the Cohen wants to forgive it, he may forgive.

משנה ד: זֶה הַכְּלָל כָּל־הַמְּשַׁלֵּם קֶרֶן וְחוֹמֶשׁ תַּשְׁלוּמִין תְּרוּמָה אִם רָצָה הַכֹּהֵן לִמְחוֹל אֵינוֹ מוֹחֵל וְכָל־הַמְּשַׁלֵּם אֶת הַקֶּרֶן וְאֵינוֹ מְשַׁלֵּם אֶת הַחוֹמֶשׁ הַתַּשְׁלוּמִין חוּלִין אִם רָצָה הַכֹּהֵן לִמְחוֹל מוֹחֵל.

Mishnah 4: This is the principle: In every case one pays the principal and the fifth, the payment is heave and although the Cohen may want to forgive, he may not forgive. In every case one pays the principal but not the fifth, the payment is profane and if the Cohen wants to forgive, he may do so.

88 *Lev.* 22:14: "If a man ate in error from the holy [food], then he has to add a fifth and hand over the holy [food] to the Cohen." In the first cases of the Mishnah, he himself does not eat; therefore, he is not covered by the verse. But minors and slaves are not responsible; they cannot be asked to pay. Heave from outside the Land is of questionable holiness. Less than the volume of an olive may be nibbling; it is not eating.

(fol. 44d) **הלכה ג**: לֹא הִסְפִּיק לְשַׁלֵּם עַד שֶׁנִּשְׁתַּחְרֵר נוֹתֵן. הָיוּ לוֹ נְכָסִים שֶׁאֵין לְרַבּוֹ רְשׁוּת בָּהֶן נוֹתֵן.

Halakhah 3: If he[89] did not have occasion to pay before he[90] was manumitted, he[90] gives. If he had property about which his master had no power, he gives[91].

89 The master who fed his slave illegitimate heave.

90 The slave.

91 In principle, anything the slave acquires, the master acquires. However, if a third person gives property to the slave with the explicit condition that the master should have no power of disposal over the property, that condition is valid and enforceable in court.

הֵיךְ עֲבִידָא. רְאוּבֵן שֶׁגָּזַל מִשִּׁמְעוֹן וְהֶאֱכִילָהּ לְלֵוִי יָצָא יְדֵי גְזֵילוֹ. תַּפְלוּגְתָא דְרִבִּי חִייָה רַבָּא וְרִבִּי יַנַּאי. דְּאִיתְפַּלְּגוּן גָּזַל מַעֲפָרְתּוֹ שֶׁל זֶה וְנָתַן לְזֶה. רִבִּי לָעְזָר בְּשֵׁם רִבִּי חִייָה רַבָּה מוֹצִיאִין מִן הָרִאשׁוֹן וְאֵין מוֹצִיאִין מִן הַשֵּׁנִי. רִבִּי יוֹחָנָן בְּשֵׁם רִבִּי יַנַּאי אַף מוֹצִיאִין מִן הַשֵּׁנִי. וְאַף רִבִּי חִייָה רוֹבָה מוֹדֵי מִכֵּיוָן שֶׁנְּתָנָהּ לְלֵוִי יָצָא בָהּ יְדֵי גְזֵילוֹ.

How is this? If Reuben robbed from Simeon and served it to Levi, is he quit for his robbery[92]? This is the disagreement between the elder Rebbi Ḥiyya and Rebbi Yannai, since they disagreed: One robbed a hooded coat from one person and gave it to someone else. Rebbi Eleazar in the name of the elder Rebbi Ḥiyya, one can collect from the first but not from the second[93]. Rebbi Joḥanan in the name of Rebbi Yannai, one can also collect from the second[94]. But the elder Rebbi Ḥiyya also agrees that when Levi gave, he is quit for his robbery[95].

92 If Levi paid Simeon, is Reuben free from the obligation of restitution? This refers to the previous paragraph which seems to imply that the payment by an ex-slave frees his former owner from the obligation of restitution for the heave taken in error.

93 By the transaction, the second owner acquired ownership and the original owners can only sue the robber for monetary damages.

94 In the Babli, *Baba Qama* 111b, it is held in the name of R. Ḥisda that a change of ownership removes the buyer from the obligation of restitution only if the original owners had given up hope to regain the robbed article. This is not the position of the Yerushalmi.

95 Even R. Ḥiyya will agree that if Levi, who cannot be sued, voluntarily pays Simeon, Reuben is freed from his obligation towards Simeon.

(fol. 44b) **משנה ה**: שְׁתֵּי קוּפּוֹת אַחַת שֶׁל תְּרוּמָה וְאַחַת שֶׁל חוּלִין שֶׁנָּפְלָה סְאָה שֶׁל תְּרוּמָה לְתוֹךְ אַחַת מֵהֶן וְאֵין יָדוּעַ לְאֵי זֶה מֵהֶן נָפְלָה הֲרֵי אֲנִי אוֹמֵר לְתוֹךְ שֶׁל תְּרוּמָה נָפְלָה.

Mishnah 5: Two boxes, one of heave and one profane. A *seah* of heave fell into one of them and it is not known into which one; I say it fell into heave.

(fol. 44d) **הלכה ד**: אַחַת טְמֵאָה וְאַחַת טְהוֹרָה אֲנִי אוֹמֵר לְתוֹךְ טְמֵאָה נָפְלָה. אַחַת מְדוּמָּעַת וְאַחַת אֵינָהּ מְדוּמָּעַת אֲנִי אוֹמֵר לְתוֹךְ מְדוּמָּעַת נָפְלָה. אַחַת יֵשׁ בָּהּ כְּדֵי לַעֲלוֹת וְאַחַת אֵין בָּהּ כְּדֵי לַעֲלוֹת אֲנִי אוֹמֵר לְאוֹתָהּ שֶׁאֵין בָּהּ כְּדֵי לַעֲלוֹת נָפְלָה.

Halakhah 4: One impure and one pure, I say it fell into the impure one[96]. One *dema'* and one not *dema'*, I say it fell into the one containing *dema'*[97]. One contains enough for lifting[96] and one does not, I say it fell into the one which does not contain enough for lifting.

96 In Tosephta 6:15 it is added that in case the two boxes contained heave, the pure heave may be formed into dough only in quantities less than the volume of an egg, to avoid possible impurities. This means that the expression "I say" implies only restrictions, not leniencies.

97 Cf. Chapter 4, Note 62.

(fol. 44b) **משנה ו**: אֵין יָדוּעַ אֵי זוֹ הִיא שֶׁל תְּרוּמָה וְאֵי זוֹ הִיא שֶׁל חוּלִין. אָכַל אֶת אַחַת מֵהֶן פָּטוּר. וְהַשְּׁנִייָה נוֹהֵג בָּהֶן כִּתְרוּמָה וְחַייֶבֶת בְּחַלָּה דִּבְרֵי רַבִּי מֵאִיר וְרַבִּי יוֹסֵי פּוֹטֵר. אָכַל אֶחָד מִן הַשְּׁנִייָה פָּטוּר. אָכַל אֶחָד מִשְּׁנֵיהֶן מְשַׁלֵּם כִּקְטַנָּה שֶׁבִּשְׁנֵיהֶן.

Mishnah 6: [98]If it is not known which [box] is heave and which one is profane, if one ate [the contents of] one of them, he is free[99]. The [contents of] the second he treats as heave but it is subject to *hallah*[100], the words of Rebbi Meïr; but Rebbi Yose declares it free[101]. If another person ate from the second [box], he is free. If he ate from both of them, he pays according to the lesser of the two[102].

98 This is a direct continuation of the previous Mishnah; in most Mishnah codices the two form a single unit.

99 In this Mishnah, "free" means free from paying for the heave.

100 *Ḥallah* is heave taken from profane dough. While one treats the contents as heave, one is not sure that it is heave. If they were profane, any dough made from them would be subject to *ḥallah* under the rules of heave. Since R. Meïr always considers all possibilities, he must require that *ḥallah* be taken.

101 R. Yose puts the second box under the rules of *dema'*. Dough made from *dema'* is free from the obligation of *ḥallah* (Mishnah *Ḥallah* 3:2).

102 Since the obligation is monetary, he has to pay only the amount certainly due.

(fol. 44d) **הלכה ה**: רִבִּי שִׁמְעוֹן בֶּן לָקִישׁ בְּשֵׁם בַּר קַפָּרָא אָמַר וְהוּא שֶׁיֵּשׁ בִּשְׁנִייָה רוֹב. רִבִּי יוֹחָנָן אָמַר אַף עַל פִּי שֶׁאֵין בִּשְׁנִייָה רוֹב. מִחְלְפָה שִׁיטָּתֵיהּ דְּרִבִּי שִׁמְעוֹן בֶּן לָקִישׁ. תַּמָּן הוּא אוֹמֵר סְפֵיקָן בָּטֵל בְּרוֹב וְהָכָא אָמַר הָכֵין. תַּמָּן בְּשֵׁם גַּרְמֵיהּ. וְהָכָא בְּשֵׁם בַּר קַפָּרָא. מִחְלְפָה שִׁיטָּתֵיהּ דְּרִבִּי יוֹחָנָן. תַּמָּן הוּא אָמַר כּוּלְּהֶם נַעֲשׂוּ הוֹכִיחַ וְהָכָא אַתְּ אָמַר הָכֵין. שַׁנְייָה הִיא הָכָא שֶׁיֵּשׁ לוֹ בְּמַה לִתְלוֹת.

Halakhah 5: Rebbi Simeon ben Laqish in the name of Bar Qappara: Only if the second [box] was larger[103]. Rebbi Johanan said, even if the second was not larger. The opinion of Rebbi Simeon ben Laqish seems inverted. There[104], he says this doubt disappears in the plurality but here, he says so? There, he said it as his own [opinion], here in the name of Bar Qappara. The opinion of Rebbi Joḥanan seems inverted. There, he says all become subject to proof but here, he says so? There is a difference because here there is a peg to hang on[105].

103 Since in biblical law, all doubts are resolved by a plurality (Chapter 4, Note 71).

104 In the case of heave figs falling into profane figs, Chapter 4, Notes 82 ff.

105 Figs all look alike, but here there are two different boxes. This is an argument valid only because we hold that the obligation of heave today is rabbinical; if it were biblical, one could not pretend to guess the place of the heave.

(fol. 44b) **משנה ז**: נָפְלָה אַחַת מֵהֶן לְתוֹךְ הַחוּלִין אֵינָהּ מְדַמְּעָתָן וְהַשְּׁנִייָה נוֹהֵג בָּהּ בִּתְרוּמָה וְחַיֶּיבֶת בְּחַלָּה דִּבְרֵי רִבִּי מֵאִיר וְרִבִּי יוֹסֵי פוֹטֵר. נָפְלָה שְׁנִיָּה לְמָקוֹם אַחֵר אֵינָהּ מְדַמְּעָתוֹ. נָפְלוּ שְׁתֵּיהֶן לְמָקוֹם אֶחָד מְדַמְּעוֹת כִּקְטַנָּה שֶׁבִּשְׁתֵּיהֶן.

Mishnah 7: [106]If one of them fell into profane [produce] it would not make it *dema'*. The [contents of] the second he treats as heave but it is subject to *ḥallah*[100], the words of Rebbi Meïr; but Rebbi Yose declares it free[101]. If the [contents of the] second [box] fell into another place, they would not make it *dema'*. If both together fell into one place they would create *dema'* relative to the smaller one[107].

106 This is still a continuation of Mishnah 5.

107 The rule is taken from Mishnah 3:2 (Note 28), where the reasoning behind it is explained.

(fol. 44d) **הלכה ו**: שְׁתֵּי קוּפּוֹת אַחַת שֶׁל תְּרוּמָה טְמֵאָה וְאַחַת שֶׁל חוּלִין טְהוֹרִין וְנָפְלָה סְאָה תְרוּמָה טְמֵאָה לְתוֹךְ אַחַת מֵהֶן וְאֵין יָדוּעַ לְאֵי זוֹ מֵהֶן נָפְלָה אֲנִי אוֹמֵר לְתוֹךְ שֶׁל תְּרוּמָה נָפְלָה. וְהַחוּלִין יֵאָכְלוּ בְטָהֳרָה. נָפְלָה סְאָה תְרוּמָה טְהוֹרָה אֲנִי אוֹמֵר לְתוֹךְ שֶׁל תְּרוּמָה טְמֵאָה נָפְלָה וְחוּלִין יֵאָכְלוּ נִיקוּדִים. שְׁתֵּי קוּפּוֹת אַחַת (fol. 45a) שֶׁל תְּרוּמָה טְהוֹרָה וְאַחַת שֶׁל חוּלִין טְמֵאָה וְנָפְלָה סְאָה

תְּרוּמָה טְהוֹרָה לְתוֹךְ אַחַת מֵהֶן וְאֵין יָדוּעַ לְאֵי זוֹ מֵהֶן נָפְלָה. אֲנִי אוֹמֵר לְתוֹךְ תְּרוּמָה נָפְלָה וְחוּלִין יֵאָכְלוּ נִיקוּדִין. נָפְלָה סְאָה תְרוּמָה טְמֵאָה שְׁתֵּיהֶן אֲסוּרוֹת. מַה נַפְשָׁךְ אִי לְתוֹךְ תְּרוּמָה נָפְלָה אָסוּר. אִי לְתוֹךְ שֶׁל חוּלִין נָפְלָה אָסוּר. לָמָּה שֶׁסָּפֵק טָמֵא טָמֵא וְסָפֵק מְדוּמָּע מוּתָּר.

Halakhah 6: [108]"Two boxes, one of impure heave and one of pure profane [grain]: a *seah* of impure heave fell into one of them and it is not known into which of them it fell, I say it fell into heave but the profane should be eaten in the form of crackers[109]. If a *seah* of pure heave fell, I say it fell into heave but the profane should be eaten as crackers.

Two boxes, one of pure heave and one of impure profane [grain]: a *seah* of pure heave fell into one of them and it is not known into which of them it fell, I say it fell into heave but the profane should be eaten as crackers. If a *seah* of impure heave fell, both of them are forbidden." In any way you look at it, if it fell into heave, it is forbidden, if it fell into the profane, it is forbidden since impurity in doubt is impure[110] but *dema'* in doubt is permitted[111].

108 Similar arguments in different formulation are in Tosephta 6:15 -17.

109 To avoid impurity, cf. Chapter 5, Note 5. We say that heave fell into heave only to avoid *dema'* which is rabbinical. Since in reality, the heave might be in the profane box, one has to take care not to contaminate it with impurity (R. Joseph Caro on Maimonides *Terumot* 15:20.)

110 Since all action is in a private domain, cf. Chapter 3, Note 9. This shows that in the second case, all is forbidden.

111 Since there is a double doubt: Maybe the heave fell into the other box, and if it fell into the box from which grain was taken, maybe all or almost all grains are profane. Cases of double doubt are permitted even for biblical prohibitions [*Yebamot* 15:1 (fol. 15c), *Ketubot* 1:1 (fol. 24d)].

אָמַר רִבִּי יוֹחָנָן סָפֵק מְדוּמָּע פָּטוּר מִן הַחַלָּה. סָפֵק דִימּוּעַ הַנֶּאֱכָל מִשּׁוּם דֶּמַע חַיָּיב בְּחַלָּה. אָמַר רִבִּי יוֹחָנָן דְּרִבִּי יוּדָה הִיא. דְּתַנִּינָן תַּמָּן אִם נִשְׁאֲלוּ בְּבַת אַחַת טְמֵאִין. בְּזֶה אַחַר זֶה טְהוֹרִין. רִבִּי יוֹסֵי אוֹמֵר בֵּין כָּךְ וּבֵין כָּךְ טְמֵאִין. בְּמָה נָן קַייָמִין. אִם בְּנִשְׁאֲלוּ שְׁנֵיהֶן כְּאַחַת טְמֵאִין וְאִם בְּזֶה אַחַר זֶה טְהוֹרִין. אֶלָּא כִּי נָן קַייָמִין בְּבָא לִשְׁאַל עָלָיו וְעַל חֲבֵירוֹ. רִבִּי יוּדָה אוֹמֵר אוֹמֵר לוֹ שְׁאוֹל דִּילָךְ וְאֵיזִיל לָךְ. וְרִבִּי יוֹסֵי אָמַר כְּמִי שֶׁנִּשְׁאֲלוּ שְׁנֵיהֶן כְּאַחַת. וְהָכָא לֹא כְּמִי שֶׁנִּשְׁאֲלוּ שְׁנֵיהֶן כְּאַחַת.

Rebbi Joḥanan said, a doubt of *dema'* is free from *ḥallah*[112] but a doubt of *dema'* which is eaten as *dema'* is subject to *ḥallah*[113]. Rebbi Joḥanan said, this follows Rebbi Jehudah, as we have stated there[114]: "If they ask together, they are impure. One after the other they are pure. Rebbi Yose says, in both cases they are impure." Where do we hold? If somebody comes to ask about himself and his friend. Rebbi Jehudah says, he says: ask about yourself[115] and go away. But Rebbi Yose said, it is as if both of them asked together[116]. And here it is as if both of them asked together[117].

112 Halakhah *Ḥallah* 1:3, on condition that the profane grain be more than the amount causing the *dema'*.

113 In the case of the two boxes, when we declare that there is no *dema'* but we require the grain to be eaten as if there were.

114 Mishnah *Ṭahorot* 5:5: "Two roads, one impure [it leads over a grave whose exact position is unknown] and one pure [and it is unknown which is which]. A person walked on one of them and prepared food in purity, another person walked on the other and prepared food in purity. Rebbi Jehudah says, if they ask together . . ."

115 Since this is a doubt of impurity in the public domain, it has to be declared pure.

116 While R. Yose must agree that singly their doubts must be resolved for purity, if there is a logical necessity ("in any way you look at it") that one of them must be impure, that logical necessity overrides the rule about doubts.

117 Even R. Jehudah must agree that in the case of the two boxes one cannot ask about one and then go away. R.

Joḥanan wants to say that the *baraita* follows not only R. Yose but even R. Jehudah.

(fol. 44b) **משנה ח**: זָרַע אֶת אַחַת מֵהֶן פָּטוּר. וְהַשְּׁנִיָּה נוֹהֵג בָּהּ כִּתְרוּמָה וְחַיֶּיבֶת בְּחַלָּה דִּבְרֵי רִבִּי מֵאִיר. וְרִבִּי (fol. 44c) יוֹסֵי פוֹטֵר. זָרַע אַחֵר אֶת הַשְּׁנִיָּה פָּטוּר. זָרַע אֶחָד אֶת שְׁתֵּיהֶן בְּדָבָר שֶׁזַּרְעוֹ כָלֶה מוּתָּר. וּבְדָבָר שֶׁאֵין זַרְעוֹ כָלֶה אָסוּר.

Mishnah 8: [118]If he sowed [the contents of] one of them, he is free. The [contents of] the second he treats as heave but it is subject to *ḥallah*[100], the words of Rebbi Meïr; but Rebbi Yose declares it free[101]. If another person sowed the second one, he is free. If one person sowed [the contents of] both of them, if it is a kind whose seeds disappear, all is permitted[119], if they do not disappear[120], it is forbidden.

118 Continuation of the previous Mishnah.

119 Since the seeds have been transformed into roots and plants, there is no longer any heave in existence which could be forbidden.

120 This cannot apply if one speaks strictly of seeds. What is meant is that small bulbs of onions or leeks, etc., are planted which grow into large plants. These plants retain the property of being heave.

(fol. 45a) **הלכה ז**: רִבִּי זְעִירָא בְּשֵׁם רִבִּי חִייָא בַּר וָוא וְהוּא שֶׁזָּרַע אֶת הַשְּׁנִיָּה עַד שֶׁלֹּא קָצַר רִאשׁוֹנָה. אִם זָרַע אֶת הַשְּׁנִיָּה עַד שֶׁלֹּא קָצַר אֶת הָרִאשׁוֹנָה אֵין תָּלוּשׁ וּמְחוּבָּר נַעֲשׂוּ הוֹכִיחַ. רִבִּי חֲנִינָא תִּירְתַיָּיה בְּשֵׁם רִבִּי יַנַּאי בָּצָל שֶׁל תְּרוּמָה שֶׁעֲקָרוֹ וּשְׁתָלוֹ מִכֵּיוָן שֶׁרָבָה עָלָיו הֶחָדָשׁ מוּתָּר. הֲתִיב רִבִּי זְעִירָא וְהָתַנִּינָן אֶת שֶׁזַּרְעוֹ כָלֶה מוּתָּר וּבְדָבָר שֶׁאֵין זַרְעוֹ כָלֶה אָסוּר. שֶׁזַּרְעוֹ כָלֶה מוּתָּר בְּמַרְבֶּה עָלָיו הֶחָדָשׁ. וְדִכְוָותָהּ דָּבָר שֶׁאֵין זַרְעוֹ כָלֶה אָסוּר וְאַף עַל פִּי שֶׁרָבָה עָלָיו הֶחָדָשׁ. רִבִּי זְעִירָא כְּדַעְתֵּיהּ דְּאָמַר רִבִּי זְעִירָא בְּשֵׁם רִבִּי יוֹנָתָן בָּצָל

שֶׁל כִּלְאֵי הַכֶּרֶם שֶׁעֲקָרוֹ וּשְׁתָלוֹ אֲפִילוּ מוֹסִיף כַּמָּה אָסוּר שֶׁאֵין גִּידוּלֵי אִיסּוּר מַעֲלִין אֶת הָאִיסּוּר.

Rebbi Zeïra in the name of Rebbi Ḥiyya bar Abba: Only if he sowed the [contents of the] second [box] before he harvested from the first. If he sowed the [contents of the] second [box] before he harvested from the first then what is cut and what is standing does not all become subject to proof[121]. Rebbi Ḥanina Eyntanaya in the name of Rebbi Yannai: An onion of heave that was uprooted and replanted becomes permitted as soon as the new growth is more [than what was planted]. Rebbi Zeïra objected: Did we not state: "If it is a kind whose seeds disappear, all is permitted, if they do not disappear, it is forbidden." If it is a kind whose seeds disappear, [it is permitted] the moment the new growth is more [than the original amount]. Similarly, if they do not disappear, [it is forbidden] even if the new growth is more! [122]Rebbi Zeïra follows his own opinion, as Rebbi Zeira said in the name of Rebbi Jonathan: An onion from *kilaim* in a vineyard that he removed from the soil and planted anew is forbidden even if it increases manifold, since growth of what is forbidden can never justify forbidden produce.

121 For this expression, that they do not prove contradictory statements, cf. Chapter 4, Note 82; Chapter 7, Halakhah 5.

122 The following sentence is from *Kilaim* Halakhah 5:7, cf. Note 76.

האשה פרק שמיני

(fol. 45a) **משנה א:** הָאִשָּׁה שֶׁהָיְתָה אוֹכֶלֶת בִּתְרוּמָה בָּאוּ וְאָמְרוּ לָהּ מֵת בַּעֲלֵיךְ אוֹ גֵירְשָׁךְ. וְכֵן הָעֶבֶד שֶׁהָיָה אוֹכֵל בִּתְרוּמָה וּבָאוּ וְאָמְרוּ לוֹ מֵת רַבָּךְ אוֹ מְכָרָךְ לְיִשְׂרָאֵל אוֹ נְתָנָךְ בְּמַתָּנָה. אוֹ עֲשָׂאָךְ בֶּן חוֹרִין. וְכֵן כֹּהֵן שֶׁהָיָה אוֹכֵל בִּתְרוּמָה וְנוֹדַע שֶׁהוּא בֶּן גְּרוּשָׁה אוֹ בֶן חֲלוּצָה רִבִּי לִיעֶזֶר מְחַייֵב קֶרֶן וְחוֹמֶשׁ. וְרִבִּי יְהוֹשֻׁעַ פּוֹטֵר. הָיָה עוֹמֵד וּמַקְרִיב עַל גַּבֵּי הַמִּזְבֵּחַ וְנוֹדַע שֶׁהוּא בֶּן גְּרוּשָׁה אוֹ בֶן חֲלוּצָה רִבִּי לִיעֶזֶר אוֹמֵר כָּל־קָרְבָּנוֹת שֶׁהִקְרִיב עַל גַּבֵּי הַמִּזְבֵּחַ פְּסוּלִין. וְרִבִּי יְהוֹשֻׁעַ מַכְשִׁיר. נוֹדַע שֶׁהוּא בַּעַל מוּם עֲבוֹדָתוֹ פְסוּלָה.

Mishnah 1: When they came to a woman who was eating heave[1] and told her your husband died, or he divorced you[2]; similarly a slave[3] who was eating heave when they came and told him your master died[4], or he sold you to an Israel or gave you as a gift, or made you a free person; similarly a Cohen who was eating heave when it became known that he was the son of a divorcee[5] or the son of a woman who had performed *ḥaliẓah*[6], Rebbi Eliezer obliges them to pay principal and fifth[7], but Rebbi Joshua frees them. If[8] he was standing on top of the altar and sacrificing when it became known that he was the son of a divorcee or the son of a woman who had performed *ḥaliẓah*, Rebbi Eliezer says that all sacrifices he performed on the altar are invalid but Rebbi Joshua declares them valid. If it became known that he has a bodily defect, his work is invalid.

1 The daughter of an Israel or a Levite married to a Cohen who may eat heave only as long as she is married to a Cohen or, if she becomes a widow,

has descendants who may eat heave.

2 Since a woman is legally divorced only if the divorce document is delivered to her or her agent, the Halakhah has to find a case in which the divorced woman may have eaten heave in error.

3 A Gentile slave owned by a Cohen who became Jewish by circumcision and immersion in a ritual bath and has to observe all rules of the Jewish religion. As long as he is owned by a Cohen, he eats heave. If he is manumitted, he becomes a full Jew but not a Cohen.

4 In case the master has no heirs who may eat heave; for example, if the master had only daughters and they are married to Israel husbands.

5 The son of a Cohen and a divorcee is desecrated (*Lev*. 21:15) and cannot eat heave.

6 The widow of a childless man who is not married by her brother-in-law but freed from him by the ceremony of drawing off her brother-in-law's shoe. While this act is not a divorce, it is considered close enough to a divorce to forbid the widow to any Cohen by rabbinic law.

7 Like everybody eating heave in error.

8 This part of the Mishnah will be explained in Halakhah 2.

הלכה א: הָאִשָּׁה שֶׁהָיְתָה אוֹכֶלֶת בִּתְרוּמָה כו׳. נִיחָא מֵת בַּעֲלֵיךְ. גֵּירְשָׁךְ. רַבָּנִין אָמְרִין כְּמִשְׁנָה רִאשׁוֹנָה. שֶׁכֵּן אֲרוּסָה בַּת יִשְׂרָאֵל אוֹכֶלֶת בִּתְרוּמָה וְאָבִיהָ מְקַבֵּל אֶת גִּיטָּהּ. רִבִּי לִיעֶזֶר אוֹמֵר וַאֲפִילוּ (fol. 45b) תֵּימַר כְּמִשְׁנָה אַחֲרוֹנָה. תִּיפְתָּר שֶׁאָמְרָה לוֹ הֲבֵא גִיטִּי מִמָּקוֹם פְּלוֹנִי וְהָיָה דַרְכּוֹ לְהָבִיא לָהּ בַּעֲשָׂרָה יָמִים וּמָצָה סוּס רָץ וְהֵבִיא לָהּ לַחֲמִשָּׁה יָמִים. וְלֹא רִבִּי לִיעֶזֶר כְּרִבִּי לָעְזָר. דְּתַנִּינָן רִבִּי לָעְזָר אוֹסֵר מִיַּד. וְלֹא מוֹדֵי רִבִּי לָעְזָר שֶׁאִם אָמְרָה הֲבֵא לִי גִיטִּי מִמָּקוֹם פְּלוֹנִי שֶׁהִיא אוֹכֶלֶת בִּתְרוּמָה עַד שֶׁמַּגִּיעַ גֵּט לְאוֹתוֹ מָקוֹם. אָמַר רִבִּי חֲנִינָה מִכֵּיוָן שֶׁאָמְרָה לוֹ הֲבֵא לִי גִיטִּי מִמָּקוֹם פְּלוֹנִי כְּמִי שֶׁאָמְרָה לוֹ לֹא יְהֵא גֵט אֶלָּא לַעֲשָׂרָה יָמִים מַה שֶׁאָכְלָה בְּהֵיתֵר אָכְלָה.

Halakhah 1: "A woman who was eating heave," etc. It is acceptable, "your husband died." "He divorced you?[2]" The rabbis say, this follows the old Mishnah[9], according to which the betrothed daughter of an Israel eats heave and her father accepts her divorce document. Rebbi Eliezer[10] says, you may even say following the later Mishnah; explain it that she said to him, bring my divorce document from place X and usually that should have taken him ten days to deliver to her but he found a galloping horse and brought it to her in five days. Rebbi Eliezer cannot follow Rebbi Eleazar, as we have stated[11]: "Rebbi Eleazar forbids her immediately." Does Rebbi Eleazar not agree that if she said, bring my divorce document from place X, that she may eat heave until the document arrives at that place[12]? Rebbi Ḥaninah said, when she said to him, bring my divorce document from place X, it is as if she had said to him, it shall become a divorce document only after ten days. What she ate, she ate with permission[13].

9 Mishnah *Ketubot* 5:3: "One gives a virgin 12 months after the bridegroom claimed her to get her trousseau . . . If that time arrived and she is not married she eats from him and she eats heave . . . , this is the old Mishnah. The later authorities said, no woman eats heave until she enters the bridal canopy." The Mishnah deals with a minor who is married off by her father. After the preliminary wedding ceremony (cf. *Peah* 6:2, Note 46) the bride really is "acquired by the husband's money" and, by biblical law (*Lev*. 22:11) she may eat heave if the husband is a Cohen. By an old rabbinic institution, she is prevented from eating heave until the date originally fixed for the actual wedding, when it was planned that she should start living with her husband. The later authorities restricted the access of the Israel bride of a Cohen to the time after the final marriage ceremony.

The final marriage ceremony emancipates the bride from her father's authority. During the time between preliminary and final ceremonies, Mishnah *Giṭṭin* 6:2 states that both the minor and her father may accept a divorce document; R. Jehudah denies the right of the minor to receive the document (cf. *Peah* Chapter 4, Note 117). The Mishnah here can refer to with a woman eating heave in error only in case the woman still is a minor and the groom did not finally marry her at the previously stipulated time. In this approach, with the decree of the later authorities the mention of a divorce in our Mishnah became meaningless.

10 He must be R. Eleazar ben Pedat, the student of R. Johanan. Probably, his name was changed here to distinguish him from R. Eleazar ben Shamua‘, the Tanna, who is quoted in the next sentence. [The changes from "R. Eliezer" to "R. Eleazar" and vice-versa in all printed editions has no basis in mss. The Yerushalmi tradition of Mishnah *Giṭṭin* 6:4 (Leyden ms. and Venice print, Mishnah ed. Low) as well as the main text of the Munich ms. of the Babli and the mss. of the later version of Maimonides's Commentary read "R. Eleazar"; the Napoli Mishnah and the early version of Maimonides's Commentary read "R. Eliezer".] Since R. Eleazar is the main authority on divorce documents, it is reasonable to read "R. Eleazar" in the Mishnah.

11 Mishnah *Giṭṭin* 6:4: "Bring me my divorce document, she eats heave until the document comes into her possession. Accept the document for me, she immediately is forbidden heave. Accept the document for me at place X, she eats heave until the document reaches place X; Rebbi Eleazar forbids her immediately." This Mishnah speaks of the adult wife appointing an agent. (A minor, even though emancipated from her father, cannot appoint an agent. She can be divorced only by delivery of the document into her hands by the husband or his duly appointed agent. If she is too young to take care of the document, she cannot be divorced.)

12 An agent who violates the terms of his appointment is not a valid agent for divorce documents. If the agent would accept the document at another place, the document would be invalid and the woman not divorced. There is no reason for her not to eat heave until the document reaches the specified place.

13 In this case, even R. Eliezer will agree that heave was eaten lawfully, there is no case of restitution of anything, and the explanation of R. Eleazar ben Pedat is contradicted.

רִבִּי חַגַּיי שָׁאַל לַחֲבֵרַייָה מְנַיִן לָאוֹכֵל בִּרְשׁוּת שֶׁהוּא פָּטוּר. מַה בֵּין סָבוּר שֶׁהוּא חוּלִין וְנִמְצָא תְרוּמָה שֶׁהוּא חַייָב. מַה בֵּין סָבוּר שֶׁהוּא יִשְׂרָאֵל וְנִמְצָא כֹּהֵן שֶׁהוּא פָּטוּר. אָמְרִין לֵיהּ מֵהוֹרַייַת בֵּית דִּין. אָמַר לוֹן עוֹד צְרִיכָה לִי. מַה בֵּין סָבוּר שֶׁהוּא חוֹל וְנִמְצָא שַׁבָּת שֶׁהוּא חַייָב. מַה בֵּין סָבוּר שֶׁהוּא פֶּסַח וְנִמְצָא שְׁלָמִים שֶׁהוּא פָּטוּר. אָמְרוּן לֵיהּ מְשׁוֹחֵט בִּרְשׁוּת. אָמַר לוֹן עוֹד צְרִיכָה לִי. מַה

בֵּין סָבוּר שֶׁהוּא שׁוּמָּן וְנִמְצָא חֵלֶב שֶׁהוּא חַייָב. מַה בֵּין סָבוּר שֶׁהוּא אָסוּר וְנִמְצָא מוּתָּר שֶׁהוּא פָטוּר. לֹא אֲגִיבוּ. אָמַר לוֹן נִמְלָכִין מִינָן אוֹ הוֹדַע אֵלָיו חַטָּאתוֹ וְהֵבִיא. הַשָּׁב מִידִיעָתוֹ חַייָב עַל שִׁגְגָתוֹ. יָצָא זֶה שֶׁאֲפִילוּ יָדַע אֵינוֹ פוֹרֵשׁ. אָעַל רִבִּי יוֹסֵי לְגַבּוֹן אָמַר לוֹן לָמָּה לֹא אַמְרִיתוּ לֵיהּ אוֹ הוֹדַע אֵלָיו חַטָּאתוֹ וְהֵבִיא. אֲמְרִין לֵיהּ הוּא קְשִׁיתָהּ וְהוּא קִייְמָהּ.

Rebbi Ḥaggai asked the colleagues, from where that he who eats with permission is free[14]? What is the difference between him who thought that it was profane but it turned out that it was heave, who is obligated[15], and him who thought that he was an Israel but it turned out that he was a Cohen, who is free? They said to him, by the declaration of the court[16]. He said to them, still I am having a problem. What is the difference between him who thought that it was a weekday but it turned out that it was a Sabbath[17], who is obligated, and him who thought that it was a Passover sacrifice but it turned out that it was a well-being offering, who is free[18]? They said to him, because he slaughtered with permission[19]. He said to them, still I am having a problem. What is the difference between him who thought that it was permitted fat but it turned out that it was forbidden fat, who is obligated, and him who thought that it was forbidden but it turned out that it was permitted, who is free[20]? They did not answer him. What did he say to them? Let us take counsel! (*Lev.* 4:23,28): "Or his transgression in which he sinned was made known to him; he has to bring.[21]" He who returns from his prior knowledge is obligated for his error; this excludes one who would not stop even if he knew!

Rebbi Assi went to see them and said, why did you not answer him (*Lev.* 4:23,28): "Or his transgression in which he sinned was made known to him; he has to bring"? They said to him, he asked the question and gave the answer[22].

14 This is not an attack on the argument of R. Ḥanina; if a person has no intention of breaking the law and is not breaking the law, obviously he is free not only of guilt but of all monetary obligations.

The parallel to this text is in *Horaiot* 1:1, fol. 45c; a text which differs in places from the text here. The commentaries assume that the text there is the better one; they take the question of R. Ḥaggai as directed against the argument of R. Ḥaninah; therefore, they are forced in the next sentence to follow the *Horaiot* text and to switch the terms "Israel" and "Cohen", an emendation not supported here by any manuscript and contradicted by the third question of R. Ḥaggai.

15 An Israel who ate what he thought was profane food. If it turns out that it was heave, he has to pay as stated in Mishnah 6:1. If it turns out that he was in fact a Cohen but did not know it, he does not have to pay even though at the time of eating he thought he was an Israel. If payment were a punishment for negligence, there is no reason why he should not be held liable.

In the Horaiot text, speaking of a person who thought he was a Cohen when he was not, the reference would be to the position of R. Joshua in the Mishnah here and the "declaration of the court" is the court decision which strips him of his priesthood, on the testimony of two cross-examined credible witnesses. The conditions under which an action of the court obligates him to bring a sacrifice are noted *Horaiot* 1:1; the reading of *Horaiot* is appropriate there, the reading of *Terumot* is appropriate here.

16 The interpretation of the biblical law quoted later.

17 The person violating the Sabbath in error has to bring an expiatory sacrifice.

18 This refers to Mishnah *Pesaḥim* 6:4. The Passover sacrifice, a lamb or kid goat, has to be sacrificed during the afternoon of Nissan 14, even if that day is a Sabbath. It also has to be designated beforehand as Passover sacrifice and is counted as a special kind of well-being offering. If the 14th falls on a weekday, a festival offering, which is a well-being offering, is also slaughtered at the same time (cf. the author's *The Scholar's Haggadah*, Northvale NJ 1995, p. 248.) On the Sabbath, any slaughtering not directly mandated by the biblical verse is forbidden. On that the Mishnah states: "If the Passover sacrifice [which is valid only if slaughtered for this particular purpose] was slaughtered not

for its purpose on the Sabbath, one is obligated for an expiatory sacrifice. For any well-being offering slaughtered as a Passover sacrifice which was not usable [a calf or an old sheep or goat], one is obligated. If it was usable, R. Eliezer obligates him for an expiatory sacrifice, R. Joshua declares him free." Why should he be free?

19 The language refers to Mishnah *Pesaḥim* 6:6: "If he slaughtered [the Passover sacrifice on a Sabbath] and it turned out to have a blemish, he is obligated [for an expiatory sacrifice]. If it turned out to be unusable because of an internal defect [which could not have been detected by inspection when the animal was alive], he is free. If he slaughtered and then it turned out that the owners had withdrawn from it [they chose another lamb as their sacrifice], or that they had died [and the sacrifice became unusable because nobody may eat from the Passover unless he joined the group before the lamb was slaughtered], or had become impure, he is free since he slaughtered with permission." Since R. Joshua declares him free and the animal could have been a valid Passover sacrifice, he slaughtered with permission.

20 He thought the fat he ate was forbidden when in fact it was permitted. Then in his mind he should be more guilty of negligence than the one who thought the fat was permitted when it was in fact forbidden.

21 The involved statement is explained to mean that one became aware of the sinful character of what he had done inadvertently. If a person never knew that certain acts are forbidden, he cannot become obligated for an expiatory sacrifice since no negligence was involved. If he knew and then did something inadvertently, he is obligated for his negligence. But if he knew beforehand that, had he known then what he knows now, his action would have been legitimate, there is no negligence and no sacrifice.

22 This paragraph is more explicit in *Horaiot*, and written in better style.

הלכה ב: רִבִּי יוֹחָנָן בְּשֵׁם רִבִּי יַנַּאי זֶה אֶחָד מִשָּׁלֹשׁ מִדְרָשׁוֹת שֶׁהֵן מְחֻוָּרִין בַּתּוֹרָה. וּבָאתָ אֶל הַכֹּהֵן אֲשֶׁר יִהְיֶה בַּיָּמִים הָהֵם. וְכִי יֵשׁ כֹּהֵן עַכְשָׁיו וְאֵין כֹּהֵן לְאַחַר זְמָן. וְאֵי זֶה זֶה שֶׁהָיָה עוֹמֵד וּמַקְרִיב עַל גַּבֵּי הַמִּזְבֵּחַ וְנוֹדַע שֶׁהוּא בֶּן גְּרוּשָׁה אוֹ בֶן חֲלוּצָה שֶׁעֲבוֹדָתוֹ כְּשֵׁירָה. אָמַר רַב וּפוֹעַל יָדָיו תִּרְצֶה כָּל־שֶׁהוּא מִזַּרְעוֹ שֶׁל לֵוִי עֲבוֹדָתוֹ כְּשֵׁירָה.

Halakhah 2[23]: Rebbi Joḥanan in the name of Rebbi Yannai: This is one of three derivations[24] which are clear from the Torah (*Deut.* 26:3): "You shall come to the Cohen who will be in those days." Is there a Cohen now who is not a Cohen after some time? Who is that? That is one who was standing sacrificing on the altar when it became known that he is the son of a divorcee or of one who had performed *ḥaliẓah*, that his work is valid[25]. Rav said, (*Deut.* 33:11) "You will want the work of his hands," that the work of everybody who is of the descendants of Levi is valid[26].

23 Here starts the discussion of the second part of Mishnah 1.

24 Cf. Chapter 1, Note 159. The parallel in the Babli to the derivations here is *Qiddušin* 66b. The argument of Rav, Rav Abba, somewhat changed, is there given in the name of Samuel's father, Abba ben Abba. Elsewhere (*Sifry Deut.* 298. Babli *Sanhedrin* 28b) the argument of R. Yannai is given in the name of R. Yose the Galilean (the Tanna); the argument of Rav is not found in tannaïtic sources.

25 In Tosephta *Roš Haššanah* 2:18, the similar verse *Deut.* 17:9 is explained that Cohen and judge in one's own time have the same authority as Aaron and Moses in their time.

26 Since the verse is addressed to the entire tribe of Levi and not only to the recognized Cohanim. Since the sons of divorcees are also descendants of Levi, they are included (if they happened to be admitted to the service.)

וְעַל דַּעְתֵּיהּ דְּרַב בִּלְבַד כֹּהֵן מַקְרִיב. וְעַל דַּעְתֵּיהּ דְּרִבִּי יוֹחָנָן וַאֲפִילוּ כָל־כֹּהֵן. עַל דַּעְתֵּיהּ דְּרַב וּבִלְבַד בְּקָדְשֵׁי מִקְדָּשׁ. עַל דַּעְתֵּיהּ דְּרִבִּי יוֹחָנָן וַאֲפִילוּ בְּקָדְשֵׁי הַגְּבוּל. עַל דַּעְתַּיְיהוּ דְּרַבָּנִין וּבִלְבַד בִּשְׁעַת מִקְדָּשׁ. עַל דַּעְתֵּיהּ דְּרִבִּי יוֹחָנָן וַאֲפִילוּ בִּזְמַן הַזֶּה.

In Rav's opinion, only a sacrificing Cohen[27]. In Rebbi Joḥanan's opinion, any Cohen[28]. In Rav's opinion, only for sacrifices in the Temple. In Rebbi Joḥanan's opinion, even holy food in the countryside. In the rabbis' opinion, only during the existence of the Temple. In Rebbi Joḥanan's opinion, even today.

27 In the preceding verse, burning of incense and sacrifices is mentioned. This restricts the verse to service in the Temple.

28 For any ceremony for which a Cohen is needed: Not only the reception of First Fruits but also the presentation of the firstling, judging skin disease, etc.

רִבִּי יִרְמְיָה בָּעֵי וְאַף לְעִנְיַן שְׁאָר הַדְּבָרִים כֵּן מְקַבֵּל וְאַחַר כָּךְ זוֹרֵק קוֹמֵץ וְאַחַר כָּךְ מַקְטִיר שׂוֹרֵף וְאַחַר כָּךְ מַזֶּה. רִבִּי יַעֲקֹב בַּר זַבְדִּי בְּשֵׁם רִבִּי יִצְחָק מִן מַה דְּתַנֵּי עָשׂוּ אוֹתָהּ כְּחַטָּאת גְּזוּלָה שֶׁלֹּא נוֹדְעָה לָרַבִּים שֶׁהִיא מְכַפֶּרֶת. הָדָה אָמְרָה שֶׁהוּא מְקַבֵּל וְאַחַר כָּךְ זוֹרֵק קוֹמֵץ וְאַחַר כָּךְ מַקְטִיר שׂוֹרֵף וְאַחַר כָּךְ מַזֶּה.

Rebbi Jeremiah asked: Does this apply even to the remaining actions[29]? If he received [the blood], does he sprinkle [the blood on the walls of the altar]; if he takes a fist full [of the flour offering], can he burn it [on the altar]; if he burned [the red cow], can he sprinkle [water mixed with its ashes, to purify]? Rebbi Jacob bar Zavdi in the name of Rebbi Isaac: Since we have stated[30]: "they made it like a purification sacrifice which atones even if obtained by robbery, as long as this fact is unknown to the public;" this means[31] that if he received, he sprinkles; if he takes a fist full, he burns; if he burned, he sprinkles.

29 If he performed an action which has to be followed by another one and he is notified of his desecrated status in the middle of the first action, can he finish the entire procedure?

30 This refers to Mishnah *Giṭṭin* 5:5, in which it is stated, as testimony from Temple times, that the priests have to accept every animal offered as a sacrifice of expiation (which has to be eaten by the priests) and are not permitted to investigate whether it was stolen or robbed, unless such defect was public knowledge. Both Talmudim

agree that this arrangement can be justified by biblical verses and that it was strictly enforced since nobody would be able to bring such a sacrifice if the priests were allowed to set their own standards of what is kosher.

31 If a questionable sacrifice is valid as a sacrifice, then a questionable Cohen's actions are counted as valid actions.

רִבִּי יַעֲקֹב בַּר זַבְדִּי בְשֵׁם רִבִּי יִצְחָק שָׁאַל הָיָה עוֹמֵד וּמַקְרִיב עַל גַּבֵּי הַמִּזְבֵּחַ וְנוֹדַע לוֹ שֶׁהוּא בֶּן גְּרוּשָׁה אוֹ בֶן חֲלוּצָה מַה אַתְּ עֲבַד לֵיהּ. כְּמִי שֶׁהוּא מֵת וְיַחֲזִיר הָרוֹצֵחַ לִמְקוֹמוֹ. אוֹ כְּמִי שֶׁנִּגְמַר דִּינוֹ בְּלֹא כֹהֵן גָּדוֹל וְאֵינוֹ יוֹצֵא מִשָּׁם לְעוֹלָם.

Rebbi Jacob ben Zavdi asked in the name of Rebbi Isaac: If he was standing sacrificing on the altar when it became known to him that he was the son of a divorcee or a woman who had performed *ḥalizah*, how do you treat him[32]? As if he had died and the homicide might return to his home town, or as if [the latter's] trial had been concluded when there was no High Priest, when he never could leave from there?[33]

32 This thoroughly theoretical case deals with a High Priest who is informed that the special court judging the status of priests has stripped him of his office because he was found to be the son of a divorcee, or of a woman who had performed *ḥalizah*, by the testimony of two reliable witnesses. The problem concerns a person found guilty of involuntary or negligent homicide sentenced to exile in a city of refuge (*Num.* 35:9-34). He may return to his home town only after the death of the High Priest during whose term of office he was sentenced (*v.* 28). This implies that if he was sentenced while there was no High Priest, he is sentenced to life in exile.

33 The answer will be given in the paragraph after the next.

נִישְׁמְעִינָהּ מִן הָדָא. מַעֲשֶׂה בִמְגוֹרֶת שֶׁל דִּיסְקוֹס בְּיַבְנֶה שֶׁנִּפְגְּמָה וְנִמְדְּדָה וְנִמְצֵאת חֲסֵירָה. וְהָיָה רִבִּי טַרְפוֹן מְטָהֵר וְרִבִּי עֲקִיבָה מְטַמֵּא. אָמַר רִבִּי טַרְפוֹן הַמִּקְוֶה הַזֶּה בְּחֶזְקַת טָהֳרָה לְעוֹלָם הוּא בְטָהֳרָתוֹ עַד שֶׁיִּוָּדַע שֶׁחָסֵר.

אָמַר רִבִּי עֲקִיבָה הַטָּמֵא הַזֶּה בְּחֶזְקַת טוּמְאָה לְעוֹלָם הוּא בְטוּמְאָתוֹ עַד שֶׁיִּוָּדַע שֶׁטָּהֵר. אָמַר רִבִּי טַרְפוֹן לְמָה זֶה דוֹמֶה לְעוֹמֵד וּמַקְרִיב עַל גַּבֵּי הַמִּזְבֵּחַ וְנוֹדַע שֶׁהוּא בֶּן גְּרוּשָׁה אוֹ בֶן חֲלוּצָה שֶׁעֲבוֹדָתוֹ כְּשֵׁירָה. אָמַר רִבִּי עֲקִיבָה לְמָה זֶה דוֹמֶה לְעוֹמֵד וְהִקְרִיב עַל גַּבֵּי הַמִּזְבֵּחַ וְנוֹדַע שֶׁהוּא בַּעַל מוּם שֶׁעֲבוֹדָתוֹ פְסוּלָה. אוֹמַר לוֹ רִבִּי טַרְפוֹן מַה עֲקִיבָה אֲנִי מְדַמֶּה לֵיהּ לְבֶן גְּרוּשָׁה וְאַתְּ מְדַמֶּה לֵיהּ לְבַעַל מוּם. נִרְאֶה לְמִי דוֹמֶה אִם לְבֶן גְּרוּשָׁה הוּא דוֹמֶה נְלַמְּדֶינּוּ מִבֶּן גְּרוּשָׁה. וְאִם לְבַעַל מוּם הוּא דוֹמֶה נְלַמְּדֶינּוּ מִבַּעַל מוּם. אָמַר לוֹ רִבִּי עֲקִיבָה מִקְוֶה פְסוּלוֹ בְגוּפוֹ וּבַעַל מוּם פְּסוּלוֹ בְגוּפוֹ. וְאַל יוֹכִיחַ בֶּן גְּרוּשָׁה שֶׁפְּסוּלוֹ מֵחֲמַת אֲחֵרִים. מִקְוֶה פְסוּלוֹ בְיָחִיד וּבַעַל מוּם פְּסוּלוֹ בְיָחִיד. וְאַל יוֹכִיחַ בֶּן גְּרוּשָׁה שֶׁפְּסוּלוֹ בְּבֵית דִּין. וְנִמְנוּ עָלָיו וְטִימְּאוּהוּ. אָמַר רִבִּי טַרְפוֹן לְרִבִּי עֲקִיבָה הַפּוֹרֵשׁ מִמְּךָ כְּפוֹרֵשׁ מֵחַיָּיו.

Let us hear from the following[34]: "It happened that the reservoir of Discus at Jabneh was damaged, measured, and found deficient[35]. Rebbi Ṭarphon declared pure and Rebbi Aqiba impure. Rebbi Ṭarphon said, the prior status of this *miqweh* was one of purity; it remains forever in its purity until it becomes known that it is deficient. Rebbi Aqiba said, the prior status of the impure is impurity, he remains forever in his impurity until it becomes known that he is pure. Rebbi Ṭarphon said, to what can this be compared? To one who was standing sacrificing on the altar when it became known that he was the son of a divorcee or of a woman who had performed *ḥaliẓah,* whose work is valid. Rebbi Aqiba said, to what can this be compared? To one who was standing sacrificing on the altar when it became known that he has a bodily defect, whose work is invalid[36]. Rebbi Ṭarphon said to him, how is that, Aqiba? I am comparing this to the son of a divorcee or of a woman who had performed *ḥaliẓah*, and you compare it to one with a bodily defect. Let us see to which case it really is similar; if to the son of a divorcee or of a woman who had performed *ḥaliẓah*, let us learn from the son of the divorcee, but if to one with a bodily defect, let us learn from the person with a bodily defect. Rebbi Aqiba said to him, the *miqweh* is invalid because of an inherent defect; the one with a bodily defect is disqualified because of an inherent defect. The son of a divorcee cannot prove anything since he is disqualified because of others[37]. The *miqweh* is invalid because of itself, the one with a bodily defect is disqualified because of himself; the son of a divorcee cannot prove anything since he is disqualified by the court[38]. They voted on the matter and declared him impure. Rebbi Ṭarphon said to Rebbi Aqiba, he who separates himself from you is as if he separated himself from his own life."

34 In slightly enlarged form, Tosephta *Miqwa'ot* 1:17-20; in much shortened form Babli *Qiddušin* 66b.

The "reservoir of Discus" according to Rashi is named either after a place or a person *Discus*, Latin proper n.

35 Because something happened to the structure, they measured the volume of the water after the accident and found it to be less than 40 *seah* and, therefore, to be unusable for purification (cf. Chapter 4, Note 112). Since earlier, the *miqweh* was a valid one, a person who had immersed himself before the accident came to ask whether he could be considered pure because of the prior validity of the *miqweh*, or whether he was impure since now the *miqweh* was invalid.

36 *Lev.* 21:16-24. Since it is stated (*v.* 17) that a person with a bodily defect "shall not come close to present the bread of his God," it is clear that this prohibition overrides the general inclusion inferred from *Deut.* 26:3 or 33:11.

37 His parents.

38 As noted below, only the court can strip him of his role as Cohen, and only after regular judicial proceedings.

אָמַר רִבִּי יוֹסֵי זֹאת אוֹמֶרֶת הָיָה עוֹמֵד וּמַקְרִיב עַל גַּבֵּי הַמִּזְבֵּחַ וְנוֹדַע שֶׁהוּא בֶּן גְּרוּשָׁה אוֹ בֶן חֲלוּצָה שֶׁעֲבוֹדָתוֹ כְּשֵׁירָה עַד שֶׁיִּפָּסֵל בְּבֵית דִּין. הָדָא אָמְרָה סָפֵק טָמֵא סָפֵק בַּעַל מוּם עֲבוֹדָתוֹ כְּשֵׁירָה. דְּאַת מְדַמֵּי לֵיהּ לְבֶן גְּרוּשָׁה לְבֶן חֲלוּצָה. אֲבָל אִם מְדַמֵּי לְבַעַל מוּם עֲבוֹדָתוֹ פְּסוּלָה. וּמִקְוֶה לֹא סָפֵק הוּא. אָמַר רִבִּי חֲנִינָא זֹאת אוֹמֶרֶת פְּסוּל מִשְׁפָּחָה צָרִיךְ בֵּית דִּין.

Rebbi Yose said, this[39] means that if he was standing sacrificing on the altar when it became known that he was the son of a divorcee or of a woman who had performed *ḥaliẓah,* his work remains valid until he is disqualified by a court[40]. That [also] means that if it was doubtful whether he was impure or had a bodily defect, his work is valid if you can compare him to the son of a divorcee [or] the son of a woman who had given *ḥaliẓah.* But if you have to compare him to a person with a bodily defect, his work is invalid. But is the case of the *miqweh* not that of a doubt[41]? Rebbi Ḥanina said, this means that any blemish on the family needs a court [judgment][42].

39 The argument of R. Aqiba, accepted by all other rabbis, that the son of a divorcee is not automatically disqualified but only by court decree.

40 For the original question, it means that the High Priest is validly officiating; therefore his removal will allow all homicides convicted during his tenure to return home.

41 The entire argument started only because it was not known at which point in time the volume of the *miqweh* fell below 40 *seah.*

42 If it was not known at his birth that he was the son of a divorcee, he remains a Cohen until disqualified by a court.

(fol. 45a) **משנה ב:** וְכוּלָּם שֶׁהָיָה תְרוּמָה לְתוֹךְ פִּיהֶם רִבִּי אֱלִיעֶזֶר אוֹמֵר יִבְלָעוּ וְרִבִּי יְהוֹשֻׁעַ אוֹמֵר יִפְלוֹטוּ. אָֽמְרוּ לוֹ נִטְמֵאתָ וְנִטְמֵאת תְּרוּמָה רִבִּי אֱלִיעֶזֶר אוֹמֵר יִבְלַע וְרִבִּי יְהוֹשֻׁעַ אוֹמֵר יִפְלוֹט. טָמֵא הָיִיתָ וּטְמֵאָה הָֽיְתָה תְרוּמָה אוֹ נוֹדַע שֶׁהוּא טֶבֶל וּמַעֲשֵׂר רִאשׁוֹן שֶׁלֹּא נִיטְּלָה תְרוּמָתוֹ אוֹ מַעֲשֵׂר שֵׁנִי וְהֶקְדֵּשׁ שֶׁלֹּא נִפְדּוּ אוֹ שֶׁטָּעֲמוֹ טַעַם פִּישְׁפֵּשׁ לְתוֹךְ פִּיו הֲרֵי זֶה יִפְלוֹט.

Mishnah 2: All of these[43], if heave was in their mouths, Rebbi Eliezer says, they should swallow it[44], Rebbi Joshua says, they should spit it out[45]. If they said to him, you and the heave have become impure, Rebbi Eliezer says, he should swallow it, Rebbi Joshua says, he should spit it out[46]. You or the heave were impure, or if it became known that it was *ṭevel*, or First Tithe of which its heave had not been taken, or Second Tithe or dedicated [food] that had not been redeemed,[47] or that he tasted the taste of a bed bug in his mouth[48], he has to spit it out[49].

43 Those mentioned in Mishnah 1 who have to stop eating heave immediately.

44 And add the value of the food swallowed to the amount to be paid as principal and fifth, according to R. Eliezer.

45 Since R. Joshua does not require payment, he cannot tolerate enjoyment of the heave for a single moment after it became forbidden.

46 This case is parallel to the previous one. "He" in this case is a Cohen of unquestioned pedigree who started to fulfill his duty eating heave, thinking he and the heave were pure.

47 In all these cases, eating the food was sinful to begin with. An impure person may not eat heave and impure heave may not be eaten (*Num.* 18:13). First Tithe remains *ṭevel* as long as the heave of the tithe was not lifted from it. Unredeemed Second Tithe can be eaten only in Jerusalem, and eating unredeemed dedicated food is larceny of Temple property.

48 Swallowing such food would be a health hazard; it is forbidden knowingly to contribute to a deterioration of one's health (*Deut.* 4:15).

49 R. Eliezer agrees that food cannot be swallowed if there never was a time when swallowing it was permitted.

(fol. 45b) **הלכה ג**: אָמַר רִבִּי יוֹחָנָן מַה פְלִיגִין בְּעֶבֶד וְאִשָּׁה. אֲבָל בִּשְׁאָר דְּבָרִים אַף רִבִּי אֱלִיעֶזֶר מוֹדֵי. אָמַר רִבִּי שְׁמוּאֵל בַּר רַב יִצְחָק מַתְנִיתָא אָמְרָה כֵן אוֹ נוֹדַע שֶׁהוּא טֶבֶל וּמַעֲשֵׂר רִאשׁוֹן שֶׁלֹּא נִיטְלָה תְרוּמָתוֹ אוֹ מַעֲשֵׂר שֵׁנִי וְהֶקְדֵּשׁ שֶׁלֹּא נִפְדּוּ וְלֵית רִבִּי לִיעֶזֶר פְּלִיג.

Halakhah 3: Rebbi Joḥanan said, where do they disagree? Concerning slave and wife. But in the other cases, even Rebbi Eliezer agrees. Rebbi Samuel ben Rebbi Isaac said, the Mishnah says so: "or if it became known that it was *ṭevel*, or First Tithe of which its heave had not been taken, or Second Tithe or dedicated [food] that had not been redeemed," and Rebbi Eliezer does not disagree[50].

50 Therefore, he will not disagree that a person disqualified as a Cohen has to spit out, including the son of a divorcee.

מַה טַעֲמָא דְרִבִּי לִיעֶזֶר מִשּׁוּם שֶׁהִתְחִיל בְּהֵיתֵר. תַּנֵּי רִבִּי נָתָן אוֹמֵר. לֹא שֶׁהָיָה רִבִּי לִיעֶזֶר אוֹמֵר מִשּׁוּם שֶׁהִתְחִיל בּוֹ בְּהֵיתֵר. אֶלָּא שֶׁהָיָה רִבִּי לִיעֶזֶר אוֹמֵר הַלָּעוּס כְּבָלוּעַ. אַף בְּשַׁבָּת כֵּן. אַף בְּפֶסַח כֵּן. אַף בְּיוֹם הַכִּיפּוּרִים כֵּן. אַף בְּנָזִיר כֵּן. אַף בִּנְבֵילוֹת כֵּן אַף בִּטְרֵיפוֹת כֵּן אַף בִּשְׁקָצִים כֵּן אַף בִּרְמָשִׂים כֵּן.

What is the reason of Rebbi Eliezer? Because he started with permission. It was stated: "Rebbi Nathan said, not that Rebbi Eliezer said because he started with permission but Rebbi Eliezer holds that chewed is like swallowed." It is the same with the Sabbath[51], Passover[52], the Day of Atonement[53], the *nazir*[54], carcasses and torn animals[55], abominations[56] and crawling things[57].

51 If somebody carries food in his mouth through the public domain on the Sabbath, he has desecrated the Sabbath. But if he chewed the food it is as if he swallowed it, it becomes part of his body and there is no desecration of the Sabbath. Since practice follows R. Joshua, these opinions are irrelevant for practice.

52 If one chews leavened matter without swallowing, it is a transgression of the commandment not to eat leavened matter on Passover. The Babli (*Pesaḥim* 39b) only forbids chewing grain kernels as a rabbinic precaution.

53 Chewing is breaking the fast.

54 If a *nazir* chews raisins, it is as if he had swallowed grapes.

55 A carcass is the body of a

permitted animal which was not killed by cutting its throat. A torn animal is a permitted animal which has an exterior or interior defect which excludes the animal's long term survival. Such an animal may not be eaten. For R. Eliezer, chewing forbidden meat is as bad as eating it.

56 Reptiles and amphibia.

57 Insects and worms.

רִבִּי חִייָה בְּשֵׁם רִבִּי יוֹחָנָן הַשּׁוֹחֵט בְּהֵמָה וּמָצָא בָהּ שֶׁקֶץ אָסוּר בַּאֲכִילָה. מַה טַעֲמָא בְּהֵמָה בַּבְּהֵמָה תֹּאכֵלוּ. וְלֹא שֶׁקֶץ בַּבְּהֵמָה תֹּאכֵלוּ.

Rebbi Ḥiyya in the name of Rebbi Joḥanan: If somebody slaughters an animal and finds in it an abomination, that is forbidden as food. What is the reason? An animal (*Lev.* 11:3) "inside an animal you may eat," but an abomination inside an animal you may not eat.[58]

58 [Sifra *Šemini* 2(9), Babli *Ḥulin* 69a] The verse reads: "All that has hoofs, with clefts through the hoofs, and that chews the cud, *inside an animal*, such you may eat." This is taken to mean that a fetus *inside an animal* may be eaten after the slaughter of the mother. {Sadducees did require separate slaughter of the fetus; MMT lines 37-38.} It is stated here that this applies only if the fetus itself is a permitted animal. The question remains open, what is meant by בהמה "animal"? A four-legged animal, a mammal, or a kosher mammal?

אָמַר רִבִּי יוֹנָה רִבִּי הוֹשַׁעְיָה בָּעֵי מַה בֵינָהּ לְבֵין זִיזִין שֶׁבָּעֲדָשִׁים לִיתוּשִׁין שֶׁבַּכְּלֵיסִים. לְתוֹלָעִים שֶׁבַּתְּמָרִים וּבַגְּרוֹגְרוֹת. תַּמָּן בְּגוּפֵיהֶן הֵן. בְּרַם הָכָא אֵינוֹ בְגוּפוֹ.

Rebbi Jonah said, Rebbi Hoshaiah asked: What is the difference between this[59] and worms in peas, squash bugs[60] in sweet vetch[61], worms in dates and dried figs? There, they are in their bodies[62]; here it is not in its body.

59 The abominations in a slaughtered animal are compared to worms in fruits and vegetables of which Tosephta 7:11 (quoted in Babli *Ḥulin* 67b)

declares that one is not guilty of a transgression if one eats them as long as they never left the fruit.

60 Usually, יתוש is translated as "mosquito", the meaning of the word in modern Hebrew. However, a mosquito cannot be in vetch, only its larva which is not called יתוש. The translation follows H. L. Fleischer, from the Arabic root نتش. The translation fits not only here, but also in the story of Titus (*Giṭṭin* 56b) who is said to have died from an enormous יתוש growing in his head.

61 Translation of Rashi (Babli *Ḥulin* 67b), supported by *Halakhot Gedolot* (ed. Hildesheimer *Hilkhot Dagim*) who translates by Arabic באקלי "legumes; portulac, fava beans". Maimonides: A kind of figs. I. Löw proposes *Prosopis Stephaniana,* also of the family of legumes.

62 They grew inside the fruit whereas the reptile found inside a slaughtered mammal must have come from the outside.

הָדֵין צִירָא מוּרְייֵסָא עַד שֶׁלֹּא יַצְלִיל שָׁרֵי. מִדְּהוּא צָלִיל אָסוּר.

Muries sauce[63], if it is not clear, is permitted; if it is clear it is forbidden.

63 Fish sauce, cf. *Demai* Chapter 1, Note 156. If the sauce is cloudy, it does not have to be checked for worms but if one can see through it, it is forbidden if it is seen to contain worms.

דַּם שֶׁעַל הַכִּכָּר גּוֹרְרוֹ וְאוֹכְלוֹ. וְאִם הָיָה מִבֵּין שִׁנָּיו אוֹכְלוֹ וְאֵינוֹ חוֹשֵׁשׁ. שֶׁקֶץ שֶׁבְּזִיזִין וּזְבוּבִין[64] וּבַהֲגָזִין וּבִשְׁקָצִים וּבִרְמָשִׂין יָכוֹל בִּזְמָן שֶׁהוּא בְּפֵרִי. תַּלְמוּד לוֹמַר טְמֵאִים הֵן בִּזְמָן שֶׁהֵן בִּפְנֵי עַצְמָן וְלֹא בִּזְמָן שֶׁהֵן בְּפֵרִי. יָכוֹל אֲפִילוּ יָֽצְאוּ וְחָֽזְרוּ. תַּלְמוּד לוֹמַר טְמֵאִים הֵם וַאֲפִילוּ יָֽצְאוּ וְחָֽזְרוּ. רַב חִייָה בַּר אַשִׁי בְשֵׁם רַב אֲפִילוּ יָֽצְאוּ עַל שְׂפַת (fol. 45c) אוֹכֶל וְחָֽזְרוּ הֲרֵי אֵלוּ אֲסוּרִין.

Blood on a loaf of bread one shaves off and eats [the bread]. If it came from between his teeth he eats and does not worry[65]. The abominations among mites, flies, wild bees, abominations and crawling things[66], I might think [that they are forbidden] while they are inside the fruit, the verse says (*Lev.* 11:26,27,28): "They are impure," when they exist independently rather than inside the fruit. I might think, even if they left and returned; the verse says "they are impure," even if they left and returned. Rav Ḥiyya bar Ashi in the name of Rav: As soon as they reach the rim of the food they are forbidden even if they return[67].

64 Reading of the Rome ms. Leyden: הבזבוזין "the spendthrifts".

65 Tosephta 7:11 (in the name of R. Joshua), Babli *Keritut* 21b. In the Babli, blood from bleeding gums has to be sucked off (it may be swallowed), in the Tosephta it has to be wiped off. Blood on the bread (no longer liquid) is only rabbinically forbidden.

66 The list is in Tosephta 7:11, Babli *Ḥulin* 67b. The derivation from the verse is only here; a different one in *Sifra Šemini* 12(1).

67 As soon as any part of a worm or insect developing inside a fruit is visible from the outside, it becomes forbidden. (In talmudic theory, worms and insects develop spontaneously, not from eggs, and, therefore, may be considered as part of the fruit.)

אַבָּא בַּר רַב חוּנָא בְּשֵׁם רִבִּי יוֹחָנָן הַשּׁוֹחֵט בְּהֵמָה וּמָצָא בָהּ חֲזִיר מוּתָּר בַּאֲכִילָה. רִבִּי יוֹנָה אָמַר אָסוּר בַּאֲכִילָה. מַה טַעֲמָא בְּהֵמָה בַּבְּהֵמָה תֹּאכֵלוּ. וְלֹא עוֹף בַּבְּהֵמָה תֹּאכֵלוּ. וְלֹא שֶׁקֶץ בָּאֲכִילָה.

Abba bar Rav Ḥuna in the name of Rebbi Joḥanan: He who slaughters an animal and found in it a pig may eat it. Rebbi Jonah said, it is forbidden to eat, what is the reason? An animal (*Lev.* 11:3) "inside an animal you may eat.[58]" You should not eat a bird inside an animal and not an abomination inside an animal[68].

68 In the Babli, *Ḥulin* 69a, R. Joḥanan is quoted forbidding a pigeon found inside a slaughtered animal. That statement must have fallen out here since the interpretation of the verse also refers to birds which were not mentioned beforehand. On the other hand, the mention of the pig must have fallen out in the Babli since that source points out that the verse permits only the consumption of ruminants with cloven hoofs found inside a slaughtered

animal. It is therefore determined, according to R. Jonah, that בהמה means only "kosher animal", cf. Note 58.

לֹא סוֹף דָּבָר פִּישְׁפֵּשׁ אֶלָּא כָּל־דָּבָר שֶׁנַּפְשׁוֹ שֶׁל אָדָם חַתָּה מִמֶּנּוּ.

Not only a bed bug, but everything a person is afraid of[69].

69 One has to spit it out even if it is sanctified food if it tastes like a health hazard.

(fol. 45a) **משנה ג**: הָיָה אוֹכֵל בְּאֶשְׁכּוֹל וְנִכְנַס מִן הַגִּינָּה לֶחָצֵר. רִבִּי לִיעֶזֶר אוֹמֵר יִגְמוֹר וְרִבִּי יְהוֹשֻׁעַ אוֹמֵר לֹא יִגְמוֹר. חֲשֵׁיכָה לֵילֵי שַׁבָּת רִבִּי לִיעֶזֶר אוֹמֵר יִגְמוֹר וְרִבִּי יְהוֹשֻׁעַ אוֹמֵר לֹא יִגְמוֹר.

Mishnah 3: If he was eating a bunch of grapes and entered from the garden into the courtyard. Rebbi Eliezer said, he should finish, but Rebbi Joshua said, he should not finish. If it got dark on Sabbath eve, Rebbi Eliezer said, he should finish, but Rebbi Joshua said, he should not finish[70].

70 Commentary of Maimonides: We have a principle that *ṭevel* becomes subject to tithes by biblical law only when the produce sees the face of the house as it was said (*Deut.* 26:13): "I removed the holy food from the house." Any fruits eaten on the field or in the garden are not subject to tithes because that is a snack. Another principle is that the Sabbath brings the obligation of tithes; it is forbidden to eat even a snack from *ṭevel* on the Sabbath since the Eternal said, (*Is.* 58:13) "you should call the Sabbath a pleasure". Therefore, all one has is prepared so that he may eat or drink from it on the Sabbath; this will be explained in Tractate *Ma'serot* (Chapter 4). And when Rebbi Eliezer says "he should finish", the meaning is that he should leave the courtyard again and finish. But in the courtyard he may not finish eating. And so they said on the Sabbath "he should finish", *i. e.*, he should leave it alone until the end of the Sabbath day and only then finish.

But on the Sabbath itself he is forbidden to eat it. And when R. Joshua said "he should not finish," it means he should not continue to eat before he tithed.

(fol. 45c) **הלכה ד**: תַּמָּן תַּנִּינָן גֶּפֶן שֶׁהִיא נְטוּעָה בֶחָצֵר נוֹטֵל אֶת כָּל־הָאֶשְׁכּוֹל. וְכֵן בָּרִימּוֹן וְכֵן בָּאֲבַטִּיחַ דִּבְרֵי רִבִּי טַרְפוֹן. רִבִּי זְעִירָא רִבִּי חִיָּיה בְשֵׁם רִבִּי יוֹחָנָן אוֹמֵר רִבִּי טַרְפוֹן כְּרִבִּי אֱלִיעֶזֶר. אוֹמֵר רִבִּי טַרְפוֹן עוֹשֶׂה קְצִיעַת הָאוֹכֶל כִּתְחִילָּתוֹ. רִבִּי אִילָא רִבִּי יָסָא בְשֵׁם רִבִּי יוֹחָנָן אוֹ רִבִּי טַרְפוֹן כְּרִבִּי לִיעֶזֶר אוֹ רִבִּי טַרְפוֹן עוֹשֶׂה אֲכִילָה אַחַת שֶׁיֵּשׁ בָּהּ שְׁתַּיִם וְשָׁלֹשׁ אֲכִילוֹת כַּאֲכִילָה אַחַת. מַה טַעֲמָא דְרִבִּי לִיעֶזֶר מִשּׁוּם שֶׁהִתְחִיל בּוֹ בְהֵיתֵר. תַּנֵּי רִבִּי נָתָן אוֹמֵר. לֹא שֶׁהָיָה רִבִּי לִיעֶזֶר אוֹמֵר מִשּׁוּם שֶׁהִתְחִיל בּוֹ בְהֵיתֵר. אֶלָּא שֶׁרִבִּי לִיעֶזֶר אוֹמֵר יַמְתִּין עַד מוֹצָאֵי שַׁבָּת אוֹ עַד שֶׁיֵּצֵא חוּץ לֶחָצֵר וְיִגְמוֹר.

Halakhah 4: There[71], we have stated: "If a vine is planted in the courtyard[72], one may take an entire bunch, and similarly for pomegranate and water melon, the words of Rebbi Ṭarphon." Rebbi Zeïra, Rebbi Ḥiyya, in the name of Rebbi Joḥanan: Rebbi Ṭarphon says following Rebbi Eliezer. Rebbi Ṭarphon says, one makes the cut[73] of food equal to its start. Rebbi Illa, Rebbi Assi in the name of Rebbi Joḥanan: Either Rebbi Ṭarphon follows Rebbi Eliezer or Rebbi Ṭarphon makes a meal consisting of two or three snacks equal to one snack[74]. What is the reason of Rebbi Eliezer? Because he started with permission. It was stated: "Rebbi Nathan said, not that Rebbi Eliezer said because he started with permission but Rebbi Eliezer holds he should wait until the end of the Sabbath or he should leave the courtyard again and finish."[75]

71 Mishnah *Ma'serot* 3:9. The entire Halakhah is reproduced, *mutatis mutandis*, in Halakhah *Ma'serot* 3:9.

72 If one harvests, the produce should be free of tithes and heave, and available for snacks, until it is brought to the house. But if it grows in the courtyard, it is immediately in front of the house. R. Ṭarphon permits taking an entire bunch, or an entire water

melon, for a snack. Rebbi Aqiba allows only a few grapes or a small piece of watermelon for a snack and requires taking heave and tithing for everything else.

73 In *Ma'serot*: עוקצין, "the stalk", what remains if everything else is eaten.

74 Since snacks can be eaten after harvest without tithing, he allows snacks as large as one wants.

75 Nevertheless, R. Joshua and R. Aqiba are greater authorities than R. Eliezer and R. Ṭarphon and Maimonides is justified in deciding following R. Joshua. However, in the Kaufman ms. of the Mishnah and many mss. of the Maimonides tradition, the names of rabbis Eliezer and Joshua are switched in the last part of the Mishnah; but cf. *Ma'serot* 2, Note 33.

(fol. 45a) **משנה ד**: יֵין תְּרוּמָה שֶׁנִּתְגַּלָּה יִשָּׁפֵךְ וְאֵין צָרִיךְ לוֹמַר שֶׁל חוּלִין. שְׁלֹשָׁה מַשְׁקִין אֲסוּרִין מִשּׁוּם גִּילּוּי הַמַּיִם וְהַיַּיִן וְהֶחָלָב וּשְׁאָר כָּל־הַמַּשְׁקִין מוּתָּרִין. כַּמָּה יִשְׁהוּ וְיִהְיוּ אֲסוּרִין כְּדֵי שֶׁיָּבֹא הָרַחַשׁ מִמָּקוֹם קָרוֹב וְיִשְׁתֶּה.

Mishnah 4: Heave wine that was left uncovered[76] should be poured out, certainly if it was profane. Three kinds of fluids are forbidden when they were uncovered, water, wine, and milk. All other fluids are permitted. How long should they be left unattended to become forbidden? So that the crawling creature[77] might come from a nearby place and drink.

76 Left uncovered while nobody was in the room. It was assumed that snake poison in the drink was poisonous to humans. While it is sinful to destroy food, it is worse not to destroy food that is potentially poisonous.

77 The reference is mostly to snakes, but included are any poisonous creatures which might put some poison into the fluid. For health reasons, none of the potentially dangerous fluids may be used for any purpose.

(fol. 45c) **הלכה ה**: רִבִּי יַעֲקֹב בַּר אָחָא רִבִּי שִׁמְעוֹן בַּר בָּא בְשֵׁם רִבִּי חֲנִינָה יַיִן שֶׁנִּתְגַּלָּה יִשָּׁפֵךְ וַאֲפִילוּ שֶׁל תְּרוּמָה. תַּבְשִׁיל שֶׁבִּישְּׁלוֹ בְמַיִם מְגוּלִּין אֲפִילוּ שֶׁל תְּרוּמָה יִשָּׁפֵךְ וְאֵין צָרִיךְ לוֹמַר שֶׁל חוּלִין. אָמַר רִבִּי יוֹסֵי מַתְנִיתָא אָמְרָה כֵן יַיִן שֶׁל תְּרוּמָה שֶׁנִּתְגַּלָּה יִשָּׁפֵךְ וְאֵין צָרִיךְ לוֹמַר שֶׁל חוּלִין. חֲבֵרַייָא בְשֵׁם רִבִּי יוֹחָנָן יַיִן שֶׁנִּתְגַּלָּה אָסוּר לְשְׁהוֹתוֹ. וְאִם שִׁיהוּ וְהֶחֱמִיץ מֵאֵילָיו אָסוּר. תְּאֵינִים וַעֲנָבִים שֶׁנִּיקְּרוּ אָסוּר לְשְׁהוֹתָן וְאִם שִׁיהָן וְצָמְקוּ מֵאֵילֵיהֶן מוּתָּרוֹת.

Halakhah 5: Rebbi Jacob bar Aḥa, Rebbi Simeon bar Abba in the name of Rebbi Ḥanina: Wine left uncovered must be poured out, even if it is heave. A dish cooked with water that was left uncovered must be thrown out, even if it is heave and certainly if it is profane. Rebbi Yose said, our Mishnah says so: "Heave wine that was left uncovered should be poured out, and certainly profane wine." The colleagues in the name of Rebbi Joḥanan: It is forbidden to keep wine that was left uncovered; if it was kept and it turned into vinegar by itself it is forbidden[78]. It is forbidden to keep figs and grapes that were pecked at; if they were kept and dried up by themselves they are permitted[79].

78 Poison in sour wine will not prevent it from turning into vinegar.

79 Poison in figs or grapes will make them rot. If they dry out (without being heated artificially), it is a sign that no poison is present (Tosephta 7:16).

מַעֲשֶׂה בְּרַתֵּיהּ[80] דְּרִבִּי חִייָה רוֹבָא הֲוָה מְנַקְּרָא בִתְאֵינַייָא בְּגִין דְּלָא יֵיכְלוּן חֲבֵירַייָא. וַהֲוָה רִבִּי חִייָה אָבוֹי אָכַל מִינְּהוֹן. וְלֵית אָסוּר. לְדַעְתֵּיהּ הֲוָה עוּבְדָא. וַאֲפִילוּ כֵן לֹא אָסִיר. לֹא כֵן תַּנֵּי רָאָה צִיפּוֹר נוֹקֶרֶת בִּתְאֵינָה וְעַכְבָּר מְנַקֵּר בְּאֲבַטִּיחַ אָסוּר. אֲנִי אוֹמֵר מָקוֹם הַנֶּקֶר אָכְלוּ. מְנַטְּרָא לָהֵין הֲוֵית.

[It happened that] the daughter of the elder Rebbi Ḥiyya punched holes into figs so that the fellows should not eat them but (his) [her] father Rebbi Ḥiyya ate from them. Is that not forbidden? He knew of the matter. Is it not forbidden anyhow, have we not stated[81]: "If somebody saw a bird pecking at a fig or a rat nibbling at a watermelon, it is forbidden for I say, they ate from the place of a pecking hole." She had been watching.

80 Reading of the Rome ms. Leyden and Venice: באחריה "At the place". That reading makes no sense. The reading of the Rome ms. is difficult since (a) R. Ḥiyya had twin daughters, Pazy and Martha, and (b) it should say "her father", not "his father." However, the Yerushalmi cannot be judged by standards of style.

81 Tosephta 7:17, Babli *Avodah Zarah* 9a/b. The Babli states that the rules for health hazards must be much stricter than those for religious obligations; cf. Halakhah 7.

רִבִּי יִצְחָק בַּר נַחְמָן בְּשֵׁם רִבִּי יְהוֹשֻׁעַ בֶּן לֵוִי הַחַד וְהַמָּר וְהַמָּתוֹק אֵין בּוֹ מִשּׁוּם גִּילּוּי. רִבִּי סִימוֹן בְּשֵׁם רִבִּי יְהוֹשֻׁעַ בֶּן לֵוִי הַחַד וְהַמָּר וְהַמָּתוֹק אֵין בָּהֶן לֹא מִשּׁוּם גִּילּוּי וְלֹא מִשּׁוּם יַיִן נֶסֶךְ. רִבִּי סִימוֹן מְפָרֵשׁ הַחַד קוֹנְדִּיטוֹן. וְהַמָּר פסתינון[82]. וְהַמָּתוֹק חַמְרָא מְבַשְּׁלָא. רִבִּי יְהוֹשֻׁעַ בַּר זֵידָל הֲוָה לֵיהּ חַמְרָא מְבַשְּׁלָא שֶׁנִּתְיַיחֵד בִּרְשׁוּת הַגּוֹי. שָׁאַל לְרִבִּי יַנַּאי בֵּי רִבִּי יִשְׁמָעֵאל אָמַר לֵיהּ כֵּן אָמַר רִבִּי שִׁמְעוֹן בֶּן לָקִישׁ מָתוֹק אֵין בּוֹ לֹא מִשּׁוּם גִּילּוּי וְלֹא מִשּׁוּם יַיִן נֶסֶךְ. רִבִּי יַנַּיי בֵּי רִבִּי יִשְׁמָעֵאל אִבְאָשׁ סָלְקוֹן לְגַבֵּיהּ רִבִּי זֵירָא רִבִּי הוֹשַׁעְיָה וְרִבִּי בּוֹן בַּר כַּהֲנָא וְרִבִּי חֲנַנְיָה חֲבֵרְהוֹן דְּרַבָּנִין מְבַקְּרָתֵיהּ. חָמוֹן לְרִבִּי יְהוֹשֻׁעַ בַּר זֵידָל יְתִיב. אָמְרִין הָא מָרֵי שְׁמוּעֲתָא וְהָא מָרֵי עוּבְדָּא אָתוֹן וְשָׁאֲלוֹן לֵיהּ. אָמַר לוֹן רִבִּי יַנַּיי בֵּי רִבִּי יִשְׁמָעֵאל כֵּן אָמַר רִבִּי שִׁמְעוֹן בֶּן לָקִישׁ מָתוֹק אֵין בּוֹ לֹא מִשּׁוּם גִּילּוּי וְלֹא מִשּׁוּם יַיִן נֶסֶךְ. אָמַר לוֹ רִבִּי זְעִירָא דְּדִילְמָא מַה אִילֵּין דְּרִבִּי שִׁמְעוֹן בֶּן לָקִישׁ דְּהָכֵן הָכִין. אָמַר לֵיהּ לֹא לְעוֹבְדָא וְסָמְכוּן עֲלוֹי. כַּד נַחְתּוֹן קָם רִבִּי אִילָּא עִם רִבִּי בּוֹן בַּר כַּהֲנָא אָמַר לֵיהּ[83] אִילוּלֵי דְּאַתּוּן מְרַחֲמִין שְׁמוּעֲתָא וְלֹא מַתְנִיתָא הִיא. דְּתַנֵּי רִבִּי חִייָה יַיִן מְבוּשָּׁל שֶׁל גּוֹיִם לָמָּה אָסוּר מִפְּנֵי שֶׁהָיָה

מִתְּחִילָּתוֹ יַיִן. חוֹמֶץ שֶׁל גּוֹיִם לָמָּה אָסוּר שֶׁהָיָה מִתְּחִילָּתוֹ יַיִן. אָמַר רִבִּי יוֹסֵי מַתְנִיתָא אָמְרָה כֵן הַיַּיִן וְהַחוֹמֶץ שֶׁל גּוֹיִם שֶׁהָיָה מִתְּחִילָּתוֹ יַיִן.

[84]Rebbi Isaac bar Naḥman in the name of Rebbi Joshua ben Levi: The hot, the bitter, and the sweet are not under the rules for being uncovered. Rebbi Simon in the name of Rebbi Joshua ben Levi: The hot, the bitter, and the sweet are not under the rules for being uncovered or under those of libation wine[85]. Rebbi Simeon explains: The hot, spice wine. And the bitter, vermouth wine. And the sweet, cooked wine[86]. Rebbi Joshua ben Zeidal[87] had cooked wine which was left unsupervised in the possession of a Gentile. He asked Rebbi Yannai ben Rebbi Ismael who said to him, so says Rebbi Simeon ben Laqish: The sweet is not under the rules for being uncovered or under those of libation wine. Rebbi Yannai ben Rebbi Ismael fell ill. Rebbi Zeïra, Rebbi Hoshaiah, Rebbi Abun bar Cahana, and Rebbi Ḥananiah the colleague of the rabbis went to visit him. They saw that Rebbi Joshua ben Zeidal was sitting [there]. They said, there is the master of the decision and the person of the happening; they went and asked him. Rebbi Yannai ben Rebbi Ismael said to them, so says Rebbi Simeon ben Laqish, the sweet is not under the rules for being uncovered or under those of libation wine. Rebbi Zeïra said to him, maybe that statement of Rebbi Simeon ben Laqish is for argument's sake? He told him no, it is for action and you can rely on me[88]. When they came back, there was Rebbi Hila standing with Rebbi Abun bar Cahana. He told him, if you did not prefer decisions, is it not a *baraita*? Since Rebbi Ḥiyya stated[89]: "Why is cooked wine of Gentiles forbidden? Because it started out as wine. Why is vinegar of Gentiles forbidden? Because it started out as wine." Rebbi Yose said, the Mishnah says so: "wine[90] and vinegar of Gentiles which originally was wine."

82 Reading of the Rome ms. פסתיטון, of the parallel in *Avodah Zarah* (and *Tanḥuma Wayešev*) פסינתטון. In the parallel in the Babli, *Avodah Zarah* 30a, אפסינתין is explained by the Gaonim and R. Ḥananel as name of the plant ἀψίνθιον, τό "wormwood, *Artemisia Absinthium*".

83 Reading of the Rome ms. Leyden and Venice: א״ר (אמר רבי) "Rabbi . . . said".

84 This and the following paragraphs also are in *Avodah Zarah* 2:3 (fol. 41a).

85 If left standing uncovered and unsupervised, they still may be consumed. If left in the hands of a Gentile, they do not become prohibited; the Gentile will not use them for libations.

86 In the Babli, there are two explanations. 1. Hot, hot *tilia* (linden tree) wine. Bitter, wine from blighted grapes. Sweet, sweetened wine. 2. Hot, pepper wine. Bitter, vermouth wine. Sweet, sweetened wine (according to *Arukh*, *carenum*; cf. Note 94)

87 A third generation Amora whose name appears only here and in the parallel in *Avodah Zarah*. In the Babli (*Avodah Zarah* 30a), he appears as R. Ismael ben Zeirod. In the Rome ms., his name is R. Joshua ben Gidul.

88 A similar statement is in Babli *Avodah Zarah* 30a.

89 A similar statement is in Babli *Avodah Zarah* 29b. In Tosephta *Avodah Zarah* 4:12, the text reads: "[Gentile] cooked wine and *olentia* are forbidden because they originally were wine."

90 "Wine which originally was wine" is cooked wine which is thickened and lost its alcohol in cooking.

רִבִּי אִימִּי הֲוָה לֵיהּ אוֹרְחִין אָמַר לוֹן אִילוּלֵי דְאִיתְגְּלִי חַמְרָא מְבַשְּׁלָא דִידִי הֲוֵינָא מַשְׁקֵי לְכוֹן מִינֵיהּ. אָמַר לֵיהּ רִבִּי בִיבַי אַיְתֵיי וַאֲנָא שָׁתֵיי. אָמַר מָאן דְּבָעֵי מֵימוֹת[91] יֵיזִיל יָמוּת גּוֹ בֵּייתֵיהּ.

Rebbi Immi had guests. He said to them, if my cooked wine had not been left uncovered, I would have served you some. Rebbi Vivian told him, bring it and I shall drink. He said, he who wants to die should go and die in his own house.

בַּר יוּדָנִי אִיגְלֵי קוֹנְדִיטוֹן דִּידֵיהּ אָתָא שָׁאַל לְרַבָּנִין אָמְרִין לֵיהּ אָסוּר. וְלֹא כֵן אָמַר רִבִּי יִצְחָק בַּר נַחְמָן בְּשֵׁם רִבִּי יְהוֹשֻׁעַ בֶּן לֵוִי הַחַד וְהַמָּר וְהַמָּתוֹק אֵין בּוֹ

מְשׁוּם גִּילּוּי. רַבָּנִין דְּקֵסָרִין בְּשֵׁם רִבִּי חִייָה בַּר טִיטֵס בְּהַהוּא דְשָׁחִיק חַד לִתְלָתָא.

The spiced wine of Bar Yudani was left uncovered. He went and asked the rabbis who told him, it is forbidden. But did not Rebbi Isaac bar Naḥman say in the name of Rebbi Joshua ben Levi: The hot, the bitter, and the sweet are not under the rules for being uncovered! The rabbis of Caesarea in the name of Rebbi Ḥiyya bar Titus[92]: One which consists of one third ground spices[93].

91 Reading of the Rome ms. and the Leyden text in *Avodah Zarah*. Leyden here: ימות.

92 He is mentioned only here and in the parallel in *Avodah Zarah*.

93 Spice wine is immune to exposure only if the spices make up one third of the volume.

בְּעוֹן קוֹמֵי רִבִּי אַבָּהוּ יַיִן שֶׁנִּתְבַּשֵּׁל שֶׁנִּתְגַּלֶּה מַהוּ. אֲמַר לוֹן קָרֵינָה צְרִיכָה לְרִבִּי יוֹחָנָן וְאַתּוּן שְׁאָלוּן לִי לֹא כָל־שֶׁכֵּן יַיִן מְבוּשָּׁל. אֲעַל שָׁאַל לְרִבִּי יִצְחָק אָמַר לֵיהּ אָסוּר. אִינְהַר רִבִּי אַבָּהוּ דְּאָמַר רִבִּי יוֹחָנָן אָסוּר.

They asked before Rebbi Abbahu: What [is the status of] cooked wine that was left uncovered? He said to them, Rebbi Joḥanan had a problem with *carenum*[94], and you are asking me? Is that not [applicable to] cooked wine? He went to ask Rebbi Isaac who told him, it is forbidden. Rebbi Abbahu [then] remembered that Rebbi Joḥanan had said, it is forbidden.

94 Wine that lost one third of its volume by cooking, Greek κάροινον. (The word may originally be Accadic, *karānu* "wine", *kurūnu* "date liquor.") It follows that "cooked wine" did not yet come to the state of *carenum*. R. Joḥanan could not decide whether the rules of uncovered fluid apply to *carenum* or not. Therefore, wine which lost less than one third of its volume in cooking certainly is forbidden.

רִבִּי יַעֲקֹב בַּר אָחָא רִבִּי אִימִּי בְּשֵׁם רִבִּי לָֽעְזָר אִם הָיָה נִכְנַס וְיוֹצֵא מוּתָּר. בַּר נְטוֹזָא אִיתְגְּלִי לֵיהּ גִּיגִיתֵיהּ. אָעַל שָׁאַל לְרִבִּי בָּא בַּר מָמָל. אָמַר לֵיהּ אִם הָיָה נִכְנַס וְיוֹצֵא מוּתָּר. רִבִּי יַעֲקֹב בַּר אָחָא רִבִּי אִימִּי בְּשֵׁם רִבִּי לָֽעְזָר אִם הָיָה יָשֵׁן מוּתָּר. רִבִּי חֲנַנְיָה וְרִבִּי יָשׁוּעַ בֶּן לֵוִי חַד אָמַר יָשֵׁן מוּתָּר. וְחָרָנָא אָמַר יָשֵׁן אָסוּר. וְלָא יָֽדְעִין מָאן אָמַר דָּא וּמָאן אָמַר דָּא. וּמִסְתַּבְּרָה דְּאָמַר רִבִּי חֲנִינָא יָשֵׁן מוּתָּר. דִּבְכָל־אָתָר רִבִּי לָֽעְזָר סָמִיךְ לְרִבִּי חֲנִינָה.

Rebbi Jacob bar Aḥa, Rebbi Ammi, Rebbi Eleazar: If he was entering and leaving it is permitted[95]. The barrel of Bar Neṭoza became uncovered. He went and asked Rebbi Abba bar Mamal, who told him, it is permitted. Rebbi Jacob bar Aḥa, Rebbi Ammi, Rebbi Eleazar: If he was sleeping it is permitted. Rebbi Ḥanina and Rebbi Joshua ben Levi, one said, if he was sleeping it is permitted; the other said, it is forbidden. We do not know who said what. It is reasonable [to infer that] Rebbi Ḥanina said, if he was sleeping it is permitted, since Rebbi Eleazar everywhere relies on Rebbi Ḥanina.

95 This is the general rule for the prohibition of wine touched by a Gentile who might have used the wine for a pagan libation. The Gentile would not use wine that was not his if he had to expect the Jewish owner or one of his Jewish employees at any moment. That rule is extended here to wine left uncovered; one does not expect a snake to venture out of its hole if there is continuous traffic in the room.

וְרִבִּי יוֹסֵי בֶּן שָׁאוּל מִשְׁתָּעֵי אֲהֵן עוּבְדָּא. חַד אִיתְתָא הֲווֹ רַחֲמְנָא מִצְוָותָא סַגִּי. חַד זְמַן סְלָק גַּבָּהּ חַד מִיסְכֵּן יְהָבַת קוֹמוֹי מֵיכֻל. מִי אָכַל אַרְגְּשָׁה בַּעֲלָהּ אִיסְלַק יְהָבְתֵיהּ גַּו עִילִיתָא. יְהָבַת קוֹמוֹי בַּעֲלָהּ דְּיוֹכוּל. אָכַל נָם וְדָמַךְ לֵיהּ. אָתָא חִיוְיָה אָכַל מִן מַה דַּהֲוָה קוֹמוֹי וַהֲוָה מִסְתַּכֵּל בֵּיהּ. מִן דְּאִיתְעָר קָם בָּעֵי מֵיכַל מִן מַה דַּהֲוָה קוֹמוֹי שָׁרֵי הַהוּא דְעִילִיתָא מַלּוּלֵי בֵּיהּ. הָדָא אָֽמְרָה יָשֵׁן מוּתָּר. בָּרִיר הֲוָה. וְאֵין אָסוּר מִשּׁוּם יִיחוּד. מִכֵּיוָן דְּלָא חָשִׁיד עַל הָדָא לֹא חָשִׁיד עַל הָדָא. כִּי נֹאֵפוּ וְדָם בִּידֵיהֶן.

Rebbi Yose ben Shaul understands it from this occurrence: A woman loved very much doing good deeds[96]. One time, a poor man came to her and she served him food. While he was eating, she noticed that her husband was coming. She put him [the poor] on the upper floor[97]. She put food before her husband who ate, took a nap, and slept. A snake came and ate from what was before him; he [the poor] saw it. When he awoke and got up he wanted to continue eating what was before him. The one on the upper floor started to talk to him. That means, if he was sleeping, it is permitted[98]. It was familiar with it[99]. Is she not forbidden for being alone [with another man?][100] Since he is not suspected in one thing, he is not suspected in the other, (*Ez.* 23:37) "For they committed adultery, blood is on their hands."[101]

96 "Good deeds" without specific identification are deeds of charity.

97 Not to be seen alone with another man. In a parallel story in Babli *Nedarim* 91b it was not a poor man but the woman's lover.

98 Since without the warning, the husband would have eaten the contaminated food.

99 The snake was used to the dwellers in the house, otherwise it would not have ventured near a sleeping person. Therefore, food near a sleeping person is permitted except for houses with a house snake. (The text in the Rome ms., the Leyden text *Avodah Zarah*, and the quote in *Arukh* read כריך "used to" instead of בריר.)

100 Since a married Jewish woman is not supposed to be alone in a house with another man, could the husband not divorce her for suspicion of adultery without paying her the *ketubah* sum? The rules for this are detailed in the last chapter of *Qiddušin*.

101 An adulterer would gladly have let the husband die. Since the person upstairs did not let the husband die, he was not an adulterer and the wife is cleared. The Babli concurs (Note 97).

מַעֲשֶׂה בְּטַבָּח בְּצִיפּוֹרִי שֶׁהָיָה מַאֲכִיל יִשְׂרָאֵל נְבֵילוֹת וּטְרֵיפוֹת. פַּעַם אַחַת שָׁתָה יַיִן בְּעֶרֶב שַׁבָּת וְעָלָה לְגַג וְנָפַל וּמֵת. וְהָיוּ כְּלָבִים מְלַקְקִין בְּדָמוֹ. אָתוּן וְשָׁאֲלוּן

לְרִבִּי חֲנִינָה מַהוּ מִירְמִיתֵי מִן קוֹמֵיהוֹן. אָמַר לוֹן כְּתִיב וּבָשָׂר בַּשָּׂדֶה טְרֵיפָה לֹא תֹאכֵלוּ לַכֶּלֶב תַּשְׁלִיכוּן אוֹתוֹ. וְזֶה הָיָה גוֹזֵל אֶת הַכְּלָבִים וּמַאֲכִיל אֶת יִשְׂרָאֵל. אָמַר לוֹן אַרְפּוּנוֹן דְּמִדִּידְהוֹן אִינּוּן אָכְלִין.

It happened that a butcher in Sepphoris sold to Jews carcasses and torn meats. Once he drank wine Friday night, went to the roof[102], fell down, and died. The dogs were licking his blood. People came and asked Rebbi Ḥanina, should we lift him from before them[103]? He said to them, it is written (*Ex*. 22:30): "Torn meat on the fields you shall not eat, you must throw it to the dogs!" This one robbed the dogs and fed it to Jews. He said to them, let them, they are eating from their own!

102 In the dark. In *Avodah Zarah*: He got drunk on Yom Kippur Eve.

103 Presumably he was lying in the street where the removal of a corpse on the Sabbath needs detailed rabbinic instruction on how to proceed without a violation of the Sabbath laws. Inside the courtyard it would not have been necessary to ask.

מַעֲשֶׂה בְּחָסִיד אֶחָד שֶׁהָיָה מְלַגְלֵג בְּגִילּוּי יַיִן. פַּעַם אַחַת לָקָה בְדַלֶּקֶת. וְרָאוּ אוֹתוֹ יוֹשֵׁב וְדוֹרֵשׁ בְּיוֹם הַכִּיפּוּרִים וּצְלוֹחִית שֶׁל מַיִם בְּיָדוֹ.

A pious person happened to be insistent[104] in [the matter of] uncovered wine. Once he was smitten with a fever. They saw him sitting and giving a sermon on the Day of Atonement with a flask of water in his hand[105].

104 This word is not the usual "to make fun of", but a direct derivative of Arabic لجّ "to be insistent", also لجلج "to repeat words in speaking"; cf. H. L. Fleischer's notes to Levy's Dictionary, *s. v.* לגלג.

105 For a medical necessity, he could take sips of less than a mouthful of water to combat his fever on the Day of Atonement. He would not let the flask out of his hands for fear it could stand unsupervised.

חַד בַּר נַשׁ אִיגְלִי לֵיהּ גֶּרֶב דַּחֲמַר. אָזַל בַּעֲרוּבָא צוֹמָא רַבָּא לְמִשְׁפְּכִינֵיהּ. חֲמְתֵיהּ חַד אָמַר לֵיהּ הֲבֵיהּ לִי נִשְׁתַּיְיָה. אָמַר לֵיהּ לָאו מִגְלֵי הוּא. אָמַר לֵיהּ הֲבֵיהּ לִי וּמָרֵיהּ דְּצוֹמָא לִיקוּם. לָא אַסְפָּק מִישְׁתֵּיהּ עַד דְּאִיתְחַלְחַל.

A person's amphora of wine became uncovered. He went on the eve of the Great Fast to pour it out. Another person saw him and said, give it to me to drink. He said to him, but was it not left uncovered? He said to him, give it to me, the Master of the Fast will support [me]. He did not finish drinking when he started shaking.

רִבִּי יִרְמְיָה בְשֵׁם רִבִּי חִייָה בַּר בָּא כָּל־הָאֲרָסִין מַעֲלִין חַטָּטִין וְאֵירֶס נָחָשׁ מֵמִית. רִבִּי יִרְמְיָה שָׁאַל לְרִבִּי (fol. 45d) זְעִירָא מָארֵיהּ שְׁמוּעָתָא שָׁאַל לֵיהּ.

Rebbi Jeremiah in the name of Rebbi Ḥiyya bar Abba: All poisons cause scab but the poison of a snake kills. [106] Rebbi Jeremiah asked Rebbi Zeïra. As the master of the ruling, could he have asked?

106 A sentence is missing here which is preserved in *Avodah Zarah*: ר' חייה אמר אין נשאלין על הגילוין "Rebbi Ḥiyya said, one is not asked about uncovered [fluids]." From the next sentence, one must assume that R. Jeremiah transmitted the statement in the name of R. Ḥiyya bar Abba.

The meaning of the statement is that in case of possible danger to life, as expressed in the preceding sentence, no logical or rabbinic arguments are admitted and everybody is supposed to exercise the utmost care which means that in matters of doubt, the fluids cannot be used. Therefore, no questions about this can be asked from any rabbi.

מִתְנַמְנֵם הָיָה רִבִּי זְעִירָא הֲוָה יְתִיב אָכִיל (וַהֲוָה דָמִיךְ) [בְּרַמְשָׁא].[107] יְהַב יָדֵיהּ עַל תּוּמַנְתָּא וְאָמַר לוֹן אַדְלְקוּן בּוֹצִינָה. אַדְלְקוּן וְאַשְׁכְּחוֹן שְׁפוֹפִינָא שֶׁהוּא דוֹמֶה לִשְׂעָרָה כָּרִיךְ עָלֶיהָ. אָמַר לֵיהּ רְשִׁיעָא לֹא הֲוֵינָא זָהִיר בָּךְ.

Rebbi Zeïra was dozing; he was sitting and eating (and was sleeping) [in the evening]. He put his hand on a toman[108] and said, kindle a light.

They lit a light and found a snakelet like a hair curled around it. He said to it: Evil one, was I not careful about you?

107 In parenthesis the reading here, in brackets the reading in *Avodah Zarah*.

108 A vessel containing one eighth of a *kab* of wine. Since it got dark, he held that being in the room with the vessel was not sufficient.

אָמַר רִבִּי אִמִּי צְרִיכִין לְמֵיחוּשׁ לְמָה דְבִירְיָיתָא חָשְׁשִׁין. אָסוּר דְּלָא מִיתַּן[109] בַּר נַשׁ פְּרִיטִין גַּו פּוּמָא. וְתַבְשִׁילָה תוֹתֵי עַרְסָא. פִּיתָּא תְּחוֹת שִׁיחְיָא. מִיצַּע סַכִּינָא גַו פּוּגְלָא. סַכִּינָא גַו אֶתְרוֹגָא. אָמַר רִבִּי יוֹסֵי בֵּי רִבִּי בּוּן כָּל־זִיעָא דְנַפְקָא מִבַּר נַשׁ סַם מָוֶת הוּא חוּץ מִזֵּיעַת הַפָּנִים.

Rebbi Ammi said, one has to be careful with what the creatures[110] are careful. It is forbidden to put a coin into the mouth, or a dish under the bed, a bread in the arm pit, a knife in the middle of a radish, a knife into an *etrog*. Rebbi Yose ben Rebbi Abun said, all sweat that comes from a human is poison except the sweat of the face.

109 In *Avodah Zarah* למיתן, avoiding the double negative.

110 People.

כַּד שְׁאָלוּן לְרִבִּי יוֹנָתָן אָמַר לֵיהּ עַרְבָא דְנַפְשָׁךְ אֲנָא. אָמַר רִבִּי יַנַּאי אִין קְטָא קְטָא שִׁיחוֹר. וְאִין אוֹבֵד אוֹבֵד מַרְגָּלִי. אָמַר רִבִּי שִׁמְעוֹן בֶּן לָקִישׁ אִלּוּ זְבַנְתְּ גַּרְמָךְ לְלוּדָנִין הֲוָה מַזְבִּין לְהוֹן בְּדָמִין יְקָרִין. וְהָכָא בְדָמִין קְלִילִין.

When they asked Rebbi Jonathan, he said: Am I the guarantor of your life[111]? Rebbi Yannai said, if you bit something off, you bit off soot. If you lose, you lose a pearl. Rebbi Simeon ben Laqish said, if you would sell yourself for the games[112], you would sell yourself at a high price; but here at a very cheap price.

111 These sayings also point out how stupid it is to consult rabbinic authorities in health matters when the alternatives are a very minor monetary loss against loss of one's life.

112 Latin *ludi*. He would sell himself as a gladiator (as R. Simeon ben Laqish had done according to Babylonian tradition, Babli *Giṭṭin* 47a).

תַּנֵּי מַיִם שֶׁנִּתְגַּלּוּ לֹא יִרְבֵּץ בָּהֶן בְּתוֹךְ בֵּיתוֹ וְלֹא יִשְׁפְּכֵם בִּרְשׁוּת הָרַבִּים וְלֹא יַשְׁקֶה לְגוֹי וְלֹא יַשְׁקֶה מֵהֶן בְּהֶמַת חֲבֵירוֹ אֲבָל מַשְׁקֶה הוּא בְּהֶמְתּוֹ. מַיִם שֶׁנִּתְגַּלּוּ לֹא יָשְׁרֶה בָהֶן אֶת הַטִּיט וְלֹא יְכַבֵּס בָּהֶן אֶת הַכֵּלִים וְלֹא יַדִּיחַ בָּהֶן קְעָרוֹת כּוֹסוֹת וְתַמְחוּיִין. וְאֵין צָרִיךְ לוֹמַר פָּנָיו יָדָיו וְרַגְלָיו. אֲחֵרִים אוֹמְרִים לֹא אָסְרוּ אֶלָּא מְקוֹם סִירְטָא. פָּנָיו כְּסִירְטָא הֵם. רָאשֵׁי אֶצְבָּעוֹת יָדָיו וְרַגְלָיו כְּסִירְטָא הֵן. מַיִם שֶׁנִּתְגַּלּוּ לֹא יְגַבֵּל בָּהֶן אֶת הָעִיסָּה. רִבִּי נְחֶמְיָה אָמַר אֲפִייָה מוּתָּר מִפְּנֵי שֶׁאֵירֶס נָחָשׁ כָּלֶה בָאוּר. רִבִּי סִימוֹן בְּשֵׁם רִבִּי יְהוֹשֻׁעַ בֶּן לֵוִי אָמַר בְּשֶׁאֵינָהּ נוֹפֶלֶת. אֲבָל אִם הָיְתָה נוֹפֶלֶת אָסוּר.

It was stated[113]: "With water that was left uncovered one should not scrub his house; one should not pour it into the public domain[114], or give it to drink to a Gentile[115], neither should one use it to water another person's animals but one may use it to water his own animals[116]. With water that was left uncovered one should not knead clay, or wash clothes, or soak pots, glasses, and food baskets[117], and certainly not wash his face, hands, and feet. Others say, they forbade only the place of a scratch. His face is always like a scratch. The tips of his fingers and toes are always like a scratch. With water that was left uncovered one should not knead dough. Rebbi Neḥemiah said, baking is permitted because snake poison is destroyed by fire." Rebbi Simon in the name of Rebbi Joshua ben Levi: That is, if it does not collapse[118], but if it collapsed it is forbidden.

113 A shorter version is in Tosephta 7:14 and Babli *Avodah Zarah* 30b, *Baba Qama* 115b. From here on, the text is missing in Yerushalmi *Avodah Zarah*.

114 The person who creates a danger in the public domain becomes

liable for all consequences (*Ex.* 21:33).

115 Even though Gentiles do not worry about water left uncovered and the Gentile would drink it on his own, the Jew may not give him anything he knows is dangerous.

116 Since the animal will not die from the poison but it will be weakened. The Babli also forbids watering his own animal.

117 Cf. *Peah* Chapter 8, Note 83.

118 If the dough collapses in baking or the bread when cooling.

הַכֹּל מוֹדִין בְּמַיִם שֶׁהוּחְמוּ שֶׁאָסוּר. מַה בֵּין פַּת וּמַה בֵּין הַמַּיִם. כָּאן הָאוּר שׁוֹלֵט וְכָאן אֵין הָאוּר שׁוֹלֵט. כָּאן הַכֵּלִי מַפְסִיק וְכָאן אֵין הַכֵּלִי מַפְסִיק. שְׁמוּאֵל אָמַר מַה יַּעֲשֶׂה לִי רָשָׁע זֶה אֵין אֲנִי שׁוֹתֶה אֶלָּא חַמִּין. מִילְתֵיהּ אָמַר צוֹנִין שֶׁנַּעֲשׂוּ חַמִּין מוּתָּרִין. אָמַר רִבִּי חֲנִינָה רָשָׁע זֶה דַּעְתּוֹ נְקִייָה וְאֵינוֹ שׁוֹתֶה חַמִּין שֶׁנַּעֲשׂוּ צוֹנִין. מִילְתֵיהּ אָמַר חַמִּין וְנַעֲשׂוּ צוֹנִין מוּתָּרִין. רִבִּי אַבָּהוּ בְשֵׁם רִבִּי יוֹחָנָן בֵּין זֶה בֵין זֶה אָסוּר. מַתְנִיתָא מְסַייְעָא לְרִבִּי יוֹחָנָן חַמִּין כָּל־זְמַן שֶׁמַּעֲלִין הֶבֶל הֲרֵי אֵלּוּ מוּתָּרִין. אֲבָל מַיִם הַמְגוּלִּין אַף עַל פִּי שֶׁמְּחַמְּמָן הֲרֵי אֵלּוּ אֲסוּרִין. מֵי כְבָשִׁין וּמֵי שְׁלָקוֹת וּמֵי תוּרְמוּסִין הֲרֵי אֵלּוּ מוּתָּרִין. מַיִם שֶׁהֵדִיחַ בָּהֶן כְּבָשִׁין וּשְׁלָקִין וְתֶרְמוּסִין הֲרֵי אֵלּוּ אֲסוּרִין. הֵדִיחַ בָּהֶן עֲנָבִים וְאוֹבְשִׁין לְחוֹלֶה אָסוּר.

Everybody agrees that water which was heated is forbidden. What is the difference between bread and water? Here the fire rules[119], there the fire does not rule. There, a vessel separates, here no vessel separates[120]. Samuel said, what can this evil one do to me? I only drink hot [water]. His word says, cold water that was heated is permitted. Rebbi Ḥanina said, this evil one has a delicate taste; he will not drink hot water that cooled. His word says, hot water that cooled is permitted. Rebbi Abbahu in the name of Rebbi Johanan: Both are forbidden. A *baraita* supports Rebbi Joḥanan: [121]"Hot water is permitted[122] as long as it is steaming. But water left uncovered is forbidden even after it was heated. Pickling, preserving[123], and lupine[124] water is permitted. Water in which he soaked [food for] pickling or preserving, or lupines, is forbidden. If he soaked wild grapes[125] for a sick person, it is forbidden."

119 The nature of bread dough is changed by heating.
120 Bread hangs in the *tannur* directly over the fire.
121 Tosephta 7:13, in different formulation and order.
122 Even if left uncovered and unsupervised.
123 Preserving by cooking in water a very long time.
124 Lupines become edible only after cooking.
125 Following R. Saul Lieberman, reading ענבים אובשים, fruits of the wild vine used in medicine (cf. Plinius, *Hist. nat.* Bk. 23, Chap. 14). The water will absorb the taste of these grapes; nevertheless, it remains forbidden if left uncovered.

הַמְשַׁמֶּרֶת שֶׁל יַיִן רִבִּי נְחֶמְיָה אוֹמֵר אִם הָיְתָה פְקוּקָה מִלְּמַעְלָה אַף עַל פִּי שֶׁהִיא פְתוּחָה מִלְּמַטָּן. רִבִּי יוּדָה אוֹמֵר אִם הָיְתָה הַתַּחְתּוֹנָה מְכוּסָּה אַף עַל פִּי שֶׁהָעֶלְיוֹן מְגוּלֶּה מוּתָּר מִפְּנֵי שֶׁאֵירֶס נָחָשׁ עוֹמֵד כִּשְׂבָכָה וְעוֹמֵד מִלְּמַעְלָן. אָמַר רִבִּי לָעְזָר בְּשֶׁלֹּא טָרַף. אֲבָל אִם טָרַף אָסוּר.

"[126]The wine filter, Rebbi Neḥemiah says, if it is blocked on top even though it is open below. Rebbi Jehudah says, if it was covered below even if the top is uncovered it is permitted since snake poison is like netting[127] and remains on top." Rebbi Eliezer[128] says, if he did not stir it. But if he did stir, it is forbidden.

126 A parallel is in Babli *Bava Qama* 115b. There (and in the Rome ms.) the opinion ascribed to R. Jehudah here is reported to be R. Neḥemiah's.
127 In the Babli, "like a sponge". We do not know what was the filtering material used to remove the dregs from the wine.
128 In the Babli, R. Simon in the name of R. Simeon ben Laqish.

לָגִין בְּתֵיקוֹ מוּתָּר מְכוּסֶּה וְאֵינוֹ פָקוּק אָסוּר. פָּקוּק וְאֵינוֹ מְכוּסֶּה אִם הָיָה פְקָקוֹ חוּץ מוּתָּר. תְּרֵין אֲמוֹרִין חַד אָמַר כְּדֵי שֶׁיִּנָּטֵל בְּפִיקוּקוֹ. וְחָרָנָה אָמַר

כְּדֵי שֶׁלֹּא יִכָּנֵס לְתוֹכוֹ רֹאשׁ הַכַּרְכָּר. אָמַר רִבִּי בָּא מָאן דַּעֲבַד טַבָּאוּת פָּקִיק לָהּ וּמְכַסֶּה לָהּ.

A flask in its casing is permitted[129]; covered but not stoppered it is forbidden. Stoppered but not covered, if the stopper appeared on the outside it is permitted. Two Amoraïm, one said if it can be taken up by its stopper[130], and the other said, so that the head of the weaver's shuttle could not enter[131]. Rebbi Abba said, he who wants to do it right, stoppers and covers it.

129 In the Tosephta (7:16): "Forbidden." For the Yerushalmi, the casing (θήκη) keeps the snake out; the Tosephta worries that a miniature snake was in the casing but not noticed.

130 The cork or other material is so tightly pushed in that the flask may be lifted by it.

131 Between the cork and the wall of the vessel.

לָגִין שֶׁהִנִּיחוֹ בְּשִׁידָּה תֵּיבָה וּמִגְדָּל וּשְׁכָחוֹ וְחָזַר וּמְצָאוֹ אָסוּר. בָּדַק וְאַחַר כָּךְ הִנִּיחוֹ מוּתָּר. חַד עוּבְדָא אֲתָא קוֹמֵי רִבִּי בְּחַד דְּחָמְתֵיהּ מְגַלֵּי וּמְכַסֵּי. אָמַר מִפְּנֵי רָשָׁע זֶה נְקַלְקֵל אֶת הַכִּיסוּיִין. אָמַר רִבִּי מָנָא לֹא מִסְתַּבְּרָא דְּלֹא דְּהַהִיא עוּבְדָא דְּהַהוּא אָסִיר.

A forgotten flask deposited in a litter, a chest, or a chassis[132] that later was found is forbidden. If he checked and afterwards put it in it is permitted. A case came before Rebbi, where it[133] was seen uncovering and covering. He said, because of that evil one should we invalidate all covers? Rebbi Mana said, it is reasonable that in that case itself[134] was forbidden.

132 All three are of wood and used for transportation.

133 The snake was seen lifting the cover, drinking, and replacing the cover. This is considered aberrant behavior by the snake.

134 If the snake was seen drinking.

אָמַר רִבִּי יִרְמְיָה חָלָב שֶׁל גּוֹי לָמָּה אָסוּר. מִפְּנֵי תַעֲרוֹבֶת בְּהֵמָה טְמֵאָה. וְתַנִּינָן עוֹמֵד הוּא גוֹי וְחוֹלֵב בְּעֶדֶר וְיִשְׂרָאֵל עוֹמֵד עַל גַּבָּיו וְאֵינוֹ חוֹשֵׁשׁ. רָבָא בְשֵׁם רַב יְהוּדָה רִבִּי סִימוֹן בְּשֵׁם רִבִּי יְהוֹשֻׁעַ בֶּן לֵוִי חָלָב שֶׁל גּוֹי לָמָּה אָסוּר. מִפְּנֵי הַגִּילּוּי. וְיַעֲמִיד אָמַר רִבִּי שְׁמוּאֵל בַּר רַב יִצְחָק מִפְּנֵי הָאֵירֶס הָעוֹמֵד בֵּין הַנְּקָבִין.

[135]Rebbi Jeremiah said, why is Gentile's milk forbidden[136]? Because of admixture from impure animals. As we have stated: "If the Gentile stands and milks the herd, if a Jew stands nearby there is no worry." Rav Abba in the name of Rav Jehudah: Why is Gentiles' milk forbidden? Because of the uncovering[137]. Let him make cheese? Rebbi Samuel ben Rav Isaac said, because of the poison between the holes[138].

135 This and the following paragraph are also in *Šabbat* 1:4, fol. 3a, and, in slightly less complete form, *Avodah Zarah* 2:9, fol. 41d; the discussion in the Babli is *Avodah Zarah* 35b-36a.

136 "Milk milked by a Gentile without a Jew seeing him" is forbidden for consumption but not for use; Mishnah *Avodah Zarah* 2:9.

137 Since Gentiles do not care about uncovered milk and snake poison.

138 In the Babli, uncovered milk is not discussed. There, it is held that impure milk (horse or donkey milk) cannot be made into cheese but a mixture may produce cheese with the impure milk remaining in the holes of the cured cheeses.

שְׁלֹשָׁה אֵירוֹסִין הֵן. אֵרֶס שׁוֹקֵעַ. וְאֵירֶס צָף. וְאֵירֶס עוֹמֵד כִּסְבָכָה מִלְּמַעְלָה. בְּיוֹמוֹי דְּרִבִּי יִרְמְיָה אִיתְגַּלְיָין גּוּגְיָיתֵיהּ דְּסִדְרָא רוּבָּה. שָׁתוֹן קַדְמִייָן וְלֹא מֵייתוֹן. אֲחָרַיָּין וּמֵייתוֹן. אֲנִי אוֹמֵר אֵירֶס שׁוֹקֵעַ הָיָה. פָּעֲלַיָּא הֲווֹן בְּחַקְלָא[139] אִיתְגַּלְיָין קוֹלָתָא דְמַיָּא וְאִישְׁתּוֹן מִינָהּ קַדְמִייָן וְלָא מֵיתוֹן. אַחֲרָיָין וּמֵיתוֹן. אֲנִי אוֹמֵר אֵירֶס שׁוֹקֵעַ הָיָה. וְתַנֵּי כֵן חָבִית שֶׁנִּתְגַּלְּתָה וְכֵן אֲבַטִּיחַ שֶׁנִּיקֵּר וְאָכְלוּ וְשָׁתוּ רִאשׁוֹנִים לֹא יֹאכְלוּ וְיִשְׁתּוּ אַחֲרוֹנִים. אֲנִי אוֹמֵר אֵירֶס שׁוֹקֵעַ הוּא. יַיִן שֶׁנִּתְגַּלָּה וְשָׁתוּ מִמֶּנּוּ עֲשָׂרָה בְנֵי אָדָם אָסוּר לוֹכַל וְלִשְׁתּוֹת אַחֲרֵיהֶן אֲנִי אוֹמֵר אֵירֶס שׁוֹקֵעַ הוּא.

There are three kinds of poison. Poison which sinks down, poison which floats on top, and poison remaining on the surface like a net[140]. In the days of Rebbi Jeremiah, the barrels of the great assembly[141] were uncovered. The first ones drank and did not die but the last ones died. I say that was sinking poison. Workers were on the field when the water pitcher was uncovered. The first ones drank from it and did not die but the last ones died. I say that was sinking poison. We have stated so[142]: An uncovered amphora or a water melon with pecking marks, even if the first ones ate or drank [from it], the later ones should not eat or drink; I say that there is sinking poison. Uncovered wine from which ten persons drank is forbidden for others to (eat or) drink after them; I say that there is sinking poison.

139 Reading of the parallel in *Avodah Zarah*. Rome ms. חֶלְקָה, same meaning. Leyden ms. חלא "vinegar".

140 In the Babli, *Avodah Zarah* 30b, it is stated that the poison of young snakes sinks down (is heavier than water), that of middle-aged snakes is suspended, and that of old snakes stays on top (is lighter than water). There is no indication that the Yerushalmi subscribes to this theory. The "poison remaining like a net" seems to be colloidal.

141 The yearly or half-yearly assembly of all rabbinic scholars.

142 Tosephta 7:17, Babli *Avodah Zarah* 30b, in different formulation.

חֲמִשָּׁה מַשְׁקִין אֵין בָּהֶן מִשּׁוּם גִּילּוּי. הַצִּיר וְהַמּוּרְיֵיס וְהַחוֹמֶץ וְהַשֶּׁמֶן וְהַדְּבָשׁ. רִבִּי שִׁמְעוֹן אוֹסֵר בִּדְבָשׁ. מוֹדִין חֲכָמִים לְרִבִּי שִׁמְעוֹן בְּשֶׁרָאוּ אוֹתוֹ נוֹקֵר. רִבִּי חִינְנָא בַּר פַּפָּא הֲוָת בְּיָדֵיהּ צְלוֹחִית דִּדְבָשׁ מְגַלְיָא. לֹא אִסְפַּק מִישְׁאוֹל עַד דְּפַעְפָּעַת בְּיָדֵיהּ.

"Five fluids are not endangered by being uncovered: Fish oil, *muries*[143], vinegar, olive oil, and honey. Rebbi Simeon forbids honey[144]. The Sages agree with Rebbi Simeon if it was seen pecking[145]." Rebbi

Ḥinena bar Pappos had an uncovered flask of honey in his hand. Before he could ask, it broke apart[146].

143 Cf. *Demay*, Chapter 1, Note 156.

144 Tosephta 7:12, Babli *Ḥulin* 49b. In both sources, R. Simeon forbids all five fluids.

145 They will agree that snakes sometimes act in a perverted way but do not agree that this is enough for a general prohibition (*loc. cit.* 144).

146 The next paragraph will show that this was a miracle to save his life.

רַב וּשְׁמוּאֵל תְּרֵיהוֹן אָֽמְרִין נִיתְּנָה רְשׁוּת לָאָרֶץ לִבָּקַע מִפָּנָיו. וְלֹא נִיתְּנָה רְשׁוּת לְכֵלִי לִיבָּקַע מִפָּנָיו. רִבִּי חִיָּיה רַבָּה וְרִבִּי שִׁמְעוֹן בְּרִבִּי הֲווֹן יָֽתְבִין בְּחַד בַּיִת אָֽזְלוּ מַרְמְרִין. אָֽמְרִין אֶיפְשַׁר דְּהוּא מִיתְחֲמֵי הָכָא וְאִיתְחֲמֵי. אָֽמְרִין בָּרוּךְ הוּא שֶׁבָּחַר בָּהֶן בַּחֲכָמִים שֶׁאָֽמְרוּ נִיתְּנָה רְשׁוּת לָאָרֶץ לִבָּקַע מִפָּנָיו. וְלֹא נִיתְּנָה רְשׁוּת לְכֵלִי לִיבָּקַע מִפָּנָיו.

Rav and Samuel both say, the earth is permitted to be broken apart before it[147], but no vessel is permitted to be broken apart before it. Rebbi Ḥiyya the Great and Rebbi Simeon ben Rebbi were sitting in a certain house[148] when murmurs went around. They said, is it possible that it will be seen here? It was seen. They said, praised be He Who chose the Sages who said, the earth is permitted to be broken apart before it, but no vessel is permitted to be broken apart before it[149].

147 A snake may tunnel under the earth. The comparison with a vessel suggests the theory that snake poison can dissolve earth but not fired clay and metals.

148 Their houses usually had dirt floors. Houses with paved (mosaic) floors usually are called "palaces".

149 Since Rav was a student of his uncle R. Ḥiyya, Rav and Samuel cannot have been the authors of the theory but they may have given the final formulation.

רִבִּי יַנַּאי הֲוָה מִידְחַל מִינֵיהּ סַגִּין וַהֲוָה יְהִיב עַרְסֵיהּ עַל אַרְבָּעָה מָרוֹשִׁין דְּמַיִין. חַד זְמָן פָּשַׁט יָדֵיהּ וְאַשְׁכְּחֵיהּ גַּבֵּיהּ. אָמַר אֲרִימוֹן מִינֵיהּ שׁוֹמֵר פְּתָאִים יי.

Rebbi Yannai feared it so much that he put his bed on four beams [standing] in water. Once he stretched out his hand and found it near himself. He said, take it away from me, (*Ps.* 116:6) "the Eternal watches over the simple-minded."

וְכַמָּה הוּא שִׁיעוּר נֶקֶב. רִבִּי יַעֲקֹב בַּר אָחָא בְּשֵׁם רִבִּי חֲנִינָה מְחַוֵּי בָהּ הָכֵין אָמַר רֹאשׁ אֶצְבָּעִי קְטַנָּה. רִבִּי יַעֲקֹב בַּר אָחָא רִבִּי שִׁמְעוֹן בַּר וָוא בְּשֵׁם רִבִּי יְהוֹשֻׁעַ בֶּן לֵוִי כְּדֵי שֶׁלֹּא תִיכָּנֵס רֹאשׁ אֶצְבַּע קְטַנָּה לְתוֹכוֹ שֶׁל תִּינוֹק בֶּן יוֹמוֹ. וַאֲפִילוּ פָּחוֹת מִיכֵּן הוּא עָלִיל. אֶלָּא דְלֹא יָדַע דְּהוּא נָפֵק לֹא עָלִיל. הָדֵין סִלְטָא אֲפִילֵי קָטָן כַּמָּה אָסוּר דְּהוּא עָלִיל בְּהָדָא וְנָפִיק בְּהָדָא. הָדָא סַלָּקוּתָא אֲפִילוּ דְהוּא תַלְיָיא כַּמָּה אֲסוּרָה דְּהוּא מִשְׁתַּלְשֵׁל.

What is the measure of a hole[150]? Rebbi Jacob bar Aḥa in the name of Rebbi Ḥanina showed it thus: he said, the tip of my small finger. Rebbi Jacob bar Aḥa, Rebbi Simeon bar Abba in the name of Rebbi Joshua ben Levi, so that the tip of the small finger of a newborn cannot enter it. Even if [the hole] were smaller, it [the snake] could enter it but since it does not know how to leave again, it does not enter. A woven basket even if very tight is forbidden for it can enter at one place and leave at another. A knapsack[151] is forbidden even if it hangs very high since it will let itself down[152].

150 When is a hole in a wall a potential hiding place of a snake so that one has to worry about fluids left uncovered? Tosephta 7:16.

151 The meaning of this word is everybody's guess. The meaning "knapsack" is R. M. Margalit's guess, identified by J. Levy as Arabic شلاق *šallāq* "beggar's knapsack". R. Eliahu Fulda writes only "some vessel". Kohout's suggestion to refer the word to Arabic صليقة *ṣalīqa* "slice of roast

beef" has to be rejected.

The word may be Greek σάλαξ, -ακος, ὁ "miner's sieve, coarse sieve, screen"; cf. text at Note 126 (E. G.).

152 The snake will climb to the ceiling and lower itself to the knapsack/sieve.

אֵי זֶהוּ מָקוֹם קָרוֹב. אָמַר רִבִּי שְׁמוּאֵל מֵאוֹזֶן חָבִית וּלְפִיהָ. וְלֹא חֲמִי לֵיהּ. אָמַר רִבִּי חֲנִינָא מִין קָטָן הוּא וּשְׁפִיפוֹן שְׁמוֹ וְהוּא דוֹמֶה לְשְׂעָרָה.

What is "close by[153]"? Rebbi Samuel said, from the handles of an amphora to its mouth. Would it not be seen[1534]? Rebbi Ḥanina said, it is a small kind called *šefifōn* and looks like a hair[155].

153 The distance mentioned in the Mishnah.

154 How can a snake hide under the handle of an amphora?

155 Cf. text after note 108.

(fol. 45a) **משנה ה**: שִׁיעוּר הַמַּיִם הַמְּגוּלִּים כְּדֵי שֶׁתֵּאָבֵד בָּהֶן הַמָּרָה. רִבִּי יוֹסֵי אוֹמֵר בַּכֵּלִים כָּל־שֶׁהֵן וּבְקַרְקָעוֹת אַרְבָּעִים סְאָה.

Mishnah 5: The measure of uncovered water, until the bitterness be lost in them[156]. Rebbi Yose said, in vessels any amount[157] and on the ground 40 *seah*[158].

156 Water left uncovered is forbidden unless it is diluted so much that the poison will become inactive.

157 Water left uncovered in a vessel is forbidden in any amount.

158 Cf. *Berakhot* Chapter 3, Note 164.

(fol. 45d) **הלכה ו**: תַּנֵּי הַמַּיִם בְּקַרְקָעוֹת אַרְבָּעִים סְאָה. רִבִּי נְחֶמְיָה אוֹמֵר כְּדֵי שֶׁתְּהֵא חָבִית שִׁיחִין מִתְמַלֵּא מֵהֶן. הַיַּיִן בֵּין בְּכֵלִים בֵּין בְּקַרְקָעוֹת כָּל־שֶׁהוּא. הַיַּיִן כָּל־זְמַן (fol. 46a) שֶׁהוּא תוֹסֵס אֵין בּוֹ מִשּׁוּם גִּילּוּי. כַּמָּה תוֹסֵס עַד שְׁלֹשָׁה

יָמִים. וּמַעֲשֶׂה וְנִמְצָא נָחָשׁ בְּצַד הַבּוֹר שֶׁל יַיִן. וּבָא מַעֲשֶׂה לִפְנֵי רִבִּי יוּדָה וְהִתִּיר. מַעְיָן כָּל־זְמַן שֶׁהוּא מוֹשֵׁךְ אֵין בּוֹ מִשּׁוּם גִּילּוּי. אָמַר רִבִּי יִשְׁמָעֵאל בְּנוֹ שֶׁל רִבִּי יוֹחָנָן בֶּן בְּרוֹקָה מַעֲשֶׂה שֶׁיָּרַד רִבִּי יוֹחָנָן בֶּן נוּרִי אֵצֶל רִבִּי יוֹחָנָן בֶּן בְּרוֹקָה אַבָּא לְבֵית שְׂרִיי. וְהֶרְאֵהוּ גּוּבִי שֶׁלֹּא הָיָה בוֹ אֶלָּא שְׁלֹשָׁה לוֹגִין מַיִם וְהָיוּ הַגְּשָׁמִים מְטַפְטְפִין וְיוֹרְדִין וְשָׁחָה וְשָׁתָה. וְאָמַר כְּזֶה אֵין בּוֹ מִשּׁוּם גִּילּוּי.

Halakhah 6: It was stated: "[159]Water on the ground forty *seah.* Rebbi Neḥemiah says, that a *Šiḥin* amphora[160] can be filled from it. Wine both in vessels and on the ground in any quantity. Wine is not under the rules of uncovering as long as it is fermenting. How long does it ferment? Three days. It happened that a snake was found near a wine vat; the case came before Rebbi Jehudah[161] and he permitted it. A source is not under the rules of uncovering as long as it is running. Rebbi Ismael the son of Rebbi Joḥanan ben Nuri said, it happened that Rebbi Joḥanan ben Beroqa went down to my father Rebbi Joḥanan ben Nuri to Bet Serii; he showed him a pool that contained only three *log*[158] of water, into which rain water was dripping. He bowed down and drank, saying this is an example of what is not under the rules of uncovering[162]."

159 Tosephta 7:14-15; in different order and slightly different language.

160 A standard measure which is not determined in any parallel source. In the Tosephta there is an additional opinion, "others say, two *seah.*"

161 In the Tosephta, R. Jehudah ben Baba.

162 As long as the pool is not stagnant but overflowing from the rain water, it is counted as a source or river and one may assume that all poison was washed away (explanation of R. S. Lieberman).

וְעַד הֵיכָן. רִבִּי מָנָא בַּר תַּנְחוּם בְּשֵׁם רִבִּי חֲנִינָה עַד כְּדֵי שֶׁתִּפָּרַח הַבִּרִית.[163] רִבִּי לָעְזָר בְּרִבִּי יוֹסֵי בְּשֵׁם רַב עַד כְּדֵי שֶׁיֵּעָשׂוּ כְּרַגְלֵי הָאַוָּז. אָמַר רִבִּי יַעֲקֹב בַּר אָחָא מִכֵּיוָן שֶׁהוּתַּר מַה שֶּׁבַּשָּׂדֶה הוּתַּר מַה שֶּׁבַּבַּיִת. תַּנֵּי רִבִּי הוֹשַׁעְיָה הַגִּילּוּיִין נוֹהֲגִין בֵּין בָּאָרֶץ בֵּין בְּחוּצָה לָאָרֶץ בֵּין בִּימוֹת הַחַמָּה בֵּין בִּימוֹת הַגְּשָׁמִים.

[164]How long? Rebbi Mana bar Tanḥum[165] said, until the soap-wort blossoms. Rebbi Eleazar ben Rebbi Yose[166] in the name of Rav: Until they[167] become like goose feet. Rebbi Jacob bar Aḥa said, when it became permitted on the field, it became permitted in the house[168]. Rebbi Hoshaiah stated: [The rules of] uncovering apply in the Land and outside the Land, in summer and in winter.

163 Reading of the parallel in *Mo'ed Qaṭan*. Text here: ברית.

164 The first two sentences, dealing with the problem of R. Joḥanan ben Beroqa, how long is a puddle considered a brook, is also in *Mo'ed Qaṭan* 1:1, fol. 80b.

165 In *Mo'ed Qaṭan*, Ḥiyya bar Abun in the name of R. Joḥanan.

166 The same name appears in *Mo'ed Qaṭan*; there he speaks in the name of R. Tanḥum ben R. Ḥiyya, an Amora of the third generation. In any case, R. Eleazar ben R. Yose cannot be the Tanna, son of R. Yose ben Ḥalaphta, who is the author in all other cases where the name is mentioned.

167 The soap-wort plants.

168 If it rains so much that puddles on the field get the status of brooks, snakes hibernate and are no danger in the house. R. Hoshaiah disagrees and declares the danger to exist everywhere, at all times.

(fol. 45a) **משנה ו**: נִיקּוּרֵי תְאֵינִים וַעֲנָבִים וְקִשּׁוּאִים וְאֲבַטִּיחִים וְדִילוּעִין וְהַמְּלַפְּפוֹנוֹת אֲפִילוּ הֵן כְּכַד אֶחָד גָּדוֹל וְאֶחָד קָטוֹן אֶחָד תָּלוּשׁ וְאֶחָד מְחוּבָּר כָּל־שֶׁיֵּשׁ בּוֹ לֵחָה אָסוּר. וּנְשִׁיכַת הַנָּחָשׁ אֲסוּרָה מִפְּנֵי סַכָּנַת נְפָשׁוֹת. וְהַמְּשַׁמֶּרֶת שֶׁל יַיִן אֲסוּרָה מִשּׁוּם גִּילּוּי וְרִבִּי נְחֶמְיָה מַתִּיר.

Mishnah 6: Pecked-at figs, grapes, green melons, water melons, gourds, and sweet melons, even large as a pitcher, large or small, separated from or connected to the ground which contain moisture are forbidden[169]. What was bitten by a snake is forbidden because of mortal danger[170].

The wine filter is forbidden when left unattended but Rebbi Neḥemiah permits it[171].

169 If these fruits show signs that they have been pecked at by an animal, we are afraid that it might have been a poisonous animal and the poison diffused through the entire fruit through its moisture. If it was pecked at while completely dry, one could cut out the affected area and eat the remainder.

For the determination of the plants' identity, see *Kilaim* Chapter 1.

170 A kosher animal bitten by a snake may not be slaughtered or its meat eaten since it may contain snake poison.

171 If a wine filter (used to filter out the dregs, cf. Note 126 ff.) was left unattended and afterwards used to filter wine, that wine becomes forbidden (unless new filter material was used) because of poison from the filter. R. Neḥemiah holds that the poison is retained by the filter.

(fol. 46a) **הלכה ז**: אָמַר רִבִּי יוּדָה בַּר פָּזִי מָאן תַּנָּא נִיקוּרִין. רַבָּן גַּמְלִיאֵל אוֹמֵר אַף הַנָּחָשׁ שֶׁהוּא מֵקִיא. אָמַר רִבִּי יוֹנָה מַה אַפָּךְ לָן מִצְוֹת גַּבֵּי נִיקוּרִין.

Halakhah 7: Rebbi Jehudah bar Pazi said, who is the Tanna of pecking? "Rabban Gamliel says, also the snake because it spits out[172]." Rebbi Jonah said, who would turn commandments into peckings for us[173]?

172 Mishnah *Parah* 9:3. The Mishnah states that water drawn for the purification rite of the ashes of the red cow becomes unusable if any animal drank from it because some of the animal's spittle will be mixed with the water. In general, reptiles are reputed not to invalidate the water. Rabban Gamliel declares the snake to invalidate the water because it always will deposit some of its poison. Since the opinion of Rabban Gamliel is a minority opinion not followed in practice, R. Jehudah bar Pazi implies that the Mishnah here does not represent practice.

173 The rules given here are rules of hygiene, rather than religious observance. Therefore, the reference to Rabban Gamliel is irrelevant and the Mishnah here does represent practice.

תַּנֵּי רָאָה צִיפּוֹר נוֹקֶרֶת בִּתְאֵינָה וְעַכְבָּר בָּאֲבַטִּיחַ הֲרֵי זֶה אָסוּר. אֲנִי אוֹמֵר מָקוֹם הַנֶּקֶר אָכְלוּ. וְאָמַר רִבִּי בָּא דְּהוּא אָמַר נָחָשׁ חוֹזֵר וּמֵקִיא. אָמַר רִבִּי יוֹנָה מַה אַכְפַּיי לָהֶן לְמִצְוֹת לְגַבֵּי נִיקוּרִין וּלְעִנְיַן טְרֵיפָה. וְאָמַר רִבִּי בָּא בְשֵׁם רַבָּנִין דְּתַמָּן שְׁחָטָהּ וְחָטְפוּ הַזְּאֵיבִים בְּנֵי מֵיעֶיהָ כְּשֵׁירָה שֶׁחֶזְקַת בְּנֵי מֵעַיִם כּוֹשֶׁר. וְחָשׁ לוֹמַר שֶׁמָּא נִיקְבוּ. חֶזְקַת בְּנֵי מֵעַיִם כּוֹשֶׁר. וְהָכָא אַתְּ אָמַר הָכֵין. חוֹמֶר הוּא בְּסַכָּנַת נְפָשׁוֹת וְיָרְדוּ בְנִיקוּרִין כְּרַבָּן גַּמְלִיאֵל.

It was stated[81]: "If somebody saw a bird pecking at a fig or a rat nibbling at a watermelon, it is forbidden [to eat from them] for I say, they might have eaten from the place of a pecking hole." Rebbi Abba said, that means that a snake spits out repeatedly. Rebbi Jonah said, who considers for us commandments for peckings[173]? But for torn [animals][174], Rebbi Abba said in the name of the rabbis from there, "if it was slaughtered and the wolves took its innards, it is in order because intestines are presumed to be in order." Should one not question whether they were pierced? Intestines are presumed to be in order. But here, you say so? It is worse if there is danger to life[175]; for peckings they went all the way with Rabban Gamliel.

174 A kosher animal, correctly slaughtered, can be eaten only if inspection shows that it was healthy. The quote here is from *Berakhot* 9:4, Notes 209 ff.

175 This is a general principle; any logical arguments and rules of decision based on probabilities and prior assumptions are inapplicable in health matters.

תַּנֵּי רִבִּי לִיעֶזֶר אוֹמֵר אוֹכֵל אָדָם תְּאֵנִים וַעֲנָבִים בַּלַּיְלָה וְאֵינוֹ חוֹשֵׁשׁ. שֶׁנֶּאֱמַר שׁוֹמֵר פְּתָאִים יי. רִבִּי יוֹנָה בְשֵׁם רַב דָּג נִיקּוֹר אָסוּר. רִבִּי חִזְקִיָּה רִבִּי טָבִי בְשֵׁם רַב דָּג נִיקּוֹר חַי אָסוּר. וּמְלִיחַ עַל יְדֵי מְלִיחָה מִתְחַלְחֵל. מֵת נוֹטֵל מְקוֹם הַנֶּקֶר.

It was stated: Rebbi Eliezer said, one may eat figs and grapes in the night without worry, since it is said (*Ps*. 116:6) "the Eternal watches over the simple-minded." Rebbi Jonah in the name of Rav: A fish with pecking marks is forbidden. Rebbi Ḥizqiah, Rebbi Tabi in the name of Rav: A living fish with pecking marks is forbidden. If it is salted, through the salt it trembles[176]. Dead[177], one cuts out the place of the pecking.

176 It is visible whether the salted fish is infected or not.

177 If it is clear that some animal pecked at the fish after it died.

רִבִּי יַעֲקֹב בַּר אָחָא בְשֵׁם רִבִּי חִייָא בַּר בָּא אֲבַטִּיחַ שֶׁנִּיקַּר שֶׁנִּתְמַסְמְסוּ בְנֵי מֵיעֶיהָ אָסוּר. חַד בַּר נַשׁ הֲוָה טָעִין מֶלַפֶּפוֹן נָקוּר וְאַכִּיל מִינֵיהּ לַעֲשָׂרָה בְנֵי נַשׁ וּמוֹתוֹן. עָבְרַת רִירִין עֲלוֹי וּפְסַקְתֵּיהּ.

Rebbi Jacob bar Aḥa in the name of Rebbi Ḥiyya bar Abba: A watermelon with pecking marks whose inside is rotten is forbidden. A person carried a sweet melon with pecking marks. He let ten people eat from it and they died. He covered it with spittle and it broke apart.

חַד בַּר נַשׁ הֲוָה סְנֵי קוּפָּד דְּאִימֶּר. חַד זְמָן הֲוָה אָכִיל קוּפָּד עֲבַר חַד וְאָמַר לֵיהּ דְּאִימֶּר הוּא וְאִיתְכַּלְעֵס וּמִית. חֲמָרַייָא שָׁרוֹן בְּפוֹנְדָּקִיָּא אָמְרִין לוֹ הָבוּ לָן טְלוֹפְחִין וִיהָבוֹן. אָמְרֵי לוֹן הָבוּ לָן תִּנְיָן וִיהָבִין. אָמְרִין לוֹן קַדְמִייָן הֲווֹן טָבִין מַה אִילֵּין. אָמְרִין לוֹן שִׁזְרָתֵיהּ דְּחִיוֵי אַשְׁכַּחְנוֹן בְּהוֹן וְאִיתְכַּלְעַסוּן וּמִיתוּן.

A person hated sheep's meat. Once he was eating red meat when a passer-by said, this is sheep's meat. He choked[178] and died. The donkey drivers stayed at an inn. They said, bring us lentils; they brought. They said, give us a second helping; they brought. They said to them, the first ones were better, what were those? They said, we found the spine of a snake in them; they choked and died.

178 According to Z. Ben-Ḥayyim, *The Literary and Oral Traditions of Hebrew and Aramaic Amongst the Samaritans*, Jerusalem 1961, vol. II, p. 442, Galilean כלעס is the equivalent of Samaritan בלעט, "to choke". This invalidates the opinion of the dictionaries which see in כלעס a scribal error for Syriac בלעס, assumed to be derived from בלע "to swallow".

כְּתִיב בִּרְצוֹת יי דַּרְכֵי אִישׁ גַּם אוֹיְבָיו יַשְׁלִים אִתּוֹ. רִבִּי מֵאִיר אוֹמֵר זֶה הַכֶּלֶב. רִבִּי יְהוֹשֻׁעַ בֶּן לֵוִי אוֹמֵר זֶה הַנָּחָשׁ. רְעַייָא חָלְבוֹן חָלָב וְאָתָא חִיוְיָא וְאָכַל מִינֵיהּ וַהֲוָה כֶּלֶב מִסְתַּכֵּל בֵּיהּ. כַּד אָתוֹן יֵיכְלוּן מִישְׁרֵי נָבַח בְּהוֹן וְלֹא אִתְבּוֹנְנוֹן בְּסוֹפָא אָכַל וּמִית. חַד בַּר נַשׁ עֲבַד תּוֹם שְׁחִיק גּוֹ בֵּיתֵיהּ וְאָתָא חִיוְיָא דְטוּר וְאָכִיל מִינֵיהּ וַהֲוָה חִיוִי דְבַיִת מִסְתַּכֵּל בֵּיהּ אָתוֹן בְּנֵי בֵיתֵיהּ מֵיכַל מִינֵיהּ. מִישְׁרֵי מְתַרְתֵּר עֲלֵיהוֹן עָפָר וְלָא אִיתְבּוֹנְנוֹן וְקָלַק גַּרְמֵיהּ גַּוֵּיהּ. חַד בַּר נַשׁ זְמִין חַד רַבָּן וְאַייתִיב כַּלְבָּא גַּבֵּיהּ. אָמַר לֵיהּ בִּיזָּיוֹן אֲנָא חַיָּיב לָךְ. אָמַר לֵיהּ רִבִּי טִיבוֹ אֲנָא מְשַׁלֵּם לֵיהּ. שַׁבְיָין עֲלוֹן לְקַרְתָּא אָעַל חַד מִינְהוֹן בְּעָא מִינְסַב אִיתְּתִי וְאָכַל בֵּיצָיו.

It is written (*Prov.* 16:6): "When the Eternal likes the conduct of a person, even his enemy will make peace with him." Rebbi Meïr says, that is the dog. Rebbi Joshua ben Levi says, that is the snake. The shepherds milked; there came a snake, ate from it, but the dog observed it. When they came to eat, he started barking at them but they did not pay attention. At the end, he ate and died. A person made ground garlic in his house. There came a mountain snake and ate from it but the house snake observed it. When the people from the house came to eat from it, it [the house snake] started to throw dust down on them[179]. When they did not pay attention, it threw itself on it. A person invited a rabbi and let the dog sit next to him [the rabbi]. He said, how did I merit this insult? He said, rabbi, I am repaying his [the dog's] good deed. Kidnappers came to town. One of them came and wanted to take my wife but he [the dog] ate his testicles.

179 Another version of the same story is in *Gen. rabba* 54(1). In that source, all authors are late Amoraïm; the snake is identified as the enemy by R. Samuel.

(fol. 45a) **משנה ז**: חָבִית שֶׁל תְּרוּמָה שֶׁנּוֹלְדָה לָהּ סָפֵק טוּמְאָה רִבִּי אֱלִיעֶזֶר אוֹמֵר אִם הָיְתָה מוּנַחַת בְּמָקוֹם הַתּוֹרְפָּה יַנִּיחֶנָּה בְּמָקוֹם הַמּוּצְנָע. וְאִם הָיְתָה מְגוּלָּה יְכַסֶּנָּה. רִבִּי יְהוֹשֻׁעַ אוֹמֵר אִם הָיְתָה מוּנַחַת בְּמָקוֹם הַמּוּצְנָע יַנִּיחֶנָּה בְּמָקוֹם הַתּוֹרְפָּה וְאִם הָיְתָה מְכוּסָּה יְגַלֶּינָּה. רַבָּן גַּמְלִיאֵל אוֹמֵר לֹא יְחַדֵּשׁ בָּהּ דָּבָר.

Mishnah 7: An amphora of heave about which a doubt of impurity arose[180]. Rebbi Eliezer says, if it was at a vulnerable place, he should move it to a hidden place. If it was uncovered, he should cover it. Rebbi Joshua said, if it was at a hidden place, he should move it to a vulnerable place. If it was covered, he should uncover it. Rabban Gamliel said, he should not change anything.

180 If it were certainly impure, heave wine could be used to settle dust on dirt floors, heave oil or grain as fuel. If there only is a doubt, the heave is called "suspended". It cannot be used as impure since it might be pure, nor as pure since it might be impure. R. Eliezer holds that one has to treat this heave according to all rules of holiness. R. Joshua holds that one has to make sure that the heave be used somehow. Since it never will be usable as pure heave, one has to make sure it will be usable impure (Rashi in *Bekhorot* 33b).

(fol. 46a) **הלכה ח**: אָמַר רִבִּי יוֹסֵי בֵּי רִבִּי בּוֹן מִדִּבְרֵי שְׁלָשְׁתָּן תְּלוּיָיה אֲסוּרָה לְשׂוֹרְפָהּ.

Halakhah 8: Rebbi Yose ben Rebbi Abun said, from the opinions of all three of them: It is forbidden to burn suspended [heave].

(fol. 45a) **משנה ח**: חָבִית שֶׁנִּשְׁבְּרָה בְּגַת הָעֶלְיוֹנָה וְהַתַּחְתּוֹנָה טְמֵאָה. מוֹדֵי רַבִּי אֱלִיעֶזֶר וְרַבִּי יְהוֹשֻׁעַ שֶׁאִם יָכוֹל לְהַצִּיל מִמֶּנָּה רְבִיעִית בְּטָהֳרָה יַצִּיל וְאִם לָאו רַבִּי אֱלִיעֶזֶר אוֹמֵר תֵּרֵד וְתִיטַּמֵּא וְאַל יְטַמְּאֶנָּה בְיָדָיו.

Mishnah 8: If an amphora[181] broke in the upper part of the wine press whose lower part was impure, Rebbi Eliezer and Rebbi Joshua agree that if one can save a *revi'it* from it, he shall save that in purity[182]. Otherwise, Rebbi Eliezer said, let it descend and become impure; he should not make it impure with his hands.

משנה ט: וְכֵן חָבִית שֶׁל שֶׁמֶן שֶׁנִּשְׁפְּכָה מוֹדֵי רַבִּי לִיעֶזֶר וְרַבִּי יְהוֹשֻׁעַ שֶׁאִם יָכוֹל לְהַצִּיל מִמֶּנָּה רְבִיעִית בְּטָהֳרָה יַצִּיל. וְאִם לָאו רַבִּי אֱלִיעֶזֶר אוֹמֵר תֵּרֵד וְתִיבָּלַע וְאַל יְבַלְּעֶנָּה בְיָדָיו.

Mishnah 9: And so if an amphora of oil broke[183], Rebbi Eliezer and Rebbi Joshua agree that if one can save a *revi'it* from it, he shall save that in purity. Otherwise, Rebbi Eliezer said, let it descend and be absorbed [in the ground]; he should not cause it to be absorbed by his hands' [action].

משנה י: עַל זוֹ וְעַל זוֹ אָמַר רַבִּי יְהוֹשֻׁעַ לֹא זוֹ תְרוּמָה שֶׁאֲנִי מוּזְהָר עָלֶיהָ מִלְּטַמֵּא אֶלָּא מִלְּאָכְלָהּ וּבַל תְּטַמְּאָהּ.

Mishnah 10: About both of these cases, Rebbi Joshua said, this is not heave for which I have been warned not to make it impure; only not to eat it and not to [intentionally] make it impure[184].

181 The amphora contains heave wine which will become useless if impure.

182 If a reasonable amount can be saved in a pure vessel, R. Eliezer agrees that one should save as much as possible even if by this action the remainder will become impure much more rapidly than if it were left alone.

183 Even though impure oil is used as fuel, one still should save as much as possible from impurity.

184 It is forbidden to make heave impure by an independent action. But one is not required to avoid impurity if the wine or oil are going to be spilled without human intervention; in that

case one may cause impurity to most of the heave if thereby one saves a small part in purity.

(fol. 46a) **הלכה ט**: חֲבֵרַייָא בְּשֵׁם רִבִּי לָעְזָר חָבִית הָרִאשׁוֹנָה כְּרִבִּי יוֹסֵי וְהַשְּׁנִיָּה כְּרִבִּי מֵאִיר. חֲבֵרַייָא אָמְרֵי הָרִאשׁוֹנָה כְּרִבִּי יוֹסֵי וְלֵית רִבִּי מֵאִיר מוֹדֶה בָהּ. וְהַשְּׁנִיָּה כְּרִבִּי מֵאִיר וְלֵית רִבִּי יוֹסֵי מוֹדֶה בָהּ. אָמַר לוֹן רִבִּי יוֹסֵי חֲמוֹן מַה אַתּוּן מְרִין. חָבִית הָרִאשׁוֹנָה כְּרִבִּי יוֹסֵי. הָא כְּרִבִּי מֵאִיר שׂוֹרְפִין וּכְרִבִּי שִׁמְעוֹן שׂוֹרְפִין. וְיִרְבּוּ רִבִּי מֵאִיר וְרִבִּי שִׁמְעוֹן עַל רִבִּי יוֹסֵי וְיִשְׂרוֹפוּ. וְעוֹד מִן הָדָא וַאֲנָא חֲמִי רַבָּנִין אָתָא עוֹבְדָא קוֹמֵיהוֹן וְאָמְרִין אֵיזִיל תְּלִי. וְהָא אַשְׁכְּחָן דְּאָמַר רִבִּי שִׁמְעוֹן שׂוֹרְפִין. דְּתַנִּינָן מוֹדֵי רִבִּי לִיעֶזֶר וְרִבִּי יְהוֹשֻׁעַ שֶׁשּׂוֹרְפִין זוֹ לְעַצְמָהּ וְזוֹ לְעַצְמָהּ. וְאָמַר רִבִּי יוֹחָנָן רִבִּי שִׁמְעוֹן שְׁנָייָהּ. וְאִין תֵּימְרוּן לֵית לְרִבִּי מֵאִיר תְּלוּיָה הָא תַנֵּי תְּרוּמָה תְלוּיָה וּטְמֵאָה שׂוֹרְפִין אוֹתָהּ עֶרֶב שַׁבָּת עִם חֲשֵׁיכָה דִּבְרֵי רִבִּי מֵאִיר. וַחֲכָמִים אוֹמְרִים בִּזְמַנָּהּ. אָמַר רִבִּי זְעִירָה קוֹמֵי רִבִּי מָנָא תִּיפְתָּר בִּתְלוּיָה שֶׁדַּעְתּוֹ לְהִישָּׁאֵל עָלֶיהָ. אָמַר לֵיהּ כֵּן אָמַר רִבִּי יוֹסֵי רַבּוֹ. כָּל־תְּלוּיָה דַאֲנָן אָמְרִין הָכָא בִּתְלוּיָה שֶׁאֵין דַּעְתּוֹ לְהִישָּׁאֵל עָלֶיהָ. אֲבָל דַּעְתּוֹ לְהִישָּׁאֵל עָלֶיהָ טְהוֹרָה הִיא. דְּתַנֵּי תְּלוּיָה שֶׁאָמַר טְהוֹרָה הִיא טְמֵאָה הִיא. הֲרֵי זוֹ טְמֵאָה. אִם אָמַר הֲרֵינִי מְנִיחָהּ עַל מְנָת שֶׁאֶישְׁאַל עָלֶיהָ טְהוֹרָה. אָמַר רִבִּי יוֹסֵי בֵּי רִבִּי בּוֹן תִּיפְתָּר שֶׁנּוֹלְדָה לָהּ סָפֵק טוּמְאָה עִם דִּמְדוּמֵי חַמָּה. וְלֵית שְׁמַע מִינָּהּ כְּלוּם.

Halakhah 9: [185]The colleagues in the name of Rebbi Eleazar: The first amphora[186] following Rebbi Yose, the second[187] following Rebbi Meïr. The colleagues say, the first amphora following Rebbi Yose but Rebbi Meïr will not agree; the second following Rebbi Meïr but Rebbi Yose will not agree. Rebbi Yose told them, be careful what you teach. The first amphora following Rebbi Yose; therefore, following Rebbi Meïr one burns[188] and following Rebbi Simeon one burns. Then Rebbi Meïr and Rebbi Simeon should form a majority against Rebbi Yose[189] and one should burn. In addition, we see that the rabbis, in cases which come before them, say, go and consider it suspended. We find that Rebbi Simeon says one burns, as we have stated[190]: "Rebbi Eliezer and Rebbi Joshua agree that one burns each one separately." On this, Rebbi Joḥanan said, Rebbi Simeon taught that[191]. And if you want to say that Rebbi Meïr does not recognize suspension[192], have we not stated: "Suspended heave and impure heave are burned on Sabbath eve when it gets dark, the words of Rebbi Meïr; but the Sages say, at its appointed time[193]." Rebbi Zeïra said before Rebbi Mana[194], explain it if it is suspended because he intends to ask about it. He said to him, so said my teacher Rebbi Assi: All suspended [heave] we are dealing with here is suspended [heave] about which he has no intention of asking[195]. But if he intends to ask about it, it has to be treated as pure. As we have stated[196]: "If he said, it is pure or impure, then it is impure. But if he said, I am keeping it in order to ask about the situation, it is pure." Rebbi Yose ben Rebbi Abun said, explain it if the doubt arose at sundown. Then you cannot infer anything[197].

185 Most of this Halakhah is from *Pesaḥim* 1:7; a parallel treatment is in Babli *Pesaḥim* 14a-21a. In the Mishnah, R. Ḥanina the Second of the Cohanim (who had to substitute when the High Priest was disabled) and R. Aqiba, who both had seen the Temple, report that the Cohanim never refrained from burning meat impure in a secondary way together with meat of original impurity, or oil becoming unusable by tertiary impurity together with impure oil of primary impurity, even though a momentary increase in impurity was inevitable. The late Tanna R. Meïr wants to infer that on Passover eve, when all leavened matter must be burned, one may burn leavened pure and impure heave together. His contemporary R. Yose (ben Ḥalaphta) objects and notes that both R. Eliezer and R. Joshua require that these heaves be burned separately. Their disagreement is that R. Eliezer requires suspended and impure heaves to be burned separately but R. Joshua permits them to be burned together.

186 The amphora of Mishnah 7, where R. Joshua only permits to put it in danger's way but not directly to

make it impure, gives R. Yose's interpretation of the position of R. Joshua.

187 The amphoras of Mishnaiot 8-10, where R. Joshua permits causing impurity if this helps a good cause.

188 One burns pure and impure heave together on the 14th of Nisan. The position of R. Simeon has to be proven since he does not appear in the Mishnah.

189 Even though singly their opinions would be disregarded when in opposition to R. Yose.

190 Mishnah *Pesaḥim* 1:7, speaking of pure and impure heave. If this is the teaching of R. Simeon, he must hold that they disagree for suspended and impure heave and, therefore, these can be burned together since practice always follows R. Joshua against R. Eliezer. But then suspended heave should be treated as impure, against Mishnah 7.

191 Tosephta *Pesaḥim* 1:5, quoted in Babli *Pesaḥim* 20b. The Tosephta is Babylonian, unknown to the Yerushalmi.

192 Since most anonymous Mishnaiot are R. Meir's formulation, Mishnah *Tahorot* 4:5, which directs burning only for six narrowly defined kinds of suspended heave, excludes most kinds of suspended heave from being treated as impure. Accordingly, R. Simeon's is an isolated opinion, rather than practice to be followed.

193 Tosephta *Pesaḥim* 3:9. Since on the Sabbath, heave may not be burned, it must be fed to animals to be disposed of.

194 R. Mana I, student of Rabbis Yannai, Joḥanan, and Assi.

195 In this case, the heave can never be used again and may be treated as impure for practical purposes.

196 A different formulation is in Tosephta 7:18: "I am keeping it; *until I* ask about the situation, it is *im*pure." That formulation does not necessarily conflict with the one here. If the heave is left unusable for an indefinite period, chances are it will become impure. But if the question to a rabbinic authority is asked within a foreseeable time, there is no reason to declare the suspended heave impure.

197 Since there is no time to burn anything, the opinion of the Sages must be followed even by their opponents. This does not prove anything about the position of R. Meïr if the heave was already suspended in the morning.

וְאַתּוּן אָֽמְרִין חָבִית הָֽרִאשׁוֹנָה כְּרִבִּי יוֹסֵי לֵית רִבִּי מֵאִיר מוֹדֶה בָהּ. וְהָתַנֵּי בְּמַה דְּבָרִים אֲמוּרִים בְּבוֹר שֶׁיֵּשׁ בָּהֶן לְהַעֲלוֹת. אֲבָל בְּבוֹר שֶׁאֵין בָּהּ כְּדֵי לְהַעֲלוֹת

אֲפִילוּ כָּל־שֶׁהוּא אָסוּר לְטַמְּאוֹת. וְאִין כְּרִבִּי מֵאִיר הָא יֵשׁ בָּהּ כְּדֵי לְהַעֲלוֹת הָא אֵין בָּהּ כְּדֵי לְהַעֲלוֹת אֲפִילוּ כָּל־שֶׁהוּא אָסוּר לְטַמְּאוֹת. וְעוֹד מִן הָדָא דְתַנִּינָן. אָמַר רִבִּי יוֹסֵי אֵינָהּ הִיא מִידָּה. וְלֵית בַּר נַשׁ אָמַר אֵינָהּ אֶלָּא דְהוּא מוֹדֵי עַל קַדְמִיָיתָא. מַיי כְדוֹן. תַּמָּן הַתּוֹרָה חָסָה עַל מָמוֹנָן שֶׁל יִשְׂרָאֵל. הָכָא מַה אִית לָךְ מֵימַר. וְהָכָא אֵינוֹ מַפְסִידוֹ מָמוֹן שֶׁהוּא צָרִיךְ עֵצִים לְשׂוֹרְפוֹ זֶה לְעַצְמוֹ וְזֶה לְעַצְמוֹ. לְהֶפְסֵד מְרוּבֶּה חָשׁוּ. לְהֶפְסֵד מְעַט לֹא חָשׁוּ. אָמַר רִבִּי יוֹסֵי בֵּי רִבִּי בוֹן תִּיפְתָּר כְּמָאן דְּאָמַר מִדִּבְרֵי רִבִּי עֲקִיבָה וּמִדִּבְרֵי רִבִּי חֲנַנְיָה סְגַן הַכֹּהֲנִים. וְלֵית שְׁמַע מִינָהּ כְּלוּם.

You say, the first amphora following Rebbi Yose, and Rebbi Meïr will not agree[198]. But did we not state: "When has this been said? Regarding a vat which contains enough to lift it. But for a vat which does not contain enough to lift it, it is forbidden to make any amount impure.[199]" And if it follows Rebbi Meïr, whether it contains enough to lift it or does not contain enough to lift it, is it forbidden to make any amount impure[200]? In addition, from what we have stated[201]: "Rebbi Yose said, this is not the implication." A person says "this is not the implication" only if he agrees with the premise . How is that? There, the Torah cares about the money of the Jews[202], here what can you say[203]? Does he not here also cayse him to lose money since he needs fire wood to burn each lot separately? They worried about a big loss, they did not worry about a small loss. Rebbi Yose bar Abun said, explain it following him who said, from the words of Rebbi Aqiba and the words of Rebbi Ḥananiah, the Second of the Cohanim[204].

198 While this is the text of R. Yose's second argument in both mss. and the early prints, it is clear from the following that the discussion is about the second part of the statement of the colleagues, "the second amphora following Rebbi Meïr, and Rebbi Yose will not agree." The discussion centers on Mishnaiot 8-9, where everybody agrees that in order to save some pure

heave one may actively bring impurity on the remainder.

199 This is the text both here and in *Pesaḥim* but it is difficult to explain. The Babli (*Pesaḥim* 21a) reads: "An amphora which broke in the upper part of the wine press while the lower part contains a hundred times as much impure (wine), Rebbi Eliezer admits to Rebbi Joshua that if he can save a *revi'it* from it, he shall save that in purity; otherwise, let it descend and he should not make it impure with his hands." The Mishnah does not explain what is in the lower part of the winepress. If there is enough profane wine to let one lift heave according to the rules of Chapter 5, not much is lost since the wine remains usable. But if heave cannot be lifted because the profane is not more than 100 times the heave all becomes forbidden and, at most, can be used as ointment or to sprinkle on a dirt floor to eliminate dust. This represents a considerable monetary loss.

200 Since R. Meïr permits to bring impurity to anything that later automatically would become impure.

201 In Mishnah *Pesaḥim* 1:7 (Note 184) the discussion between R. Meïr and R. Yose is formulated not as a clash of traditions but of logical arguments, with R. Yose disputing R. Meïr's inference but not his premise. The problem, as pointed out in the Babli, is that it is not clear whether the basis of the argument is the common statement of R. Ḥanina, the Second of the Cohanim, and R. Aqiba in the Mishnah there, or the partial agreement of R. Eliezer and R. Joshua in the Mishnah here. For the moment, we assume that R. Meïr and R. Yose refer to R. Eliezer and R. Joshua.

202 Mishnah *Nega'im* 12:5. The difference between large and small losses is also noted in Babli *Pesaḥim* 20b.

203 This shows that the origin of the text is in *Pesaḥim*. "There" means *Terumot*, where potentially an entire harvest may be lost in the winepress. "Here" means *Pesaḥim*, where the question is only whether different kinds of leavened matter may be burned together or have to be burned separately.

204 Cf. Note 184. In their cases, no monetary loss is incurred and nothing can be inferred for our case.

רִבִּי אִילָא וְרִבִּי זְעִירָא תְּרֵיהוֹן בְּשֵׁם רִבִּי יוֹחָנָן חָבִית הָרִאשׁוֹנָה כְּרִבִּי יוֹסֵי.
וְהַשְּׁנִייָה בֵּין כְּרִבִּי מֵאִיר בֵּין כְּרִבִּי יוֹסֵי. אָמַר רִבִּי זְעִירָא קוֹמֵי רִבִּי מָנָא וְלֵית

הָדָא פְלִיגָא עַל רִבִּי מֵאִיר. אָמַר לֵיהּ נֹאמַר דְּלֹא כְרִבִּי מֵאִיר וְנֹאמַר דְּלֹא כְרִבִּי יוֹסֵי. לְפִי שֶׁמָּצִינוּ רִבִּי מֵאִיר שׂוֹרֵף תְּלוּיָה בְּכָל־מָקוֹם. אָמַר רִבִּי מָנָא אֲזָלִית לְקֵיסָרִין שָׁמְעִית רִבִּי זְרִיקָן בְּשֵׁם זְעִירָה[205] רִבִּי מֵאִיר שׂוֹרֵף בְּכָל־מָקוֹם תְּלוּיָה. וְאָמְרִית לֵיהּ בְּגִין שֶׁהִיא תְלוּיָה דְּבַר תּוֹרָה. אָמַר לִי[206] אֵין אֲנִי פָתַר לָהּ שֶׁנִּיטְמְאָה בְּמָדוֹר שֶׁל גּוֹיִם. מַה אִית לָךְ. (fol. 46b) דְּתַנֵּי מָדוֹר שֶׁל גּוֹיִם תּוֹלִין. רִבִּי יוֹסֵי בֵּי רִבִּי יְהוּדָה אוֹמֵר שׂוֹרְפִין. רִבִּי הוּנָא בְּשֵׁם רִבִּי יִרְמְיָה רִבִּי מֵאִיר שׂוֹרֵף תְּלוּיָה בִּשְׁאָר יְמוֹת הַשָּׁנָה. דְּתַנֵּי תְּרוּמָה תְלוּיָה וּטְמֵאָה שׂוֹרְפִין אוֹתָהּ עֶרֶב שַׁבָּת עִם חֲשֵׁיכָה דִּבְרֵי רִבִּי מֵאִיר. וַחֲכָמִים אוֹמְרִים בִּזְמַנָּהּ. וְיִשְׂרוֹף בְּשַׁחֲרִית. תִּיפְתָּר בְּשֶׁנִּתְעַצֵּל וְלֹא שָׂרַף. תֵּדַע לָךְ שֶׁהוּא כֵן דְּלָא תַנִּינָן שַׁחֲרִית. וְלֹא בְּשֶׁנִּתְעַצֵּל וְלֹא שָׂרַף. אָמַר רִבִּי אַבָּא מָרִי אָחוֹי דְּרִבִּי יוֹסֵי תִּיפְתָּר שֶׁנּוֹלַד לָהּ טוּמְאָה בְּאוֹתָהּ שָׁעָה וְלֵית שְׁמַע מִינָּהּ כְּלוּם.

Rebbi Ila and Rebbi Zeïra, both in the name of Rebbi Joḥanan: The first amphora[186] follows Rebbi Yose, the second[187] both Rebbi Meïr and Rebbi Yose. Rebbi Zeïra asked before Rebbi Mana: Does it not disagree with Rebbi Meïr? He said to him, we may say it follows neither Rebbi Meïr nor Rebbi Yose since we find that Rebbi Meïr burns suspended [heave] in all cases[207]. Rebbi Mana said, I went to Caesarea and heard Rebbi Zeriqan in the name of Zeïri: Rebbi Meïr burns suspended [heave] in all cases. I said to him, because he considers suspended [heave] from the words of the Torah[208]. He said to me, do I not explain that it became impure in Gentiles' dwellings? For we have stated[209]: "From Gentiles' dwellings one suspends; Rebbi Yose ben Rebbi Jehudah says, one burns[210]." Rebbi Huna in the name of Rebbi Jeremiah: Rebbi Meïr burns suspended [heave] any day of the year, as we have stated: "Suspended heave and impure heave are burned on Sabbath eve when it gets dark, the words of Rebbi Meïr; but the Sages say, at its appointed time[193]." Should he not burn it during the morning hours[211]? Explain it if he was lazy and did not burn it [then]. Know that this is so, for he did not state "during the morning hours." Is that not because he was lazy and did not burn [then]? Rebbi Abba Mari, the brother of Rebbi Yose said, explain it if impurity was created at that time, and you cannot infer anything[195].

205 Reading of the text in *Pesahim*. Text here: חזקיה בשם ר' ירמיה "Hizqiah in the name of R. Jeremiah." If "Hizqiah" is correct, then "R. Jeremiah" must refer to the Babylonian Rav Jeremiah, cf. *Berakhot* 1, Note 13; neither of whom is connected with Caesarea. One cannot read "R. Hizqiah" since R. Mana II was his student, not in Caesarea.

206 Reading of the text in *Pesahim*. Text here: לו "him".

207 This implies that he treats suspended heave as impure and does not object to an increase in its impurity.

208 If there is a doubt of impurity in biblical law, the doubt has to be resolved in a restrictive manner and there is no reason not to treat suspended heave as impure.

209 Tosephta *Ahilut* 18:7. Since Gentiles bury their stillborn babies in their houses, Gentile dwellings in the Holy Land are potential sources of impurity of a tent (cf. *Kilaim* Chapter 6, Note 25). Any heave in such a permanent dwelling is therefore automatically suspended. However, since it is questionable whether impurity of the dead extends to Gentiles, that impurity is purely rabbinic.

210 R. Meïr is supposed to follow R. Yose ben R. Jehudah.

211 If Passover eve falls on a weekday, leavened matter must be eliminated before noon since the Passover sacrifice must be slaughtered in a leaven-free environment (*Ex.* 23:18, 34:25). Therefore, even if Passover eve falls on a Sabbath, the elimination of leavened matter preferably should take place on Friday before noontime.

אָמַר רִבִּי יוֹחָנָן רִבִּי יְהוֹשֻׁעַ וְרִבִּי שִׁמְעוֹן שְׁנֵיהֶן אָמְרוּ דָבָר אֶחָד. אָמַר רִבִּי אִילָא רִבִּי שִׁמְעוֹן דִּבְכּוּרוֹת וְרִבִּי יְהוֹשֻׁעַ דִּתְרוּמוֹת לֹא הָדֵין מוֹדֵי לָדֵין וְלֹא הָדֵין מוֹדֵי לָדֵין. אָמַר רִבִּי זְעִירָא מִסְתַּבְּרָא רִבִּי שִׁמְעוֹן מוֹדֵי לְרִבִּי יְהוֹשֻׁעַ וְרִבִּי יְהוֹשֻׁעַ לֹא מוֹדֵי לְרִבִּי שִׁמְעוֹן. רִבִּי בּוּן בַּר חִיָּיה בְּעָא קוֹמֵי רִבִּי זְעִירָא עַל דַּעְתָּךְ דְּתֵימַר רִבִּי שִׁמְעוֹן יוֹדֵי לְרִבִּי יְהוֹשֻׁעַ וְהָתַנִּינָן מוֹדִין רִבִּי לִיעֶזֶר וְרִבִּי יְהוֹשֻׁעַ שֶׁשּׂוֹרְפִין זוֹ לְעַצְמָהּ וְזוֹ לְעַצְמָהּ. וְיִשְׂרוֹף שְׁתֵּיהֶן כְּאַחַת. אָמַר לֵיהּ תַּמָּן

טְהוֹרָה הִיא דְּבַר תּוֹרָה תְּרוּמָה בְּעֵייְנָהּ הִיא אַתָּה הוּא שֶׁגָּזַרְתָּה לְשׂוֹרְפָהּ בְּכָל־מָקוֹם לֹא נִפְסְלָה בְהֵיסַח הַדַּעַת. לֹא כֵן אָמַר רִבִּי יוֹחָנָן הֵיסַח הַדַּעַת דְּבַר תּוֹרָה. חָבִית שְׁנִייָה כְּרִבִּי מֵאִיר תּוֹרָה. אֲחִיזַת דָּם כְּרִבִּי שִׁמְעוֹן תּוֹרָה. אָמַר לֵיהּ שֶׁהוּא[212] מְשַׁמְּרָהּ שֶׁלֹּא תִגַּע בִּטְהוֹרוֹת אֲחֵרוֹת. הָתִיב רִבִּי יִצְחָק בְּרֵיהּ דְּרִבִּי חִייָה כְתוֹבָה[213] הַגַּע עַצְמָךְ שֶׁהָיְתָה[214] נְתוּנָה עַל גַּבֵּי גֶחָלִים. אָמַר לֵיהּ לִכְשֶׁיִּתְּנֶנָּה. אָמַר רִבִּי מָנָא לְרִבִּי שַׁמַּי אַתּוּן אָמְרִין יוֹדֵי רִבִּי שִׁמְעוֹן[215] לְרִבִּי יְהוֹשֻׁעַ וַאֲפִילוּ רִבִּי יְהוֹשֻׁעַ לֵית הִיא רִבִּי יְהוֹשֻׁעַ. אָמַר לֵיהּ תַּנָּיִין אִינּוּן. תַּמָּן רִבִּי מֵאִיר בְּשֵׁם רִבִּי יְהוֹשֻׁעַ. בְּרַם הָכָא רִבִּי שִׁמְעוֹן בְּשֵׁם רִבִּי יְהוֹשֻׁעַ.

Rebbi Joḥanan said, Rebbi Joshua and Rebbi Simeon[216] both said the same thing[217]. Rebbi Ilaï said: Rebbi Simeon in *Bekhorot* and Rebbi Joshua in *Terumot*, neither of them will agree with the other[218]. Rebbi Abun bar Ḥiyya asked before Rebbi Zeïra: Is it not reasonable that Rebbi Simeon agrees with Rebbi Joshua but Rebbi Joshua will not agree with Rebbi Simeon? Did we not state[190]: "Rebbi Eliezer and Rebbi Joshua agree that each batch should be burned separately.[191]" Could one not burn the two together[219]? He said to him, there [the heave] is pure; by Torah law the heave is still in existence; you are the person who decided to burn it[220]. In any case, would it not become unusable by being left unattended? Did not Rebbi Joḥanan say, leaving unattended is from the Torah[221]? The second amphora for Rebbi Meïr follows the Torah[222], coughing blood for Rebbi Simeon follows the Torah[223]! He said to him, one still watches it so it should not come in contact with other pure [heave][224]. Rebbi Isaac, the son of Rebbi Ḥiyya the scribe: Think about it, if it was put on coals[225]? He said to him, after if was put there. Rebbi Mana said to Rebbi Shammai: You who say that Rebbi Simeon agrees with Rebbi Joshua! Even Rebbi Joshua does not agree with Rebbi Joshua[226]! He said to him, these are Tannaïm[227]. There, Rebbi Meïr in the name of Rebbi Joshua, but here Rebbi Simeon in the name of Rebbi Joshua[203].

212 Reading of the text in *Pesaḥim*. Here: שהיא.

213 Reading of the text in *Pesaḥim*. Here: בחירה.

214 Reading of the text in *Pesaḥim*. Here: שהוא.

215 Reading of the Rome ms. and the text in *Pesaḥim*. Here: ר' ליעזר.

216 Mishnah *Bekhorot* 5:2, quoted in the next paragraph. While a firstling calf or lamb has to be treated as a sacrifice, R. Simeon permits any surgical operation if the health of the animal requires it, even if it is clear that by the operation the animal will become unfit as a sacrifice.

217 R. Joshua permits to bring impurity to heave in order to save some part in purity; R. Simeon permits to make a blemish on a firstling calf in order to save its life.

218 R. Joshua permits to bring impurity to heave in order to save food. In the case of *Bekhorot*, the Mishnah states that one may not slaughter the firstling because of the man-induced blemish; the animal cannot become food for anybody. Therefore, it is not necessary that R. Joshua agree with R. Simeon. On the other hand, R. Simeon holds that pure and impure heave cannot be burned together; it is forbidden to make heave impure even if it must be burned (Note 190). Therefore, R. Simeon cannot be shown to agree with R. Joshua in *Terumot*.

219 Since the pure heave also must be destroyed by biblical decree.

220 By biblical decree, leavened matter is permitted on the 14th of Nisan until the time of the slaughter of the Passover lamb, which is shortly after noon (Note 210). However, by rabbinic decree no leavened matter may be eaten two hours before noontime and all leavened matter must be eliminated at least one hour before noon. Therefore, at the time of burning, the heave would still be good heave according to biblical law for another hour and could not be considered as being lost automatically.

221 Heave must be eaten in purity, which can be guaranteed only if the heave is guarded at all times or at least kept at a place locked away from possible impurities (cf. *Šeqalim* 7:2, fol. 50c; Babli *Pesaḥim* 34a). Since on the 14th of Nisan, leavened heave cannot be eaten after 10 a.m. local time, there is no need to watch it any longer and, by being released from supervision, it

should become invalid immediately even by biblical standards.

222 As just shown, the lack of attention makes everything impure for practical purposes.

223 In the next paragraph, R. Simeon's interpretation of the biblical text is given.

224 Therefore, the argument of Note 221 is inapplicable in our situation.

225 If one starts the fire to burn the heave, guarding against impurity certainly is unnecessary. The answer is that this argument is irrelevant since we deal with the moment before the fire is started.

226 The positions of R. Joshua in *Pesaḥim* 1:7 and *Terumot* 8:8-10 do not necessarily coincide, as explained by R. Ilaï.

227 It is impossible to fully reconstruct the original position of R. Joshua since the only knowledge we have of his statements is through the interpretations of the students of R. Aqiba.

תַּמָּן תַּנִּינָן בְּכוֹר שֶׁאֲחָזוֹ דָּם אֲפִילוּ מֵת אֵין מַקִּיזִין לוֹ אֶת הַדָּם דִּבְרֵי רִבִּי יוּדָה. וַחֲכָמִים אוֹמְרִים יַקִּיז וְאַף עַל פִּי שֶׁעָשָׂה בוֹ מוּם. וְאִם עָשָׂה בוֹ מוּם הֲרֵי זֶה לֹא יִשְׁחוֹט עָלָיו. רִבִּי שִׁמְעוֹן אוֹמֵר יַקִּיז וְאַף עַל פִּי שֶׁעָשָׂה בוֹ מוּם. רִבִּי אַבָּהוּ בְשֵׁם רִבִּי לָעְזָר אַתְיָיה דְרִבִּי יוּדָה [228]כְּרַבָּן גַּמְלִיאֵל. דְּרַבָּנָן כְּרִבִּי לִיעֶזֶר. וּדְרִבִּי שִׁמְעוֹן כְּרִבִּי יְהוֹשֻׁעַ. וְתַנֵּי רִבִּי שִׁמְעוֹן יַקִּיז וְאַף עַל פִּי שֶׁהוּא מִתְכַּוֵּן לַעֲשׂוֹת בּוֹ מוּם. וְאַתְיָיה כְרִבִּי יְהוֹשֻׁעַ אַחֲרַייָה. רִבִּי אַבָּהוּ בְשֵׁם רִבִּי שִׁמְעוֹן בֶּן לָקִישׁ טַעֲמָא דְרִבִּי יוּדָה לֹא תֹאכְלֶנּוּ עַל הָאָרֶץ תִּשְׁפְּכֶנּוּ כַּמָּיִם. לֹא הִתַּרְתִּי לָךְ דָּמוֹ אֶלָּא לְשָׁפְכָם. מָתִיב רִבִּי אַבָּא מָרִי אָחוֹי דְרִבִּי יוֹסֵי. וְהָא פְסוּלֵי מוּקְדָּשִׁין כְּתִיב לֹא תֹאכְלֶנּוּ עַל הָאָרֶץ תִּשְׁפְּכֶנּוּ כַּמָּיִם. אָמַר רִבִּי חִיָּיה בַּר אַבָּא לְהֶכְשֵׁר אַתְּ אֲמְרַתְּ. מַה מַּיִם מַכְשִׁירִין אַף דָּם מַכְשִׁיר. רִבִּי אַבָּהוּ בְשֵׁם רִבִּי יוֹחָנָן וּשְׁנֵיהֶם מִקְרָא אֶחָד דָּֽרְשׁוּ. תָּמִים יִהְיֶה לְרָצוֹן כָּל־מוּם לֹא יִהְיֶה בּוֹ. רִבִּי שִׁמְעוֹן דָּרַשׁ בְּשָׁעָה שֶׁהוּא לְרָצוֹן אֵין אַתְּ רַשַּׁאי לִיתֵּן בּוֹ מוּם. בְּשָׁעָה שֶׁאֵינוֹ לְרָצוֹן אַתְּ רַשַּׁאי לִיתֵּן בּוֹ מוּם. וַחֲכָמִים אוֹמְרִים אֲפִילוּ כוּלּוֹ מוּמִין אֵין אַתְּ רַשַּׁאי לִיתֵּן בּוֹ מוּם.

There[229], we stated: "A firstling afflicted by blood, even if it is going to die, cannot be bled, the words of Rebbi Jehudah. But the Sages say, it should be bled even if this causes a blemish. If it did cause a blemish, it should not be slaughtered because of it. Rebbi Simeon says, he should bleed it even if he makes a blemish."

Rebbi Abbahu in the name of Rebbi Eleazar: Rebbi Jehudah parallels Rabban Gamliel, the Rabbis parallel Rebbi Eliezer, Rebbi Simeon parallels Rebbi Joshua[230]. But we have stated: "Rebbi Simeon says, he should bleed it even if he knows he will cause a blemish." This parallels the later opinion of Rebbi Joshua[231].

Rebbi Abbahu in the name of Rebbi Simeon ben Laqish: The reason of Rebbi Jehudah (*Deut.* 12:24): "You shall not eat it; spill it onto the ground like water." I permitted you its blood only to spill it[232]. Rebbi Abba Mari, the brother of Rebbi Yose, objected: That is written about [blood of] invalid sacrifices: "You shall not eat it; spill it onto the ground like water." Rebbi Ḥiyya bar Abba said, you get from it for preparation[233]. Just as water prepares, so blood prepares.

Rebbi Abbahu in the name of Rebbi Joḥanan: Both of them explained the same verse (*Lev.* 22:21): "Perfect it[234] shall be for goodwill; any blemish shall not be on it." Rebbi Simeon explains: As long as it is for goodwill, you may not induce a blemish. If it is no longer for goodwill, you may induce a blemish. But the Sages say, even if it is all blemishes, you may not add a blemish[235].

228 Reading of the text in *Pesaḥim*. Here ר' יודה כחכמים כר"ג.

229 Mishnah *Bekhorot* 5:2. Since a firstling is a sacrifice by birth, it has to be treated according to the rules of sacrifices. The only difference is that a dedicated sacrifice which develops a blemish must be redeemed to become profane whereas a firstling in the hands of a Cohen which develops a

blemish automatically becomes quasi profane and may be eaten by everybody and in impurity. Therefore, Cohanim are suspected to induce blemishes on the firstlings in their possession.

230 In Mishnah 7 (the "first amphora"). The Babli (*Bekhorot* 35b) identifies the position of the Sages with that of Rebbi Joshua (i. e., the operative opinion in *Bekhorot* with the operative opinion in *Terumot*.) The Yerushalmi implies that practice should follow Rebbi Simeon.

231 His opinion about the "second amphora", where he permits to induce impurity on most of the heave in order to save a small portion in purity.

232 One would have expected R. Jehudah to use *Deut*. 15:23, speaking of the firstling: "Only its blood you shall not eat; spill it onto the ground like water." The verse used gives the rules for animals which develop blemishes after being dedicated. This also includes firstlings.

233 Blood is one of the fluids that prepare dry food to accept impurity (cf. *Demay* Chapter 2, Notes 136, 141). Since the rules for preparation are spelled out for water (*Lev*. 11:38), other fluids have this property of water only if there is a biblical verse which compares them to water.

234 Any sacrifice.

235 As Rashi explains in *Bekhorot* 35b, the Sages hold that R. Simeon would be justified if the verse read "*no blemish* shall be on it." But the involved language, *any blemish*, forbids the imposition of a new blemish on existing blemishes.

Here ends the parallel in *Pesaḥim*.

רִבִּי חָמָא בַּר עוּקְבָּא בְשֵׁם רִבִּי יוֹסֵי בֵּי רִבִּי חֲנִינָה. כְּלִי שֶׁתּוֹכוֹ טָהוֹר וַאֲחוֹרָיו טְמֵאִין אֵין מְטַמְּעִין בּוֹ דָבָר מְמוּעָט אֲפִילוּ לְהַצִּיל בּוֹ דָבָר מְרוּבָּה. וְהָתַנִּינָן תֵּרֵד וְתִיטָּמֵא וְאַל יְטַמְּאֶנָּה בְיָדָיו. אָמַר רִבִּי שְׁמוּאֵל בַּר בְּרֶכְיָה תִּפְתָּר בִּשְׁנֵי כֵלִים. אֶחָד תּוֹכוֹ טָהוֹר וַאֲחוֹרָיו טְמֵאִין וְאֶחָד תּוֹכוֹ טָמֵא וַאֲחוֹרָיו טְהוֹרִין. מֶהָדֵי מַתְנִיתָא בִּכְלִי אֶחָד טָמֵא. אָמַר רִבִּי מָנָא תִּיפְתָּר בְּבוֹר טָהוֹר. מַה דְמַתְנִיתָא בְּבוֹר טָמֵא. וְהָתַנִּינָן תֵּרֵד וְתִיבָּלַע וְאַל יִבְלָעוּהָ בְיָדָיו. תִּיפְתָּר שֶׁנִּתְגַּלְגְּלָה לְבֵית הַפְּרָס.

Rebbi Ḥama bar Uqba in the name of Rebbi Yose ben Rebbi Ḥanina: With a vessel which inside is pure but impure outside one does not defile a small amount even to save a large amount[236]. But did we not state: "Let it descend and become impure; he should not make it impure with his hands?[237]" Rebbi Samuel bar Berekhiah said, explain for two vessels, one pure inside and impure outside, the other impure inside and pure outside[238]. But that Mishnah speaks of one impure vessel! Rebbi Mana said, explain it if the vat is pure; the Mishnah deals with an impure vat[239]. Did we not state: "Let it descend and be absorbed [into the ground]; he should not cause it to be absorbed by his hands' [action]." Explain it if it rolled onto to a *bet happĕrās*[240].

236 This discussion seems to center on the position of R. Eliezer, who does not permit defiling heave under any circumstances, even in order to save some heave in purity. In biblical law, pottery can become impure only from the inside; once the inside is impure by primary impurity, the outside also is impure. The outside of a pottery vessel can be impure only by rabbinic decree, not by biblical law. A metal vessel can become impure from the outside; such a vessel, if touched by a fluid from outside, becomes impure; cf. *Berakhot*, Chapter 8, Note 46.

Whether the discussion is about the position of R. Eliezer or R. Joshua and the kind of impurity of vessels involved is a matter of controversy in Babli *Pesaḥim* 21a.

237 This suggests that making impure indirectly, by a vessel, is permitted.

238 The statement of R. Yose ben R. Ḥanina does not refer to the position of R. Eliezer (who is not to be followed in practice) but to that of R. Joshua (whom practice follows). It is stated that if there is a chance that the wrong vessel will be chosen, which would make everything impure, nothing should be done.

239 The Mishnah speaks of the "lower part of the winepress". If that is a cistern built in the ground, it is part of the ground and cannot become impure. In that case, if the cistern is empty, the heave should be left to flow into it. This is the case considered by R. Yose ben R. Ḥanina. The Mishnah must speak of a winepress whose receptacle is movable and therefore can become impure together with its contents.

240 בית הפרס is a ploughed field where a grave had been. It is possible that some bones were dug up; the entire field is impure by rabbinic practice. Therefore, the rules are less strict than for biblical impurity and according to everybody the vessel may be used if only its interior is pure.

עַל דַּעְתֵּיהוֹן דַּחֲבֵרַיָּא חָבִית רִאשׁוֹנָה וְחָבִית שְׁנִיָּה. עַל דַּעְתֵּיהּ דְּרִבִּי יוֹסֵי חָבִית שֶׁל יַיִן וְחָבִית שֶׁל שֶׁמֶן.

In the opinion of the colleagues, first and second amphoras. In the opinion of Rebbi Yose, an amphora of wine and one of oil[241].

241 This refers back to the beginning of the Halakhah, notes 184 ff. The colleagues make an essential difference between "first" and "second" amphoras, as explained there. R. Yose (the Amora) may hold that R. Joshua permits exposing heave to impurity only for wine, which cannot be used if it is unclear whether it is pure or impure. Olive oil *can* be used as fuel for lamps even if pure; it *must* be used as fuel once it becomes impure. It follows that suspended heave of oil is usable and the Amora R. Yose holds that it should not be exposed to impurity even according to R. Joshua.

(fol. 45a) **משנה יא**: הָיָה עוֹבֵר מִמָּקוֹם לְמָקוֹם וְכִכְּרוֹת תְּרוּמָה בְיָדוֹ אָמַר לוֹ נָכְרִי תֵּן לִי אַחַת מֵהֶן וַאֲטַמְּאֶהָ וְאִם לָאו הֲרֵינִי מְטַמֵּא אֶת כּוּלָּהּ רִבִּי אֱלִעֶזֶר אוֹמֵר יְטַמֵּא אֶת כּוּלָּהּ וְאַל יִתֵּן לוֹ אַחַת מֵהֶן. רִבִּי יְהוֹשֻׁעַ אוֹמֵר יַנִּיחַ לְפָנָיו עַל הַסֶּלַע. וְכֵן נָשִׁים שֶׁאָמְרוּ לָהֶן גּוֹיִם תְּנוּ לָנוּ אַחַת מִכֶּם וּנְטַמְּאֶהָ וְאִם לָאו הֲרֵי אָנוּ מְטַמְּאִין כּוּלְּכֶם יְטַמְּאוּ אֶת כּוּלָּם וְאַל יִמְסְרוּ לָהֶן נֶפֶשׁ אַחַת מִיִּשְׂרָאֵל.

Mishnah 11: If somebody was on the road[242] with loaves of heave and a Gentile said to him, give me one of them that I may defile it, otherwise I shall defile all of them, Rebbi Eliezer says, he shall defile all of them but one should not hand over any to him. Rebbi Joshua said, he should put it on a rock before him[243]. Similarly, women to whom Gentiles said, give us one of you that we may defile her[244], otherwise we shall defile all of you, they should defile all of them but no Jewish person should be handed over[245].

242 Alone, with no help in sight.

243 On a rock, not in the dirt, to preserve the loaf as food. R. Joshua agrees that heave cannot be handed over to be made impure but an effort should be made within the letter of the law to preserve as much as possible in purity.

244 Rape her.

245 This principle is agreed to by everybody.

(fol. 46b) **הלכה י**: לֹא מִסְתַּבְּרָא אִם הָיְתָה כְּבָר טְמֵאָה. לֹא מִסְתַּבְּרָא אִם הָיְתָה שִׁפְחָה אַחַת.

Halakhah 10: It is not reasonable if one already was impure[246]. It is not reasonable if one was a slave girl[247].

246 In one of the heave cakes was impure, it is reasonable to hold that that cake might be handed over to the Gentile to give him the impression that he was defiling when in fact his actions had no effect.

247 Since slaves cannot marry, a slave girl (of Gentile origin, becoming quasi Jewish by immersion in a ritual bath) is barred from having sex with Jews for whom extramarital relations are sinful. [Sexual relations of a Jew with a person whom he could not marry are criminal acts, punishable by the courts.] Therefore, since sex is a fundamental human right, a slave girl is free to have guiltless sexual relations with slaves and Gentiles; she cannot be defiled by sexual relations with Gentiles. Since a freed slave girl can marry any Jew except a Cohen, her sleeping with these Gentiles would not impair her marriage chances if she should be manumitted later. Therefore, her being given to the Gentiles is similar to the impure heave being handed over.

תַּנֵּי סִיעוֹת בְּנֵי אָדָם שֶׁהָיוּ מְהַלְּכִין בַּדֶּרֶךְ וּפָגְעוּ לָהֶן גּוֹיִם. וְאָמְרוּ תְּנוּ לָנוּ אֶחָד מִכֶּם וְנַהֲרוֹג אוֹתוֹ וְאִם לָאו הֲרֵי אָנוּ הוֹרְגִין אֶת כּוּלְּכֶם. אֲפִילוּ כּוּלָּן נֶהֱרָגִים

אַל יִמְסְרוּ נֶפֶשׁ אַחַת מִיִּשְׂרָאֵל. יִיחֲדוּ לָהֶן אֶחָד כְּגוֹן שֶׁבַע בֶּן בִּכְרִי יִמְסְרוּ אוֹתוֹ וְאַל יֵיהָרֵגוּ. אָמַר רִבִּי שִׁמְעוֹן בֶּן לָקִישׁ וְהוּא שֶׁיְּהֵא חַייָב מִיתָה כְּשֶׁבַע בֶּן בִּכְרִי. וְרִבִּי יוֹחָנָן אָמַר אַף עַל פִּי שֶׁאֵינוֹ חַייָב מִיתָה כְּשֶׁבַע בֶּן בִּכְרִי. עוּלָּא בַּר קוֹשַׁב תְּבַעְתֵּיהּ מַלְכוּתָא. עָרַק וְאָזַל לֵיהּ לְלוֹד גַּבֵּי רִבִּי יוֹשׁוּעַ בֶּן לֵוִי. אָתוּן וְאַקְפּוּן מְדִינְתָא. אָמְרוּ לָהֶן אִין לֵית אַתּוּן יְהָבוּן לֵיהּ לָן אֲנָן מַחֲרְבִין מְדִינְתָא. סְלַק גַּבֵּיהּ רִבִּי יְהוֹשֻׁעַ בֶּן לֵוִי וּפַייְסֵיהּ וִיהָבֵיהּ לוֹן. וַהֲוָה אֵלִיָּהוּ זָכוּר לַטּוֹב יְלִיף מִיתְגְּלֵי עֲלוֹי וְלָא אִיתְגְּלֵי. וְצָם כַּמָּה צוֹמִין וְאִיתְגְּלֵי עֲלוֹי. אָמַר לֵיהּ וְלִמְסוֹרוֹת אֲנִי נִגְלָה. אָמַר לֵיהּ וְלֹא מִשְׁנָה עָשִׂיתִי. אָמַר לֵיהּ וְזוֹ מִשְׁנַת הַחֲסִידִים.

It was stated[248]: "A group of people on the road were met by Gentiles who said to them, give us one of you that we may kill him, otherwise we shall kill all of you; even if all of them are killed they should not hand over a Jewish person. If they designated one, like Sheba ben Bikhri[249], they should hand him over so as not to be killed." Rebbi Simeon ben Laqish said, on condition that he be guilty of a capital crime like Sheba ben Bikhri; but Rebbi Johanan said, even if he is not guilty of a capital crime like Sheba ben Bikhri. Ulla bar Qoshav[250] was proscribed by the government. He fled and went to Lydda to Rebbi Joshua ben Levi. They came and surrounded the city. They said to them, if you do not hand him over to us, we shall destroy the city. Rebbi Joshua ben Levi went to him and talked him into being handed over to them. Elijah, may be be remembered for good things, used to appear to him[251]; he[252] stopped appearing. He[251] fasted may fasts; he[252] appeared to him and said, do I appear to informers? He[251] said to him, did I not act according to a *baraita*? He[252] said to him, is that a statement for the pious?

248 Tosephta 7:20; *Gen. rabba* 94(9).

249 Even though Sheba ben Bikhri revolted against David and the entire affair was intra-Jewish (*2S*. 20), the

action of the people of Abel Bet Maakhah is taken as legal precedent in all cases.

250 In the Rome ms. and *Gen. rabba*: Qoshar.

251 R. Joshua ben Levi.

252 Elijah.

רִבִּי אִיסִּי אִיתְצַיָּד בְּסַפְסוּפָה. אָמַר רִבִּי יוֹנָתָן יִכָּרֵךְ הַמֵּת בְּסַדִּינוֹ. אָמַר רִבִּי שִׁמְעוֹן בֶּן לָקִישׁ עַד דַּאֲנָא קַטִיל וַאֲנָה מִיתְקְטִיל אֲנָא אֵיזִיל וּמְשֵׁיזִיב לֵיהּ בְּחֵיילָא. אָזַל וּפַיְיסוֹן וִיהָבוֹנֵיהּ לֵיהּ. אָמַר לוֹן וְאָתוּן גַּבִּי סַבִּין וְהוּא מַצְלֵי עֲלֵיכוֹן. אָתוּן גַּבֵּי רִבִּי יוֹחָנָן. אָמַר לוֹן מַה דַהֲוָה בִּלְבַבְכוֹן אִיעֲבַד לֵיהּ יִתְעֲבִיד לוֹן יִמְטָא לְהַהוּא עַמָּא. לָא מַטוֹן אפיפסרוס עַד דְּאָזְלוֹן כּוּלְהוֹן.

Rebbi Issi was captured in Safsufa[253]. Rebbi Jonathan said, may the dead be wrapped in his shroud[254]. Rebbi Simeon ben Laqish said, even if I should kill or be killed, I shall go and save him by force. He went and negotiated; they handed him over to him. He said to them, come to our old man, he shall pray for you. They came to Rebbi Joḥanan. He said to them, what was in your mind to do to him shall be done to these people. They did not reach **אפיפסרוס**[255] when all of them were gone[256].

253 In the next story, the place is under the dominion of Zenobia, queen of Palmyra. The extent of her dominion in Syria in not well documented. There are some places *al-Safsūf* in Galilee. Note Arabic سفسف "to sift", سفساف "matter of little value, importance."

254 He considers him as dead. In the Rome ms., after R. Jonathan, R. Joḥanan is quoted in the same sense. Since in the following R. Joḥanan is described as "old man", and R. Issi (Assi) was a student of R. Joḥanan, the mention of R. Jonathan is an anachronism.

255 In the Rome ms., **אפיפסרון**. Cf. Greek ἄποψις, -εως, ἡ, "outlook, tower from which one looks out". Perhaps "they did not reach the lookout" or "they had not vanished from sight." (E. G.)

256 They all had died.

זְעִיר בַּר חִינְנָא אִיתְצַיַּד בְּסַפְסוּפָא. סְלַק רִבִּי אִימִּי וְרִבִּי שְׁמוּאֵל מְפַייְסָה עֲלוֹי. אָמְרָה לְהוֹן זְנֹבִיָּה מַלְכְּתָא יְלִיף הוּא בָּרְיֵיכוֹן עֲבַד לְכוֹן נִיסִּין מְעַשִּׂיקִין בֵּיהּ. עָלַל חַד סַרָקַיי טְעִין חַד סַפְסֵר. אָמַר לוֹן בְּהָדָא סַפְסֵירָא קְטַל בַּר נִיצוֹר לְאָחוֹי. וְאִישְׁתֵּיזִיב זְעִיר בַּר חִינְנָא.

Zeïr bar Ḥinena was captured at Safsufa. Rebbi Ammi and Rebbi Samuel went to negotiate for him. Queen Zenobia said to them, your Creator usually does wonders for you; put Him under pressure! There came a Saracen carrying a sabre. He said to them, with this sabre did Odenathus[257] kill his brother. Zeïr bar Ḥinena was saved.

257 Zenobia's husband. In the Babli, his name is בר נצר . It is not clear whether Odenathus killed his own brother or the brother of the Saracen.

רִבִּי יוֹחָנָן אָמַר אִקְפַּח בַּעֲלֵי קַנְייָה. סְלִיק לְבֵית וַועֲדָא וַהֲוָה רִבִּי שִׁמְעוֹן בֶּן לָקִישׁ שְׁאִיל לֵיהּ וְלָא מֵגִיב. שְׁאִיל לֵיהּ וְלָא מֵגִיב. אָמַר לֵיהּ מַהוּ הָכֵין. אָמַר לֵיהּ כָּל־הָאֵיבָרִין תְּלוּיִין בְּלֵב וְהַלֵּב תָּלוּי בַּכִּיס. אָמַר לֵיהּ וּמַהוּ כֵן. אָמַר לֵיהּ וּמַה אַתְּ כֵן. אָמַר לֵיהּ אִיקְפָּחַת בַּעֲלֵי קַנְייָה. אָמַר לֵיהּ חֲמוֹ לִי זְוִיתָא. נְפַק מְחַוֵּי לֵיהּ. חֲמִיתוּן מִן רָחוֹק וְשָׁרֵי מְצַלְצֵל. אָמְרִין אִין רִבִּי יוֹחָנָן הוּא יְסַב פַּלְגָּא. אָמַר לוֹן חַיֵּיכוֹן כּוּלָּהּ אֲנָא נְסִיב וּנְסַב כּוּלָּהּ.

Rebbi Joḥanan said, I was robbed by the people of Qanah. He went to the assembly hall where Rebbi Simeon ben Laqish was asking him repeatedly but he did not answer. He said, what happened? He said, what can you do? He said, all limbs depend on the heart and the heart depends on the wallet. He said, I was robbed by the people of Qanah. He said, what do you have? He said to him, show me their corner[258]. He went out to show him. They saw him from afar and started to chirp. They said, if that is Rebbi Joḥanan, may he take half of it[259]. He said to them, by your life I am taking all of it; he took all.

258 Their quarter in Tiberias.

259 The Rome ms. adds: ואין ריש לקיש הוא יסוב כולה "when it is R. Simeon ben Laqish, he will take everything".

דִּיקְלוֹט חֲזִירָא מְחַוְנֵיהּ טַלְיֵי דְרִבִּי יוּדָה נְשִׂייָא. אִיתְעֲבִיד מֶלֶךְ נְחַת לְפַמַּייָס. שְׁלַח כְּתָבִין בָּתַר רַבָּנִין תֵּיהֲווֹן גַּבֵּיי בְּמַפְקֵי שׁוּבְתָא מִיַּד. אֲמַר לֵיהּ לִשְׁלוּחֵיא לֹא תִתֵּן לָהֶן כְּתָבִין אֶלָּא בְּעֲרוּבְתָא עִם מְטַמְעֵי שִׁמְשָׁא. וְאָתָא שְׁלִיחָא גַּבְּהוֹן בְּעֲרוּבְתָא עִם מְטַמְעֵי (fol. 46c) שִׁמְשָׁא. וַהֲוָה רִבִּי יוּדָן נְשִׂייָא וְרִבִּי שְׁמוּאֵל בַּר נַחְמָן נַחְתִּין לְמִיסְחֵי בְּדֵימוֹסִין דְּטִיבֵּרְיָא. אָתָא אנגיטריס גַּבְּהוֹן וּבְעָא רִבִּי יוּדָן נְשִׂייָא לְמִינְזַף בֵּיהּ. אֲמַר לֵיהּ רִבִּי שְׁמוּאֵל בַּר נַחְמָן אַרְפֵּי לֵיהּ לְנִסָּיוֹן מִיתְחַמֵּי. אֲמַר לוֹן מַה רַבָּנִין עָבְדִין תַּנּוּן לֵיהּ עוּבְדָא. אֲמַר לוֹן סְחוֹן. דְּבָרְיֵיכוֹן עֲבִיד נִיסִּין בְּמַפְקֵי שׁוּבְתָא. טָעַן יַתְהוֹן וְאָעִיל יַתְהוֹן. אָמְרוּ לֵיהּ הָא רַבָּנִין לְבַר. אֲמַר לָא יֶיחֱמוּן אַפֵּיי עַד דְּאִינוּן סַחְיָין. הֲוָה הַהוּא בֵּי בָנֵי אֲזִייָהּ שִׁבְעָה יוֹמִין וְשִׁבְעָה לֵילְוָן. נְפַק וְאַצְנָהּ[260] קָדֳמֵיהוֹן וְעָלְלוֹן וְקָמוּן לֵיהּ קַדְמֵיהוֹן. אֲמַר לוֹן בְּגִין דְּבָרְיֵיכוֹן עֲבִיד לְכוֹן נִיסִּין אַתּוּן מְבַזִּין מַלְכוּתָא. אָמְרִין לֵיהּ דִּיקְלוֹט חֲזִירָא בְזִינָן. דִּיקְלֶיטִאָנוּס מַלְכָּא לָא בְזִינָן. וַאֲפִילוּ כֵן לָא מַכְסֵי לָא בְּרוֹמֵי זְעִיר וְלָא בְּחָבֵר זְעִיר.

[261]The boys of Rebbi Jehudah Neśia hit Diocles[262] the swine-herd. He became king and descended to Paneas. He sent letters to the rabbis that they should be at his place immediately after the end of the Sabbath. He said to his courier, do not deliver the letters before the evening, near sundown. The courier came to them in he evening, near sundown. Rebbi Jehudah Neśia and Rebbi Samuel bar Naḥman had gone to bathe in the public baths of Tiberias. An אנגיטרוס[263] came to them; Rebbi Jehudah Neśia wanted to scold him[264]. Rebbi Samuel bar Naḥman said, let him; he appears for wonders. He said to them, how are the rabbis? They told him about their problem. He said to them, go and bathe; your Creator will perform a miracle for you at Sabbath's end. He[265] carried them and brought them up. They[266] said to him, the rabbis are outside. There was

that bathhouse, he[267] let it be heated for seven days and seven nights. He[268] went out and cooled it before them. They went in and then appeared before him[267]. He[267] said to them: Because your Creator performs miracles for you, you insult the majesty! They said, we insulted Diocles the swine-herd; we do not insult Diocletianus the king. Even so, one should never vex a little Roman or a little Gueber[269].

260 Reading of the Rome ms. In *Gen. rabba* מזגה (*Yalqut* מזגא) "mixed (with cold water)". Leyden and Venice: מנצחת "directs, is victorious".

261 A more complete version is in *Gen. rabba* 63(24); *Yalquṭ Šim'oni* #110.

262 *Diocles*, reportedly the original name of *Diocletianus* before he became a general and then emperor. דיוקלוט *Dioclot* perhaps reflects contemporary spelling pronunciation.

263 Rome ms.: אנטיגרס; *Gen. rabba* (Theodor-Albeck) ארגינטין, ארגנטין, ארגנטי, also ארגינט, ארגינטי, אגרנטין; *Yalquṭ* ארגינטין. The name of this friendly demon has not been determined.

Since *Gen. rabba* clearly is the primary source, (א)רגנטי may mean "guiding spirit" from Latin *rego* "to lead; conduct; guide"; cf. *regens, -ntis* "prince, ruler", *rectus, -a, -um* "led straight; direct; in a straight line" (E. G.).

264 In *Gen. rabba*, the demon danced before them. The corresponding sentence must have been lost here.

265 The friendly demon, after Sabbath's end. Diocletian descended to Paneas from the North or East; the demon had to bring them up from South and West.

266 Diocletian's staff.

267 Diocletian.

268 The demon.

269 The tribe of the Sassanid kings in Persia. In *Gen. rabba* and *Yalquṭ*: גוליירי cf. *galearii, -orum*, "a kind of soldier's servants."

הזורע פרק תשיעי

(fol. 46c) **משנה א:** הַזּוֹרֵעַ תְּרוּמָה שׁוֹגֵג יוֹפַּךְ וּמֵזִיד יְקַייֵם. וְאִם הֵבִיאָה שְׁלִישׁ בֵּין שׁוֹגֵג בֵּין מֵזִיד יְקַייֵם. וּבְפִשְׁתָּן מֵזִיד יוֹפַּךְ.

Mishnah 1: If somebody sows heave in error it should be ploughed under; if intentionally it must be kept[1]. If it is one third ripe it must be kept, whether in error or intentionally[2]. But flax must be ploughed under when [sown] intentionally[3].

1 The entire harvest will be heave. In case of unintentional use of heave grain, if the error is discovered early enough, the farmer has a chance for a new crop. If it was intentional, the field cannot be used for commercial produce the entire growing season.

2 As explained earlier, "one third ripe" means that the grains are well formed and one third ripe, not that only one third of the entire growing season has passed. The grain is heave and may not be destroyed.

3 The reason is explained in the Halakhah: To avoid that the flax stalks (which are not food but the most valuable part of the plant) could be used.

הלכה א: הַזּוֹרֵעַ תְּרוּמָה שׁוֹגֵג יוֹפַּךְ כו'. לֹא מִסְתַּבְּרָא דְלָא חִילוּפִין קְנָסוּ בוֹ שֶׁתִּיבָּטֵל שָׂדֵהוּ עַל גַּב תְּרוּמָה.

Halakhah 1: "If someone sows heave in error it should be ploughed under;" etc. Would it not be reasonable to switch[4]? They fined him that his field should be worthless under the heave[5].

4 Should not the crop sown intentionally be ploughed under and the one sown unintentionally be left standing?

5 Since the yield will be heave,

the farmer sowing intentionally will be deprived of the use of his field for the entire growing season.

רִבִּי שְׁמוּאֵל בַּר אֶבוּדַימִי בָּעֵי. מַהוּ שֶׁיְּהֵא נֶאֱמָן לוֹמַר מֵזִיד הָיִיתִי. וְאָמְרוּ לוֹ אִם כְּשֶׁהָיוּ אֲחֵרִים[6] מַכִּירִין לֹא כָּל־הֵימֶנּוּ וְאִם לָאו הַפֶּה שֶׁאָסַר הוּא הַפֶּה שֶׁהִתִּיר.

Rebbi Samuel bar Eudaimon asked: Can he be trusted if he says, I did it intentionally[7]? They said to him, if other people knew, it is not on his [word]; otherwise, the mouth which forbade is the mouth that permitted[8].

6 Reading of the Rome ms. It is possible to see in this word an explanatory gloss which entered the text.

7 If he prefers to have a field of heave to having to plough it under.

8 A general legal principle that if somebody testifies to something, not known from other sources, which would put him at a disadvantage, he himself may offer additional information which explains away the pejorative aspects. This rule is accepted in both Talmudim.

רִבִּי בִּנְיָמִין בַּר גִּידּוֹל בָּעֵי זָרַע תְּרוּמָה כַּרְשִׁינִין זָרַע תְּרוּמַת חוּצָה לָאָרֶץ. וְאָמְרוּ לוֹ גְּזֵירָה הִיא וְאֵין גְּזֵירָה לִגְזֵירָה.

Rebbi Benjamin ben Gidul asked: If he had sown vetch? If he had sown heave from outside the Land[9]? They said to him, it is a "fence", and there is no "fence" for a "fence"[10].

9 Vetch is animal feed; it is subject to heave only by rabbinic usage. Produce from outside the Land is subject to heave only by rabbinic decree.

10 Reading גדירה for Babylonian גזירה; the rules of the Mishnah are rabbinic decrees promulgated as a "fence around the Law" to safegard the Biblical institution of heave. Rabbinic heave needs no "fence".

הָדָא אָמְרָה שֶׁהַקְּדוּשָּׁה חָלָה עָלֶיהָ כְּשֶׁהוּא מְחוּבָּר. הָדָא אָמְרָה הִפְרִישׁ מִפֵּירוֹת שֶׁלֹּא הֵבִיאוּ שְׁלִישׁ לֹא קָדְשׁוּ.

That means[11] that sanctity falls on it when it is still standing[12]. That means, if he separated before it was one third ripe it did not become holy[13].

11 This refers to the Mishnah stating that produce one third ripe should be left standing in any case.

12 If the illegally grown produce would acquire the status of heave only after harvesting, there would be no difference before and after it is one third ripe.

13 If heave would be holy when taken from produce not one third ripe then it would always be forbidden to plough under any produce from heave since one may not destroy heave.

וּבְמֵזִיד יוּפַּךְ. קָנְסוּ בוֹ שֶׁלֹּא יֵיהָנֶה בְקִיסְמִין.

"[It] must be ploughed under when [sown] intentionally[14]." They fined him lest he profit from the wooden parts[3].

14 Quote from the Mishnah, speaking of flax heave sown.

משנה ב: וְחַיֶּיבֶת בְּלֶקֶט וּבְשִׁיכְחָה וּבְפֵיאָה וַעֲנִיֵּי יִשְׂרָאֵל וַעֲנִיֵּי כֹהֲנִים מְלַקְּטִין וַעֲנִיֵּי יִשְׂרָאֵל מוֹכְרִין אֶת שֶׁלָּהֶן לָעֲנִיִּים כֹּהֲנִים בִּדְמֵי תְרוּמָה וְהַדָּמִין שֶׁלָּהֶן. רִבִּי טַרְפוֹן אוֹמֵר אֵין מְלַקְּטִין אֶלָּא עֲנִיֵּי כֹהֲנִים שֶׁמָּא יִשְׁכְּחוּ וְיִתְּנוּ לְתוֹךְ פִּיהֶן. אָמַר לוֹ רִבִּי עֲקִיבָה אִם כֵּן לֹא יִלְקְטוּ אֶלָּא טְהוֹרִים.

Mishnah 2: But it is subject to gleanings, forgotten sheaves, and *peah*[15]. Israel poor and poor Cohanim collect; the Israel poor must sell to the Cohanim poor for the value of heave but the proceeds are theirs[16]. Rebbi Ṭarphon says, only Cohanim poor may collect; maybe they would forget and put some in their mouths[17]. Rebbi Aqiba said to him, if that is so, then only pure persons should collect[18].

15 Since the new crop grown from heave seed is heave only by rabbinic decree, it is not freed from the biblical obligations.

16 What is collected must be treated as heave but since it is intrinsically profane, the proceeds are profane in the hand of the poor non-Cohen.

17 The poor non-Cohen will incur guilt eating what was declared to be heave.

18 Since eating heave when impure is a deadly sin.

הלכה ב: רִבִּי יוֹסֵי בָּעֵי הִפְרִישׁ עֳמָרִין שֶׁלּוֹ וְנִתְחַלְּפוּ לוֹ אֲפִילוּ כֵן עֲנִיֵּי יִשְׂרָאֵל וַעֲנִיֵּי כֹהֲנִים מְלַקְּטִין.

Halakhah 2: Rebbi Yose asked: If he dedicated sheaves of his [harvest][19] and they were switched[20], do even so poor Israel and poor Cohanim collect?

19 He dedicated some sheaves as heave even though the duty of heave starts only after threshing. It is implied by the preceding Halakhah that any heave dedicated from grain that was at least one third ripe is legal heave. Hence, the sheaves are legal heave.

20 They were mixed up with profane sheaves. Gleanings from profane sheaves are for the poor. The question implies that practice follows R. Meïr in Mishnah *Peah* 4:8 that in cases of doubt, the gleanings belong to the poor. Nevertheless, grain falling from heave sheaves is heave; since the heave sheaves are no longer identifiable, all gleanings are potential heave and have to be sold to Cohanim as heave. Since there is no answer given, R. Yose's hypotheses are accepted.

תַּנֵּי אִשְׁתּוֹ שֶׁל עַם הָאָרֶץ טוֹחֶנֶת עִם אִשְׁתּוֹ שֶׁל חָבֵר בִּזְמָן שֶׁהִיא טְמֵאָה. אֲבָל בִּזְמָן שֶׁהִיא טְהוֹרָה לֹא תִטְחוֹן שֶׁהִיא מַחֲזֶקֶת עַצְמָהּ טְהוֹרָה מִמֶּנָּה. וּכְדִבְרֵי רִבִּי טַרְפוֹן אֲפִילוּ בִּזְמָן שֶׁהִיא טְמֵאָה לֹא תִטְחוֹן שֶׁמָּא תִשְׁכַּח וְתִתֵּן לְתוֹךְ פִּיהָ.

It was stated[21]: "The wife of a vulgar may grind with the wife of a Fellow when she is impure[22]. But when she is pure she should not grind, for she will hold herself more pure that the other." Following the words of Rebbi Ṭarphon she should not grind even when she is impure lest she forget and put some into her mouth[23]!

21 Tosephta *Ṭahorot* 8:4.

22 The notions of "vulgar" and "fellow" are explained in the Introduction to *Demay*. The grain to be ground must be prepared to accept impurity, cf. *Demay* Chapter 2, Note 141. If the wife of the vulgar considers herself impure, she will refrain from touching the grain. If she holds herself to be pure she still is impure by Fellows' standards but will not refrain from touching the grain and will make it impure by Fellows' standards.

In the Tosephta, R. Simeon disagrees and forbids grinding together with the wife of a vulgar since the latter, while careful herself in the days of her impurity, will not care if her friends touch the grain.

23 Since this is not mentioned in the Tosephta, the teaching of R. Ṭarphon cannot represent practice.

הלכה ג: כֵּן הִיא מַתְנִיתָא אִם כֵּן לֹא יְלַקְּטוּ אֶלָּא טְהוֹרִים.

Halakhah 3: So is the Mishnah: "If that is so, then only pure persons should collect.[24]"

24 In this version, both Cohanim and non-Cohanim may collect if they are pure. This text is in most Mishnah mss., except most of the Maimonides tradition. Cf. J. N. Epstein, מבוא לנוסח המשנה [2], p. 448; N. Sacks, ed. משנה עם שנויי נוסחאות, זרעים ב, p. קעב.

משנה ג: וְחַיֶּיבֶת בְּמַעֲשֵׂר וּבְמַעֲשַׂר עָנִי וַעֲנִיֵּי יִשְׂרָאֵל וַעֲנִיֵּי כֹהֲנִים נוֹטְלִין. וַעֲנִיֵּי
יִשְׂרָאֵל מוֹכְרִין אֶת שֶׁלָּהֶן לַכֹּהֲנִים בִּדְמֵי תְרוּמָה וְהַדָּמִין שֶׁלָּהֶן. הַחוֹבֵט מְשׁוּבָּח

וְהַדָּשׁ כֵּיצַד יַעֲשֶׂה תּוֹלֶה כְּפִיפוֹת בְּצַוְּארֵי בְהֵמָה וְנוֹתֵן לְתוֹכָן מֵאוֹתוֹ הַמִּין וְנִמְצָא לֹא זוֹמֵם אֶת הַבְּהֵמָה וְלֹא מַאֲכִיל אֶת הַתְּרוּמָה.

Mishnah 3: Also, it is subject to tithe and the tithe of the poor[25]. Poor Israel and poor Cohanim may take; the poor Israel must sell to Cohanim for the value of heave but the proceeds are theirs[16]. He who flails[26] is praiseworthy; he who threshes, what shall he do? He hangs baskets over the neck of the animal and fills it from the same kind[27]. In that way, he will not muzzle the animal or feed it heave.

25 Since the new crop grown from heave seed is heave only by rabbinic decree, it is not freed from the biblical obligations.

26 He removes the grains from the ears by hitting with a flail. He is praiseworthy because he does not use an animal. Since grain is human food, its heave may not be used as animal feed. On the other hand, muzzling a threshing animal is forbidden (*Deut.* 25:4).

27 So that the animal may eat from the basket while threshing.

הלכה ד: כֵּן הִיא מַתְנִיתָא חַיֶּיבֶת בִּתְרוּמָה וּבְמַעְשְׂרוֹת וּבְמַעֲשֵׂר עָנִי.

Halakhah 4: So is the Mishnah: "It is subject to heaves[28], tithes[29], and the tithe of the poor."

28 Great Heave and Heave of the Tithe.

29 First tithe (always), second tithe (in years 1, 2, 4, 5 of the Sabbatical cycle) and the tithe of the poor (in years 3, 6 of the Sabbatical cycle.) The special mention of the tithe of the poor is needed only as introduction to the next sentence, that non-Cohanim are entitled to the tithe of the poor in case of doubt.

לִיטְרָא בְצָלִים שֶׁל מַעֲשֵׂר רִאשׁוֹן שֶׁנְּטָעָהּ וַהֲרֵי בָהּ עֶשֶׂר לִיטְרִין הֲרֵי אֵלּוּ חַיָּיבוֹת בְּמַעְשְׂרוֹת. וְאוֹתוֹ מַעֲשֵׂר רִאשׁוֹן שֶׁלָּהֶן שֶׁהוּא מַפְרִישׁ עַל תְּרוּמַת מַעֲשֵׂר וְעַל מַה שֶּׁנָּטַע. לִיטְרָא בְצָלִים שֶׁל מַעֲשֵׂר שֵׁנִי שֶׁנְּטָעָהּ הֲרֵי בָהּ עֶשֶׂר לִיטְרִין חַיֶּיבֶת בְּמַעְשְׂרוֹת וְחוֹזֵר וּפוֹדֶה אֶת מַעֲשֵׂר שֵׁנִי שֶׁנָּטַע.

[30]If he[31] planted one pound of onions of First Tithe and it became ten pounds, these are subject to tithes[32]. Its First Tithe is given for the heave of the tithe and for what he planted[33]. If he[34] planted one pound of onions of Second Tithe and it became ten pounds, these are subject to tithes[35] and he still has to redeem the second tithe from what he planted.

30 Tosephta 8:5-6.

31 The Levite planted the onions before he gave Heave of the Tithe; when all is still *ṭevel*. After Heave of the Tithe has been given, the tithe is totally profane in the hand of the Levite.

32 In the Tosephta: "Subject to heave and First and Second Tithes." Since onions do not disappear in the new growth, the entire harvest is *ṭevel* by biblical law.

33 For the Heave of the Tithe that should have been given before the onions were planted.

34 Any Jew who illegally planted Second Tithe that was not redeemed. Unredeemed Second Tithe may only be used as food inside the walls of Jerusalem.

35 In the Tosephta: "Subject to heave and First and Second Tithes."

הַחוֹבֵט מְשׁוּבָּח. מִן מִי מְשׁוּבָּח. מִן הַדָּשׁ. הַדָּשׁ כֵּיצַד הוּא עוֹשֶׂה. תַּנֵּי בְשֵׁם רִבִּי שִׁמְעוֹן תּוֹלֶה לָהּ כַּרְשִׁינִין וְהֵן יָפִין לָהּ מִן הַכֹּל. אָמַר רִבִּי יוֹסֵי זֹאת אוֹמֶרֶת עָשָׂה כֵן בְחוּלִין אֵינוֹ עוֹבֵר עָלָיו מִשּׁוּם בַּל תַּחְסוֹם.

""He who flails is praiseworthy." Praiseworthy in relation to whom? To him who threshes. "He who threshes, what shall he do?" It was stated[36] in the name of Rebbi Simeon: "He hangs vetch for her and she likes it better than anything." Rebbi Yose said, this implies that if he did this with profane [grain][37] he does not transgress "do not muzzle."

36 Tosephta 8:3; quoted Babli *Baba Meẓi'a* 90a.

37 Even if it is permitted to feed the animal from the grain to be threshed, vetch may be substituted for the grain (*Deut.* 25:4).

הַמְרַכֵּין בְּקִטְנִיּוֹת וּבְתִלְתָּן אֵינוֹ עוֹבֵר מִשּׁוּם בַּל תַּחְסוֹם שׁוֹר בְּדִישׁוֹ. אֲבָל אָסוּר מִפְּנֵי מַרְאִית הָעַיִן. אִית תַּנּוֹיֵי תַּנֵּי בְּדַיִישׁ שֶׁהוּא מוּתָּר לָךְ. וְאִית תַּנּוֹיֵי תַּנֵּי בְּדַיִישׁ שֶׁהוּא אָסוּר לָךְ.

"[38]One does not transgress 'do not muzzle' while softening legumes or fenugreek[39], but it is forbidden because of the bad impression." Some Tannaïm state: "Threshing which is permitted to you[40]." But some Tannaïm state: "Threshing which is not permitted to you."

38 A different *baraita* is quoted in Babli *Baba Meẓi'a* 89b: "Cows trampling on grain or threshing heave and tithes are not subject to 'do not muzzle' but because of the bad impression one brings some of the same kind and hangs it around their necks; R. Simeon says, he hangs vetch for her and she likes it better than anything." The translation follows the interpretation of Maimonides.

39 It is not clear how cattle were used in these cases.

40 *Deut.* 25:4 applies only to threshing profane grain. The opposing opinion applies the verse both to profane and sanctified food; this is the basis for the Mishnah.

אָמַר רִבִּי בָּא בַּר מָמָל מַתְנִיתִין בְּשֶׁנְּתָנוֹ מִשֶּׁהוֹצִיאוּ עֲדָשִׁים מֵימֵיהֶן. עֲדָשִׁין צוֹפְרוֹת אוֹתוֹ שֶׁלֹּא יִתֵּן. אֲבָל אִם נְתָנוֹ עַד שֶׁלֹּא הוֹצִיאוּ עֲדָשִׁין לֹא בְדָא. וּכְמָה דְאַתְּ אָמַר עֲדָשִׁים צוֹפְרוֹת אוֹתוֹ שֶׁלֹּא יִתֵּן. וְדִכְוָותָהּ עֲדָשִׁים צוֹפְרוֹת אוֹתוֹ (fol. 46d) שֶׁלֹּא יִבְלַע. הֵיךְ עֲבִידָא בָּצָל שֶׁל חוּלִין שֶׁנְּתָנוֹ לְתוֹךְ עֲדָשִׁים שֶׁל תְּרוּמָה אֲפִילוּ כֵן עֲדָשִׁים צוֹפְרוֹת אוֹתוֹ שֶׁלֹּא יִבְלַע. הָדָא דְתֵימַר בְּיָבֵשׁ אֲבָל בְּלַח אָסוּר. בְּבָצָל וּבְקֶפְלוֹט בֵּין לַח בֵּין יָבֵשׁ בֵּין שָׁלֵם בֵּין מְחוּתָּךְ אָסוּר. הֶעֱבִיר פְּטוֹמְתוֹ כִּמְחוּתָּךְ הוּא. הָיוּ שְׁנַיִם שְׁלֹשָׁה כִּמְחוּתָּכִין הֵן.

[41]Rebbi Abba bar Mamal said, our Mishnah[42] after the lentils lost their sap; [then] the lentils shrink[43] it that it will not give [any taste]. But if he gave it before the lentils gave their sap; it does not deal with that case[44]. And just as you say, the lentils shrink it that it will not give[45], so the lentils shrink that it will not absorb[46]. How is that? If he put a profane

onion into lentils of heave, the lentils shrink it that it will not absorb. That means, if it is dry, but if it[47] is moist it is forbidden. Onions and leeks are forbidden moist or dry, whole or cut up. If he removed the top it is as if cut up. If they are two or three they are as if cut up[48].

41 This paragraph belongs to the discussion of Mishnah 10:1 and is partially repeated in Halakhah 10:1.

42 10:1, speaking of onions stored with lentils when one of the kinds is heave and the other profane. In that case the profane food will become legal heave if it has absorbed the taste of the heave.

43 In Halakhah 10:1, the reading of both mss. is צופדות; this has been translated here (cf. *Thr.* 4:8). In Halakhah 9:4, both sources read צופרות "deflect".

44 If the lentils are moist, a dry outer skin of the onion will not be impermeable.

45 The taste of the onions into the lentils.

46 The onion will not absorb the taste of the lentils.

47 The onion.

48 Since Mishnah 10:1 mentions "onion" in the singular.

הָדָא דְתֵימַר בְּשֶׁאֵין בִּקְלִיפָּה הַחִיצוֹנָה בְּנוֹתֵן טַעַם. אֲבָל אִם יֵשׁ לָהּ אִית תַּנָּיֵי תַּנֵּי בְּדַיִישׁ שֶׁהוּא מוּתָּר לָךְ. מַתְנִיתָא תַּמָּן דְּאָמַר אַף בְּדַיִישׁ שֶׁהוּא אָסוּר לָךְ דְּתַנִּינָן תּוֹלֶה כְּפִיפוֹת בְּצַוָּאר בְּהֵמָה.

This all is if the outer skin[49] does not impart taste. But if it does, there are Tannaïm who state: "Threshing which is permitted to you." The Mishnah there[50] implies also threshing which is not permitted to you, since we have stated: "He hangs baskets over the neck of the animal.[51]"

49 Of the onion. The outer skin of a dry onion is not usually used as food. Therefore, it should not have the sanctity of heave.

50 This is the Mishnah here, 9:3.

51 Since the Mishnah forbids muzzling the animal, it considers the grain to be heave. Normally, the obligation of heave starts only after threshing. This means that the Mishnah considers growth from heave as heave in biblical law (negated by the Babli,

Baba Meẓi'a 90a). By analogy, since the outer skin of green onions is food, the dry outer skin of an onion of heave also retains its quality of heave. In addition, practice follows those who prohibit the muzzling of threshing animals under all circumstances.

בְּדִישׁוֹ וְלֹא בְדוֹרְכוֹ. רִבִּי לִיעֶזֶר בֶּן יַעֲקֹב אוֹמֵר אַף בְּדוֹרְכוֹ.

"When it threshes," not when it tramples on it. Rebbi Eliezer ben Jacob says, even if it tramples on it[52].

52 It is not clear what "trampling" means. Maimonides (*Śekhirut* 12:6) seems to read it as "stepping on" and permits muzzling cattle when driven from one place to another. Here, "trampling" must refer to some agricultural work; a detailed definition of the conditions imposed by the biblical use of "threshing", based on *Sifry Deut.* 287, is in *Ma'serot* 2:6 and its parallel Babli *Baba Meẓi'a* 89a.

Most commentators refer the disagreement here to the earlier statement that there is no prohibition of muzzling if vegetables are crushed (Notes 38-39).

אָמַר רִבִּי אָבוּן רִבִּי עֲקִיבָה שָׁאַל רִבִּי שִׁמְעוֹן בֶּן יוֹחַי מִבְדְּקִינֵיהּ. חָסַם מִבְּחוּץ וְהִכְנִיס מִבִּפְנִים. אָמַר לֵיהּ בְּבוֹאֲכֶם אֶל אוֹהֶל מוֹעֵד. מִבּוֹאֲכֶם אֶל אוֹהֶל מוֹעֵד. אָמַר רִבִּי עֶזְרָא לֹא תַחְסוֹם שׁוֹר בְּדִישׁוֹ. לֹא תָדוּשׁ בְּשׁוֹר חָסוּם.

Rebbi Abun said: Rebbi Aqiba asked Rebbi Simeon ben Ioḥai[53] in order to examine him: If somebody muzzled outside and then brought [the animal] inside[54]? He said to him (*Lev.* 10:9): "When you come to the tent of meeting;" from when you come to the tent of meeting[55]. Rebbi Ezra[56] said, (*Deut.* 25:4) "Do not muzzle an ox at his threshing;" do not thresh using a muzzled ox.

53 In the Babli, *Baba Meẓi'a* 90b, R. Jonathan asked R. Simai.

54 Reading the verse as: "Do not muzzle an ox while he is threshing", does this imply that one may use a muzzled ox for threshing when the act of muzzling was done away from the threshing floor?

55 The Babli is more explicit: Since the paragraph forbids priests to serve in the Temple when they have alcohol in their system, it implies that it is forbidden for a priest, who had come to the Temple while sober, to drink alcohol during his service. Therefore, as a matter of biblical style, *Deut.* 25:4 has to be interpreted following R. Ezra.

56 He is R. Azariah.

(fol. 44c) **משנה ד**: גִּידּוּלֵי תְרוּמָה תְרוּמָה. וְגִידּוּלֵי גִידּוּלִין חוּלִין. אֲבָל הַטֵּבֶל וּמַעֲשֵׂר רִאשׁוֹן וּסְפִיחֵי שְׁבִיעִית וּתְרוּמַת חוּצָה לָאָרֶץ וְהַמְּדוּמָּע וְהַבִּיכּוּרִים גִּידּוּלֵיהֶן חוּלִין. גִּידּוּלֵי הֶקְדֵּשׁ וּמַעֲשֵׂר שֵׁנִי חוּלִין וּפוֹדֶה אוֹתָם בִּזְמַן זַרְעָם.

Mishnah 4: The growth from heave is heave[57]; the growth from their growth is profane. But the growths from *ṭevel*[58], First Tithe, aftergrowth of the Sabbatical[59], heave from outside the Land, *dema'*[60], and First Fruits are profane. Growths from dedicated[61] [seeds] and Second Tithe are profane; one redeems them corresponding to the time of sowing[62].

57 By rabbinic decree. In the opinion of the Babli (*Šabbat* 13c) this is one of the "eighteen decrees" which the House of Shammai forced on the House of Hillel; according to the Yerushalmi (*Šabbat* 3c), it might be one of these decrees. The reason given is that one wants to prevent a Cohen from keeping impure heave for sowing since in the meantime he might inadvertently eat from it.

58 Seed grain is exempt from heave and tithes.

59 The entire prohibition of aftergrowth of the Sabbatical year is rabbinical, as is heave from outside the Land.

60 Since in biblical law, a minority of forbidden food disappears in the majority, if the *ṭevel* content of *dema'* is strictly less than 50%, the prohibition is rabbinical.

61 Dedicated to the Temple to be sold and its proceeds used for the Temple.

62 The language implies that grains from Second Tithe or dedicated grain were sown without being redeemed,

otherwise these would be totally profane. One has to redeem from next year's crop only an amount equal to the original seed grain. The reading of the Rome ms. and the Munich ms. of the Babli is: בדמי זרעם "for the value of their seeds;" the meaning is the same.

(fol. 44d) **הלכה ה**: וְתַנֵּי עֲלָהּ בְּמַה דְּבָרִים אֲמוּרִים. בְּדָבָר שֶׁזַּרְעוֹ כָלֶה. אֲבָל בְּדָבָר שֶׁאֵין זַרְעוֹ כָלֶה גִּידּוּלֵי גִידּוּלִין אֲסוּרִין. אֲבָל הַטֵּבֶל שֶׁרוּבּוֹ חוּלִין. וּמַעֲשֵׂר רִאשׁוֹן שֶׁרוּבּוֹ חוּלִין. וּסְפִיחֵי שְׁבִיעִית שֶׁאֵין מְצוּיִין וּתְרוּמַת חוּצָה לָאָרֶץ שֶׁאֵינָהּ מְצוּיָה. וְהַמְּדוּמָּע רוּבּוֹ חוּלִין. וְהַבִּיכּוּרִים שֶׁאֵין מְצוּיִין.

Halakhah 5: We have stated on this[63]: When has this been said? Anything whose seeds disappear. But in produce whose seeds do not disappear[64], the growth from their growth is forbidden. But *ṭevel* is mostly profane[65], First Tithe is mostly profane[66], aftergrowth of the Sabbatical is infrequent[67], heave from outside the Land is infrequent[68], most of *dema‘* is profane[60], First Fruits are infrequent.

63 Referring to growth of heave.

64 Bulbous plants.

65 88% is profane if neither heave nor First Tithe were taken.

66 90% is profane. If heave of the tithe is taken, the resulting grain is totally profane and is no longer called "First Tithe".

67 That one would be able to collect enough grain from aftergrowth to serve as seed grain.

68 Even from countries bordering on the Land where there is a rabbinic heave; that heave should not be brought into the Land.

וְגִידּוּלֵי הֶקְדֵּשׁ וּמַעֲשֵׂר שֵׁנִי חוּלִין וּפוֹדֶה אוֹתָם בִּזְמַן שֶׁזְּרָעָן. רִבִּי אַבָּהוּ בְּשֵׁם רִבִּי יוֹחָנָן פוֹדֶה אֶת כָּל־הָאוֹצָר בִּדְמֵי אוֹתָהּ סְאָה. הֶפְרֵישׁ הֶקְדֵּשׁ לְמַעֲשֵׂר שֵׁנִי. מַעֲשֵׂר שֵׁנִי בֵּין דָּבָר שֶׁזַּרְעוֹ כָלֶה וּבֵין דָּבָר שֶׁאֵין זַרְעוֹ כָלֶה נִפְדֶּה בְּשַׁעַר הַזּוֹל. אֶלָּא דָּבָר שֶׁזַּרְעוֹ כָלֶה נִפְדֶּה בְּשַׁעַר שֶׁהוּא עוֹמֵד בּוֹ. דָּבָר שֶׁאֵין זַרְעוֹ כָלֶה נִפְדֶּה בְּשַׁעַר הָרִאשׁוֹן. הֶקְדֵּשׁ בֵּין דָּבָר שֶׁזַּרְעוֹ כָלֶה וּבֵין דָּבָר שֶׁאֵין זַרְעוֹ כָלֶה אֵין לוֹ אֶלָּא מְקוֹמוֹ וְשַׁעְתוֹ. אֲבָל דָּבָר שֶׁזַּרְעוֹ כָלֶה פּוֹדֶה אֶת כָּל־הָאוֹצָר בִּדְמֵי אוֹתָהּ סְאָה שֶׁזָּרַע. וְדָבָר שֶׁאֵין זַרְעוֹ כָלֶה פּוֹדֶה אֶת כָּל־הָאוֹצָר.

"Growths from dedicated [seeds] and Second Tithe are profane; one redeems them corresponding to the time he sowed." Rebbi Abbahu in the name of Rebbi Joḥanan: He redeems the entire storage for the value of that *seah*[69]. The difference between dedicated [produce] and Second Tithe: Second Tithe, whether produce whose seeds disappear or whose seeds do not disappear, is redeemed by the wholesale price[70]; only that produce whose seeds disappear is redeemed by current prices, produce whose seeds do not disappear is redeemed following the early price[71]. Dedicated [produce], whether produce whose seeds disappear or whose seeds do not disappear, is treated in its place and time[72]; only that one redeems the entire storage of produce whose seeds disappear for the value of that *seah*, but for produce whose seeds do not disappear he has to redeem the [contents of] the entire storage.

69 One has to redeem only the value of the seed grain, not the entire harvest.

70 Mishnah *Ma'aser Šeni* 4:2. The Babli (*Baba Meẓi'a* 57a) holds that redemption may be done below the wholesale value; this is never mentioned in the Yerushalmi.

71 The wholesale price at the time and place of sowing.

72 The wholesale price at time and place of redemption is the operative price.

(fol. 44c) **משנה ה**: מֵאָה לַגֵּינָה שֶׁל תְּרוּמָה וְאַחַת שֶׁל חוּלִּין כּוּלָּן מוּתָּרִין בְּדָבָר שֶׁזַּרְעוֹ כָלָה אֲבָל בְּדָבָר שֶׁאֵין זַרְעוֹ כָלֶה אֲפִילוּ מֵאָה שֶׁל חוּלִּין וְאַחַת שֶׁל תְּרוּמָה כּוּלָּן אֲסוּרִין.

Mishnah 5: One hundred *lagenae*[73] of heave and one profane are all permitted for produce whose seeds disappear[74]; but for produce whose seeds do not disappear[64], even if there are one hundred profane and one of heave they all are forbidden[75].

73 Name of a vessel and a measure of grain, Greek λάγυνος, λάγηνος, Latin *lagena, lagaena, lagoena, lagona*, Accadic *lignu, liginnu*; used here for the surface area from which one *liginnu* can be harvested. The size of a *lagena/liginnu* in Mishnaic times is unknown (cf. *Demay* Chapter 7, Note 85). The Halakhah assumes that each *lagena* is a separate plot but the farmer forgot what he sowed where.

74 If a field (probably the standard field of one *bet seah*) is sown to yield 101 *lagenae*, and 100 parts of the seeds were profane and one part heave, then all the yield is profane and usable by everybody since even the growth from heave seed is forbidden only by rabbinic degree. (This would make 1 *lagena* = 4.975 square cubits.)

75 Since the original heave is still in existence, it is forbidden by biblical decree and the entire crop is available only to Cohanim.

(fol. 44d) **הלכה ו**: אָמַר רִבִּי יוֹסֵי זֹאת אוֹמֶרֶת הָיוּ לְפָנָיו מֵאָה סְאָה הָעוֹלוֹת מִתּוֹךְ מֵאָה סְאָה. וְאַחַת שֶׁל חוּלִין נִתְחַלְּפָה לוֹ מוּתָּרוֹת.

Halakhah 6: Rebbi Yose said: This implies that if there were 100 *seah*, each one lifted from 100 *seah*[76], and one profane was switched with one of them, all would be permitted.

76 In a hundred cases, one *seah* of heave fell into 100 *seah* profane grain and one *seah* was lifted as replacement heave. That replacement is now treated as heave and the remaining 100 *seah* as profane. But if now one of the 100 *seah* of heave was accidentally exchanged for a *seah* of profane grain and it is impossible to identify which grain is profane, all 100 *seah* (99 replacement heave and one profane) are permitted to everybody since the holiness of replacement heave is rabbinical, just as the holiness of growth from heave seeds is rabbinical.

תַּמָּן אָמַר רִבִּי יוֹחָנָן סְאָה תְרוּמָה שֶׁעָלַת מִתּוֹךְ מֵאָה חוּלִין כָּל־שֶׁהֵן מְבַטְּלִין אוֹתָהּ. וְהָכָא לִיקֵּט וְנָפַל לְתוֹכָן חוּלִין כָּל־שֶׁהֵן מוּתָּרִין. כְּמוֹ דְרִבִּי יוֹחָנָן אָמַר

תַּמָּן טוֹחֵן וּמַתִּיר אַף הָכָא כֵן. תַּמָּן מִזֶּה וּמִזֶּה עָלָה בְיָדוֹ. בְּרַם הָכָא כָּל הַטֶּבֶל עָלָה בְיָדוֹ. כְּשֶׁלִּקֵּט מֵאַחַת. אֲבָל אִם לִיקֵּט מִשְּׁתֵּיהֶן מִזּוֹ וּמִזּוֹ עָלָה בְיָדוֹ.

There[77], Rebbi Joḥanan said if a *seah* of heave was lifted from 100 of profane produce, anything will cause it to become insignificant. And here, if he collected and some profane produce fell into it, should it not be permitted[78]? As Rebbi Joḥanan said there[79], he mills and it is permitted, so also here. There, both kinds came into his hands. But here, only *ṭevel* came into his hands if he collected from one [*lagena*]. But if he collected from two, both kinds[80] came into his hands.

77 Halakhah 5:6, Note 77.

78 Even if the seeds do not disappear.

79 The statement is from Mishnah 5:9 that different kinds are considered as one if they are ground together and now are indistinguishable.

80 Growth from profane and heave seeds. In the Tosephta (8:4) it is formulated that the particular stringencies for vegetables whose seeds do not disappear are eliminated once the vegetables are harvested and R. Simeon even permits harvesting for the express purpose of eliminating the stringencies. It is clear that this Tosephta was not known to the authors of the Yerushalmi.

(fol. 44c) **משנה ו**: הַטֶּבֶל גִּידּוּלָיו מוּתָּרִין בְּדָבָר שֶׁזַּרְעוֹ כָלֶה אֲבָל בְּדָבָר שֶׁאֵין זַרְעוֹ כָלֶה גִּידּוּלֵי גִידּוּלִין אֲסוּרִין. אֵי זֶהוּ דָבָר שֶׁאֵין זַרְעוֹ כָלֶה כְּגוֹן הַלּוּף הַשּׁוּם וְהַבְּצָלִים רִבִּי יְהוּדָה אוֹמֵר הַשּׁוּם כִּשְׂעוֹרִים.

Mishnah 6: Growth from *ṭevel* is permitted[81] for anything whose seeds disappear, but if the seeds do not disappear even the growth from the growth is forbidden. What is one whose seeds do not disappear? For example arum, garlic, and onions. Rebbi Jehudah says, garlic is like barley.

81 Usually, grain becomes forbidden food as *ṭevel* (cf. *Peah* Chapter 1, Note 303) after threshing and cleaning until heave and tithes are taken. Before threshing, one may eat the grains from single ears. However, for produce whose seeds do not disappear, the quality of *ṭevel* is never removed and such produce is forbidden even as occasional snack before heave and all tithes are taken. (However, tithes for any produce other than grain, grapes, and olives are rabbinic in character.)

(fol. 44d) **הלכה ז**: עַד הֵיכָן. רִבִּי יַעֲקֹב בַּר אִידִי בְּשֵׁם רִבִּי יוֹחָנָן עַד שָׁלֹשׁ גְּרָנוֹת אֲסוּרוֹת. עַד גּוֹרֶן הָרְבִיעִית אָסוּר וְהָרְבִיעִית מוּתָּר. רִבִּי שְׁמוּאֵל בַּר אֶבוּדַּמָא בְּעָא קוֹמֵי רִבִּי מָנָא בִּתְרוּמָה עַד כַּמָּה. אָמַר לֵיהּ עָשׂוּ גּוֹרֶן הָרְבִיעִית כְּגוֹרֶן הָרִאשׁוֹנָה. מַה גּוֹרֶן הָרִאשׁוֹנָה דָּבָר שֶׁזַּרְעוֹ כָלֶה בִּתְרוּמָה אָסוּר וּבְטֶבֶל מוּתָּר. אַף גּוֹרֶן הָרְבִיעִית בְּדָבָר שֶׁאֵין זַרְעוֹ כָלֶה בִּתְרוּמָה אָסוּר וּבְטֶבֶל מוּתָּר.

Halakhah 7: How far[82]? Rebbi Jacob bar Idi in the name of Rebbi Joḥanan: It is forbidden for three harvests[83]; it is forbidden up to the fourth harvest, but the fourth is permitted. Rebbi Samuel ben Eudaimon asked before Rebbi Mana: How far for heave[84]? He said to him, they made the fourth harvest like the first harvest. Just as the first harvest of growth whose seeds disappear is forbidden for heave and permitted for *ṭevel*, so the fourth harvest of growth whose seeds do not disappear is forbidden for heave[85] and permitted for *ṭevel*.

82 The growth from *ṭevel* whose seeds do not disappear is forbidden. The Mishnah does not spell out the status of the second year's growth.

83 R. Simson does not have this clause; it seems that the sentence is the confluence of two parallel traditions. The second clause does not add anything to the first.

84 Heave planted from bulb vegetables whose first growth retains the status of heave (Mishnah 4).

85 But the fifth harvest would be permitted (R. Simson).

מַה אִית לָךְ. אָמַר רִבִּי יוֹסֵי בֵּי רִבִּי בּוּן כְּגוֹן הַכלובסין.

What do you have[86]? Rebbi Yose ben Rebbi Abun said, e. g., bulb plants[87].

86 What are plants whose seeds do not disappear?

87 The word כלובסין is unexplained. For the translation, I am reading בּוֹלְבָּסִין "bulbs"; cf. *Demay* Chapter 2, Note 42 {but compare Greek κολοβός, όν "stunted, undersized" (E. G.)}.

רִבִּי אַבָּהוּ בְּשֵׁם רִבִּי יוֹסֵי בֶּן חֲנִינָה הַשּׁוּם עַד כִּשְׂעוֹרִין לְדָבָר שֶׁזַּרְעוֹ כָלֶה. מִכָּן וְהֵילַךְ לְדָבָר שֶׁאֵין זַרְעוֹ כָלֶה. רִבִּי יוֹסֵי בֵּי רִבִּי בּוּן בְּשֵׁם רִבִּי יוֹסֵי בֶּן חֲנִינָה הַשּׁוּם עַד כִּשְׂעוֹרִים לְכָל־דָּבָר.

Rebbi Abbahu in the name of Rebbi Yose ben Ḥanina: Garlic up to the size of a barley corn is a plant whose seeds disappear[88]. Larger than that, it is a plant whose seeds do not disappear. Rebbi Yose ben Rebbi Abun in the name of Rebbi Yose ben Ḥanina: Garlic is like barley in every respect.

88 The dispute is about the statement of R. Jehudah in the Mishnah that garlic is like barley for these rules. That the statement of R. Jehudah is discussed in practical terms signifies for Rashi (*Pesaḥim* 34a) that practice follows him; this is denied by Maimonides.

(fol. 44c) **משנה ז**: הַמְנַכֵּשׁ עִם הַנָּכְרִי בְּחִסִּיּוֹת אַף עַל פִּי שֶׁפֵּירוֹתָיו טֶבֶל אוֹכֵל מֵהֶן עֲרַאי. שְׁתִלֵי תְרוּמָה שֶׁנִּיטְמְאוּ שְׁתָלָן טָהֲרוּ מִלְּטַמֵּא וַאֲסוּרִין מִלּוֹכַל עַד שֶׁיָּגוֹם אֶת הָאוֹכֶל. רִבִּי יְהוּדָה אוֹמֵר עַד שֶׁיָּגוֹם וְיִשְׁנֶה.

Mishnah 7: He who weeds with a Non-Jew among bulb plants[89], even though his vegetables are *ṭevel* one may eat a snack from them[90].

Saplings of heave that became impure[91] if planted become pure not to transmit impurity[92] but they remain forbidden to be eaten until he removes what is edible[93]. Rebbi Jehudah says, until he removes a second time.

89 Defined by the Tosephta (9:3) as arum, garlic, onions, and leeks; cf. *Kilaim* Chapter 2, Note 126.

90 A snack can be eaten from anything that grows until it is harvested in bulk and ready for storage. This Tanna holds that a Gentile's real estate in the Holy Land is still subject to the obligations of heave and tithes before Jews may eat from its yield (cf. *Peah* Chapter 4, Notes 129-131).

91 They are forbidden as food and should have been burned.

92 Nothing in the ground can be impure. But nevertheless impure heave is forbidden as food and, since the growth from heave is heave, this prohibition is transmitted to the new growth. This is the interpretation of Maimonides (*Terumot* 11:23). R. Abraham ben David holds that once the impurity has been removed, the heave becomes food for Cohanim. His opinion is well supported in the Babli (*Menaḥot* 70a) which quotes as a Mishnah the statement that nothing connected to the ground can be heave. That statement is not in the Mishnah texts and is incompatible with the Yerushalmi here (Notes 99 ff.).

For the anonymous Tanna, the second growth is permitted, for R. Jehudah the third growth.

93 And burns it.

(fol. 44d) **הלכה ח**: רַב חִייָא בַּר אַשִׁי בְּשֵׁם רִבִּי אַבָּהוּ בְּשֵׁם רִבִּי יוֹחָנָן דְּרִבִּי שִׁמְעוֹן הִיא. אִין כְּרִבִּי שִׁמְעוֹן לָמָּה לִי עֲרַאי אֲפִילוּ קֶבַע. אֶלָּא בְגִין דְּאָמַר רִבִּי יִרְמְיָה רִבִּי חִיָּיה בְּשֵׁם רִבִּי יוֹחָנָן מוֹדֶה רִבִּי שִׁמְעוֹן שֶׁהוּא מַפְרִישׁ מַעַשְׂרוֹתָיו מֵהֲלָכָה לְפוּם כֵּן צָרְכִינָן מֵימַר דְּרִבִּי שִׁמְעוֹן הִיא.

Halakhah 8: Rav Ḥiyya bar Ashi in the name of Rebbi Abbahu in the name of Rebbi Joḥanan: This follows Rebbi Simeon[94]. If it follows Rebbi Joḥanan, even a full meal! But since Rebbi Jeremiah, Rebbi Ḥiyya said in the name of Rebbi Joḥanan[95]: Rebbi Simeon agrees that nevertheless he must separate tithes as a matter of practice; therefore we have to say that this follows Rebbi Simeon[96].

94 Who with R. Jehudah holds that Gentiles' possessions in the Land are free from obligations of heave and tithes. Since R. Jehudah and R. Simeon are greater authorities than R. Meïr who holds that Gentiles' possessions are subject to heave and tithes, it is difficult to understand the Mishnah following our rules.

95 *Demay* Chapter 3, Note 132.

96 The rule given by the Mishnah is rabbinical; for R. Meïr it would be biblical.

תַּנֵּי הַמְנַכֵּשׁ עִם הַכּוּתִי מוּתָּר בִּדְמַאי. הָא בְוַדַּאי לֹא. לָמָּה. שֶׁהַדְּמַאי בָטֵל בִּמְחוּבָּר לְקַרְקַע וְאֵין גִּידּוּלֵי אִיסּוּר מַעֲלִין אוֹתוֹ.

It was stated: *Demay* is permitted to him who weeds with a Samaritan[97]. Therefore, not if it is certain! Why? For *demay* disappears when it is in the ground but the growth of forbidden produce[98] cannot lift it.

97 On the Samaritan's property. If he only suspects the Samaritan not to have tithed the plants used to produce the seeds, he may eat snacks from the fruits but not if he is sure that the Samaritan used untithed fruit. One has to wonder about the entire paragraph since Samaritans are Sadducees following only the written law. For them, the only produce subject to heave and tithes are grains, grapes, and olives. Therefore, Samaritan onions, etc., are certainly not tithed. This is the position of the Tosephta (8:7) which treats all Samaritan bulb plants as growths from *ṭevel* except after a Sabbatical year.

98 If the seeds were certain *ṭevel*, the new growth goes under the rules of Mishnah 6.

רִבִּי אַבָּהוּ בְשֵׁם רִבִּי יוֹחָנָן שִׁיתְלֵי תְרוּמָה שֶׁנִּטְמֵאת שְׁתָלָן וְעוֹשֶׂה אוֹתָן תְּרוּמָה. וְאִם הָיוּ תְרוּמָה מֵעִיקָּרָן כְּבָר נִדְחוּ. רִבִּי אַבָּהוּ בְשֵׁם רִבִּי יוֹחָנָן מַיִם שֶׁנִּיטְמְאוּ מַשִּׁיקָן וְעוֹשֶׂה אוֹתָן מֵי חַג וְאִם הָיוּ מֵי חַג מֵעִיקָּרָן כְּבָר נִדְחוּ. רִבִּי אַבָּהוּ בְשֵׁם

רִבִּי יוֹחָנָן תְּאֵינִים וַעֲנָבִים שֶׁנִּיטְמְאוּ סוֹחֲטָן וְעוֹשֶׂה אוֹתָן תְּרוּמָה. וְאִם הָיוּ תְּרוּמָה מֵעִיקָּרָן כְּבַר נִדְחוּ. רִבִּי זְעִירָא רִבִּי יַסָּא בְשֵׁם רִבִּי לָעְזָר סוֹחֲטָן עַד פָּחוֹת מִכְּזֵיתִים וְיֵינוֹ כָּשֵׁר אֲפִילוּ לִנְסָכִים. אָמְרִין רִבִּי שִׁמְעוֹן בֶּן לָקִישׁ פְּלִיג. מַה בֵּין לְקוּלָּה בֵּין לְחוּמְרָא. אִין תֵּימַר לְקוּלָּה נִיחָא. אִין תֵּימַר לְחוּמְרָא הָא תַנִּינָן עַד שֶׁיְּגוֹם אֶת הָאוֹכְלִים.

Rebbi Abbahu in the name of Rebbi Joḥanan: Saplings of heave that had become impure he may plant and make them heave but if they were heave from before they already were pushed aside[99]. Rebbi Abbahu in the name of Rebbi Joḥanan: Water that became impure is made to touch and may be used as water for Tabernacles but if it was water for Tabernacles from before it already is pushed aside[100]. Rebbi Abbahu in the name of Rebbi Joḥanan: Figs and grapes that had become impure one may squeeze and make them heave but if they were heave from before they already were pushed aside[101]. Rebbi Zeïra, Rebbi Assi, in the name of Rebbi Eleazar, one squeezes less than the volume of olives[102] and his wine is good even for libations. They said, Rebbi Simeon ben Laqish disagrees. Both about leniency and restriction? If you say about leniency, this is understandable[103]. If you say about restriction[104], did we not state: "Until he removes what is edible?"

99 If they were impure and he planted them to free them from impurity, he may then declare the growth to be heave and it is permitted for Cohanim. But if it was impure heave before planting, the new growth cannot be eaten by anybody (Note 92).

100 Flowing water or standing water of at least 40 *seah* removes impurity (Chapter 4, Note 112). Impure water in a vessel can be purified by immersing the vessel in a *miqweh* so that the surface of the water in the vessel barely touches ("kisses") the water of the *miqweh*. Water of Tabernacles is the water used as a libation on the altar (*Ševi'it* Chapter 1, Notes 51-52). Before being used, it has to be dedicated in a Temple vessel.

The Babli (*Pesaḥim* 34b) concludes

from the parallel treatment of heave and libations that dedication in or for the Temple is as strong and permanent a designation as heave.

101 Grape juice is considered a new food; if there is less than the volume of a chicken egg, the fluid cannot accept impurity. But if the grapes were impure heave, they are not food and no food can come from them. Grape juice squeezed from these grapes is not a drink, pure or impure.

102 An indefinite plural means 2, as smallest integer >1 [cf. H. Guggenheimer, *Seder Olam* (Northvale NJ 1998), p. 6]. Since a chicken egg is not smaller than the convex hull of two olives touching one another (*Tosaphot Yešenim Yoma* 80a), squeezing not more than the volume of two olives will keep the volume safely below the minimal volume that might lead to impurity. The Babli (*Pesaḥim* 34b) does not define what is "less than the volume of a chicken egg."

103 R. Simeon ben Laqish does not agree that juice squeezed from a fruit becomes a new kind of food; it is the fluid form of the previous fruit and remains impure even if squeezed in amounts less than a chicken egg.

104 R. Simeon ben Laqish cannot deny that impure heave remains forbidden as food for everybody; even if he would accept the trick of squeezing small quantities he could not accept that this would make impure heave drinkable.

רִבִּי אַבָּהוּ בְשֵׁם רִבִּי יוֹחָנָן כֵּינִי מַתְנִיתָא עַד שֶׁיְּגוֹם בֶּעָלִים וְיִשְׁנֶה.

Rebbi Abbahu in the name of Rebbi Joḥanan: so is the Mishnah, "until he removes the leaves a second time.[105]"

105 R. Jehudah requires only that the leaves (and flowers) be removed twice before the new fruit is allowed to grow; after that the growth is permitted to Cohanim (Maimonides *Terumot* 11:24). {This כיני מתניתא is not discussed by J. N. Epstein.}

בצל פרק עשירי

(fol. 46d) **משנה א**: בָּצָל שֶׁנְּתָנוֹ בְּתוֹךְ עֲדָשִׁים אִם שָׁלֵם מוּתָּר. אִם חִיתְּכוֹ בְּנוֹתֵן טַעַם. וּשְׁאָר כָּל־הַתַּבְשִׁיל בֵּין שָׁלֵם בֵּין מְחוּתָּךְ בְּנוֹתֵן טַעַם. רִבִּי יְהוּדָה מַתִּיר בְּצַחֲנָה שֶׁאֵינוֹ אֶלָּא לִיטּוֹל אֶת הַזּוּהֲמָה.

Mishnah 1: An onion which one added to lentils, if whole it is permitted, if cut up it depends on transferring taste[1]. Any other cooked food, whether whole or cut up, depends on transferring taste. Rebbi Jehudah permits in anchovies[2] where it only serves to remove pollutants.

1 Profane onion in cooked but cold heave lentils; if the heave changes the taste of the profane food everything has to be eaten by a Cohen under the rules of heave. Otherwise, the profane remains profane and permitted to everybody.

2 In translation and interpretation, one has the choice between biblical "stinking dish" (*Joel* 2:20) or mishnaic "small salted fish in brine" (Mishnah *Nedarim* 5:5), Arabic צחן. Maimonides chooses the first alternative, R. Simson the second. One has to wonder that the medical doctor Maimonides would think of saving spoiled food.

If an entire onion of heave is put into the brine to absorb impurities, the anchovies remain profane according to R. Jehudah.

(fol. 47a) **הלכה א**: בָּצָל שֶׁנְּתָנוֹ בְּתוֹךְ עֲדָשִׁים כו׳. רִבִּי חִזְקִיָּה רַב אָחָא בְשֵׁם רִבִּי בָּא בַּר מָמָל מַתְנִיתִין בְּשֶׁהוֹצִיאוּ עֲדָשִׁים מֵימֵיהֶן שֶׁעֲדָשִׁים צוֹפְדוֹת אוֹתוֹ שֶׁלֹּא יִבְלַע. וּכְמָה דְתֵימַר עֲדָשִׁים צוֹפְדוֹת אוֹתוֹ שֶׁלֹּא יִבְלַע. וְדִכְוָותָהּ עֲדָשִׁין צוֹפְדוֹת אוֹתוֹ שֶׁלֹּא יִתֵּן.

"An onion which one added to lentils," etc. Rebbi Ḥizqiah, Rav Aḥa in the name of Rebbi Abba bar Mamal[3] said, our Mishnah [in case] after the lentils lost their sap; [then] the lentils shrink it so it will not absorb [any taste]. (As you say, lentils shrink it so it will not absorb.) Similarly, lentils shrink it so it will not give.

3 This paragraph is a shortened version of the discussion in Chapter 9, Halakhah 4, Notes 41-46. The sentence in parentheses is superfluous. Its text follows the Rome ms. Venice and Leyden read: דאמר אמר.

מַתְנִיתִין בְּבָצָל שֶׁל חוּלִין שֶׁנְּתָנוֹ לְתוֹךְ עֲדָשִׁין שֶׁל תְּרוּמָה. אֲבָל בְּבָצָל שֶׁל תְּרוּמָה שֶׁנְּתָנוֹ לְתוֹךְ עֲדָשִׁין שֶׁל חוּלִין לֹא בְדָא. בְּיָבֵשׁ אֲבָל בְּלַח אָסוּר. בְּבָצָל אֲבָל בְּקֶפַלּוֹטוֹת בֵּין לַח בֵּין יָבֵשׁ בֵּין שָׁלֵם בֵּין מְחוּתָּךְ אָסוּר.

The Mishnah speaks about a profane onion which he put into heave lentils; but not the case of a heave onion put into profane lentils[4]. If it is dry, but moist is forbidden. An onion, but leeks are forbidden moist or dry, entire or cut up.

4 In that case, the lentils have to be eaten by a Cohen in purity. In all these discussions, "forbidden" means forbidden to the layman and the impure.

הֶעֱבִיר פְּטוּמָתוֹ כִמְחוּתָּךְ הוּא. הָיוּ שְׁנַיִם שְׁלֹשָׁה קְטַנִּים כִּמְחוּתָּכִין הֵן. הָדָא דְתֵימַר בְּשֶׁאֵין קְלִיפָּתוֹ הַחִיצוֹנָה כְּדֵי לִיתֵּן טַעַם. אֲבָל אִם יֵשׁ בִּקְלִיפָּתוֹ הַחִיצוֹנָה כְּדֵי לִיתֵּן טַעַם אָסוּר.

If he removed the tip[5] it is as if cut up. If there were two or three small ones, they are as if cut up. Only if the outer shell does not transmit taste[6]. But if the outer shell transmits taste, it is forbidden.

5 Of the onion.

6 The onion mentioned in the Mishnah is dry, with an inert brown outer skin. Green onions are like leeks.

תַּמָּן תַּנִּינָן דָּגִים שֶׁנִּתְבַּשְּׁלוּ עִם הַקֶּפַלּוֹטוֹת שֶׁל מַעֲשֵׂר שֵׁנִי וְהִשְׁבִּיחוּ הַשֶּׁבַח לְפִי חֶשְׁבּוֹן. אָמַר רִבִּי הוֹשַׁעְיָה מַתְנִיתִין דְּלֹא כְרִבִּי יוּדָה דְּתַנִּינָן רִבִּי יוּדָה מַתִּיר בְּצַחֲנָה שֶׁאֵינוֹ אֶלָּא לִיטּוֹל אֶת הַזּוֹהֲמָה.

There[7], we have stated: "If fish improved in value when cooked with leeks of second tithe, the increase is proportional[8]." Rebbi Hoshaia said, that Mishnah does not follow Rebbi Jehudah, since we have stated: "Rebbi Jehudah permits in anchovies where it only serves to remove pollutants[9]."

7 Mishnah *Ma'aser Šeni* 2:1.

8 If the leeks were worth a and the fish b before cooking but now the whole is worth $c > a + b$, then some of the proceeds of the dish, $ac/(a+b)$, has to be used to buy food to be consumed according to the rules of second tithe.

9 Even though cleaned anchovies in brine fetch more on the market than uncleaned ones.

רַבָּנִין דְּקַיְסָרִין בְּעָיָן. וְהָדָא דְאָמַר רִבִּי אַבָּהוּ בְשֵׁם רִבִּי יוֹחָנָן כָּל־הָאִיסּוּרִין מְשַׁעֲרִין אוֹתָן כִּילּוּ בָּצָל כִּילּוּ קֶפַלּוֹט דְּלֹא כְרִבִּי יוּדָה. מוֹדֵי רִבִּי יוּדָה בְּבָצָל שֶׁל הֶקְדֵּשׁ וּמוֹדֵי רִבִּי יוּדָה בְּבָצָל שֶׁל עֲבוֹדָה זָרָה.

The rabbis of Caesarea asked: The saying of Rebbi Abbahu in the name of Rebbi Joḥanan[10], that all forbidden [food] is estimated as if it were onion, as if it were leeks[11], does this contradict Rebbi Jehudah[12]? Rebbi Jehudah will agree regarding an onion of the Temple or an onion of idol worship.

10 This Yerushalmi standard is quoted in *Ma'aser Šeni* 2:1 (fol. 53b), *Orlah* 1:4 (fol. 61a), 2:6 (fol. 62b), *Nazir* 6:1 (fol. 54d), 6:10 (fol. 55b). It is quoted in Babli *Ḥulin* 97b where the more lenient standard of 1 part forbidden in 61 permitted is established.

11 Forbidden food that fell into permitted is permitted if the taste of the forbidden food could not be tasted in the permitted, assuming the forbidden items were onion or leeks.

12 Since R. Jehudah allows the use of heave onion to improve non-heave fish.

(fol. 46d) **משנה ב**: תַּפּוּחַ שֶׁרִיסְקוֹ וּנְתָנוֹ לְתוֹךְ עִיסָּה וְחִימִיצָהּ הֲרֵי זוֹ אֲסוּרָה. שְׂעוֹרִים שֶׁנָּפְלוּ לְתוֹךְ הַבּוֹר שֶׁל מַיִם אַף עַל פִּי שֶׁהִבְאִישׁוּ מֵימָיו מוּתָּרִין.

Mishnah 2: If a mashed apple[13] is added to dough and it soured, [the dough] is forbidden[4]. But if barley grains fell into a cistern of water, even though they made it stink, [the water] is permitted[14].

13 The heave apple's influence makes the entire profane dough change nature; even if the amount of apple is negligible, its action is not and it cannot be disregarded.

14 Since anything that destroys the taste does not make forbidden.

(fol. 47a) **הלכה ב**: תַּפּוּחַ שֶׁרִיסְקוֹ וּנְתָנוֹ לְתוֹךְ עִיסָּה וְחִימִיצָהּ הֲרֵי זוֹ אֲסוּרָה. תַּנֵּי וְרִבִּי יוֹסֵי מַתִּיר. רִבִּי אָחָא רִבִּי אַבָּהוּ בְּשֵׁם רִבִּי יוֹסֵי בֶּן חֲנִינָה מַה פְּלִיגִין בִּמְחַמֵּץ בְּמֵימָיו אֲבָל בִּמְחַמֵּץ בְּגוּפוֹ מוּתָּר. כְּמָה דְרִבִּי יוֹסֵי אָמַר תַּמָּן אֵין חִימּוּצוֹ חִימּוּץ בָּרוּר. כֵּן הוּא אָמַר הָכָא אֵין תַּבְשִׁילוֹ תַּבְשִׁיל בָּרוּר.

Halakhah 2: [15]"If a mashed apple is added to dough which soured, [the dough] is forbidden" It was stated[16]: Rebbi Yose permits it. Rebbi Aḥa, Rebbi Abbahu in the name of Rebbi Yose ben Ḥanina: They disagree when it becomes sour from the juice [of the apple]. But if it becomes sour from its solid substance it is permitted[17]. Just as Rebbi Yose says there[18], its souring is not clearly souring, so he says here[19], its cooking is not clearly cooking.

15 The main place of the paragraph is in *Šabbat* 3, fol. 5d. The text is also in *Ḥallah* 1:1 (fol. 57a), *Pesaḥim* 2:4 (fol. 29b).

16 In Tosephta 8:9, the language is: "Rebbi Yose says, what is induced by [the apple] is not souring." This is the position of the Babli in *Pesaḥim* 36a/b. According to the Yerushalmi it is not clear whether what is induced by fruit juice falls under the legal category of "to turn sour;" this is the position of the Babli in *Menaḥot* 54a. In any case, the quote here cannot be from the Tosephta.

17 Even the anonymous Sages

admit that dry mixing of a mashed apple with flour will not induce souring.

18 Here in *Terumot*. R. Yose will not agree that what happens if a dough is kneaded with pure apple juice is souring; therefore he holds that mixing dough with apple juice can have no legal consequences.

19 Mishnah *Šabbat* 3:3: "One may not put an egg next to the samowar [that it should become a soft-boiled egg on the Sabbath] and one may not break it on [hot, exposed to the sun] towels [to make a fried egg on the Sabbath], but Rebbi Yose permits it."

כָּל־נוֹתְנֵי טַעַם בֵּין לִשְׁבָח בֵּין לִפְגָּם אָסוּר דִּבְרֵי רִבִּי מֵאִיר. רִבִּי שִׁמְעוֹן אוֹמֵר לִשְׁבָח אָסוּר לִפְגָּם מוּתָּר. אָמַר רִבִּי שִׁמְעוֹן בֶּן לָקִישׁ מַה פְלִיגִין בְּשֶׁהִשְׁבִּיחַ וְאַחַר כָּךְ פָּגַם. אֲבָל אִם פָּגַם וְאַחַר כָּךְ הִשְׁבִּיחַ אַף רִבִּי מֵאִיר מוֹדֶה. רִבִּי יוֹחָנָן אָמַר לֹא שַׁנְיָיא הִיא פָּגַם הִיא הִשְׁבִּיחַ. הִיא הִשְׁבִּיחַ הִיא פָּגַם הִיא מַחְלוֹקֶת. תַּמָּן תַּנִּינָן שְׂעוֹרִים שֶׁנָּפְלוּ לְתוֹךְ בּוֹר שֶׁל מַיִם אַף עַל פִּי שֶׁהִבְאִישׁוּ מֵימָיו מֵימָיו מוּתָּרִין. הָדָא מַתְנִיתִין מַה הִיא. רִבִּי יוֹחָנָן אָמַר בְּמַחְלוֹקֶת. רִבִּי שִׁמְעוֹן בֶּן לָקִישׁ אָמַר דִּבְרֵי הַכֹּל. רִבִּי יוֹסֵי בֵּי רִבִּי בּוּן אָמַר אִילֵּין שְׁמוּעָתָא הָכָא רִבִּי יוֹחָנָן אָמַר בְּמַחְלוֹקֶת. רִבִּי שִׁמְעוֹן בֶּן לָקִישׁ אָמַר דִּבְרֵי הַכֹּל.

"[20]Everything that can be smelled is forbidden[21], whether it improves or spoils, the words of Rebbi Meïr. Rebbi Simeon says, if it improves it is forbidden, if it spoils it is permitted." Rebbi Simeon ben Laqish[22] said, in what do they disagree? If it first improved but then spoiled. But if it spoiled and later improved, even Rebbi Meïr will agree. Rebbi Joḥanan said, there is no difference whether it spoiled and improved or improved and spoiled, it is a disagreement. There[23], we have stated: "If barley grains fell into a cistern of water, even though they made it stink, the water is permitted." What is the status of that Mishnah? Rebbi Joḥanan said it is a disagreement; Rebbi Simeon ben Laqish said it is the opinion of everybody. Rebbi Yose ben Rebbi Abun said this tradition here[24]: Rebbi Joḥanan said it is a disagreement; Rebbi Simeon ben Laqish said it is the opinion of everybody.

20 Tosephta 8:9, in slightly different wording. The main source of this paragraph is *Orlah* 2:5 (fol. 62a); a slightly shortened version is in *Avodah Zarah* 5:3 (fol. 44d); Babli *Avodah Zarah* 67b/68a.

21 If forbidden food is mixed with permitted food, the mixture is forbidden as long as the forbidden substance changes the taste of the food. According to R. Simeon, whose opinion is the majority opinion in the Babli, this holds only if the admixture does not spoil the taste of the permitted food.

22 In the Babli, that author is Ulla (Rebbi La).

23 Here, in *Terumot*.

24 He refers to the Mishnah, not the Tosephta.

(fol. 46d) **משנה ג**: הָרוֹדֶה פַּת חַמָּה וּנְתָנָהּ עַל פִּי חָבִית שֶׁל יַיִן שֶׁל תְּרוּמָה רִבִּי מֵאִיר אוֹסֵר וְרִבִּי יְהוּדָה מַתִּיר. רִבִּי יוֹסֵי מַתִּיר בְּשֶׁל חִטִּים וְאוֹסֵר בְּשֶׁל שְׂעוֹרִים מִפְּנֵי שֶׁהַשְּׂעוֹרִים שׁוֹאֲבוֹת.

Mishnah 3: If somebody takes hot pitta bread out of the oven and deposits it on the mouth of an amphora of heave wine[25], Rebbi Meïr forbids[26] and Rebbi Jehudah permits. Rebbi Yose permits in the case of wheat and forbids in the case of barley because barley absorbs[27].

25 The hot flat bread absorbs the taste of the wine.

26 For the lay person and the impure.

27 It absorbs smells and particles.

(fol. 47a) **הלכה ג**: אָמַר רִבִּי זְעִירָא בְּעוֹן קוֹמֵי רִבִּי יַנַּאי נְתָנוֹ עַל פִּי מְגוּפַּת חָבִית מַהוּ. אָמַר לוֹן יַגִּיד עָלָיו רֵיעוֹ. מַהוּ יַגִּיד עָלָיו רֵיעוֹ. אָמַר רִבִּי יוֹסֵי כְּהָדָא דְתַנִּינָן תַּמָּן חָבִית מְלֵיאָה פֵירוֹת וּנְתוּנָה לְתוֹךְ הַמַּשְׁקִין אוֹ שֶׁמְּלֵיאָה מַשְׁקִין וּנְתוּנָה לְתוֹךְ הַפֵּירוֹת. כְּמַה דְאַתְּ אָמַר תַּמָּן וְהוּא שֶׁיְּהֵא הַמַּשְׁקִין נוֹגְעִין בְּחָבִיּוֹת. וְהָכָא וְהוּא שֶׁתְּהֵא כִכָּר נוֹגַעַת בִּמְגוּפָה. אָמַר רִבִּי מָנָא וּמִינָהּ כְּמַה

דְתֵימָא וְהוּא שֶׁיְּהוּ מַשְׁקִין נוֹגְעִין בְּחָבִיּוֹת עַצְמָהּ. וְאַף הָכָא וְהוּא שֶׁתְּהֵא כִכָּר נוֹגַעַת בִּמְגוּפָּה עַצְמָהּ. מִילְתֵיהּ אָמַר אֲפִילוּ בְצוֹנֶנֶת. אָמַר רִבִּי בָא בְּצוֹנֶנֶת הֲוָה עוּבְדָא. וְהָא תַנִּינָן חַמָּה. אָמַר רַב חִסְדָּא שֶׁלֹּא תֹאמַר הוֹאִיל וְהַהֶבֶל כּוֹבֵשׁ יְהֵא מוּתָּר.

Halakhah 3: Rebbi Zeïra said, they asked before Rebbi Yannai: What [are the rules] if he put it on the plug[28] of the amphora? He said to them (*Job* 36:33): "Its neighbor[29] will inform about it." What means, "its neighbor will inform about it"? Rebbi Yose said, that which we have stated there[30]: "An amphora full of fruits added to fluids, or one full of fluids added to fruits." As you say there, only if the fluids touch the amphora; so here only if the loaf touches the plug. Rebbi Mana said, from this it follows as you say there, only if the fluids touch the amphora itself; so here only if the loaf touches the plug itself[31]. His opinion implies, even [if the pitta] is cold. Rebbi Abba said, the problem was about a cold one[32]. But did we not state "hot"? Rav Ḥisda said, that one should not say since the vapor absorbs it should be permitted.

28 A clay plug that closes the open top of the amphora and forms a barrier for the smell.

29 In the verse, ריע is derived from רוע "to sound the trumpet."

30 Mishnah *Makhširin* 3:2-3: "2. An amphora full of fruits added to fluids, or one full of fluids added to fruits; if they absorbed, all those which absorbed are prepared. They spoke about water, wine, and vinegar, but the rest of the fluids are pure. R. Neḥemiah declares legumes pure because legumes do not absorb. 3. If somebody takes hot pitta bread out of the oven and deposits it on the mouth of an amphora of wine, Rebbi Meïr declares it impure but Rebbi Jehudah declares it pure. Rebbi Yose declares it pure in the case of wheat and impure in the case of barley because barley absorbs."

For preparation of solid food for impurity, cf. *Demay*, Chapter 2, Note 141. For the impurity of fluids, *Demay*, Chapter 2, Notes 136-137.

The amphora contains fruit not prepared for impurity. Since the walls of a clay amphora are porous, the fruits inside (or outside) may get moist. Since human action puts the amphora into the fluid, the moisture prepares for impurity. This applies only to water and wine; the rest of the impure fluids (olive oil, date honey, and human body fluids) are viscous and do not penetrate a clay wall. In Mishnah 3, the wine is impure. Bread, being made with water, is always prepared for impurity. R. Meïr holds that the bread will receive the taste of the wine by absorbing particles evaporated from the wine. Since he holds that all smells transfer prohibitions and impurity, the bread must be impure.

31 Since the plug sits on the narrowest part of the neck of the amphora, in most cases a pitta deposited on top of the rim will not touch the plug. As noted in the next sentence, this argument is valid only if the pitta is almost cold since a hot pitta will sink down and always touch the plug.

32 The original question directed to R. Yannai.

כְּמָה רִבִּי שִׁמְעוֹן בֶּן לָקִישׁ מַיִם עוֹשִׂין פֵּירוֹת וּמַשְׁקִין אֵין עוֹשִׂין פֵּירוֹת דְּלֹא כְרִבִּי יוּדָה. אֶלָּא רִבִּי שִׁמְעוֹן בֶּן לָקִישׁ אָמַר מַיִם עוֹשִׂין פֵּירוֹת וַחֲסֵירִין וּמַשְׁקִין עוֹשִׂין פֵּירוֹת וְאֵינָן חֲסֵירִין. רִבִּי יְהוּדָה אוֹמֵר אֵין מַשְׁקִין עוֹשִׂין פֵּירוֹת כָּל־עִיקָּר.

Following Rebbi Simeon ben Laqish, water acts on fruits, [other] fluids do not act on fruits, against Rebbi Jehudah[33]! But Rebbi Simeon ben Laqish says, water acts on fruits and loses fluid volume, [other] fluids act on fruits and do not lose volume[34]. Rebbi Jehudah says, [other] fluids do not act on fruits at all[35].

33 This refers to the part of Mishnah *Makhširin* 3:2 not quoted in our text, that only water and wine (table wine or vinegar) can influence the status of fruits through a clay wall. Everybody agrees that viscous fluids cannot act through the clay wall. The only problem is wine, which in the anonymous Mishnah 2 is equated with water but in Mishnah 3, R. Jehudah denies that it can act on bread. "Other fluids" here means the fluids excluded in Mishnah 2 plus wine. The statement of R. Simeon ben Laqish seems to point

to an inconsistency in the position of R. Jehudah.

34 Since for R. Meïr it is enough that the fruits absorb some of the smell of the wine even if they do not become moistened.

35 Mishnah 2 is R. Meïr's alone; R. Jehudah would classify wine as "other fluid." Mishnah 2 is anonymous; therefore practice follows R. Meïr in this instance.

וּמַה דְאָמַר רִבִּי יוֹחָנָן כְּשֶׁהָיִינוּ הוֹלְכִין אֶצֶל רִבִּי הוֹשַׁעְיָה רַבָּה לְקַיְסָרִין לִלְמוֹד תּוֹרָה הָיוּ נוֹתְנִין חֲמִטָתֵינוּ עַל גַּבֵּי קִבּוֹטִין שֶׁל מוּרְיֵיס וְהָיוּ טוֹעֲמִין בָּהּ טַעַם מוּרְיֵיס דְּלָא כְרִבִּי יוּדָה. מַהֲלִימִין הָיוּ. וְאֵין אָסוּר מִשּׁוּם גֶּזֶל בַּעַל הַבַּיִת. נוֹטְלִין הָיוּ רְשׁוּתוֹ שֶׁל בַּעַל הַבַּיִת.

And what Rebbi Joḥanan said, when we went to Caesarea to study Torah with the Great Rebbi Hoshaia, we put our flat-cake on boxes[36] of fish sauce and we tasted there the taste of fish sauce. Is this against Rebbi Jehudah[37]? They put it into the brine[38]. Is that not forbidden because they rob the owner? They had obtained the owner's permission.

36 Greek κιβώτιον "box, chest". For *muries*, cf. *Demay* p. 384.

37 Then R. Joḥanan would agree with R. Simeon ben Laqish that Mishnah *Makhširin* 3:2 determines practice following R. Meïr, against our rules that R. Jehudah is the greater authority than R. Meïr.

38 Greek ἁλμεύω "to put into brine".

חִיטִּין מִלְּמַטָּן וּשְׂעוֹרִין מִלְּמַעְלָן כְּשֵׁם שֶׁאֵין חִיטִּין שׁוֹאֲבוֹת כָּךְ אֵין הַשְּׂעוֹרִין שׁוֹאֲבוֹת. שְׂעוֹרִין מִלְּמַטָּן וְחִיטִּים מִלְּמַעְלָן כְּשֵׁם שֶׁהַשְּׂעוֹרִין שׁוֹאֲבוֹת כָּךְ הַחִיטִּין שׁוֹאֲבוֹת.

Wheat below and barley above[39]; just as wheat does not absorb so the barley will not absorb. Barley below and wheat above, just as barley absorbs so wheat will absorb.

39 This discusses the statement of R. Yose in the Mishnah whom practice has to follow not only because he is the highest authority but also because he gives a reasoned decision partially following each of the opponents in the matter. One deals with a two-layer dough made from two different grains.

(fol. 46d) **משנה ד**: תַּנּוּר שֶׁהִסִּיקוֹ בְּכָמוֹן שֶׁל תְּרוּמָה וְאָפָה בוֹ אֶת הַפַּת הַפַּת מוּתָּר שֶׁאֵין טַעַם כָּמוֹן אֶלָּא רֵיחַ כָּמוֹן.

Mishnah 4: If an oven was heated with heave cumin and one baked bread in it, the bread is permitted since it absorbs not the taste of cumin but the smell[40] of cumin.

40 In contrast to taste, smell is considered immaterial.

(fol. 47a) **הלכה ד**: מַהוּ לִצְלוֹת שְׁנֵי שְׁפוּדִין אֶחָד שֶׁל בָּשָׂר שְׁחוּטָה וְאֶחָד שֶׁל בָּשָׂר (fol. 47b) נְבֵילָה בְּתַנּוּר אֶחָד. רַב יִרְמְיָה אָמַר בְּשֵׁם רַב אָסוּר. וּשְׁמוּאֵל אָמַר בְּשֵׁם לֵוִי מוּתָּר. פְּלִיגָא מַתְנִיתִין עַל רַב. אֵין צוֹלִין שְׁנֵי פְסָחִים בְּתַנּוּר אֶחָד מִפְּנֵי הַתַּעֲרוֹבוֹת. לֹא אָמְרוּ אֶלָּא מִפְּנֵי הַתַּעֲרוֹבוֹת. הָא שֶׁלֹּא מִפְּנֵי הַתַּעֲרוֹבוֹת לֹא.

Halakhah 4: May one roast two spits together in one oven[41], one of kosher meat and one of carcass meat[42]? Rav Jeremiah said in the name of Rav, it is forbidden. Samuel said in the name of Levi, it is permitted. A *baraita*[43] disagrees with Rav: "One may not roast two Passover sacrifices together in one oven because they could be mixed up[44]." They said only, because they could be mixed up; therefore, not if they could not be mixed up[45].

41 This oven has the form of a conical frustrum and is open at the top; the hot air and the particles of meat it might carry escape with the draft through the open top. It is clear that in an enclosed oven one may not cook kosher and nonkosher food together.

42 Meat from an animal not killed in a ritually acceptable way.

43 Tosephta *Pisḥa* 5:11.

44 The Passover sacrifice must be eaten by its subscribers. A person who was not part of the party at the time of slaughter is prohibited from eating of the sacrifice. The Tosephta notes that roasting the two sacrifices together is forbidden only because they should not accidentally be switched but not because particles of one could be carried by the hot air onto the other sacrifice.

The Passover sacrifice has to be "roasted over the fire," *Ex.* 12:8,9. It is permitted to roast the sacrifice in an oven because the oven serves only to intensify the fire. It is forbidden to roast the sacrifice in a closed oven since then it also would be roasted by the heat stored in the walls.

45 The parallel is in Babli *Pesaḥim* 96a/b. In both Talmudim, practice follows Levi.

מֵי צִתְרִי רַב אָמַר אָסוּר וּשְׁמוּאֵל אָמַר מוּתָּר. אַייְכוֹל שְׁמוּאֵל לְרַב מֵי צִתְרִי.

Calamint water, Rav said it is forbidden, Samuel said it is permitted. Samuel served Rav calamint water[46].

46 *Ṣitra* has been defined as calamint at the end of *Ševi'it* 7:2. Calamint is a weed that may be used as spice. Since it is food only by the intent of the person collecting it, it is not subject to heave, certainly not outside the Land. So if somebody in Babylonia gave heave from calamint, any drink made from it is permitted to everybody. We have a principle that if a person thinks of something permitted as forbidden, another person may not serve him what he thinks is forbidden. If Samuel disregarded this injunction, he must have thought that Rav's position did not merit attention, or he managed to convince Rav of his error.

הָדֵין טַוויָּה רַב חִייָה בַּר אַשִׁי בְּשֵׁם רַב מַשְׁגַּר לֵיהּ בְּחָרוּתָא.

That inner part[47], Rav Ḥiyya bar Ashi in the name of Rav: One fires it with dry branches.

47 טויה II in Levy's dictionary is explained from Arabic طوي "to be hidden". This refers back to Rav's statement that roasting kosher and non-kosher meats together in an open oven makes the kosher meat forbidden. Rav requires even that afterwards the oven be kashered by burning dry branches in the empty oven, to remove any particles of nonkosher meat from the walls. (Explanation of R. M. Margalit.)

(fol. 46d) **משנה ה**: תִּלְתָּן שֶׁנָּפְלָה לְתוֹךְ הַבּוֹר שֶׁל מַיִם בִּתְרוּמָה וּבְמַעֲשֵׂר שֵׁנִי אִם יֵשׁ בְּזֶרַע כְּדֵי לִיתֵּן טַעַם אֲבָל לֹא בְעֵץ. וּבַשְּׁבִיעִית וּבְכִלְאֵי הַכֶּרֶם וְהֶקְדֵּשׁ אִם יֵשׁ בְּזֶרַע וּבְעֵץ כְּדֵי לִיתֵּן טַעַם.

Mishnah 5: Fenugreek that fell into a water cistern, for heave and second tithe if the seeds are enough to impart taste, disregarding the wood[48]. But for the Sabbatical, *kilaim* in a vineyard, and dedicated seeds, if seeds and wood together impart taste[49].

משנה ו: מִי שֶׁהָיוּ לוֹ חֲבִילֵי תִלְתָּן שֶׁל כִּלְאֵי הַכֶּרֶם יִדָּלֵקוּ. הָיוּ לוֹ חֲבִילֵי תִלְתָּן שֶׁל טֶבֶל כּוֹתֵשׁ וּמְחַשֵּׁב כַּמָּה זֶרַע (fol. 46d) יֵשׁ בָּהֶן וּמַפְרִישׁ אֶת הַזֶּרַע וְאֵינוֹ צָרִיךְ לְהַפְרִישׁ אֶת הָעֵץ. אִם הִפְרִישׁ לֹא יֹאמַר אֶכְתּוֹשׁ וְאֶטּוֹל אֶת הָעֵץ וְאֶתֵּן אֶת הַזֶּרַע אֶלָּא נוֹתֵן אֶת הָעֵץ עִם הַזֶּרַע.

Mishnah 6: If somebody had bundles of fenugreek of *kilaim* from a vineyard, they should be burned. If he had bundles of fenugreek from *ṭevel*[50], he pounds them and computes how much seed this contains and separates the seeds but not the wood. If he separated, he should not say I shall pound, take the wood, and give the seeds but he gives seeds with the wood.

48 The wooden parts of fenugreek give less taste than the seeds but may be used as cheap substitute. Nevertheless, the wood is not subject to heave and tithes and cannot be counted in matters of heave and tithes.

49 For these, all that can be used as spice must be counted and makes the water forbidden.

50 The Yerushalmi holds (Notes 54-57) that, while the wood in itself is not subject to heave and tithes, bundles of fenugreek on the stalk are objects of trade. Therefore, the making of bundles is the end of the harvest and fenugreek is subject to heave and tithes in the hand of the farmer as soon as it was bundled for sale. The Mishnah speaks both of the Geat Heave and Heave of the Tithe.

For the Babli (*Beẓah* 13a), stalks of fenugreek are not subject to heave and tithes; the obligation of heave starts only after the separation of seeds from the stalks by threshing ("pounding" in the Mishnah.) Therefore, the situation of the Mishnah can happen only if no heave was given but the farmer irregularly gave First Tithe to the Levite before separating the seeds from the stalks. The tithe bundles in the hand of the Levite are now *ṭevel* for Heave of the Tithe; the Levite has to prepare them by pounding and then give the Cohen his due. But if he simply hands one bundle out of ten to the Cohen, it becomes heave and he may not go back on his word and try to take the stalks for himself.

(fol. 47b) **הלכה ה**: וְאֵין עֵץ פּוֹגֵם וְחוֹזֵר וּפוֹגֵם. מַתְנִיתִין כְּמָאן דְּאָמַר נוֹתֵן טַעַם לִפְגָם אָסוּר. וַאֲפִילוּ כְּמָאן דְּאָמַר נוֹתֵן טַעַם לִפְגָם מוּתָּר מוֹדֵי הוּא הָכָא שֶׁהוּא אָסוּר. לָמָּה כָּל־דָּבָר שֶׁנֶּפְלָה לְתוֹכָהּ תִּילְתָּן הוּא מַשְׁבִּיחַ.

Halakhah 5: Does not the wood spoil repeatedly? Our Mishnah follows him who says that anything that spoils is forbidden[51]. But even according to him who says anything that spoils is permitted, he agrees here that it is forbidden. Why? Fenugreek improves anything into which it falls.

51 If the action is to spoil, why should the water be forbidden at all?

וְכַמָּה הִיא חֲבִילָה עֶשְׂרִים וַחֲמִשָּׁה זֵירִין. אָמַר רִבִּי יוֹחָנָן וְאַרְבָּעָה מִינְהוֹן מִיטָּה.

How much is a bundle? 25 plants[52]. Rebbi Johanan said, four to a bed[53].

52 In the technical sense, a "bundle of fenugreek" is only a bundle of at least 25 plants (cf. Mishnah *Orlah* 3:6). Also, a contract for delivery of bundles of fenugreek requires delivery of bundles of 25 each.

53 If the expression חבילה is used for impurity of beds (Mishnah *Kelim* 18:9), it means groups of four.

מִילְתֵיהּ אָמְרָה עַד שֶׁהֵן בַּחֲבִילוֹת הֵן נִטְבָּלוֹת. מֵעַתָּה וַאֲפִילוּ שִׁבָּלִים. אֵין מַכְנִיסִין לָכֵן. וַהֲלֹא חַבִּיּוֹת מַכְנִיסָן לְכֵן. אֵין גִּידּוּלֵיהֶן לָכֵן. וְאֵלּוּ מַכְנִיסָן לְכֵן וְגִידּוּלֵיהֶן לְכֵן.

It[54] implies that they become *tevel* in bundles[55]. Why not single ears? One never gathers for that. But may grains be gathered thus[56]? One does not grow for that. But these[57], one gathers for this, one grows for this.

54 The Mishnah.

55 Without "threshing."

56 Arabic حَبّ "grain". The commentators are at a loss to connect Hebrew חבית (Arabic خابية) "amphora" in this context.

57 Bundles of 25 stalks of fenugreek.

(fol. 47a) **משנה ז**: זֵיתֵי חוּלִין שֶׁכְּבָשָׁן עִם זֵיתֵי תְרוּמָה פִּיצוּעֵי חוּלִין עִם פִּיצוּעֵי תְרוּמָה פִּיצוּעֵי חוּלִין עִם שְׁלֵימֵי תְרוּמָה אוֹ בְמֵי תְרוּמָה אָסוּר. אֲבָל שְׁלֵימֵי חוּלִין עִם פִּיצוּעֵי תְרוּמָה מוּתָּר.

Mishnah 7: Profane olives preserved[58] with heave olives, if they were broken profanes with broken heaves, broken profanes with whole heaves, or preserves in heave fluid[59], are forbidden[60]. But whole profanes[61] with broken heaves are permitted[60].

58 Preserved in brine, oil, or vinegar.

59 Water in which heave olives were preserved; cf. Halakhah 7.

60 For non-Cohanim.

61 Whole olives are considered as non-absorbing.

(fol. 47b) **הלכה ו**: אָמַר רִבִּי יוֹנָה זֹאת אוֹמֶרֶת פְּצוּעִין בּוֹלְעִין וּפוֹלְטִין וְחוֹזְרִין וּבוֹלְעִין. שְׁלֵימִים בּוֹלְעִין וּפוֹלְטִין וְעוֹד אֵינָן בּוֹלְעִין. הָדָא אָמְרָה לֹא לְשְׁבָח וְלֹא לִפְגָם אָסוּר. מַתְנִיתִין דְּרִבִּי שִׁמְעוֹן דְּרִבִּי שִׁמְעוֹן אוֹמֵר נוֹתֵן טַעַם לִפְגָם אָסוּר. וְהָא רִבִּי שִׁמְעוֹן אָמַר נוֹתֵן טַעַם לִפְגָם מוּתָּר. כְּהָדָא רִבִּי שִׁמְעוֹן אוֹמֵר כְּרוּב שֶׁל שְׁקָיָא שֶׁשְּׁלָקוֹ עִם כְּרוּב שֶׁל בַּעַל אָסוּר מִפְּנֵי שֶׁהוּא בוֹלֵעַ.

Halakhah 6: Rebbi Jonah said, this implies that broken [olives] absorb, release, and absorb again; whole [olives] absorb, release, but do not absorb again[62]. That means, if it is neither improving nor spoiling it is forbidden[63]. The Mishnah is Rebbi Simeon's, for Rebbi Simeon says if its taste spoils, it is forbidden. But did Rebbi Simeon not say, if its taste spoils, it is permitted[20]? Following what Rebbi Simeon says[64], irrigated cabbage preserved with unirrigated cabbage is forbidden because it absorbs.

62 It is axiomatic that anything put in a fluid environment absorbs from the environment. But then the fluid also absorbs what is released from the solid food. Since one cannot say that whole olives do not absorb from their environment (they certainly absorb salt from the surrounding brine), one has to say that they release the taste acquired from heave back into the surrounding fluid and then no longer absorb.

63 Since the Mishnah implies that preserving profane and heave olives of equal quality together makes every

thing forbidden to laymen.

64 Mishnah 11. One assumes that the cabbage from the unirrigated field is heave. If it is cooked together with the more expensive and better cabbage from an irrigated garden plot, the result is forbidden to laymen even though the admixture of standard cabbage can only reduce the quality of the garden cabbage.

(fol. 47a) **משנה ח**: דָּג טָמֵא שֶׁכְּבָשׁוֹ עִם דָּג טָהוֹר וְכָל־גָּרָב שֶׁהוּא מַחֲזִיק סְאָתַיִם אִם יֵשׁ בּוֹ מִשְׁקַל עֲשָׂרָה זוּזֵי בִּיהוּדָה שֶׁהֵן חָמֵשׁ סְלָעִים בַּגָּלִיל דָּג טָמֵא צִירוֹ אָסוּר. רִבִּי יְהוּדָה אוֹמֵר רְבִיעִית בְּסָאתַיִם. רִבִּי יוֹסֵי אוֹמֵר אֶחָד מִשִּׁשָּׁה עָשָׂרֵה שֶׁבּוֹ.

Mishnah 8: If an impure fish[65] was preserved with a pure fish, if in any keg[66] containing two *seah* the impure fish weighed ten *zuz* in Judea which are five tetradrachmas[67] in Galilee, the sauce is forbidden[68]. Rebbi Jehudah says, a quarter [*log*] in two *seah*[69]. Rebbi Yose said, one sixteenth of it[70].

משנה ט: חֲגָבִים טְמֵאִים שֶׁנִּכְבְּשׁוּ עִם חֲגָבִים טְהוֹרִים לֹא פָּסְלוּ אֶת צִירָן. הֵעִיד רִבִּי צָדוֹק עַל צִיר חֲגָבִים טְמֵאִים שֶׁהוּא טָהוֹר.

Mishnah 9: Impure locusts preserved with pure locusts do not forbid the fluid exuding[71] from the latter. [72]Rebbi Ẓadoq[73] testified that the fluid exuding from impure locusts[74] is pure.

65 Any aquatic animal without scales and fins. While the non-kosher fish cannot be eaten and cannot be knowingly preserved with kosher fish, fishsauce, whose biblical status is unclear, may be used if the admixture was not intentional and the forbidden amount is minute.

66 In Syriac, גרב is a vessel containing exactly 1 *seah*.

67 In *Sifra Šemini Parašah* 3(9), "Ten *zuz* in Judea which equal ten

tetradrachmas in Galilee."

68 The contents of the keg are forbidden food. "Sauce" here is not the fluid in which the fish is preserved but the fluid oozing out of the fish.

69 Since a *seah* equals 24 *log*, this is $^1/_{196}$ whereas the first Tanna allows only $^1/_{960}$ of contamination (Note 81).

70 If the forbidden fluid is at least $^1/_{16}$ of the kosher fish fluid, the mixture is forbidden. In this interpretation, R. Yose does not express a separate opinion on the impure fish itself.

According to R. Abraham ben David (whose interpretation is accepted by R. S. Lieberman), R. Yose refers to the *garab* as "it". Since the *garab* contains 9600 *zuz* (Notes 78-81), $^1/_{16}$ of it would be 600 *zuz* and the 10 *zuz* given in the Mishnah are $^1/_{60}$ of this quantity. Therefore, R. Yose asserts that in this case also the mixture is permitted if the kosher food is as least 60 times the quantity of the forbidden.

71 This fluid, which can exist only in minute quantities, is disregarded. The list of kosher locusts is in *Lev.* 11:22.

72 This text is also in *Idiut* 7:2

73 A student of the House of Shammai who survived the fall of Jerusalem and became a follower of the rules of the House of Hillel. When Rabban Johanan ben Zakkai defected to the Romans, one of the favors he asked from Vespasian was medical attention for R. Ẓadoq. The meaning of R. Ẓadoq's testimony is explained in the last paragraph of the Halakhah.

74 Any locust not on the list of *Lev.* 11:22. The only Jewish group with a continued tradition of identification of the edible locust is Yemenite Jewry. In Yemen, locusts were only eaten roasted.

(fol. 47b) **הלכה ז**: תַּנֵּי רִבִּי יוּדָה בַּר פָּזִי דְּבַר דְּלָיָה דָּג טָהוֹר טָפֵל שֶׁכְּבָשׁוֹ עִם דָּג טָמֵא מְלִיחַ אָסוּר. וְהָתַנֵּי רִבִּי חִיָּיה מַדִּיחוֹ וּמוּתָּר. אָמַר רִבִּי מָנָא מָאן דְּאָמַר מוּתָּר שֶׁכְּבָשָׁן שְׁתֵּיהֶן כְּאַחַת. מָאן דְּאָמַר אָסוּר שֶׁכְּבָשָׁן זֶה אַחַר זֶה. תֵּדַע לָךְ שֶׁהוּא כֵן דְּתַנִּינָן אוֹ בְמֵי תְרוּמָה אָסוּר לֹא בְּשֶׁכְּבָשָׁן זֶה אַחַר זֶה.

Rebbi Jehudah bar Pazi stated from Bar Delaiah[75]: "Unsalted pure fish preserved with salted impure fish is forbidden". But did we not state: "He washes it and it is permitted"[76]? Rebbi Mana said, he who said it is permitted, when he preserved them simultaneously; he who said it is prohibited when he preserved them one after the other. You can understand that this is so, since we have stated "in heave fluid[59] it is forbidden;" [is that] not when he preserved one after the other[77]?

75 A similar text is in Tosephta 9:2

76 In the Tosephta (9:2), this is stated for the case when the fish are either both unsalted or both salted. In *Sifra Šemini Parashah* 3(6) it is stated: (*Lev.* 11:9) "Those you shall eat," to include pure fish preserved with impure.

The Babli (*Avodah Zarah* 40a) reports on a disagreement on whether the fluid oozing out from non-kosher seafood is forbidden. It decides that it is forbidden; a decision accepted by R. Zeïra.

77 This really proves only R. Mana's second statement.

וְכָל־גָּרָב שֶׁמַּחֲזִיק סְאָתַיִם. כַּמָּה סְאָתָה עֲבְדָא עֲשָׂרָה וְאַרְבָּעָה לוֹגִין. וְכַמָּה לוֹגָא עֲבִיד תַּרְתֵּין לִיטְרִין. וְכַמָּה לִיטְרָא עֲבְדָא מֵאָה זִינִין נִמְצָה כָּל־זִין וְזִין אַחַת מִתְּשַׁע מֵאוֹת וְשִׁשִּׁים. הוֹרֵי רִבִּי יוֹסֵי בֵּי רִבִּי בּוּן בְּעַכְבָּרָא חַד לְאֶלֶף.

"Any keg containing two *seah*". How much is in a *seah*? [24] (14) *log*[78]. How much is in a *log*? 2 pounds[79]. How much is in a pound? 100 *zin*[80]. It turns out that each single *zin* corresponds to one in 960[81]. Rebbi Yose ben Rebbi Abun instructed at Akhbara[82]: one in a thousand.

78 Both mss. have "14", but this number is not a divisor of 960. R. Solomon ibn Adrat, *Responsa* vol. 1, No. 281, reads "24". A *seah* is 6 *qab*, each *qab* is 4 *log*.

79 Of the 25 mss. collated in *The Mishnah with variant readings* (Jerusalem 1975), 11 read *zin*, 1 *ziz* (reading also of the Rome ms. in the Halakhah), and 12 *zuz* in the Mishnah text. Therefore, *zin* here equals *zuz* in the Mishnah.

80 Since *log* refers to volume and pound to weight, one has to assume that the volume of 1 *log* of water weighs 2 Jerusalem pounds. Under the Julian-Claudian dynasty, a denar (*zuz*) was $^1/_{96}$ of a Roman lb. of 12 Troy oz., (about 345 g). It follows from the text that this denar was $^1/_{100}$ of a smaller pound.

81 Since 1 *zin* = $^1/_{9600}$ of 2 *seah*,

and 10 *zin* of impure fish make the 2 *seah* forbidden, it follows that each single *zin* of impure fish contaminates 960 times its weight or volume. (Explanation of R. Solomon ibn Adrat.)

82 The place of R. Yose bar Abun's academy. For practical purposes, he replaced 960 by 1000.

רִבִּי אַבָּהוּ בְּשֵׁם רִבִּי יוֹסֵי בַּר חֲנִינָה רוֹבַע צִיר בְּסָאתַיִם צִיר. וַהֲלֹא אֵין צִיר דָּג טָמֵא מַצִּיל. אָמַר רִבִּי אַבָּהוּ חֲשַׁבְתִּית יָתָהּ קָרוֹב לְמָאתַיִם. רִבִּי אִילָא בְּשֵׁם רִבִּי שִׁמְעוֹן בַּר חִייָה רוֹבַע צִיר בְּסָאתַיִם דָּגִים וְצִיר. אֲתָא עוֹבְדָא קוֹמֵי רִבִּי יֹאשִׁיָּה וְהוֹרֵי כֵן.

Rebbi Abbahu in the name of Rebbi Yose bar Ḥanina: A quarter [*log*][83] of fish sauce in two *seah* of fish sauce[84]. But the sauce of an impure fish never can save[85]! Rebbi Abbahu said, I computed that close to 200[86]. Rebbi Ila in the name of Rebbi Simeon bar Ḥiyya[87], a quarter [*log*] of fish sauce in two *seah* of fish and fish sauce. A case came before Rebbi Joshia and he instructed accordingly[88].

83 Usually, רובע means "a quarter *qab*" which is a dry measure equal to one *log* in liquid measure. But since the Yerushalmi here follows R. Jehudah in the Mishnah, one has to understand "quarter *log*".

84 Fish sauce is permitted if the proportion of impure fish (in an inadvertent contamination) is less than 1 in 196 (replaced for practical purposes by 1 in 200 by R. Abbahu.)

85 Fish sauce is forbidden only as "sweat exuding from the fish" (Babli *Ḥulin* 99b). It never can contribute to the 196 times the permitted food has to exceed the forbidden.

86 R. S. Lieberman (*Tosefta ki-fshutah* 2, p. 440) accepts an explanation that R. Abbahu determined that the sauce exuded by 10 *zin* impure fish will be about $^1/_{200}$ of a *garab* of fish and sauce. In the Babli (*Ḥulin* 99b), R. Yose bar Ḥanina implies that the anonymous Tanna also accepts R. Jehudah's opinion about fish sauce and requires $^1/_{960}$ only for the fish itself. This also is the position of the Yerushalmi which distinguishes between the impure fish, discussed in the preceding paragraph, and fish sauce.

87 In the Babli, he appears without a title. He was a student of Rav in

Babylonia who immigrated into Galilee.

88 Practice is decided following R. Jehudah in a lenient way. The Babli (*Ḥulin* 99b) accepts the ruling of R. Jehudah in the interpretation of R. Abbahu which counts only the amount of sauce.

וְתַנֵּי כֵן בְּמַה דְבָרִים אֲמוּרִים בִּזְמַן שֶׁשּׁוֹלֶה רִאשׁוֹן רִאשׁוֹן וּמַנִּיחַ לְפָנָיו שֶׁמּוּתָּר לַעֲשׂוֹת כְּסֶדֶר הַזֶּה. אֲבָל אִם הָיָה שׁוֹלֶה רִאשׁוֹן רִאשׁוֹן וּמַנִּיחַ לַאֲחָרָיו אֲפִילוּ יוֹתֵר מִכְּסֶדֶר הַזֶּה מוּתָּר.

עַל יְדֵי עִילָּה גְּבוּנְתָּא אִיקַלְקֶלֶת. שָׁאַל רִבִּי חַגַּיי לְרִבִּי בָּא בַּר זַבְדָּא אָמַר לֵיהּ דָּבָר שֶׁל רַבִּים אֵינוֹ נֶאֱסָר. רִבִּי יַעֲקֹב בַּר זַבְדִּי אָמַר רִבִּי יִצְחָק שָׁאַל וְאִילֵּין אִיגַּרְתָּא לֹא גַייס לוּקָס כְּתִיב בְּהֶן וְאַתְּ אָמַר עַל יְדֵי עִילָּה.

We have stated thus[89]: "When has this been said? If he scoops out piece by piece and puts them before himself, he has to proceed in the way indicated[90]. But if he scoops out piece by piece and throws them away, even more than was indicated is permitted."

[91]By some pretext, cheese was mixed up[92]. Rebbi Ḥaggai asked Rebbi Abba bar Zavda. He said to them, the property of the public cannot be forbidden[93]. Rebbi Jacob bar Zavdi said, Rebbi Isaac asked: Is not Caius Lycus written on these documents, and you say, by a pretext[94]?

89 A similar text in Tosephta 9:1, in the name of R. Yose ben R. Jehudah.

90 If he scooped out from the barrel to prepare the fish as food and found 10 *zin* of impure fish, all is forbidden. But if he scooped out and threw the impure away, so that at no time there are 10 *zin* of impure fish before him, the fish fluid itself is bland and does not forbid anything even if the total sum of impure fish would have been greater than 10 *zin*. (Explanation of R. S. Lieberman.)

91 The same paragraph appears in *Avodah Zarah* 2:10 (fol. 42a). In that text, instead of גבונתא one reads זבונתא "merchandise". Since both texts speak about food that possibly is forbidden, the reading here seems preferable (but גבונתא possibly does not mean "cheese".) In *Avodah Zarah*, the paragraph follows a lenient ruling of Rebbi referring

to a shipload of wine amphoras. In both cases, it is not clear whether the expression "by some pretext" refers to the previous very lenient statement (and should be translated "as a subterfuge") or to the following. Therefore, it is left to the reader to decide where or whether to split both paragraphs.

92 The percentages of forbidden cheese could no longer be ascertained for each individual piece.

93 This argument usually is used for public property, such as public baths dedicated to a pagan deity; cf. *Ševi'it* Chapter 8, Note 132. Here it is extended to mixed cargo on a common carrier. This is a subterfuge.

94 This refers to a statement in *Giṭṭin* 1:1 (fol. 43b) that a divorce document is valid even if its witnesses sign with Roman (Caius) or Greek (Λύκος "wolf") names. It is stated there that this refers only to divorce documents executed outside the Land since the Jews of the diaspora have Gentile names and, therefore, there is a presumption that the document was signed by Jews. Since without the document the divorced wife could never remarry, it is the duty of the rabbinic court of her home town to find ways to validate a divorce document for which no replacement could be demanded from overseas. This is a situation in which the rabbis would be forced to find pretexts to declare the document valid. However, the statement is an absolute one, valid also for cases in which there is no urgency.

הֵעִיד רִבִּי צָדוֹק עַל צִיר חֲגָבִים טְמֵאִים שֶׁהוּא טָהוֹר. מַהוּ טָהוֹר טָהוֹר מִלְּהַכְשִׁיר. הָא לְטַמֵּא אֲפִילוּ כָּל־שֶׁהוּא מְטַמֵּא.

"Rebbi Ẓadoq testified that the fluid exuding from impure locusts is pure.[95]" In what respect is it pure? It is pure not to prepare. But to make impure[96], the most minute amount makes impure.

95 Locust fluid is not a fluid that can prepare food for impurity; cf. *Demay* Chapter 2, Note 141.

96 This means, forbidden as food. (Commentary of R. Abraham ben David to *Idiut* 7:2.)

(fol. 47a) **משנה י**: כָּל־הַנִּכְבָּשִׁין זֶה עִם זֶה מוּתָּרִין אֶלָּא עִם הַחִיסִית. חִיסִית שֶׁל חוּלִין עִם חִיסִית שֶׁל תְּרוּמָה יָרָק שֶׁל חוּלִין עִם חִיסִית שֶׁל תְּרוּמָה אָסוּר. אֲבָל חִיסִית שֶׁל חוּלִין עִם יָרָק שֶׁל תְּרוּמָה מוּתָּר.

Mishnah 10: All those which are pickled one with the other are permitted[97] except with bulb plants[98]. Profane bulb plant with heave bulb plant, profane vegetable with heave bulb plant, are forbidden[99]. But profane bulb plant with heave vegetable is permitted.

משנה יא: רִבִּי יוֹסֵי אוֹמֵר כָּל־הַנִּשְׁלָקִין עִם הַתְּרָדִין אֲסוּרִין מִפְּנֵי שֶׁהֵן נוֹתְנִין טַעַם. רִבִּי שִׁמְעוֹן אוֹמֵר כְּרוּב שֶׁל שִׁיקְיָא עִם כְּרוּב שֶׁל בַּעַל אָסוּר מִפְּנֵי שֶׁהוּא בוֹלֵעַ. רִבִּי עֲקִיבָה אוֹמֵר כָּל־הַמִּתְבַּשְּׁלִין זֶה עִם זֶה מוּתָּרִין אֶלָּא עִם הַבָּשָׂר.

Mishnah 11: Rebbi Yose says, all that is cooked in water with white beets is forbidden[100] because it imparts taste. Rebbi Simeon says[64], irrigated cabbage [preserved] with unirrigated cabbage is forbidden because it absorbs. Rebbi Aqiba[101] says, all those which are cooked together are permitted except with meat[102].

97 They do not impart taste.

98 Defined in Chapter 9, Note 89.

99 For laymen.

100 For laymen if the beets were heave.

101 This is the reading of all mss. of the Mishnah. For some reason, the Venice Babli and Mishnah have "R. Jehudah".

102 Any meat cooked with vegetables will improve in taste. Therefore, meat cooked with any heave vegetables will become forbidden for laymen.

(fol. 47b) **הלכה ח**: אָמַר רִבִּי יוֹחָנָן לֵית כָּאן נִכְבָּשִׁין אֶלָּא נִשְׁלָקִין. כָּבוּשׁ כְּרוֹתֵחַ הוּא.

Halakhah 8: Rebbi Joḥanan said, one does not speak of pickled [food] but of that cooked in water[103]. Pickled is like being hot[104].

103 Since Mishnah 11 records the dissent of Tannaïm from Mishnah 10, the two Mishnaiot must speak about the same procedures.

104 In the Babli, R. Joḥanan is reported to hold that being preserved in salt is like being cooked over a flame. There, he explains that being pickled is not like being cooked in water (implicitly stated here) but Samuel holds that pickling and cooking in water are the same as far as dietary laws are concerned.

רִבִּי חֲנִינָה תִּירְתָא בְשֵׁם רִבִּי הוֹשַׁעְיָה חִסִּית בְּחִסִּית מִין בְּמִינוֹ רִבִּי עֲקִיבָה מַתִּיר וַחֲכָמִים אוֹסְרִין. רִבִּי יָסָא בְשֵׁם רִבִּי יוֹחָנָן מוֹדִין חֲכָמִים לְרִבִּי עֲקִיבָה בְּבָשָׂר בְּבָשָׂר שֶׁהוּא מוּתָּר. אָמַר רִבִּי זְעִירָא לְרִבִּי יָסָא וְאִילּוּ לֹא אִתְאֲמָרַת הָדָא לֹא הֲוֵינָן יָדְעוּן דְּהוּא כֵן. וְדִילְמָא לֹא אִתְאֲמָרַת אֶלָּא מוֹדֵי רִבִּי עֲקִיבָה לַחֲכָמִים בְּבָשָׂר בְּבָשָׂר שֶׁהוּא אָסוּר. אָתָא רִבִּי אַבָּהוּ בְשֵׁם רִבִּי יוֹחָנָן מוֹדֵי רִבִּי עֲקִיבָה לַחֲכָמִים בְּבָשָׂר בְּבָשָׂר שֶׁהוּא אָסוּר. רִבִּי חִינְנָה שָׁמַע לָהּ מִן דְּבַתְרָהּ רִבִּי עֲקִיבָה אוֹמֵר כָּל־הַמִּתְבַּשְּׁלִין זֶה עִם זֶה מוּתָּרִין חוּץ מִן הַבָּשָׂר. הָא בָּשָׂר בְּבָשָׂר אָסוּר. דִּילְמָא אִתְאֲמָרַת אֶלָּא מוֹדִין חֲכָמִים לְרִבִּי עֲקִיבָה בְּבָשָׂר בְּבָשָׂר שֶׁהוּא אָסוּר. רִבִּי חֲנַנְיָה רִבִּי אַבָּהוּ בְשֵׁם רִבִּי יוֹחָנָן מוֹדִין חֲכָמִים לְרִבִּי עֲקִיבָה בְּבָשָׂר בְּבָשָׂר שֶׁהוּא אָסוּר.

Rebbi Ḥanina Tortayya in the name of Rebbi Hoshaiah: Bulb vegetables with bulb vegetables, a kind with itself[105], Rebbi Aqiba permits but the Sages forbid. Rebbi Assi in the name of Rebbi Joḥanan: The Sages agree with Rebbi Aqiba that meat with meat is permitted[106]. Rebbi Zeïra said to Rebbi Assi: If that had not been said, we would not know that it is so, but maybe it was said as follows: Rebbi Aqiba agrees with the Sages that meat with meat is forbidden[107]. Rebbi Abbahu came in the name of Rebbi Joḥanan: Rebbi Aqiba agrees with the Sages that meat with meat is forbidden. Rebbi Ḥinena understood it from the next Mishnah: "Rebbi Aqiba says, all those which are cooked together are permitted except with meat." Therefore, "meat with meat is forbidden[108]."

Maybe it was formulated as: The Sages agree with Rebbi Aqiba that meat with meat is forbidden. Rebbi Ḥinena: Rebbi Abbahu in the name of Rebbi Joḥanan, the Sages agree with Rebbi Aqiba that meat with meat is forbidden[109].

105 Heave and profane cooked together.

106 Following R. Joḥanan's stand that Mishnah 10 also speaks of cooking different foods together in water, he asserts that cooking meat forbidden to laymen (Note 102) with other meat does not extend the prohibition.

107 He denies that R. Joḥanan holds that pickling and cooking have the same rules. Since Mishnah 10 only states "all those which are pickled together", it follows that the same is not true for "all" that are cooked together; in particular, not for meat.

108 Tosephta 9:4.

107 R. Joḥanan still holds that pickling and cooking follow the same rules and that pickling or cooking kosher and non-kosher meat together makes everything forbidden, unless the amount of non-kosher meat is negligible.

אָמַר רִבִּי יוֹסֵי הֲוֵינָן סָבְרִין מֵימַר שֶׁל בַּעַל בּוֹלֵעַ מִן מַה דְאָמַר רַב חוּנָא סַב מִן אִיבָּהּ וְהַב לִפְלוּפָהּ. הָא אָמְרָה שֶׁל שַׁקִּי בּוֹלֵעַ.

Rebbi Yose said, we were of the opinion that the unirrigated [cabbage] absorbs[108]. Since Rav Huna said, take away its growing parts and get moisture; this shows that the irrigated absorbs.

108 That the statement of R. Simeon in the Mishnah refers only to irrigated heave and profane unirrigated cabbage. The obscure saying of Rav Huna implies that R. Simeon's statement holds for all kinds of cabbage.

(fol. 47a) **משנה יא**: רִבִּי יוֹחָנָן בֶּן נוּרִי אוֹמֵר כָּבֵד אוֹסֶרֶת וְאֵינָהּ נֶאֱסֶרֶת מִפְּנֵי שֶׁהִיא פוֹלֶטֶת וְאֵינָהּ בוֹלַעַת.

Mishnah 11: Rebbi Johanan ben Nuri says, liver makes forbidden but will not become forbidden, for it releases but does not absorb[109].

109 Liver is so full of blood that only blood oozes out and nothing is absorbed. But the blood will make anything cooked with it forbidden.

(fol. 47b) **הלכה ט**: רִבִּי יִרְמְיָה בָּעֵי שְׁלָקָהּ בְּחָלָב מַהוּ. רִבִּי זְעִירָא לֹא אָכַל כָּבֵד מִיָּמָיו. שְׁלָקָהּ רִבִּי בָּא וְאָכְלָה לָהּ. וְאִית דְּאָמַר מְלָחָהּ רִבִּי בָּא וְאָכְלָה לָהּ.

Halakhah 9: Rebbi Jeremiah asked: What is the rule if he cooked it in milk[110]? Rebbi Zeïra never in his life ate liver[111]. Rebbi Abba cooked it in water and ate it; some say Rebbi Abba salted and ate it.

110 The milk is certainly forbidden because it is mixed with blood. But if R. Johanan ben Nuri is correct, the liver did not absorb any milk; when taken out of the milk and washed it might be permitted even though the act of cooking itself is forbidden by biblical law. This is one of the impossible questions of R. Jeremiah, cf. *Ma'serot* 3:10, Note 156, Babli *Baba Batra* 23b. In this case, it proves that the rule of R. Johanan ben Nuri leads to an impossible consequence; it cannot possibly be true.

111 Since he was a posthumous child whose mother died in childbirth, he never could see how his mother handled liver. Since he was a Babylonian, he would have seen that in Babylonia liver was broiled to stop it from oozing blood (*Ḥulin* 111a).

(fol. 47a) **משנה יב**: בֵּיצָה שֶׁנִּיתַּבְּלָה בְתַבְלִין אֲסוּרִין אֲפִילוּ חֶלְמוֹן שֶׁלָּהּ אָסוּר מִפְּנֵי שֶׁהוּא בוֹלֵעַ. מֵי כְּבָשִׁים וּמֵי שְׁלָקוֹת שֶׁל תְּרוּמָה אֲסוּרִין לְזָרִים.

Mishnah 12: If an egg was treated with forbidden spices, even its yolk is forbidden because it absorbs. Pickling and cooking fluid of heave is forbidden to laymen.

(fol. 47b) **הלכה י**: חֶלְמוֹן אָסוּר מִפְּנֵי שֶׁהוּא בוֹלֵעַ. תַּנֵּי בַּר קַפָּרָא חֶלְמוֹן אָסוּר וְכָל־שֶׁכֵּן חֲלֵב בֵּיצִים.

Halakhah 10: "Yolk is forbidden because it absorbs." Bar Qappara stated: Yolk is forbidden and certainly egg white.

יִצְחָק רַבָּה בְּשֵׁם רִבִּי שִׁמְעוֹן בֶּן לָקִישׁ בֵּיצִים שֶׁשְּׁלָקָן וּמָצָה בָהֶן אֶפְרוֹחַ בְּנוֹתֵן טַעַם.

Isaac Rabba[112] in the name of Rebbi Simeon ben Laqish: If eggs were cooked in water and a chick was found in one of them, it is [judged] by the taste it gives[113].

112 It seems that this is a misattribution since R. Isaac Rabba was a student of Rebbi, cf. Z. Frankel, מבוא הירושלמי, p. 105b-106a. It seems that the tradent is R. Isaac (Napaḥa), of the students of R. Joḥanan, or that the source of the statement was Rebbi, not R. Simeon ben Laqish. The text as it stands is confirmed by the quote of this and the following two paragraphs in *Or Zarua'* I #452. The Rome ms. has Jacob Rabba; possibly the source had only י"ר as metathesis from ר"י

An equivalent statement is in Tosephta 9:5; that Tosephta clearly was unknown to the compilers of the Yerushalmi.

113 If the taste of the cooked chick is noticeable in the food it was cooked with, all is forbidden since the chick in the egg was not ritually slaughtered. The definition of "giving taste" is discussed in the next paragraph. An equivalent statement is in Tosephta 9:5. The Yerushalmi does not consider the possibility of having the food tasted by a Gentile; its definition of "giving taste" is purely numerical and independent of any actual taste. Therefore, the question whether a chick inside an undamaged shell can impart any taste is irrelevant.

רִבִּי זְעִירָא רִבִּי שִׁמְעוֹן בַּר אַבָּא בְשֵׁם רִבִּי יוֹחָנָן אָדָא בַּר גֵּרְשׁוֹן רִבִּי בִּירַיי רִבִּי לֵוִי בַּר פְּלָטָא זָקֵן אֶחָד בְּשֵׁם רִבִּי שִׁשִּׁים וְאַחַת אֲסוּרוֹת. שִׁשִּׁים וּשְׁתַּיִם מוּתָּרוֹת. רִבִּי שְׁמוּאֵל בַּר נַחְמָן בְּשֵׁם רִבִּי יוֹנָתָן הֵעִיד אָדָא חֲבֵירֵינוּ לְפָנֵינוּ בְּשִׁשִּׁים. וְאָמַר מִי שֶׁיָּבִיא לִי יוֹתֵר מִשִּׁשִּׁים מַכְשֵׁר אָנָא. אָמְרִין לְשִׁמְעוֹן בַּר וָוא אָמַר אַתְּ הָכֵין וְאִינּוּן אָמְרִין הָכֵין. אָמַר לוֹן אֲנָא מַה דִּשְׁמָעִית וְאִינּוּן מַה דִּשְׁמָעוּן. שִׁמְעוֹן בַּר וָוא אָמַר קוֹמֵי רִבִּי חֲנִינָה [בְּשֵׁם רִבִּי חִיָּה רַבָּה עַד שְׁלֹשִׁים וְאָמַר לֵיהּ גִּיזְמָה שִׁמְעוֹן בַּר בָּא בְּשֵׁם רִבִּי חֲנִינָה][115] מַעֲשֶׂה בָא לִפְנֵי רַבָּן גַּמְלִיאֵל בְּרִבִּי אָמַר לֵיהּ אֲנָא[116] לֹא מוֹדֵי בְּאַרְבָּעִים וְשֶׁבַע וַאֲנָא מוֹדֶה בְּאַרְבָּעִים וְחָמֵשׁ. רִבִּי חִיָּה בְּשֵׁם רִבִּי חֲנִינָה מַעֲשֶׂה בָא לִפְנֵי רִבִּי אָמַר אִית תַּמָּן חֲמִשִּׁין.

Rebbi Zeïra, Rebbi Simeon bar Abba in the name of Rebbi Joḥanan; Ada bar Gershon[117], Rebbi Birai[118], Rebbi Levi bar Plautus[119], an elder[120] in the name of Rebbi: 61 are forbidden[121], 62 are permitted. Rebbi Samuel bar Naḥman in the name of Rebbi Jonathan: Our colleague Ada[122] testified before us: 60[123]. He said, if somebody brings before me more than 60, I shall declare it kosher. They said to Simeon bar Abba, you say this, but the others say otherwise! He said to them, I [said] what I heard, they what they heard. Simeon bar Abba said before Rebbi Ḥanina in the name of the elder Rebbi Ḥiyya: Up to thirty[124]. He said, an exaggeration. Simeon bar Abba in the name of Rebbi Ḥanina: A case came before Rabban Gamliel ben Rabbi. He said, my father[116] did not agree to 47, I agree to 45. Rebbi Ḥiyya in the name of Rebbi Ḥanina: A case came before Rebbi; he asked: Are there 50[125]?

115 Reading of the Rome ms. In *Or Zarua'*: בְּשִׁשִּׁים אָמַר גּוּזְמָא שִׁמְעוֹן בַּר בָּא בְּשֵׁם רִבִּי חֲנִינָא. The details of the spelling of *Or Zarua'* are Babylonian, not to be taken as testimony of Yerushalmi spelling. The omission in the Leyden ms. is by oversight from 'ר חנינה to 'ר חנינה.

116 In *Or Zarua'*: אבא. This reading has been translated.

117 He is mentioned only here. In the parallel, Babli *Ḥulin* 98a, he appears as R. Idi bar Gershom; in *Or Zarua'* as R. Ada bar Gershom. [The reading in the printed Babli, R. Idi bar Idi bar Gershom, is not confirmed by any ms.]

118 He is otherwise unknown. In *Ḥulin* 98a, he appears as R. Biriam.

119 An Amora of the second generation (רִבִּי לֵוִי בַּר פְּרֹטָא); almost all of his sayings are aggadic and quoted in the old Galilean Midrashim. His father's name is either Latin *Plautus* or Greek πρῶτος "first", used as name of a first-born son. For other examples of names in Greek corresponding to Jewish but not Greek usage, cf. E. and H. Guggenheimer, *Jewish Family Names and Their Origins*, Hoboken NJ 1992; *Etymologisches Lexikon der jüdischen Familiennamen*, München 1996.

120 In *Ḥulin* 98a, "an elder by the name of R. Jacob."

121 If one part of the total is forbidden and 60 are permitted, for a total of 61, then everything is forbidden. But if more than 60 are permitted, for a total of approximately 62, then the mixture is permitted. This is practice accepted by the Babli.

122 He is the Ada bar Gershon quoted earlier.

123 This dissenting testimony is the Babylonian version. *Ḥulin* 98a. The food is permitted if not more than one part in 60 is forbidden.

124 In *Or Zarua'*: 60. It is impossible to determine the correct version; R. Ḥanina thinks either that 30 is much too small or that 60 is much too large.

125 He would permit a mixture of 50 parts permitted and one part forbidden food.

רִבִּי חִייָא בְּשֵׁם רִבִּי חֲנִינָה וְהַיֶּרֶק וְהַקְּלִיפִּין וְהַמַּיִם מִצְטָרְפִין. אָמַר רִבִּי זְעִירָא וְאִיסּוּר מִתּוֹכָן. אָמַר רַב חוּנָא קְלִיפֵּי אִיסּוּר מַעֲלִין אֶת הַהֵיתֵר. רִבִּי זְעִירָא הָדָא דְתֵימַר וְהוּא שֶׁשְּׁלָקָן בִּקְלִיפֵּיהֶן שְׁלוּקוֹת בִּשְׁלוּקוֹת אֲבָל שְׁלָקָן בֵּיצִים קְלוּפוֹת בִּשְׁאֵינָן קְלוּפוֹת אוֹ שְׁאֵינָן קְלוּפוֹת בִּקְלוּפוֹת שְׁלוּקוֹת בִּשְׁאֵינָן שְׁלוּקוֹת צְרִיכִין שִׁיעוּר אַחֵר.

Rebbi Ḥiyya in the name of Rebbi Ḥanina: Vegetables, shells, and water are counted[126]. Rebbi Zeïra said, even if the inside is forbidden. Rav Huna said, the shells of the forbidden help the permitted[127]. Rebbi

Zeïra: That is, if he cooked them in their shells, cooked with cooked. But if he cooked shelled eggs with unshelled in water, or unshelled with shelled, cooked with uncooked[128], that needs a different measure[129].

126 To establish that there is 45, 47, or 50 times more permitted food than the forbidden chick.

127 Even the shell of the egg in which the chick was found is counted as permitted.

128 If uncooked eggs are cooked with shelled, it is clear that the shelled had been cooked first, otherwise the shelled eggs would not preserve their shape. Therefore, the meaning of the sentence is: uncooked unshelled eggs with cooked shelled.

129 A minimum of 60 times, not 45, 47 or 50.

גִּיעוּלֵי בֵיצִים מוּתָּרִין שׁוֹרוֹ עִיבַּר וְלֹא יַגְעִיל. בֵּיצִים שֶׁהִקְרִימוּ הֲרֵי אֵלּוּ אֲסוּרוֹת מוּזָרוֹת הַנֶּפֶשׁ הַיָּפָה תֹאכַל. מָצָא בָּהֶן דָּם קוֹלֵף מְקוֹם הַדָּם.

Unimpregnated eggs are permitted: (*Job* 21:10) "His steer made pregnant, he will not miss impregnating.[130]" Eggs that started developing[131] are forbidden. Twisted ones, he who likes it may eat them[132]. If one found blood in them[133], one shaves off the place of the blood.

130 The verse is quoted to show that the verb געל used here does not mean "to loathe" but "to miss impregnation."

131 In Babylonian spelling, this would be שהרקימו. The paragraph has a parallel in Tosephta 9:5, but this one sentence is missing there.

132 Eggs in which the yolk does not form a ball and which will not develop even if the hen sits on them a long time. These may be eaten by people who are not repelled by them.

133 Boiled eggs.

רִבִּי זְעִירָא סְלַק מְבַקְרָה לְרִבִּי חִייָא בְּרֵיהּ דְּרִבִּי יִצְחָק עֲטוֹשַׁייָא אַשְׁכְּחֵיהּ יְתִיב. אָמַר לֹא שָׁנוּ אֶלָּא בְּלוּבַן חֶלְמוֹן אֲבָל בְּלוּבַן חֶלְבּוֹן מוּתָּר. הוּא סָבַר דְּהוּא גַּבֵּיהּ מִן אַבְהָתֵיהּ. (fol. 47c) אֲתָא רִבִּי אַבָּהוּ בְּשֵׁם רִבִּי יוֹחָנָן בֵּין חֶלְבּוֹן

בֵּין חֶלְמוֹן אָסוּר. תַּנֵּי רִבִּי חֲלַפְתָּא בֶּן שָׁאוּל חֶלְמוֹן אָסוּר חֶלְבּוֹן מוּתָּר. אָמַר רִבִּי זְעִירָא הֵן דְּאָמַר חֶלְמוֹן אָסוּר בְּשֶׁנִּמְצָא בִּמְקוֹם זְכָרוּתוֹ שֶׁל חֶלְמוֹן וַאֲפִילוּ חֶלְמוֹן וְהוּא שֶׁנִּמְצָא בִּמְקוֹם זְכָרוּתוֹ שֶׁל מוֹחַ שֶׁמִּמֶּנּוּ אֶפְרוֹחַ נוֹצָר.

Rebbi Zeïra went to visit Rebbi Ḥiyya[134], the son of Rebbi Isaac Aṭoshiyya. He found him sitting. He said, they taught only for yolk, but in the egg white[135] it is permitted. He thought that he had heard it from his ancestor. Rebbi Abbahu came in the name of Rebbi Johanan: Both egg white and yolk are forbidden. Rebbi Ḥalaphta ben Shaul stated: Yolk is forbidden, egg white permitted[136]. Rebbi Zeïra said, he who says yolk is forbidden if it is found at the male part of the yolk; this applies even to yolk, but only if it is found on its male part since from there the development of the chick starts[137].

134 A sick-bed visit.

135 The language here is a confluence of two texts. לובן means the white, חלבון the egg white. At the start of the Halakhah, egg white was called "egg water" (at least of uncooked eggs.) לובן חלבון is a double expression; inלובן חלמון the first word should be deleted. In the quote in Tosaphot (*Ḥulin* 64b, והוא), לובן is missing altogether but this cannot be used as a witness to the text.

136 A similar *baraita* is in the Babli, *Ḥulin* 64b, in the name of R. Dositheos ben Patricius.

137 This text is badly transmitted; in its present form it is self-contradictory. In Tosaphot (*loc. cit.* 135), the text reads: "Rebbi Zeïra said, what was said about yolk being forbidden [with a blood spot], if it is found at the male part of the yolk." The second part seems to be another version of the same tradition. The "male part" of the yolk is the place where the yolk meets the thicker part of the egg white strung from a vertex to the yolk.

תַּמָּן תַּנִּינָן אֵלּוּ פוֹסְלִין וְלֹא מַעֲלִין. הַמַּיִם בֵּין טְהוֹרִין בֵּין טְמֵאִין. מֵי כְּבָשִׁים מֵי שְׁלָקוֹת וְהַתֶּמֶד עַד שֶׁלֹּא הֶחֱמִיץ. הָכָא אַתְּ עֲבַד לֵיהּ אוֹכֶל וְהָכָא אַתְּ עֲבַד לֵיהּ מַשְׁקֶה. אָמַר רִבִּי מָנָא כָּאן בְּקָשִׁין כָּאן בְּרַכִּין. כָּאן בְּאוֹכֶל כָּאן בְּמַשְׁקֶה.

אָמַר רִבִּי יוֹסֵי בֵּי רִבִּי בּוּן אֲפִילוּ תֵימַר כָּאן וְכָאן בְּקָשִׁים וְכָאן וְכָאן בְּרַכִּין. נוֹתְנִין טְעָמִים בִּתְרוּמָה וְאֵין נוֹתְנִין טְעָמִים בְּמִקְוֶה.

There[138], we have stated: "The following disable and do not fill[139]: Water, whether pure or impure[140], pickling water, cooking water, afterwine[141] before it became vinegar." Here[142], you treat it as food, there as fluid[143]. Rebbi Mana said, here when it is thick, there when it is thin. Rebbi Yose ben Rebbi Abun said, you may even say in both cases thick or thin. Taste counts for heave[144] but not for a *miqweh*.

138 Mishnah *Miqwa'ot* 7:2.

139 A *miqweh*, or ritual bath, must contain at leat 40 *seah* of natural water, cf. Chapter 4, Note 112. Fluids other than water have no influence on the *miqweh* but water either drawn in a vessel or used for other purposes in the volume of at least three log makes the *miqweh* unusable. If there were 40 *seah* minus 2 *log* in the *miqweh*, adding 2 *log* of water as described in the Mishnah will not produce 40 *seah* of usable water, it does not "fill", and the *miqweh* is still deficient.

140 In a vessel.

141 Obtained by pouring water over husks of grapes. This is water, not wine.

142 The only heave from fluids is from wine and olive oil. If the water described in the Mishnah is forbidden for laymen, then it must have the status of solid food.

143 If the fluids considered food for heave were also food in regard of the laws of the *miqweh*, they would neither disable nor fill.

144 The taste particles in the fluid make it forbidden for laymen, regardless of its status as food.

אין נותנין פרק אחד עשר

(fol. 47c) **משנה א**: אֵין נוֹתְנִין דְּבֵילָה וּגְרוֹגְרוֹת לְתוֹךְ הַמּוּרְיֵיס מִפְּנֵי שֶׁהוּא מְאַבְּדָן אֲבָל נוֹתְנִין אֶת הַיַּיִן לְמוּרְיֵיס וְאֵין מְפַטְּמִין אֶת הַשֶּׁמֶן אֲבָל עוֹשִׂין אֶת הַיַּיִן יֵינוֹמֵילִין. אֵין מְבַשְּׁלִין יַיִן שֶׁל תְּרוּמָה מִפְּנֵי שֶׁהוּא מְמַעִיטוֹ. רִבִּי יְהוּדָה מַתִּיר מִפְּנֵי שֶׁהוּא מַשְׁבִּיחוֹ.

Mishnah 1: One does not put a fig cake or figs[1] into *muries*[2] because he would destroy them[3] but one may add wine to *muries*. One does not use olive oil as base for perfume[4] but one may use wine as base for οἰνόμελι[5]. One may not cook heave wine because he diminishes it; Rebbi Jehudah permits it because he improves it.

1 Of heave. The entire Mishnah deals only with heave.

2 Fish sauce, cf. *Demay*, Chapter 1, Note 156.

3 Fig sap is used as a spice; the figs are then discarded. It is forbidden to use heave for anything but food. Spices which are consumed in their entirety are permitted.

4 This is no longer food.

5 "Wine-honey", a mixture of wine, honey, and spices. The Greek has been hebraized, showing the relationship between יין (Arabic יַיִן "black raisin") and Ϝοιν-.

הלכה א: אֵין נוֹתְנִין דְּבֵילָה וּגְרוֹגְרוֹת לְתוֹךְ הַמּוּרְיֵיס כו'. תַּנֵּי נוֹתֵן דְּבֵילָה וּגְרוֹגְרוֹת לְתוֹךְ הַמּוּרְיֵיס כְּדֶרֶךְ שֶׁנּוֹתֵן תַּבְלִין וּבִלְבַד שֶׁלֹּא יִסְחֲטֵם לְהוֹצִיא מֵימֵיהֶם. וּבְתַבְלִין מוּתָּר שֶׁכָּךְ הִיא מְלַאכְתָּן. צְרוֹר תַּבְלִין שֶׁנְּתָנוֹ לְתוֹךְ קְדֵירָה זוֹ וְחָזַר וּנְתָנָהּ לְתוֹךְ קְדֵירָה אַחֶרֶת אִם יִבָּטֵל טַעֲמוֹ מוּתָּר וְאִם לָאו אָסוּר.

Halakhah 1: "One does not put fig cake or figs into *muries*", etc. It was stated[6]: "One puts fig cake or figs into *muries* in the way one uses spices on condition he not squeeze them to extract their juice[7]. But spices are permitted, for that is what they are used for. A bundle of spices put into one pot and then transferred to another, if their taste is lost they are permitted[8], otherwise forbidden."

6 Tosephta 9:7 where, however, the last sentence is completely different.

7 A rabbinic prohibition, that one should not treat heave figs as he would profane figs and throw them away after squeezing out the juice.

8 If heave spices are used repeatedly, they reach a stage where they will no longer act as spices and are permitted to lay people.

מַה בֵּינָהּ לְבֵין שֶׁבֶת. לֹא כֵן תַּנֵּי הַשֶּׁבֶת שֶׁנָּתַן טַעַם בְּקְדֵירָה אֵין בָּהּ מִשּׁוּם תְּרוּמָה. וְאֵינָהּ מְטַמְּאָה טוּמְאַת אוֹכְלִין. מִשֶּׁלָּךְ נָתְנוּ לָךְ בְּדִין הוּא שֶׁלֹּא תְטַמֵּא טוּמְאַת אוֹכְלִין וְהֵן אָמְרוּ שֶׁתְּטַמֵּא טוּמְאַת אוֹכְלִין. וְהֵן אָמְרוּ מִכֵּיוָן שֶׁנָּתְנָה טַעַם בְּקְדֵירָה בָּטְלָה.

What is the difference between this and dill? Did we not state[9]: "Dill which gave its taste [to a dish] in a pot no longer is under the rules of heave and does not accept the impurity of food." They gave to you from your own. From biblical law it should not accept the impurity of foodstuffs[10]; they said that it should accept the impurity of foodstuffs and they said that after it transferred its taste it is disregarded.

9 Mishnah *Uqeẓin* 3:4.

10 In the opinion of the Babli, dill was never used for cooking but only as raw addition to a dessert. Solid food used only raw is not subject to impurity. Since the impurity of dill is rabbinical, it cannot be considered for inferences about other substances.

רִבִּי חִייָה בְּשֵׁם רִבִּי יוֹחָנָן דְּרִבִּי הִיא דְּתַנֵּי יַיִן לְמוּרְיֵיס רִבִּי מַתִּיר וְרִבִּי אֶלְעָזָר בֵּי רִבִּי שִׁמְעוֹן אוֹסֵר. לְפִיכָךְ אִם עָבַר וְנוֹתְנוֹ רִבִּי אוֹסֵר לְזָרִים. וְרִבִּי אֶלְעָזָר בֵּי רִבִּי שִׁמְעוֹן מַתִּיר לְזָרִים.

Rebbi Ḥiyya in the name of Rebbi Joḥanan: This[11] is Rebbi's, as we have stated[12]: "Wine in *muries*, Rebbi permits but Rebbi Eleazar ben Rebbi Simeon forbids[13]. Therefore, if somebody transgressed and put it in, Rebbi forbids it to laymen but Rebbi Eleazar ben Rebbi Simeon permits to laymen."

11 The sentence in the Mishnah which permits heave wine in fish sauce. This and the following paragraphs are also in *Avodah Zarah* 2:6 (fol. 41c).

12 The last sentence of this *baraita* is similar to a statement of Tosephta 9:6.

13 In his opinion, wine is not usually added to *muries* since it will ruin the taste.

רִבִּי מָנָא בְּרִבִּי תַנְחוּם בָּעֵי כְּדִבְרֵי מִי שֶׁמַּתִּיר לְזָרִים. מוּרְיֵיס שֶׁל גּוֹיִם לָמָּה אָסוּר. רִבִּי יִרְמְיָה בְשֵׁם רִבִּי חִייָא בַּר וָוא מִשּׁוּם בִּישׁוּלֵי גוֹיִם הֵן אֲסוּרִין. הָתִיב רִבִּי יוֹסֵי וְהָתַנֵּי חמין[14] מוּתָּר וּשֶׁאֵינוֹ חמין אָסוּר. חמין מוּתָּר לֹא אֲפִילוּ מְבוּשָּׁלִם וְדִכְוָותָהּ וּשֶׁאֵינוֹ חמין אָסוּר וַאֲפִילוּ שֶׁאֵינוֹ מְבוּשָּׁל. וְאָמַר רִבִּי יוֹחָנָן בַּר מַרְיָה וַאֲפִילוּ כְּמָאן דְּאָמַר חמין מוּתָּר וּבִלְבַד בְּיוֹדֵעַ. הָדָא אָמְרָה הֲנָיַית תְּרוּמָה מוּתֶּרֶת. הֲנָיַית עֲבוֹדָה זָרָה אֲסוּרָה.

Rebbi Mana ben Rebbi Tanḥum asked: Following him who permits to laymen, why is *muries* of Gentiles forbidden[15]? Rebbi Jeremiah in the name of Rebbi Ḥiyya bar Abba, it is forbidden as being cooked by Gentiles[16]. Rebbi Yose objected: Did we not state: "From a professional it is permitted, not from a professional it is forbidden.[17]" From a professional it is permitted even if it is cooked; similarly, from a non-professional[18] it is forbidden even if not cooked. Rebbi Joḥanan bar Maria said, even according to him who says from a professional it is permitted, only if he knows[19]. This implies that usufruct of heave is permitted[20], usufruct of paganism is forbidden[21].

14 In *Avodah Zarah*: אומן. That word has been translated.

15 In Mishnah *Avodah Zarah* 2:5, everybody agrees that Gentile *muries* is forbidden. R. Meïr forbids usufruct from Gentile *muries*, the Sages forbid *muries* only as food.

16 Forbidden in Mishnah *Avodah Zarah* 2:9.

17 Tosephta 4:13, Babli *Avodah Zarah* 34b, state only: "One may buy *muries* only from a professional." Rashi explains that this refers to a Gentile professional producer. The Babli specifies that this holds only for good quality *muries* made with fish fat, which would be spoiled by the addition of wine.

18 A Gentile; he might use wine to clarify the *muries* as explained in the parallel in *Avodah Zarah* 2:6. Tosephta (*loc. cit.*) and Babli (39b) note that at a non-professional Jew's one may eat *muries* without asking.

19 He knows for sure that the seller is a professional in the *muries* trade.

20 If the heave wine cannot be tasted, it is permitted to laymen.

21 If libation wine cannot be tasted, or even if it spoils the taste, it still is forbidden to all Jews.

רִבִּי לֶעְזָר וְרִבִּי יוֹחָנָן חַד אָמַר מִפְּנֵי שֶׁמְּמַעֲטוֹ מִמִּידָּתוֹ. וְחָרָנָה אָמַר מִפְּנֵי שֶׁמְּמַעֲטוֹ מִשּׁוֹתָיו. וְלֹא יָדְעִין מָאן אָמַר דָּא וּמָאן אָמַר דָּא. מִן מַה דְּאָמַר (fol. 47d) רִבִּי יוֹחָנָן מְחַלְּפָה שִׁיטָּתֵיהּ דְּרִבִּי יְהוּדָה. וְאָמַר רִבִּי לָעְזָר אֵינָהּ מוּחְלֶפֶת תַּמָּן בְּכֹהֵן כָּאן בִּבְעָלִים. הֲוֵי רִבִּי יוֹחָנָן הוּא דְאָמַר מִפְּנֵי שֶׁמְּמַעֲטוֹ מִשּׁוֹתָיו.

Rebbi Eleazar and Rebbi Johanan, one of them said because he diminishes its volume, the other says because he reduces the number of drinkers[22]. We did not know who said what. Since Rebbi Johanan said, Rebbi Jehudah inverted his reasoning but Rebbi Eleazar said, Rebbi Jehudah did not invert his reasoning, there for the Cohen, here for the owners, it follows that Rebbi Joḥanan said because he reduces the number of drinkers.

22 The paragraph discusses the statement of the Sages who in the Mishnah prohibit cooking heave wine because "it diminishes." The paragraph was explained in Chapter 2, Halakhah 5, Notes 118-119.

יְהוּדָה בֶּן כֵּינִי רִבִּי אִימִּי בְשֵׁם רִבִּי שִׁמְעוֹן בֶּן לָקִישׁ מִפְּנֵי שֶׁמְּמַעֲטוֹ מִשּׁוֹתָיו.

Jehudah ben Keni[23], Rebbi Ammi in the name of Rebbi Simeon ben Laqish: Because he reduces the number of drinkers.

23 This name probably is an error of transmission. The sentence is not in the parallel in *Avodah Zarah*, nor in Chapter 2.

(fol. 47c) **משנה ב**: דְּבַשׁ תְּמָרִים וְיֵין תַּפּוּחִין וְחוֹמֶץ סִיתְוָנִיּוֹת וּשְׁאָר כָּל־מֵי פֵּירוֹת שֶׁל תְּרוּמָה. רִבִּי לִיעֶזֶר מְחַייֵב קֶרֶן וְחוֹמֶשׁ. וְרִבִּי יְהוֹשֻׁעַ פּוֹטֵר. רִבִּי לִיעֶזֶר מְטַמֵּא מִשּׁוּם מַשְׁקֶה אָמַר רִבִּי יְהוֹשֻׁעַ אוֹמֵר לֹא מָנוּ חֲכָמִים שִׁבְעָה מַשְׁקִין כְּמוֹנֵי פַּטָּמִין אֶלָּא אָמְרוּ שִׁבְעָה מַשְׁקִין טְמֵאִין וּשְׁאָר כָּל־הַמַּשְׁקִין טְהוֹרִין.

Mishnah 2: Date honey, apple wine, vinegar from winter grapes[24], and any other fruit juices from heave, Rebbi Eliezer subjects to [repayment of] value and fifth[25], but Rebbi Joshua frees [from payment]. Rebbi Eliezer declares them impure as drinks[26]. Rebbi Joshua said, the Sages did not enumerate seven fluids as one counts raw materials for perfumes[27] but they said, seven fluids are impure, all other fluids are pure.

24 Late grapes that never became sweet enough to be eaten or used to make wine.

25 If consumed by a non-Cohen in

error, cf. Mishnah 6:1.

26 "Impure" means (a) potentially impure if exposed to impurity and (b) able to prepare solid food for impurity; "pure" means not subject to impurity; cf. *Demay*, Chapter 2, Note 141. The seven fluids subject to impurity are enumerated in Mishnah *Makhširin* 6:4: Dew, water (including human body fluids), wine, olive oil, blood, milk, bees' honey. These fluids are called "drinks", following the verse *Lev.* 11:34.

27 Which the perfumer chooses according to his own wishes.

(fol. 47d) **הלכה ב**: הֲוון בָּעֵי מֵימַר מַה פְלִיגִין בְּחוֹמֶשׁ אֲבָל בְקֶרֶן אַף רִבִּי יְהוֹשֻׁעַ מוֹדֵי. מַה פְלִיגִין לְשֶׁעָבַר הָא בַתְּחִילָּה אַף רִבִּי יְהוֹשֻׁעַ מוֹדֵי. וְתַנִּינָן דְּבַשׁ תְּמָרִים רִבִּי לִיעֶזֶר מְחַייֵב בְּמַעְשְׂרוֹת וְרִבִּי יְהוֹשֻׁעַ פּוֹטֵר. כָּאן שֶׁזָּכוּ מִשֶּׁנִּטְבְּלוּ. וְכָאן שֶׁזָּכוּ עַד שֶׁלֹּא נִטְבְּלוּ.

Halakhah 2: They want to say that they differ about the fifth but Rebbi Joshua agrees about the principal[28]. They differ after the fact[29], but before the fact Rebbi Joshua agrees[30]. But we have stated[31]: "Rebbi Eliezer subjects date honey to tithes, but Rebbi Joshua frees it." Here, when they obtained it after it became *ṭevel*, there before it became *ṭevel*[32].

28 Since the statement is formulated as tentative, if the farmer uses his own date honey from dates destined for the Cohen, he does not pay at all. But if a third person uses it, he has to pay its value as he would for any robbery (Maimonides and R. Abraham ben David, *Terumot* 11:2).

29 About the amount the transgressing layman has to pay.

30 That date honey made from heave dates is forbidden to laymen.

31 Tosephta 9:8; only the statement of R. Eliezer and that of R. Nathan in the next paragraph.

32 If the date honey was taken before the dates themselves became subject to heave and tithes as explained in the first chapter of *Ma'serot*, R. Joshua holds that date honey itself cannot become subject to heave and tithes. But if the honey exuded from the dates after the dates were given as heave, R. Joshua agrees that it remains heave and is forbidden to laymen. The answer is thoroughly impractical since

Mishnah *Ma'serot* 1:2 states that dates become subject to tithes as soon as they contain moisture; it is difficult to see how honey could exude from dates harvested dry even if they were left to ripen in storage.

מוֹדֶי רִבִּי לִיעֶזֶר שֶׁאִם עִישֵּׂר עַל הַתְּמָרִים אֲפִילוּ בְּאִסְפַּמְיָא דִּבְשָׁן מוּתָּר. מִילְתֵיהּ אָמַר שֶׁהוּא מְעַשֵּׂר מִן הַתְּמָרִים עַל הַדְּבָשׁ לְפִי תְּמָרִים. רִבִּי לִיעֶזֶר מְחַייֵב בְּמַעְשְׂרוֹת. תַּנֵּי רִבִּי נָתָן אוֹמֵר לֹא שֶׁרִבִּי לִיעֶזֶר מְחַייֵב בְּמַעְשְׂרוֹת אֶלָּא שֶׁרִבִּי לִיעֶזֶר אוֹמֵר שֶׁלֹּא יֹאכַל מִן הַתְּמָרִים עַד שֶׁיְּעַשֵּׂר עַל הַדְּבָשׁ. מִילְתֵיהּ אָמַר שֶׁהוּא מְעַשֵּׂר מִן הַתְּמָרִים עַל הַדְּבָשׁ לְפִי דְבָשׁ וּלְפִי תְּמָרִים.

Rebbi Eliezer agrees that if he tithed the dates, their honey is permitted even in Spain[33]. This implies that he tithes dates including honey proportional to the dates. "Rebbi Eliezer subjects date honey to tithes." We have stated[31]: "Rebbi Nathan says, not that Rebbi Eliezer subjects it to tithes but Rebbi Eliezer says he should not eat from the tithes until he also tithed the honey." This implies that he tithes dates including honey proportional[34] to honey and dates.

33 If the dates were tithed when dry and the honey was produced later from exported dates, the honey remains permitted. (Since the text is not punctuated, it would be possible to read: If he tithed the dates even in Spain, their honey would be permitted. However, this interpretation is impossible since fruits of the Land cannot be tithed in Spain, not even in Apamea in Syria.)

34 In volume.

רִבִּי לִיעֶזֶר מְטַמֵּא מִשּׁוּם מַשְׁקֶה. תַּנֵּי רִבִּי נָתָן אוֹמֵר לֹא שֶׁרִבִּי לִיעֶזֶר מְטַמֵּא מִשּׁוּם מַשְׁקֶה עַל מַה נֶחְלְקוּ עַל שֶׁנָּפַל לְתוֹכוֹ מַשְׁקֶה. שֶׁרִבִּי לִיעֶזֶר מְטַמֵּא מִשּׁוּם מַשְׁקֶה. וַחֲכָמִים אוֹמְרִים הוֹלְכִין אַחַר הָרוֹב.

"Rebbi Eliezer declares it[35] impure as drink." It was stated: "Rebbi Nathan said, Rebbi Eliezer does not declare it impure as drink; what did they disagree about? If some drink[36] fell into it, then Rebbi Eliezer declares it impure as drink but the Sages say, it follows the majority[37]."

35 The Tosephta (9:8) makes it clear that only date honey is being discussed.

36 In the Tosephta: "Water".

37 It is not a "drink" as long as there is more than 50% date honey.

עַל דַּעְתֵּיהּ דְּרִבִּי נָתָן רִבִּי מֵאִיר וְרִבִּי לִיעֶזֶר בֶּן יַעֲקֹב וְרִבִּי לִיעֶזֶר שְׁלָשְׁתָּן אָמְרוּ דָּבָר אֶחָד. רִבִּי מֵאִיר דּוּ אָמַר אֵין מֵי פֵּירוֹת בְּטֵילִין לְעוֹלָם. רִבִּי לִיעֶזֶר בֶּן יַעֲקֹב דְּתַנֵּי רִבִּי לִיעֶזֶר בֶּן יַעֲקֹב אוֹמֵר צִיר טָהוֹר שֶׁנָּפַל לְתוֹכוֹ מַיִם כָּל־שֶׁהוּא טָמֵא. וְהָדֵין רִבִּי לִיעֶזֶר דְּהָכָא.

In the opinion of Rebbi Nathan, Rebbi Meïr, Rebbi Eliezer ben Jacob, and Rebbi Eliezer, all three said the same. Rebbi Meïr, for he says[38], "fruit juice never is disregarded." Rebbi Eliezer ben Jacob as we have stated[39]: "Pure fish sauce into which fell the smallest amount of water is impure." And Rebbi Eliezer here.

38 It seems that this refers to the anonymous Mishnah *Miqwa'ot* 7:2, presumed to be R. Meïr's teaching, which states that if a *miqweh* is short one half *seah* of the required 40 *seah* of water (cf. Chapter 4, Note 112, Chapter 19, Note 139), if one half of a *seah* of fruit juice fell in, the status of the *miqweh* is not changed. If the character of fruit juice could be disregarded (being less than 1 in 60 of the total amount), then the watered down fruit juice could make up the difference.

39 Mishnah *Makhširin* 6:3. Usually, fish sauce is impure since fish, coming out of the water, is always prepared for impurity (*Demay*, Chapter 2, Note 141.) If it is known that the fish sauce was extracted from pure fish by people strictly keeping the laws of purity, then the fish sauce is pure and, since it is not one of the "seven fluids" (Note 26), cannot become impure. But if any amount of water is added, it is prepared for impurity.

טַעֲמָא דְּרִבִּי לִיעֶזֶר וְכָל־מַשְׁקֶה. מַה טַעֲמָא דְּרַבָּנִין אֲשֶׁר יִשָּׁתֶה. מָה רִבִּי לִיעֶזֶר כְּרִבִּי יִשְׁמָעֵאל דְּרִבִּי יִשְׁמָעֵאל דּוּ אָמַר כְּלָל וּפְרָט הַכֹּל בִּכְלָל. וְרוּבָּה מִדְּרִבִּי יִשְׁמָעֵאל דּוּ אָמַר אֲפִילוּ כְּלָל וּפְרָט וְחָזַר וְכָלַל הַכֹּל בִּכְלָל. רִבִּי פֶּרֵיגוֹרִי דְקַיְסָרִין אָמַר רִבִּי לִיעֶזֶר בֵּי רִבִּי יִשְׁמָעֵאל אֶלָּא כָּךְ מֵשִׁיב רִבִּי לִיעֶזֶר לַחֲכָמִים מַה דְאִית לְכוֹן אֲשֶׁר יֵאָכֵל פְּרָט לְאוֹכֶל סָרוּחַ. כֵּן אִית לִי אֲשֶׁר יִשָּׁתֶה פְּרָט לְמַשְׁקֶה סָרוּחַ. אָמַר לוֹ לֹא דוֹמִין אוֹכְלִין לְמַשְׁקִין. לֹא אִם אָמַרְתָּ בְּאוֹכְלִין שֶׁכֵּן אוֹכֶל סָרוּחַ מֵעִיקָּרוֹ טָהוֹר. תֹּאמַר בְּמַשְׁקִין שֶׁכֵּן מַשְׁקֶה סָרוּחַ מֵעִיקָּרוֹ טָמֵא. דָּבָר אַחֵר לֹא אִם אָמַרְתָּ בְּאוֹכְלִין שֶׁכֵּן אוֹכְלִין הַמְּיוּחָדִין לְאָדָם אֵין צְרִיכִין מַחֲשָׁבָה. תֹּאמַר בְּמַשְׁקִין שֶׁכֵּן מַשְׁקִין הַמְּיוּחָדִין לְאָדָם צְרִיכִין מַחֲשָׁבָה. וּמִפְּנֵי שֶׁצְּרִיכִין מַחֲשָׁבָה יְהֵא מַשְׁקִין סָרוּחַ מֵעִיקָּרוֹ טָמֵא. הוֹאִיל וְהֵן צְרִיכִין מַחֲשָׁבָה יְהֵא מַשְׁקֶה סָרוּחַ מֵעִיקָּרוֹ טָהוֹר. דָּבָר אַחֵר אָמְרוּ לוֹ לֹא אִם אָמַרְתָּ בְּאוֹכְלִין שֶׁכֵּן אוֹכְלֵי בְהֵמָה לְאָדָם אֵינָן בָּאִין בְּמַחֲשָׁבָה. תֹּאמַר בְּמַשְׁקִין שֶׁכֵּן מַשְׁקֶה בְהֵמָה לְאָדָם בָּאִין בְּמַחֲשָׁבָה. וְתַנֵּי כֵן כָּל־מַשְׁקֶה מַה תַלְמוּד לוֹמַר אֲשֶׁר יִשָּׁתֶה פְּרָט לְמַשְׁקֶה סָרוּחַ דִּבְרֵי רִבִּי לִיעֶזֶר. אָמְרוּ לוֹ אֵין מַשְׁקִין יוֹצְאִין לֹא עַל יְדֵי עוֹפוֹת וְלֹא עַל יְדֵי פָּרָה.

The reason of Rebbi Eliezer (*Lev.* 11:34): "Any drink." What is the reason of the rabbis? "That can be drunk.[40]" Does Rebbi Eliezer hold with Rebbi Ismael, that for a particular statement after a general one, everything is included[41]? He assumes more than Rebbi Ismael, in that even if there is a second general statement, all is included[42]. Rebbi Paregoros from Caesarea[43]: Rebbi Eliezer ben Rebbi Ismael said: So did Rebbi Eliezer answer the Sages: Since you interpret (*Lev.* 11:34): "That can be eaten," to exclude stinking food[44], so I hold "that can be drunk," to exclude stinking drinks. They said to him, solid food and drinks are not comparable. If you argue about food, which is pure if stinking from the start[45], what can you infer for drinks since drinks stinking from the start can become impure[46]? Another approach: If you argue about food, when human food does not need thinking about, what can you infer for drinks since human drink needs thinking about[47]? Because they need thinking about them, should drinks stinking from the start become impure? Because they need thinking about them, drinks stinking from the start should be pure[48]! Another approach. They said to him: If you argue about food, animal feed for humans is not created by thought[49], what can you infer for drinks since animal drinks for humans need thought? We have stated thus[50]: (*Lev.* 11:34) "Any drink," why does the verse have to add "that can be drunk"? This excludes stinking drinks, the words of Rebbi Eliezer. They said to him, no drink is rejected by birds or a cow.

40 *Lev.* 11:34: "Any food that can be eaten, if water comes upon it it may become impure, and any drink that can be drunk can become impure in any vessel." For the notion of preparation for impurity based on this and the nearby verses, cf. Note 26.

The argument ascribed here to the rabbis is difficult to understand and is not found in any of the parallel sources; it is not followed up and is superseded later by the documented opinion of the rabbis. The emphasis is only on the arguments of R. Eliezer, to show that R. Eliezer's position in the Mishnah is not practice, even if R. Eliezer's position in the Tosephta would be accepted because he is supported by R. Meïr and R. Eliezer ben Jacob. {Maimonides, *Hilkhot Ṭum'at Okhlin* 2:14, follows R. Eliezer; the interpretation here follows R. Abraham ben David *ad loc.*}

In *Sifra Šemini Parašah* 8(1), fruit juices are excluded since the verse speaks only of "water". It is concluded that only drinks described by a single noun can be meant. Blood is included [*loc. cit.* 8(4)] since it is compared to water in *Ps.* 110:7. Fruit juices are excluded since they are called "fruit water".

41 "A general statement followed by a particular one" is the heading of one of the 13 hermeneutical rules of R. Ismael, listed in the Introduction to *Sifra*. The detailed description of the rule, that a general statement followed by a particular one applies only to that particular one, is no longer connected with the name of R. Ismael; it represents the opinion of the Sages. For an application, cf. *Kilaim* Chapter 8, Note 20.

It is asserted here and in *Nazir* 6:2 that R. Ismael disagrees with the interpretation of the Sages and holds that the particular statement is only an illustration. The concurrence of both mss. here and the one available ms. in *Nazir* shows that the statement cannot be amended away and that in the Introduction to *Sifra*, only paragraphs 1 and 2 are attributable to R. Ismael.

In our case, "any drink" is taken as a general statement, "that can be drunk" as a particular one.

42 This is a theoretical statement, not of relevance here, since the particular is not followed by a second general statement. However, it opens a window for a possible study of the development of the hermeneutical rules.

43 He is mentioned only here. Greek παρήγορος "comforting", a sobriquet for Menaḥem; cf. E. and H. Guggenheimer, *Jewish Family Names and their Origins* (Hoboken, NJ, 1992; *Etymologisches Lexikon der jüdischen Familiennamen*, München 1996), entry Perigord.

44 *Sifra Šemini Pereq* 9(1). Since spoiled food is no longer food, it is not subject to the impurity of food.

45 The expression is unclear since foodstuffs spoiled when coming into being never were food and, therefore, never subject to impurity of food.

46 This argument refers to the quote from *Sifra*, Note 50, that water is subject to impurity as long as it is acceptable to animals and birds.

47 Mishnah *Uqeẓin* 3:1: "All that is exclusively human food needs preparation [for impurity] but no thought." Once prepared for impurity it automatically is ready to accept impurity. Tosephta *Ṭevul Yom* 1:5: "Foodstuffs [in certain aspects] have more restrictive rules than drinks, and drinks [in certain aspects] have more restrictive rules than foodstuffs. Food may have handles [the peduncles of apples, pears, etc. become impure with the fruit], they do not need thought to be food." Any fluid other than water is a "drink" only if made for human consumption.

48 Since nobody will want them as human drink.

49 This refers to vetch which is human food only in times of famine and, according to R. Jehudah in Tosephta *Uqeẓin* 3:13, and the Sages in Mishnah *Ḥallah* 4:10, is treated as standard food if prepared as such. This means that vetch becomes human food only by a combination of intent and action, never by intent alone, in contrast to drinks.

50 *Sifra Šemini Parašah* 8(4).

חֲבֵרַייָא בְשֵׁם רִבִּי לָֽעְזָר מוֹדֶה רִבִּי לִיעֶזֶר לַחֲכָמִים בְּמַשְׁקֶה סָרוּחַ מֵעִיקָּרוֹ שֶׁהוּא טָמֵא. וְהָתַנִּינָן הַמּוֹהַל הַיּוֹצֵא מֵהֶן רִבִּי לִיעֶזֶר מְטַהֵר וַחֲכָמִים מְטַמְּאִין. רִבִּי אִילָא בְשֵׁם רִבִּי לָֽעְזָר מוֹדֶה רִבִּי לִיעֶזֶר לַחֲכָמִים בְּמֵי יַם הַגָּדוֹל שֶׁאֲפִילוּ הֵן סְרוּחִין הַתּוֹרָה קָרָא אוֹתָן מַיִם. וּלְמִקְוֵה הַמַּיִם קָרָא יַמִּים. רִבִּי יַעֲקֹב בַּר זַבְדִּי בְשֵׁם רִבִּי אַבָּהוּ מוֹדֵי רִבִּי לִיעֶזֶר לַחֲכָמִים בְּמֵי תְּרָדִין וּבְמֵי שְׁלָקוֹת שֶׁאֵינָן מַכְשִׁירִין.

The colleagues in the name of Rebbi Eleazar: Rebbi Eliezer agrees with the Sages that if a drink is stinking from the start it is impure. But did we not state[51]: "The fluid oozing out from them Rebbi Eliezer declares pure but the Sages impure"? Rebbi Ila in the name of Rebbi Eleazar: Rebbi Eliezer agrees with the Sages about the waters of the ocean; even if they are stinking the Torah calls them water (*Gen.* 1:10): "The collection of water He called oceans." Rebbi Jacob bar Zavdi in the name of Rebbi Abbahu: Rebbi Eliezer agrees with the Sages that beet juice[52] does not prepare.

51 Mishnah *Ṭahorot* 9:3, speaking of the sap of olives which is not oil but fruit juice. Even though it does not smell badly, it is useless and we see that R. Eliezer declares useless fruit sap to be impure.

In the Mishnah, R. Simeon disagrees with the anonymous Tanna and holds that R. Eliezer declares olive sap pure. Since the Yerushalmi lacks this statement, it seems to reject the statements of R. Simeon and the colleagues.

52 תרד (Hebrew) and שלק (Arabic) are the same; cf. *Kilaim* Chapter 1, Note 64.

רִבִּי יוֹחָנָן בְּשֵׁם רִבִּי שִׁמְעוֹן בֶּן יוֹחַי אִם יֹאמַר לָךְ אָדָם שְׁמוֹנָה מַשְׁקִין הֵן אֱמוֹר לוֹ הֲרֵי טַל וּמַיִם מִין אֶחָד הֵן וּמָנוּ אוֹתָן חֲכָמִים שְׁנַיִם. אִילּוּ הֲוָה לָן חוֹרָן לֹא מְנִינֵיהּ וְאִין הֲוָה חוֹרָן לֹא הֲוָה מְנִינֵיהּ.

Rebbi Joḥanan in the name of Rebbi Simeon ben Ioḥai: If somebody would say to you there are eight drinks[53], tell him, are not dew and water the same? But they counted them as two! If we had another[54], would they not have counted it? If another did exist[55], would they not have counted it?

53 The seven drinks which prepare for impurity (Note 26) and fruit juice.

54 Fruit juice, known to us from the controversy of R. Eliezer and the Sages.

55 Unknown to us.

(fol. 47c) **משנה ג**: אֵין עוֹשִׂין תְּמָרִים דְּבָשׁ וְלֹא תַפּוּחִין יַיִן וְלֹא סִתְוָנִיּוֹת חוֹמֶץ וּשְׁאָר כָּל־הַפֵּירוֹת אֵין מְשַׁנִּין אוֹתָן מִבִּירְיָיתָן בִּתְרוּמָה וּבְמַעֲשֵׂר שֵׁנִי אֶלָּא זֵיתִים וַעֲנָבִים בִּלְבַד. אֵין סוֹפְגִין אַרְבָּעִים מִשּׁוּם עָרְלָה אֶלָּא עַל הַיּוֹצֵא מִן הַזֵּיתִים וּמִן הָעֲנָבִים. וְאֵין מְבִיאִין בִּכּוּרִים מַשְׁקִין אֶלָּא הַיּוֹצֵא מִן הַזֵּיתִים וּמִן הָעֲנָבִים. אֵינוֹ מְטַמֵּא מִשּׁוּם מַשְׁקֶה אֶלָּא הַיּוֹצֵא מִן הַזֵּיתִים וּמִן הָעֲנָבִים. וְאֵין מַקְרִיבִין עַל גַּבֵּי הַמִּזְבֵּחַ אֶלָּא הַיּוֹצֵא מִן הַזֵּיתִים וּמִן הָעֲנָבִים.

Mishnah 3: One does not make honey from dates, or wine from apples, or vinegar from winter grapes, nor does one change any fruit of heave or second tithe from the way it grew except olives and grapes[58]. Nobody endures the forty[57] because of *'orlah*, except for produce of olives and grapes[58]; one does not bring First Fruits as drinks except for products from olives and grapes. Nothing makes impure as a drink except what comes from olives and grapes[59]. Nothing is presented on the altar except what comes from olives and grapes.

משנה ד: עוּקְצֵי תְאֵינִים וּגְרוֹגְרוֹת וְהַכְּלָסִים וְהֶחָרוּבִים אֲסוּרִין לְזָרִים.

Mishnah 4: The stalks of fresh figs, dried figs, *kelisin*[60], and carobs are forbidden to laymen[61].

56 Since heave is due from oil and wine by biblical decree, olives and grapes may be (or should be) processed into oil and wine. All other fruits of heave have to be consumed in their natural state even if they are preferable in processed state. Winter grapes do not contain enough sugar to produce wine.

57 Is whipped 39 times if convicted of breaking a biblical law.

58 The verse *Lev.* 29:23 declaring the fruits of the first three years after planting a tree forbidden for all use refers to "fruit-bearing trees"; in Mishnah *Kilaim* 7:6 there is an opinion that exludes all trees except olive trees, vines, and fig trees from this category.

59 In the Babli, *Ḥulin* 120b, all these rules are said to follow R. Joshua who derives all rules from those of heave.

60 The Gaonic commentary to *Uqeẓin* 1:6 reads קליסין and defines these as pears. Maimonides: small figs. Rashi (*Ḥulin* 67a) about בלונס, adopted here by R. Simson: cedar kernels. Rashi's definition clearly does not fit here. Maimonides's interpretation seems to be a guess. Löw thinks of licorice. {Cf. Greek κέρασος, Latin *cerasus*, "cherry tree, cherry" (E. G.).}

61 If the fruit itself is heave.

(fol. 47d) **הלכה ג**: רִבִּי אִילָא בְשֵׁם רִבִּי לָעְזָר כֵּינִי מַתְנִיתָא אֵין מְבִיאִין בִּכּוּרִים מַשְׁקִין אֶלָּא הַיּוֹצֵא מִן הַזֵּיתִים וּמִן הָעֲנָבִים. וַאֲפִילוּ מִשֶּׁזָּכוּ בָהֶן בְּעָלִים. וְהָתַנֵּי דָּרַךְ בִּיכּוּרִים מַשְׁקֶה לַהֲבִיאָן מְנַיִין שֶׁיָּבִיא תַּלְמוּד לוֹמַר תָּבִיא. מִשֶּׁלְּקָטָן מִשָּׁעָה רִאשׁוֹנָה עַל מְנָת כָּךְ. בְּרַם הָכָא בְּשֶׁלֹּא לְקָטָן מִשָּׁעָה רִאשׁוֹנָה עַל מְנָת כָּךְ.

Halakhah 3: [62]Rebbi Ila in the name of Rebbi Eleazar: So says the Mishnah, "one does not bring First Fruits as drinks except for those made from olives and grapes," even after it became property of the owners[63]. But did we not state: "If he pressed First Fruits as a drink, from where that he should bring them? The verse says (*Ex.* 23:19, 34:26), 'bring!'[64]". That is, if he harvested them from the start for this purpose. But here, if he did not harvest them from the start for this purpose[65].

62 The main occurrence of this paragraph is in *Ḥallah* 4:12, on the Mishnah: "Joseph the Cohen brought his First Fruits as olive oil and wine and these were not accepted in the Temple." That Mishnah seems to contradict the Mishnah here; cf. *Šiṭṭah Mequbeẓet*, *Ḥulin* 120b, Note 11.

63 The priests serving in the Temple. Since First Fruits were designated as such while still growing, they were already dedicated when harvested and never were property of the farmer.

64 Since the commandment is repeated, it means "bring in any shape or form."

65 In the interpretation of the Babli, the entire discussion is only about grapes. It is difficult to decide whether this is also the point of view of the Yerushalmi.

זֵיתִים שֶׁל תְּרוּמָה טְהוֹרִים יֵיעָשׂוּ שֶׁמֶן. טְמֵאִין לֹא יֵיעָשׂוּ. וַעֲנָבִים בֵּין טְמֵאוֹת בֵּין טְהוֹרוֹת לֹא יֵיעָשׂוּ דִּבְרֵי רִבִּי מֵאִיר. רִבִּי יַעֲקֹב אוֹמֵר מִשְּׁמוֹ לֹא נֶחְלְקוּ רִבִּי לִיעֶזֶר וְרִבִּי יהוֹשֻׁעַ עַל זֵיתִים טְהוֹרִין שֶׁיֵּיעָשׂוּ עַל מַה נֶּחְלְקוּ עַל הַטְּמֵאִים שֶׁרִבִּי לִיעֶזֶר אוֹמֵר לֹא יֵיעָשׂוּ וְרִבִּי יוֹשׁוּעַ אוֹמֵר יֵיעָשׂוּ וַעֲנָבִים טְהוֹרוֹת יֵיעָשׂוּ. טְמֵאוֹת לֹא יֵיעָשׂוּ. אָמַר רִבִּי יוּדָן מוֹדֶה רִבִּי לִיעֶזֶר וְרִבִּי יהוֹשֻׁעַ בְּזֵיתִים טְהוֹרִין שֶׁיֵּיעָשׂוּ עַל מַה נֶּחְלְקוּ עַל הַטְּמֵאִים שֶׁרִבִּי לִיעֶזֶר אוֹמֵר לֹא יֵיעָשׂוּ וְרִבִּי יוֹשׁוּעַ אוֹמֵר יֵיעָשׂוּ וַעֲנָבִים בֵּין טְהוֹרוֹת בֵּין טְמֵאוֹת יֵיעָשׂוּ. אָמַר רִבִּי יוֹחָנָן מוֹדֶה רִבִּי לִיעֶזֶר וְרִבִּי יְהוֹשֻׁעַ בְּזֵיתִים טְהוֹרִין שֶׁיֵּיעָשׂוּ וַעֲנָבִים טְמֵאוֹת שֶׁלֹּא יֵיעָשׂוּ. וְעַל מַה נֶּחְלְקוּ עַל זֵיתִים טְמֵאִים וְעַל עֲנָבִים טְהוֹרוֹת שֶׁרִבִּי לִיעֶזֶר אוֹמֵר לֹא יֵיעָשׂוּ וְרִבִּי יְהוֹשֻׁעַ אוֹמֵר יֵיעָשׂוּ. כָּל־עַמָּא רַבִּיָן עַל דְּרִבִּי מֵאִיר בַּעֲנָבִים טְהוֹרוֹת שֶׁיֵּיעָשׂוּ וְלָמָּה אָמַר לֹא יֵיעָשׂוּ. חֲשׁוּבוֹת הֵן לְאוֹכֶל יוֹתֵר מִן הַמַּשְׁקֶה. כָּל־עַמָּא רָבִין עַל דְּרִבִּי יוּדָן בַּעֲנָבִים טְמֵאוֹת שֶׁלֹּא יֵיעָשׂוּ. וְלָמָּה אָמְרוּ שֶׁיֵּיעָשׂוּ בִּשְׁבִיל לֵיהָנוֹת מִן הַחַרְצָנִים וּמִן הַזָּגִין. זֵיתִים טְמֵאִים רִבִּי וְרִבִּי מֵאִיר חַד רִבִּי יַעֲקֹב וְרִבִּי יוּדָה חָדָא. הֵיךְ עָבְדִין עוּבְדָא.

"[66]Pure heave olives should be made into oil, impure should not; grapes either pure or impure should not be processed [into wine], the words of Rebbi Meïr. Rebbi Jacob says in his name, Rebbi Eliezer and Rebbi Joshua did not disagree that pure olives should be processed; they disagreed about impure ones where Rebbi Eliezer says they should not be processed, but Rebbi Joshua said they should be processed, and pure grapes should be processed, but not impures ones. Rebbi Jehudah said, Rebbi Eliezer and Rebbi Joshua did not disagree that pure olives should be processed; they disagreed about impure ones where Rebbi Eliezer says they should not be processed, but Rebbi Joshua said they should be processed, and grapes should be processed, whether pure or impure[67]. Rebbi (Joḥanan)[68] said, Rebbi Eliezer and Rebbi Joshua did not disagree that pure olives should be processed and impure grapes should not be processed; they disagreed about impure olives and pure grapes where Rebbi Eliezer says they should not be processed, but Rebbi Joshua said they should be processed." They all form a majority against Rebbi Meïr about pure grapes, that they should be processed. Why does he say, they should not be processed? They are more valuable as food than as drink. They all form a majority against Rebbi Jehudah about impure grapes, that they should not be processed. Why does he say, they should be processed? To be able to use seeds and skins[69]. About impure olives, Rebbi and Rebbi Meïr form one group, Rebbi Jacob and Rebbi Jehudah another one. How does one act[70]?

66 Tosephta 9:9, in slightly different formulation.

67 In the Tosephta: Rebbi Jehudah said, Rebbi Eliezer and Rebbi Joshua did not disagree that pure olives *and grapes* should be processed, they disagreed about impure ones which Rebbi Eliezer says should not be processed, but Rebbi Joshua said they should be.

68 This is clearly in error since the entire statement is tannaïtic and in the discussion, as well as in the Tosephta, it is labelled Rebbi's. The error is an old one since it is in both mss.

69 The grape juice clearly has to be discarded since it is impure and cannot be used as drink. Since it is fresh and unfermented, it cannot be used as spray. But the seeds and the

skins can be used as fuel.

70 No answer is given; the decision is prorogated for the Sages at the time of the Messiah.

רִבִּי זְעִירָא בְשֵׁם רִבִּי לָעְזָר אָמַר[71] מַתְנִיתִין בְּמוּבְלַעַת בְּאוֹכֶל. רִבִּי זְעִירָא כָּל־דִּתְרוּמוֹת וְטָהֳרוֹת שְׁמוּעָה בְשֵׁם רִבִּי לָעְזָר.

Rebbi Zeïra in the name of Rebbi Eleazar said, our Mishnah[72] if they stick in the food. All [statements] by Rebbi Zeïra about heaves and purity are traditions in the name of Rebbi Eleazar.

71 Reading of the Rome ms., R. Simson, and R. S. Adani. Venice and Leyden: **אם**

72 Mishnah 4. If the pedicles are not part of the fruit they are considered as wood and not included in the sanctity of heave.

(fol. 47c) **משנה ה**: גַּרְעִינֵי תְרוּמָה בִּזְמַן שֶׁהֵן מְכַנְּסָן הֵן אֲסוּרוֹת וְאִם הִשְׁלִיכָן מוּתָּרוֹת. וְכֵן עֲצָמוֹת שֶׁל קֳדָשִׁים בִּזְמַן שֶׁהוּא מְכַנְּסָן אֲסוּרִין וְאִים הִשְׁלִיכָן מוּתָּרִין. הַמּוּרְסָן מוּתָּר. סוּבִּין שֶׁל חֲדָשׁוֹת אֲסוּרוֹת וְשֶׁל יְשָׁנוֹת מוּתָּרוֹת. נוֹהֵג בִּתְרוּמָה כְדֶרֶךְ שֶׁהוּא נוֹהֵג בְּחוּלִין. הַמְסַלֵּת קַב אוֹ קַבַּיִים לַסְּאָה לֹא יֹאבֵד אֶת הַשְּׁאָר אֶלָּא יַנִּיחֶנּוּ בְּמָקוֹם הַמּוּצְנָע.

Mishnah 5: The seeds of heave, as long as they are collected[73], are forbidden but if they are thrown away they are permitted. And so bones of sacrifices, as long as they are collected[73], are forbidden but if they are thrown away they are permitted. Coarse bran is permitted; fine bran of new grain is forbidden, of old it is permitted. One treats heave as one treats profane food[74]. If one makes fine flour, one or two *qab* from a *seah*, he should not throw away the remainder but put it down in a hidden place[75].

73 As food.

74 An example is given in the next sentence.

75 Since the remainder is coarse flour, it is food for somebody else and may not be thrown away.

(fol. 47d) **הלכה ד**: אָמַר רִבִּי יוֹחָנָן בְּגַלְעִינֵי אַגַּסִּין וּקְרוּסְטוּמֵלִין הִיא מַתְנִיתָא. אָמַר רִבִּי לִיעֶזֶר וַאֲפִילוּ תֵימַר בְּגַלְעִינֵי הָרוֹטֶב. בִּמְחוּסָּרוֹת לְמַצְמֵץ. וְהָא תַנִּינָן וְכֵן[75] עֲצָמוֹת הֶקְדֵּשׁ אִית לָךְ מֵימַר בִּמְחוּסָּרוֹת לְמַצְמֵץ. לֹא בְּרָאשֵׁי כְנָפַיִם הַסְּחוּסִין. אָתָא רִבִּי אָבָהוּ בְּשֵׁם רִבִּי יוֹחָנָן בְּרָאשֵׁי כְנָפַיִם הַסְּחוּסִין הוּא מַתְנִיתָא.

Halakhah 4: Rebbi Joḥanan, the Mishnah deals with seeds of pears and paradise pears[76]. Rebbi Eleazar said, you can even say the pit of unripe dates if they have not been sucked[77]. But did we not state, "and so bones of sacrifices;" can you say if they have not been sucked[78]? No, about cartilage[79] in wings. Rebbi Abbahu came in the name of Rebbi Joḥanan: The Mishnah speaks of cartilage in wings.

76 Greek χρυστουμῖνος, Latin *crustuminus* "Crustumerian pear"; cf. *Kilaim* Chapter 1, Note 73. Their seeds are eaten with the fruits.

77 If these are separated from the dates, some fruit flesh will cling to the pits. This will have to be eaten before the pit loses its sanctity.

78 If the bones contain marrow, they may not be discarded. If they contain no marrow and are clean, nothing can be taken from them.

79 Which is edible.

וְאֵלּוּ הֵן הַחֲדָשׁוֹת כָּל־זְמָן שֶׁהַבְּרִיּוֹת רְגִילִים לַחֲבוֹט. רִבִּי אָחָא אָמַר עַד שְׁלֹשִׁים יוֹם.

"These are the new ones, all the time people regularly mash them. Rebbi Aḥa said, up to thirty days.[80]"

80 Tosephta 10:4. This refers to the Mishnah stating that new fine bran is forbidden to laymen. The Tanna R. Aḥa (Aḥai) mentioned here is one of the students of R. Aqiba.

רִבִּי אַבָּהוּ בְשֵׁם רִבִּי יוֹחָנָן כֵּן הִיא שִׁיעוּרָהּ. וְהָתַנֵּי מְסַלֵּת בְּחִטִּין כָּל־שֶׁהוּא רוֹצֶה. וּמְנַקֵּב בְּיָרָק כָּל־שֶׁהוּא רוֹצֶה. רִבִּי אַבָּהוּ בְשֵׁם רִבִּי יוֹחָנָן בְּמַעֲמִידוֹ עַל תְּרוּמָתוֹ. רִבִּי יִרְמְיָה (fol. 48a) בְּשֵׁם רִבִּי אִילָא כָּאן בִּשְׁנֵי רְעָבוֹן כָּאן בִּשְׁנֵי שׂוֹבַע.

Rebbi Abbahu in the name of Rebbi Joḥanan: That is its measure[81]. But did we not state[82]: "One produces fine flour from wheat as he wants it, he cleans vegetables[83] as he wants it." Rebbi Abbahu in the name of Rebbi Joḥanan: When he reduces it to its heave[84]. Rebbi Jeremiah in the name of Rebbi Ila: Here in years of famine[85], there in years of plenty.

81 One or two *qab* of fine flour per *seah* of wheat grain.

82 *Sifra Emor Pereq* 4:11, on the verse *Lev.* 22:7: "For it is his food." This is interpreted that the Cohen may treat heave as he would treat profane food. If he eats profane bread only from the whitest flour and vegetables only if they are free from all blemishes, he does not have to lower his standards for heave.

83 The Cohen may remove the outer leaves of heave vegetables and eat only the perfect ones.

84 While the standard is 1 *qab* per *seah*, i. e., a yield of 16.67%, a very selective Cohen will be able to refine it to a yield of only 10%, corresponding to heave of the tithe.

85 The standard of the Mishnah has to be followed in years of famine; any refinement is possible in a year of plenty.

תַּמָּן תַּנִּינָן מְעֵי אֲבַטִּיחַ וּקְנִיבַת יָרָק שֶׁל תְּרוּמָה. רִבִּי דוֹסָא מַתִּיר לְזָרִים וַחֲכָמִים אוֹסְרִים. רִבִּי אַבָּהוּ בְשֵׁם רִבִּי יוֹחָנָן לֹא שָׁנוּ אֶלָּא בִקְנִיבַת יָרָק שֶׁל גַּנָּנִין. אֲבָל בִּקְנִיבַת יָרָק שֶׁל בַּעֲלֵי בָתִּים אַף רַבָּנִין מוֹדִיין. רִבִּי בּוּן בָּעֵיין. לֹא מִסְתַּבְּרָא בִתְרוּמָה גְדוֹלָה אֲבָל בִּתְרוּמַת מַעֲשֵׂר אֵין הֶעָלִין תְּלוּשִׁין עַל הֶעָלִין וְלֹא הַקְּלָחִין תְּלוּשִׁין עַל הַקְּלָחִין.

There[86], we have stated: "The center parts of water melon and what is cleaned from vegetables of heave, Rebbi Dosa permits to laymen but the

Sages forbid." Rebbi Abbahu in the name of Rebbi Joḥanan: They taught that only for what is cleaned from vegetables of gardeners[87]. But for what is cleaned from vegetables of private people, even the rabbis will agree. Rebbi Abun asked: Is it not reasonable that this refers only to the Great Heave, but for heave of the tithe[88] torn-off leaves do not count for leaves, neither do torn-off stems for stems?

86 Mishnah Idiut 3:3, Tosephta 10:2.

87 Since they clean large quantities of vegetables for the market, they will find a use for the leaves taken off. If they are of heave, they do not lose their status. But in private households, the cleanings of vegetables are garbage and garbage of heave is profane (R. Abraham ben David, Commentary to *Sifra Šemini Pereq* 4:2.)

88 Which has to be exactly 10%. Therefore, the leaves to be discarded never were sanctified as heave and the Sages agree with R. Dosa in that case.

(fol. 47c) **משנה ו**: מְגוֹרָה שֶׁפִּינָּה מִמֶּנָּה חִיטֵּי תְרוּמָה אֵין מְחַייְבִין אוֹתוֹ לִהְיוֹת יוֹשֵׁב וּמְלַקֵּט אַחַת אַחַת אֶלָּא מְכַבֵּד כְּדַרְכּוֹ וְנוֹתֵן לְתוֹךְ הַחוּלִין.

Mishnah 6: If someone removed heave wheat from a chest, one does not oblige him to sit down and pick out the last grains but he sweeps it as usual and then fills it with profane grain[89].

משנה ז: וְכֵן הֶחָבִית שֶׁל שֶׁמֶן שֶׁנִּשְׁפְּכָה אֵין מְחַייְבִין אוֹתוֹ לִהְיוֹת יוֹשֵׁב וּמְטַפֵּחַ אֶלָּא נוֹהֵג בָּהּ כְּדֶרֶךְ שֶׁהוּא נוֹהֵג בְּחוּלִין.

Mishnah 7: Similarly, if someone empties an amphora of oil, one does not oblige him to sit down and clean it with his fingers but he treats it as he treats profane vessels.

משנה ח: הַמְּעָרֶה מִכַּד לְכַד וְנוֹטֵף שָׁלֹשׁ טִיפִּין וְנוֹתֵן לְתוֹךְ הַחוּלִין הִרְכִּינָהּ וּמִיצָּת הֲרֵי זוֹ תְרוּמָה. וְכַמָּה תְּהֵא בִתְרוּמַת מַעֲשֵׂר שֶׁל דְּמַאי וְיוֹלִיכֶנָּהּ לַכֹּהֵן אֶחָד מִשְּׁמוֹנֶה לִשְׁמִינִית.

Mishnah 8: If one pours from pitcher to pitcher one lets drip three drops and then may fill it with profane [wine][90]. If he turned it and it accumulated, that is heave. How much should heave of the tithe of *demay*[91] be that he is required to deliver it to a Cohen? An eighth of an eighth[92].

89 Most Mishnah mss. read לתוכה חולין, but the text of the Leyden mss. and Venice print is supported by some of the best ms. evidence, the Mishnah edited by Low, the Munich ms. of the Babli, and the Parma ms. of the Mishnah. The text does not mean that the grains collected in sweeping the storage bin can be added to profane grain.

90 If one empties a pitcher of heave oil or wine, one holds it until at the end three distinct drops have fallen out. Then one may assume that the pitcher is empty. But if instead of refilling the pitcher with profane fluid one lets it lie on its side, then any fluid that accumulates is heave.

91 The only gift to the Cohen from *demay*; cf. *Demay*, Introduction.

92 $^1/_{64}$ of a *log*, or about 8.33 cm^3. Less than this amount he burns or leaves for a Cohen to pick it up himself.

(fol. 48a) **הלכה ה**: תַּמָּן תַּנִּינָן הִרְכִּינָהּ וּמִצָּה הֲרֵי הוּא שֶׁל מוֹכֵר. אָמַר רִבִּי יוֹחָנָן לֵית כָּאן שֶׁל מוֹכֵר אֶלָּא שֶׁל לוֹקֵחַ וְהָכָא אַתְּ אָמַר הָכֵין. אָמַר רִבִּי יִצְחָק בַּר אֶלְעָזָר מִשּׁוּם יֵאוּשׁ. וְאַף בְּקוֹדֶשׁ כֵּן. אָתָא רִבִּי אַבָּהוּ בְּשֵׁם רִבִּי יוֹחָנָן וְאַף בְּקוֹדֶשׁ כֵּן.

Haslakhah 5: There[93], we have stated: "If he turned it and it accumulated, that belongs to the seller." Rebbi Joḥanan said, there is no "belongs to the seller" but "belongs to the buyer", as you say here[94]. Rebbi Isaac bar Eleazar said, it is because of abandonment[95]. Is it the same for consecrated food? Rebbi Abbahu came in the name of Rebbi Joḥanan: It is the same for consecrated food[96].

93 *Baba Batra* 5:9. If somebody buys wine or oil and the grocer filled a measuring pitcher, he has to empty his pitcher into the buyer's vessel until three separate drops fall out at the end.

94 Since what would accumulate is heave.

95 Since the buyer does not expect more than what he had when three drops fell out, the remainder that could be picked up after waiting several hours is not part of the sale contract and belongs to the seller. In the Babli, *Baba Batra* 87b, this argument is credited to R. Abbahu.

96 Oil and wine for sacrifices have to be poured out until three separate drops fall out.

אָמַר רִבִּי הוֹשַׁעְיָה לֹא שָׁנוּ אֶלָּא בְּקֳדָשִׁים שֶׁיֵּשׁ לָהֶן מַתִּירִין. אֲבָל בְּקֳדָשִׁים שֶׁאֵין לָהֶן מַתִּירִין אֲפִילוּ כָּל־שֶׁהוּא צָרִיךְ לְהַחֲזִיר. רִבִּי בּוּן בַּר חִיָּה בָּעֵי. הָדֵין לוֹג שֶׁמֶן שֶׁל מְצוֹרָע צָרִיךְ לְהַחֲזִיר אוֹ אֵינוֹ צָרִיךְ לְהַחֲזִיר. אִין תֵּימַר צָרִיךְ לְהַחֲזִיר לֹא הֶחֱזִיר עוֹבֵר מִשּׁוּם חִסָּרוֹן. אִין תֵּימַר אֵינוֹ צָרִיךְ לְהַחֲזִיר וְהֶחֱזִיר עוֹבֵר מִשּׁוּם יִתָּרוֹן. רִבִּי חִינְנָא לֹא אָמַר כֵּן אֶלָּא אָמַר רִבִּי הוֹשַׁעְיָה לֹא שָׁנוּ אֶלָּא בְּקֳדָשִׁים שֶׁיֵּשׁ לָהֶן מַתִּירִין. אֲבָל בְּקֳדָשִׁים שֶׁאֵין לָהֶן מַתִּירִין אֲפִילוּ כָּל־שֶׁהוּא צָרִיךְ לְהַחֲזִיר. וְהָדֵין לוֹג שֶׁמֶן שֶׁל מְצוֹרָע לֹא כְקֳדָשִׁים שֶׁיֵּשׁ לָהֶן מַתִּירִין הֵן וְתֵימַר צָרִיךְ לְהַחֲזִיר. הָדָא אָמְרָה צָרִיךְ לְהַחֲזִיר וְאִם לֹא הֶחֱזִיר עוֹבֵר מִשּׁוּם חִסָּרוֹן.

Rebbi Hoshaia said, this was taught only for consecrated food which can be permitted[97]. But of consecrated food which cannot be permitted one has to give back even the most minute amount. Rebbi Abun bar Ḥiyya asked: That *log* of oil of the leper, must he give it back or not[98]? If you say he must give it back, and he did not, he transgresses by default. If you say he need not give it back, and he did, he transgresses by excess[99] Rebbi Ḥinena did not say so[100], but Rebbi Hoshaia said, this was taught only for consecrated food which can be permitted. But of consecrated food which cannot be permitted one has to give back even the most minute amount. That *log* of oil of the leper belongs to those [consecrated foods] which can be permitted and you say he must give it back? That means, he must give back and if he did not, he transgresses by default.

97 Consecrated foods which can be permitted are those which must be eaten by Cohanim after certain actions have been taken. In general, a flour offering must be eaten by Cohanim after a handful of the offering and its incense have been burned on the altar. Between dedication and burning, the flour and its accompanying oil are forbidden for everybody. However, the flour offering of a Cohen must be completely burned on the altar; it is consecrated food which never can be permitted. Also, wine offerings are poured completely on the altar; they never can be permitted.

98 The person healed from *ẓara'at* (commonly translated as "leprosy") has to bring a sacrifice including one *log* of oil (*Lev.* 14:10,21). No instructions are given in the text what to do with the oil left over after the conclusion of the purification ceremony. "Giving back" means waiting until all remaining oil has collected at the bottom of the flask and then emptying it.

99 In both cases it will not be an exact *log* if the rules are not followed.

100 For him it is not an unresolved question but a straightforward conclusion.

תַּנֵּי רִבִּי חֲלַפְתָּא בֶּן שָׁאוּל קְדֵירָה שֶׁבִּישֵּׁל בָּהּ תְּרוּמָה מַגְעִילָהּ בְּחַמִּין שְׁלֹשָׁה פְעָמִים וְדַיוֹ. אָמַר רִבִּי בָּא וְאֵין לְמֵידִין מִמֶּנָּה לְעִנְייַן נְבֵילָה. אָמַר רִבִּי יוֹסֵי קַשִּׁייתָהּ קוֹמֵי רִבִּי בָּא תְּרוּמָה בַּעֲוֹן מִיתָה וּנְבֵילָה בְּלֹא תַעֲשֶׂה וְאַתְּ אָמַר הָכֵין. אָמַר לִי כְּמָאן דְּאָמַר מֵאֵילֵיהֶן קִיבְּלוּ עֲלֵיהֶן אֶת הַמַּעְשְׂרוֹת.

Rebbi Ḥalaphta ben Shaul stated: A pot[101] in which heave was cooked[102] is cleansed three times with boiling water and that is enough. Rebbi Abba said, one does not learn from this for carcass meat[103]. Rebbi Yose said, I objected before Rebbi Abba: Heave implies a deadly sin, carcass meat is a simple prohibition, and you say so? He said to me, it follows him who says, they accepted tithes voluntarily[104].

101 A clay pot. In general, one deduces from *Lev.* 6:21 that clay vessels cannot be cleansed from impurities.

102 In order to use the same pot for profane food available to Non-Cohanim, the remains of heave which entered the porous walls have to be removed.

103 A clay pot in which non-kosher meat was cooked cannot be rehabilitated to be used for kosher food.

104 R. Eleazar in *Ševi'it* Chapter 6, Notes 11-13. It is the operative opinion of the Yerushalmi that the duties upon the Land have rabbinic character only as long as the entire Jewish people do not live in the Land and the land distribution of Joshua has not been re-established. Therefore, eating carcass meat which is a biblical prohibition is a much more severe sin than unauthorized use of rabbinic heave.

רִבִּי יוּסְטֵי בַּר שׁוּנֶם בְּעָא קוֹמֵי רִבִּי מָנָא. תַּנִּינָן הִרְכִּינָהּ וּמִיצֵּת הֲרֵי זוֹ תְרוּמָה וְאַתְּ אָמַר הָכֵין. אָמַר לֵיהּ כָּאן עַל יְדֵי הָאוֹר נִגְעַל וְיוֹצֵא.

Rebbi Justus bar Shunem asked before Rebbi Mana: We have stated: "If he turned it and it accumulated, that is heave," and here you say so? He said to him, here through the fire it becomes inedible and disappears[105].

105 Repeated heating of boiling water will not only destroy the remaining heave as food, when it loses its sanctity, but also remove it. This cannot be compared to the Mishnah where the heave oil accumulates in the cold vessel.

שְׁמָרִים שֶׁל תְּרוּמָה הָרִאשׁוֹן וְהַשֵּׁנִי אָסוּר. וְהַשְּׁלִישִׁי מוּתָּר. בְּמַה דְבָרִים אֲמוּרִים בְּשֶׁנָּתַן לְתוֹכָן מַיִם. אֲבָל לֹא נָתַן לְתוֹכָן מַיִם אֲפִילוּ שְׁלִישִׁי אָסוּר. שְׁמָרִים שֶׁל מַעֲשֵׂר שֵׁנִי רִאשׁוֹן אָסוּר וְשֵׁנִי מוּתָּר. רִבִּי מֵאִיר אוֹמֵר הַשֵּׁנִי בְּנוֹתֵן טַעַם. רִבִּי יוֹחָנָן בְּשֵׁם רִבִּי שִׁמְעוֹן בֶּן יוֹצָדָק הַקּוֹדֶשׁ כְּמִיצוּוֹ.[106]

"[107]Yeast of heave, the first and second are forbidden, the third is permitted. When has this been said? If he added water. But if he did not add water, even the third is forbidden[108] Yeast of second tithe, the first is forbidden but the second permitted. Rebbi Meïr said, the second by imparting taste[109]." Rebbi Joḥanan in the name of Rebbi Simeon ben Yoẓadaq, the consecrated is like the accumulated[110].

106 Reading of the Leyden ms. The Venice print has an unintelligible כמי גוי. The Rome ms: כמינויין "the holy corresponds to its count;" since consecrated food of the Temple can become impure in the 1st, 2nd, 3rd, or 4th degrees, it is implied that for them afterwine is forbidden to the fourth degree. This reading was already conjectured by R. Moses Margalit; it was accepted by R. S. Lieberman. Since this reading parallels the interpretation of the Babli, it has to be rejected.

107 Tosephta 10:12, Babli *Baba Batra* 97a. Each of the three texts represents a different tradition.

108 It is difficult to understand what "first, second, third" means if no fresh water was added to the wine barrel. The reference is to afterwine obtained by pouring water over the pomace remaining in the vat after the wine was drained. It is assumed that the volume of afterwine obtained does not exceed the volume of water put in; in that case the afterwine is presumed not to contain any heave wine and the prohibition of the first and second afterwines is only rabbinical.

109 The second afterwine transmits the holiness of second tithe as long as it can be tasted in a mixture; cf. Halakhah 2.

110 All afterwine made from grapes that are intrinsically sacred (in that they belong to the altar and cannot be redeemed) remains sacred in any amount. There is no other source indicating that afterwine was ever made from intrinsically sacred grapes.

חַרְסָן[111] שֶׁל זָב רִאשׁוֹן טָמֵא וְשֵׁנִי טָהוֹר. בְּמַה דְבָרִים אֲמוּרִים שֶׁלֹּא נָתַן לְתוֹכָן מַיִם. אֲבָל נָתַן לְתוֹכָן מַיִם אֲפִילוּ עֲשִׂירִי טָמֵא.

"[112]The clay pot of the sufferer from discharge, the first is impure but the second pure. When has this been said? If he did not put water in it, but if he put water in it even the tenth is impure."

111 Reading of the Rome ms. Leyden and Venice: הרוסן "the bridle".

112 Tosephta *Ṭahorot* 5:4 and Babli *Zebaḥim* 79b: The clay pot of the

sufferer from gonorrhoea, the first and second rinses are impure but the third is pure. When has this been said? If he did put water in it, but if he did not put water in it, even the tenth is impure. Rebbi Eliezer ben Jacob said, even if no water was put in (but other, not impure people, used it), the third is pure.

It is clear that the Yerushalmi tradition cannot be reconciled with the Tosephta-Babli tradition. The concurrence of the mss. shows that the tradition is original. The Yerushalmi holds that water in a clay chamberpot becomes impure with the original impurity of the urine of a sufferer from gonorrhoea (*Lev*. 15); hence, presence or absence of remainders of the urine in the walls of the chamberpot becomes irrelevant.

רִבִּי יוּדָן בַּר אַחְתֵּיהּ דְּרִבִּי יוֹסֵי בַּר חֲנִינָה בְּשֵׁם רִבִּי יוֹסֵי בַּר חֲנִינָה פָּחוּת מִכֵּן נוֹתְנוֹ בְּנֵירוֹ. רִבִּי יַנַּאי בְּשֵׁם רִבִּי יוּדָן בְּאוֹכֶל כְּדֵי לְבַשֵּׁל בֵּיצָה קַלָּה. הָדָא דְתֵימַר הַךְ כְּבֵיצָה. בְּטֻמְאָה. אֲבָל טָהוֹר אֲפִילוּ כָּל־שֶׁהוּא צָרִיךְ לְהַחֲזִיר. בִּדְמַאי. אֲבָל בְּוַדַּאי בֵּין טָמֵא בֵּין טָהוֹר בֵּין רַב בֵּין מוּעָט צָרִיךְ לְהַחֲזִיר.

[113]Rebbi Yudan, the son of Rebbi Yose ben Ḥanina's sister, in the name of Rebbi Yose ben Ḥanina: Less than that he puts in his fire[114]. Rebbi Yannai in the name of Rebbi Jehudah: "Solid food corresponding to a cooked easy egg[115]. That means that the volume of an egg[116] is valid in impurity, but pure the minutest amount must be delivered. If it is *demay*; but if it is certain it must be delivered impure or pure, much or little."

113 This paragraph deals with the amounts of heave of the tithe of *demay* to be delivered to the Cohen.

114 This sentence also is in Tosephta 10:6, which more or less parallels the statement attributed to R. Jehudah in this paragraph.

115 "Easy egg", mentioned in Mishnah *Šabbat* 8:5, is defined in the Babli (*Šabbat* 80b) as a chicken egg, reputed to be quickest to be cooked among all kosher eggs.

116 Even a small chicken egg has a volume of at least 3.5 times $^1/_{64}$ *log* ≈ 29 cm^3.

(fol. 47c) **משנה ט**: כַּרְשִׁינֵי תְרוּמָה מַאֲכִילִין אוֹתָן לִבְהֵמָה וּלְחַיָּה וּלְתַרְנְגוֹלִין. יִשְׂרָאֵל שֶׁשָּׂכַר פָּרָה מִכֹּהֵן מַאֲכִילָהּ כַּרְשִׁינֵי תְרוּמָה. וְכֹהֵן שֶׁשָּׂכַר פָּרָה מִיִּשְׂרָאֵל אַף עַל פִּי שֶׁמְּזוֹנוֹתֶיהָ עָלָיו לֹא יַאֲכִילֶנָּה כַּרְשִׁינֵי תְרוּמָה. יִשְׂרָאֵל שֶׁשָּׁם פָּרָה מִכֹּהֵן לֹא יַאֲכִילֶנָּה כַּרְשִׁינֵי תְרוּמָה. וְכֹהֵן שֶׁשָּׁם פָּרָה מִיִּשְׂרָאֵל מַאֲכִילָהּ כַּרְשִׁינֵי תְרוּמָה.

Mishnah 9: Heave vetch may be fed to domestic animals, wild animals, and chickens[117]. An Israel who rented a cow from a Cohen feeds it heave vetch. A Cohen who rented a cow from an Israel may not feed it heave vetch even if he is required to feed it. An Israel who received a cow from a Cohen by appraisal[118] may not feed it heave vetch. A Cohen who received a cow from an Israel by appraisal may feed it heave vetch.

117 If these animals are possessions of the Cohen, as explained in the Halakhah. The determining factor is ownership.

118 At the time of transfer of ownership, the value of the cow was appraised but not paid. The Israel will fatten the cow. If it is finally sold, the original owner will receive the appraised value and part of the added value. Since there is transfer of ownership, some rules will have to be observed to avoid giving the Cohen's part of the added value the status of forbidden interest.

(fol. 48a) **הלכה ו**: מְנַיִין לְפָרָתוֹ שֶׁל כֹּהֵן שֶׁהָיְתָה שׁוּמָה אֶצֶל יִשְׂרָאֵל שֶׁאֵינָהּ מַאֲכִילָהּ בִּתְרוּמָה. תַּלְמוּד לוֹמַר וְכֹהֵן כִּי יִקְנֶה נֶפֶשׁ קִנְיַין כַּסְפּוֹ וגו'. יָכוֹל לֹא יַאֲכִילֶנָּהּ בְּכַרְשִׁינִין. תַּלְמוּד לוֹמַר הֵם. אִית תַּנָּיֵי תַנֵּי יָכוֹל לֹא תֹאכַל בְּכַרְשִׁינִין וּבִתְלְתָּן. רִבִּי חִזְקִיָּה רִבִּי יִרְמְיָה רִבִּי חִיָּיה בְשֵׁם רִבִּי יוֹחָנָן לֵית כָּאן תִּלְתָּן דְּבַר תּוֹרָה. לֹא כֵן תַּנֵּי מְנַיִין לְכֹהֵן שֶׁקָּנָה עֶבֶד וּלְיִשְׂרָאֵל בּוֹ שׁוּתָפוּת אֲפִילוּ אֶחָד מִמֵּאָה בּוֹ שֶׁאֵינוֹ מַאֲכִילוֹ בתרוּמָה. תַּלְמוּד לוֹמַר וְכֹהֵן כִּי יִקְנֶה. תַּנֵּי בַּר קַפָּרָא אֶחָד זוֹ וְאֶחָד זוֹ לֹא תֹאכַל בִּתְרוּמָה.

Halakhah 6: From where that a cow of a Cohen which was appraised at an Israel's cannot be fed vetch? The verse says (*Lev.* 22:11): "If a Cohen buys a living being with his money, etc.[119]" I could think, he may not feed it vetch, the verse says, "they"[120]. Some Tannaïm state: I could think, he may not feed it vetch or fenugreek. Rebbi Ḥizqiah, Rebbi Jeremiah, Rebbi Ḥiyya, in the name of Rebbi Joḥanan: The word of the Torah is that here, there is no "fenugreek"[121]. Did we not state: From where that a Cohen who bought a slave in partnership with an Israel, even if the latter has only a one percent interest, cannot feed him heave[122]? The verse says, "If a Cohen buys." Bar Qappara stated: Neither one of them may eat heave[123].

119 (*Lev*. 22:11): "If a Cohen buys a living being with his money, he may eat of it; whoever is born in his house, they shall eat of his bread." The ownership must be 100% the Cohen's.

120 The argument is elliptic. It is a little more explicit in *Sifra Emor Parašah* 5:6: "They shall eat," they but not an animal. I could think an animal could not eat [heave] vetch? The verse says, "a living being".

121 Vetch is human food only in times of famine; fenugreek is human food. R. Joḥanan follows the argument of Note 117 to exclude feeding animals heave of human food.

122 Why should an animal given to the Cohen on appraisal be fed heave vetch if the Israel has a continuing monetary stake in the animal?

123 Bar Qappara (and the editors of the Yerushalmi) disagree with the Mishnah and forbid heave vetch in all cases of an animal given on appraisal.

(fol. 47c) **משנה י**: מַדְלִיקִין שֶׁמֶן שְׂרֵיפָה בְּבָתֵּי כְנֵיסִיּוֹת וּבְבָתֵּי מִדְרָשׁוֹת וּבִמְבוֹאוֹת אֲפֵילִין וְעַל גַּבֵּי הַחוֹלִים בִּרְשׁוּת הַכֹּהֵן. בַּת יִשְׂרָאֵל שֶׁנִּישֵּׂאת לְכֹהֵן וְהִיא לִימוּדֶת לָבוֹא אֶצֶל אָבִיהָ אָבִיהָ מַדְלִיק בִּרְשׁוּתָהּ. מַדְלִיקִין בְּבֵית הַמִּשְׁתֶּה אֲבָל לֹא בְּבֵית הָאֵבֶל דִּבְרֵי רִבִּי יְהוּדָה. רִבִּי יוֹסֵי אוֹמֵר בְּבֵית הָאֵבֶל אֲבָל לֹא בְּבֵית הַמִּשְׁתֶּה. רִבִּי מֵאִיר אוֹסֵר כָּאן וְכָאן וְרִבִּי שִׁמְעוֹן מַתִּיר כָּאן וְכָאן.

Mishnah 10: One lights "oil to burn"[124] in synagogues, houses of study, dark passageways, and near the sick with permission of the Cohen. If the daughter of an Israel married to a Cohen is used to visit her father[125], her father puts up lights with her permission. One puts up lights at a wedding but not in a house of mourning, the words of Rebbi Jehudah; Rebbi Yose says, in a house of mourning but not at a wedding. Rebbi Meïr forbids in both cases, Rebbi Simeon permits in both cases[126].

124 Impure olive oil of heave which must be burned. It may be used for lighting. Since Cohanim also use public institutions such as synagogues, houses of study, and public roads, their consent to the use of impure oil for the institutions is implied.

125 She is a member of the Cohen's family and stands in his stead in matters of heave.

126 The Halakhah will discuss the four possible opinions.

(fol. 48a) **הלכה ז**: מַדְלִיקִין שֶׁמֶן שְׂרֵיפָה בְּבָתֵּי כְּנֵיסִיּוֹת וּבְבָתֵּי מִדְרָשׁוֹת כו'. שִׁמְעוֹן בַּר בָּא בְּשֵׁם רִבִּי יוֹחָנָן כֵּן הִיא מַתְנִיתָא וְעַל גַּבֵּי הַחוֹלִים בִּרְשׁוּת כֹּהֵן. הָא מַתְנִיתָא קַדְמִייָתָא אֲפִילוּ שֶׁלֹּא בִרְשׁוּת כֹּהֵן. תַּנֵּי רִבִּי חִיָּיה בִּיקּוּר הַחוֹלִים אֵין לוֹ שִׁיעוּר. אָמַר רִבִּי חִיָּיא בַּר אָדָא מַתְנִיתָא אָמְרָה כֵן וְעַל גַּבֵּי הַחוֹלִים בִּרְשׁוּת כֹּהֵן.

"One lights 'oil to burn' in synagogues, houses of study; etc." Simeon bar Abba in the name of Rebbi Joḥanan, so is the Mishnah: "and near the sick with permission of the Cohen.[127]" That means, the earlier parts of the Mishnah even without the permission of a Cohen. Rebbi Ḥiyya stated: "Sickbed visits have no measure[128]." Rebbi Ḥiyya bar Ada said, the Mishnah says so: "and near the sick with permission of the Cohen."

127 The permission of the Cohen is needed only for burning at the bedside of a Non-Cohen; public buildings can be lit since the utility for some Cohen is assured.

128 One may visit the sick at all

times, even after dark; therefore, the sick may need light after dark. The Babli, *Nedarim* 26b, is not quite sure about the meaning of the statement.

רִבִּי יִרְמְיָה בְּעָא קוֹמֵי רִבִּי זְעִירָא עַד כְּדוֹן בִּתְרוּמָה שֶׁנָּֽפְלָה לוֹ מִבֵּית אֲבִי אִמּוֹ כֹּהֵן. וַאֲפִילוּ בִּתְרוּמַת גּוֹרְנוֹ. אָמַר לֵיהּ מָאן יֵימַר (fol. 48b) לָךְ בִּתְרוּמַת גּוֹרְנוֹ. רִבִּי יוֹנָה וְרִבִּי יוֹסֵי. רִבִּי יוֹנָה כְּרִבִּי יִרְמְיָה וְרִבִּי יוֹסֵי כְּרִבִּי זְעִירָא. מָאן דְּאָמַר בִּתְרוּמַת גּוֹרְנוֹ נִדְלַק[129] וְאָתֵי אַתְיָיא לְמָאן דְּאָמַר בִּתְרוּמָה שֶׁנָּֽפְלָה לוֹ מִבֵּית אֲבִי אִמּוֹ כֹּהֵן בְּלֹא כֵן בְּשֶׁאֵינוֹ צָרִיךְ זְכִייָה. אָמַר לוֹ בִּמְזַכֶּה לוֹ עַל יְדֵי אַחֵר.

Rebbi Jeremiah asked before Rebbi Zeïra: So far heave that fell to him from the house of his maternal grandfather, a Cohen[130]. Perhaps also from the heave of his own threshing floor[131]? He said to him, who could tell you, from the heave of his own threshing floor? Rebbi Jonah and Rebbi Yose; Rebbi Jonah followed Rebbi Jeremiah[132], Rebbi Yose followed Rebbi Zeïra. He who says, from the heave of his own threshing floor, may he go and light a lamp? [133]Following him who said, heave that fell to him from the house of his maternal grandfather, a Cohen, would he not need empowering anyhow[134]? He said to him, when he transfers it to him through a third party[135].

129 Reading of the Rome ms. Leyden: נחלק "split, distributed".

130 This refers to the part of the Mishnah speaking of the father of a Cohen's wife. The Mishnah presupposes that the Israel is the rightful owner of some impure heave oil. One possibility is that it came to him as an inheritance.

131 Maybe he is an olive grower and the oil is his from his own oilpress. "Threshing floor", referring to grain, simply denotes the place and moment the obligation of heave was created.

132 That an Israel may use impure heave from his own harvest to the benefit of a Cohen without ever transferring ownership.

133 The Rome ms. has here a lengthy addition: ר' בא בר כהן בעא קומי ר' יוסי ולמאן דאמר בתרומה שנפלה לו מבית אבי אמו כהן בלא כך שאינו . . . "Rebbi Abba bar Cohen asked before Rebbi Yose: According to him who said, heave that

fell to him from his maternal grandfather, a Cohen, without that would he not . . ."

134 Since he is an Israel and you said that an Israel cannot use his own heave for the benefit of a Cohen, he should not be able to use his inheritance without transferring ownership to his son-in-law.

135 He cannot transfer the ownership of his own possessions without actually performing some act of transfer but he may tell a third person to accept disposal rights of this heave for his daughter. Then he can use the oil for her benefit.

תַּנֵּי יִשְׂרָאֵל וְכֹהֵן שֶׁהָיוּ שׁוּתָּפִין בְּחָנוּת. מְמַלֵּא יִשְׂרָאֵל אֶת הַנֵּר שֶׁמֶן שְׂרֵיפָה וְעוֹלֶה לָעֲלִיָּה וְיוֹרֵד לֶחָנוּת לַעֲשׂוֹת צְרָכָיו שֶׁל כֹּהֵן. אֲבָל לֹא שֶׁל יִשְׂרָאֵל. כֹּהֵן שֶׁבָּא אֵצֶל יִשְׂרָאֵל לַעֲשׂוֹת עִמּוֹ חֶשְׁבּוֹן מַדְלִיק[136] עַל גַּבָּיו שֶׁמֶן שְׂרֵיפָה אַף עַל פִּי כֵן זְכִייָה אָמַר לָהֶן בִּמְזַכֶּה לָהֶן עַל יְדֵי אַחֵר.

It was stated[137]: "If an Israel and a Cohen were partners in a store, the Israel may fill the lamp with oil to burn and go to the upper floor and down into the store in the business of the Cohen, but not his own. If a Cohen came to an Israel to help him with his accounts[138], the latter may light oil to burn for him." Where is the empowering? He[139] said to them, when he transfers it to them through a third party.

136 Reading of the Rome ms. Leyden: והדליק "if he lit"; this language is proper for the quote of the same *baraita* below.

137 A somewhat similar text is in Tosephta 10:9, but there the Israel is the employee of the Cohen and it is clear that what he does in the store is for the benefit of his employer. In the *baraita* here, "the business of the Cohen" means anything in which the Cohen has some monetary interest; it only excludes private affairs of the Israel.

138 The visit of the Cohen is for the benefit of the Israel. In this case, the same problem arises as in the previous case of inherited oil, cf. Notes 131-132.

139 R. Zeïra, the author of the preceding paragraph.

תַּנֵּי בַּת יִשְׂרָאֵל שֶׁנִּכְנְסָה לַעֲשׂוֹת צְרָכָיו שֶׁל כֹּהֵן אֲבָל לֹא שֶׁל יִשְׂרָאֵל.

It was stated: An Israel woman who came to work for a Cohen, but not for an Israel[140].

140 This *baraita* fragment must have stated that she may use left-over oil for some personal use, cf. Tosephta 10:9 and the two following paragraphs.

תַּנֵּי בַּת יִשְׂרָאֵל שֶׁנִּכְנְסָה לְהַדְלִיק מִכֹּהֶנֶת טוֹבֶלֶת פְּתִילָהּ שֶׁמֶן שְׂרֵיפָה וּמַדְלֶקֶת. רִבִּי חוּנָה בְשֵׁם דְּבֵי רִבִּי יַנַּאי שְׁעַת מִשְׁלַחַת זְאֵבִים הָיְתָה וְלֹא עָמַד בֵּית דִּין וּבִיטֵּל. כְּמָה דְתֵימַר תַּמָּן לֹא עָמַד בֵּית דִּין וּבִיטֵּל אַף הָכָא לֹא עָמַד בֵּית דִּין וּבִיטֵּל.

[141]It was stated: "An Israel woman who comes to a priestly woman to get fire dips her wick into oil to burn and lights." Rebbi Ḥuna in the name of the house of Rebbi Yannai: It was a time of wolf packs; there was no court which disestablished. (As you say there, there was no court which disestablished, so here there was no court which disestablished!)[142]

141 This entire paragraph is taken from *Ševi'it* Chapter 4, Notes 39-42. A somewhat similar statement is in Tosephta 10:9. From here to the start of the discussion about weddings, the text is also in *Šabbat*, Chapter 2, fol. 4c/d.

142 This sentence, which embodies the essence of the argument in *Sevi'it*, is out of place here. As R. S. Lieberman notes, it seems from the Tosephta that the Israel woman needs the light to go home in the night from the Cohen's house. This kind of use is generally accepted by popular practice since it is necessary if the Cohen should have any kind of social life.

בְּקָרוֹ שֶׁל כֹּהֵן שֶׁהָיָה מַאֲכִיל אֶצֶל יִשְׂרָאֵל. וְכֵן בִּגְדוֹ שֶׁל כֹּהֵן שֶׁהָיָה נֶאֱרָג אֶצֶל יִשְׂרָאֵל מַדְלִיק עַל גַּבָּיו שֶׁמֶן שְׂרֵיפָה וְאֵינוֹ חוֹשֵׁשׁ. כֹּהֵן שֶׁבָּא לַעֲשׂוֹת חֶשְׁבּוֹן עִם יִשְׂרָאֵל וְהִדְלִיק עַל גַּבָּיו שֶׁמֶן שְׂרֵיפָה וְעָמַד לוֹ וְהָלַךְ לוֹ. אַף עַל פִּי כֵן אֵין מְחַייְבִין אוֹתוֹ לְכַבּוֹתוֹ עַד שֶׁיִּכְבֶּה מֵאֵילָיו. רִבִּי חֲנַנְיָה בַּר עַכְבָּרִי הֲוָה עֲבַד עוֹבְדְּתָא גַּבֵּי רִבִּי חִיָּה צִיפּוֹרַיָּא. מִי אֲזִיל לֵיהּ מַלֵּי לֵיהּ בּוֹצִינָא שֶׁמֶן שְׂרֵיפָה.

לֹא כֵן סָבְרִין[143] מֵימַר לַעֲשׂוֹת צְרָכָיו שֶׁל כֹּהֵן אֲבָל לֹא שֶׁל יִשְׂרָאֵל. אָמְרִין דִּי לָא הֲוָה עֲבַד לֵיהּ כֵּן לָא הֲוָה אָתֵי. סָבְרִין מֵימַר כַּד יַמְטֵי בֵּייתֵיהּ הֲוָה מַטְפֵּי לֵיהּ. אָמַר רִבִּי חִינְנָא עַל יָדֵי כֵן הֲוָה שְׁהַר וְעַל יָדֵי הֲוָה כֵן קְרֵץ.

"[144]If cattle of a Cohen was fed at an Israel's, or the garment of a Cohen being woven at an Israel's, he lights for this oil to burn without hesitation. If a Cohen came to an Israel to help him with his accounts[138] and he lit oil to burn for him, even after [the Cohen] left one does not require him to extinguish it before it burns out by itself." Rebbi Ḥanania from Akhbar[145] worked at R. Ḥiyya's from Sepphoris. When he left, the latter filled him a lamp full of oil to burn. Were we not of the opinion to say, "to work for a Cohen, but not for an Israel"? They said, if he had not done this for him, he would not have come. They thought, when he arrived at his house, he had to extinguish it. Rebbi Ḥinena said, this happened to me; by this he awoke, by this he got up early.

143 Reading of the Rome ms. and the parallel in *Šabbat*. Leyden: שֶׁבְּקִינָן "we abandon".

144 Tosephta 10:9.

145 He appears only here (and in the parallel in *Šabbat*). His employer, R. Ḥiyya from Sepphoris, is also quoted in *'Orlah* in a discussion with R. Ammi. Therefore, both men belong to the third generation of Galilean Amoraim. It follows from the story that this R. Ḥiyya was a Cohen; he might be identical with R. Ḥiyya bar Abba.

אָדָא שַׁמָּשָׁא שָׁאַל לְרִבִּי אִימִּי בְּגִין דַּאֲנָא צְבַע פְּתִילָה מִן חוֹלָא. אָמַר לֵיהּ בָּטֵל הוּא עַל גַּב פְּתִילוֹת. הוֹרֵי רִבִּי יוּדָה בֶּן פָּזִי בְּאִילֵין דְּבַר נְחֶמְיָה כֵן. רִבִּי אִימִּי נְסַב פְּתִילָה. רִבִּי אִילָּא לֹא נְסַב פְּתִילָה. לֵית לְרִבִּי אִילָּא הָדָא דְּרִבִּי אִימִּי. סָבַר רִבִּי אִילָּא מִשּׁוּם גֶּזֶל וּבְלָא מִן הָדֵין שַׁמָּשָׁא מְבַזְבְּזָא בָהּ קְדוּשָׁה.

Ada the nurse asked Rebbi Ammi: Since I am dipping wicks at a sick person's[146]? He said to him, it becomes insignificant in the wick. Rebbi Jehudah ben Pazi instructed those of Bar Neḥemiah in this way. Rebbi

Immi took a wick, Rebbi Ila did not take a wick[147]. Did Rebbi Ila not agree with Rebbi Immi? Rebbi Ila thought because of robbery; in addition, the nurse will spoil the consecrated food[148].

146 The question is elliptic, so is the answer. It is not even clear whether R. Immi ruled to permit (R. Eliahu Fulda) or prohibit (R. Moses Margalit). It seems, with R. Eliahu Fulda, that the paragraph refers to the statement in the Mishnah that oil to burn may be used for all sick persons with the consent of the Cohen. The question now is whether from this oil the nurse can light for himself. The answer is that the value of the oil is insignificant.

147 Dipped in oil for burning given to the sick.

148 Will not treat it with due respect but will use it in dirty places.

גַּמְלִיאֵל זוּגָא שָׁאַל לְרִבִּי יָסָא מַהוּ לְהוֹסִיף שֶׁמֶן חוּלִין וּלְהַדְלִיק. אָמַר לֵיהּ לֹא תַנֵּי רִבִּי הוֹשַׁעְיָה אֶלָּא אֵין מְחַייְבִין אוֹתוֹ לְמַצּוֹתוֹ.

Gamliel the twin asked Rebbi Yasa: May one add profane oil and light[149]? He said to him, Rebbi Hoshaia stated only that one is not required to squeeze it out[150].

149 May one add profane oil to oil for burning and use it to light for a healthy Israel with no connection to any Cohen?

150 In the *baraita*/Tosephta quoted above, Note 142, the Israel does not have to extinguish the light when the Cohen leaves, but he is not permitted to start burning oil for burning in the absence of the Cohen. Therefore, Gamliel's question has to be answered in the negative.

אָמַר רִבִּי אַבָּהוּ שָׁנָה לִי יוֹנָתָן בֶּן עַכְמַאי. בַּת כֹּהֵן שֶׁהָיְתָה עוֹמֶדֶת עֶרֶב שַׁבָּת עִם חֲשֵׁיכָה וּבְיָדָהּ נֵר וּבְתוֹכוֹ שֶׁמֶן שְׂרֵיפָה הֲרֵי זוֹ מוֹסִיפָה לְתוֹכוֹ שֶׁמֶן שֶׁל חוּלִין וּמַדְלִיקָה. אָמַר לֵיהּ רִבִּי זְעִירָא מַה טִבְיָיהּ. אָמַר לוֹ אָדָם גָּדוֹל הָיָה וּבָקִי בְמִשְׁנָתֵינוּ הָיָה. פִּרְשֵׁיהּ רִבִּי חִייָא דִכְפַר תְּחוּמִין קוֹמֵי רַבִּי וּמַנִּיתֵיהּ חֲכִים.

Rebbi Abbahu said, Jonathan ben Akhmai did teach me: The daughter of a Cohen standing Sabbath eve with a light filled with oil for burning, adds some profane oil and lights[151]. Rebbi Zeïra said, what is the nature of this[152]? He said to him, he was a great personality, well versed in the Mishnah. Rebbi Ḥiyya from Kefar Teḥumin explained this to Rabbi and he appointed him rabbi[153].

151 Mishnah *Šabbat* 2:2 states that Sabbath lamps may not be filled with oil for burning. It is now stated that this refers only to lamps filled exclusively with oil for burning, not to a mixture of that with profane oil.

152 Can this statement be trusted? Since the Babli does not mention the possibility of adding profane oil, it certainly must disagree.

153 R. Ḥiyya from Kefar Teḥumin was a third generation Amora in Galilee. Therefore, "Rabbi" mentioned here cannot be Rebbi; it must be R. Jehudah II Neśia, or possibly R. Joḥanan. The person given the title "rabbi" seems to have been Jonathan ben Akhmai.

Here ends the parallel in *Šabbat* 2.

מַדְלִיקִין בְּבֵית הַמִּשְׁתֶּה אֲבָל לֹא בְּבֵית הָאֵבֶל דִּבְרֵי רִבִּי יוּדָה. רִבִּי יוֹסֵי אוֹמֵר בְּבֵית הָאֵבֶל אֲבָל לֹא בְּבֵית הַמִּשְׁתֶּה. רִבִּי מֵאִיר אוֹסֵר כָּאן וְכָאן. רִבִּי שִׁמְעוֹן מַתִּיר כָּאן וְכָאן. מַה טַעֲמָא דְרִבִּי יְהוּדָה. בֵּית הַמִּשְׁתֶּה עַל יְדֵי דְמָנֵיהוֹן נְקִיִּים לֹא מִתְעַסְּקִין. בְּבֵית הָאֵבֶל עַל יְדֵי דְמָנֵיהוֹן צָאִין מִתְעַסְּקִין בֵּיהּ. מַה טַעֲמָא דְרִבִּי יוֹסֵי. בֵּית הָאֵבֶל עַל יְדֵי דְאִינּוּן כְּנִיעִין לֹא מִתְעַסְּקִין בֵּיהּ. בֵּית הַמִּשְׁתֶּה עַל יְדֵי דְאִינּוּן פְּחִיזִין מִתְעַסְּקִין בֵּיהּ. מַאי טַעֲמָא דְרִבִּי מֵאִיר בְּבֵית הָאֵבֶל עַל יְדֵי דְמָנֵיהוֹן צָאִין מִתְעַסְּקִין בּוֹ. בֵּית הַמִּשְׁתֶּה עַל יְדֵי דְאִינּוּן פְּחִיזִין מִתְעַסְּקִין בֵּיהּ. מַאי טַעֲמָא דְרִבִּי שִׁמְעוֹן בֵּית הָאֵבֶל עַל יְדֵי דְאִינּוּן כְּנִיעִין לֹא מִתְעַסְּקִין בֵּיהּ. בֵּית הַמִּשְׁתֶּה עַל יְדֵי דְמָנֵיהוֹן נְקִיִּין לֹא מִתְעַסְּקִין בֵּיהּ. אָמְרִין דְּבֵי רִבִּי יַנַּאי הֲלָכָה כְרִבִּי שִׁמְעוֹן. רִבִּי יַעֲקֹב בַּר אָחָא בְּשֵׁם רִבִּי יוֹשִׁיָּה הֲלָכָה כְרִבִּי שִׁמְעוֹן. רִבִּי יוֹסֵי צַיְדָנַיָּא בְּעָא קוֹמֵי רִבִּי יִרְמְיָה. דְּלֹא כֵן מַה נָן אָמְרִין. רִבִּי מֵאִיר וְרִבִּי שִׁמְעוֹן אֵין הֲלָכָה כְרִבִּי שִׁמְעוֹן. אָמַר לֵיהּ שֶׁל בֵּית קוֹדְמִין הִיא.

וְהָא רִבִּי יוּדָה אוֹמֵר מֵעֵין שְׁנֵיהֶן. וְרִבִּי יוֹסֵי אוֹמֵר מֵעֵין שְׁנֵיהֶן. וְרִבִּי יוּדָה וְרִבִּי יוֹסֵי הֲלָכָה כְרִבִּי יוֹסֵי.

"One puts up lights at a wedding but not in a house of mourning, the words of Rebbi Jehudah; Rebbi Yose says, in a house of mourning but not at a wedding. Rebbi Meïr forbids in both cases, Rebbi Simeon permits in both cases." What is the reason of Rebbi Jehudah? At a wedding, since their garments are clean, they will not touch it[154]. In a house of mourning, since their garments are dirty, they will touch it. What is the reason of Rebbi Yose? In a house of mourning, since they are subdued, they will not touch it. At a wedding, since they are unrestrained, they will touch it. What is the reason of Rebbi Meïr? In a house of mourning, since their garments are dirty, they will touch it. At a wedding, since they are unrestrained, they will touch it. What is the reason of Rebbi Simeon? In a house of mourning, since they are subdued, they will not touch it. At a wedding, since their garments are clean, they will not touch it.

In the house of Rebbi Yannai they said, practice follows Rebbi Simeon. Rebbi Jacob bar Aḥa in the name of Rebbi Joshia: Practice follows Rebbi Simeon. Rebbi Yose from Sidon asked before Rebbi Jeremiah: Otherwise, what would we say? Rebbi Meïr and Rebbi Simeon, does practice not follow Rebbi Simeon[155]? He said to him, it is from the preceding paragraph. Rebbi Jehudah says similar to these two, Rebbi Yose says similar to those two, between Rebbi Jehudah and Rebbi Yose, practice follows Rebbi Yose[156].

154 Since they will not touch it, there is no danger that any oil will be used for other than approved purposes.

155 This is false, cf. Chapter 3, Note 25.

156 If the disagreement between RR. Meïr and Simeon is taken as fundamental, practice should follow one of the opinions intermediate between the fundamental opinions. This would lead

one to declare that practice must follow R. Yose. Therefore, the decision to follow R. Simeon for a wedding is not trivial.

מַהוּ לְהַדְלִיק שֶׁמֶן שְׂרֵיפָה בַּחֲנוּכָּה. אָֽמְרִין דְּבֵי רִבִּי יַנַּאי מַדְלִיקִין שֶׁמֶן שְׂרֵיפָה בַּחֲנוּכָּה. אָמַר רִבִּי נִיסָּא אֲנָא לָא אֲנָא חֲכִים לְאַבָּא. אִימָּא הֲוָה אָֽמְרָה לִי אָבוּךְ הֲוָה אֲמַר מִי שֶׁאֵין לוֹ שֶׁמֶן חוּלִּין מַדְלִיק שֶׁמֶן שְׂרֵיפָה בַּחֲנוּכָּה.

May one use oil for burning on Hanukkah? They said in the name of Rebbi Yannai: One uses oil for burning on Hanukkah. Rebbi Nasa said, I never knew my father. My mother told me, your father said that he who has no profane oil may use oil for burning on Hanukkah[157].

157 Even without permission of a Cohen (Maimonides *Terumot* 11:18). In the Babli, *Šabbat* 21a/b, this is a matter of controversy. The Yerushalmi's position there is represented by R. Zeïra in the name of Rav Mattanah or Rav, the opposite position is taken by Rav Huna.

Introduction to Tractate Ma'serot

The Tractate is devoted not to the manner in which heave and tithes are given; that topic was dealt with in tractates *Demay* and *Terumot*. Its main topic is the determination of (a) which agricultural produce is subject to heave and tithes and (b) at which point in time heave and tithes are due. Subject (a) is purely rabbinic in character since both in the Torah and in *Nehemiah* 10:25, tithes are restricted to grain, wine, and olive oil. The topic is discussed mainly in Chapters One and Five.

Most of the Tractate is devoted to subject (b). As a matter of principle, only the completion of the harvest activates the duty of heave and tithes. Before the end of processing, any produce may be eaten untithed (and without heave) as a snack. However, prior sale and a number of other actions may cause an earlier start of the obligation of heave. The bulk of the discussions in the Tractate centers on the circumstances under which produce may be consumed without the obligation of giving heave or tithes.

The agricultural worker who eats from the produce which he is harvesting (*Deut.* 23:25-26) always eats untithed. In the later part of Chapter Two, the obligations of the farmer and the rights of his workers are detailed.

For the interpretation, as always the main guides are Maimonides and R. Simson of Sens. Of the Eighteenth Century commentators, the most useful is R. Eliahu Fulda; the least useful are R. Moses Margalit (פני משה), R. Eliahu Wilna and, from the Twentieth Century, R. H. Kanievski, all of whom tend to emend away the difficult portions and the disagreements with Babylonian tradition. Similarly, the preliminary translation and explanation by J. Neusner and Martin S. Jaffee (Chicago, 1989) heavily depend on the emended Wilna text and a presumed but untenable identification of the Tosephta underlying the Yerushalmi with the Tosephta in our hands. The manuscript evidence, while meager, definitely excludes most emendations. Of modern commentaries, that by R. Saul Lieberman (*Tosefta ki-fshutah,* New York, 1955) and R. Y. Qafeḥ's commented edition and translation of Maimonides's Commentary are most useful. Other sources are quoted by name when used.

כלל אמרו פרק ראשון

(fol. 48c) **משנה א:** כְּלָל אָֽמְרוּ בַּמַּעְשְׂרוֹת כָּל־שֶׁהוּא אוֹכֶל וְנִשְׁמָר וְגִידּוּלָיו מִן הָאָרֶץ חַיָּיב בְּמַעְשְׂרוֹת. וְעוֹד כְּלָל אַחֵר אָֽמְרוּ כָּל־שֶׁתְּחִילָּתוֹ אוֹכֶל וְסוֹפוֹ אוֹכֶל אַף עַל פִּי שֶׁשִּׁימְּרוֹ לְהוֹסִיף אוֹכֶל חַיָּיב קָטוֹן וְגָדוֹל וְכָל־שֶׁאֵין תְּחִילָּתוֹ אוֹכֶל אֲבָל סוֹפוֹ אוֹכֶל אֵינוֹ חַיָּיב עַד שֶׁיֵּעָשֶׂה אוֹכֶל.

Mishnah 1: They declared a principle for tithes: Anything that is food[1], is guarded[2], and grows from the earth[3], is subject to tithes. They declared another principle: Anything that is food from start to end[4], even though it was kept to grow, is subject to tithes small or large. But anything that is not food from the start but at the end is food[5], is not subject to tithes until it becomes food.

1 But not industrial crops such as indigo.

2 This excludes wild growing berries, etc.

3 This excludes mushrooms and truffles which take their nourishment from decaying plants.

4 For example lettuce and most vegetables which could be eaten even if very small. These are subject to tithes when harvested.

5 Such as fruits, inedible in the early stages of development.

הלכה א: כְּלָל אָֽמְרוּ בְמַעְשְׂרוֹת[6] כו׳. כְּתִיב עַשֵּׂר תְּעַשֵּׂר אֵת כָּל־תְּבוּאַת זַרְעֶךָ. הָיִיתִי אוֹמֵר כָּל־הַדְּבָרִים יְהוּ חַייָבִין בְּמַעְשְׂרוֹת. תַּלְמוּד לוֹמַר אֵת כָּל־תְּבוּאַת זַרְעֶךָ רִיבָּה. וְרִיבָּה שְׁאָר זֶרְעוֹנֵי גִינָּה שֶׁאֵין נֶאֱכָלִין. כְּתִיב תְּבוּאַת זַרְעֶךָ.

וּכְתִיב הַיּוֹצֵא הַשָּׂדֶה שָׁנָה שָׁנָה. הָא כֵיצַד. טוֹל מִבֵּנְתַיִים דָּבָר שֶׁהוּא אוֹכֶל וְנִשְׁמָר.

Halakhah 1: "They declared a principle for tithes, etc." It is written (*Deut*. 14:22): "You should certainly tithe all produce of your seed." I would say, everything is subject to tithes. The verse says, "*all* produce of your seed," this includes. Does it include garden seeds that are not eaten? It is written: "produce of your seed," and it is written: "which your field produces every year." How is that? Take from among them anything that is food and is guarded[7].

6 Reading of the Rome ms. Leyden and Venice: בשביעית "in the Sabbatical."

7 The argument is rather cryptic since it also involves v. 23 which is not mentioned in the text. The full text of the verses is: "You should certainly tithe all produce of your seed which your field produces every year. Then you should eat before the Eternal, your God, at the place He will choose to let His Name dwell there, the tithe of your grain, your cider, and your oil, as well as the firstborn of your cattle and sheep, so that you shall learn to fear the Eternal, your God, all the days." While the second verse refers only to Second Tithe, the insistence of the first verse. עַשֵּׂר תְּעַשֵּׂר, "you should certainly tithe", is taken to mean that the rules apply to both tithes equally (*Sifry Deut*. 105). The Babli frequently (*Berakhot* 36b, *Pesaḥim* 44a, *Beẓah* 3b, *Yebamot* 81b, *Nedarim* 51a, *Bekhorot* 54b, *Ḥulin* 120b) insists that the second verse restricts tithes in biblical law to grain, grapes and wine, and olives and olive oil. All other tithes are considered only rabbinic. The Yerushalmi here, by not quoting the second verse explicitly, extends biblical obligations of tithe to all fruits. However, for practical purposes the Yerushalmi declares all tithes, including grain, wine, and oil, as voluntary (rabbinic) obligations in force since the return from Babylonian captivity (*Ševi'it* Chapter 6, Notes 11-13). Therefore, the biblical law as explained here is applicable only to the past, from Joshua to the destruction of the first Temple, and the future, the

days of the Messiah.

The paragraph here is shorthand for the detailed discussion, transmitted, e. g., in *Sifry Deut.* 105. Since v. 22 speaks of *all* produce, one could think that all produce is subject to tithes, including industrial crops like indigo and madder. Since v. 23 requires the tithe to be eaten, industrial crops are excluded. Nevertheless, the expression "all" must include produce not otherwise mentioned. Since v. 23 speaks only of grain, wine, and oil, it follows that v. 22 includes all other fruits and seeds. However, v. 23 excludes seeds that are not food. The *Sifry* goes on to include vegetables that are not seeds from the verse *Lev.* 27:30: "All tithe from the earth, from seeds of the earth, from fruits of trees, belongs to the Eternal." Here, "from the earth" is taken to denote vegetable food that is neither seed nor tree fruit. While *Lev.* 27:30 is discussed in the next paragraph in parallel to *Deut.* 14:22-23, the argument of the *Sifry* is not mentioned and in the Yerushalmi it is the generally accepted opinion that tithes of vegetables are purely rabbinical, cf. Note 17.

אִית דְּבָעֵי מִישְׁמְעִינָהּ מִן הָדָא. עַשֵּׂר תְּעַשֵּׂר כְּלָל. אֵת כָּל־תְּבוּאַת זַרְעֶךָ פְּרָט. כְּלָל וּפְרָט אֵין בִּכְלָל אֶלָּא מַה שֶׁבִּפְרָט. אֵין לִי אֶלָּא תְבוּאָה. קִיטְנִית מְנַיִין. תַּלְמוּד לוֹמַר וְכָל־מַעְשַׂר הָאָרֶץ מִזֶּרַע הָאָרֶץ מִפְּרִי הָעֵץ לַיי הוּא. לְרַבּוֹת זֶרַע שׁוּם שַׁחְלִים וְגַרְגֵּר. אוֹ יָכוֹל שֶׁאֲנִי מַרְבֶּה לוּף הָעֶלְיוֹן וְזֶרַע כְּרֵישִׁין זֶרַע בְּצָלִים זֶרַע לֶפֶת וּצְנוֹנוֹת וּשְׁאָר זֶרְעוֹנֵי גִינָּה שֶׁאֵין נֶאֱכָלִין. תַּלְמוּד לוֹמַר מִזֶּרַע הָאָרֶץ. וְלֹא כָל־זֶרַע הָאָרֶץ. פְּרִי הָעֵץ לְרַבּוֹת כָּל־פֵּירוֹת הָאִילָן. יָכוֹל שֶׁאֲנִי מַרְבֶּה חָרוּבֵי שִׁיטָּה וְצַלְמוֹנָה וְחָרוּבֵי גְדוֹרָה. תַּלְמוּד לוֹמַר מִפְּרִי הָעֵץ לֹא כָּל־פֵּירוֹת הָאִילָן.

Some want to understand it from the following[8]: (*Deut.* 14:22): "You should certainly tithe," a general statement. "All grain[9] of your seed," a detail. For every general statement followed by a detail, the general statement only implies the detail. That means, only grain. From where legumes? The verse says (*Lev.* 27:30): "All tithe from the earth, from seeds of the earth, from the fruit of the tree, belongs to the Eternal." This includes seeds of garlic, cress[10] and rocket[11]. I might think to add the upper part of arum[12] and the seeds of vetch, the seeds of onions, the seeds of turnips and radishes, and all other garden seeds that are not eaten; the verse says, "from[13] seeds of the earth," and not all seeds of the earth. (*Lev.* 27:30) "From fruits of trees," to include all fruits of trees. I might think to add acacia[14] and *ṣalmona*[15] pods, and carobs from dry land[16]; the verse says, "from[13] fruits of trees," not all fruits of trees.

8 *Sifra Beḥuqotai Pereq* 12(9); *Sifry Deut.* 105.

9 While תבואה in biblical Hebrew means "yield" in general, its meaning in rabbinic legal texts is limited to "grain".

10 This is the meaning of Syriac תחלא and of Maimonides' (*Ma'serot* 4:6) Arabic חב אל-רשאד.

11 Cf. *Ševi'it* 9:1.

12 The inedible part carrying the seeds.

13 Talmudic interpretation gives to a prefix מ a partitive meaning.

14 Some *Sifra* and *Sifry* sources read שקמה "sycamore".

15 The commentators take צלמונה as a place name. {A place צלמון is mentioned in Mishnah *Yebamot* 16:6. Cf. also *Sulmo*, later *Sulmona*, birth place of Ovid (E. G.).} However, since the other two kinds are trees, the word also must denote a tree, possibly connected with Accadic *ṣulmu* "black (tree)".

16 *Sifra* reads גרידה "(earth) dry and hard". This is the basis of the translation, rather than גדורה "fenced in". In *Sifry* most mss. read גירודה (variant of גרידה, cf. Levy's Dictionary, vol. 1, p. 357a); one ms. reads גירוגא "willow basket".

יְרָקוֹת מְנַיִין. אִיסִּי בֶּן יְהוּדָה אוֹמֵר הַמַּעְשְׂרוֹת לִירָקוֹת מִדִּבְרֵיהֶן.

Vegetables from where? Issy ben Jehudah says, tithes of vegetables are from their words[17].

17 It is not clear whether the obligation to tithe the vegetables is an original institution of Ezra or an addition from later times.

רַב חִסְדָּא אָמַר הִבְקִיר קָמָה וְחָזַר וְזָכָה בָהּ וְעָבַר וְהִפְרִישׁ מֵהֶן תְּרוּמָה הֲרֵי זוֹ תְּרוּמָה. מַה בֵּין קָמָה לַשִּׁיבֳּלִין. קָמָה עַד שֶׁלֹּא הִבְקִירָהּ עָבַר וְהִפְרִישׁ מִמֶּנָּה תְּרוּמָה אֵינָהּ תְּרוּמָה. שִׁבֳּלִין עַד שֶׁלֹּא הִבְקִירָהּ עָבַר וְהִפְרִישׁ מֵהֶן תְּרוּמָה הֲרֵי זוֹ תְּרוּמָה. רַב חִינְנָא בְשֵׁם רַב חִסְדָּא אַף בְּהֶקְדֵּשׁ כֵּן. מִילֵּיהוֹן דְּרַבָּנִין פְּלִיגִן. דְּאָמַר רִבִּי יוֹחָנָן בְּשֵׁם רִבִּי יַנַּאי. וּבָא הַלֵּוִי כִּי אֵין לוֹ חֵלֶק וְנַחֲלָה עִמָּךְ. מִמָּה שֶׁיֵּשׁ לָךְ וְאֵין לוֹ אַתְּ חַיָּב לִיתֵּן לוֹ. יָצָא לֶקֶט שֶׁיָּדָךְ וְיָדוֹ שָׁוִין בּוֹ. הִיא לֶקֶט הִיא שִׁכְחָה הִיא פֵּיאָה הִיא הֶבְקֵר. אָמַר רִבִּי יוֹחָנָן חֲבוּרָה הָיָה מַקְשָׁה הֲרֵי הֶקְדֵּשׁ הֲרֵי אֵין יָדָךְ וְיָדוֹ שָׁוִין כְּמִי שֶׁיָּדָךְ וְיָדוֹ שָׁוִין. אָמַר רִבִּי אִילָא מַה נָן קַייָמִין. (fol. 48d) אִם בְּשֶׁנִּתְמָרֵחַ הַכְּרִי בִּרְשׁוּת הַהֶבְקֵר וּבִרְשׁוּת הַהֶקְדֵּשׁ אָמְרָה תוֹרָה רֵאשִׁית דְּגָנְךָ וְלֹא שֶׁל הֶבְקֵר רֵאשִׁית דְּגָנְךָ וְלֹא שֶׁל הַהֶקְדֵּשׁ. אֶלָּא כִי נָן קַייָמִין בְּשֶׁהִבְקִיר שִׁיבֳּלִין וְחָזַר וְזָכָה בָהֶן. בְּהֶבְקֵר פָּטוּר. בְּהֶקְדֵּשׁ חַיָּב. בְּהֶבְקֵר פָּטוּר מִן הַהִיא דְּאָמַר רִבִּי יוֹחָנָן בְּשֵׁם רִבִּי יַנַּאי. וּבָא הַלֵּוִי כִּי אֵין לוֹ חֵלֶק וְנַחֲלָה עִמָּךְ. בְּמָה שֶׁיֵּשׁ לָךְ וְאֵין לוֹ אַתְּ חַיָּב לִיתֵּן לוֹ. יָצָא הֶבְקֵר שֶׁיָּדָךְ וְיָדוֹ שָׁוִין בּוֹ. בְּהֶקְדֵּשׁ חַיָּב. מִן הָדָא הִקְדִּישׁ קָמָה וּפָדָה קָמָה חַיָּב. מַה בֵּין הֶבְקֵר וּבֵין הֶקְדֵּשׁ. הֶבְקֵר יָצָא יְדֵי הַכֹּל. הֶקְדֵּשׁ לֹא יָצָא מִידֵי הַגִּזְבָּר. אָמַר רִבִּי אָבִין אֲפִילוּ יְדֵי הַבְּעָלִים לֹא יָצָא. מֵאַחַר שֶׁאָמַר לוֹ פְּדֵה אַתְּ רִאשׁוֹן.

Rav Ḥisda said, if somebody declared his standing grain ownerless, came back and retook possession, and illegally gave heave, that is heave[18]. What is the difference between standing grain and ears of grain? Standing grain, if he illegally gave heave before he declared it ownerless, that is not heave. Ears, if he illegally gave heave before he declared them ownerless, that is heave. Rav Ḥinena in the name of Rav Ḥisda, the same applies to a dedicated crop[19]. The words of the rabbis disagree, since Rebbi Joḥanan said in the name of Rebbi Yannai[20]: (*Deut.* 14:29) "The Levite shall come, because he has neither part nor inheritance with you." You are obliged to give him from what you have but he has not. This excludes gleanings for which your and his hands are equal. Gleanings, forgotten sheaves, *peah*, and abandoned property are all equal. Rebbi Joḥanan said, the company did ask: But dedications, where your and his hands are not equal, are treated[21] as if your and his hands were equal. Said Rebbi Ila, what are we talking about? If the heap was made when it was ownerless or dedicated, the Torah said (*Deut.* 18:4) "the first of *your* grain", not the ownerless, "the first of *your* grain", not Temple property. But we must be talking about ears that he declared ownerless and of which he retook possession. If they were ownerless, he would be free, if dedicated, he would be obligated. If they were ownerless, he would be free, since Rebbi Joḥanan said in the name of Rebbi Yannai: (*Deut.* 14:29) "The Levite shall come, because he has neither part nor inheritance with you." You are obligated to give him from what you have but he has not. This excludes gleanings for which your and his hands are equal. If dedicated, he would be obligated, from the following[22]: "If somebody dedicated standing produce and redeemed it standing, it is obligated." What is the difference between ownerless and dedicated? Ownerless [property] is outside the power of everybody, dedicated [property] is not outside the power of the Temple treasurer. Rebbi Abin said, it did not even go outside the power of its owners since he must say to him you redeem first[23].

18 Produce collected from ownerless property is not subject to heave and tithes, as deduced later in this paragraph from *Deut.* 18:4. In general, if somebody gives heave and tithes from exempt produce, his action is invalid and no sanctity is attached to the heave given. Standing grain is not under any obligation of heave. The obligation of heave and tithes falls on

the grain when it is stored after threshing but there is a latent obligation from the time it is cut since then it is potential commercial produce. Therefore, if heave was given from standing grain, that is an invalid act; if heave was given from cut ears of grain, this is against the rules but valid. If the exempt produce was cut while in the possession of its owner, a latent obligation is on it which can be activated by his giving heave and tithes "illegally", i. e., against the rules.

In the Babli (*Nedarim* 44b, *Baba Qama* 28a,94a, *Temurah* 6a, *Ḥulin* 134b, *Niddah* 51a), a similar principle is established using the grape harvest as an example. The entire argument disregards the opinion of R. Yose [*Peah* 6:1 (fol. 19b), *Demay* 3:2 (fol. 23b), *Nedarim* 4:10 (fol. 38d)] who rejects the concept of ownerless property and holds that the owner has full responsibility for his abandoned property until it is taken up and acquired by another person.

19 As indicated below, a crop which is Temple property is exempt from heave and tithes, as well as from the gifts to the poor. Rav Ḥisda wants to extend this exemption to standing grain which was dedicated to the Temple and redeemed while standing. In that case, there certainly is no exemption from the gifts to the poor, *Peah* Mishnah 4:5.

20 *Terumot* 1:5 (fol. 40d), *Ḥallah* 1:3 (fol. 57c), *Nedarim* 4:10 (fol. 38d); as tannaïtic statement *Sifry Deut.* 109.

21 By Rav Ḥisda. One continues to show that Rav Ḥisda's statement is wrong.

22 Mishnah *Peah* 4:5.

23 The prior owner of dedicated property retains the right of first refusal when the Temple wants to sell the property (*Sifra Beḥuqotay Pereq* 10).

רִבִּי זְעִירָא רִבִּי יָסָא בְּשֵׁם רִבִּי לָעְזָר הַזּוֹרֵעַ שְׂדֵה הֶבְקֵר חַיָּיב בְּמַעְשְׂרוֹת. רִבִּי יוֹנָה מַפִּיק לִישְׁנָא בְּזָכָה בִשְׂדֵה הֶבְקֵר וְגִידוּלֶיהָ.

Rebbi Zeïra, Rebbi Yasa in the name of Rebbi Eleazar: If somebody sowed an ownerless field, the crop is subject to tithes. Rebbi Jonah offers the language: Because he acquired the ownerless field and its growth[24].

24 Any agricultural work on an ownerless field is an acquisition (Babli *Baba Qama* 54a/b). Therefore, sowing a field (including preparing it for sowing) is an act of acquisition and the grain never grows as ownerless.

רִבִּי חִייָא בַּר אָדָא בְּעָא קוֹמֵי רִבִּי יוֹחָנָן כְּמֵהִין וּפִטְרִיּוֹת מָהוּ שֶׁיְּהוּ חַייָבִין בְּמַעְשְׂרוֹת. אָמַר לֵיהּ רִבִּי יוֹחָנָן בְּשֵׁם רִבִּי סִימַיי[25] כְּתִיב עַשֵּׂר תְּעַשֵּׂר אֵת כָּל־תְּבוּאַת זַרְעֶךָ. דָּבָר שֶׁהוּא נִזְרָע וּמַצְמִיחַ. יָצְאוּ כְּמֵהִין וּפִטְרִיּוֹת שֶׁאֵינָן נִזְרָעוֹת וּמַצְמִיחוֹת. רִבִּי יוֹנָה מַפִּיק לִישְׁנָא מִפְּנֵי שֶׁהָאָרֶץ פּוֹלְטָתָן.

Rebbi Ḥiyya bar Ada asked before Rebbi Joḥanan: Are truffles and mushrooms obligated for tithes? Rebbi Joḥanan said to him in the name of Rebbi Simai, it is written (*Deut.* 14:22): "You should certainly tithe all produce of your seed." Anything which is sown and grows. This excludes truffles and mushrooms which grow but are not sown[26]. Rebbi Jonah offers the language: Because the earth extrudes them[27].

25 Reading of the Rome ms. Leyden and Venice: סיסיי, an otherwise unknown name.

26 They reproduce by spores, not seeds.

27 Lacking chlorophyll, they live not on air and earth but on decaying organic matter.

אַף עַל פִּי שֶׁהוּא שׁוֹמְרוֹ לְהוֹסִיף אוֹכֶל חַייָב קָטוֹן וְגָדוֹל. הָא אִם אֵינוֹ שׁוֹמְרוֹ לְהוֹסִיף אוֹכֶל. אֵינוֹ חַייָב קָטוֹן וְגָדוֹל. רִבִּי אִימִּי בְּשֵׁם רִבִּי שִׁמְעוֹן בֶּן לָקִישׁ זוֹ לְהוֹצִיא מִדִּבְרֵי רַבָּן גַּמְלִיאֵל. דְּתַנִּינָן תַּמָּן רַבָּן גַּמְלִיאֵל אוֹמֵר תְּמָרוֹת שֶׁל תִּלְתָּן שֶׁל חַרְדָּל וְשֶׁל פּוֹל לָבָן חַייָבוֹת בְּמַעְשְׂרוֹת. אָמַר רִבִּי יוֹסֵי וְכִי מֵחֲמַת הָאוֹכֶל רַבָּן גַּמְלִיאֵל מְחַייֵב מֵעַתָּה אֲפִילוּ יַרְקָן. אֶלָּא רַבָּן גַּמְלִיאֵל אוֹמֵר חֲשׁוּבוֹת הֵן לְאוֹכֶל. וְרַבָּנִין אָמְרֵי אֵין חֲשׁוּבוֹת לְאוֹכֶל. וְעוֹד מִן הָדָא דְּתַנֵּי אוֹמֵר רִבִּי יוֹשֻׁעַ מִיָּמַי לֹא מְלָאַנִי לִבִּי לוֹמַר לְאָדָם צֵא וּלְקוֹט לָךְ תְּמָרוֹת שֶׁל תִּלְתָּן וְשֶׁל חַרְדָּל וְשֶׁל פּוֹל הַלָּבָן וּשְׁלוֹק לְפוֹטְרוֹ מִן הַמַּעְשְׂרוֹת.

"Even though it was kept to grow it is subject to tithes small or large.[28]" Does this imply that if it was not kept to grow it is not subject to tithes small or large? Rebbi Immi in the name of Rebbi Simeon ben Laqish: To exclude the words of Rabban Gamliel as we have stated there: "Rabban Gamliel says, flower buds of fenugreek, mustard, and white beans are subject to tithes." Rebbi Yasa said, did Rabban Gamliel obligate them because of food[29]? If it were so, what about their greenery? But Rabban Gamliel says, they are important as food, but the rabbis say, they are not important as food. In addition, from what we are stating[30]: "Rebbi Joshua said, I never wanted to tell anybody go, collect flower buds of fenugreek, mustard, and white beans and cook them, to free them from tithes[31]."

28 Quote from the Mishnah.

29 The seeds of fenugreek, mustard, and beans are food and subject to heave and tithes. Should this imply that any other part of these plants is also subject to heave and tithes? By the time the seeds are ripe and edible, the remainder of the chalice, developed from the flower buds, has turned into wood and is inedible. This is the opposite of the case of the Mishnah, parts of plants that are food at the beginning but non-food at the end.

30 Tosephta 3:7. There, the name is R. Joshua ben Qabusai.

31 While he agrees with the rabbis that these flower buds (which, it seems, have to be cooked to become edible) are free from tithes, he did not want to state this publicly since Rabban Gamliel objected.

תַּנֵּי כָּל־שֶׁתְּחִילָּתוֹ אוֹכֶל וְאֵין סוֹפוֹ אוֹכֶל מַה אִית לָךְ כְּהָדָא דְתַנֵּי הַמְקַיֵּים מְלֵיאָה שֶׁל אַכְרוּעַ לְזֶרַע בָּטְלָה דַעְתּוֹ קְלָחִין יְחִידִין לֹא בָטְלָה דַעְתּוֹ וְאָמַר רִבִּי יוֹנָה וְהוּא שֶׁלִּיקֵּט יָרָק. אֲבָל לֹא לִקֵּט יָרָק כָּךְ אָנוּ אוֹמְרִים עֵצִים חַייָבִין בְּמַעְשְׂרוֹת.

It was stated[32]: "Everything that is food at the start but not at the end." What is this? As we stated: "He who keeps the castor plant[33] for seeds, his opinion is inoperative[34]; for single stalks it is not inoperative[35]." Rebbi Jonah said, only if he collected greens[36]. But if he did not collect greens, do we say that wood is subject to tithes?

32 Tosephta 1:1. In the Vienna ms., the Tosephta is rudimentary as quoted here. In the Erfurt ms., it continues: For example, if somebody keeps vegetables for their seeds, they are obligated at the start and free at the end.

33 Arabic חִרוע, identification by H. L. Fleischer.

34 Since nobody plants an entire field for seeding (not to extract industrial oil from the seeds), his action does not follow agricultural practice and does not free from tithes.

35 Since every farmer will produce some seeds for next year's crop.

36 If he never used the plant as food when it still was edible, it is not food and is free from heave and tithes in all respects.

וְכָל־שֶׁאֵין תְּחִילָּתוֹ אוֹכֶל אֲבָל סוֹפוֹ אוֹכֶל אֵינוֹ חַייָב עַד שֶׁיֵּעָשֶׂה אוֹכֶל. מַה אִית לָךְ בַּהֲדָה. דְּתַנִּינָן דְּבַתְרָא מֵאֵימָתַי פֵּירוֹת חַייָבִין בְּמַעְשְׂרוֹת תְּאֵינִים מִשֶּׁיַּבְחִילוּ.

"But anything that is not food from the start but at the end is food, is not subject to tithes until it becomes food." What is that? That is what we have stated next: "From when are fruits subject to tithes? Figs from the moment they start to ripen.[37]"

37 The last sentence of the first Mishnah is the introduction to the following Mishnaiot.

(fol. 48c) **משנה ב**: מֵאֵימָתַי הַפֵּירוֹת חַייָבִין בְּמַעְשְׂרוֹת תְּאֵינִים מִשֶּׁיַּבְחִילוּ. וְהָעֲנָבִים וְהַבְּאוּשִׁין מִשֶּׁהִבְאִישׁוּ. הָאוֹג וְהַתּוּתִים מִשֶּׁיַּאְדִימוּ וְכָל־הָאֲדוּמִים מִשֶּׁיַּאְדִימוּ. הָרִימּוֹנִים מִשֶּׁיִּמַּסּוּ. הַתְּמָרִים מִשֶּׁיַּטִּילוּ שְׂאוֹר. הַפֶּרְסִיקִין מִשֶּׁיַּטִּילוּ גִידִין. וְהָאֶגוֹזִים מִשֶּׁיֵּעָשׂוּ מְגוּרָה. רִבִּי יְהוּדָה אוֹמֵר הָאֶגוֹזִים וְהַשְּׁקֵידִים מִשֶּׁיֵּעָשׂוּ קְלִיפָּה.

Mishnah 2: From when are fruits subject to tithes? Figs from the moment they start to ripen, grapes and wild grapes when they start to produce sap. Sumac and mulberries when they start to become red, and all red fruits when they start to become red. Pomegranates when they become soft, dates when they start to become bloated. Peaches when they get stripes, walnuts when they form a container. Rebbi Jehudah says, walnuts and almonds when they develop a shell.

(fol. 48b) **הלכה ב**: בִּיחִילוּ רִבִּי חִייָה בַּר וָא אָמַר חָיְתָה. כְּמַה דְתֵימַר וְגַם נַפְשָׁם בָּחֲלָה בִי. רִבִּי אַבָּא בַּר יַעֲקֹב מִשֵּׁם רִבִּי יוֹחָנָן מִשֶּׁיַּאֲדִימוּ פְּנֵיהֶם. וְכָל־הַתְּאֵינִים פִּיהֶם מַאֲדִימוֹת. רִבִּי תַנְחוּם בַּר מָרְיוֹן בְּשֵׁם רִבִּי יוֹחָנָן לוֹקֵחַ אַחַת וּמַנִּיחַ. אִם בְּשֵׁלָה בְתוֹךְ מֵעֵת לְעֵת חַייָבוֹת וְאִם לָאו פְּטוּרוֹת.

Halakhah 2: What means ביחילו? Rebbi Ḥiyya bar Abba said, if it comes alive, as you say (*Zach.* 11:8): "And their souls were too much for me.[38]" Rebbi Abba bar Jacob in the name of Rebbi Joḥanan: When they start to become red outside[39]. Do all figs become red on the outside? Rebbi Tanḥum bar Marion said in the name of Rebbi Joḥanan: He takes one and puts it somewhere. If that one ripens within 24 hours they are obligated, otherwise they are free.

38 Cf. *Ševi'it* Chapter 7, Note 84. "Coming alive" means getting some moisture in the fruit.

39 Here and in the paragraph on

mulberries, "red" means any color other than green. Figs are either green or dark violet.

פיסקא. הָעֲנָבִים וְהַבְּאוּשִׁין מִשֶּׁהִבְאִישׁוּ. רִבִּי זְעִירָא בְּשֵׁם רִבִּי יָסָא מִשֶּׁיִּקְרְאוּ בְּאִישָׁה. רִבִּי אַיְיבוֹ בַּר נַגָּרִי רִבִּי תַנְחוּם בַּר עִילַאי בְּשֵׁם רִבִּי נָחוּם בַּר סִימַאי שֶׁתְּהֵא חַרְצַנָּהּ שֶׁלָּהֶן נִרְאֵית מִבְּחוּץ.

New section. "Grapes and wild grapes when they start to produce sap." Rebbi Zeïra in the name of Rebbi Yasa: When they are called wretched grapes[40]. Rebbi Ayvo bar Nagari[41], Rebbi Tanḥum bar Ilaï[42] in the name of Rebbi Naḥum bar Simai: Only if their seeds are visible from the outside[43].

40 Bad but edible. R. Isaac Simponti notes that such grapes are called *uve malate* in Italian, paralleling the language of the Mishnah.

41 Tiberian Amora, student of R. Ḥiyya bar Abba and R. Ila.

42 Elsewhere, he is called R. Tanḥum bar Ḥanilaï or bar Ḥanina; a student of R. Joshua ben Levi and teacher of R. Levi.

43 The skin becomes transparent.

אָמַר רִבִּי יוֹחָנָן רְכִיב הֲוִינָא עַל כִּיתְפֵי דְסַבִּי וְשָׁמְעִית קָלֵיהּ דְּרִבִּי שִׁמְעוֹן בֶּן אֶלְעָזָר יְתִיב מַתְנֵי. מַכְנִיסִין בִּמְעֵי מְלַפְּפוֹן וְאֵין מַכְנִיסִין בִּמְעֵי אֲבַטִּיחַ. מָה בֵין מֵיעֵי מְלַפְּפוֹן לִמְעֵי אֲבַטִּיחַ. אָמַר רִבִּי שִׁמְעוֹן בַּר בַּרְסָנָא מֵיעֵי מְלַפְּפוֹן לָאֲכִילָה. מְעֵי אֲבַטִּיחַ לִזְרִיעָה. אִם אוֹמֵר אַתְּ כֵּן נִמְצֵאתָ מְכַבֵּד אֶת הַקַּרְקַע בְּשַׁבָּת.

Rebbi Joḥanan said: I was riding on my grandfather's shoulder when I heard the voice of Rebbi Simeon ben Eleazar who was sitting and stating: "One collects the insides of a sweet melon[44] but one does not collect the insides of a water melon." What is the difference between the insides of a sweet melon and those of a water melon? Rebbi Simeon ben Barsana[45] said, the insides of a sweet melon are for eating, those of a water melon for sowing. If you would say so, you will end up sweeping the ground on the Sabbath[46].

44 The seeds and the loose tissue in which they are embedded.

45 In *Terumot* 2, Note 72, he is called ben Karsana, in the Rome ms. ben Parsana.

46 It is difficult to understand what the entire paragraph means and how much to trust the testimony of a toddler. It is not known which kind of melon corresponds to *melopepo*; it must be a kind whose seeds, similar to pumpkin seeds, are food after roasting. Water melon seeds with their thick, black shell are not treated as food and never subject of separate tithe. Sweeping the floor on the Sabbath is forbidden, cf. *Šabbat* 3:4 (fol. 6a), Tosephta *Šabbat* 16:20. One has to assume that R. Simeon ben Eleazar permits to collect (for roasting during the week) on the Sabbath the seeds of sweet melon eaten with the Sabbath dinner; the commentary of the editors of the Talmud is that in that case, people will come to sweep their dirt floors, קרקע, to collect the seeds, which may be forbidden by biblical law. (The sweeping of stone floors, ריצפה, is only forbidden by rabbinic decree as a weekday occupation.)

פיסקא. כָּל־הָאֲדוּמִים מִשֶּׁיַּאֲדִימוּ. מְיָישָׁא תַּנֵּי רִימוֹן שֶׁנִּיקְרָה בוֹ אֲפִילוּ פְּרִידָה אַחַת כּוּלָּהּ חִיבּוּר לְמַעֲשֵׂר. אֶשְׁכּוֹל שֶׁבִּישֵּׁל בּוֹ אֲפִילוּ גַּרְגֵּר יְחִידִי כּוּלּוֹ חִיבּוּר לְמַעְשְׂרוֹת. אָמַר רִבִּי חֲנִינָה פֶּשְׁטוּ הוּא לָן כָּל־אוֹתָהּ הַגֶּפֶן כָּל־אוֹתָן הַמִּין. חָזְרוּ וּפָשְׁטוּ לוֹ כָּל־אוֹתָהּ הָרוּחַ. רִבִּי יוֹסֵי בֵּי רִבִּי בּוּן אוֹמֵר כָּל־אוֹתוֹ הַכֶּרֶם. הָיָה כֶּרֶם קָטָן וַעֲשָׂאוֹ גָדוֹל. גָּדוֹל וַעֲשָׂאוֹ קָטָן אֶחָד וַעֲשָׂאוֹ שְׁנַיִם שְׁנַיִם וַעֲשָׂאוֹ אֶחָד.

New section. "All red fruits when they start to become red." Miasha[47] stated: Even if only one pomegranate was soft, all[48] is connected for tithe. "A bunch of grapes one berry of which became red is all connected for tithes.[49]" Rebbi Ḥanina said, they[50] made it clear to us, [this refers to] the entire vine, even to the entire strain[51]. They[50] added and made it clear, all this direction[52]. Rebbi Yose ben Rebbi Abun said, the entire vineyard. If it was a small vineyard and he made it large, large and he made it small, one and he split in into two, two which he united[53]?

47 Usually he is called Rebbi Miasha. R. S. Lieberman (*Tosefta ki-fshutah Zeraïm* p. 667), who holds that R. Ḥanina mentioned later is the first generation Amora, takes מיישא to be the sugar-berry-tree, *Celtis australis*, mentioned as illustration of the Mishnah. Then he starts a new sentence: "It was stated . . ."

48 The entire pomegranate tree is now subject to tithes. The Hebrew text is difficult, the interpretation follows Maimonides (*Ma'serot* 2:5).

49 A similar statement, in the name of R. Ismael ben R. Yose, is in *Demay* 1:1 (Note 53) and Tosephta *Ma'serot* 1:1.

50 The missing subject must be R. Miasha and his school. This shows that "R. Ḥanina" here is the fourth generation Amora who usually is called R. Ḥanania.

51 All vines of the same strain in the vineyard.

52 All vines of this strain in this direction as seen from the dwelling of the owner.

53 Small and large vineyards are defined in *Kilaim* Chapter 4. Since one now agrees that one berry makes the entire vineyard subject to tithes, the question is whether the legal definition of the vineyard refers to the time the first berry became red or to the time of tithing. The question is not answered, probably because it never arose in a practical case.

שְׁמוּאֵל אָמַר דְּלַעַת שֶׁנִּיקְּרָה בְּבֵית אָבִיהָ כָּל־אוֹתָהּ הַגּוּמָא אֲסוּרָה. אַף בְּמַכְבֵּדוֹת תְּמָרָה כֵן. אָמַר רִבִּי יוֹסֵי שָׁאַל יוֹנָתָן בֶּן חֲרָשָׁא אִישׁ גִּינָּסַר אֶת רַבָּן גַּמְלִיאֵל וַחֲכָמִים בְּיַבְנֶה. נִיקּוּרֵי רֶטֶב בָּאֲבִיהֶן מָה הֵן. אָמְרוּ לוֹ כָּל־אוֹתוֹ הַדֶּקֶל אָסוּר. אָמַר רִבִּי יוֹסֵי לָכֵן צְרִיכָה בְּשֶׁנִּיקְּרוּ כּוּלָּן. שֶׁלֹּא תֹאמַר הוֹאִיל וְאֵין דֶּרֶךְ הַנָּחָשׁ לַעֲשׂוֹת כֵּן. אֲנִי אוֹמֵר עָנָן שֶׁל צִיפּוֹרִין שֶׁכָּן עֲלֵיהֶן וְנִיקְּרוּ. רִבִּי

יוֹנָה בְשֵׁם רִבִּי שִׁמְעוֹן חֲסִידָא נִיקוּרֵי רֶטֶב בְּאֲבִיהֶן אָסוּר וְהָרַבִּים נָהֲגוּ בָהֶן הֵיתֵר וְאֵינָן נִיזוֹקִין.

Samuel said, if a pumpkin was punctured, all that grows in that depression is forbidden[54]. The same holds for bunches of dates[55]. "[56]Rebbi Yose said, Jonathan ben Ḥarasha from Genezareth[57] asked Rabban Gamliel and the Sages at Jabneh: What is the status of punctured soft dates on their tree? They said to him, that entire date palm is forbidden." Rebbi Yose[58] said, that statement is needed if all [dates] are punctured; you should not say, since a snake does not usually do this, a cloud of birds rested on them and pecked at them. Rebbi Jonah in the name of Rebbi Simeon the Pious: Punctured soft dates on their tree are forbidden, but people behave as if they were permitted and they are not hurt.

54 It was the practice to plant several pumpkins at opposite corners of a depression and to make them grow in different directions, cf. *Kilaim* 3:1.

33 The entire bunch is forbidden if one date shows a puncture mark that might come from a snake bite; cf. *Terumot* 8:4-5.

56 Tosephta *Kelim Baba Batra* 5:6.

57 Nothing else is known about him.

58 The Amora.

פיסקא. הָרִימּוֹנִים מִשֶּׁיִּמַּסּוּ. רִבִּי זְעִירָא בְשֵׁם רִבִּי יָסָא מִשֶּׁיִּתְמָעֵךְ הָאוֹכֶל תַּחַת יָדָיו. רִבִּי יוּדָה בַּר פָּזִי בְשֵׁם רִבִּי יְהוֹשֻׁעַ בֶּן לֵוִי מִשֶּׁיַּכְנִיסוּ מֶחֱצָה. רִבִּי יוֹנָה בָּעֵי דִּילְמָא מִן רַבָּנִין דַּאֲגַדְתָּא הוּא שָׁמַע לָהּ. אַחֵינוּ הֵמַסּוּ אֶת לְבָבֵינוּ. פַּלְגוֹן לְבָבֵינוּ.

New section. "Pomegranates when they get soft." Rebbi Zeïra in the name of Rebbi Assi: When the food gets soft in his hand. Rebbi Jehudah bar Pazi in the name of Rebbi Joshua ben Levi: From when half the juice is in them. Rebbi Jonah asked: Maybe he understood that from teachers of homilies? (*Deut.* 1:28) "Our brethren made our hearts melt," they split our hearts in two[59].

59 This interpretation, taking the *hiph'il* of מסס as Greek ἥμισυς "half", is not recorded in any Targum or known Midrash. From the homily one might infer that the local pronunciation of הֵמַסּוּ was הֵמִסּוּ or that the short vowels *a, i* were practically indistinguishable.

R. Jonah's objection determines practice according to R. Zeïra.

הַתְּמָרִים מִשֶּׁיַּטִּילוּ שְׂאוֹר. רִבִּי חִיָּיה בַּר וָוא אָמַר מִשֶּׁיִּתְמַלֵּא הַחֶרֶץ. רִבִּי יוֹנָה בָּעֵי מַה נָן קַיָּמִין אִם כְּשֶׁיִּתְמַלֵּא הַחֶרֶץ נוֹבֶלֶת הִיא. אִם מִשֶּׁתִּפְרוֹשׁ גַּרְעִינָהּ בְּשֵׁילָה הִיא כָל־צוֹרְכָהּ. רַבָּנָן דְּקֵיסָרִין אָמְרֵי וְיִהְיוּ יָפוֹת לָאֲכִילָה.

"Dates when they start to become bloated." Rebbi Ḥiyya bar Abba said, when the indentation is straightened out[60]. Rebbi Jonah asked: How do we hold? If the indentation is straightened out, it is wind-fall[61]! If the pit can be separated, it is fully ripe[62]! The rabbis from Caesarea say, when they are ready to be eaten.

60 If the shape of the date is convex all around.

61 A normal date is concave around the pedicle. If it is bloated there also, is it unsound and not food.

62 In that case, one does not need a special rule.

הַפֶּרְסִיקִין מִשֶּׁיַּטִּילוּ גִידִים. רִבִּי זְעִירָא בְּשֵׁם אִיסִּי מִשֶּׁיַּטִּילוּ גִידִין אֲדוּמִין.

"Peaches when they get stripes." Rebbi Zeïra in the name of Assi: When they get red stripes.

הָאֱגוֹזִים וְהַשְּׁקֵדִים מִשֶּׁיַּעֲשׂוּ מְגוּרָה. רִבִּי יוּדָה אוֹמֵר הָאֱגוֹזִים וְהַשְּׁקֵידִים מִשֶּׁיַּעֲשׂוּ קְלִיפָּה. אָמְרוּ בִּקְלִיפָּה הַתַּחְתּוֹנָה שֶׁהִיא סְמוּכָה לָאוֹכֶל. מוֹדִין

חֲכָמִים לְרִבִּי יוּדָה בָּאַלְצָרִין וּבְאִיפִּסְטָקִין וּבְאִיצְטְרוֹבֵּילִין מִשֶּׁיַּעֲשׂוּ קְלִיפָּה.

"Walnuts and almonds when they form a container[63]. Rebbi Jehudah says, walnuts and almonds when they develop a shell. They said, the inner skin close to the edible part. The Sages agree with Rebbi Jehudah regarding filberts[64], pistachios, pine nuts, when they develop a shell.[65]"

63 A hard shell acting as a container for the edible nut.

64 Determination of I. Löw and S. Liebermann (*Tosefta ki-fshutah* p. 667-668). Following Payne-Smith, the same word in Syriac denotes pistachios, but this cannot be the meaning in Hebrew since pistachios are mentioned separately.

65 Tosephta *Ma'serot* 1:1: "Filberts, pistachios, pine nuts, when they develop a shell. Walnuts and almonds when they form a container, Rebbi Jehudah says, when they develop a shell. What shell did they talk about? The inner skin close to the edible part." In this formulation, practice follows R. Jehudah; in the formulation of the Yerushalmi it follows the Sages.

(fol. 48c) **משנה ג:** הֶחָרוּבִין מִשֶּׁיְּנַקֵּידוּ וְכָל־הַשְּׁחוֹרִים מִשֶּׁיְּנַקֵּידוּ. וְהָאֲגָסִים וְהַקְּרוּסְטוֹמֵלִין וְהַפָּרִישִׁין וְהַחִזְרָרִין מִשֶּׁיְּקָרֵיחוּ וְכָל־הַלְּבָנִים מִשֶּׁיְּקָרֵחוּ. הַתִּלְתָּן כְּדֵי שֶׁתִּצְמַח. הַתְּבוּאָה וְהַזֵּיתִים מִשֶּׁיַּכְנִיסוּ שְׁלִישׁ.

Carobs from when they become spotted, and all black ones when they become spotted[66]. Pears, golden apples, quince, and sorbs[67], when they get bald[68], and all white ones when they get bald. Fenugreek so that a new plant grows[69]. And olives when they contain a third[70].

66 When the originally green pods start developing black spots.

67 These trees have been identified in *Kilaim* 1:4, Notes 73,74.

68 When they lose their down-like small hairs.

69 When the fenugreek seeds will produce new plants.

70 This has been explained in *Ševi'it* 4:9, Note 104. It really means that the olives, when pressed, yield one ninth of the amount of oil recoverable from ripe fruits.

(fol. 48b) **הלכה ג**: תַּנֵּי רִבִּי חִינְנָא בַּר פַּפָּא חֲרוּבִין שֶׁלְּשׁוּלָן הוּא חֲנָטָן. וְכָל־הַשְּׁחוֹרִין כְּגוֹן עִינְּבֵי הֲדַס וְעִינְּבֵי סְנֶה מִשֶּׁיִּנָּקֵידוּ. תַּנֵּי רִבִּי חִינְנָא בַּר פַּפָּא מִשֶּׁיֵּעָשׂוּ נְקוּדוֹת שְׁחוֹרוֹת. הַפְּרִישִׁין אִיסְפַּרְגְּלִין וְלָמָּה נִקְרָא שְׁמָן פְּרִישִׁין שֶׁאֵין לָךְ מִין אִילָן פָּרִישׁ לִקְדֵירָה אֶלָּא מִין זֶה בִּלְבָד.

Halakhah 3: Rebbi Ḥinena bar Pappa stated, for carob trees their forming clusters means their sprouting[71]. "All black ones", e. g., bunches of the myrtle and bunches of senna [berries]. Quince, quince[72]. Why are they called "prepared", because there is no tree only producing for the pot except that kind.

71 This sentence is from *Ševi'it* Halakhah 4:10.

72 The same meaning; the first word is in Hebrew, the second in Syriac. This statement and the next sentence are from *Kilaim* 1:4, Notes 78-79.

פיסקא א. וְכָל־הַלְּבָנִים. כְּגוֹן אִילֵין מרפייתא. מִשֶּׁיִּקָּרֵיחוּ. רִבִּי חִינְנָא בַּר פַּפָּא אָמַר מִשֶּׁיֵּעָשׂוּ קְרָחוֹת קְרָחוֹת לְבָנוֹת. תַּנֵּי רִבִּי שִׁמְעוֹן בֶּן יוֹחַי מִשֶּׁיַּזְחִילוּ מַיִם. אָתָא עוּבְדָא קוֹמֵי רִבִּי חֲנִינָה וּבְעָא לְמֵיעֲבַד כְּרִבִּי חִינְנָא בַּר פַּפָּא. חָזַר וְאָמַר וְכִי מֵחֲמַת הָאוֹכֶל הֵן מַקְרִיחוֹת. לֹא מֵחֲמַת הַתּוֹלַעַת שֶׁיֵּשׁ בָּהֶן.

New section 1. "All white ones," e. g. מרפייתא[73]. Rebbi Ḥinena bar Pappa said, when they get white bald spots. Rebbi Simeon ben Yoḥai stated, when water starts to flow in them[74]. There came a case before

Rebbi Ḥanina and he wanted to act following Rebbi Ḥinena bar Pappa. He had second thoughts and said, do they get bald because of the edible part? Rather it is because a worm is in them!

73 This fruit has not been identified. The Rome ms. has מספייתא which Löw reads as מספילתא "medlars".

74 When juice can be extracted from the fruit.

פיסקא ב. הַתִּלְתָּן מִשֶּׁתִּצְמַח. כֵּינִי מַתְנִיתָא כְּדֵי שֶׁתִּזָּרַע וְתִצְמַח. כֵּיצַד הוּא (fol. 49a) בּוֹדֵק. רִבִּי שְׁמוּאֵל בַּר נַחְמָן בְּשֵׁם רִבִּי יוֹנָתָן נוֹטֵל מְלֹא קוּמְצוֹ וְנוֹתֵן לְתוֹךְ הַסֵּפֶל שֶׁל מַיִם אִם שָׁקַע רוּבָּהּ חַייֶבֶת. וְאִם לָאו פְּטוּרָה. רִבִּי יוֹנָה בָּעֵי מֵעַתָּה מַה שֶּׁשִּׁיקַע יְהֵא חַייָב. וּמַה שֶּׁלֹּא שִׁיקַע יְהֵא פָּטוּר. אֶלָּא בְּרוֹב כָּל־פְּרִידָה וּפְרִידָה אִיתְאֲמָרַת. אָמַר רִבִּי יוֹסֵי בֵּי רִבִּי בּוּן וְכֵינִי בְּרוֹב כָּל־פְּרִידָה וּפְרִידָה אִיתְאֲמָרַת.

New paragraph 2. "Fenugreek so that a new plant grows." So is the Mishnah: So that it would grow if sown[75]. How can one check? Rebbi Samuel bar Naḥman in the name of Rebbi Jonathan: He takes a handful and puts it into a pot full of water. If the greater part of it will sink down, it is obligated; otherwise it is exempt. Rebbi Jonah asked: In this case, should not that which sank down be obligated, what did not sink down be exempted[76]? But it must have been said about the greater part of each single ear[77]. Rebbi Yose ben Rebbi Abun confirmed: It has been said about the greater part of each single ear.

75 The criterion is obviously impractical for fenugreek grown for sale. Hence, it must be formulated as hypothetical.

76 Since fenugreek seeds are extremely small and valuable, a handful of seeds will come from many plants and, therefore, all seeds from one ear can sink or float. This would make the ear either subject to tithes or exempt.

The advice to take a handful is impractical.

77 The basic method of checking is correct; it leads to the determination whether there is an obligation or not. But it must be applied to each ear separately (as long as there is any doubt.)

אָמַר רִבִּי זְעִירָא כְּתִיב עַשֵּׂר תְּעַשֵּׂר אֵת כָּל־תְּבוּאַת זַרְעֶךָ. דָּבָר שֶׁהוּא נִזְרָע וּמַצְמִחַ יָצָא פָּחוּת מִשְּׁלִישׁ שֶׁאֵינוֹ נִזְרָע וּמַצְמִחַ. רִבִּי חִינְנָא בְּשֵׁם רִבִּי זֵיתִים וַעֲנָבִים שֶׁלֹּא הֵבִיאוּ שְׁלִישׁ אַף הַמַּשְׁקִין הַיּוֹצְאִין מֵהֶן. לְהַכְשִׁיר אֵין מַכְשִׁירִין.

Rebbi Zeïra said: It is written (*Deut* 14:22): "You shall certainly tithe all your seed-yield." Anything which will grow when sown[78]; this excludes seeds less than one-third ripe which will not grow when sown. Rebbi Ḥinena in the name of Rebbi: The fluids from grapes or olives which are not one-third ripe will not prepare [for impurity[79]].

78 Is subject to tithes. This paragraph starts the discussion of the last part of the Mishnah, about olives. This interpretation of the verse, universally accepted in the Yerushalmi (cf. *Ševi'it* 2:7, fol. 34a, *Ḥallah* 1:4, fol. 57d), is in the Babli (*Sukkah* 36a) ascribed to R. Simeon only, as a minority opinion.

79 Cf. *Demay* Chapter 2, Notes 136,141.

רִבִּי חִייָה בְּשֵׁם רִבִּי חֲנִינָה זֵיתִים מֵאֵימָתַי חַייָבוֹת בְּמַעְשְׂרוֹת מִשֶּׁיְּבַכֵּר צַמְיָיא קַייְטָא. לֹא בִיכֵּר צַמְיָיא קַייְטָא. מִשֶּׁבִּיכְּירוּ בְּנוֹת שֶׁבַע. לֹא בִיכִּירוּ בְּנוֹת שֶׁבַע. מִשֶּׁיּוּרוּ מֶרְוִיוֹת שְׁנִייָה שֶׁבִּמּוּקְצֶה. רִבִּי לָעְזָר בֵּי רִבִּי יוֹסֵי בְּשֵׁם רִבִּי תַּנְחוּם בַּר חִייָה מִשֶּׁיְּבַכְּרוּ בְּנוֹת שֶׁבַע לְבָנוֹת. אָמַר רִבִּי יוֹסֵי בֵּי רִבִּי בוּן וּבִלְבַד בְּנוֹת שֶׁבַע שֶׁבְּאוֹתוֹ הַמָּקוֹם.

Rebbi Ḥiyya[80] in the name of Rebbi Ḥanina: From when are olives subject to tithes[81]? When the quickly growing summer fruit[82] first ripens. If no quickly growing summer fruit ripens, when white figs[83] first ripen. If there are no white figs to ripen, when the second batch is seen in the *muqẓeh*[84]. Rebbi Eleazar ben Rebbi Yose said in the name of Rebbi Tanḥum bar Ḥiyya, when the first really white white figs ripen. Rebbi Yose ben Rebbi Abun said, this refers only to white figs of the same place.

80 The Great Rebbi Ḥiyya.

81 As a practical criterion.

82 These fruits have not been identified.

83 Cf. Mishnah *Demay* 1:1, *Ševi'it* 4:1. These figs stay on the tree for three years; one looks at the first ripe fruits of the third year.

84 This is the place where cut-up (קצה) figs are left to ferment to be made into fig cakes. {Since during the fermentation process the figs are inedible, the term *muqẓeh* is transferred (regarding the rules of Sabbath and holidays) to denote anything unusable which, therefore, may not be moved on the Sabbath or the holiday.}

(fol. 48c) **משנה ד:** וּבְיָרָק הַקִּשּׁוּאִין וְהַדִּילּוּעִין וְהָאֲבַטִּיחִין וְהַמֶּלַפְפוֹנוֹת הַתַּפּוּחִים וְהָאֶתְרוֹגִים חַיָּבִין גְּדוֹלִים וּקְטַנִּים. רִבִּי שִׁמְעוֹן פּוֹטֵר אֶת הָאֶתְרוֹגִין בְּקוֹטְנָן. הַחַיָּב בִּשְׁקֵדִים הַמָּרִים פָּטוּר מִן הַמְּתוּקִים הַחַיָּב בַּמְּתוּקִין פָּטוּר מִן הַמָּרִים.

Mishnah 4: Of vegetables green melons[85], pumpkins, water melons, sweet melons[85], [also] apples and cedrats[86] are obligated large and small. Rebbi Simeon frees cedrats when they are small[87]. What is obligated among bitter almonds[88] is free among sweet almonds[89]; what is obligated among the sweet is free among the bitter.

85 Cf. *Kilaim* 1:2, Notes 38, 39.

86 Definition of Maimonides from the Arabic אתרוג; *Citrus medica cedrata R*. This *citrus medica* is sweet with very thin skin; the thick-skinned variety which is inedible unless cooked is

forbidden for use on the holiday of Tabernacles by R. Aqiba, see below.

87 In Mishnah *Sukkah* 3:5, a "small" cedrat is defined as one the size of a walnut (R. Meïr) or a chicken egg (R. Jehudah).

88 These might be edible only if they are extremely young, before they become poisonous. Later they are only used in small quantities for cooking or baking.

This sentence is also in Mishnah *Ḥulin* 1:5. The interpretation follows Maimonides and Rashi *Ḥulin* 25b.

89 They are not usually eaten when they are undeveloped.

(fol. 49a) **הלכה ד**: תַּמָּן תַּנִּינָן הַלּוֹקֵחַ שְׂדֵה יָרָק בְּסוּרְיָא עַד שֶׁלֹּא בָאוּ לְעוֹנַת הַמַּעְשְׂרוֹת חַייָב. מִשֶּׁבָּאוּ לְעוֹנַת הַמַּעְשְׂרוֹת פָּטוּר וְלוֹקֵט כְּדַרְכּוֹ וְלוֹקֵחַ. וְכָא אַתְּ אָמַר הָכֵין. חִזְקִיָּה אָמַר בִּשְׂדֵה שֶׁל קִשּׁוּאִין וְשֶׁל דִּילוּעִין הִיא מַתְנִיתָא. אָמַר רִבִּי זְעִירָא אֲפִילוּ תֵימַר בִּשְׂדֵה יָרָק עַצְמוֹ עוֹד הוּא יֵשׁ לוֹ גְבוּל מִשֶּׁיָּבִיא שָׁלֹשׁ פְּתִילוֹת.

Halakhah 4: There[90], we have stated: If somebody buys a vegetable field in Syria[91], if this was before the start of the season of tithes, he is obligated. But if it was after the start of the season of tithes, he is free. And here, you say so[92]? Ḥizqiah said, the Mishnah[93] speaks of a field of green melons or pumpkins. Rebbi Zeïra said, even if you hold this about a general field of vegetables, there still is a limit, only after it grew three twisted leaves[94].

90 Mishnah 5:5.

91 The obligation of tithes in Syria is purely rabbinical. If the field was a Gentile's possession when theoretically the obligation of tithes started, it remains free at all times (Mishnah 5:5). In Mishnaiot 1 - 4, the start of the obligation is only potential; the actual obligation starts only when the harvest is stored, as explained in Mishnah 5.

92 Our Mishnah here states that once the vegetable starts growing, it is potentially subject to (rabbinic) tithes; there never would be a time "before the season of tithes."

93 The Mishnah here which denies

a time before the season of tithes.

94 Even if all vegetables are held to be always in the season of tithes, as long as there are no vegetables to be used there can be no tithes. The expression פתילה "wick" used here in an agricultural sense is not recognized in the dictionaries and not explained in the commentaries. In Arabic, فتل is either a wick or a pod of seeds of certain shrubs.

נְהוֹרַאי בַּר שִׁינְיָא אָמַר מִשּׁוּם רִבִּי שִׁמְעוֹן תַּפּוּחִים קְטַנִּים פְּטוּרִין. תַּפּוּחִין גְּדוֹלִים חַיָּבִין. תַּפּוּחֵי מֶלִּימֵילָה בֵּין גְּדוֹלִים בֵּין קְטַנִּים חַיָּבִין. וְדָא מַתְנִיתָא מָהִיא מָאן דְּאָמַר קְטַנִּים בְּמַחְלוֹקֶת. מָאן דְּאָמַר תַּפּוּחֵי מֶלִּימֵילָה דִּבְרֵי הַכֹּל.

"[95]Nehorai bar Shania said in the name of Rebbi Simeon: Small apples are exempt, large apples are obligated. Honey apples[96] are obligated large or small." What is the status of the Mishnah[97]? One may say small ones are in dispute, one may say honey apples in agreement with everybody[98].

95 Tosephta 1:1. Nehorai bar Shanaia (שָׁנְיָיה, vocalized reading of a Geniza fragment) appears in *Rosh Hashanah* 2:1, fol. 57d, as one of the sages of the Synhedrion at Usha.

96 Greek μελίμηλον, τό. ("Summer apple", *pyrus praecox*. In Greek authors, the word is also used for a drink made from the fruit. According to I. Löw, the fruit of an apple-tree on quince stock.) In the Tosephta, edited outside the Greek-speaking world, the word is corrupted to נמילה, נמילא, מי נמלה.

97 Since the Mishnah declares all apples to be potentially subject to tithes, whether commercially usable or not.

98 According to this opinion, "apples" in the Mishnah means only "honey apples".

אֶתְרוֹג הַבּוֹסֶר רִבִּי עֲקִיבָה אוֹמֵר אֵינוֹ פֶּרִי. וַחֲכָמִים אוֹמְרִים פֶּרִי. רִבִּי אִילָא רִבִּי יָסָא בְּשֵׁם רִבִּי לָעְזָר אַתְיָא דְּרִבִּי שִׁמְעוֹן בְּשִׁיטָּה רִבִּי עֲקִיבָה רַבּוֹ. כְּמַה דְּרִבִּי עֲקִיבָה אוֹמֵר אֵינוֹ פֶּרִי כֵּן רִבִּי שִׁמְעוֹן אוֹמֵר אֵינוֹ פֶּרִי. אָמַר רִבִּי יוֹסֵי

כָּל־שֶׁהוּא כָשֵׁר לְלוּלָב חַיָּיב בְּמַעְשְׂרוֹת וְכָל־שֶׁאֵינוֹ כָשֵׁר לְלוּלָב אֵינוֹ חַיָּיב בְּמַעְשְׂרוֹת. הָתִיבוֹן הֲרֵי גָדֵל בְּטֵפוּס. הֲרֵי עָשׂוּי כְּכַדּוּר. הֲרֵי הוּא פָּסוּל לְלוּלָב וְחַיָּיב בְּמַעְשְׂרוֹת. מִסְתַּבְּרָא רִבִּי שִׁמְעוֹן יוֹדֵי לְרִבִּי עֲקִיבָה וְרִבִּי עֲקִיבָה לֹא יוֹדֵי לְרִבִּי שִׁמְעוֹן. רִבִּי שִׁמְעוֹן יוֹדֵי לְרִבִּי עֲקִיבָה דִּכְתִיב פְּרִי וְאֵינוֹ פֶרִי. רִבִּי עֲקִיבָה לֹא יוֹדֶה לְרִבִּי שִׁמְעוֹן הֲרֵי מְנוּמָּר. הֲרֵי גָדֵל בְּטֵפוּס הֲרֵי עָשׂוּי כְּכַדּוּר הֲרֵי הוּא פָּסוּל לְלוּלָב וְחַיָּיב בְּמַעְשְׂרוֹת.

[99]Rebbi Aqiba says an unripe cedrat[100] is not a fruit[101], but the Sages say it is a fruit. Rebbi Hila, Rebbi Yasa, in the name of Rebbi Eleazar: It follows that Rebbi Simeon[102] follows the argument of his teacher, Rebbi Aqiba. Just as Rebbi Aqiba said it is not a fruit, so Rebbi Simeon said it is not a fruit. Rebbi Yasa[103] said, is everything usable for *lulab*[104] subject to tithes and everything not usable for *lulab* not subject to tithes? Did they not object, there is one that grew in a form[105] or one shaped like a ball; it is not usable for *lulab* but subject to tithes! It is reasonable [to hold that] Rebbi Simeon agrees with Rebbi Aqiba but Rebbi Aqiba does not agree with Rebbi Simeon. Rebbi Simeon agrees with Rebbi Aqiba since it is written (*Lev.* 23:40) "fruit[106]" and it is not a fruit. Rebbi Aqiba does not agree with Rebbi Simeon, there is the spotted one, one that grew in a form, or one shaped like a ball; it is not usable for *lulab* but subject to tithes.

99 This is a copy of the text in *Sukkah* 3:7, fol. 57d. The parallel, but different, discussion in the Babli is *Sukkah* 36a/b.

100 Since בוסר originally means "unripe grape berry", Rashi in *Sukkah* 36a defines אתרוג בוסר as a small cedrat the size of a grape berry. This seems to contradict the Mishnah, cf. Note 87.

101 He frees apples from tithes if their seeds will not sprout. A different argument about this subject in the Babli is between Rabba (bar Naḥmani), Abbai, and Rava (bar Rav Joseph bar

Ḥama).

102 Following the text in *Sukkah*: . . . אמר ר׳ יסה וכי כל

103 Since its seeds will not sprout.

104 The "four kinds" taken for the festival of Tabernacles, *Lev*. 23:40.

105 Greek τύπος "form". It grows in an unnatural shape.

106 Cedrat is called "fruit of the *hadar* tree", implying that its seeds should be fertile.

הַחַיָּב בִּשְׁקֵדִים הַמָּרִים פָּטוּר בִּמְתוּקִים קְטַנִּים. הַחַיָּב בַּמְּתוּקִין פָּטוּר בְּמָרִים גְּדוֹלִים. תַּנֵּי רִבִּי יִשְׁמָעֵאל בֵּי רִבִּי יוֹסֵי מִשּׁוּם אָבִיו שְׁקֵידִים הַמָּרִים הֲרֵי אֵלּוּ פְטוּרִין. וּמְתוּקִין אֵינָן חַיָּבִין עַד שֶׁתִּפְרוֹשׁ קְלִיפָּתָן הַחִיצוֹנָה. הוֹרֵי רִבִּי חֲנִינָה בְצִיפּוֹרִי כְּהָדָא דְרִבִּי יִשְׁמָעֵאל בֵּי רִבִּי יוֹסֵי. בְּמַה הוֹרֵי. צִיפּוֹרָאֵי אָמְרֵי בְּמָרִים. רִבִּי זְעִירָא אָמַר בִּמְתוּקִים. אָמַר רִבִּי יוֹחָנָן יָרְדוּ לְכָאן נִתְחַיְּיבוּ. עָלוּ כְּבָר נִפְטְרוּ. הוֹרֵי רִבִּי פִינְחָס כֵּיוָן שֶׁרָאָה שְׁלֹשָׁה שֶׁפֵּירְשָׁה קְלִיפָּתָן הַחִיצוֹנָה שֶׁהוּא תוֹרֵם אֶת כָּל־הַקּוּפָּה. אָמַר רִבִּי מָנָא וּבִלְבַד שֶׁלֹּא יִתְרוֹם מִקּוּפָּה עַל חֲבֵירָתָהּ.

"What is obligated among bitter almonds is free among sweet almonds", small ones; "what is obligated among the sweet is free among the bitter", large ones[107]. "[108]Rebbi Ismael ben Rebbi Yose stated in the name of his father: Bitter almonds are free; sweet ones are not obligated before the outer shell separates." Rebbi Ḥanina instructed in Sepphoris following that statement of Rebbi Ismael ben Rebbi Yose. What did he instruct about? The people of Sepphoris said, about bitter ones[109]. Rebbi Zeïra said, about sweet ones. Rebbi Joḥanan said, if they came down here they would become obligated[110]. If they are brought up, they already are free[111]. Rebbi Phineas instructed: After one saw three with detached outer shell[112], he gives heave for the entire box. Rebbi Mana said, only he may not give heave from one box for another[113].

107 The entire sentence may be tannaïtic; a similar formulation is in Tosephta *Ḥulin* 1:24.

108 Tosephta 1:2: "Rebbi Ismael ben Rebbi Yose stated in the name of his father: Bitter almonds are *obligated* both small and large; sweet ones are not obligated before the outer shell separates." The Babli (*Eruvin* 28b, *Ḥulin* 25b) quotes both statements, "some people say free, some people say obligated."

109 This is the only explanation given in the Babli, *Ḥulin* 25b.

110 R. Joḥanan in Tiberias usually disagrees with the practical rulings of R. Ḥanina in Sepphoris, cf. *Ševi'it* Chapter 1, Notes 24-26. He follows the Mishnah, that small bitter almonds are subject to tithes.

111 Even if bitter almonds from the mountain region were temporarily at Tiberias, when they return to Sepphoris one has to follow the ruling of R. Ḥanina.

112 The soft, green outer shell containing the wooden shell of ripe almonds.

113 As long as there is a question whether all almonds are subject to tithes.

(fol. 48c) **משנה ה:** וְאֵי זֶהוּ גוֹרְנָן לְמַעְשְׂרוֹת הַקִּישׁוּאִין וְהַדִּילוּעִין מִשֶּׁיְּפַקֵּיסוּ[114] וְאִם אֵינוֹ מְפַקֵּס מִשֶּׁיַּעֲמִיד עֲרֵימָה. אֲבַטִּיחַ מִשֶּׁיְּשַׁלֵּק. וְאִם אֵינוֹ מְשַׁלֵּק מִשֶּׁיַּעֲשֶׂה מוּקְצֶה. יָרָק הַנֶּאֱגַד מִשֶּׁיּוּגָד. וְאִם אֵינוֹ אוֹגֵד מִשֶּׁיְּמַלֵּא אֶת הַכֶּלִי וְאִם אֵינוֹ מְמַלֵּא אֶת הַכֶּלִי מִשֶּׁיִּלְקוֹט כָּל־צוֹרְכוֹ. כַּלְכָּלָה מִשֶּׁיְּחַפֶּה וְאִם אֵינוֹ מְחַפֶּה מִשֶּׁיְּמַלֵּא אֶת הַכֶּלִי וְאִם אֵינוֹ מְמַלֵּא אֶת הַכֶּלִי מִשֶּׁיִּלְקוֹט כָּל־צוֹרְכוֹ. בַּמֶּה דְבָרִים אֲמוּרִים בְּמוֹלִיךְ לַשּׁוּק. אֲבָל בְּמוֹלִיךְ לְבֵיתוֹ אוֹכֵל מֵהֶן עֲרַאי עַד שֶׁהוּא מַגִּיעַ לְבֵיתוֹ.

Mishnah 5: What is their threshing floor for tithes[115]? Green melon and pumpkins from when they are cleaned[116]; if they are not cleaned, when one makes a heap. Water melons, when they are cleaned[117]; if they are not cleaned, when he puts them in storage. Vegetables sold in bundles, when they are bundled. When he makes no bundles, when he is finished filling the vessel; if he does not fill the vessel, when he is finished harvesting. A fig basket when he covers it; if he does not cover it when the vessel is completely filled; if he does not completely fill the vessel, when he has collected all he wants. When has this been said? When he brings it to market. But if he brings it to his house, he may eat snacks from it until he reaches his house.

114 Reading of the Leyden ms. The Mishnah mss. of the Maimonides tradition have active משיפקס, most other Mishnah sources and the Rome ms. have משיפקסו.

115 Since heave and tithes have to be given "from the threshing floor and the wine cellar" (*Num.* 18:27), the obligation starts only when the finished produce is stored. Before that time, one is permitted to eat snacks from the harvest without tithing since permission to eat snacks on the field is explicitly granted the agricultural worker (*Deut.* 23:26). Vegetables, which need neither threshing nor wine making, become subject to heave and tithes as soon as they are brought into storage, as noted at the end of the Mishnah. The problem discussed here is that of the farmer who brings his vegetables directly from the field to market. Since he will sell his vegetables on the way to the market in case he finds a buyer, the obligation starts as soon as the fruits and vegetables are ready to be transported from the field.

The Mishnah deals with fruits and vegetables that do not ripen together; they are collected and sold over an extended period of time.

116 Since نقوس means a melon in Arabic, it is reasonable to explain פקס as Semitic "preparing a melon as food."

Oriental sources (Maimonides, Rabbenu Ḥananel) explain that the reference is to the fine hair (פקסוס) growing on very young melons, zucchini, and cucumbers. For Rashi (*Beẓah* 13b, *Baba Meẓi'a* 88b), פקס is the remainder of the flower which falls off by itself when the melon is harvested. The fine hair disappears from the ripening fruit without intervention by the farmer. In his Code (*Ma'aser* 3:8), Maimonides remains true to his active reading in the Mishnah and formulates: "After he (the farmer, actively) rubs them clean."

117 Maimonides and R. Ḥananel both explain that שלק is the technical term for watermelon corresponding to פקס for sweet melon, without connection to שלק "preserving by prolonged cooking." Levy explains the word here as meaning: fully ripened by the sun. The Tosephta, 1:6, mentions cooking only for sweet melons, *melopepones*; if they are collected to be cooked they become subject to tithes only after cooking.

(fol. 49a) **הלכה ה**: מָאן דִּי יָרִים פֶּקְסוֹסֵיהּ מָאן דִּי יָרִים שֶׁלְקוֹקֵיהּ. הָיָה מְפַקֵּס רִאשׁוֹן רִאשׁוֹן וּמְשַׁלֵּק רִאשׁוֹן רִאשׁוֹן לֹא נִטְבְּלוּ עַד שֶׁיְּפַקֵּס כָּל־צָרְכּוֹ וְיִשְׁלוֹק כָּל־צָרְכּוֹ. פִּיקֵּס וְשִׁילֵּק בִּרְשׁוּת הַהֶקְדֵּשׁ וּפְדָיוֹ אֲגְדוֹ צִינוֹק גָּדוֹל לַשָּׂדֶה. אֲבָל אִם אֲגְדוֹ צִינוֹק קָטוֹן לַשּׁוּק נִטְבָּל. רִבִּי עֶזְרָא בָּעֵי אֲדַייִן לֹא נִגְמְרָה מְלֶאכֶת הַשָּׂדֶה וְאַתְּ אָמַר הָכֵין. אֶלָּא כֵינִי אֲגְדוֹ צִינוֹק גָּדוֹל בַּשָּׂדֶה וְהוּא עָתִיד לְאוֹגְדוֹ צִינוֹק קָטָן לַשּׁוּק נִטְבָּל.

Halakhah 5: When[118] its *peksos* is removed, when its *šelqoq*[119] is removed. "[120]When he continued removing *peksos* or *šelqoq*, it becomes *ṭevel* only when he finished with all he needs." When he removed *peksos* or *šelqoq* when it was property of the Temple and redeemed it[121], if he made a large bundle in the field[122]. But if he made a small bundle for the market, it became *ṭevel*." Rebbi Ezra[123] asked: The work on the field is not yet finished and you say so? But so it must be: If he made a large bundle in the field and he intends later to make it into small bundles for the market, it became *ṭevel*[124].

118 In *Hayerushalmi Kifshuto*, p. כג, S. Lieberman accepts the determination by H. Yalon that מאן in the Yerushalmi may have the meaning מִן "from the time that". This sentence is one of his examples. It is possible to read the sentence: "[יפקס and ישלק mean:] he removes *peksos* and *šelqoq*."

119 *Peksos* and *šelqoq* are the nouns corresponding to פקס, שלק meaning either small hairs or the remainder of the flower, cf. Note 116.

120 Tosephta 1:5. There, the verb is מפקיץ instead of מפקס, a purely dialectal variant. The text supports the interpretation of Maimonides.

121 Temple property is exempt from heave and tithes. If, however, the yield of the Temple's fields was redeemed at a stage when for fully profane produce no tithes were yet due, the tithes will become due as if it had been profane from the start.

122 Then no tithes are due until the produce is stored. The revision later shows that the *baraita* is elliptic, not defective.

123 In the Rome ms: ר' זעירא.

124 Since he wants to sell without bringing his fruits first to the house, he would also sell if he finds a buyer on the field. Therefore, for him the harvest is completed.

הָיְתָה כַלְכָּלָה אַחַת וּבְדַעְתּוֹ לְמַלְאוֹת אֶת חֶצְיָיהּ כֵּיוָן שֶׁמִּילֵּא חֶצְיָיהּ נִטְבְּלָה. בְּדַעְתּוֹ לְמַלְאוֹת אֶת כּוּלָּהּ לֹא נִטְבְּלָה עַד שֶׁיְּמַלֵּא אֶת כּוּלָּהּ. הָיוּ שְׁתַּיִם וּבְדַעְתּוֹ לְמַלְאוֹת שְׁתֵּיהֶן לֹא נִטְבְּלוּ עַד שֶׁיְּמַלֵּא שְׁתֵּיהֶן. בְּמַה דְבָרִים אֲמוּרִים בְּמוֹלִיךְ לַשּׁוּק. אֲבָל בְּמוֹלִיךְ לְבֵיתוֹ אוֹכֵל מֵהֶן עֲרַאי עַד שֶׁהוּא מַגִּיעַ לְבֵיתוֹ. מַה בֵּין הַמּוֹלִיךְ לַשּׁוּק. מַה בֵּין הַמּוֹלִיךְ לְבֵיתוֹ. בְּשָׁעָה שֶׁהוּא מוֹלִיךְ לְבֵיתוֹ בְּדַעְתּוֹ הַדָּבָר תָּלוּי. וּבְשָׁעָה שֶׁהוּא מוֹלִיךְ לַשּׁוּק לֹא בְדַעְתּוֹ הַדָּבָר תָּלוּי בְּדַעַת הַלְּקוּחוֹת הַדָּבָר תָּלוּי שֶׁמָּא יִמְצָא לְקוּחוֹת וְנִטְבְּלוּ מִיַּד.

"If he had one basket and he intended to fill half of it, it became *ṭevel* once it was half filled. If he intended to fill it completely, it does not become *ṭevel* until it is completely filled. If there were two and he intended to fill both of them, they do not become *ṭevel* until he filled both of them. When has this been said? When he brings it to market. But if be brings it to his house, he may eat snacks from it until he reaches his house.[125]" What is the difference between him who brings to market and him who brings to his house? When he brings to his house, it depends on his intention. But if he brings to market, it does not depend on his intention but on that of his customers. Maybe he will find a customer; therefore, it becomes *ṭevel* immediately.

125 A *baraita* from a collection that has not come down to us. The paragraph has been explained in Note 115.

(fol. 48c) **משנה ו:** הַפֶּרֶד וְהַצִּימּוּקִין וְהֶחָרוּבִין מִשֶּׁיַּעֲמִיד עֲרֵימָה. הַבְּצָלִים מִשֶּׁיְּפַקֵּילוּ. וְאִם אֵינוֹ מְפַקֵּל מִשֶּׁיַּעֲמִיד עֲרֵימָה. הַתְּבוּאָה מִשֶּׁיְּמָרֵחַ וְאִם אֵינוֹ מְמָרֵיחַ מִשֶּׁיַּעֲמִיד עֲרֵימָה. הַקִּטְנִיּוֹת מִשֶּׁיְּכַבּוֹר וְאִם אֵינוֹ כוֹבֵר עַד שֶׁיְּמָרֵחַ. אַף עַל פִּי שֶׁמֵּירֵחַ נוֹטֵל מִן הַקּוּטָּעִים וּמִן הַצְּדָדִים וּמִמַּה שֶּׁבְּתוֹךְ הַתֶּבֶן וְאוֹכֵל.

Mishnah 6: Dried pomegranate cells, raisins, and carob when he makes them into a pile. Onions when they are cleaned, if he does not clean when he makes them into a pile. Grain when it is in smooth piles, if he does not smoothe when he makes it into a pile. Legumes when they are sifted, if he does not sift when he makes smooth piles. Even though he made smooth piles, he may take from the broken ones, from the sides, and from what is in the chaff and eat.

משנה ז: הַיַּיִן מִשֶּׁיְּקַפֶּה אַף עַל פִּי שֶׁקִּיפָּה קוֹלֵט מִן הַגַּת הָעֶלְיוֹנָה וּמִן הַצִּינּוֹר וְשׁוֹתֶה. הַשֶּׁמֶן מִשֶּׁיֵּרֵד לָעוּקָה אַף עַל פִּי שֶׁיָּרַד נוֹטֵל מִן הָעֶקֶל וּמִן הַמַּמָּל וּמִבֵּין הַפַּצִּים וְנוֹתֵן לַחֲמִיטָה וּלְתוֹךְ הַתַּמְחוּי אֲבָל לֹא יִתֵּן לְלָפָּס וְלִקְדֵירָה כְּשֶׁהֵן מְרוּתָּחִין. רִבִּי יְהוּדָה אוֹמֵר לַכֹּל הוּא נוֹתֵן חוּץ מִדָּבָר שֶׁיֵּשׁ בּוֹ חוֹמֶץ וְצִיר.

Mishnah 7: Wine after he cleaned it[126]. Even after he cleaned it he may collect from the upper part of the winepress or the pipe[127] and drink. Oil after it descended into the barrel. Even after it descended, he may take from the press, the weight, and between the beams[128] and put it on a pizza or into a bowl but he should not add it to a hot pan or pot[129]. Rebbi Jehudah says, he may put it anywhere except into anything containing vinegar or fish sauce.

126 From the fermenting yeast and the membrane which formed on top of the fermenting wine. It is clear from the Tosephta quoted later that this cleaning comes after the removal of seeds and skins from the fermenting wine; the removal is called שׁוֹלֶה "fishing out".

127 Any fluid that is not in the fermentation vat will not be wine and, therefore, is not subject to tithes.

128 Oil clinging to these places can never be stored; it is exempt from tithes.

129 Cooking is an action that should come after storing. Therefore, cooking itself makes any produce liable to heave and tithing (cf. Halakhah 4:1). R. Jehudah disagrees and restricts the rule to cooking in a reacting medium.

(fol. 49a) **הלכה ו**: תַּנֵּי מִשֶּׁיַּעֲמִיד עֲרֵימָה בְּרֹאשׁ גַּגּוֹ. רִבִּי יוֹנָה בָּעֵי הָא בַשָּׂדֶה לֹא. אָמַר רִבִּי חִינְנָא דְּרוּבָּהּ אָתָא אֵימוֹר לָךְ אֲפִילוּ מִשֶּׁיַּעֲמִיד עֲרֵימָה בְּרֹאשׁ גַּגּוֹ.

Halakhah 6: It was stated: When he makes a pile on his roof top. Rebbi Jonah asked: Therefore, not on his field? Rebbi Ḥinena said, it tells you something additional: even if he makes a pile on his roof top[130].

130 One cannot make a pile on the roof without bringing the fruits to the house. Nevertheless, if the intention is to dry the fruits, they become subject to tithes only when the dried raisins or pomegranates are stored.

הַבְּצָלִים מִשֶּׁיְּפַקֵּלוּ. מִן דּוּ יָרִים פּודגרה.

"Onions when they are cleaned," when he removes what is clinging to them[131].

131 The reading פודגרה "podagra, gout" of the Leyden ms. and the Venice print makes no sense, neither does the Rome ms.'s איגורה "stone heap". The translation follows R. M. Margalit in reading פורגרה, cf. *Peah* Chapter 3, Note 71.

תְּבוּאָה מִשֶּׁיִּתְמָרֵחַ. רִבִּי חֲנַנְיָה בְּשֵׁם רִבִּי יוֹחָנָן מִן דּוּ יְשַׁפֵּר אַפּוֹי דִּכְרֵיהּ. וְהָא תַּנֵּי רִבִּי יַעֲקֹב בַּר סִיסִין מֵאֵימָתַי הוּא תוֹרֵם אֶת הַגּוֹרֶן מִשֶּׁתֵּיעָקֵר הָאֵלָה. כָּאן בְּשֶׁיֵּשׁ בְּדַעְתּוֹ לִימָרֵחַ. וְכָאן בְּשֶׁאֵין בְּדַעְתּוֹ לִימָרֵחַ. תַּנֵּי אֲבָל כּוֹבֵר הוּא מִקְצָת וְתוֹרֵם מִן הַכָּבוּר עַל שֶׁאֵינוֹ כָבוּר. אָמַר רִבִּי אִילָא שֶׁכֵּן דֶּרֶךְ בַּעֲלֵי בָתִּים לִהְיוֹת מַכְנִיסִין לְתוֹךְ בָּתֵּיהֶן. מַה טַעֲמָא וְהָאֲלָפִים וְהָעֲיָרִים עוֹבְדֵי הָאֲדָמָה בְּלִיל חָמִיץ יֹאכֵלוּ. כָּבַר בִּרְשׁוּת הַהֶקְדֵּשׁ וּפְדָיוֹ מֵאַחַר שֶׁהוּא יָכוֹל לוֹכַל מִמֶּנּוּ עֲרַאי. וְאַכְשָׁיו שֶׁאֵינוֹ יָכוֹל לוֹכַל מִמֶּנּוּ עֲרַאי כְּמִי שֶׁעָשָׂה מַעֲשֶׂה בִּרְשׁוּת הַהֶקְדֵּשׁ וְהוּא חַיָּיב. הָתִיב רִבִּי חִינְנָא וְהָתַנֵּי שִׁילָּה וְקִיפָּה בִּרְשׁוּת הַהֶקְדֵּשׁ פָּטוּר. אָמַר רִבִּי יוּדָן תַּמָּן אִי אֵיפְשַׁר לוֹ שֶׁלֹּא יִכְבּוֹשׁ וְשֶׁלֹּא לִשְׁלוֹק. בְּרַם הָכָא אֵיפְשַׁר לוֹ שֶׁלֹּא לְמָרֵחַ. דְּאָמַר רִבִּי אִילָא וְהָאֲלָפִים וְהָעֲיָרִים וכו'.

"Grain when it is in smooth piles." Rebbi Ḥanania in the name of Rebbi Joḥanan: When he straightens his heap. But did not Rebbi Jacob ben Sisin[132] state: "When does he start to give heave from his threshing floor? When he removes the pitchfork[133]." Here, when he intends to smoothe, there if he did not intend to smoothe. It was stated[134]: "He sifts part and gives heave from the sifted part for what is not sifted." Rebbi Ila said, for this is the way of householders to bring it into their houses. What is the reason? (*Is.* 30:24) "The bulls and young donkeys which work the soil will eat sour mix[135]." If he sifted [grain] dedicated to the Temple and then redeemed it; since he was able to eat from it as a snack and now he cannot eat, it is as if he did it with the permission of the Temple and he is obligated[136]. Rebbi Ḥinena objected: Did we not state[137], "if he took out and cleaned what was dedicated to the Temple, he is free?" Rebbi Yudan said[138], there it is not impossible for him not to preserve or not to cook a long time[140]. But here it is impossible for him not to smooth it, as Rebbi Ila said, the bulls and young donkeys, etc.[141]

132 Usually called R. Jacob bar Sisi; cf. *Berakhot* Chapter 4, Note 121.

133 Tosephta *Terumot* 3:11. For the definition of אלה as "pitchfork", used to turn around the grain, cf. S. Lieberman, *Tosephta ki-fshutah*, p. 327.

134 Tosephta *Terumot* 3:11.

135 The argument is from the end of the verse which was not quoted: "Which had been winnowed with shovel and fork."

136 The argument is elliptic. If a person dedicated his crop to the Temple and then redeemed it, if the dedication was of grain on the stalk and the redemption was after that grain was threshed and sifted, the completion of the work on the harvest was while the grain was the Temple's and, therefore, the grain is exempt from heave and tithes. However, if the grain was dedicated threshed and redeemed sifted, since sifting is not done with commercial grain where a certain amount of impurities is permitted (Mishnah *Baba Batra* 6:2, cf. *Kilaim* Chapter 2, Note 1), sifting brings an exemption only if done by Temple personnel, not by another person.

137 Tosephta 1:7, speaking of wine dedicated when in the fermenting vat.

138 The argument of R. Yudan is from Halakhah 4:1; there, the language is easier to understand since he uses only איפשר "impossible". Yerushalmi אֵיפשר "impossible", contracted from אי אפשר, is not Babylonian and modern Hebrew אֶפשר "possible"; cf. *Peah* Chapter 7, Note 170.

140 Mishnah 4:1 speaks of a person who preserves somebody else's produce possibly without the owner's consent.

141 Since they certainly will eat unsifted grain, sifting in general is unimportant for determining the point when heave and tithes are due.

תְּנָן אֲבָל קוֹלֵט הוּא מִתַּחַת הַכְּבָרָה וְאוֹכֵל. רַב חִסְדָּא אָמַר שֶׁהֵן מְחוּסָּרִין לָרוּחַ. רִבִּי אִילָא בְּשֵׁם רִבִּי יָסָא שֶׁהֵן מְחוּסָּרִין נִיחָה. וְהָתַנִּינָן הַיַּיִן מִשֶּׁיִּקַּפֶּה.

מָאן דְּאָמַר שֶׁהֵן מְחוּסָּרִין נִיחָא. מָאן דְּאָמַר שֶׁהֵן מְחוּסָּרִין לְרוּחַ מְחוּסָּר הוּא בִּשְׁמָרָיו. הָתִיב רִבִּי בִּנְיָמִין בַּר גִּידוּל וְהָא תַנִּינָן הַשֶּׁמֶן מִשֶּׁיֵּרֵד לָעוּקָה. מָאן דְּאָמַר שֶׁהֵן מְחוּסָּרִין נִיחָא. מָאן דְּאָמַר שֶׁהֵן מְחוּסָּרִין לְרוּחַ מְחוּסָּר הוּא לְהַצִּיל.

We have stated[142]: "But he collects from under the sieve and eats." Rav Ḥisda said, because it misses the action of the wind[143]. Rebbi Ila in the name of Rebbi Yasa: It misses rest[144]. But did we not state: "Wine after he cleaned it?" For him who says because it misses rest [it is understandable][145]. For him who says because it misses the action of the wind, it still misses [removal of] its yeast. Rebbi Benjamin ben Gidul objected: Did we not state: "Oil after it descended into the barrel?" For him who says because it misses rest [it is understandable]. For him who says because it misses the action of the wind, it still misses clearing up[146].

142 Tosephta 1:6 a similar formulation, referring to legumes. The Rome ms. has תני instead of תנן which at least in Babylonian style is required for a tannaïtic statement which is not a Mishnah. When legumes (peas or beans) are sifted, if one grabs some peas in the air, they are permitted as snack without tithing.

143 The sieve will retain coarse impurities, the wind will carry away light impurities. Therefore, taking peas directly under the sieve is taking before the processing of the harvest is finished.

144 Processing is only finished if all legumes are at rest in some pile.

145 In both cases where this argument occurs a word fell out because it looked like a duplication: מָאן דְּאָמַר שֶׁהֵן מְחוּסָּרִין נִיחָה נִיחָא. "For him who says because it misses [rest] (Hebrew root נוח), it is understandable (Aramaic root ניח)."

The objection is from the statement of the Mishnah that one may take wine from the funnel leading from the press to the vat, which corresponds to taking peas when they fall down from the sieve.

146 Following R. Eliahu Fulda, deriving הציל from the root צלל "to become (optically) clear", not from נצל "to save".

הָיָה אוֹכֵל וַחֲשֵׁיכָה לֵילֵי שַׁבָּת אוֹ שֶׁנְּתָנוֹ לְאָדָם אַחֵר לֹא נִטְבָּלוֹ. רִבִּי יִרְמְיָה סָבַר מֵימַר בְּנָתוּן בַּחֲמִיטָה וּבְתַמְחוּי אֲבָל בְּנָתוּן בִּצְלוֹחִית נִטְבָּל. אָמַר רִבִּי יוֹסֵי (fol. 49b) אֲפִילוּ נָתוּן בִּצְלוֹחִית לֹא נִטְבָּל. אָמַר לֵיהּ רִבִּי יִרְמְיָה וְאֵין שַׁבָּת טוֹבֶלֶת. אָמַר לֵיהּ וְאֵין מֶקַח טוֹבֵל. אָמַר לֵיהּ כְּהַהִיא דְאָמַר רִבִּי יוֹסֵי בְשֵׁם רִבִּי זְעִירָא רִבִּי יוֹנָה רִבִּי זְעִירָא בְּשֵׁם רִבִּי לָעְזָר אַף מַה שֶׁבְּלָגִין לֹא נִטְבָּל מִפְּנֵי שֶׁהוּא עָתִיד לְהַחֲזִירוֹ בְּדָבָר שֶׁלֹּא נִגְמְרָה מְלַאכְתּוֹ. חֵיילֵיהּ דְּרִבִּי יִרְמְיָה מִן הָדָא. וְעוֹד אָמַר רִבִּי לִיעֶזֶר עוֹמֵד אָדָם הוּא עַל הַמּוּקְצֶה עֶרֶב שַׁבָּת בִּשְׁבִיעִית וְאוֹמֵר מִכָּן אֲנִי אוֹכֵל לְמָחָר. לֹא אָמַר אֶלָּא בִּשְׁבִיעִית הָא שְׁאָר שְׁנֵי שָׁבוּעַ לֹא. מָה עָבַד לֵיהּ רִבִּי יִרְמְיָה לְהַחֲזִירוֹ לִמְקוֹמוֹ אֵי אַתְּ יָכוֹל שֶׁהוּא עוֹשֶׂה מוּקְצֶה לְפִיכָךְ נִטְבָּל. מַתְנִיתָא פְלִיגָא עַל רִבִּי יִרְמְיָה אֵין עֲרַאי לְשַׁבָּת. פָּתַר לָהּ וּבִלְבַד דָּבָר שֶׁיֵּשׁ לוֹ מוּקְצֶה. עַל דַּעְתֵּיהּ דְּרִבִּי יִרְמְיָה לֹא שַׁנְיָא הִיא דָּבָר שֶׁיֵּשׁ לוֹ מוּקְצֶה הִיא דָּבָר שֶׁאֵין לוֹ מוּקְצֶה.

"If he was eating[147] when night fell Friday evening or when he gave it to another person it did not become *ṭevel*." Rebbi Jeremiah wanted to say, when it[148] was put on pitta bread or into a bowl, but when it was in a flask[149] it became *ṭevel*[150]. Rebbi Yose said, even in a flask it did not become *ṭevel*. Rebbi Jeremiah said to him, does not the Sabbath create *ṭevel*? He answered him, does not buying create *ṭevel*? He retorted, following what Rebbi Yose said in the name of Rebbi Zeïra, Rebbi Jonah, Rebbi Zeïra in the name of Rebbi Eleazar, even what is in a flask did not become *ṭevel*, in case it was not fully processed, since he would in the end return it[151]. The strength of Rebbi Jeremiah is from the following[152]: "In addition, Rebbi Eliezer said a person may stand near the *muqẓeh*[84] on a Friday of a Sabbatical year and say, from here I shall eat tomorrow." He mentioned only the Sabbatical year; that exludes the other years of the Sabbatical cycle[153]. How does Rebbi Jeremiah argue about this? You cannot return it to its place as *muqẓeh*[154], therefore it creates *ṭevel*. A *baraita* disagrees with Rebbi (Jeremiah)[155]: There are no snacks on the Sabbath. He explains it, anything that has *muqẓeh*[154]. In the opinion of Rebbi Jeremiah, whether it has *muqẓeh* or does not have *muqẓeh*.

147 A snack of produce not subject to heave and tithes. Since for the Sabbath it is a biblical commandment to "prepare what one brings" (*Ex.* 16:5), no food on the Sabbath can have the legal status of a casual snack, as formulated later in this paragraph. Therefore, one would assume that at nightfall all produce automatically becomes subject to heave and tithes and will be forbidden as food since no heave or tithes may be declared on the Sabbath. The formulation of the Tosephta, 1:8, is: "If he ate Friday evening and had leftovers, after nightfall it remains permitted."

Similarly, transfer of property in general presupposes completion of processing and requires heave and tithes. The exemption given here refers only to leftovers of snacks. In the Tosephta it is stated explicitly that these leniencies do not apply if it was clear from the start that the quantities were so large that the person could not finish eating his snack.

148 The examples show that now one speaks of olive oil, mentioned in Mishnah 6.

149 The usual vessel to keep cooking oil.

150 The Rome ms. has " did not become *ṭevel*," a clear scribal error.

151 To be fully processed.

152 Mishnah *Beẓah* 4:7.

153 The figs, grapes, or pomegranates in the *muqzeh* were not yet removed from there; the processing was not yet finished.

154 If after drying it is edible, the processing is finished.

155 This is the reading in both mss., but it must be רבי יוסי since the *baraita* spells out the position of R. Jeremiah. One may conjecture that a common *Vorlage* of both mss. was copied from a text in which the name was simply given as ר״י which was wrongly read as ר׳ ירמיה. In copies of the Babli, ר״י can only mean R. Jehudah, R. Yose, or R. Johanan.

רִבִּי מָנָא בָּעֵי הָיְתָה צְלוֹחִית מְלֵיאָה וּנְתוּנָה בֵּין פַּצִּים לַחֲבֵירוֹ נִטְבְּלָה אוֹ מֵאַחַר שֶׁהִיא נְתוּנָה בְּמָקוֹם שֶׁלֹּא נִגְמְרָה מְלַאכְתּוֹ לֹא נִטְבְּלָה.

Rebbi Mana asked: If it was a full flask put between two beams it became *ṭevel* or maybe since it was deposited at a place where processing was not finished it did not become *ṭevel*[156]?

156 This refers to the statement in Mishnah 6 that oil between the beams of the oil press is not subject to tithes. The question is not answered, probably because the answer is obvious that oil in a flask is not oil clinging to any part of the oil press.

עַד הֵיכָן רִבִּי יוּדָה בַּר פָּזִי רִבִּי סִימוֹן בְּשֵׁם רִבִּי יוֹסֵי בַּר חֲנִינָה עַד כְּדֵי שֶׁיְּהֵא נִתּוּן יָדוֹ לְתוֹכָהּ וְהִיא נִכְוֵית. הַכֹּל מוֹדִין בִּכְלִי שֵׁנִי שֶׁהוּא מוּתָּר. מַה בֵּין כְּלִי רִאשׁוֹן מַה בֵּין כְּלִי שֵׁנִי. אָמַר רִבִּי יוֹסֵי בֵּי רִבִּי בּוּן כָּאן הַיָּד שׁוֹלֶטֶת. כָּאן אֵין הַיָּד שׁוֹלֶטֶת. אָמַר רִבִּי יוֹנָה כָּאן וְכָאן[157] אֵין הַיָּד שׁוֹלֶטֶת אֶלָּא עָשׂוּ הֶרְחֵק לִכְלִי רִאשׁוֹן וְלֹא עָשׂוּ הֶרְחֵק לִכְלִי שֵׁנִי. אָמַר רִבִּי מָנָא הָהֵן פִּינְכָּא[158] דְאוֹרִיזָא[159] מְסַייֵעַ[158] לְאַבָּא הָהֵן פִּינְכָּא דִגְלוּסָא[160] מְסַייֵעַ לְאַבָּא דְּאַתְּ מְפַנֵּי לֵיהּ מִן אֲתַר לַאֲתַר וְעוֹד כְּדוֹן הוּא רָתַח.

[161]How far? Rebbi Jehudah bar Pazi, Rebbi Simon, in the name of Rebbi Yose bar Ḥanina: Unless he would burn his hand if he put it in[162]. Everybody agrees that a second vessel[163] is permitted. What is the difference between first and second vessels? Rebbi Yose bar Abun said, here the hand holds, there the hand does not hold. Rebbi Jonah said, in both cases the hand does not hold but they decreed removal for a first but not a second vessel[164]. Rebbi Mana said, that platter of rice supports my father[165], that platter of grits supports my father since you remove it from place to place and it is still boiling[166].

157 In a Geniza fragment, the spelling is always בַּן.

158 Vocalization from the Geniza fragment; Greek πίναξ "platter", cf. *Berakhot* 9:3, Note 130.

159 Reading of the Rome ms. and the parallel in *Šabbat* 6b; Greek ὄρυζα "rice", cf. *Berakhot* 6:1, Note 74. In the Geniza fragment, דְּאוֹרְזָה. Leyden and Venice: דאריא.

160 The Rome ms. and the parallel in *Šabbat* 6b read דגרוסא without change in meaning. Genizah: דְּגְרִיסָה.

161 This and the next three sections are copied from *Šabbat* Chapter 3, in the discussion of Mishnah 5: "If a (still hot) samowar was emptied, one may not fill it (on the Sabbath) with water to heat the water but one may fill it with (a large quantity of) water to make the water lukewarm." The problem is, what larger category of vessel does the samowar represent regarding cooking on the Sabbath? For that category it will then be forbidden to use untithed oil as specified in our Mishnah.

162 In the Babli (e. g., *Šabbat* 40b), the vessel is forbidden if היד סולדת בו, the hand jumps off (or trembles) when it touches. One may assume that Galilean שולטת "rules over", which had lost the /*š*/, sounded in Babylonian ears like Biblical (*Job* 6:10) סוֹלדת "trembles". This required a switch between "permitted" (if שולטת) and "forbidden" (if סולדת).

163 A vessel into which the hot food was poured. According to Rashi, a "first vessel" is one whose walls heat the food, a "second vessel" one whose walls are heated by the food, as, e. g., a thermos bottle. "Permitted" here means that cold water or food can be put into it without restriction. "Everybody" is R. Meïr and R. Jehudah who in the Halakhah in *Šabbat* disagree on the technicalities of turning cold water into lukewarm.

164 In his opinion, once the fire under the samowar is extinguished there cannot be any biblical prohibition of cooking; the entire Mishnah is rabbinic.

165 R. Jonah.

166 Being far from the fire, it is no longer a "first vessel".

מַהוּ לִיתֵּן תַּבְלִין מִלְּמַטָּן וְלַעֲרוֹת עֲלֵיהֶן מִלְּמַעְלָן. רִבִּי יוֹנָה אָמַר אָסוּר וְעִירוּי[165] כִּכְלִי רִאשׁוֹן הוּא. חֵילֵיהּ דְּרִבִּי יוֹנָה מִן הָדָא אֶחָד שֶׁבִּישֵּׁל בּוֹ וְאֶחָד

שֶׁעִירָה עָלָיו רוֹתֵחַ.[166] וְכָא אַתְּ אָמַר הָכֵין. אָמַר רִבִּי יוֹסֵי תַּמָּן כְּלִי חֶרֶס בּוֹלֵעַ. תַּבְלִין אֵינָן מִתְבַּשְּׁלִין. הָתִיב רִבִּי יוֹסֵי בֵּי רִבִּי בּוּן וְהָתַנֵּי אַף בִּכְלֵי נְחוֹשֶׁת כֵּן. אִית מֵימַר כְּלִי נְחוֹשֶׁת בּוֹלֵעַ.

May one put spices at the bottom and pour[167] on them from above? Rebbi Jonah said, it is forbidden and pouring acts as first vessel. The force of Rebbi Jonah comes from this[168]: "Both vessels used for cooking or into which it was poured boiling." (And here, you say so?)[169] Rebbi Yose said, there a pottery vessel absorbs; spices are not cooked[170]. Rebbi Yose bar Rebbi Abun objected: Did we not state[171], "the same holds for brass vessels." Can one say that brass vessels absorb?

165 In the Genizah fragment: וְעָרוּי.

166 In the Genizah fragment: רותָח.

167 Boiling water. Is this cooking on the Sabbath and cooking in the sense of Mishnah 7 here? The question arises because of Mishnah *Šabbat* 3:6: "One may not put spices into a hot pan or a pot taken from the fire, but one may put them on a plate or a bowl." This is similar to using oil as described in Mishnah 7 here.

168 Mishnah *Zebaḥim* 11:7. *Lev.* 6:21 precribes that pottery vessels after being used to cook a *ḥaṭṭat* sacrifice must be broken and metal vessels cleansed and washed. The Mishnah explicitly includes pouring hot water in the biblical definition of "cooking".

169 This sentence is missing in the *Šabbat* text and is out of place here.

170 It is generally agreed that pottery must be broken because it absorbs particles from the sacrifice which on the following day become forbidden. Cf. J. Milgrom, *Leviticus* 1-16, pp. 404-407, New York 1991.

171 *Sifra Ẓaw, Pereq* 7(1). The argument is that *Lev.* 6:21 reads a passive "a pottery vessel in which something has been cooked", not "in which one cooked". This is taken to mean that one cooks *in*, not *by* the vessel. In that case, the vessel is really "second vessel" (cf. Note 163) since its walls do not transfer heat to the meat being cooked. The only case one can think of is pouring boiling water into the vessel. Since the argument of R. Yose does not work for metal pots, R. Jonah is justified.

מַהוּ לְהַעֲרוֹת עִם[172] הַקִּילוּחַ. אָמַר רִבִּי חֲנִינָה בְּרֵיהּ דְּרִבִּי הִילֵּל מַחְלוֹקֶת רִבִּי יוֹנָה וְרִבִּי יוֹסֵי. רִבִּי יִצְחָק בַּר גּוּפְתָּה בָּעֵי קוֹמֵי רִבִּי מָנָא עָשָׂה כֵן בַּשַּׁבָּת חַייָב מִשּׁוּם מְבַשֵּׁל. עָשָׂה כֵן בְּבָשָׂר בְּחָלָב חַייָב מִשּׁוּם[173] מְבַשֵּׁל. אָמַר לֵיהּ כַּיי דָּמַר רִבִּי זְעִירָא אֵי זֶהוּ חָלוּט בָּרוּר כָּל־שֶׁהָאוֹר מְהַלֵּךְ תַּחְתָּיו. וְכָא אֵי זֶהוּ תַּבְשִׁיל בָּרוּר כָּל־שֶׁהָאוֹר מְהַלֵּךְ תַּחְתָּיו.

Can one pour in from a stream[174]? Rebbi Ḥanina, the son of Rebbi Hillel, said, the disagreement of Rebbi Jonah and Rebbi Yose. Rebbi Isaac bar Gufta[175] asked before Rebbi Mana: If he did this on the Sabbath, is he guilty because of cooking? If he did this with meat and milk[176], is he guilty because of cooking? He said to him, parallel to what Rebbi Zeïra said, what is certainly a dumpling[177]? Only if fire burned underneath it. So here also, what is certainly a cooked dish? Only if fire burned underneath it[178].

172 Genizah fragment: מן.

173 Genizah fragment: מִשֶּׁם. The Leyden/Venice text shows intrusion of Babylonian usage.

174 If boiling water was poured in a stream coming from a vessel much higher than the receiving one, do we say that the water in the receiving pot is certainly no longer boiling?

175 A fifth generation Galilean Amora who is only mentioned for his questions to R. Mana.

176 The prohibition of combining milk and meat together is given three times (*Ex.* 23:19, 34:26, *Deut.* 14:21) with emphasis on cooking.

177 Flour balls cooked in boiling water.

178 Pouring hot water over food on the Sabbath or pouring boiling milk over meat not over the fire are rabbinical prohibitions.

עַל דַּעְתֵּיהּ דְּרִבִּי יְהוּדָה מֶלַח כַּצִּיר יַיִן כְּחוֹמֶץ.

In the opinion of R. Jehudah, salt is like fish sauce and wine like vinegar[179].

179 Both in the Mishnah here and in Sabbath 3:5, R. Jehudah holds that vinegar and fish sauce cure and, therefore, act as if cooking.

(fol. 48c) **משנה ח:** הָעִיגּוּל מִשֶּׁיַּחֲלִיקֶינּוּ. מַחֲלִיקִין בִּתְאֵינִים וּבָעֲנָבִים שֶׁל טֶבֶל. רִבִּי יְהוּדָה אוֹסֵר. הַמַּחֲלִיק בָּעֲנָבִים לֹא הוּכְשַׁר. רִבִּי יְהוּדָה אוֹמֵר הוּכְשַׁר. וּגְרוֹגְרוֹת מִשֶּׁיִּדּוֹשׁ וּמְגוּרָה מִשֶּׁיְּעַגֵּל. הָיָה דָשׁ בֶּחָבִית וּמְעַגֵּל בַּמְּגוּרָה נִשְׁבְּרָה הֶחָבִית וְנִפְתְּחָה הַמְּגוּרָה לֹא יֹאכַל מִמֶּנּוּ עֲרַאי. רִבִּי יוֹסֵי מַתִּיר.

Mishnah 8: The round fig cake when he smoothes it[180]. One may smoothe *ṭevel* figs and grapes, Rebbi Jehudah forbids it[181]. If one smoothes grapes they are not prepared[182]; Rebbi Jehudah says, they are prepared. Dried figs when he presses them and in a bin if he planes with a roller. If, while he presses in an amphora or planes in a bin, the amphora broke or the bin collapsed, he may not eat from the contents as a snack[183], but Rebbi Yose permits it.

180 Maimonides translates by Arabic ימלסה "he polishes it", by rubbing with the palm of his hand. For the anonymous Tanna, the obligation of tithes starts with the beginning of the polishing action.

181 Since polishing is done by squeezing some juice out of the fruit, R. Jehudah considers this to be commercial use of the juice which requires prior taking of the heave.

182 Prepared for impurity of foodstuffs, cf. *Demay* Chapter 2, Note 141. Wine is one of the fluids preparing for impurity. R. Jehudah considers the juice pressed out from grapes or raisins as wine; the anonymous Tanna considers it as useless fluid (Maimonides) or as food, not juice (R. Ḥananel).

183 Without tithing since by starting he activated the obligation of heave and tithes.

(fol. 49a) **הלכה ז**: חֲנַנְיָה בְּרֵיהּ דְּרִבִּי יָסָא אָמַר מַה פְלִיגִין רִבִּי יוּדָה וְרַבָּנִין בְּטֶבֶל שֶׁנִּטְבַּל מִדִּבְרֵיהֶן. אֲבָל טֶבֶל שֶׁנִּטְבַּל דְּבַר תּוֹרָה אוּף רַבָּנִין מוֹדֵיי.

Ḥananiah the son of Rebbi Yasa said, where do Rebbi Jehudah and the rabbis disagree[184]? If it is *ṭevel* by their words[185]. But for *ṭevel* by biblical decree, the rabbis also will agree.

184 That working on *ṭevel* produce should be permitted.

185 All the cases discussed in later chapters which trigger the duty of heave and tithes when the harvest is not yet stored when the biblical obligation starts; cf. Note 115.

רִבִּי מָנָא אָמַר לֵיהּ סְתָם. רִבִּי אָבוּן בְּשֵׁם רִבִּי יוֹחָנָן רִבִּי יוּדָן כְּדַעְתֵּיהּ וְרַבָּנִין כְּדַעְתּוֹן דְּתַנֵּי זֵיתִ שֶׁפִּיצְּעוֹ בְּיָדַיִם מְסוֹאָבוֹת לֹא הוּכְשְׁרוּ. לְסוֹפְגָן בְּמֶלַח הוּכְשְׁרוּ. לֵידַע אִם יֵשׁ בּוֹ מַיִם לֹא הוּכְשְׁרוּ. רִבִּי יוּדָן אוֹמֵר הוּכְשְׁרוּ. רַבָּנִין אָמְרִין בְּמֵימָיו הוּא בוֹדֵק. רִבִּי יוּדָה אוֹמֵר בְּגוּפוֹ הוּא בוֹדֵק. וְהָכָא רַבָּנִין אָמְרִין בְּמֵימָיו הוּא מַחֲלִיק. רִבִּי יוּדָה בְּשֶׁיֵּשׁ שֶׁלּוֹ מַחֲלִיק.

Rebbi Mana said it without attribution, Rebbi Abun [said it] in the name of Rebbi Joḥanan: Rebbi Jehudah stays with his opinion, the rabbis stay with their opinion[186], as we have stated[187]: "Olives which somebody crushed with impure hands are not prepared[188], to let them soak up salt they are prepared[189], to know whether they contain sap they are not prepared; Rebbi Jehudah says they are prepared[190]." The rabbis say, he checks their sap. Rebbi Jehudah says, he checks their body. Here, the rabbis say he polishes with their sap, Rebbi Jehudah says, he polishes with what he has.

186 In the second part of the Mishnah, polishing raisin cakes.

187 Tosephta *Ṭahorot* 10:11, Babli *Šabbat* 145a.

188 In the Babli: "prepared." While olive oil is one of the fluids which

prepare for impurity, for the Tannaïm of Yerushalmi and Tosephta the sap which oozes out of the broken olives is not oil and is discarded. For the Tanna of the Babli, breaking olives before pressing produces virgin oil. For unclean hands, cf. *Demay* Chapter 2, Note 136.

189 In the Babli: "not prepared." For Yerushalmi and Tosephta, the wetness of the olives is desirable since salt will not dissolve and enter the olives when they are completely dry. In addition, it is asserted that in this case the fluid has the status of oil since pickled olives are eaten for their oil.

190 The three sources all have different formulations but they agree that checking whether the olives already contain oil does not turn the sap into oil since it is not collected, but for R. Jehudah it is oil. Similarly, the grape fluid used to glaze the raisin cake is not wine for the anonymous Tanna but is wine for R. Jehudah.

רִבִּי אָמַר לְרִבִּי שִׁמְעוֹן בְּרֵיהּ עֲלֵה וְהָבֵא לָנוּ גְּרוֹגְרוֹת מִן הֶחָבִית. אָמַר לֵיהּ וְאֵינוֹ אָסוּר מִשּׁוּם מוּקְצֶה. אָמַר לֵיהּ וַאֲדַייִן אַתְּ לְזוֹ אֵין לָךְ אָסוּר מִשּׁוּם מוּקְצֶה אֶלָּא תְאֵינִים וַעֲנָבִים בִּלְבַד. אָמַר רִבִּי שְׁמוּאֵל בַּר סִיסָרְטַאי מִפְּנֵי שֶׁהֵן מַסְרִיחוֹת בֵּינְתַיִים. רִבִּי זְעִירָא בָּעֵי קוֹמֵי רִבִּי יָסָא לֹא מִסְתַּבְּרָא בְּאִילֵּין פְּצוּלַיְיָה[191] הֲוָה עוּבְדָא. אָמַר לֵיהּ אוּף אֲנָא סָבַר כֵּן. אָתָא רִבִּי יוֹסֵי בֵּי רִבִּי בּוּן רִבִּי יִצְחָק בַּר בִּיסְנָא בְּשֵׁם רִבִּי יוֹחָנָן בְּאִילֵּין פְּצוּלַיְיָא הֲוָה עוּבְדָא.

[192]Rebbi said to his son Rebbi Simeon, climb up and bring us dried figs from the barrel. He said to him, is it not forbidden because of *muqzeh*[84]? He retorted, are you still holding that? Nothing but figs and grapes can be forbidden because of *muqzeh*[193]! Rebbi Samuel bar Sisarta: Because they stink in between. Rebbi Zeïra asked before Rebbi Assi: Is it not reasonable to hold that the case involved split dates[194]? He said to him, that is my opinion also. Rebbi Yose ben Rebbi Abun, Rebbi Isaac bar Bisna[195] in the name of Rebbi Johanan: The case involved split dates.

191 Reading of the Rome ms. Reading of the text in *Beẓah* and in Venice/Leyden later in this paragraph: פְּצוּלַיָּא.

192 The main place of this and the following paragraphs is *Beẓah* 4:1, fol. 62b.

193 In the Babli (*Šabbat* 45a) this is a statement of Samuel in the tradition of R. Simeon ben Iohai.

194 Since Rebbi asked his son "to climb up", the dried figs were still on the roof, the usual drying place for figs. Since the status of these figs was not checked before the holiday began, it is not clear whether it was known before the start of the Sabbath that the dried figs already had reached a state in which they were edible before the start of the holiday. But unripe (or never ripe) dates which are spread out on the roof to mature and become sweet never pass through a phase during which they are inedible. They would be a prime example for food left to dry which is never *muqzeh*.

In the Babli (*loc. cit.*) Rebbi Simeon ben Rebbi is quoted asking Rebbi about the status of פצעילי, which are identical with פציליא here.

194 A Galilean Amora, student of rabbis Ammi and Assi (Immi and Yasa), and colleague of R. Zeïra. He is mentioned several times in the Babli.

אָמַר לֵיהּ אֵין לָךְ אָסוּר מִשּׁוּם מוּקְצֶה אֶלָּא תְאֵינִים בִּלְבַד. רִבִּי יַעֲקֹב בַּר זַבְדִּי בְּשֵׁם רִבִּי אַבָּהוּ הָדָא דְתֵימָא לְעִנְייַן שַׁבָּת. אֲבָל לְעִנְייַן מַעְשְׂרוֹת כָּל־הַדְּבָרִים יֵשׁ לָהֶן מוּקְצֶה. אָמַר רִבִּי יוֹסֵה[195] מַתְנִיתָא אָמְרָה כֵן גְּרוֹגְרוֹת מִשֶּׁיִּדּוֹשׁ וּמְגוּרָה מִשֶּׁיְּעַגֵּל.

"He said to him, nothing but figs[196] can be forbidden because of *muqzeh*!" Rebbi Jacob bar Zavdi in the name of Rebbi Abbahu: that is, concerning the Sabbath. But concerning tithes, everything may pass through a stage of *muqzeh*. Rebbi Yose said, the Mishnah said so: "Dried figs when he presses them and in a bin if he planes with a roller.[197]"

195 Reading of the Rome ms. and the text in *Beẓah*. Word missing in Venice print.

196 "And grapes" has fallen out by a scribal error; grapes are also mentioned in the parallel in *Šabbat*.

197 While dried figs can be used as soon as they are edible again, if he had the intention from the start to store the finished produce in an amphora or a bin, the treatment in a case of *muqzeh* is irrelevant for tithes. Similarly, any produce put out to dry is free from tithes until it is brought to its final storage.

אָמַר רִבִּי יוֹחָנָן דִּבְרֵי שׁוֹנֶה רִאשׁוֹן לֹא הַתַּחְתּוֹן צָרִיךְ לָעֶלְיוֹן וְלֹא הָעֶלְיוֹן צָרִיךְ לַתַּחְתּוֹן. דִּבְרֵי שׁוֹנֶה אַחֲרוֹן צָרִיךְ לָעֶלְיוֹן וְלֹא הָעֶלְיוֹן צָרִיךְ לַתַּחְתּוֹן. אָמַר רִבִּי לָעְזָר דְּרִבִּי מֵאִיר הִיא. אָמַר לֵיהּ דְּלֹא תִיסְבּוֹר מֵימַר סְתָמָא דְּרִבִּי יוֹסֵי הִיא הֲלָכָה כִסְתָמָה. לְפוּם כֵּן צָרִיךְ מֵימַר דְּרִבִּי מֵאִיר הִיא. דְּרִבִּי מֵאִיר וְרִבִּי יוֹסֵי הֲלָכָה כְּרִבִּי יוֹסֵי.

Rebbi Joḥanan said: The words of the first teacher imply that neither does the bottom need the top nor the top the bottom[198]. The words of the last teacher, [the bottom] needs the top but not the top the bottom[199]. Rebbi Eleazar said, that is Rebbi Meïr's. He said to him, that you should not think to say it is an anonymous opinion and, against Rebbi Yose, practice follows the anonymous opinion. Therefore, one needs to say that this is Rebbi Meïr's and between Rebbi Meïr and Rebbi Yose practice follows Rebbi Yose[200].

198 This refers to the disagreement between the anonymous Tanna and R. Yose about dried figs being pressed into an amphora. The first Tanna holds that the start of pressing brings on the obligation of tithes since there is no longer any processing involved.

199 This sentence is corrupt in both mss.; the complete sentence is only paraphrased by R. Simson. R. Isaac Simponti has a complete sentence which, however, does not seem to be correct. The argument can best be reconstructed from Tosephta 1:11: " If, while he presses into an amphora or planes in a bin, the amphora broke or the bin collapsed, he may not eat from the contents as a snack, but Rebbi Yose permits it because the bottom needs the top." R. Yose holds that pressing dried

figs into an amphora is processing, that pressed figs are different from loose dried figs and, therefore, the end but not the start of the operation counts for tithes.

200 Maimonides in his Commentary and his Code (*Ma'aser* 3:16) treats this statement as a disagreement between Rebbis Joḥanan and Eleazar and holds that practice follows the anonymous teacher.

היה עובר בשוק פרק שני

(fol. 49b) **משנה א:** הָיָה עוֹבֵר בַּשּׁוּק וְאָמַר טְלוּ לָכֶם תְּאֵינִים אוֹכְלִין וּפְטוּרִין. לְפִיכָךְ אִם הִכְנִיסוּ לְבָתֵּיהֶן מְתַקְּנִין וַדַּאי. טְלוּ וְהַכְנִיסוּ לְבָתֵּיכֶם לֹא יֹאכְלוּ מֵהֶן עֲרַאי לְפִיכָךְ אִם הִכְנִיסוּ לְבָתֵּיהֶן אֵינָן מְתַקְּנִין אֶלָּא דְמַאי.

Mishnah 1: If somebody[1] passed by the market place and said: "take some figs[2]," one may eat without tithing[3]. Therefore, if they brought to their houses, they must put in order as certain produce. "Take some figs and bring them home," one should not eat them as a snack[4]. Therefore, if they brought to their houses, they have to put in order only as *demay*.

1 A person not certified as trustworthy or a Fellow, see the Introduction to *Demay*. A trustworthy person will not give away anything not fully tithed.

2 As is a gift, cf. Note 5.

3 Since he offers single figs, we assume that they are freshly harvested and never were near the offerer's house. Therefore, they are not yet under the obligation of heave and tithes. When they become obligated upon being brought to the recipient's house, they must be treated as fully untithed.

4 If the vulgar offers figs as fully tithed, one has to assume that only heave was given but not tithes as explained in Tractate *Demay*.

(fol. 49c) **הלכה א:** שְׁמוּאֵל אָמַר דְּרִבִּי מֵאִיר הִיא דְּרִבִּי מֵאִיר אוֹמֵר אֵין מַתָּנָה כְּמֶכֶר. אָמַר רִבִּי יוֹסֵי דִּבְרֵי הַכֹּל הִיא. אִישְׁתְּאָלִית לְאִילֵּין דְּבֵי רִבִּי יַנַּאי. וְאָמְרִין נָהֲגִין הֲוֵינָן יְהָבִין אִילֵּין לְאִילֵּין בְּחַקְלָא וְאָכְלִין וְלֹא מְתַקְּנִין. מַיי כְדוֹן. כְּמָאן דְּאָמַר מֵאֵילֵיהֶן קִבְּלוּ עֲלֵיהֶן הַמַּעְשְׂרוֹת.

Halakhah 1: Samuel said, this is Rebbi Meïr's opinion since Rebbi Meïr says a gift is not like a sale[5]. Rebbi Yose said, it is the opinion of everybody. This was asked of those from Rebbi Yannai's house and they said, we used to give to one another in the fields and ate without putting in order[6]. How can this be? Following him who held that they accepted tithes voluntarily[7].

5 It is stated in Halakhah 4:1 that produce which would become obligated when brought to storage also becomes obligated if it is sold on the field; the buyer may not eat a snack without giving heave and tithes. In general, we hold that the formal rules of transfer of property by a gift are the same as by sale in all respects. R. Meïr is quoted here and in *Ma'ser Šeni* 1:1 to hold that, while a gift is only valid if it were valid also as a sale, a gift does not induce the obligations of heave and tithes.

6 Since practice follows the Mishnah, the Mishnah cannot describe a minority opinion. R. Yose is proven correct.

7 Following R. Eleazar, *Ševi'it* 6:1, Notes 11-13.

מַתְנִיתִין בְּמָקוֹם שֶׁרוֹב מַכְנִיסִין לְבָתִּים אֲבָל בְּמָקוֹם שֶׁרוֹב מַכְנִיסִין לַשּׁוּק אֵינָן מְתַקְּנִין אֶלָּא דְמַאי. אִם בְּמָקוֹם שֶׁרוֹב מַכְנִיסִין לְבָתִּים כְּדָא דְתַנִּינָן טְלוּ וְהַכְנִיסוּ לְבָתֵּיכֶם לֹא יֹאכְלוּ מֵהֶן עֲרַאי. מִכֵּיוָן שֶׁאָמַר טוֹל וְהַכְנֵיס כְּמִי שֶׁאָמַר טוֹל אֲנִי מְעַשֵּׂר עַל יָדֶיךָ. אֲבָל בְּמָקוֹם שֶׁרוֹב מַכְנִיסִין לַשּׁוּק אֵינוֹ נֶאֱמָן לוֹמַר לוֹ עִישַּׂרְתִּי וְאֵינוֹ נֶאֱמָן לוֹמַר לוֹ לְתוֹךְ בֵּיתִי אֲנִי מַכְנִיסָן.

Our Mishnah[8] [deals with] the case that most people bring to their houses but in case most people bring directly to market one has to put in order only as *demay*. If we were dealing with the case that most people bring to their houses[9], is that not what we have stated[10]: "'Take some figs and bring them home,' one should not eat them as a snack?" Since he said, "take some figs and bring them home," it is as if he said, "take, I am taking care of the tithes for you[11]." But if most people bring directly to market he is not trusted if he says to somebody, I did tithe, nor is he trusted if he says to him, I am bringing mine to my house[12].

8 This refers to the first part of the Mishnah. If the farmer is a Fellow and he brings his figs directly to market he has to tithe (by the rules of fellowship) so that the vulgar who buys from him will not become guilty when he takes the figs home. Therefore, if the seller is not trustworthy, he still can be assumed to have given heave even if the figs never got near the house since collecting the figs is the last act of harvest, comparable to threshing for grains.

9 Before going to market. Then the fruits are subject to heave and tithes by biblical standards.

10 The second part of the Mishnah. Therefore, the first part cannot refer to the same case.

11 Since the giver is not trustworthy, the recipient still has to treat the gift as *demay*.

12 If he were trustworthy, in the first case one would also require tithing only as *demay*, not as certain as required by the Mishnah.

נָתַן לוֹ דָבָר מְרוּבָּה אֲפִילוּ אָמַר לוֹ טוֹל וֶאֱכוֹל כְּמִי שֶׁאָמַר לוֹ טוֹל וְהַכְנֵס. נָתַן לוֹ דָבָר שֶׁאֵין דַּרְכּוֹ לְהֵיאָכֵל חַי אֲפִילוּ אָמַר לוֹ טוֹל וֶאֱכוֹל כְּמִי שֶׁאָמַר לוֹ טוֹל וְהַכְנֵס. הָיָה אָדָם גָּדוֹל וְאֵין דַּרְכּוֹ לוֹכַל בַּשּׁוּק וְאָמַר לוֹ טוֹל אֱכוֹל כְּמִי שֶׁאָמַר לוֹ טוֹל וְהַכְנֵס. הָיוּ שְׁנַיִם לְזֶה אָמַר לוֹ טוֹל וֶאֱכוֹל לְזֶה אָמַר טוֹל וְהַכְנֵס. זֶה שֶׁאָמַר לוֹ טוֹל וֶאֱכוֹל פָּטוּר. וְזֶה שֶׁאָמַר לוֹ טוֹל וְהַכְנֵיס חַיָּב. אָמַר רִבִּי יוֹסֵי וְלָאו מַתְנִיתִין הִיא. אוֹכְלִין וּפְטוּרִין וּבַעַל הַשַּׁעַר וּבַעַל הֶחָנוּת חַיָּבִין. אָמַר רִבִּי יוֹנָה דִּבְרֵי הַכֹּל הִיא. כָּאן בִּדְמַאי כָּאן בְּוַדַּאי.

If he gave much, even if he said, take and eat, it is as if he said, take and store[13]. If he gave him anything that usually is not eaten raw, even if he said, take and eat, it is as if he said, take and store. If [the recipient] was an important personality who does not usually eat in public, if he said, take and eat, it is as if he said, take and store. If there were two people; to one he said, take and eat; to the other he said, take and store. The one to whom he said, take and eat, is free[14]; the one to whom he said, take and store, is obligated[15]. Rebbi Yose said, is that not a Mishnah (2:2): "They eat and are free but the owners of the gate or the store are obligated?[16]" Rebbi Jonah said, it is everybody's opinion[17]; here for *demay*, there for certain.

13 Even if he uses the language specified in the Mishnah for the first case, the rule to be followed is that of the second case if a typical person will not be able to eat all of it on the spot. Similar arguments hold for the next two cases.

14 The first case of the Mishnah.

15 The second case.

16 If a passer-by gives fruits to a group of people gossiping at a place where the owner's own produce would become obligated, the visitors may eat them as a snack but not the owners. R. Jehudah also permits the owners to eat as long as they stay in the group. He must disagree with the rules just given.

17 Mishnah 2 speaks of untithed fruits, Mishnah 1 of *demay*. R. Yose's argument is invalid; the rules must be spelled out and cannot be inferred from the Mishnah.

צֵא וְלַקֵּט לָךְ עֶשְׂרִים תְּאֵינִים מִשֶּׁלִּי וַאֲנִי מְמַלֵּא כְרֵיסִי מִשֶּׁלָּךְ הַמְּמַלֵּא אֶת כְּרֵיסוֹ פָּטוּר. וְהָאוֹכֵל בְּמִנְייָן חַייָב. רִבִּי בּוּן בַּר חִייָה בְּעָא קוֹמֵי רִבִּי זְעִירָא וְאֵין אָדָם אוֹכֵל אַחַת אַחַת בִּרְשׁוּת הַכֹּל וּפָטוּר. אָמַר לוֹ אִין. הָכָא לָמָּה הוּא חַייָב. אָמַר לוֹ בִּמְצָרֵף. אִם בִּמְצָרֵף אֲפִילוּ הַמְּמַלֵּא אֶת כְּרֵיסוֹ יְהֵא חַייָב. וְאֵינוֹ אָסוּר מִשּׁוּם חֲלִיפִין. אָמַר רִבִּי שַׁמַּיי אֵין לוֹ חֲלִיפִין שֶׁלֹּא נִתְכַּוֵּן הָאִישׁ הַזֶּה אֶלָּא לְהַגֵּס אֶת לִבּוֹ שֶׁיֹּאכַל.

[18]"'Go and collect for yourself 20 figs from my tree and I will eat my fill from yours,' he who eats his fill is free[19] and he who eats a fixed number is obligated[20]." Rebbi Abun bar Ḥiyya asked before Rebbi Zeïra: Can a person not eat one by one with permission and be free? He said to him, yes. Then why is he obligated here? He said to him, when he takes them together[21]. If he takes them together, even he who eats his fill should be obligated[22]! Is he not forbidden because of barter[23]? Rebbi

Shammai said, there is no barter since this man only wanted to make him hungry that he should eat[24].

18 Tosephta 2:6.

19 He eats as a snack, untithed.

20 The fixed number makes it a business deal for which the fruits have to be tithed.

21 If he first collects 20 figs and then eats them, he must tithe first. If he eats every fig before he picks the next one, it is a snack and needs no tithing.

22 If the answer stands, the Tosephta is misleading. It should say, he who eats while collecting is free but he who collects and then eats is obligated.

23 There is no difference whether one picks and then eats or eats while picking. The person who gets 20 figs gets them by barter and has to tithe in any case; the question of R. Abun bar Ḥiyya seems irrelevant.

24 20 figs to eat in one sitting is a large amount. The person who wants to eat his fill is afraid the other person, who probably is poor, would not eat enough. So he induces him to eat a large quantity; there are two snacks and no barter. The objection of R. Abun bar Ḥiyya is supported; the Tosephta cannot represent practice.

צֵא וְלַקֵּט לָךְ עֶשְׂרִים תְּאֵינִים מִשֶּׁלִּי אוֹכֵל כְּדַרְכּוֹ וְהוּא פָּטוּר. צֵא וּמַלֵּא אֶת הַכַּלְכָּלָה לֹא יֹאכַל עַד שֶׁיְּעַשֵּׂר. בַּמֶּה דְבָרִים אֲמוּרִים בְּעַם הָאָרֶץ. אֲבָל בְּחָבֵר אוֹכֵל וְאֵינוֹ צָרִיךְ לְעַשֵּׂר דִּבְרֵי רַבִּי. רַבָּן שִׁמְעוֹן בֶּן גַּמְלִיאֵל אוֹמֵר בַּמֶּה דְבָרִים אֲמוּרִים בְּעַם הָאָרֶץ. אֲבָל בְּחָבֵר מְתַקְּנָן וַדַּאי. שֶׁלֹּא נֶחְשְׁדוּ חֲבֵרִים לִתְרוֹם שֶׁלֹּא מִן הַמּוּקָף. אָמַר רַבִּי רוֹאֶה אֲנִי אֶת דְּבָרַי מִדִּבְרֵי רַבָּן שִׁמְעוֹן בֶּן גַּמְלִיאֵל. מוּטָּב שֶׁיִּתְרוֹמוּ שֶׁלֹּא מִן הַמּוּקָף וְלֹא לְהַאֲכִיל לְעַמֵּי הָאָרֶץ טְבָלִים. אָמַר רַבִּי זְעִירָא מִדִּבְרֵי שְׁנֵיהֶן אֲפִילוּ חָבֵר שֶׁשּׁוֹלֵחַ לְחָבֵר צָרִיךְ לְעַשֵּׂר. הֲוֹון בָּעֵיי מֵימַר מָאן דְּאָמַר שֶׁלֹּא נֶחְשְׁדוּ חֲבֵרִים לִתְרוֹם שֶׁלֹּא מִן הַמּוּקָף וְזֶה חָבֵר צָרִיךְ הוּא לְעַשֵּׂר. וּמָאן דְּאָמַר מוּטָּב שֶׁיִּתְרוֹמוּ שֶׁלֹּא מִן הַמּוּקָף וְלֹא לְהַאֲכִיל עַמֵּי הָאָרֶץ טְבָלִים וְזֶה חָבֵר צָרִיךְ הוּא לְעַשֵּׂר. רַבִּי יוֹנָה בָּעֵי הָכָא אַתְּ עֲבִיד לֵיהּ חָבֵר. וְהָכָא אַתְּ עֲבִיד לֵיהּ עַם הָאָרֶץ. אָמַר רַבִּי יוֹסֵי כָּאן וְכָאן עַם הָאָרֶץ הוּא. אֶלָּא בִּשְׁבִיל אֶחָד שֶׁהוּא מְתַקֵּן הוּא נִקְרָא חָבֵר.

[25]"'Go and collect for yourself 20 figs from my tree', he eats as usual and is free[26]. 'Go and fill a basket,' he should not eat before tithing[27]. When has this been said? About a vulgar. But from a Fellow he can eat and does not have to tithe, the words of Rebbi. Rabban Simeon ben Gamliel says, when has this been said? About a vulgar. But from a Fellow he has to put it in order as certainly untithed since Fellows are not suspected to tithe what is not earmarked[28]. Rebbi said, I prefer my words to those of Rabban Simeon ben Gamliel[29]. It is preferable that they should tithe what is not earmarked[30] than to feed *ṭevel* to the vulgar[31]." Rebbi Zeïra said, from both their opinions [it follows that] even a Fellow who sends to another Fellow must tithe[32]. They ventured to say, he who said that Fellows are not suspected to tithe what is not earmarked, when somebody is a Fellow he has to tithe[33]. And he who said, it is better to tithe what is not earmarked than to feed *ṭevel* to the vulgar, if he is a Fellow he has to tithe[34]. Rebbi Jonah asked: Here you declare him to be a Fellow, there you declare him to be a vulgar[35]. Rebbi Yose said, in both cases, he is a vulgar. But because of the rare one who puts in order he is called a Fellow[36].

25 Tosephta 2:5, Babli *Eruvin* 32a.

26 In the Tosephta and Babli (printed editions and Munich ms.): "He may eat a snack and tithes as certainly untithed." But R. Ḥananel reads in the Babli: "He may eat a snack and tithes as *demay*." The Yerushalmi does not deal with the problem; the *baraita* simply states that he "is free" to eat an untithed snack.

27 In the Tosephta and Babli: He may eat a snack and tithes as *demay*"; since the giver specifies a measure he might have given tithes for his gift from another batch. Here R. Ḥananel reads: "tithes as certainly untithed." The Yerushalmi does not deal with the problem: According to Mishnah 1:5, a filled basket subjects all figs in it to heave and tithes. It is clear that then the figs cannot be eaten untithed. But the status of the tithing, whether *de*

may or certain, is not determined.

28 See *Terumot* 4:3, Note 21; 2:1, Notes 3,6.

29 This is the formulation of the editor. Rebbi would have said "my father".

30 Transgressing a positive biblical injunction.

31 Committing the grave sin of "putting a stone in the path of a blind man." Rabban Simeon ben Gamliel holds that the just should never sin to save the wicked; this is his position everywhere, cf. *Demay* 3:8, Note 135, Mishnah *Ma'aser Šeni* 5:1; Babli *Baba Qama* 69a.

32 See *Demay* 2:2, Note 125 (R. Zeïra in the name of R. Joḥanan). In Halakhah 5:1, the rule is attributed to R. Simeon ben Laqish.

33 The recipient has to tithe as certainly untithed if circumstances indicate that the produce could not have been tithed by the giver, as in the case here since the figs collected in the recipient's basket could not have been delineated by the giver; cf. *Demay* 3:3, Notes 79 ff.

34 The giver has to tithe by the rule of Rebbi; the recipient has to tithe by the rules of *demay*.

35 The recipient is treated as a Fellow since he is required to tithe *demay*. On the other hand, he is treated as a vulgar in Rebbi's argument.

36 If somebody is not a Fellow, he nevertheless may not be a vulgar in the legal sense of the word.

רִבִּי יוֹסֵי בְּשֵׁם רִבִּי שֵׁשֶׁת רִבִּי לָֽעְזָר בְּשֵׁם רִבִּי יוֹסֵי בְּשֵׁם רַב אָבִין הָאוֹמֵר לַחֲבֵירוֹ אֲנִי מְעַשֵּׂר עַל יָדֶיךָ אֵינוֹ צָרִיךְ לַעֲמוֹד עִמּוֹ. תַּמָּן תַּנִּינָן נְתָנוֹ בְּאִילָן לְמַעְלָה מֵעֲשָׂרָה טְפָחִים אֵינוֹ עֵירוּב. לְמַטָּה מֵעֲשָׂרָה טְפָחִים הֲרֵי זֶה עֵירוּב. אָמַר רִבִּי לָֽעְזָר וְצָרִיךְ לַעֲמוֹד עִמּוֹ. וְהָכָא אַתְּ אָמַר הָכֵין. אָמַר רִבִּי חִיָּיה בַּר אָדָא כַּאן בְּגָדוֹל כָּאן בְּקָטוֹן. רִבִּי חֲנַנְיָה בְשֵׁם רִבִּי חֲנִינָא אֲפִילוּ תֵימַר כָּאן וְכָאן בְּגָדוֹל. כָּאן וְכָאן בְּקָטוֹן. תַּמָּן בְּאוֹמֵר לוֹ עֲרֵב עַל יָדַיי.[37] בְּרַם הָכָא בְּאוֹמֵר לוֹ אֲנִי מְעַשֵּׂר עַל יָדֶיךָ.[38] הָדָא יָֽלְפָה מִן הַהִיא וְהַהִיא יָֽלְפָה מִן הָדָא. הָדָא יָֽלְפָה מִן הַהִיא בְּאוֹמֵר לוֹ אֲנִי מְעָרֵב עַל יָדֶיךָ שֶׁאֵינוֹ צָרִיךְ לַעֲמוֹד עִמּוֹ. וְהַהִיא יָֽלְפָה מִן הָכָא שֶׁאוֹמֵר לוֹ עֲשֵׂר עַל יָדַי שֶׁהוּא צָרִיךְ לַעֲמוֹד עִמּוֹ.

[39]Rebbi Yose[40] in the name of Rebbi Sheshet, Rebbi Eleazar in the name of Rebbi Yose in the name of Rebbi Abin: If somebody says to

another I shall tithe for you, he does not have to be with him. There[41], we have stated: "If he put it in a tree, higher than ten hand-breadths it is not an *eruv*, lower than ten hand-breadths it is an *eruv*." Rebbi Eleazar said, he has to be with him[42]. And here, you say so? Rebbi Ḥiyya bar Ada said, here about an adult, there about a minor. Rebbi Ḥananiah said in the name of Rebbi Ḥanina, you may even say in both cases we deal with an adult or in both cases we deal with a minor. There, when he says, make an *eruv* for me! But here, he says I shall tithe for you[43]. This learns from that and that learns from this. This learns from that, if he says I shall make an *eruv* for you, he does not have to be with him. That learns from this, if he says tithe for me, he has to be with him.

37 Reading of the Rome ms. and the Leyden and Venice texts in *Eruvin* 3. Leyden and Venice here: אֲנִי מְעָרֵב עַל יָדֶיךָ.

38 Reading of the Rome ms. and the Leyden and Venice texts in *Eruvin* 3. Leyden and Venice here: עֲשֵׂר עַל יָדִי.

39 The paragraph has a parallel in *Eruvin* 3, fol. 20d.

40 This must be R. Yose ben R. Ḥanina since R. Eleazar quotes in his name. No Rebbi Sheshet is known from another source; Rav Sheshet holds in Babli *Eruvin* 32a that one always may trust an agent to fulfill the duties of his agency. This is rejected here. The older R. Yose ben Ḥanina is not likely to quote from the younger Rav Sheshet.

41 Mishnah *Eruvin* 3:3. For the notion of *eruv*, cf. *Peah* 8, Note 56.

42 The previous Mishnah states: "An *eruv* sent through an insane, a deaf and dumb, or a minor is invalid. If the *eruv* will be delivered to a competent person, it is valid." In the interpretation of the Yerushalmi, the two Mishnaiot belong together; the person who puts the *eruv* into a tree at the border of the Sabbath domain is an agent of the person who intends to use the *eruv*. The latter has to check that the agent executed the terms of his agency.

43 The initiative is the agent's, not the beneficiary's.

צֵא וְלַקֵּט לָךְ עֶשְׂרִים תְּאֵינִים מִשֶּׁלִּי אוֹכֵל וְהוֹלֵךְ וְהוּא פָּטוּר. צֵא וּמַלֵּא אֶת הַכַּלְכָּלָה. רִבִּי אוֹמֵר אוֹמֵר אֲנִי שֶׁהוּא צָרִיךְ לְהַרְאוֹת לוֹ אֶת הַכַּלְכָּלָה. וְכַמָּה הוּא שִׁיעוּר הַכַּלְכָּלָה. רִבִּי שְׁמוּאֵל בַּר נַחְמָן בְּשֵׁם רִבִּי יוֹנָתָן סְתָם כַּלְכָּלָה אַרְבַּעַת קַבִּין. וּגְדוֹלָה סְאָה. וּקְטַנָּה שְׁלֹשָׁה קַבִּין. רִבִּי יוֹנָה בָּעֵי לְמַעְשְׂרוֹת אִיתְאֲמָרַת אוֹ לְמִידַּת הַדִּין. אִין (fol. 49d) תֵּימַר לְמַעְשְׂרוֹת אִיתְאֲמָרַת כָּל־שֶׁכֵּן לְמִידַּת הַדִּין. אִין תֵּימַר לְמִידַּת הַדִּין אִיתְאֲמָרַת הָא לְמַעְשְׂרוֹת לֹא. רִבִּי יוֹסֵי פְּשִׁיטָא לֵיהּ לְמַעְשְׂרוֹת אִיתְאֲמָרַת כָּל־שֶׁכֵּן לְמִידַּת הַדִּין.

"'[25]Go and collect for yourself 20 figs from my tree', he eats one after the other and is free. 'Go and fill a basket.'" Rebbi says, I say that he has to show him the basket[44]. What is the measure of a basket? Rebbi Samuel bar Naḥman in the name of Rebbi Jonathan[45]: A standard basket is four *qab*, a large one a *seah*, a small one three *qab*[46]. Rebbi Jonah asked: Has this been said for tithes or for contract law[47]? If you say for tithes[48], then certainly also for contracts. If for contracts, then not for tithes. It was obvious to Rebbi Yose that this was said for tithes, and certainly also for contracts.

44 He follows the Tosephta and disagrees with the Amoraïm who fix standard sizes of baskets.

45 In the Rome ms: R. Joḥanan in the name of R. Simeon ben Yehoẓadaq.

46 In Tosephta 2:7, a large basket is ≥ a *seah*, an average one ≥ three *qab*, a small one ≥ two *qab*. For the volumes of *seah* and *qab*, cf. *Peah* 3:7, Note 108.

47 If the seller contracts to deliver a basket of a commodity, is he bound to deliver the standard volume even if this is not specified in the contract? The question is impossible for the Tannaïm who specify only minimal sizes; for them, the measures must refer to tithes.

48 For Rebbi, it gives the donor an indication which quantity to tithe for his gift to be collected.

(fol. 49b) **משנה ב:** הָיוּ יוֹשְׁבִין בְּשַׁעַר אוֹ בְחָנוּת וְאָמַר טְלוּ לָכֶם תְּאֵינִים אוֹכְלִין וּפְטוּרִין. וּבַעַל הַשַּׁעַר וּבַעַל הֶחָנוּת חַייָבִים. רִבִּי יְהוּדָה פוֹטֵר עַד שֶׁיַּחְזוֹר אֶת פָּנָיו אוֹ עַד שֶׁיְּשַׁנֶּה מְקוֹם יְשִׁיבָתוֹ.

Mishnah 2: If they were sitting in a gate or in a store and he[49] said, take some figs, they may eat and are free, but the owners of the gate or the store are obligated[50]. Rebbi Jehudah frees them[51] unless they turn their faces away or change their places[52].

49 The person of Mishnah 1 who is giving away figs.

50 Since for them "the figs see the house" and, therefore, are subject to heave and tithes.

51 Since one is not supposed to be eating in public, he defines the house which induces the duty of tithes as a place in which the owner can eat without embarassment.

52 In order to eat in privacy.

(fol. 49d) **הלכה ב:** הָדָא אָמְרָה שֶׁבֵּיתוֹ טוֹבֵל לוֹ אֲבָל לֹא לַאֲחֵרִים. אָמַר רִבִּי לָעְזָר רִבִּי יוּדָה וְרִבִּי נְחֶמְיָה שְׁנֵיהֶן אָמְרוּ דָבָר אֶחָד דְּתַנִּינָן תַּמָּן רִבִּי נְחֶמְיָה אוֹמֵר כָּל־שֶׁאֵין אָדָם בּוֹשׁ מִלּוֹכַל בְּתוֹכָהּ חַייֶבֶת. אָמַר רִבִּי יוֹסֵי הֲוֵינָן סָבְרִין מֵימַר מִפְלְגוֹן רִבִּי נְחֶמְיָה וְרַבָּנִן בְּחָצֵר שֶׁהוּא בוֹשׁ לוֹכַל בְּכוּלָּהּ. הָא מִקְצָתָהּ בּוֹשׁ וּמִקְצָתָהּ לֹא בוֹשׁ לֹא. מִן דְּאָמַר רִבִּי לָעְזָר רִבִּי יוּדָה וְרִבִּי נְחֶמְיָה שְׁנֵיהֶן אָמְרוּ דָבָר אֶחָד הָדָא אָמְרָה מָקוֹם שֶׁהוּא בוֹשׁ פָּטוּר מָקוֹם שֶׁאֵינוֹ בוֹשׁ חַייָב.

Halakhah 2: That means[53] that the house creates *ṭevel* for its owner but not for others. Rebbi Eleazar said, Rebbi Jehudah and Rebbi Neḥemiah said the same thing as we have stated[54]: "Rebbi Neḥemiah says, every [courtyard] in which a person is not ashamed to eat obligates." Rebbi Yose said, we thought that Rebbi Neḥemiah and the other rabbis disagree about a courtyard in which he would be ashamed to eat anywhere. That means, not one in which he would be ashamed at some place but not at another. Since Rebbi Eleazar said Rebbi Jehudah and Rebbi Neḥemiah said the same thing, this implies that a place where he would be ashamed is free and one where he would not be ashamed is obligated.

53 The opinion of the anonymous majority.

54 Mishnah 3:5, reporting the opinions of various rabbis about the definition of a courtyard which induces the obligation of heave and tithes. R. Jehudah also is quoted in this Mishnah in a statement which does not necessarily conflict with R. Eleazar's opinion.

אָמַר רִבִּי יוֹחָנָן דִּבְרֵי רִבִּי יְהוּדָה עָשׂוּ אוֹתוֹ כְּייחוּר שֶׁהוּא נוֹטֶה לֶחָצֵר. עַל דַּעְתֵּיהּ דְּרִבִּי יוֹחָנָן בְּאוֹכֵל אַחַת אַחַת וּבְאוֹכֵל בִּרְשׁוּת הַכֹּל וּבִמְשַׁיֵּיר. עַל דַּעְתֵּיהּ דְּרִבִּי לָעְזָר אֲפִילוּ אֵינוֹ אוֹכֵל אַחַת אַחַת אֲפִילוּ אֵינוֹ אוֹכֵל בִּרְשׁוּת הַכֹּל וְלֹא שִׁיֵּיר.

Rebbi Joḥanan said, Rebbi Jehudah implies that they made it like a branch hanging into the courtyard[55]. In the opinion of Rebbi Joḥanan, if he eats single ones, eats in a public place, and leaves some remainder. In the opinion of Rebbi Eleazar, even if he does not eat single ones, even if he does not eat in a public place and leaves no remainder[56].

55 As long as the fruits hang on the branch, they are not obligated. Once harvested, they become immediately obligated unless they are eaten as snack singly (Note 21), in a place free according to Rebbis Jehudah and Neḥemiah, and before the harvest is completed, i. e., while some fruits remain on the branch.

56 The character of the courtyard alone determines the obligation.

משנה ג: הַמַּעֲלֶה פֵּירוֹת מִגָּלִיל לִיהוּדָה אוֹ עוֹלֶה לִירוּשָׁלַם אוֹכֵל עַד שֶׁהוּא מַגִּיעַ לְמָקוֹם שֶׁהוּא הוֹלֵךְ וְכֵן בַּחֲזִירָה. רִבִּי מֵאִיר אוֹמֵר עַד שֶׁהוּא מַגִּיעַ (fol. 49b)

לְמְקוֹם הַשְּׁבִיתָה. הָרוֹכְלִים הַמְחַזְּרִים בָּעֲייָרוֹת אוֹכְלִין עַד שֶׁהֵן מַגִּיעִין לִמְקוֹם הַלִּינָה. רִבִּי יְהוּדָה אוֹמֵר בַּיִת הָרִאשׁוֹן הוּא בֵּיתוֹ.

Mishnah 3: If somebody brings fruits from Galilee to Judea or if he is on a pilgrimage to Jerusalem, he may eat[56] until he reaches his destination; the same holds for the return journey[57]. Rebbi Meïr says, until he reaches the place where he stays for the Sabbath[58]. Peddlers who make the tour of villages may eat[56] until they come to the place where they will stay for the night. Rebbi Jehudah says, the first house[59] is his house.

56 Untithed fruits as a snack.

57 Untithed fruits collected just before his departure.

58 Since no untithed fruit may be eaten on the Sabbath; see below and Mishnah 3:2.

59 In the village where he wants to stay overnight.

(fol. 49d) **הלכה ג**: פֵּירוֹת שֶׁלְּקָטָן שֶׁלֹּא לְצוֹרֶךְ הַשַּׁבָּת וְקִדֵּשׁ עֲלֵיהֶן הַשַּׁבָּת רִבִּי יוֹחָנָן אָמַר הַשַּׁבָּת טוֹבֶלֶת. רִבִּי שִׁמְעוֹן בֶּן לָקִישׁ אָמַר אֵין הַשַּׁבָּת טוֹבֶלֶת. מָתִיב רִבִּי שִׁמְעוֹן בֶּן לָקִישׁ לְרִבִּי יוֹחָנָן עַל דְּתֵימַר הַשַּׁבָּת טוֹבֶלֶת וְהָתַנִּינָן הַמַּעֲלֶה פֵּירוֹת מִן הַגָּלִיל לִיהוּדָה אוֹ עוֹלֶה לִירוּשָׁלַם אוֹכֵל עַד שֶׁהוּא מַגִּיעַ לִמְקוֹם שֶׁהוּא הוֹלֵךְ וְכֵן בַּחֲזִירָה. וְתַנֵּי עֲלָהּ אֲפִילוּ לָן אֲפִילוּ שָׁבַת. אָמַר לוֹ בְּרוֹצֶה לִשְׁבּוֹת. תֵּדַע לָךְ שֶׁהוּא כֵן. דְּתַנֵּי עֲלָהּ אֲפִילוּ שָׁבַת בְּשֵׁנִי. וְיֵשׁ שְׁבִיתָה בְּשֵׁנִי. אֶלָּא בְּרוֹצֶה לִשְׁבּוֹת אַף הָכָא בְּרוֹצֶה לִשְׁבּוֹת.

Halakhah 3: When fruits were collected not for use on the Sabbath and the Sabbath started, Rebbi Joḥanan said, the Sabbath makes it *ṭevel*, Rebbi Simeon ben Laqish said, the Sabbath does not make it *ṭevel*. Rebbi Simeon ben Laqish objected to Rebbi Joḥanan, since you say the Sabbath makes it *ṭevel*, did we not state: "If somebody brings fruits from Galilee to Judea or if he is on a pilgrimage to Jerusalem, he may eat until he reaches his destination; the same holds for the return journey?" We stated about this: Even if he stayed overnight, even if he stayed over the Sabbath! He said to him, when he wants to stay for the Sabbath[60]. You should know that this is so since we have stated about this: "Even if he stayed for the Sabbath on Monday[61]." Can you have the Sabbath on a Monday? It must be that he wants to stay for the Sabbath; here also if he wants to stay for the Sabbath.

60 The Sabbath causes *ṭevel* if he stays by choice, not by necessity. If he stays over Sabbath at one place during a trip, it is not creating *ṭevel*, if he stays in one place on a vacation or for work, his room becomes his house and induces *ṭevel*. In the Babli, *Bezah* 35a, R. Johanan restricts this to produce fully processed.

61 In Tosephta 2:1, the formulation is: "R. Meïr says, if he arrives at the place of his choice for the Sabbath he must tithe even if it is a Monday."

הַכֹּל מוֹדִין בְּלִינָה שֶׁאֵינָהּ טוֹבֶלֶת. מַה בֵּין לִינָה מַה בֵּין שְׁבִיתָה. אָדָם מְגַלְגֵּל בְּלִינָה וְאֵין אָדָם מְגַלְגֵּל בִּשְׁבִיתָה. בְּכָל־מָקוֹם אָדָם לָן וְאֵין אָדָם שׁוֹבֵת בְּכָל־מָקוֹם.

Everybody agrees that staying overnight does not induce *ṭevel*. What is the difference between staying overnight and staying during the Sabbath? A person happens to stay overnight[62], nobody happens to stay during the Sabbath. A person will stay anywhere overnight, nobody stays everywhere during the Sabbath[63].

62 For this meaning of the root גלגל, cf. H. L. Fleischer in Levy's Dictionary, vol. I, p. 434, referring to p. 329a.

63 Since the choice for staying over the Sabbath is deliberate, that place takes the quality of home.

תַּנֵּי מַעֲשֶׂה בְּרִבִּי יְהוֹשֻׁעַ שֶׁהָיָה מְהַלֵּךְ אַחַר רַבָּן יוֹחָנָן בֶּן זַכַּאי לִבְנֵי חַיִל וְהָיוּ בְּנֵי אוֹתָן הָעֲיָירוֹת מְבִיאִין לָהֶן פֵּירוֹת. אָמַר לָהֶן רִבִּי יְהוֹשֻׁעַ אִם לָנוּ כָּאן אָנוּ

חַיָּבִין לְעַשֵּׂר. וְאִם לָאו אֵין אָנוּ חַיָּבִין לְעַשֵּׂר. אָמַר רִבִּי זְעִירָא רִבִּי יְהוֹשֻׁעַ דַּעְתּוֹ נְקִייָה. אָמַר לוֹ רִבִּי מָנָא וְכָל־עַמָּא שַׁטְיֵי. אֶלָּא רִבִּי יְהוֹשֻׁעַ דִּלְוִייָתֵיהּ שְׁכִיחָה לֵיהּ הֲוֵ דוּ אָמַר הַלִּינָה טוֹבֶלֶת. וּשְׁאַר בְּנֵי אָדָם דְּלֵית אַלְוִייָתֵיהּ שְׁכִיחָה לוֹן אֵין לִינָה טוֹבֶלֶת. וְהָתַנִּינָן רוֹכְלִין הַמַּחֲזִירִין בָּעֲייָרוֹת אוֹכְלִין עַד שֶׁהֵן מַגִּיעִין לִמְקוֹם הַלִּינָה. מַהוּ מְקוֹם הַלִּינָה בֵּיתוֹ. רִבִּי שִׁמְעוֹן בֶּן לָקִישׁ בְּשֵׁם רִבִּי הוֹשַׁעְיָה כְּגוֹן אִילֵּין דִּכְפַר חֲנַנְיָה דְּנָפְקִין וְסַחֲרִין אַרְבַּע וְחָמֵשׁ קוּרִייָן וְעַיְילִין דָּמְכִין בְּבָתֵּיהֶן.

It was stated[64]: "It happened that Rebbi Joshua went to Rabban Joḥanan ben Zakkai in Bene Ḥayil[65], and some local people brought them fruits. Rebbi Joshua said to them, if we stay overnight[66], we are obligated to tithe; otherwise, we are not obligated to tithe." Rebbi Zeïra said, Rebbi Joshua insists on cleanliness[67]. Rebbi Mana said to him, are all others insane[68]? But Rebbi Joshua, who frequently was attended to[69], says that staying overnight induces *ṭevel*. For all others, who are not frequently attended to, staying overnight does not induce *ṭevel*. But did we not state: "Peddlers who make the tour of villages may eat[56] until they come to the place where they will stay for the night." Where is their overnight stay? In their house! Rebbi Simeon ben Laqish in the name of Rebbi Ḥanina: Like those of Kefar Ḥanina[70] who go out, trade in four or five villages, return, and sleep in their houses.

64 Tosefta 2:1, *Demai* 3:1, Note 5.

65 In the other sources, the place of Rabban Joḥanan ben Zakkai is Beror Ḥayil.

66 Reading לנו as contracted from לנין אנו found in the other sources. The Tosephta seems to contradict the Mishnah.

67 He will stay only in a clean room. Therefore, for him staying overnight is comparable to staying during the Sabbath and counted as if he stayed in his own house.

68 To want to stay in dirty, unhealthy surroundings.

69 He was so famous that people

prepared his lodgings specially for him; the lodgings could be considered his personally.

70 Cf. *Ševi'it* 9:2, Note 40.

תַּנֵּי רִבִּי חֲלַפְתָּא בֶּן שָׁאוּל רוֹצֶה הוּא אָדָם לִפְגּוֹעַ עֲסָקָיו בַּבַּיִת הָרִאשׁוֹן שֶׁהוּא פוֹגֵעַ וְלָלוּן שָׁם.

Rebbi Ḥalaphta ben Shaul stated: A person wants to unload his wares in the first house he encounters and stay overnight there[71].

71 This is an attempt at explaining the position of R. Jehudah in the Mishnah, that a traveler is obligated from the moment he arrives at the first house of the place in which he intends to stay overnight.

(fol. 49b) **משנה ד:** פֵּירוֹת שֶׁתְּרָמָן עַד שֶׁלֹּא נִגְמְרָה מְלַאכְתָּן רִבִּי לִיעֶזֶר אוֹסֵר מִלּוֹכַל מֵהֶן עֲרַאי וַחֲכָמִים מַתִּירִין חוּץ מִכַּלְכָּלַת הַתְּאֵינִים. כַּלְכָּלַת תְּאֵינִים שֶׁתְּרָמָהּ רִבִּי שִׁמְעוֹן מַתִּיר וַחֲכָמִים אוֹסְרִין.

Mishnah 4: Fruits from which he gave heave before they were completely processed[72], Rebbi Eliezer prohibits to eat snacks from them[73] but the Sages permit it except for harvesting-baskets of figs[74]. Rebbi Simeon permits from a harvesting-basket of figs from which heave was taken but the Sages forbid.

72 As explained in Chapter 1, Mishnaiot 2 ff.

73 He holds that once heave was given, tithes also must be given even though the obligation of heave and tithes never starts before the end of processing.

74 Most figs are harvested for processing into fig cakes and dried figs. But, as the preceding two Mishnaiot show, some figs are used or sold directly from the basket used when harvesting the figs.

(fol. 49d) **הלכה ד:** מַה נָן קַייָמִין אִם בְּכַלְכָּלָה שֶׁל תְּאֵינִים דִּבְרֵי הַכֹּל אָסוּר. אִם בְּזֵיתִים עַל הַשֶּׁמֶן וַעֲנָבִים עַל הַיַּיִן דִּבְרֵי הַכֹּל מוּתָּר. אֶלָּא כִּי נָן קַייָמִין בִּתְמָרִים וְהוּא עָתִיד לְדוֹרְסָן. בִּגְרוֹגְרוֹת וְהוּא עָתִיד לְדוּשָׁן. רִבִּי לִיעֶזֶר אוֹמֵר תְּרוּמָה טוֹבֶלֶת בְּפֵירוֹת שֶׁלֹּא נִגְמְרָה מְלַאכְתָּן. וְרַבָּנִין אָמְרִין אֵין תְּרוּמָה טוֹבֶלֶת בְּפֵירוֹת שֶׁלֹּא נִגְמְרָה מְלַאכְתָּן.

Halakhah 4: Where do we hold? If about a harvesting-basket of figs, everybody agrees that it is forbidden[75]. If about oil olives and wine grapes, everybody agrees that it is permitted. But we deal with dates intended for pressing[76], dried figs intended for pressing[77]. Rebbi Eliezer says, heave creates *ṭevel*[78] of fruits not completely processed but the Sages say, heave does not create *ṭevel* of fruits not completely processed.

75 In the discussion between the Sages and R. Eliezer, disregarding the opinion of R. Simeon.

76 Into date cakes.

77 Into fig cakes. Tosephta 2:2 explicitly states that the disagreement between R. Eliezer and the Sages refers to these cases only. That Tosephta cannot have been the basis of the Yerushalmi.

78 Since heave was already given, this *ṭevel* refers only to tithes and the heave of the tithe contained in the First Tithe.

רִאשׁוֹן מַהוּ שֶׁיִּטְבּוֹל. מַה נָן קַייָמִין אִם בִּכְרִי שֶׁנִּתְמָרֵחַ דִּבְרֵי הַכֹּל אָסוּר. אִם בְּמַעֲשֵׂר רִאשׁוֹן שֶׁהִקְדִּימוֹ בְּשִׁבֳּלִין דִּבְרֵי הַכֹּל מוּתָּר. אֶלָּא כִּי נָן קַייָמִין בִּתְמָרִים וְהוּא עָתִיד לְדוֹרְסָן. בִּגְרוֹגְרוֹת וְהוּא עָתִיד לְדוּשָׁן. וְהִפְרִישׁ מֵהֶן תְּרוּמָה גְדוֹלָה וְנִמְלַךְ לַהֲנִיחָן כְּמוֹת שֶׁהֵן. וְעָבַר וְהִפְרִישׁ מֵהֶן רִאשׁוֹן. אִין תֵּימַר לְמַפְרֵיעַ נִטְבְּלוּ תְּרוּמָה שֶׁהִיא טוֹבֶלֶת. אִן תֵּימַר מִכָּן וְלָבֹא רִאשׁוֹן הוּא שֶׁהוּא טוֹבֵל.

Can First Tithe induce *ṭevel*[79]? Where do we hold? If about a grain heap that was smoothed, everybody holds that it is forbidden. If First Tithe was given from ears, everybody agrees[80] that it is permitted. But we deal with dates intended for pressing[76], large figs intended for pounding[77], of which he gave the Great Heave and then changed his mind to store them as they were. Then he transgressed[81] and gave First Tithe. If you say that *ṭevel* was created retroactively, the heave induces *ṭevel*. If you say that *ṭevel* is created from there onwards, the First Tithe induces *ṭevel*.

79 For Second Tithe or the tithe of the poor, depending on the year in the Sabbatical cycle.

80 Tosephta 2:2: "R. Eliezer concedes to the Sages that if somebody gave heave from ears but intends to thresh the grain, from grapes but intends to make wine, from olives but intends to make oil, he can eat snacks from them." The reason is that heave and tithes of grain are always referred to as "from the threshing floor" (*Num.* 15:20; 18:27,30) or "from flour" (*Deut.* 12:17, 14:23, 18:4). By biblical decree, nothing preceding the threshing may induce *ṭevel*. Similarly, the obligations on the grape and olive harvests are referred to as heave of "cider and oil" (*Deut.* 12:17, 14:23, 18:4).

81 Since he gave heave when it was not due, he should first give heave when it is due before giving First Tithe.

הַלּוֹקֵחַ תְּמָרִים וְהוּא עָתִיד לְדוֹרְסָן גְּרוֹגְרוֹת וְהוּא עָתִיד לְדוּשָׁן אָסוּר לוֹכַל מֵהֶן עֲרַאי. מְתַקְּנָן דְּמַאי דִּבְרֵי רִבִּי מֵאִיר. וַחֲכָמִים אוֹמְרִים אוֹכֵל מֵהֶן עֲרַאי וּמְתַקְּנָן וַדַּאי דִּבְרֵי רִבִּי יוֹסֵי. רִבִּי הִילָא רִבִּי לָעְזָר בְּשֵׁם חִילְפַיי. אָמַר רִבִּי יוֹנָה אַשְׁכְּחוֹן כְּתַב בְּפִינַקְסֵיהּ דְּחִילְפַיי אוֹכֵל מֵהֶן עֲרַאי וּמְתַקְּנָן וַדַּאי. וְקַשְׁיָא אִם אוֹכֵל מֵהֶן עֲרַאי מְתַקְּנָן וַדַּאי. אִם מְתַקְּנָן דְּמַאי יְהֵא אָסוּר לוֹכַל מֵהֶן עֲרַאי. רִבִּי יוֹסֵי בְּשֵׁם רִבִּי הִילָא אוֹכֵל מֵהֶן עֲרַאי מִשּׁוּם דָּבָר שֶׁלֹּא נִגְמְרָה מְלַאכְתּוֹ. וּמְתַקְּנָן וַדַּאי מִתּוֹךְ שֶׁיּוֹדֵעַ שֶׁבֵּיתוֹ טוֹבֵל אַף הוּא מַפְרִישׁ תְּרוּמָה מִשָּׁעָה רִאשׁוֹנָה.

"[82]If somebody buys dates to press them, dried figs to pound them, he may not eat a snack from them and must tithe as *demay*, the words of Rebbi Meïr. But the Sages say, he may eat a snack from them and must give tithes as certain, the words of Rebbi Yose[83]." Rebbi Hilai, Rebbi Lazar in the name of Hilfai; Rebbi Jonah said, it was found on the writing tablet of Hilfai[84]: He may eat a snack from them and gives tithes as certain[85]. This is difficult! If he may eat a snack from them[86], he should give certain tithes. If he tithes as *demay*[87], he should be forbidden to eat them as a snack! Rebbi Yose in the name of Rebbi Hila: He may eat them as snack because their processing is not finished[88]; he gives certain tithes[85] since he [the seller][89] knows that his house induces *ṭevel*, he will separate heave from the start.

82 Tosephta 2:3., reading of the Erfurt ms.

83 The last clause is missing in the Tosephta. The text here seems to be the conflation of a Tosephta in the name of the Sages and a *baraita* in the name of R. Yose. Since R. Yose (ben Ḥalaphta) determines practice, there is no difference in fact between Tosephta and *baraita*.

84 Two different opinions on the chain of transmission, whether oral or written.

85 This is the reading in both mss. and the *editio princeps*. However, the text requires that one read "tithes as *demay*".

86 This implies that the fruits are not yet processed; the obligation of tithes has not yet started and, therefore, the seller could not have given heave and tithes.

87 The seller certainly gave heave; the buyer may not eat from the produce before separating the heave of the tithe.

88 The obligation of heave did not start yet.

89 The vulgar seller knows that the house induces *ṭevel* because this is a biblical commandment. He does not know the requirement that the processing has to be finished since that is only a rabbinic interpretation of the verse.

אָמַר רִבִּי לְעָזָר בְּכַלְכָּלָה שֶׁלְּכָל־דָּבָר הִיא מַתְנִיתָא. רִבִּי שִׁמְעוֹן מַתִּיר מִקַּל וָחוֹמֶר. וּמַה אִם בְּשָׁעָה שֶׁיֵּשׁ עָלֶיהָ זִיקַת שְׁלֹשָׁה מַעְשְׂרוֹת אַתְּ אָמַר מוּתָּר. בְּשָׁעָה שֶׁאֵין עָלֶיהָ אֶלָּא זִיקַת שְׁנֵי מַעְשְׂרוֹת לֹא כָּל־שֶׁכֵּן. רִאשׁוֹן מַה הוּא

שֶׁיִּטְבּוֹל לַשֵּׁנִי. וּמָה אִם בְּשָׁעָה שֶׁיֵּשׁ עָלֶיהָ זִיקַת שְׁנֵי מַעְשְׂרוֹת אַתְּ אָמַר מוּתָּר. בְּשָׁעָה שֶׁאֵין עָלֶיהָ אֶלָּא זִיקַת מַעֲשֵׂר אֶחָד לֹא כָל־שֶׁכֵּן.

Rebbi Eleazar said, the Mishnah[90] deals with any harvesting-basket[91]. [92]"Rebbi Simeon permits by a reasoning *a fortiori*: Since you say it is permitted if it carries the potential obligation of three tithes[93], so much more if it carries only the potential obligation of two tithes.[94]" Does the First Tithe create *ṭevel* for the Second? Since you say it is permitted if it carries the potential obligation of two tithes, so much more if it carries only the potential obligation of one tithe.

90 The statement of R. Simeon in the last sentence of the Mishnah.

91 Not only of figs.

92 Tosephta 2:2; instead of the Yerushalmi stereotype לא כל שכן the Tosephta has the Babylonian דין הוא.

93 Great Heave, First and Second Tithes.

94 For him, heave does not create *ṭevel* for any produce whose processing was completed outside the farmhouse as long as the farmer intends to bring the produce to the house for storage.

(fol. 49b) **משנה ה:** הָאוֹמֵר לַחֲבֵירוֹ הֵילָךְ אִיסָּר זֶה וְתֵן לִי בוֹ חָמֵשׁ תְּאֵינִים לֹא יֹאכַל עַד שֶׁיְּעַשֵּׂר דִּבְרֵי רִבִּי מֵאִיר. רִבִּי יְהוּדָה אוֹמֵר אוֹכֵל אַחַת אַחַת וּפָטוּר וְאִם צֵירַף חַיָּב. אָמַר רִבִּי יְהוּדָה (fol. 49c) מַעֲשֶׂה בְּגִינַּת וְורָדִים שֶׁהָיְתָה בִירוּשָׁלַם וְהָיוּ תְאֵינֶיהָ נִמְכָּרוֹת מִשָּׁלֹשׁ וּמֵאַרְבַּע בְּאִיסָּר וְלֹא הִפְרִישׁוּ מִמֶּנָּה תְּרוּמָה וּמַעֲשֵׂר מֵעוֹלָם.

Mishnah 5: If somebody says to another person, here take this *as*[95] and give me five figs for it, he should not eat before he tithed, the words of Rebbi Meïr[96]. Rebbi Jehudah says, if he eats them singly he is free, if he takes them together[97] he is obligated. Rebbi Jehudah said, there is a story that a rose garden was in Jerusalem whose figs were sold three or four for an *as* and nobody ever gave heave and tithes for them[98].

95 A Roman coin, one twenty-fourth of a denar.

96 Since a sale induces *ṭevel*; cf. Note 5.

97 If he holds at least two figs simultaneously; cf. Note 21.

98 They were only used as single snacks.

(fol. 49d) **הלכה ה:** רִבִּי זְעִירָא בְשֵׁם רִבִּי יוֹחָנָן רִבִּי הִילָא בְשֵׁם רִבִּי לָעְזָר מַה פְלִיגִין בְּלוֹקֵט וְנוֹתֵן לוֹ. אֲבָל בְּלוֹקֵט לְאוֹכֶל כָּל־עַמָּא מוֹדֵיי שֶׁהוּא אוֹכֵל אַחַת אַחַת וּפָטוּר. וְאִם צֵירֵף חַייָב.

Halakhah 5: Rebbi Zeïra in the name of Rebbi Joḥanan, Rebbi Hila in the name of Rebbi Eleazar: They disagree if he gathers and delivers[99]. But if he gathers for [his own] food, everybody agrees that he eats one by one and is free, but if he takes them together he is obligated.

99 R. Meïr holds that a sale creates *ṭevel* if the gatherer collected to sell without knowing what the buyer would do. But if the figs are picked by the person who eats them, even R. Meïr will agree that the sale does not induce *ṭevel*.

רִבִּי הִילָא בְשֵׁם רִבִּי לָעְזָר כְּשֵׁם שֶׁהֵן חֲלוּקִין כָּאן כָּךְ חֲלוּקִין בַּחֲצַר בֵּית שְׁמִירָה דְּאָמַר רִבִּי יוֹחָנָן מִקַּח בְּחָצֵר בְּשַׁבָּת אֵינָהּ תּוֹרָה. רִבִּי אִימִּי בְשֵׁם רִבִּי שִׁמְעוֹן בֶּן לָקִישׁ הַמְחוּוָּר מִכּוּלָּן זוֹ חֲצַר בֵּית שְׁמִירָה.

Rebbi Hila in the name of Rebbi Eleazar: Just as they differ here they differ about a secure courtyard[100] since Rebbi Joḥanan said that [the rules of] buying, courtyard, and Sabbath are not biblical[101]. Rebbi Immi in the name of Rebbi Simeon ben Laqish, the most reasonable of these is the secure courtyard[102].

100 In Mishnah 3:5, R. Ismael declares that a Tyrian courtyard, defined as one where vessels are safe from being stolen, acts like a house for *ṭevel.*

101 Since they induce *ṭevel* only by rabbinic decree, R. Jehudah insists that leniencies are possible which would be impossible for biblical obligations. The problem here is that all tithes except those of grain, wine, and oil are rabbinical. R. Eliahu Fulda notes that the basic hypothesis in all tractates of *Zeraïm* is that the covenant of Nehemiah stipulates that all obligations on the Land be kept as if they were biblical.

For מִקַּח בְּחָצֵר בְּשַׁבָּת one should read מִקַּח וְחָצֵר וְשַׁבָּת . The mss. presuppose that both β and ו were pronounced */v/;* cf. S. Baer, סידור עבודת ישׂראל p. 565.

102 In the Babli, *Baba Meẓi'a* 88a, R. Joḥanan proves from *Deut.* 26:12: "they shall eat in your gates and be satiated," that any place inside the city gates, including courtyards, are places where food can be eaten which by necessity must be tithed. While this is incompatible with the position of R. Joḥanan here in the Yerushalmi, it may underlie the position of R. Simeon ben Laqish.

חֲבֵרַיָּה בְּשֵׁם רִבִּי יוֹחָנָן כָּךְ מֵשִׁיב רִבִּי יוּדָה אֶת רִבִּי מֵאִיר אֵין אַתְּ מוֹדֶה לִי בְּנוֹתֵן לִבְנוֹ שֶׁהוּא פָּטוּר. מַה לִי הַלּוֹקֵט וְנוֹתֵן לִבְנוֹ מַה לִי הַלּוֹקֵט וְנוֹתֵן לְאַחֵר. רִבִּי יוּדָן בָּעֵי מַה חֲמִית מֵימַר בְּלוֹקֵט וְנוֹתֵן לוֹ. אוֹ נֵימַר בְּלוֹקֵט וְאוֹכֵל. אָמַר רִבִּי מָנָא לֵית כָּאן בְּלוֹקֵט וְאוֹכֵל אֶלָּא בְּלוֹקֵט וְנוֹתֵן לוֹ. מִן הָדָא גִּינַּת וְוָרְדִין. אִית לָךְ מֵימַר גִּינַּת וְוָרְדִין בְּלוֹקֵט וְאוֹכֵל לֹא בְּלוֹקֵט וְנוֹתֵן לוֹ. אַף הָכָא בְּלוֹקֵט וְנוֹתֵן לוֹ דוּ אָמַר לֵיהּ אִין אַתְּ עֲלִיל אַתְּ מְקַלְקֵל וְוָרְדֶיהָ. מַתְנִיתָא פְלִיגָא עַל הֲוָיָה דְּרִבִּי מָנָא כַּרְמָא אֲנִי מוֹכֵר לָךְ אַף עַל פִּי שֶׁאֵין בּוֹ גְּפָנִים הֲרֵי זֶה מָכוּר שֶׁלֹּא מָכַר לוֹ אֶלָּא שְׁמוֹ. פַּרְדֵּיסָא אֲנִי מוֹכֵר לָךְ אַף עַל פִּי שֶׁאֵין בּוֹ אִילָנוֹת הֲרֵי זֶה מָכוּר שֶׁלֹּא מָכַר לוֹ אֶלָּא (fol. 50a) שְׁמוֹ.

The colleagues in the name of Rebbi Joḥanan: So did Rebbi Jehudah disprove Rebbi Meïr['s argument]: Do you not concede to me that one who gives to his son is free? What is the difference between gathering and giving to his son or gathering and giving to another person[103]? Rebbi Yudan asked: What did you see to say 'if he gathers and delivers,' can we not say 'if he gathers and eats'[104]? Rebbi Mana said, there cannot be "if he gathers and eats", only "if he gathers and delivers," because of that rose garden[105]. Can you say the rose garden [is a case of] gathering and eating? No, gathering and delivering! There also, he gathers and delivers because he[106] would say to him, if you enter you will damage its roses! A *baraita*[107] disagrees with Rebbi Mana's argument: "'I am selling you the vineyard', this is a valid sale even if there are no vines since he sells him [the real estate] by description. 'I am selling you the orchard', this is a valid sale even if there are no trees since he sells him [the real estate] by description[108].""

103 Since it was agreed in the first paragraph of this Halakhah that R. Meïr frees from tithes if not the fruits themselves but the right to gather them was bought, the fact that money changes hands between the farmer and a stranger but not between himself and his son becomes irrelevant.

104 In this case, R. Jehudah's reputed argument becomes irrelevant.

105 According to R. Mana, Rebbis Johanan and Eleazar cannot be correct.

106 The owner of the rose garden to the buyer of figs.

107 Tosephta *Baba Batra* 6:18 (in different order), Yerushalmi *Ketubot* 8:7 (fol. 32b), Babli *Baba Batra* 7a, *Baba Meẓi'a* 104a (both parallel the Tosephta).

108 The Babli adds a clarification: Only if the properties were known as "orchard" or "vineyard". In any case, it is shown that the "rose garden" need not contain any roses; R. Mana's argument is invalid and the statement of Rebbis Johanan and Eleazar stands.

(fol. 49c) **משנה ו:** הָאוֹמֵר לַחֲבֵירוֹ הֵילָךְ אִיסָּר זֶה בְּעֶשְׂרִים תְּאֵינִים שֶׁאָבוֹר לִי בּוֹרֵר וְאוֹכֵל. בְּאֶשְׁכּוֹל שֶׁאָבוֹר לִי מְגַרְגֵּר וְאוֹכֵל. בְּרִימּוֹן שֶׁאָבוֹר לִי פּוֹרֵט וְאוֹכֵל. בַּאֲבַטִּיחַ שֶׁאָבוֹר לִי סוֹפֵת וְאוֹכֵל. אֲבָל אִם אָמַר לוֹ בְּעֶשְׂרִים תְּאֵינִים

אֵילּוּ בִּשְׁנֵי אֶשְׁכּוֹלוֹת אֵילּוּ בִּשְׁנֵי רִימּוֹנִים אֵילּוּ בִּשְׁנֵי אֲבַטִּיחִים אֵילּוּ אוֹכֵל כְּדַרְכּוֹ וּפָטוּר מִפְּנֵי שֶׁקָּנָה בִּמְחוּבָּר לַקַּרְקַע.

Mishnah 6: If somebody says to another person, here take this *as* for twenty figs that I shall choose[109], he chooses and eats; for the bunch of grapes that I shall choose, he selects single grape berries and eats; for the pomegranate that I shall choose, he picks single kernels and eats; for the watermelon that I shall choose, he bites off and eats. But if he said, for these twenty figs, for these two bunches, for these two pomegranates, for these two watermelon, he eats as he is used to and he is free since he bought when it was still connected to the ground.

109 In this entire Mishnah, the fruits are still on the tree or, in the case of the watermelon, on the ground connected to their roots. In the first scenario, the fruits are chosen after the deal is closed; they are bought and, since buying induces *ṭevel*, when harvested are subject to heave and tithes. In order to avoid the heave, it is necessary that they not be harvested. This means that only single berries may be plucked, not the entire bunch, not even two grapes together; small slices must be cut off the watermelon and be eaten when the watermelon still sits on the ground connected to its root; the entire watermelon will be eaten. In most cases, this means that heave and tithes cannot be avoided if the fruit is not specified at the time of the sale.

In the second case the sale was concluded when there was no possibility of an obligation of heave and tithes; it is as if somebody buys an entire field of standing grain; when he harvests he is in the place of the original farmer and his produce will become subject to heave and tithes only when it is brought to storage after full processing.

(fol. 50a) **הלכה ה:** רִבִּי יוֹסֵי בְּשֵׁם רִבִּי יוֹחָנָן מְגַרְגֵּר אַחַת אַחַת וְהוֹלֵךְ וְאוֹכֵל. אָמַר לוֹ רִבִּי חִייָה בַּר וָוא וְכֵן רִבִּי עֲבִיד. תַּנֵּי בְּשֵׁם רִבִּי יוֹסֵי אֲבַטִּיחַ שֶׁשָּׁפַת בּוֹ אֲפִילוּ כָּל־שֶׁהוּא קְנָייו. רִבִּי יוֹנָה בָּעֵי אַף בְּרִמּוֹן כֵּן.

Halakhah 5: '[110]Rebbi Yose in the name of Rebbi Joḥanan: He plucks single berries[111] and eats. Rebbi Ḥiyya bar Abba said, that is what my teacher did. It was stated in the name of Rebbi Yose: If he bit off the minutest amount from a watermelon, he acquired it. Rebbi Jonah asked, does this also hold for a pomegranate[112]?

110 In the Leyden ms. and Venice print, this is the end of Halakhah 5.

111 But never two together.

112 The positive answer is too obvious to be noted since otherwise the fruit is lost.

(fol. 49c) **משנה ז**: הַשּׂוֹכֵר אֶת הַפּוֹעֵל לִקְצוֹת בִּתְאֵינִים אָמַר לוֹ עַל מְנָת שֶׁאוֹכַל תְּאֵינִים הוּא אוֹכֵל וּפָטוּר. עַל מְנָת שֶׁאוֹכַל אֲנִי וּבְנִי אוֹ שֶׁיֹּאכַל בְּנִי בִשְׂכָרִי הוּא אוֹכֵל וּפָטוּר וּבְנוֹ אוֹכֵל וְחַיָּיב. עַל מְנָת שֶׁאוֹכַל בִּשְׁעַת הַקְּצִיעָה וּלְאַחַר הַקְּצִיעָה. בִּשְׁעַת הַקְּצִיעָה אוֹכֵל וּפָטוּר לְאַחַר הַקְּצִיעָה אוֹכֵל וְחַיָּיב שֶׁאֵינוֹ אוֹכֵל מִן הַתּוֹרָה. זֶה הַכְּלָל הָאוֹכֵל מִן הַתּוֹרָה פָּטוּר וְשֶׁאֵינוֹ אוֹכֵל מִן הַתּוֹרָה חַיָּיב.

Mishnah 7: If somebody hires a worker to slice figs; if that one told him, on condition that I may eat from the figs, he eats and is free; on condition that I and my son will eat, or that my son may eat in lieu of my wages, he may eat and is free, and his son may eat but is obligated; on condition that I may eat while cutting and after cutting, while cutting he eats and is free, after cutting he eats and is obligated since he does not eat because of the Torah. That is the principle: He who eats because of the Torah is free[113]; if he does not eat because of the Torah he is obligated.

113 The agricultural worker is always permitted to eat from the produce he is harvesting or processing, *Deut*. 23:25,26. But after he is finished

working he has no right to eat, nor has his son, unless he pays for the produce. But then he eats because of a commercial transaction and is obligated for heave and tithes.

(fol. 50a) **הלכה ו:** לָמָּה לִי עַל מְנָת אֲפִילוּ שֶׁלֹּא עַל מְנָת. רִבִּי אָבִין בְּשֵׁם רִבִּי שַׁמַּי לָכֵן צְרִיכָה אֲפִילוּ אָמַר לוֹ עַל מְנָת.

Halakhah 6: Why do I need "on condition"? Even without "on condition"[114]! Rebbi Avin in the name of Rebbi Shammai: It is necessary, even if he says "on condition"[115]!

114 Since he eats by biblical decree, there is no need to stipulate.

115 The Mishnah does not state a condition, that the worker may only eat if he stipulates so, but a leniency: Even if the worker stipulates and it looks like a commercial transaction, that stipulation, being unnecessary, is being disregarded and he eats by biblical decree, not by buying. This naturally means that the worker must stay within the bounds of the biblical decree, whose details are explained in the following paragraphs, in order to remain free from heave and tithes.

תַּמָּן תַּנִּינָן הָיָה עוֹשֶׂה בְּיָדָיו אֲבָל לֹא בְּרַגְלָיו. בְּרַגְלָיו אֲבָל לֹא בְּיָדָיו אֲפִילוּ עַל כְּתֵיפוֹ הֲרֵי זֶה יֹאכַל. וְתַנֵּי כֵן בְּיָדָיו אוֹגֵד בְּרַגְלָיו מְקַמֵּץ.[116] אֲפִילוּ עַל כְּתֵיפוֹ טוֹעֵן. רִבִּי יוֹסֵי בֵּי רִבִּי יְהוּדָה אוֹמֵר עַד שֶׁיַּעֲשֶׂה בְּיָדָיו וּבְרַגְלָיו וּבְגוּפוֹ כְּדַיִישׁ מַה דַּיִישׁ שֶׁהוּא עוֹשֶׂה בְּיָדָיו וּבְרַגְלָיו וּבְגוּפוֹ אַף כָּל־דָּבָר שֶׁהוּא עוֹשֶׂה בְּיָדָיו וּבְרַגְלָיו וּבְגוּפוֹ. דַּיִישׁ מַה דַּיִישׁ מְיוּחָד שֶׁהוּא בְּתָלוּשׁ אַף כָּל־שֶׁהוּא בְּתָלוּשׁ. יָצָא הַמְנַכֵּשׁ בְּשׁוּם וּבִבְצָלִים וְהַמְסַמֵּךְ בִּגְפָנִים וְהָעוֹדֵר תַּחַת הַזֵּיתִים. דַּיִישׁ מַה דַּיִישׁ מְיוּחָד שֶׁגִּידּוּלָיו מִן הָאָרֶץ אַף כָּל־דָּבָר שֶׁגִּידּוּלָיו מִן הָאָרֶץ. יָצָא הַחוֹלֵב וְהַמְגַבֵּן וְהַמְחַבֵּץ. דַּיִישׁ מַה דַּיִישׁ מְיוּחָד דָּבָר שֶׁלֹּא נִגְמְרָה מְלַאכְתּוֹ אַף כָּל־דָּבָר שֶׁלֹּא נִגְמְרָה מְלַאכְתּוֹ. יָצָא הַבּוֹדֵל בִּתְמָרִים וְהַמְפָרֵד בִּגְרוֹגְרוֹת וְהַיַּיִן מִשֶּׁיִּקְפֶּה וְהַשֶּׁמֶן מִשֶּׁיֵּרֵד לְעוּקָה. דַּיִישׁ מַה דַּיִישׁ מְיוּחָד שֶׁלֹּא בָא לְזִיקַת הַמַּעְשְׂרוֹת. אַף כָּל־דָּבָר שֶׁלֹּא בָא לְזִיקַת הַמַּעְשְׂרוֹת. יָצָא הַלָּשׁ וְהַמְקַטֵּף וְהָאוֹפֶה.

There[117], we have stated: "If he worked with his hands but not with his feet, with his feet but not with his hands, even on his shoulder, he eats." We have stated about this, with his hands he makes bundles, with his feet he creates support, even on his shoulder he carries. "Rebbi Yose ben Rebbi Jehudah says, only if he works with his hands, feet, and body," as in threshing where he works with his hands, feet, and body, so for anything he works with his hands, feet, and body.

[118]Threshing, just as threshing is particular in that it applies to plucked [grain], so for anything plucked. This excludes him who thins among garlic and onions, makes supports for vines, and weeds under an olive tree.

Threshing, just as threshing is particular in that it applies to growth from the earth, so for anything growing from the earth. This excludes him who milks, makes cheese, or churns milk.

Threshing, just as threshing is particular in that it does not apply after processing, so for anything not after processing. This excludes him who separates dates or dried figs[119], wine after it is fermented and olive oil when it descends into the vat.

Threshing, just as threshing is particular in that it applies before the obligation of tithes, so for anything before the obligation of tithes[120]. This excludes him who kneads dough, separates[121], or bakes.

116 Reading of the Rome ms. and the parallel in *Baba Meẓi'a* 7:2, fol. 11b. Leyden and Venice: מסמיך "makes supports".

117 Mishnah *Baba Meẓi'a* 7:4.

118 Threshing refers to *Deut*. 25:4: "You may not muzzle an ox while he is threshing." This is discussed in the Yerushalmi (here and *Baba Meẓi'a* 7:2, fol. 11b), the Babli *Baba Meẓi'a* 89a, Sifry *Deut*. 287, and the Tosephta *Baba Meẓi'a* 8:7. The Yerushalmi sources (Yerushalmi, Sifry, and part of the Tosephta) take "threshing" as the catch

word; Babylonian sources (Babli and part of the Tosephta) refer to "an ox". The Yerushalmi part of the Tosephta, a text lacking the rethorical formulas, is reproduced in Yerushalmi *Baba Meẓi'a* 7:2. The list of exclusions, without its justification, is Mishnah *Baba Meẓi'a* 7:2.

Tosephta 2:16 allows the workers to eat the onion or garlic plants which they remove for thinning.

119 According to Rashi (*Baba Meẓi'a* 89a) using an instrument.

120 Babylonian sources add "the obligation of *ḥallah*", referring to countries outside the Land. Since flour is not under the obligation of *ḥallah* as long as it is not kneaded as dough, the expression "before the obligation of" is shorthand for "anything not under the obligation at the start of work." This applies also to the Yerushalmi version since the farmhand who turns threshed and winnowed grain into an orderly heap may eat from the grain even though at the end of his work the heap is subject to heave and tithes.

121 Separates the dough into smaller loaves for baking.

כְּתִיב כִּי תָבֹא בְּקָמַת רֵעֶךָ. יָכוֹל בִּשְׁאָר כָּל־אָדָם הַכָּתוּב מְדַבֵּר. תַּלְמוּד לוֹמַר וְחֶרְמֵשׁ לֹא תָנִיף עַל קָמַת רֵעֶךָ. אֶת שֶׁיֵּשׁ לוֹ רְשׁוּת לְהָנִיף וְאֵי זֶה זֶה הַפּוֹעֵל. אִיסִּי בֶּן עֲקַבְיָה אוֹמֵר בִּשְׁאָר כָּל־אָדָם הַכָּתוּב מְדַבֵּר מַה תַלְמוּד לוֹמַר וְחֶרְמֵשׁ לֹא תָנִיף מִכָּאן שֶׁאֵין לוֹ רְשׁוּת לֶאֱכוֹל אֶלָּא בִשְׁעַת הֲנָפַת מַגָּל. תַּנֵּי רִבִּי שִׁמְעוֹן בֶּן יוֹחַי אוֹמֵר עַד אֵיכָן דִּקְדְּקָה הַתּוֹרָה בְגֶזֶל שֶׁצְּרִיכָה לָדוּן בֵּין אָדָם לַחֲבֵירוֹ עַד כְּדֵי הֲנָפַת מַגָּל כֵּן גְּדוֹלָה מְלָאכָה שֶׁלֹּא חָרַב דּוֹר הַמַּבּוּל אֶלָּא עַד מִפְּנֵי הַגֶּזֶל. וּפוֹעֵל עוֹשֶׂה בִּמְלַאכְתּוֹ וְאוֹכֵל וּפָטוּר מִן הַגֶּזֶל.

[122]It is written (*Deut.* 23:26): "If you come into your neighbor's standing grain." I could think that this means everybody; the verse says "do not swing a sickle over your neighbor's standing grain," he who has permission to swing a sickle, that means the laborer. Issy ben Aqabiah says, the verse speaks about everybody. Why does the verse say, "do not swing a sickle over your neighbor's standing grain?" He has no right except at the time of swinging the sickle[123]. It was stated[124]: Rebbi Simeon ben Iohai says, how far was the Torah careful about robbery that

it judged between a human and his neighbor about a swing of the sickle! How great is labor, since the generation of the Flood was destroyed only because of robbery, but the laborer does his work, eats, and is free of any robbery!

122 Similar texts in Sifry *Deut.* 266, 267; Babli *Baba Meẓi'a* 87b.

123 It seems that Issy ben Aqabiah's text is corrupt. The Rome text reads: אִיסִי בֶּן עֲקַבְיָה אוֹמֵר בִּשְׁאָר כָּל־אָדָם הַכָּתוּב מְדַבֵּר מַה פּוֹעֵל יֵשׁ לוֹ רְשׁוּת לְהָנִיף אַתְּ אָמוּר וּשְׁאָר כָּל־בְּנֵי אָדָן שֶׁאֵין לָהֶם רְשׁוּת לְהָנִיף לֹא כָּל־שֶׁכֵּן מַה תַּלְמוּד לוֹמַר וְחֶרְמֵשׁ לֹא תָנִיף מִכָּאן שֶׁאֵין לוֹ רְשׁוּת לֶאֱכוֹל אֶלָּא בִּשְׁעַת הֲנָפַת מַגָּל. . . "Issy ben Aqabiah says, the verse speaks about everybody. Since you speak about the laborer who has the right to swing the sickle, so much more other people who have no right to swing the sickle. The verse says 'do not swing a sickle over your neighbor's standing grain,' he has no right except at the time of swinging the sickle."

In this version, Issy ben Aqabiah agrees that only the laborer has the right to eat from the farmer's harvest and only at harvest time; this is the position of Aqabiah ben Mehalalel, *Midrash Haggadol Deut.*, ed. S. Fish (Jerusalem 1975) p. 533 = *Midrash Tannaïm*, ed. Hoffmann, p. 153.

124 This *baraita* is not found in any other source.

כְּתִיב לֹא תַחְסוֹם שׁוֹר בְּדִישׁוֹ. אֵין לִי אֶלָּא שׁוֹר בְּתָלוּשׁ וְאָדָם בִּמְחוּבָּר אָדָם מַהוּ שֶׁיֹּאכַל בְּתָלוּשׁ. מַה אִם הַשּׁוֹר שֶׁאֵינוֹ אוֹכֵל בִּמְחוּבָּר הֲרֵי הוּא אוֹכֵל בְּתָלוּשׁ. אָדָם שֶׁהוּא אוֹכֵל בִּמְחוּבָּר אֵינוֹ דִין שֶׁיֹּאכַל בְּתָלוּשׁ. תַּלְמוּד לוֹמַר לֹא תַחְסוֹם שׁוֹר בְּדִישׁוֹ. שׁוֹר בְּלֹא תַחְסוֹם וְאֵין אָדָם בְּלֹא תַחְסוֹם. שׁוֹר מַהוּ שֶׁיֹּאכַל בִּמְחוּבָּר. מַה אָדָם שֶׁאֵינוֹ אוֹכֵל בְּתָלוּשׁ אוֹכֵל בִּמְחוּבָּר שׁוֹר שֶׁהוּא אוֹכֵל בְּתָלוּשׁ אֵינוֹ דִין שֶׁיֹּאכַל בִּמְחוּבָּר. אוֹ מַה כָּאן בְּלֹא תַחְסוֹם אַף כָּאן בְּלֹא תַחְסוֹם. תַּלְמוּד לוֹמַר לֹא תַחְסוֹם שׁוֹר בְּדִישׁוֹ. בְּדִישׁוֹ אֵין אַתְּ חוֹסְמוֹ. אֲבָל חוֹסְמוֹ אַתְּ בִּמְחוּבָּר לְקַרְקַע.

[125]It is written (*Deut.* 25:4): "Do not muzzle an ox while he is threshing." Is there only an ox in the cut and a human in the standing[126]?

May a human eat from the cut[127]? If an ox which does not eat from the standing may eat from the cut, a human who may eat from the standing should *a fortiori* be able to eat from the cut. The verse says, "do not muzzle an ox while he is threshing." To an ox applies "do not muzzle"; to a human "do not muzzle" does not apply.

May an ox eat from the standing[128]? If a human who does not eat from the cut may eat from the standing, an ox which may eat from the cut should *a fortiori* be able to eat from the standing. This means, if "do not muzzle" applies to one case, it also should apply to the other. The verse says, "do not muzzle an ox while he is threshing." You may not muzzle him when he is threshing but you may muzzle him for what is standing on the ground.

125 A similar argument is in Babli *Baba Meẓi'a* 88b.

126 Only cut grain can be threshed, so the ox certainly eats from cut grain when threshing. Since it was established that the laborer may eat during the harvest, there is no reason to require that he eat only from the remaining standing grain and not from the ears already cut. Therefore, he certainly may eat from cut grain on condition that some be still standing; Mishnah *Baba Meẓi'a* 7:2.

127 After the harvest has been completed.

128 May an ox be muzzled working the field?

מִכָּן אָֽמְרוּ קוֹצֵץ הוּא אָדָם עַל יְדֵי עַצְמוֹ עַל יְדֵי בְנוֹ וּבִתּוֹ הַגְּדוֹלִים וְעַל יְדֵי עַבְדּוֹ וְשִׁפְחָתוֹ הַגְּדוֹלִים וְעַל יְדֵי אִשְׁתּוֹ מִפְּנֵי שֶׁיֵּשׁ בָּהֶן דַּעַת. אֲבָל אֵינוֹ קוֹצֵץ לֹא יְדֵי בְנוֹ וּבִתּוֹ הַקְּטַנִּים וְלֹא עַל יְדֵי עַבְדּוֹ וְשִׁפְחָתוֹ הַקְּטַנִּים וְלֹא עַל יְדֵי בְהֶמְתּוֹ מִפְּנֵי שֶׁאֵין בָּהֶן דַּעַת.

From here[129] they said, [130]"a person may renounce for himself, his adult son or daughter, or his adult male or female slave, or his wife, because they have a mind. But he may not renounce for his minor son or daughter, or his minor male or female slave, or his animal[131], because they have no mind."

129 The Mishnah which states that a laborer can sign away his right to eat from the harvest for a financial consideration. Then he can also hire out his adult children or slaves without right to eat for additional payment. If he would sell himself as a Hebrew slave (assuming that the Jubilee laws are in effect, cf. *Ševiït* 1:1, Note 7), he could stipulate in exchange for a lump sum payment that his wife would not be supported by his master.

130 Mishnah *Baba Meẓi'a* 7:6. That Mishnah is not discussed in either Talmud.

131 He cannot rent out his animal for threshing and stipulate that it may be muzzled.

לֹא צְרִיכָא הָאוֹכֵל מִן הַתּוֹרָה יְהֵא חַיָּב. אָמַר רִבִּי יוֹנָה הַתּוֹרָה פְּטָרָה אוֹתוֹ.

He who eats by biblical decree, should he not be obligated[132]? Rebbi Jonah said, the Torah freed him[133].

132 Since the laborer may eat from the harvest as the result of a contract between himself and the farmer, did he not acquire the right to eat by executing the contract (even if oral) and should he not be treated as buyer of the fruit he is eating and be obligated for heave and tithes?

133 Since the verses treat his eating as integral part of the harvest, the (rabbinic) obligation of a buyer cannot be applied here.

(fol. 49c) **משנה ח:** הָיָה עוֹשֶׂה בַּלְּבָסִים לֹא יֹאכַל בִּבְנוֹת שֶׁבַע. בִּבְנוֹת שֶׁבַע לֹא יֹאכַל בַּלְּבָסִים. אֲבָל מוֹנֵעַ הוּא אֶת עַצְמוֹ עַד שֶׁהוּא מַגִּיעַ לִמְקוֹם הַיָּפוֹת וְאוֹכֵל. הַמַּחֲלִיף עִם חֲבֵירוֹ זֶה לוֹכַל וְזֶה לוֹכַל. זֶה לִקְצוֹת וְזֶה לִקְצוֹת. זֶה לוֹכַל וְזֶה לִקְצוֹת חַיָּב. רִבִּי יְהוּדָה אוֹמֵר הַמַּחֲלִיף לוֹכַל חַיָּב וְלִקְצוֹת פָּטוּר.

Mishnah 8: If he was working with *lĕbāsîm*[134] he should not eat *benôt ševa'*[135] and vice-versa. But he may hold back until he reaches the place of good ones and eat there. If somebody switches with another person[136] so that each one eats directly, or each one cuts[137], or one eats and one cuts, he is obligated. Rebbi Jehudah says, he who exchanges to eat is obligated, to cut is free.

134 The Mishnah mss. have לבסים, לובסים, לכסים, בלוסים, כלופסין. These are cooking quality figs irrespective of the strain, cf. Arabic بَلَس *balas* "cooking dates".

135 Light green delicacy figs. Since these two qualities are distinct for commercial purposes, they are distinct for the laborer.

136 Two tree owners; their barter is a commercial transaction and induces *ṭevel*.

137 He prepares the figs to be dried into fig cakes. R. Jehudah holds that in this case the processing is not completed and a commercial transaction does not induce *ṭevel*, cf. Note 80.

(fol. 50a) **הלכה ז**: תַּמָּן תַּנִּינָן הָיָה עוֹשֶׂה בִתְאֵינִים לֹא יֹאכַל בַּעֲנָבִים. בַּעֲנָבִים לֹא יֹאכַל בִּתְאֵינִים. וְתַנֵּי עֲלָהּ הָיָה עוֹשֶׂה בְּיִיחוּר זֶה לֹא יֹאכַל בְּיִיחוּר אַחֵר. וְתַנִּינָן הָיָה עוֹשֶׂה בִּכְלוּסִין לֹא יֹאכַל בִּבְנוֹת שֶׁבַע. בִּבְנוֹת שֶׁבַע לֹא יֹאכַל בִּכְלוּסִין לֹא כֵן צְרִיכָה אֲפִילוּ שְׁתֵּיהֶן בְּיִיחוּר אֶחָד.

Halakhah 7: There[138], we have stated: "When he is working on figs he should not eat grapes, on grapes he should not eat figs." On that, we stated: If he is working on one branch, he should not eat from another branch[139]. Also, we have stated: "When he is working with *lĕbāsîm* he should not eat *benôt ševa'* and vice-versa." This is needed, even if both are on the same branch.

138 Mishnah *Baba Meẓi'a* 7:4.

139 The Babli, *Baba Meẓi'a* 91b, only notes that if he is working on one vine, he should not eat from another vine.

כְּתִיב כִּי תָבֹא בְּכֶרֶם רֵעֶךָ. יָכוֹל בִּשְׁאָר כָּל־הָאָדָם הַכָּתוּב מְדַבֵּר תַּלְמוּד לוֹמַר וְאֶל כֶּלְיְךָ לֹא תִתֵּן. אֲבָל נוֹתֵן אַתְּ לְכֵילָיו שֶׁל חֲבֵירְךָ. וְאֵי זֶה זֶה הַפּוֹעֵל. וְאָכַלְתָּ עֲנָבִים. וְכִי אֵין אָנוּ יוֹדְעִין שֶׁאֵין בְּכֶרֶם לוֹכַל אֶלָּא עֲנָבִים. מַה תַּלְמוּד לוֹמַר וְאָכַלְתָּ עֲנָבִים. אֶלָּא מִכָּן שֶׁאִם הָיָה עוֹשֶׂה בִּתְאֵנִים לֹא יֹאכַל בַּעֲנָבִים. בַּעֲנָבִים לֹא יֹאכַל בִּתְאֵנִים. כְּנַפְשְׁךָ. כָּל־דָּבָר שֶׁהַיֶּצֶר תָּאֵב. כְּנַפְשְׁךָ כָּל־דָּבָר שֶׁהוּא פָּטוּר מִן הַמַּעְשְׂרוֹת. מַה אַתְּ אוֹכֵל וּפָטוּר אַף פּוֹעֵל אוֹכֵל וּפָטוּר. כְּנַפְשְׁךָ מִיכָּן שֶׁלֹּא יֹאכַל הַפּוֹעֵל יוֹתֵר עַל שְׂכָרוֹ. מִיכָּן הָיָה רִבִּי אֶלְעָזָר חִסְמָא אוֹמֵר לֹא יֹאכַל הַפּוֹעֵל יוֹתֵר עַל שְׂכָרוֹ וַחֲכָמִים מַתִּירִין.[140]. מְנַיִין שֶׁנַּפְשׁוֹ קְרוּיָה שְׂכָרוֹ. רִבִּי אַבָּהוּ בְּשֵׁם רִבִּי[141] יוֹסֵי בֶּן חֲנִינָה נֶאֱמַר כָּאן נַפְשׁוֹ וְנֶאֱמַר לְהַלָּן נַפְשׁוֹ דִּכְתִיב וְאֵילָיו הוּא נוֹשֵׂא אֶת נַפְשׁוֹ. מַה נַּפְשׁוֹ הָאֲמוּרָה לְהַלָּן שְׂכָרוֹ אַף כָּאן שְׂכָרוֹ. שָׂבְעֶךָ. שֶׁלֹּא יְהֵא אוֹכֵל וּמֵקִיא. שָׂבְעֶךָ שֶׁלֹּא יְהֵא מְקַלֵּף בִּתְאֵינִים וּמְצַמֵּץ בָּעֲנָבִים.

[142]It is written (*Deut.* 23:25): "If you come into your neighbor's vineyard[143]." I could think that this means everybody; the verse says: "Do not put into your own vessel," but you may put into somebody else's vessel. Who is this? This is the laborer[144]. "You may eat grapes." Do we not know that in a vineyard there is nothing to eat but grapes? Why does the verse say, you may eat *grapes*[145]? From here [it follows] that if he works fig trees he cannot eat grapes, vines he cannot eat figs. "All your soul's desire," all that your inclination may be. "All your soul's desire," anything that is free from tithes. What you eat without obligation also the laborer may eat without obligation[146]. "All your soul's desire," from here that the laborer should not eat more than the value of his wages. From here did Rebbi Eleazar Ḥisma[147] deduce that the laborer should not eat more than the value of his wages, but the Sages permit it. From where that his wages are called his soul? Rebbi Abbahu in the name of Rebbi Yose ben Ḥanina, it says here "his soul" and it says at another place "his soul" as it is written (*Deut.* 24:15): "For that he carries his soul." Just

as "his soul" there means his wages, so here "his soul" means his wages. "Until you are satiated," that he should not eat and vomit[148]. "Until you are satiated," that he should not peel figs or suck out grapes[149].

140 Reading of the Rome ms. and all parallel texts; missing in Leyden ms. and Venice print.

141 Reading of the Rome ms. Leyden and Venice: רבי חנינה יוסי בן חנינה.

142 A different text with similar meaning in *Sifry Deut.* 266; a different *baraita* Babli *Baba Meẓi'a* 87b.

143 The verse reads: If you come into your neighbor's vineyard you may eat grapes to all your soul's desire until you are satiated, but do not put anything into your own vessel.

144 Who harvests into the farmer's vessel.

145 What is the practical difference between "you may eat in the vineyard" and "you may eat grapes in the vineyard"? The same argument Yerushalmi *Baba Meẓi'a* 7:5.

146 This and the following parallel argument refer כנפשך to the employer's soul and desire, not the laborer's. This interpretation is also in all parallel sources.

147 A Tanna of the third generation, student of R. Joshua in the Academy of Jabneh. His statement is in Mishnah *Baba Meẓi'a* 7:4, Tosephta *Baba Meẓi'a* 8:8.

148 He should not induce vomiting to free his stomach for more food.

149 Tosephta *Baba Meẓi'a* 8:8. The laborer has to eat all that is edible.

רַשָּׁאִין הַפּוֹעֲלִין לְטַבֵּל פִּתָּן[150] בְּצִיר בִּשְׁבִיל שֶׁיֹּאכְלוּ עֲנָבִים הַרְבֵּה. רַשַּׁאי בַּעַל הַבַּיִת לְהַשְׁקוֹתָן יַיִן בִּשְׁבִיל שֶׁלֹּא יֹאכְלוּ עֲנָבִים הַרְבֵּה. רַשַּׁאי בַּעַל הַפָּרָה לְהַרְעִיבָהּ בַּלַּיְלָה בִּשְׁבִיל שֶׁתֹּאכַל הַרְבֵּה בְּשָׁעָה שֶׁהִיא דָשָׁה. רַשַּׁאי בַּעַל הַבַּיִת לְהַאֲכִילָהּ פְּקִיעֵי עָמִיר שֶׁלֹּא תֹאכַל הַרְבֵּה בְּשָׁעָה שֶׁהִיא דָשָׁה. רִבִּי אַבָּהוּ אָמַר הִתְרִיגוּ לַבְּהֶמִין. רִבִּי חֲנַנְיָה מֵייכְלוֹן דְּבֵילָה. רִבִּי מָנָא מֵיכְלוֹן אִיסְטָפֵנִינֵי.

[151]"The laborers are permitted to dip their bread in sauce so they should eat more grapes. The employer is permitted to give them wine to drink so they should eat less grapes. The owner of a cow is permitted to starve her through the night so she should eat much while threshing. The

employer is permitted to feed her bundles of straw so she should not eat much while threshing." Rebbi Abbahu said, give citrus to the animals! Rebbi Ḥanania fed them fig cake. Rebbi Mana fed them carrots[152].

150 Reading of the Rome ms., the Tosephta and the Babli. Leyden and Venice: עמו.

151 Tosephta *Baba Meẓi'a* 8:3,4; Babli *Baba Meẓi'a* 89a, 90b.

152 Cf. *Demay* 2, Note 63.

תַּנֵּי רִבִּי חִיָּיה אוֹכֵל פּוֹעֵל אֶשְׁכּוֹל רִאשׁוֹן. תַּנֵּי אֶשְׁכּוֹל אַחֲרוֹן. רִבִּי שְׁמוּאֵל בְּשֵׁם רִבִּי הִילָא נְתָנוֹ לְסַל אָסוּר. אָמַר רִבִּי יוֹסֵי לֹא כֵן צְרִיכָה בְּשֶׁהָיָה הוּא בוֹצֵר וְאַחֵר מוֹלִיךְ. אֲבָל אִם הָיָה הוּא בוֹצֵר הוּא מוֹלִיךְ בִּתְחִילָּה אוֹכֵל מִשּׁוּם הִילְכוֹת מְדִינָה. וְלִבְסוֹף אוֹכֵל מִשּׁוּם הַפּוֹעֲלִין אוֹכְלִין בַּהֲלִיכָתָן מֵאוּמָן לְאוּמָן. וּבַחֲזִירָתָן לְגַת וּבַחֲמוֹר שֶׁתְּהֵא פוֹרֶקֶת.

Rebbi Ḥiyya stated: The laborer may eat the first bunch of grapes[153]. It was stated, the last bunch. Rebbi Samuel in the name of Rebbi Hila: If he put it in the basket it is forbidden. Rebbi Yose said, that needs to be said if he harvests and another transports[154]. But if he harvests and transports originally[155] he eats because of local usage[156]. At the end he eats because of "[157]the laborers eat when they go from one row to the next and when they return to the winepress, and the donkey[158] until it is unloaded."

153 Even before he harvested one bunch for his employer. A similar text in Tosephta *Baba Meẓi'a* 8:8. Therefore, R. Ḥiyya is R. Ḥiyya the elder.

154 In that case, his work on the bunch is finished the moment it is put into the basket; it no longer is his harvest.

155 From one vine to the next or to the winepress.

156 Not by biblical decree. Therefore, this rule is valid only where it is included in the standard labor contract by local custom.

157 Mishnah *Baba Meẓi'a* 7:5. This rule is justified in the Babli (*Baba Meẓi'a* 91b) as being in the employer's interest, so that the laborers are free to

work when they arrive at the next row. This means that this rule also may be modified according to local custom.

158 If an animal carries food and if it can turn its head and eat from it, one is forbidden by biblical law to prevent it from eating.

תַּנֵּי מַעֲרִים אָדָם עַל פּוֹעֲלָיו לִהְיוֹת אוֹכְלִין תֵּשַׁע וְקוֹצִין אַחַת. אִית תַּנָּיֵי תַּנֵּי קוֹצִין תֵּשַׁע וְאוֹכְלִין אַחַת. נִיחָא אוֹכְלִין תֵּשַׁע וְקוֹצִין אַחַת. קוֹצִין תֵּשַׁע וְאוֹכְלִין אַחַת. אָמַר רִבִּי אָבִין שֶׁלֹּא תֹאמַר יֵעָשֶׂה כִּלְאַחַר גְּמַר מְלָאכָה וִיהֵא חַייָב.

It was stated: A person may use a trick so his workers will eat ten and cut one[159]. Some Tannaïm stated: That they will cut ten and eat one. We understand "that they will eat ten and cut one." But "that they will cut ten and eat one"[160]? Rebbi Abin said, that you should not say it is as if done after the end of their work, and it should be obligated[161].

159 Explanation of R. Eliahu Fulda: If somebody wants to give figs to another person he employs him pro forma. Then the other may eat as much as he likes without tithing as long as he cuts a fig from the tree, i. e., harvests something for the giver.

160 If the recipients perform real work, what is the trick?

161 Since the other person is not a real laborer, without the trick it would be a gift which is subject to heave and tithes.

נִיחָא לֶאֱכוֹל חַייָב לִקְצוֹת חַייָב. אָמַר רִבִּי לָעְזָר רִבִּי מֵאִיר הִיא דְּרִבִּי מֵאִיר אוֹמֵר מִקַּח טוֹבֵל בְּפֵירוֹת שֶׁלֹּא נִגְמְרָה מְלַאכְתָּן. אָמַר (fol. 50b) רִבִּי לָעְזָר רִבִּי מֵאִיר וְרִבִּי לִיעֶזֶר שְׁנֵיהֶן אָמְרוּ דָבָר אֶחָד. כְּמָה דְרִבִּי לִיעֶזֶר אָמַר תְּרוּמָה טוֹבֶלֶת בְּפֵירוֹת שֶׁלֹּא נִגְמְרָה מְלַאכְתָּן. כֵּן רִבִּי מֵאִיר אָמַר מִקַּח טוֹבֵל בְּפֵירוֹת שֶׁלֹּא נִגְמְרָה מְלַאכְתָּן.

We understand that eating may be obligated, but should cutting be obligated? Rebbi Eleazar said, this is Rebbi Meïr's since Rebbi Meïr says trade induces *ṭevel* in produce not completely processed[162]. Rebbi Eleazar said, Rebbi Meïr and Rebbi Eliezer both said the same[163]. As Rebbi Eliezer said, heave induces *ṭevel* in produce not completely processed so Rebbi Meïr said trade induces *ṭevel* in produce not completely processed.

162 This paragraph refers back to the Mishnah which states that if people exchange their harvests they are obligated for tithes according to the Sages.

163 It is not really the same. R. Eleazar proclaims that R. Eliezer and R. Meïr will rule the same way in both cases.

המעביר תאנים פרק שלישי

(fol. 50b) **משנה א**: הַמַּעֲבִיר תְּאֵנִים בַּחֲצֵירוֹ לִקְצוֹת בָּנָיו וּבְנֵי בֵיתוֹ אוֹכְלִין וּפְטוּרִין. וְהַפּוֹעֲלִין שֶׁעִמּוֹ בִּזְמַן שֶׁאֵין לָהֶן עָלָיו מְזוֹנוֹת. אֲבָל אִם יֵשׁ לָהֶם עָלָיו מְזוֹנוֹת הֲרֵי אֵילּוּ לֹא יֹאכֵלוּ.

Mishnah 1: If somebody transports figs through his courtyard to cut them into pieces[1], his children and companions[2] may eat and they are free[3]; the same holds for laborers who work for him[4] as long as they cannot claim their meals from him. But those who can claim their meals from him may not eat.

1 They are not fully processed and the courtyard does not induce *ṭevel.*

2 This certainly includes his wife; it may also include hired domestic servants.

3 Since the figs are not fully processed there is no reason to require them to tithe.

4 They work on other tasks, not in processing the figs. Therefore, there is no biblical law that permits them to eat. If their meals are part of their wages the employer would pay his debts with untithed fruits and this is forbidden.

(fol. 50b) **הלכה א**: הוּא עַצְמוֹ מַהוּ שֶׁיֹּאכַל. רַב אָמַר הוּא אָסוּר לוֹכַל. עוּלָּא בְּרִבִּי יִשְׁמָעֵאל בְּשֵׁם רִבִּי לָעְזָר הַהוּא מוּתָּר לוֹכַל. רַב כְּרִבִּי מֵאִיר. רִבִּי לָעְזָר כְּרַבָּנָן. רַב כְּרִבִּי מֵאִיר אִין כְּרִבִּי מֵאִיר אֲפִילוּ בָּנָיו וּבְנֵי בֵיתוֹ יְהוּ אֲסוּרִין. אֶלָּא רַב כְּרִבִּי וְרִבִּי לָעְזָר כְּרַבָּנִין. דְּאָמַר רִבִּי סִימוֹן בְּשֵׁם רִבִּי יְהוֹשֻׁעַ בֶּן לֵוִי רִבִּי יוֹסֵי בֶּן שָׁאוּל בְּשֵׁם רִבִּי אֵין אוֹכְלִין עַל הַמּוּקְצֶה אֶלָּא עַל מְקוֹמוֹ דִּבְרֵי חֲכָמִים. רִבִּי יַעֲקֹב בַּר אִידִי בְּשֵׁם רִבִּי יְהוֹשֻׁעַ בֶּן לֵוִי אוֹכְלִין עַל הַמּוּקְצֶה בֵּין עַל מְקוֹמוֹ בֵּין שֶׁלֹּא עַל מְקוֹמוֹ. מוֹתִיב רִבִּי יוֹסֵי בֶּן שָׁאוּל לְרִבִּי וְהָתַנִּינָן

הֶחָרוּבִין עַד שֶׁלֹּא כִינְסָן לְרֹאשׁ הַגָּג. אָמַר לוֹ לֹא תְתִיבֵינִי חָרוּבִין. חָרוּבִין מַאֲכַל בְּהֵמָה הֵן.

Halakhah 1: May he himself eat[5]? Rav said, he is forbidden to eat; Ulla ben Rebbi Ismael said in the name of Rebbi Eleazar, this one is permitted to eat. Rav follows Rebbi Meïr[6], Rebbi Eleazar the rabbis. Does Rav follow Rebbi Meïr? Then even his children and domestics should be forbidden! But Rav follows Rebbi, Rebbi Eleazar the rabbis. As Rebbi Simon said in the name of Rebbi Joshua ben Levi, Rebbi Yose ben Shaul in the name of Rebbi: The Sages say, one eats from what is going to the *muqẓeh* only in its place[7]. Rebbi Jacob ben Idi in the name of Rebbi Joshua ben Levi: one eats from what is going to the *muqẓeh* in its place and in other places. Rebbi Yose ben Shaul objected to Rebbi: Did we not state[8], "carob pods until he collected them on top of his roof?" He said to him, do not object to me about carobs; carobs are animal feed[8].

5 Without tithing since his status is not mentioned in the Mishnah.

6 Who declares a sale before the end of processing to induce the status of *ṭevel*. Certainly he will hold that the presence of produce in the courtyard makes it *ṭevel*.

7 At the place where the cut-up figs are fermenting and drying, everybody sees that processing is not finished and one may eat without tithing. But at other places, sliced figs may look like finished food subject to tithing.

8 Mishnah 4: As long as the carob pods have not been stored on the roof, they may be used as animal feed without tithing. Since nobody by looking at a carob can tell whether it has been stored or not, the distinction which Rebbi makes is not applied uniformly.

8 They need human action to become human food.

עַל דַּעְתֵּיהּ דְּרַב מַה בֵּין הוּא מַה בֵּין בָּנָיו. הוּא עַל יְדֵי שֶׁהוּא תָלוּי בְּמוּקְצֶה אָסוּר. בָּנָיו עַל יְדֵי שֶׁאֵינָן תְּלוּיִין בְּמוּקְצֶה מוּתָּרִין. נִיחָא בָנָיו. וּבְנֵי בֵיתוֹ. וְאֵין לָהּ עָלָיו מְזוֹנוֹת. כְּמָאן דְּאָמַר אֵין מְזוֹנוֹת לְאִשָּׁה דְּבַר תּוֹרָה. כְּהָדָא דְתַנֵּי

אֵין בֵּית דִּין פּוֹסְקִין מְזוֹנוֹת לְאִשָּׁה מִדְּמֵי שְׁבִיעִית. אֲבָל נִיזוֹנֶת הִיא אֵצֶל בַּעֲלָהּ שְׁבִיעִית. וְיֵעָשׂוּ אוֹתָהּ כְּפוֹעֵל שֶׁאֵינוֹ יָפֶה שָׁוֶה פְרוּטָה. הָדָא אָמְרָה שֶׁלֹּא יֵעָשׂוּ אוֹתָהּ כְּפוֹעֵל שֶׁאֵינוֹ יָפֶה שָׁוֶה פְרוּטָה. אֲפִילוּ כְּמָאן דְּאָמַר אֵין לָהּ עָלָיו מְזוֹנוֹת אֵין לָהּ עָלָיו בֵּית דִּירָה. כְּהָדָא דְתַנֵּי אֲנָשִׁים שֶׁשִּׁיתְּפוּ שֶׁלֹּא מִדַּעַת הַנָּשִׁים[9] שִׁיתּוּפָן שִׁיתּוּף נָשִׁים שֶׁשִּׁיתְּפוּ שֶׁלֹּא מִדַּעַת אֲנָשִׁים אֵין שִׁיתּוּפָן שִׁיתּוּף.

According to Rav, what is the difference between himself and his children? He is forbidden because he depends on *muqẓeh*[10]. His children who do not depend on *muqẓeh* are permitted. We understand his children, but his wife? Does she not have a claim for food against him[11]? Following him who says, the wife's food is not from the Torah. Following what we have stated: "The court will not determine food[12] for a wife from Sabbatical money, but she may be given Sabbatical produce to eat at her husband's." Can she not be considered like a worker whose work is not worth a *peruṭah*[13]? It implies that she is not considered like a worker whose work is not worth a *peruṭah*. Even according to him who says, the wife's food is not from the Torah, does she not have a claim to a dwelling[14]? Following what we stated: "If men participate[15] with food without the knowledge of their wives, the participation is valid. But if wives participate without the knowledge of their husbands, the participation is invalid[16]".

9 Reading of the Rome ms. Venice and Leyden: אנשים.

10 Since he is the owner of the courtyard, without the evidence of continued processing the courtyard would induce *ṭevel* and the duty of tithes.

11 It is forbidden to pay one's debts with untithed produce. The marriage contract explicitly notes that the husband will "work for, honor, feed, and provide for" his bride "in the manner of Jewish husbands." The language seems to imply that this is a contract following rabbinic guidelines; this is the position of Nachmanides and R. Asher ben Iehiel (*Rosh Ketubot* Chap. 13, Sec. 6.) Maimonides holds

that nevertheless the obligation is biblical, *Hilkhot Išut* 12:2.

12 Tosephta *Ševiit* 5:22, quoted also in Yerushalmi *Ketubot* 7:1 (fol. 31b), 13:1 (fol. 34d). The husband left for an overseas trip, stayed longer than anticipated, and now the wife needs money to survive. She may sell some of the husband's property or take a loan under the supervision of the court. She may not sell Sabbatical produce for her needs since Sabbatical produce may not be used to pay debts of any kind. But if the husband is present, she may eat of his Sabbatical fruits; since his obligation to feed his wife is only rabbinical, this is not considered paying his debts with Sabbatical produce. Similarly here, her eating from figs destined for *muqẓeh* is not considered paying a debt with untithed fruit.

13 The smallest bronze coin, about 2 grams in weight. Amounts less than a *peruṭah* are not recognized in law. The worker cannot eat according to biblical law; what he gets is a gift and the rabbis agreed earlier that a gift has the status of a sale for the obligation of tithes. Even though the obligation of the husband to feed his wife might not be biblical, it is the consequence of a contract volontarily entered upon and it should not be possible to discharge the obligation with untithed produce (except when the wife's income from her work is more than what she would get from her husband, in which case she is free to stipulate that she will keep her earnings for herself and not be fed by him.)

14 Since she has the biblical right to live in her husband's house and courtyard, if the courtyard creates *ṭevel* for him it should do the same for her; this seems to contradict Rav's position.

15 In order to turn the dead-end street where they live into a space in which one may carry on the Sabbath, cf. *Demay* Chapter 1, Note 193.

16 Tosephta *Eruvin* 6:4. The wife's right to the dwelling is derivative; there is no reason that the courtyard should create *ṭevel* for her. This argument is peculiar to the Yerushalmi; in the Babli (*Eruvin* 80a) the Tosephta is restricted to the case where the husband disapproved of participation beforehand.

תַּנֵּי וְכוּלָּן שֶׁנִּכְנְסוּ מִשָּׂדֶה לָעִיר נִטְבְּלוּ. מַתְנִיתָא דְּרַבִּי. דְּתַנֵּי הֵבִיא תְאֵנִים מִן הַשָּׂדֶה לְאוֹכְלָן בַּחֲצֵירוֹ שֶׁאֵינָהּ מִשְׁתַּמֶּרֶת וְשָׁכַח וְהִכְנִיסָן לְתוֹךְ בֵּיתוֹ אוֹ שֶׁהִכְנִיסוּם הַתִּינוֹקוֹת (fol. 50c) הֲרֵי זֶה מַחֲזִירָן לִמְקוֹמָן וְאוֹכֵל. לֹא אָמְרוּ אֶלָּא

שׁוֹגֵג הָא מֵזִיד אָסוּר. מָאן תַּנִּיתָהּ רִבִּי. דְּתַנֵּי הֵבִיא תְאֵנִים מִן הַשָּׂדֶה וְהֶעֱבִירָן לַחֲצֵירוֹ לְאוֹכְלָן בְּרֹאשׁ גַּגּוֹ רִבִּי מְחַייֵב רִבִּי יוֹסֵי בְּרִבִּי יְהוּדָה פּוֹטֵר. הֲוֵי מָאן תַּנָּא הַמַּעֲבִיר תְּאֵינִים בַּחֲצֵירוֹ לִקְצוֹת. הָא לֹא לִקְצוֹת חַייָב.

It was stated: All that was brought from the field to town became *ṭevel*. The *baraita* is Rebbi's, as it was stated: "[17]If somebody brought figs from the field to eat them in his unprotected courtyard[18], then forgot and brought them into his house or the children brought them[19], he may bring them back to their intended place and eat." They said that only concerning error; therefore, if intentional it is forbidden. Who stated this? Rebbi! As it was stated: "[20]If somebody brought figs from the field to eat them on his roof, Rebbi obligates[21], Rebbi Yose ben Rebbi Jehudah frees." It is as it was stated, "if somebody transports figs through his courtyard to cut them into pieces[1];" therefore, if it is not to cut into pieces he is obligated.

17 Tosephta 2:8: "If somebody brought figs from the field to eat them in a courtyard exempt from tithes, then forgot and brought them into his house, he may bring them back to their intended place and eat."

18 Which does not belong to a house and does not induce *ṭevel*.

19 Without his knowledge.

20 A different text in Tosephta 2:10. There, the opinion ascribed here to Rebbi is anonymous.

21 Being exposed to the birds, this is no place of storage; the intention is to eat the figs more or less immediately. Since the figs are transported through the courtyard of the house, Rebbi declares them to be *ṭevel*; R. Yose ben R. Jehudah frees them since there was no intention of storing. It is also implied that the figs were lifted to the roof directly from the back of the house, so that they never were in the house, not even in front of the entrance door. In this case, they never can become *ṭevel* and are permanently exempt from heave and tithes according to everybody, as made explicit in the next paragraph.

רִבִּי עוּלָּא בְּרִבִּי יִשְׁמָעֵאל בְּשֵׁם רִבִּי לָעְזָר רִבִּי וְרִבִּי יוֹסֵי בֵּי רִבִּי יְהוּדָה הָיוּ מַכְנִיסִים אֶת הַכַּלְכָּלָה לַאֲחוֹרֵי הַגַּנּוֹת. רָאָה אוֹתָן רִבִּי יוּדָה בֵּי רִבִּי אִלָּעַאי אָמַר לָהֶן רְאוּ מַה בֵּינֵיכֶם לָרִאשׁוֹנִים. רִבִּי עֲקִיבָה הָיָה לוֹקֵחַ שְׁלֹשָׁה מִינִין בִּפְרוּטָה בִּשְׁבִיל לְעַשֵּׂר מִכָּל־מִין וּמִין וְאַתֶּם מַכְנִיסִין אֶת הַכַּלְכָּלָה לַאֲחוֹרֵי הַגַּנּוֹת. מַה לִי לַאֲחוֹרֵי הַגַּנּוֹת אֲפִילוּ הִכְנִיסָם בַּחֲצֵירוֹ לְאוֹכְלָן בְּרֹאשׁ גַּגּוֹ. וְלֹא רִבִּי יוֹסֵי בְּרִבִּי יְהוּדָה הִיא. בְּגִין רִבִּי דַהֲוָה עִימֵּיהּ. חַמְתּוֹן חַד סַבָּא אֲמַר לוֹן יְהָבוֹן לִי אַתּוּן אֲמְרוּן לֵיהּ אִין. אֲמַר לוֹן לַאֲבוּכוֹן דִּבְשְׁמַיָּא לֹא יְהַבְתּוֹן אֶלָּא לִי.

Rebbi Ulla ben Rebbi Ismael in the name of Rebbi Eleazar: Rebbi and Rebbi Yose ben Rebbi Jehudah brought the harvesting basket over the back of the roofs[22]. Rebbi Jehudah ben Rebbi Ilaï saw them and said, look what the difference is between you and the earlier generations. Rebbi Aqiba bought three different kinds for a *peruṭah* in order to tithe every kind separately but you bring the harvesting basket over the back of the roofs[23]! Why over the back of the roofs, even if he brings them into his courtyard with the intention to eat them on the roof! Is that not the opinion of Rebbi Yose ben Rebbi Jehudah? Because of Rebbi who was with him[21]. An old man saw[24] them and said to them, would you give me some of these? They said, yes. He said to them, you did not give to your father in Heaven, only to me!

22 Reading גגות for גנות "the gardens" in both mss. and the *editio princeps*.

23 A similar story, also in the name of R. Jehudah bar Ilaï, in Babli *Berakhot* 35b. In the Yerushalmi, the change from earlier to later generations is from before and after the war of Bar Kokhba. In the Babli, R. Jehudah considers his own generation (before and after the war) as late, the generations in the time of the Temple as early. Since his own son uses the subterfuge, he cannot object to the latter as a matter of law.

24 Speaking Aramaic, he is characterized as ignorant. He disapproves of rabbinical subterfuges.

רַבִּי יוֹחָנָן כְּרַבִּי וְרַבִּי שִׁמְעוֹן בֶּן לָקִישׁ כְּרַבִּי יוֹסֵי בֵּי רַבִּי יְהוּדָה. רַבִּי יוֹחָנָן כְּרַבִּי אֲפִילוּ דְיִסְבּוֹר כְּרַבִּי יוֹסֵי בֵּי רַבִּי יְהוּדָה חוֹמֶר הוּא בְּשַׁבָּת שֶׁכֵּן נְשָׁרִים שֶׁנָּשְׁרוּ מֵאֵילֵיהֶן אֲסוּרִין. רַבִּי שִׁמְעוֹן בֶּן לָקִישׁ כְּרַבִּי יוֹסֵי בֵּי רַבִּי יוּדָה אֲפִילוּ דְיִסְבּוֹר כְּרַבִּי חוֹמֶר הוּא בְּחָצֵר בֵּית שְׁמִירָה דְּאָמַר רַבִּי יוֹחָנָן מִקַּח בְּחָצֵר בְּשַׁבָּת אֵינָן תּוֹרָה. רַבִּי אִימִּי בְּשֵׁם רַבִּי שִׁמְעוֹן הַמְּחוּוָר שֶׁבְּכוּלָּן זֶה חֲצַר בֵּית שְׁמִירָה.

Rebbi Johanan follows Rebbi, Rebbi Simeon ben Laqish Rebbi Yose ben Rebbi Jehudah[25]. Does Rebbi Johanan follow Rebbi? Even if he would hold with Rebbi Yose ben Rebbi Jehudah, the Sabbath is more powerful since windfall which falls by itself is forbidden[26]. Does Rebbi Simeon ben Laqish follow Rebbi Yose ben Rebbi Jehudah? Even if he would follow Rebbi, since a secure courtyard[27] is more powerful as Rebbi Johanan said, buying, courtyard, and Sabbath are not biblical. Rebbi Immi in the name of Rebbi Simeon [ben Laqish], the most reasonable of these is the secure courtyard.

25 This refers to the discussion in Chapter 2, Notes 99-102, whether the Sabbath or a secure courtyard induce *ṭevel* independent of any intention of the owner.

26 Since food for the Sabbath has to be prepared beforehand (*Ex.* 16:5), fruits which fall from a tree on the Sabbath are forbidden even though collecting them is not harvesting.

27 Chapter 2, Note 101. The rest of the paragraph is also found there, Notes 101-102.

רַבִּי יוֹחָנָן בְּשֵׁם רַבִּי שִׁמְעוֹן בֶּן יוֹחַי הָיוּ לוֹ שְׁתֵּי חֲצֵירוֹת אַחַת בְּמִגְדָּלָא וְאַחַת בְּטִיבֶּרְיָא הֶעֱבִירוֹ בְּזוֹ שֶׁבְּמִגְדָּלָא לְאוֹכְלָן בְּזוֹ שֶׁבְּטִיבֶּרְיָא מִכֵּיוָן שֶׁהֶעֱבִירָן דֶּרֶךְ הֶתֵּיר מוּתָּר. אַתְיָא רַבִּי שִׁמְעוֹן בֶּן יוֹחַי כְּרַבִּי יוֹסֵי בֵּי רַבִּי יוּדָה וְרוּבָּה מִן דְּרַבִּי יוֹסֵי בֵּי רַבִּי יוּדָה. מַה דְאָמַר רַבִּי יוֹסֵי בֵּי רַבִּי יוּדָה בְּעוֹמֵד בְּמָקוֹם פָּטוּר. וּמַה דְאָמַר רַבִּי שִׁמְעוֹן בֶּן יוֹחַי[32] בְּעוֹמֵד בְּמָקוֹם חִיּוּב. מִכֵּיוָן שֶׁהֶעֱבִירָן דֶּרֶךְ הֶתֵּיר מוּתָּר. וְרַבִּי אֱלִיעֶזֶר רוּבָּה מִן דִּתְרֵיהוֹן דְּרַבִּי אֱלִיעֶזֶר אָמַר מִכֵּיוָן שֶׁהִתְחִיל בָּהֶן דֶּרֶךְ הֶתֵּיר מוּתָּר.

Rebbi Joḥanan in the name of Rebbi Simeon ben Ioḥai: If someone had two courtyards[28], one in Magdala[29] and one in Tiberias, and transported it to the one in Magdala intending to eat them in Tiberias; since he transported it in a permitted[30] way it is permitted. It turns out that Rebbi Simeon ben Ioḥai holds with Rebbi Yose ben Rebbi Jehudah but is stronger than the latter since Rebbi Yose ben Rebbi Jehudah speaks about an exempt place[31] but Rebbi Simeon ben Ioḥai about a place of obligation[32], but since he transported it in a permitted way it is permitted[30]. Rebbi Eliezer's statement[33] is stronger than either of them, since Rebbi Eliezer said, since he started in a permitted way it is permitted.

28 Both enclosed and guarded, potential sources of *ṭevel.*

29 On Lake Genezareth, less than 2000 cubits from Tiberias.

30 Since the storage in Magdala is provisional, the processing is not finished and the courtyard does not induce *ṭevel.* Since one courtyard is inactive, so is the second and the fruits become *ṭevel* only when brought into storage in house or barn.

31 The roof which never induces *ṭevel.*

32 A courtyard which usually induces *ṭevel.*

In the Venice print and the Leyden ms., the reference is to R. Simeon ben Laqish. In the Rome ms. it is correctly R. Simeon ben Ioḥai.

33 *Terumot* 8:4, Note 74, about a person who started eating a bunch of grapes as a snack and with them entered his courtyard.

(fol. 50b) **משנה ב:** הַמּוֹצִיא פוֹעֲלָיו לַשָּׂדֶה בִּזְמַן שֶׁאֵין לָהֶן עָלָיו מְזוֹנוֹת אוֹכְלִין וּפְטוּרִין. אֲבָל אִם יֵשׁ לָהֶן עָלָיו מְזוֹנוֹת אוֹכְלִין אַחַת אַחַת מִן הַתְּאֵנָה אֲבָל לֹא מִן הַסַּל וְלֹא מִן הַקּוּפּוֹת וְלֹא מִן הַמּוּקְצֶה.

Mishnah 2: If somebody takes his workers out to the field, if they have no claim to meals from him, they eat and are free[34]. But if they can claim meals from him they may eat single fruits from the fig tree but not from the basket or the box or the *muqẓeh*[35].

34 They do not work on the fig trees and do not eat by biblical decree. The farmer may offer them figs on the field but this does not have the status of a gift or a sale and does not create *ṭevel*.

35 Since any food they eat between meals reduces the amount he has to give to them, the owner cannot discharge a monetary obligation using heave and tithes. Therefore, they may eat only in the way a recipient of a gift may eat untithed food.

(fol. 50c) **הלכה ב**: נִיחָא לֹא מִן הַסַּל וְלֹא מִן הַקּוּפָּה וְלֹא מִן הַמּוּקְצֶה כְּמָה דְתֵימַר תַּמָּן מְלַקֵּט אַחַת אַחַת וְאוֹכֵל וְאִם צֵירַף חַייָב. וֶאֱמוֹר אוּף הָכָא כֵּן. אָמַר רִבִּי יִצְחָק מוּקְצֶה עָשׂוּ אוֹתוֹ כִמְצוּרָף.

Halakhah 2: We understand "not from the basket or the box[36]", but "or the *muqẓeh*?[37]" Not "[38]he eats one by one and if he takes them together he is obligated"? Rebbi Isaac said, they considered *muqẓeh* as being taken together[40].

36 Since the harvested fruits are assembled there, they cannot be eaten as a snack; cf. Chapter 2, Note 21.

37 The cut-up figs are lying there singly.

38 Mishnah 3.

40 A *muqẓeh* of figs is like a heap of grain.

(fol. 50b) **משנה ג**: הַשּׂוֹכֵר אֶת הַפּוֹעֵל לַעֲשׂוֹת עִמּוֹ בְּזֵיתִים אָמַר לוֹ עַל מְנַת לוֹכַל זֵתִים אוֹכֵל אַחַת אַחַת וּפָטוּר וְאִם צֵירַף חַייָב. לְנַכֵּשׁ בִּבְצָלִים אָמַר לוֹ עַל מְנַת לוֹכַל יָרָק מְקָרְטֵם עָלֶה עָלֶה וְאוֹכֵל. וְאִם צֵירַף חַייָב.

Mishnah 3: If somebody hires a laborer to work with him on olive trees and said to him "on condition to be able to eat olives,[41]" he eats one by one and if he takes them together he is obligated. To thin out onions, if he said to him "on condition to be able to eat vegetables" he snips off leaf by leaf and eats but if he takes them together he is obligated.

41 The Halakhah will explain that the laborer is hired to work around the tree but not on the tree itself. He cannot eat by biblical law; therefore his contract is treated as a sale and is subject to heave and tithes if he takes more than one piece at a time.

(fol. 50c) **הלכה ג**: תַּנֵּי דְבֵי רִבִּי אוֹכֵל כְּדַרְכּוֹ וּפָטוּר. רִבִּי יוֹנָה בָּעֵי מַה נָן קַייָמִין אִם בְּשֶׁשְּׂכָרוֹ לַעֲשׂוֹת עִמּוֹ בַּזֵּתִים כָּל־עַמָּא מוֹדֵיי שֶׁהוּא אוֹכֵל כְּדַרְכּוֹ וּפָטוּר. וְאִם שֶׁשְּׂכָרוֹ לַעֲשׂוֹת עִמּוֹ בְּגוּפָן שֶׁל זֵיתִים כָּל־עַמָּא מוֹדֵיי שֶׁהוּא אוֹכֵל אַחַת אַחַת וּפָטוּר וְאִם צֵירַף חַייָב. אֶלָּא כִּי נָן קַייָמִין בְּשֶׁשְּׂכָרוֹ לְנַכֵּשׁ עִמּוֹ בַּזֵּתִים. מִן דְּבַתְרָהּ לְנַכֵּשׁ בִּבְצָלִים אָמַר לוֹ עַל מְנַת לוֹכַל יָרָק מְקָרְטֵם עָלֶה עָלֶה וְאוֹכֵל וְאִם צֵירַף חַייָב.

The house of Rebbi stated: He eats normally[42] and is free. Rebbi Jonah asked, where do we hold? If he hired him to work with him on the olives[43], everybody agrees that he eats normally and is free. If he hired him to work the olive trees, everybody agrees that he eats one by one and if he takes them together he is obligated[44]. But we must hold that he hired him to thin out the olives[45]. Since the latter part is about thinning out onions, if he said to him "on condition to be able to eat vegetables" he tears them out leaf by leaf and eats but if he takes them together he is obligated.

42 If he is hired to work on olives. This statement is not in the Tosephta.

43 To harvest them.

44 Since it is not harvest time, he cannot eat by biblical law and must eat under the rules of commercial trans-

actions.

45 To remove those whose growth is below normal in order to direct the sap of the olive tree to the good olives. Since he removes olives he can be said to harvest and eat them by biblical decree; this is the position of the House of Rebbi. But since the thinning is a long time before the real harvest, this cannot be considered harvesting: the position of the Tanna of the Mishnah. The House of Rebbi holds that a poor worker will be ready to eat unripe, bitter, raw olives.

(fol. 50b) **משנה ד:** מָצָא קְצִיצוֹת בַּדֶּרֶךְ אֲפִילוּ בְּצַד שָׂדֶה קְצִיצוֹת וְכֵן תְּאֵינָה שֶׁהִיא נוֹטָה עַל הַדֶּרֶךְ וּמָצָא תַּחְתֶּיהָ תְאֵנִים מוּתָּרוֹת מִשּׁוּם גֶּזֶל וּפְטוּרוֹת מִן הַמַּעְשְׂרוֹת. הַזֵּיתִים וְהֶחָרוּבִין חַייָבִין. מָצָא גְּרוֹגְרוֹת אִם דָּֽרְסוּ רוֹב בְּנֵי אָדָם חַייָב וְאִם לָאו פָּטוּר. מָצָא פִילְחֵי דְבֵילָה חַייָב בְּיָדוּעַ שֶׁמִּדָּבָר גָּמוּר. הֶחָרוּבִין עַד שֶׁלֹּא כִּינְסָן לְרֹאשׁ הַגַּג מוֹרִיד מֵהֶן לִבְהֵמָה וּפָטוּר מִפְּנֵי שֶׁהוּא מַחֲזִיר אֶת הַמּוֹתָר.

Mishnah 4: If he found single fruits[46] on the road, even next to a field from which the single fruits may have come, or a fig tree that extends over the road and he found figs under it[47] they are permitted under the category of robbery[48] and free from tithes. Olives and carobs are obligated[49]. If he found dried figs, if most people are pressing theirs he is obligated, otherwise he is free[50]. If he found slices of a fig-cake it is obvious that this is post-processing[51]. Carobs, as long as he did not make heaps on his roof he may take down for his animals and is free because he will return the excess[52].

46 This is the reading of all Yerushalmi sources. The Babli mss. here and in *Baba Meẓi'a* 21b read קציעות "cut-up figs."

47 The figs which overhang the public domain are not public property but the owners, knowing some figs will fall down and be spoiled, are resigned to their being taken by passers-by. Therefore, these figs are abandoned property.

48 Eveybody is free to take them.

Abandoned property is not "your harvest"; therefore, they are exempt from heave and tithes.

49 They usually do not fall down from the tree, and if they do they are recognizable as fruits from a specific tree. Therefore, the owners have reasonable hope of recovering all of them at harvest time and do not abandon them (Explanation of the Babli, *Baba Meẓi'a* 21b).

49 If the figs have been dried and pressed into fig cakes in the field, their processing is finished and the finder has to tithe them as *demay*. If people of that region do not press their fig cakes in the field, the dried figs are like any other figs found on the road.

51 They have to be tithed as *demay*.

52 While, in general, the roof is not a storage place for food, it is used for carob pods which are so hard as to be virtually safe from birds. These pods are first spread out for drying; the end of processing is that they are collected into orderly heaps. If during the drying process some carobs are taken as animal feed, this does not imply that even for these the processing is completed since the remainder will be returned to be used as food for both humans and animals.

(fol. 50c) **הלכה ג**: רִבִּי חַגַּיי שָׁאַל לַחֲבֵרַיָּא מַהוּ אָהֵן פָּטוּר דְּתַנִּינָן הָכָא אָמַר לֵיהּ מִשּׁוּם אוֹכֵל עֲרַאי בַּשָּׂדֶה וְהוּא פָּטוּר. אָמַר לוֹן וְכָא אֲתִינָן מַתְנִיתִין מִשּׁוּם אוֹכֵל עֲרַאי בַּשָּׂדֶה וְהוּא פָּטוּר אֶלָּא מִשּׁוּם הֶבְקֵר שֶׁכֵּן אִם הִכְנִיסוֹ לַבַּיִת פָּטוּר. דְּתַנֵּי מָצָא כַלְכָּלָה מְחוּפָּה בֶּעָלִין אֲסוּרָה מִשּׁוּם גֶּזֶל וְחַייֶבֶת בְּמַעְשְׂרוֹת. אֲסוּרָה מִשּׁוּם גֶּזֶל מִשּׁוּם דָּבָר שֶׁיֵּשׁ בּוֹ סִימָנִין. וְחַייָבִין בְּמַעֲשֵׂר שֶׁעַד עַכְשָׁיו דַּעַת בְּעָלִים עָלֶיהָ. עַד הֵכִין. עַד כְּדֵי שֶׁיָּכוֹל לִתְרוֹם מִן הַמּוּבְקָר. לֹא הָיָה יָכוֹל לִתְרוֹם מִן הַמּוּבְקָר עוֹשֶׂה אוֹתָהּ דָּמִים וְאוֹכְלָהּ.

Rebbi Ḥaggai asked the colleagues: What is the reason we stated here that "he is free"[53]? They said to him, because he is eating a snack in the field and is free. He said to them, is our Mishnah needed for that, because he is eating a snack in the field and is free[54]? It must be because of abandoned property since if he brings it to his house he still is free. As it is stated[55]: "If somebody found a harvesting basket covered with leaves, that is forbidden because of robbery and is subject to tithes." It is forbidden because of robbery since it is something with distinguishing marks[56]. It is subject to tithes since the owners still have it in mind[57]. How far, that he could give heave from abandoned property[58]? He cannot give heave from abandoned property[59]! "He turns it into money's worth and eats.[60]"

46 When he eats from the fruits.

54 This was already stated in Mishnah 1:4 and often since.

55 Tosephta 2:17.

56 An object found belongs to its original owner if it carries a distinguishing mark which the owner could indicate as proof of ownership; Mishnah *Baba Meẓi'a* 2:1.

57 It is not abandoned but subject to heave and tithes as private property.

58 Does he have to wait before eating the fruits until it is clear that the owners will not come back and have abandoned the fruits? Probably the fruits will have spoiled by that time.

59 Since fruits abandoned before the end of processing can never become subject to heave and tithes and it is forbidden to tithe what is obligated from what is not obligated (*Terumot* 1:5).

60 He estimates the commercial value of the fruits due to the owners should they return for their property.

רִבִּי יוֹנָה בָּעֵי דָּמִים מַהוּ שֶׁיִּטְבְּלוּ בְּמִקָּח. אוֹ מֵאַחַר שֶׁהַבְּעָלִים מוֹצִיאִין אוֹתָהּ לֹא נִטְבְּלָה. רִבִּי מָנָא בָּעֵי הֲגַע עַצְמָךְ שֶׁהָיְתָה נְתוּנָה בְּפִיו. לֹא כְּמָאוּס הוּא יָכוֹל הוּא לְהַחֲזִירָהּ. אִם אוֹמֵר אַתְּ כֵּן לֹא נִמְצָא אוֹכֵל טֶבֶל לְמַפְרֵיעוֹ הָדָא אָמְרָה דָּמִים כְּמִקָּח הֵן.

Rebbi Jonah asked: Does the fixing of the price create *ṭevel* in a sale[61]? Or maybe, since the owners can take it back there is no *ṭevel*? Rebbi Mana asked: Think of it if one was put[62] in his mouth! Is it not unappetizing? Can he give it back? If you say so, is he not eating *ṭevel* retroactively? That means, the fixing of the price is like a sale.

61 This is a general question since a sale of movables is consummated only by taking possession, not by paying the amount agreed on (cf. *Kilaim* 8, Note 46). This is held to be a rabbinic decree; by biblical law a sale can be concluded also by paying the amount agreed on. In no case does the fixing of a price conclude the sale. The particular question here is what are the legal implications of the finder putting a monetary value on the fruits he found.

62 The queer formulation as a passive is necessary here since if the finder takes one fruit by all opinions he is taking possession, becomes the owner irrevocably, and incurs a monetary debt to the original owner. For the question to have meaning, a third, uninterested, person must have put the fruit into the finder's mouth.

מְצָאָהּ כַּלְכָּלָה בְּמָקוֹם שֶׁהָרוֹב מַכְנִיסִין לַשּׁוּק אָסוּר לוֹכַל מִמֶּנּוּ עֲרַאי וּמְתַקְּנָהּ דְּמַאי. בְּמָקוֹם שֶׁרוֹב מַכְנִיסִין לַבָּתִּים מוּתָּר לוֹכַל מִמֶּנּוּ עֲרַאי וּמְתַקְּנָהּ וַדַּאי. מֶחֱצָה עַל מֶחֱצָה מְתַקְּנָהּ דְּמַאי. מַכְנִיסָהּ לַבַּיִת מְתַקְּנָהּ וַדַּאי. רִבִּי יוֹנָה בָּעֵי דְּמַאי מַהוּ שֶׁיִּטְבּוֹל לְוַדַּאי. אִם אוֹמֵר אַתְּ כֵּן לֹא נִמְצֵאת מַקְדִּים. רִבִּי יוֹסֵי בֵּי רִבִּי בּוּן רִבִּי יוֹחָנָן בְּשֵׁם רִבִּי שִׁמְעוֹן בֶּן יוֹצָדָק צָרִיךְ לְהַתְנוֹת וְלוֹמַר אִם מֵאוֹתָהּ שֶׁמַּכְנִיסִים לַשּׁוּק הִיא מַה שֶּׁעָשִׂיתִי עָשׂוּי. וְאִם לָאו לֹא עָשִׂיתִי כְּלוּם. שֶׁלֹּא תְּהֵא מֵאוֹתָהּ שֶׁמַּכְנִיסִין לַבָּתִּים וְנִמְצֵאת תְּרוּמַת מַעֲשֵׂר טְבוּלָה לִתְרוּמָה גְדוֹלָה. מֶחֱצָה עַל מֶחֱצָה בַּשָּׂדֶה מְתַקְּנָהּ דְּמַאי. מַכְנִיסָהּ לַבַּיִת מְתַקְּנָהּ וַדַּאי. וְחָשׁ לוֹמַר שֶׁמָּא מֵאוֹתָהּ שֶׁמַּכְנִיסִין לַבַּיִת הִיא וְנִמְצֵאת תְּרוּמָה גְדוֹלָה טְבוּלָה לִתְרוּמַת מַעֲשֵׂר. אָמַר רִבִּי מַתַּנְיָה בְּקוֹרֵא שֵׁם עַל מַעְשְׂרוֹתָיו.

'If he found a harvesting basket in a place where most people bring to market[63], it is forbidden to eat a snack from them and he must put it in order as *demay*. In a place where most people bring to their houses[64], it is permitted to eat a snack from them and he must put it in order as certain. Half and half, he puts in order as *demay*[65] but if he brings it to his house he must put it in order as certain.' Rebbi Jonah asked, does *demay* create *ṭevel* for certain[66]? If you would say so, does he not invert the order? Rebbi Yose ben Rebbi Abun, Rebbi Joḥanan in the name of Rebbi Simeon ben Yoẓadaq, he must spell out a condition and say: "If this is from those who bring to market, what I did is valid, otherwise, I did not do anything," so that heave of the tithe should not contain *ṭevel* of the Great Heave[67]. 'Half and half on the field he puts in order as *demay* but if he brings it to his house he must put it in order as certain.' Should one not be afraid that it was from those who bring to their houses and its Great Heave would contain *ṭevel* of heave of the tithe[68]? Rebbi Mattaniah said, if he gives a name to his tithes[69].

63 Then the processing is completed and is subject to heave and tithes. Since the owner might have tithed before he lost that basket, it must be tithed as *demay*.

64 Then the obligation starts only when the harvest is brought to storage. In this case, one assumes that it was not tithed at all.

65 As spelled out later, this is if he wants to eat in the field.

66 The rule given for a harvest basket found in a place where 50% move to market makes sense only if either all or none of the fruits are eaten in the field. If some are eaten in the field and tithed as *demay*, how can they then lose their status as profane and return to that of *ṭevel* for Great Heave. This seems to be impossible; cf. *Terumot* 1:4.

67 If heave of the tithe was taken as *demay* on the field under the reservation spelled out here and the great heave and another heave of the tithe in the house, the three heaves may be eaten by a Cohen and the remainder is fully profane. If there were no reservation made the first heave of the tithe would be forbidden even to the Cohen as *ṭevel*.

68 This is the text in both mss. and the *editio princeps* but it is difficult to accept since in this case the first heave of the tithe has been declared to be profane and is given to the Cohen only because of the doubt. All commentators emend the text but their emendations do not help much. One has to say that the (slightly varied) text of the *baraita* introduces a new argument (in preparation for the answer of R. Mattaniah) which does not take the stipulation of R. Joḥanan into account. It is pointed out that not only does one run into difficulty if the basket was destined for the market but even if it was destined for the house.

In that case, the first heave of the tithe (given as *demay*) is *ṭevel* for the Great Heave and cannot be eaten by the Cohen.

69 Since Great Heave has no minimum volume by biblical standards, if the basket which was put in order as *demay* now is tithed as certain, it is sufficient to declare that some minute amount of the heave of the tithe is to be eaten as Great Heave. Since for the Cohen the rules of both are identical, no difficulty is created and the solution of R. Johanan is unnecessary.

עַד כְּדוֹן דָּבָר שֶׁאֵין לוֹ גוֹרֶן אֲבָל דָּבָר שֶׁיֵּשׁ לוֹ גוֹרֶן מַפְרִישִׁין תְּרוּמַת מַעֲשֵׂר וְאֵין צָרִיךְ לְהַפְרִישׁ תְּרוּמָה גְדוֹלָה. כְּהָדָא דְתַנֵּי מָצָא פֵּירוֹת מְמוּרָחִין בַּשָּׂדֶה מְכוּנָּסִין אֲסוּרִין מִשּׁוּם גֶּזֶל. מְפוּזָּרִין מוּתָּרִין מִשּׁוּם גֶּזֶל. בֵּין כָּךְ וּבֵין כָּךְ חַייָבִין בְּמַעְשְׂרוֹת וּפְטוּרִין מִתְּרוּמָה גְדוֹלָה. שֶׁאִי אֶפְשַׁר לְגוֹרֶן שֶׁתֵּיעָקֵר אֶלָּא אִם כֵּן נִתְרְמָה.

So far something that has no threshing floor; but of produce from the threshing floor one separates heave of the tithe but does not need to give Great Heave as it was stated: "[70]If he found cleaned[71] grain on the field, in a heap it is forbidden because of robbery, dispersed it is permitted because of robbery[72]. In any case it is subject to tithes but free from Great Heave because no threshing floor is cleared unless Great Heave was taken."

70 A related text in Tosephta 2:17. According to the Tosephta, the question in the next paragraph is pointless since tithes may be taken either from the grain or from storage.

71 Cleaned from chaff after threshing.

72 These grains are leftovers from threshing which were not collected. Therefore, they are abandoned property and legally may be taken up by any passer-by.

מַעְשְׂרוֹת מֵהֵיכָן נִיטָּלוֹת מִן הַבַּיִת אוֹ מִן הַשָּׂדֶה. נִישְׁמְעִינָהּ מִן הָדָא חָבֵר שֶׁמֵּת וְהִנִּיחַ מְגוּרָה מְלֵיאָה פֵּירוֹת אֲפִילוּ בוֹ בַיּוֹם הִכְנִיסָן הֲרֵי אֵילּוּ בְחֶזְקַת מְתוּקָּנִים. וְאֵיפְשַׁר שֶׁלֹּא נִטְרְפָה דַעְתּוֹ שָׁעָה אַחַת. אָמַר רִבִּי בּוּן בַּר חִייָה תִּפְתָּר שֶׁמֵּת

מִתּוֹךְ יִישּׁוּב. רִבִּי חֲנַנְיָה בְּשֵׁם רִבִּי פִּינְחָס שָׁמַע לָהּ מִן הָכָא עִישּׂוּר אֶחָד שֶׁאֲנִי עָתִיד לָמוּד נָתוּן לַעֲקִיבָה בֶּן יוֹסֵף שֶׁיְּזַכֶּה בוֹ לַעֲנִיִּים. הָדָא אָמְרָה מִן הַבַּיִת. רִבִּי חִייָה בַּר אַבָּא שָׁמַע לָהּ מִן הָכָא מִי שֶׁהָיוּ פֵּירוֹתָיו בִּמְגוּרָה וְנָתַן סְאָה לְבֶן לֵוִי וּסְאָה לְעָנִי הָדָא אָמַר מִן הַבַּיִת. רִבִּי אַבָּא מָרִי שָׁמַע לָהּ מִן הָכָא מִן הַבַּיִת זוֹ חַלָּה. הָדָא אָמְרָה מִן הַשָּׂדֶה.

From where are tithes taken, from the house or from the field[73]? Let us hear from the following[74]: If a fellow died and in his estate was a chest full of grain, even if he filled it the same day it is supposed to be in order. Is it impossible that he should not have been of clouded mind at least for an hour[75]? Rebbi Abun bar Ḥiyya said, explain it if he died with a clear mind. Rebbi Ḥananiah in the name of Rebbi Phineas understood it from the following[76]: "One tenth which I shall separate in the future is given to Aqiba ben Joseph that he should distribute it to the poor." That means, from the house. Rebbi Ḥiyya bar Abba understood it from the following[77]: "If somebody's produce was in a storage bin and he gave a *seah* to a Levite and a *seah* to a poor person;" that means, from the house. Rebbi Abba Mari understood it from the following[78]: "(*Deut.* 26:13) 'From the house', that is *ḥallah*." That means, from the field.

73 The question is difficult to understand since it was shown in *Terumot* 2:1 that only Great Heave must be given from the harvest at a well defined place but tithes and the Heave of the Tithe may be given from any untithed produce of the same kind. The question seems to be whether the grain collected after somebody else's threshing is subject to tithes as a biblical law, in which case it can be used to tithe others and other grains can tithe for it, or it is rabbinic and a special case which needs special handling.

74 This *baraita* is quoted in Babli *Pesaḥim* 4b,9a; *Avodah Zarah* 41b, *Niddah* 15b. It is asserted there that the fact that the grain is in a chest is in itself proof that the grain was fully tithed before storage. In contrast, the Yerushalmi seems to permit a fellow to

deposit his grain in the chest and tithe from it.

75 Then the grain might be untithed even though it belonged to a fellow who was true to his obligations.

76 Mishnah *Ma'aser Šeni* 5:9, speaking of Rabban Gamliel and his entourage on a voyage from Rome to the Land of Israel who had to tithe his grains before the holiday and did this by a promise of future delivery from storage. This proves that, in general, tithes can be given from anywhere, also from storage for grain found on the road.

77 Mishnah *Terumot* 4:2, cf. Note 14. It is implied by the Mishnah that both for R. Meïr and the Sages, tithes can be given from another storage facility.

78 Mishnah *Ma'aser Šeni* 5:10. The Mishnah contains a *midrash* on *Deut.* 26:13: "I did remove the sanctified food" refers to Second Tithe and the fourth-year growth, "from the house," refers to *ḥallah*, "and also gave it" refers to heave and heave of the tithe, "to the Levite," refers to the Levite's tithe, "the sojourner, the orphan, and the poor," refers to the tithe of the poor, "following all commandments You commanded me;" therefore, if he gave heave of the tithe before the Great Heave he cannot recite the declaration, "I did not transgress Your commandments and I did not forget." Since the house is mentioned in connection with *ḥallah* heave from dough, it is clear that heaves and tithes are supposed to be taken outside the house, i. e., in the field.

הלכה ד: אָמַר רִבִּי יוֹנָה לֹא אָמְרוּ אֶלָּא לַדֶּרֶךְ. הָא בֵינוֹ לְבֵין חֲבֵירוֹ לֹא. אָמַר רִבִּי יוֹנָה וְהוּא שֶׁמָּצָא זֵיתִים תַּחַת זֵיתִים. וְחָרוּבִין תַּחַת חָרוּבִין. אֲבָל אִם מָצָא זֵיתִים תַּחַת חָרוּבִין וְחָרוּבִין תַּחַת זֵיתִים לֹא בְדָא.

Halakhah 4: Rebbi Jonah said; only on a road, not between a person and his neighbor[79]. Rebbi Jonah said; only olives under an olive tree, carobs under a carob tree, but not olives under a carob tree, carobs under an olive tree[80].

79 There the olives remain property of the owner of the tree.

80 These belong to the finder.

הלכה ה: וְלֹא בַבָּתִּים הֵן (fol. 50d) נִדְרָסוֹת. אָמַר רִבִּי בּוּן בַּר חִיָּיה תִּפְתָּר שֶׁרוֹב דּוֹרְסִין בַּשָּׂדוֹת. רִבִּי זְעִירָא בָּעֵי וְאֵינָהּ נִיכֶּרֶת אִם דְּרוּסָה הִיא אִם אֵינָהּ דְּרוּסָה. אָמַר רִבִּי שָׁאוּל פְּעָמִים שֶׁהִיא פוֹקַעַת תַּחַת הַגַּלְגָּל וְהִיא דְּרוּסָה וְהִיא נִרְאֵית שֶׁאֵינָהּ דְּרוּסָה. פְּעָמִים שֶׁהָרֶגֶל דּוֹרְסָתָהּ וְהִיא אֵינָהּ דְּרוּסָה וְנִרְאֵית כִּדְרוּסָה. אָמַר רִבִּי לָעְזָר הָדָא דְתֵימָא בְּמָקוֹם שֶׁאֵין רוֹב דּוֹרְסִין בְּשָׂדוֹת. אֲבָל בְּמָקוֹם שֶׁרוֹב דּוֹרְסִין בְּשָׂדוֹת אוֹתָן שֶׁדָּֽרְסוּ אוֹתָן הַמִּיעוּט הָעֲתִידִין לִדְרוֹס מִצְטָֽרְפִין.

Halakhah 5: Are they not pressed in the houses[81]? Rebbi Abun bar Ḥiyya said, explain it where most people press in the fields. Rebbi Zeïra asked: Is it not recognizable whether it is pressed or not[82]? Rebbi Saul[83] said, sometime it jumps from under the roller[84], then it is pressed[85] and looks as if not pressed. Sometimes a foot squeezes it, then it is not pressed and looks like pressed. Rebbi Eleazar said, that is[86], at a place where most people are not pressing in the fields. But at a place where most people are pressing in the fields, those who pressed and the minority who will press in the future are added together.

81 This refers to the statement of the Mishnah that a dried fig is subject to tithes "if most people already pressed their figs." It is agreed that for figs taken to be dried, the end of processing is the formation of fig cakes but it is not stated where the figs were pressed. If the final processing is done in the houses, a dried fig found in the fields is a forgotten fig which may be eaten as a snack untithed.

82 In that case, the Mishnah should have stated that "if it was pressed, it is obligated, if not pressed, it may be eaten as a snack."

83 No R. Shaul is known from any other Talmudic source. The reading of the Rome ms.: R. Samuel, seems to be preferable.

84 During the pressing process.

85 It is not pressed but it has the legal status of "pressed", i. e., processed.

86 There the legal status of a found dried fig is questionable. But if

in the end most people will have pressed their fig cakes in the fields, even in the midst of the processing period any dried fig found in the fields is considered to be processed and subject to tithes.

אִית תַּנָּיֵי תַנֵּי שֶׁאֵין שִׁבְחוֹ שֶׁל תַּלְמִיד חָכָם לִהְיוֹת אוֹכֵל בַּשּׁוּק. כְּהָדָא רִבִּי לְעָזָר בְּרִבִּי שִׁמְעוֹן הֲוָה אֲכִיל בְּשׁוּקָא חֲמְתֵיהּ רִבִּי מֵאִיר אֲמַר לֵיהּ בַּשׁוּקָא אַתְּ אֲכִיל. וּבָטַל גַּרְמֵיהּ.

Some Tannaïm state[87]: Because it is not proper for a learned person to eat in public[88]. As for example, Rebbi Eleazar ben Rebbi Simeon who was eating in public and was seen by Rebbi Meïr who asked him, are you eating in public[89]? He effaced himself.

87 This refers to the last statement of the Mishnah, that carobs may be used for animal feed without tithing. The language of the Mishnah implies that humans may not eat these carobs as untithed snacks. But since it is stated that processing is not finished, neither courtyard nor house should make it subject to tithes as human food.

88 A learned person, for whom the Mishnah was formulated, would not take the carobs to eat them outside the house or a walled-in courtyard. But in house or walled courtyard, the particular carob pod would be processed and subject to heave and tithes.

This paragraph is quoted in paraphrased form in Tosaphot *Qiddušin* 40b, *s. v.* ויש, and in a different form by R. Asher ben Iehiel *Qiddušin* 1, #65. The Babylonian version (Babli *Qiddušin* 40b, *Derekh Ereẓ* 10) reads: He who eats in public is the companion of the dog; some say he is unacceptable as a witness." This belongs to the Babylonian tradition of enmity towards the vulgar, cf. the Introduction to *Demay*, or to a tradition which accuses cynics of contempt for courts. A confluence of the Yerushalmi and Babli texts appears in *Sefer Ha'iṭṭur* p. 116, a prime example why quotes of early Medieval authors cannot be used as testimonies for the text. Cf. also *Maimonides, Edut* 11:5, *Ṭur* and *Šulḥan Arukh, Ḥošen Mišpaṭ* 34, and their commentators. The text of R. Ḥananel reads (as quoted by R. Yom Ṭob ben Abraham al-Išbili, *Qiddušin* 40b): "Rebbi Eleazar ben Rebbi Simeon was eating in public and was seen by Rebbi Meïr who said to him, it is not proper for a learned person to eat in public of his own food." This must belong to a text tradition of the Yerushalmi quite different from the two extant mss.

89 He made a point of addressing the learned rabbi in Aramaic, the language of the uneducated.

(fol. 50b) **משנה ה:** וְאֵי זוֹ הִיא חָצֵר שֶׁהִיא חַייֶבֶת בְּמַעְשְׂרוֹת רִבִּי יִשְׁמָעֵאל אוֹמֵר חָצֵר הַצּוֹרִית שֶׁהַכֵּלִים נִשְׁמָרִים בְּתוֹכָהּ. רִבִּי עֲקִיבָה אוֹמֵר כָּל־שֶׁאֶחָד פּוֹתֵחַ וְאֶחָד נוֹעֵל פְּטוּרָה. רִבִּי נְחֶמְיָה אוֹמֵר כָּל־שֶׁאֵין אָדָם בּוֹשׁ מִלּוֹכַל בְּתוֹכָהּ חַייֶבֶת. רִבִּי יוֹסֵי אוֹמֵר כָּל־שֶׁנִּכְנָס לָהּ וְאֵין אוֹמֵר לוֹ מַה אַתְּ מְבַקֵּשׁ פְּטוּרָה. רִבִּי יְהוּדָה אוֹמֵר שְׁתֵּי חֲצֵירוֹת זוֹ לִפְנִים מִזּוֹ הַפְּנִימִית חַייֶבֶת וְהַחִיצוֹנָה פְּטוּרָה.

Mishnah 5: Which courtyard is obligated for tithes? Rebbi Ismael says, a Tyrian courtyard[90] in which vessels are guarded. Rebbi Aqiba says, one where one person opens and another one locks it[91], is free. Rebbi Neḥemiah says, [a courtyard] where one is not ashamed to eat is obligated. Rebbi Yose says, one into which anybody may enter and nobody asks, what are you doing here, is free. Rebbi Jehudah says, if one courtyard is inside another, the inner one is obligated[92], the outer one is free.

90 Defined in the Halakhah and the Babli (*Niddah* 47b) as having a permanent doorman.

91 If the courtyard opens into two dwellings and the occupants use the common yard independently, the courtyard is not comparable to a house and cannot be considered an extension of the house.

92 It may be obligated if it belongs just to one house. Since the inhabitants of the inner yard have a right-of-way through the outer one, the outer one is free by R. Aqiba's criterion.

(fol. 50d) **הלכה ו:** וְאֵי זוֹ הִיא חָצֵר. תַּנֵּי רִבִּי יִשְׁמָעֵאל אוֹמֵר כָּל־שֶׁהַשּׁוֹמֵר יוֹשֵׁב עַל פִּיתְחָהּ וּמְשַׁמֵּר.

Halakhah 6: Which courtyard is obligated? It was stated: Rebbi Ismael says, any with a watchman sitting and watching at the door.

רִבִּי שְׁמוּאֵל בַּר נַחְמָן בְּשֵׁם רִבִּי יוֹנָתָן כּוּלְּהוֹן מִן הַבַּיִת לָמְדוּ. בַּיִת טוֹבֵל דְּבַר תּוֹרָה אָמַר בִּיעַרְתִּי הַקּוֹדֶשׁ מִן הַבַּיִת.

Rebbi Samuel ben Naḥman in the name of Rebbi Jonathan: All of them learned it from the house[93]. The house creates *ṭevel* by biblical decree; it says (*Deut*. 26:13) "I removed the holy food from the house[94]."

93 A courtyard induces *ṭevel* if and only if a house would induce *ṭevel* under the same circumstances.

94 This means that the heave, the sanctified food, is in the house, not in the open.

שָׁמְעוּן קוֹמֵי רִבִּי יוֹחָנָן אָמַר לוֹן הֲלָכָה כְּדִבְרֵי כוּלְּהֹן לְהַחֲמִיר. וְלָמָּה לֹא אָמְרִין לֵיהּ מִשְּׁמֵיהּ דְּלֵיתֵיהּ מִילְּתָא דְּרִבִּי יוֹחָנָן פְּלִיגָא עַל מִילְּתָא. תַּנֵּי רִבִּי שִׁמְעוֹן בֶּן אֶלְעָזָר אוֹמֵר מִשּׁוּם רִבִּי עֲקִיבָה כָּל־שֶׁאֶחָד פּוֹתֵחַ וְאֶחָד נוֹעֵל פָּטוּר. בִּשְׁנֵי שׁוּתָּפִין לֹא בִשְׁנֵי דִיוּרִין. מַה בֵּין שׁוּתָּף מַה בֵּין דִיוּר. כְּשֵׁם שֶׁהַשּׁוּתָּף מְמַחֶה כָּךְ הַדִּיוּר מְמַחֶה. אָמַר רִבִּי יוֹנָה בְּבַעַל הַבַּיִת וְדִיוּרוֹ הִיא מַתְנִיתָא. בַּעַל הַבַּיִת מְמַחֶה עַל יְדֵי דַיָּיר וְאֵין דַּיָּיר מְמַחֶה עַל יַד בַּעַל הַבַּיִת. עֲלֵיהּ שָׁמְעוּן קוֹמֵי רִבִּי יוֹחָנָן הֲלָכָה כְּרִבִּי שִׁמְעוֹן בֶּן אֶלְעָזָר דְּרִבִּי עֲקִיבָה. רִבִּי יוֹנָה אָמַר זְעִירָה וְרִבִּי אִימִּי תְּרֵיהוֹן בְּשֵׁם רִבִּי יוֹחָנָן הֲלָכָה כְּרִבִּי שִׁמְעוֹן בֶּן אֶלְעָזָר דְּרִבִּי עֲקִיבָה. אָמַר רִבִּי אִימִּי הוֹרֵי דְּבֵית רִבִּי יַנַּיי[95] הֲלָכָה כְּרִבִּי שִׁמְעוֹן בֶּן לָעְזָר דְּרִבִּי עֲקִיבָה.

They heard before Rebbi Joḥanan that he said to them, practice follows all of them restrictively[96]. Why do they not say it in his name[97]? That not a word of Rebbi Joḥanan should disagree with another word of his. It was stated[98]: "Rebbi Simeon ben Eleazar said in the name of Rebbi Aqiba, one where one person opens and another one locks it is free; two partners but not two tenants." What is the difference between a partner and a tenant? Just as a partner may object so a tenant may object[99]! Rebbi Jonah said, the Mishnah refers to a landlord and his tenant. The landlord may object to the tenant, the tenant may not object to the landlord. About that they heard before Rebbi Joḥanan, practice follows Rebbi Simeon ben Eleazar in the name of Rebbi Aqiba[100]. Rebbi Jonah said, Zeïra and Rebbi Immi in the name of Rebbi Joḥanan: Practice follows Rebbi Simeon ben Eleazar in the name of Rebbi Aqiba. Rebbi Immi said, the house of Rebbi Yannai instructed that practice follows Rebbi Simeon ben Eleazar in the name of Rebbi Aqiba.

95 Reading of the Rome ms. Leyden and Venice: רִבִּי יוֹחָנָן כְּאִילֵּין דְּבֵי רִבִּי אִימִּי "Rebbi Joḥanan instructed those of the house of Rebbi Immi."

96 A courtyard creates *ṭevel* except if it is exempt according to everybody.

97 Why is the statement not directly attributed to R. Yoḥanan? In the Babli, *Niddah* 47b, the statement is a *baraita* attributed to Rebbi.

98 Tosephta 2:20. There, the reading is: For example two partners, two tenants.

99 R. Aqiba seems to indicate that the courtyard is only free if one party may open or close over the objections of the other party. This excludes both the text of the *baraita* here and the Tosephta.

100 The interpretation of R. Joḥanan is more lenient than what would follow from the logical argument of (the much later) R. Jonah. It follows that on the same subject, R. Joḥanan is both restrictive and lenient.

רִבִּי בּוּן בַּר חִיָּא בְּעָא קוֹמֵי רִבִּי זְעִירָא מַה בָּא רִבִּי יְהוּדָה לְהוֹסִיף עַל דִּבְרֵי רִבִּי עֲקִיבָה רַבּוֹ. אָמַר לוֹ לֹא כְלוּם.

Rebbi Abun bar Ḥiyya asked before Rebbi Zeïra: What does Rebbi Jehudah add to the words of his teacher Rebbi Aqiba? He said to him, nothing.

(fol. 50b) **משנה ו:** הַגַּגּוֹת פְּטוּרִין אַף עַל פִּי שֶׁהֵן שֶׁל חָצֵר חַייֶבֶת. בֵּית שַׁעַר וְאֶכְסֶדְרָא וּמִרְפֶּסֶת הֲרֵי אֵלּוּ כְּחָצֵר אִם חַייֶבֶת חַייָבִין וְאִם פְּטוּרָה פְּטוּרִין.

Mishnah 6: Roofs are exempt even if they are in an obligated courtyard. A porter's lodge, a covered walkway[101], and a gallery[102] are like the courtyard: obligated if the latter is obligated and free if the latter is free[103].

משנה ז: הַצְּרִיפִין וְהַבּוּרְגּוֹנִין וְהָאַלִּיקְטִיּוֹת פְּטוּרִין. סוּכַּת גִּינּוֹסַר אַף עַל פִּי שֶׁיֵּשׁ בּוֹ רֵיחַיִם וְתַרְנְגוֹלִין פְּטוּרִין. סוּכַּת הַיּוֹצְרִים הַפְּנִימִית חַייֶבֶת וְהַחִיצוֹנָה פְּטוּרָה. רִבִּי יוֹסֵי אוֹמֵר כָּל־שֶׁאֵינָהּ דִּירַת הַחַמָּה וְדִירַת הַגְּשָׁמִים פְּטוּרָה. סוּכַּת הֶחָג בֶּחָג רִבִּי יְהוּדָה מְחַייֵב וַחֲכָמִים פּוֹטְרִין.

Mishnah 7: Sheds[104], watchtowers[105], and summer shelters[106] are free. Genezareth huts[107] even though they contain a hand mill or chickens are free. Potter's huts[108], the inner one is obligated, the outer one free. Rebbi Yose says, any which is not a dwelling in summer and winter is free[109]. A holiday hut on the holiday[110] Rebbi Jehudah obligates but the Sages free.

101 Greek ἐξέδρα, a covered walkway in front of the house.

102 To which the apartments of the upper floor open, connected by a stair to the courtyard.

103 If fully processed produce is brought there.

104 A wooden shed with a slanted roof (Gaonic Commentary *Ahilut* 18:10; Maimonides).

105 Greek πύργος, ὅ, "tower"; Syriac בָּרְגְּנָן "small tower".

106 Permanent huts to live there the entire summer (Maimonides).

107 Permanent huts during harvest time (Maimonides). R. Simson identifies Genezareth huts with summer huts.

108 A double hut; the outer one being the workshop, the inner one dwelling and storage facility.

109 In Maimonides's autograph Mishnah and some mss. of the Maimonides tradition: Either in winter or in summer.

110 A greenery-covered hut, or *sukkah*, for the festival of *Sukkot* (*Lev.* 23:42-43).

(fol. 50d) **הלכה ז**: אָמַר רִבִּי לָעְזָר לְגַג מְבוּצָּר לַאֲוִיר חָצֵר הִיא מַתְנִיתָא. מִכֵּיוָן שֶׁהֶעֱבִירָן דֶּרֶךְ חָצֵר לֹא נִטְבְּלוּ. תִּיפְתָּר אִי כְרִבִּי יוֹסֵי בֵּי רִבִּי יוּדָה אִי כְרִבִּי בְּשֶׁהָיָה בְדַעְתּוֹ לַעֲשׂוֹתָן מוּקְצֶה וְנִמְלַךְ שֶׁלֹּא לַעֲשׂוֹתָן.

Rebbi Eleazar said, the Mishnah deals with a roof surrounded by the airspace of the courtyard[111]. Did [the produce] not become *ṭevel* when it was transported through the courtyard? Explain it either following Rebbi Yose ben Rebbi Jehudah or Rebbi[112], when he wanted to cut them up for drying and then changed his mind not to cut.[113]

111 Even if it is impossible to bring anything to the roof without crossing the courtyard.

112 Halakhah 1, Notes 21 ff.

113 This condition is needed only for Rebbi; for R. Yose ben R. Jehudah it suffices if he intends to store everything on the roof.

אָמַר רִבִּי אָבִין וְהוּא שֶׁהָיָה בְגַג אַרְבַּע עַל אַרְבַּע. מַה הַבַּיִת אֵינוֹ טוֹבֵל עַד שֶׁיְּהֵא בוֹ אַרְבַּע עַל אַרְבַּע אַף הַגָּג אֵינוֹ פוֹטֵר עַד שֶׁיְּהֵא בוֹ אַרְבַּע עַל אַרְבַּע. דְּתַנֵּי בַּיִת שֶׁאֵין בּוֹ אַרְבַּע אַמּוֹת עַל אַרְבַּע אַמּוֹת פָּטוּר מִן הַמְּזוּזָה. וּמִן הַמַּעֲקָה. וּמִן הָעֵירוּב. וְאֵינוֹ טוֹבֵל לְמַעְשְׂרוֹת. וְאֵין עוֹשִׂין אוֹתוֹ חִיבּוּר לָעִיר. וְהַנּוֹדֵר מִן הַבַּיִת מוּתָּר לֵישֵׁב בּוֹ. וְאֵין נוֹתְנִין לוֹ אַרְבַּע אַמּוֹת לִפְנֵי פִתְחוֹ. וְאֵין צָמִית בְּיוֹבֵל. וְאֵינוֹ מְטַמֵּא בִנְגָעִים. וְאֵין הַבְּעָלִים חוֹזְרִין עָלָיו מֵעוֹרְכֵי הַמִּלְחָמָה.

Rebbi Abin said, only if the roof is at least four [cubits] square. Just as a house does not induce *ṭevel* unless it is at least four [cubits] square, so the roof does not exempt unless it is at least four [cubits] square, as it is stated[114]: A house less than four [cubits] square is free from the obligations of *mezuzah*[115] and the parapet[116], from the obligation of *eruv*[117], does not induce *ṭevel*, is not counted as a connection to a town[118]; he who makes a vow not to be in a house may sit there; one does not give it four cubits before its entrance door[119]; it does not remain with the buyer in the Jubilee[120]; it cannot become impure by scale disease[121], and its owner does not return from the army because of it[122].

114 A similar *baraita* in Babli *Sukkah* 3a/b.

115 *Deut.* 6:9, 11:20.

116 *Deut.* 22:8.

117 If a courtyard belongs to a single owner except that a hut enclosing an area less that four cubits square belongs to another person, that courtyard may be used on the Sabbath by the majority owner without an *eruv* (cf. *Demay* 1, Notes 192-193).

118 On the Sabbath, one may not go outside one's town more than 2000 cubits (cf. *Peah* 8, Note 56). Any house which is within 70 cubits of a house of the town is also counted as part of the town; the count of 2000 cubits starts only at the outermost house. A small building does not count as a house.

119 In a courtyard belonging to several owners, the four cubits in front of the entrance of each house are the private domain of this house, to be used to load and unload. This does not apply to a small hut.

120 *Lev.* 25:30.

121 *Lev.* 14:34 ff.

122 *Deut.* 20:5.

מַהוּ שֶׁיִּטְבְּלוּ לְבַעַל הַבּוּרְגָּנִין. מִן מַה דְּתַנֵּי בֵּית סֵפֶר וּבֵית תַּלְמוּד טוֹבְלִין לְסֹפֵר וּלְמַשְׁנֶה.[123] אֲבָל לֹא לָאֲחֵרִים. הָדָא אָמְרָה שֶׁהֵן טוֹבְלִין לְבַעַל הַבּוּרְגָּנִין.

Do they[124] induce *ṭevel* for the dweller in watch towers? From what it is stated[125]: An elementary school and a Talmud school induce *ṭevel* for the elementary and the Mishnah teacher, but not for others. That means, they induce *ṭevel* for the dweller in watch towers.

123 Reading of the Rome ms. Leyden and Venice: ולא למשנה.

124 The watchtowers mentioned in Mishnah 7.

125 Tosephta 3:20: "One does not eat a snack in a synagogue or in a Talmud school if they also contain a dwelling; otherwise, one may eat a snack there."

רַבִּי אוֹמֵר אַרְבַּע אַמּוֹת אַף עַל פִּי שֶׁאֵין שָׁם אַרְבַּע דַּפְנוֹת. רַבִּי שִׁמְעוֹן אוֹמֵר אַרְבַּע דַּפְנוֹת אַף עַל פִּי שֶׁאֵין שָׁם אַרְבַּע אַמּוֹת. רַבִּי יְהוּדָה אוֹמֵר אַרְבַּע אַמּוֹת וְאַרְבַּע דַּפְנוֹת. וְכֵן הָיָה רַבִּי יוּדָה מְחַייֵב בִּמְזוּזָה. מִסְתַּבְּרָא רַבִּי יוּדָה יוֹדֵי לְאִילֵּין רַבָּנִין. אִילֵּין רַבָּנִין לֹא יוֹדוּן לְרַבִּי יוּדָה. אַף עַל פִּי שֶׁיֵּשׁ שָׁם אַרְבַּע אַמּוֹת וְאַרְבַּע דַּפְנוֹת שֶׁהוּא פָּטוּר מִן הַמְּזוּזָה וְאֵינוֹ טוֹבֵל לְמַעְשְׂרוֹת.

[126]Rebbi says, four cubits even though there are not four walls. Rebbi Simeon says, four walls even though there are not four cubits. Rebbi Jehudah says, four walls and four cubits[127]. Similarly, Rebbi Jehudah requires it to have a *mezuzah*. It is reasonable that Rebbi Jehudah agrees with these rabbis[128], but these rabbis will not agree with Rebbi Jehudah: Even if it has four cubits and four walls it is not required to have a *mezuzah* and it does not create *ṭevel* for tithes[129].

126 This paragraph explains why R. Jehudah holds that a *sukkah* creates *ṭevel*; for him a *sukkah* must be a complete house since one is required to dwell in it. The paragraph is also in *Sukkah* 1:1, fol. 52a; Rebbi's standpoint is quoted Babli *Sukkah* 3b.

127 He requires that a *sukkah* be a complete dwelling; quoted in Babli *Sukkah* 3b, *Yoma* 10a.

128 He does not agree but he requires everything any other authority requires.

129 Since it must be temporary.

(fol. 50b) **משנה ח:** תְּאֵינָה שֶׁהִיא עוֹמֶדֶת בֶּחָצֵר אוֹכֵל אַחַת אַחַת וְאִם צֵירַף חַייָב. רַבִּי שִׁמְעוֹן אוֹמֵר אַחַת בִּימִינוֹ וְאַחַת בִּשְׂמֹאלוֹ וְאַחַת בְּפִיו. עָלָה לְרֹאשָׁהּ מְמַלֵּא חֵיקוֹ וְאוֹכֵל.

Mishnah 8: From a fig tree standing in a courtyard[130], one may eat one by one and if he took them together he is obligated. Rebbi Simeon says, one in his right hand, one in his left hand, and one in his mouth[131].

If he climbed to the top of the tree[132] he may fill the fold of his toga[133] and eat.

130 If the figs are collected for eating raw, their processing is completed with picking and the courtyard obligates for heave and tithes.
131 If no two figs are simultaneously in a hand or in a vessel, they are not "taken together."
132 Then he is no longer in the courtyard. The top of the tree is supposed to be more than 10 handbreadths above the ground; cf. *Kilaim* 6, Note 31.
133 Hebrew חיק "bosom" is used as an equivalent of Latin *sinus, ūs, m.*, which in addition to "bosom" also means "fold, pocket, purse" (E. G.).

(fol. 50d) **הלכה ח**: תַּנֵּי נוֹתְנִין לוֹ שָׁהוּת לְפַצֵּעַ בָּהּ פַּעַם רִאשׁוֹנָה שְׁנִיָּיה וּשְׁלִישִׁית. רִבִּי יוֹנָה בְּשֵׁם רִבִּי זְעִירָא שֶׁאִים לִיקֵּט אֶת הַשְּׁנִיָּיה בְּתוֹךְ כְּדֵי שָׁהוּת רִאשׁוֹנָה[134] נִטְבְּלוּ שְׁתֵּיהֶן.

Halakhah 8: It was stated: One gives him time to hit it a first, second, and third time. Rebbi Jonah in the name of Rebbi Zeïra: If he collected the second one during the time allotted for the first, both became *ṭevel*[135].

134 Reading of the Rome ms. Leyden and Venice: השנייה.
135 The meaning of this paragraph is unclear; the subject is not mentioned in Maimonides's Code.

According to R. Eliahu Fulda, one speaks of unripe figs which need to be softened to become edible. The new information would be that in order to eat a fruit as a snack, it is not necessary to swallow it as soon as it is taken but one may take all the time necessary to make it edible. However, if the second is picked while the first one is still there, both become *ṭevel*.

According to R. Moses Margalit, there is a standard time allotted for the eating of each fig (irrespective of its ripeness). According to him, if the second fig is picked while the first still exists, both become *ṭevel*. Then one wonders what the statement of R. Zeïra means.

According to R. Eliahu Kramer of Wilna, if the second fig is picked during the time allotted to the first, if the first still exists, both become *ṭevel*. But if he second fig is picked after the time allotted to the first, even if the first still exists, only the second one becomes *tevel*; the first remains permitted.

According to *Sefer Nir*, the first sentence refers to Tosephta 2:22: "A fig tree standing in a garden which extends a branch into a window, he (mss: eats) (*editio princeps*: picks) it normally and is free. If he picked and put it on a table, even a single one is obligated." The first sentence of the paragraph states that even if he did not put it on a table but waited after softening the fig three times, he is obligated. This interpretation is the only one giving the Mishnaic expression "one gives him time" the usual restrictive meaning of "so much but not more." The second sentence is then taken to mean that if the second fig is picked after the time allotted for the first, if the first is not yet completely eaten the existing remainder becomes obligated but the second remains free unless held together with the first.

רִבִּי יִרְמְיָה בָּעֵי זָרַק אֶת הָרִאשׁוֹנָה לְמַעְלָה מֵאֲוִיר עֲשָׂרָה לֹא הִסְפִּיקָה לֵירֵד לְמַטָּה מֵאֲוִיר עֲשָׂרָה עַד שֶׁלִּיקֵּט אֶת הַשְּׁנִייָה נִטְבְּלוּ שְׁתֵּיהֶן.

Rebbi Jeremiah asked: If he threw the first higher in the air than 10 [hand-breadths[132]] and it did not descend below 10 [hand-breadths] when he collected the second one, did both of them become *tevel*[136]?

135 This is one of R. Jeremiah's famous hair-splitting questions which deserves no answer. If the first fig comes to rest on a ledge, it becomes obligated by the Tosephta quoted in the preceding Note. If it descends, the second fig was collected within the time allotted to the first and both become *tevel*. The statement can be taken as supporting the interpretation of the preceding paragraph given by *Sefer Nir*.

רִבִּי לָעְזָר בֵּי רִבִּי שִׁמְעוֹן אוֹמֵר שָׁלֹשׁ בִּימִינוֹ וְשָׁלֹשׁ בִּשְׂמֹאלוֹ וְשָׁלֹשׁ בְּפִיו. רִבִּי לָעְזָר בֵּי רִבִּי שִׁמְעוֹן עַל יְדֵי דַהֲוָה אָכְלָן הֲוָה מְשָׁעֵר גַּרְמֵיהּ כֵּן. רִבִּי לָעְזָר בֵּי רִבִּי שִׁמְעוֹן אֲזַל לְגַבֵּיהּ רִבִּי יוֹסֵי בַּר לַקוֹנְיָא חָמוֹי הֲוָה מְזַג לֵיהּ וְהוּא שָׁתֵי. מְזַג לֵיהּ וְהוּא שָׁתֵי. אָמַר לֵיהּ לֹא שְׁמַעַת מִן אָבוּךְ כַּמָּה אָדָם צָרִיךְ לְגַמּוֹת בַּכּוֹס. אָמַר לֵיהּ כְּמוֹת שֶׁהִיא אַחַת. בְּצוֹנִין שְׁתַּיִם. בְּחַמִּין שָׁלֹשׁ וְלֹא

שִׁיעֲרוּ חֲכָמִים לֹא בְּיֵינָךְ שֶׁהוּא נָאֶה וְלֹא כְּכוֹסָךְ שֶׁהוּא קָטָן וְלֹא בִּכְרֵיסִי שֶׁהִיא רְחָבָה.

Rebbi Eleazar ben Rebbi Simeon says, three in his right hand, three in his left hand, and three in his mouth[137]. Since Rebbi Eleazar ben Rebbi Simeon was a glutton, he estimated so for himself. [138]Rebbi Eleazar ben Rebbi Simeon went to his father-in-law Rebbi Simeon ben Rebbi Yose ben Laqonia who repeatedly mixed wine for him which he gulped down. He said to him, did you not hear from your father how one swallows from a cup? He said to him, one gulp if it is unmixed, two gulps [if mixed] with cold water, three with hot water. But the Sages did not estimate this with your wine which is good, or with your cup which is small, or with my belly which is large.

137 He extends his father's rule from one to three figs each, in contradiction to our general rule that even two at the same place become obligated.

138 A slightly extended version of this story is in *Pesiqta deRav Kahana*, p. 91a/b. The Babli (*Pesaḥim* 86b) has a similar story attributed to R. Ismael ben R. Yose, who had a reputation of being as obese as R. Eleazar ben R. Simeon.

וַהֲוָה רִבִּי יְהוֹשֻׁעַ בֶּן קָרְחָה צְוַוח לֵיהּ חַלָּא בַּר חַמְרָא. אֲמַר לֵיהּ לָמָּה אַתְּ צְוַוח לִי כֵן. אֲמַר לֵיהּ עַד דַּעֲרַקְתְּ וַאֲזַלְתְּ לָךְ לְלַדִיקְיָא. אֲמַר לֵיהּ לֹא קוֹצִין כְּסִיחִין כִּסַּחְתִּי. אֲמַר לֵיהּ וְלָא הֲוָה לֵילֵיךְ לָךְ לְסוֹף הָעוֹלָם לְהַנִּיחַ בַּעַל הַגִּינָּה שֶׁיִּקּוֹץ אֶת קוֹצָיו.

[139]Rebbi Joshua ben Qorḥah called him "vinegar son of wine." He said to him, why do you call me that? He said to him, you should have gone to Laodicea. He said to him: Do I not mow mowable thorns from the garden[140]? He said to him, you should have gone to the end of the world to let the owner of the garden cut his thorns.

139 The first part from the story in Babli *Baba Meẓi'a* 83b is missing : R. Eleazar ben R. Simeon, known for his psychological profiling of thieves, was forced by the Roman government to act as a detective to discover thieves and robbers. R. Joshua objected: the Roman government executed all robbers and thieves while Jewish law only required double restitution in the case of a thief and simple restitution in the case of a robber. Therefore, collaboration with the Roman Government would be possible murder.

140 The people of Israel. The imagery is from the Song of Songs.

נִתְגַּלְגְּלָה מֵאֵילֶיהָ מַהוּ מַחֲזָרְתָהּ כְּמַה דְתֵימַר תַּמָּן מַחֲזִירָן לִמְקוֹמָן וְאוֹכֵל. וְאוּף הָכָא כֵן. תַּמָּן מַחֲזִירָן בְּמָקוֹם פְּטוֹר. בְּרַם הָכָא בְּמַחֲזִירָן לְמָקוֹם חִייוּב. מַה דָמִי לָהּ הָיָה עוֹמֵד בְּרֹאשׁ הַתְּאֵינָה מַה אַתְּ עֲבִיד לָהּ כְּעוֹמֵד בָּעִיר כְּעוֹמֵד בַּשָּׂדֶה. יֵיבָא כְהָדָא הָיָה עוֹמֵד בָּעִיר וְאָמַר יוֹדֵעַ אֲנִי שֶׁהַפּוֹעֲלִין שׁוֹכְחִין עוֹמֶר שֶׁבְּמָקוֹם פְּלוֹנִי וּשְׁכָחוּהוּ אֵינוֹ שִׁכְחָה. הָיָה עוֹמֵד בַּשָּׂדֶה וְאוֹמֵר יוֹדֵעַ אֲנִי שֶׁהַפּוֹעֲלִין שׁוֹכְחִין עוֹמֶר שֶׁבְּמָקוֹם פְּלוֹנִי וּשְׁכָחוּהוּ הֲרֵי זֶה שִׁכְחָה דִּכְתִיב בַּשָּׂדֶה וְשָׁכַחְתָּ וְלֹא בָעִיר וְשָׁכַחְתָּ.

If it[141] rolled away by itself, can he bring it back as you say there[142], may he bring them back to their intended place and eat? Is it the same here? There, he brings it back to an exempt place but here he brings it back to a place of obligation. To what do you compare if he stood in the crown of a fig tree[143], to one who stands in town or in a field? It refers to the following[144]: If he stood in town and said: I know that the workers are forgetting a sheaf at place X; if they forgot it is not a forgotten sheaf. If he stood in a field and said: I know that the workers are forgetting a sheaf at place X; [if they forgot] it is a forgotten sheaf, since it says (*Deut.* 24:19): "In your field and you forget a sheaf." In the field you forget, but in town you do not forget.

141 A fig from a tree in a walled courtyard which he picked with the intention of eating it right away. Now the fig is lying in the courtyard subject

to heave and tithes.

142 Halakhah 1, about figs from an exempt courtyard which were brought into the house by error; Notes 17-19.

143 Which is an exempt domain by itself.

144 *Peah* 5:6, Note 123. No answer is given. It is difficult to understand the quote since the case in *Peah* is not decided on the basis of logic but of a narrow biblical decree restricted to the case of a forgotten sheaf.

(fol. 50b) **משנה ט**: גֶּפֶן שֶׁהִיא נְטוּעָה בֶּחָצֵר נוֹטֵל אֶת כָּל־הָאֶשְׁכּוֹל וְכֵן בָּרִמּוֹן וְכֵן בָּאֲבַטִּיחַ דִּבְרֵי רִבִּי טַרְפוֹן. רִבִּי עֲקִיבָה אוֹמֵר מְגַרְגֵּר בָּאֶשְׁכּוֹל וּפוֹרֵט בָּרִמּוֹן וְסוֹפֵת בָּאֲבַטִּיחַ. כּוּסְבָּר שֶׁהִיא זְרוּעָה בֶּחָצֵר מְקַרְטֵם עָלֶה עָלֶה וְאוֹכֵל וְאִם צֵירַף חַיָּיב. סִיאָה וְהָאֵזוֹב וְהַקּוֹרְנִית שֶׁבְּחָצֵר אִם הָיוּ נִשְׁמָרִין חַיָּבִין.

Mishnah 9: From a vine planted in a courtyard one may take an entire bunch; the same holds for a pomegranate and a watermelon, the words of Rebbi Ṭarphon. Rebbi Aqiba says, he takes single grape berries, single seeds of a pomegranate, and picks[145] from the watermelon. Of coriander sown in the courtyard[146] he snips off leaf by leaf and eats; when he takes them together they are obligated. Calamint, hyssop, and thyme in the courtyard are obligated if they are guarded.

145 Enough for one bite; cf. Mishnah 2:6, Note 109.

146 The restriction does not apply to coriander growing as a weed. For the other three spice plants mentioned, it is enough that they be guarded as valuable plants even if they started as weeds and were not sown by the owners of the courtyard; cf. *Ševiït* 7:7, Note 51; 8 Mishnah 1.

(fol. 50d) **הלכה ט**: תַּמָּן תַּנִּינָן הָיָה אוֹכֵל אֶת הָאֶשְׁכּוֹל וְנִכְנַס מִן הַגִּינָּה לֶחָצֵר. רִבִּי לִיעֶזֶר אוֹמֵר יִגְמוֹר רִבִּי יְהוֹשֻׁעַ אוֹמֵר לֹא יִגְמוֹר. רִבִּי זְעִירָה בְּשֵׁם רִבִּי יוֹחָנָן אוֹ רִבִּי טַרְפוֹן כְּרִבִּי אֱלִיעֶזֶר אוֹ דְּרִבִּי טַרְפוֹן עֲבַד עוּקְצַת הָאוֹכֶל

מִתְּחִילָּתוֹ. רִבִּי אִילָּא רִבִּי אִיסִּי בְשֵׁם רִבִּי יוֹחָנָן אוֹ רִבִּי טַרְפוֹן כְּרִבִּי לִיעֶזֶר. אוֹ רִבִּי טַרְפוֹן עֲבַד אֲכִילָה שְׁתַּיִם שָׁלֹשׁ אֲכִילוֹת כַּאֲכִילָה אַחַת. מַה טַעֲמָא דְרִבִּי לִיעֶזֶר מִשּׁוּם שֶׁהִתְחִיל בּוֹ בְהֵיתֵר. אָמַר רִבִּי נָתָן לֹא שֶׁרִבִּי אֱלִיעֶזֶר אוֹמֵר מִשּׁוּם שֶׁהִתְחִיל בּוֹ בְהֵיתֵר. אֶלָּא שֶׁרִבִּי לִיעֶזֶר אוֹמֵר יַמְתִּין עַד שֶׁיֵּצֵא שַׁבָּת אוֹ עַד שֶׁיּוֹצִיא חוּץ לַחֲצֵרוֹ וְיִגְמוֹר.

Halakhah 9: There[147], we have stated: "If he was eating a bunch of grapes and entered into the courtyard from the garden. Rebbi Eliezer said, he should finish, but Rebbi Joshua said, he should not finish." Rebbi Zeïra in the name of Rebbi Joḥanan: Either Rebbi Ṭarphon says following Rebbi Eliezer or Rebbi Ṭarphon says, one makes the cut of food equal to its start. Rebbi Illa, Rebbi Assi in the name of Rebbi Joḥanan: Either Rebbi Ṭarphon follows Rebbi Eliezer or Rebbi Ṭarphon makes one snack containing two or three snacks equal to one snack. What is the reason of Rebbi Eliezer? Because he started with permission. It was stated: "Rebbi Nathan said, not that Rebbi Eliezer said because he started with permission but Rebbi Eliezer holds he should wait until the end of the Sabbath or he should leave the courtyard again and finish."

147 *Terumot* 7, Mishnah 3, Halakhah 4; Notes 73-75, the entire paragraph with slight variations in wording.

(fol. 50b) **משנה י:** תְּאֵינָה שֶׁהִיא עוֹמֶדֶת בֶּחָצֵר וְנוֹטָה לַגִּינָּה אוֹכֵל כְּדַרְכּוֹ וּפָטוּר. עוֹמֵד בַּגִּינָּה וְנוֹטָה לֶחָצֵר אוֹכֵל אַחַת אַחַת וְאִם צֵירַף חַיָּיב. עוֹמֶדֶת בָּאָרֶץ וְנוֹטָה בְחוּצָה לָאָרֶץ אוֹ עוֹמֶדֶת בְּחוּצָה לָאָרֶץ וְנוֹטָה לָאָרֶץ הַכֹּל הוֹלֵךְ אַחַר הָעִיקָּר. וּבְבָתֵּי עָרֵי חוֹמָה הַכֹּל הוֹלֵךְ אַחַר הָעִיקָּר. בְּעָרֵי מִקְלָט הַכֹּל הוֹלֵךְ אַחַר הַנּוֹף. וּבִירוּשָׁלֵם הַכֹּל הוֹלֵךְ אַחַר הַנּוֹף.

Mishnah 10: If a fig tree was standing in a courtyard but its crown was hanging over a vegetable garden, one eats[148] as usual and is free. If it was standing in a vegetable garden but its crown was hanging over a courtyard, one eats one by one and if he takes them together he is obligated. If it was standing in the Land and hanging over outside the Land or standing outside the Land and hanging over the Land, everything is determined by the stem. For houses of walled cities[149], everything is determined by the stem. For cities of refuge[150], all goes by the crown, for Jerusalem[151] all goes by the crown.

148 Standing in the unwalled garden and picking the fruit there, as explained in the Mishnah.

149 Which can be bought back by the seller only during the first year of the sale, *Lev.* 25:29-30. The rule given there for houses is extended to trees growing in the city.

150 *Num.* 35. If the homicide reaches the crown of a tree whose stem is inside 2000 cubits from the wall of a city of refuge, he is safe.

151 Second tithe can be redeemed outside Jerusalem; in Jerusalem it must be consumed in purity. Once it is brought under the crown of a tree of Jerusalem, it cannot any longer be redeemed. The Babli (*Makkot* 12a) notes that the two last statements are parallel but the reasons are different.

(fol. 50d) **הלכה י:** תַּנֵּי בְשֵׁם רִבִּי נְחֶמְיָה חָצֵר שֶׁהִיא נֶעֱדֶרֶת הֲרֵי הִיא כְגִינָּה (fol. 51a) אוֹכְלִין בְּתוֹכָהּ עֲרַאי. אָמַר רִבִּי שִׂמְלַאי הֲלָכָה כְּרִבִּי נְחֶמְיָה. תַּנֵּי זָרַע רוּבָּהּ חַייָב. נָטַע רוּבָּהּ פְּטוּרָה. אָמַר רַב חִסְדָּא וְהוּא שֶׁנְּטָעָהּ לְנוֹייָהּ שֶׁל חָצֵר. הָדָא יָלְפָא מִן הַהִיא. וְהַהִיא יָלְפָא מִן הָדָא. הָדָא יָלְפָא מִן הַהִיא זָרַע רוּבָּהּ חַייֶבֶת וְהִיא שֶׁתְּהֵא נֶעֱדֶרֶת. וְהַהִיא יָלְפָא מִן הָדָא שֶׁאִם הָיְתָה נֶעֱדֶרֶת שֶׁהִיא כְשֵׁירָה וְהוּא שֶׁעִידֵּר רוּבָּהּ.

Halakhah 10: It was stated[152] in the name of Rebbi Neḥemiah: "A courtyard which regularly is being weeded is like a vegetable garden." Rebbi Simlai said, practice follws Rebbi Neḥemiah. It was stated: If most of it was sown it is obligated, if planted it is free[153]. Rav Ḥisda said, only if he planted to embellish the courtyard. This infers from that and that infers from this. This infers from that, if most of it was sown, it is obligated if[154] it is weeded. That infers from this, if it was weeded[155] it is acceptable only if most of it was weeded.

152 Tosephta 2:20.

153 This is a very difficult text but it is confirmed by Maimonides (*Ma'aser* 4:14), R. Abraham ben David (*ad loc.*) and *Caphtor va-Pherach* (Chap. 32, p. 504). R. Joseph Caro (*Kesef Mishneh ad loc.*) explains that a courtyard is always obligated except if it is planted with trees for its beautification since this (a) is permanent and (b) establishes the courtyard as a separate entity, rather than as working space for the house. Since the biblical law requires tithing only when produce is brought to the house, the transformation of the courtyard into a pleasure garden removes the obligation of tithing. The emendation of R. Abraham ben David, followed by R. S. Cirillo, is unnecessary.

154 Even if.

155 The pleasure garden was tended regularly.

הָדָא דְתֵימַר אוֹכֵל כְּדַרְכּוֹ פָּטוּר בְעוֹמֵד בְּגִינָּה. הֵן דְּתֵימַר אוֹכֵל אֶחָד אֶחָד פָּטוּר וְאִם צֵירַף חַיָּב בְּעוֹמֵד בְּחָצֵר.

This means "one eats as usual and is free", when he is standing in the garden; this means "if one eats one by one he is free but if he takes them together he is obligated" if he stands in the courtyard[156].

156 Explanation of the Mishnah. The text here is that of most Mishnah mss. and the Mishnah in the Munich ms. of the Babli.

רִבִּי יִרְמְיָה בְּעָא קוֹמֵי רִבִּי זְעִירָא הָיְתָה נִיטֶּלֶת בְּדוּקְנִי. דִּלְמָא רִבִּי זְעִירָא וְרִבִּי אַבָּא בַּר כַּהֲנָא וְרִבִּי לֵוִי הֲווֹן יָתְבִין וַהֲוָה רִבִּי זְעִירָא מְקַנְתֵּר לְאִילֵּין דְּאַגַּדְתָּא וְצָווַח לְהוֹן סִפְרֵי קוֹסְמֵי. אֲמַר לֵיהּ רִבִּי בָּא בַּר כַּהֲנָא לָמָּה אַתְּ מְקַנְתֵּר לוֹן שְׁאַל וְאִינּוּן מְגִיבִין לָךְ. אֲמַר לֵיהּ מַהוּ הָדֵין דִּכְתִיב כִּי חֲמַת אָדָם

תּוֹדֶךָּ שְׁאֵרִית חֵמוֹת תַּחְגּוֹר. אָמַר לוֹ חֲמַת אָדָם תּוֹדֶךָּ בְּעוֹלָם הַזֶּה. שְׁאֵרִית חֵמוֹת תַּחְגּוֹר לְעוֹלָם הַבָּא. אֲמַר לֵיהּ אוֹ נֵימַר חֲמַת אָדָם תּוֹדֶךָּ בְּעוֹלָם הַבָּא. שְׁאֵרִית חֵמוֹת תַּחְגּוֹר בָּעוֹלָם הַזֶּה. אָמַר רִבִּי לֵוִי כְּשֶׁתִּתְעוֹרֵר חֲמָתְךָ עַל הָרְשָׁעִים צַדִּיקִים רוֹאִין מַה אַתְּ עוֹשֶׂה לָהֶן וְהֵן מוֹדִין לְשִׁמְךָ. אָמַר רִבִּי זְעִירָא הִיא הֲפָכָה וְהִיא מְהַפְּכָה לֹא שְׁמָעִינָן מִינָּהּ כְּלוּם. יִרְמְיָה בְּנִי אֵזֵל לְצוֹר[157] צוֹר דקניתָךְ דְּהִיא טָבָא מִן כְּלוּם.

Rebbi Jeremiah asked before Rebbi Zeïra: If it was taken with a *dwqny*[158]? Example[159]: Rebbi Zeïra, Rebbi Abba bar Cahana, and Rebbi Levi were sitting together when Rebbi Zeïra was goading[160] those of *Agadah*[161] and called them books of sorcery. Rebbi Abba bar Cahana said to him, why are you goading us? Ask and they will answer you. He said to him, what means that which is written (*Ps.* 76:11): "For the rage of man brings thanks to You, the leftover rages You will gird?" He said to him, for the rage of man brings thanks to You in this world, the leftover rages You will gird in the future world. He said to him, why can we not say, for the rage of man brings thanks to You in the future world, the leftover rages You will gird in this world? Rebbi Levi said, when You awaken Your rage on the wicked, they will see what You are doing and they will bring thanks to Your name[162]. Rebbi Zeïra said, the same turns and turns around and one does not understand anything from it[163]. Jeremiah my son, go to Tyre, wrap your *dwqny* because it is better than anything.

157 Reading of the Rome ms. Venice and Leyden: צור "Tyre".

158 The meaning of the word is unclear. The consensus of the commentators is that it is some instrument to harvest fruits that plucks more than one fruit at a time. The question is whether then the fruits are automatically obligated for heave and tithes even if the primary intent was to get one only as a snack. The negative answer is obvious. This is another

example of R. Jeremiah's questions; cf. *Terumot* 10, Note 110.

Possibly דוקני is corrupted from דוקרני "pitchfork", cf. *Kilaim* 4:4, Note 60.

159 *Berakhot* 1:1, Note 72.

160 *Berakhot* 2:3, Note 96.

161 The allegorical explanation of Scripture which is not based on anything.

162 *Midrash Psalms* (ed. Bóber, p. 342) explains: 'For the rage, man brings thanks to You', when You decreed judgment on Israel by dispersing them, they have to thank You that You did not punish them with all Your Divine might, but 'the leftover rages You will gird' to judge the Gentiles on the Day of Judgment.

163 None of the explanations is necessary.

הלכה יא: תַּמָּן תַּנִּינָן כָּל־שֶׁהוּא לִפְנִים מִן הַחוֹמָה הֲרֵי הִיא כְבָתֵּי עָרֵי חוֹמָה חוּץ מִן הַשָּׂדוֹת. רִבִּי מֵאִיר אוֹמֵר אַף הַשָּׂדוֹת. מַה טַעֲמָה דְּרַבָּנִין וְקָם בַּיִת אֵין לִי אֶלָּא בַּיִת מְנַיִין לְרַבּוֹת בָּתֵּי בַדִּין וּבוֹרוֹת שִׂיחִין וּמְעָרוֹת וּמֶרְחַצִּיּוֹת וְשׁוֹבְכוֹת וּמִגְדָּלוֹת. תַּלְמוּד לוֹמַר אֲשֶׁר בָּעִיר. יָכוֹל אַף הַשָּׂדוֹת. תַּלְמוּד לוֹמַר בַּיִת. מַה בַּיִת מְיוּחָד שֶׁהוּא בֵּית דִּירָה. יָצְאוּ שָׂדוֹת שֶׁאֵינָן בֵּית דִּירָה. מַה טַעֲמָה דְּרִבִּי מֵאִיר וְקָם הַבַּיִת אֵין לִי אֶלָּא בַּיִת מְנַיִין לְרַבּוֹת בָּתֵּי בַדִּין וּבוֹרוֹת שִׂיחִין וּמְעָרוֹת וּמֶרְחַצִּיּוֹת וְשׁוֹבְכוֹת וּמִגְדָּלוֹת וְהַשָּׂדוֹת. תַּלְמוּד לוֹמַר אֲשֶׁר בָּעִיר.

Halakhah 11: There[164], we have stated: "Everything inside the wall is like houses of a walled city except fields[165]. Rebbi Meïr says, including fields." "[166]What is the reason of the rabbis? (*Lev.* 25:30) 'The house stands.' Not only houses; from where do we include oilpresses, cisterns, ditches, caves, bathhouses, dovecots, and towers? The verse says, 'which is in the city'. I could think, also fields? The verse says, 'the house.' The house is special in that it is a dwelling, that excludes fields which are not for dwelling[167]. What is the reason of Rebbi Meïr? 'The house stands.' Not only houses; from where do we include oilpresses, cisterns, ditches, caves, bathhouses, dovecots, towers, and fields? The verse says, 'which is in the city'."

164 Mishnah *Arakhin* 9:5, Babli *Arakhin* 32a. Here starts the discussion of the last two sentences of the Mishnah, Notes 149-151.

165 In *Sifra Behar Parašah* 4(5), the statement is attributed to R. Jehudah. This is confirmed by Babli *Arakhin* 32a.

166 *Sifra Behar Parašah* 4(5-6).

167 According to the opinion of Rav Ḥisda in Babli *Arakhin* 32a, even R. Meïr will agree that an agricultural field is excluded. The only "fields" he includes are sand quarries and fish ponds which have the character of "ditches and caves". In the Tosephta, *Arakhin* 5:14, R. Meïr admits gardens and orchards as entities which cannot be reclaimed by the seller later than one full year after the sale.

אֲשֶׁר לוֹ חוֹמָה פְּרָט לְבַיִת הַבָּנוּי לְחוֹמָה דִּבְרֵי רִבִּי יְהוּדָה. רִבִּי שִׁמְעוֹן אוֹמֵר כּוֹתְלָהּ הַחִיצוֹן הוּא הַחוֹמָה. רִבִּי יְהוּדָה דָּרַשׁ אֲשֶׁר לוֹ חוֹמָה. רִבִּי שִׁמְעוֹן אֲשֶׁר לֹא חוֹמָה.

(*Lev.* 25:30) [168]"'Which has a wall', this excludes a house which is built as a wall, the words of Rebbi Jehudah. Rebbi Simeon says, its outer wall is the city wall." Rebbi Jehudah explains 'which has a wall[169]'; Rebbi Simeon explains 'which has no wall'.

168 Mishnah *Arakhin* 9:5, Babli *Arakhin* 32a, Tosephta *Arakhin* 5:14, *Sifra Behar Parašah* 4(5-7).

169 The *Qere* in the verse; the *Ketib* is "the house in a city which has no wall." Since עיר is feminine and לו masculine, the relative pronoun should belong to בית : The house in the city which (i. e., the house) has/does not have a wall. In this interpretation, the positions of R. Jehudah and R. Simeon should be interchanged. In the Babli, the difference between the authors is explained by their different interpretations of the description of Rahab's house (*Jos.* 2:15).

אָמַר רִבִּי חִינְנָא וְהוּא שֶׁעָלָה דֶרֶךְ הַנּוֹף אֲבָל אִם עָלָה דֶרֶךְ הָעִיקָּר כְּבָר קְלָטוֹ הָעִיקָּר.

Rebbi Ḥinena said, this is only if he arrived by the crown. But if he arrived by the stem, the stem already received him[170].

170 This refers to the cities of refuge. As Maimonides puts it in his Commentary, the Mishnah should be read as: For cities of refuge, the crown *also* counts.

מַתְנִיתָא דְבֵית שַׁמַּאי אוֹמְרִין הַכֹּל כִּלְפְנִים. תַּנֵּי הֶחֱזִיר אֶת הַנּוֹף מִבִּפְנִים כּוּלּוֹ כִּלְפְנִים. וְאִית בָּהֶן תַּנַּיָּיא קַדְמִיָּא כְּבֵית שַׁמַּאי.

Our Mishnah[171] follows the House of Shammai who say[172], all has the status of inside. It was stated[173]: If he turned the crown towards the inside, all is counted as inside. The earlier Tannaïm follow the House of Shammai[174].

171 The last statement, that ritual Jerusalem is bordered by the wall and all crowns of trees overhanging the wall.

172 Mishnah *Ma'aser Šeni* 3:7; Tosephta *Ma'aser Šeni* 2:12: "Oil presses [built into the wall] open towards the city whose building extends outside, or built inside and opening to the outside, the House of Shammai say, all is counted as inside but the House of Hillel say, what is in the wall and the interior is inside, what is outside is outside."

173 A similar statement in Tosephta *Ma'aser Šeni* 2:12: "If a tree stands inside with its crown extending outside, its Second Tithe can be redeemed (as being harvested outside Jerusalem). If one turned the crown to be inside, its Second Tithe cannot be redeemed. If [the tree] was standing outside with its crown extending inside, its Second Tithe cannot be redeemed (as being harvested inside Jerusalem). If he turned the crown so as to be outside, its Second Tithe can be redeemed."

174 Tosephta *Ma'aser Šeni* 2:12: "Rebbi Yose said, this (the preceding statements about trees and olive presses) are the teachings of R. Aqiba. The earlier Mishnah: The House of Shammai [say] one does not redeem there (in or at the oil presses) as if it were inside and one does not eat sacrifices there as if it were outside. But the House of Hillel say, what is open to the inside is inside, what is open to the outside is outside." For the earlier Mishnah, the Mishnah here is not following the House of Shammai.

הכובש פרק רביעי

(fol. 51a) **משנה א:** הַכּוֹבֵשׁ הַשּׁוֹלֵק הַמּוֹלֵחַ בַּשָּׂדֶה חַיָּיב. הַמְכַמֵּר בָּאֲדָמָה פָּטוּר. הַמְטַבֵּל בַּשָּׂדֶה פָּטוּר. הַפּוֹצֵעַ זֵיתִים שֶׁיֵּצֵא מֵהֶן הַשְּׂרָף פָּטוּר. הַטּוֹחֵט זֵיתִים עַל בְּשָׂרוֹ פָּטוּר וְאִם סָחַט וְנָתַן לְתוֹךְ יָדוֹ חַיָּיב. הַמְקַפֶּה לְתַבְשִׁיל פָּטוּר וְלִקְדֵירָה חַיָּיב מִפְּנֵי שֶׁהוּא כְבוֹר קָטָן.

Mishnah 1: He who pickles, cooks, or salts in the field is obligated[1]. He who stores in the ground[2] is free. He who dips[3] in the field is free. He who pounds olives to remove the resin is free. He who squeezes olives on his skin is free but if he squeezed and put into his hand[4] he is obligated. He who prepares wine sauce for a dish[5] is free but in a pot[6] it is obligated for it is like a small cistern.

1 All these activities are considered final processing, as explained in the Halakhah. "Cooking" means preserving by prolonged cooking; "salting" is salting to preserve.

2 Unripe produce to ripen during storage.

3 Fruits in salt, salt water, or vinegar, to eat them on the spot as a snack.

4 Since the oil is collected, it is as if pressed in an oil-press and considered processed.

5 A small amount of thickened wine added to a dish already on a plate does not induce the obligation of tithes.

6 If the pot is on the fire, the obligation is induced by the fire. If the pot is empty and cold, the obligation is explained in the Mishnah; the pot acts as miniature vat.

הלכה א: אוֹר טוֹבֵל מִקָּח טוֹבֵל מֶלַח טוֹבֶלֶת תְּרוּמָה טוֹבֶלֶת. שַׁבָּת טוֹבֶלֶת. חָצֵר בֵּית שְׁמִירָה טוֹבֶלֶת. דְּאָמַר רִבִּי יוֹחָנָן מִקָּח בְּשַׁבָּת אֵינָהּ תּוֹרָה. רִבִּי אִמִּי בְּשֵׁם רִבִּי שִׁמְעוֹן בֶּן לָקִישׁ הַמְחוּוָּר מִכּוּלָּן זוֹ חָצֵר בֵּית שְׁמִירָה.

Fire creates *ṭevel*, buying creates *ṭevel*, salt creates *ṭevel*, heave creates *ṭevel*, the Sabbath creates *ṭevel*, a secure courtyard creates *ṭevel*,[7] but Rebbi Joḥanan said that buying and Sabbath are not biblical. Rebbi Immi in the name of Rebbi Simeon ben Laqish, the most reasonable of these is the secure courtyard.

7 This refers to the discussion Chapter 2:2-3. For the statements of R. Joḥanan and R. Simeon ben Laqish, cf. Chapter 2, Notes 101-102.

הַכּוֹבֵשׁ עַד שֶׁיִּכְבּוֹשׁ כָּל־צָרְכּוֹ הַשּׁוֹלֵק עַד שֶׁיִּשְׁלוֹק כָּל־צָרְכּוֹ. נִשְׁמְעִינָהּ מִן הָדָא הַמְהַבְהֵב שִׁיבֳּלִין בָּאוּר נִטְבְּלוּ. בְּלֹא כָךְ אֵינָן מְחוּסָּרִין מְלָאכָה עַל יְדֵי הָאוּר. שַׁנְיָיא הִיא שֶׁהוּא גְמַר מְלַאכְתּוֹ. וְיֵידָא אֲמְרָה דָא הַמְקַטֵּף שִׁיבֳּלִין לְעִיסָּתוֹ לְאוֹכְלִין מְלִילוֹת נִיטְבְּלוּ לַעֲשׂוֹתָן עִיסָּה לֹא נִטְבְּלוּ.

He who pickles, only if he pickles completely[8]? He who cooks, only if he cooks thoroughly? Let us hear from the following: If one singes ears of grain in the fire they become *ṭevel*[9]. Without that, would they not need to be worked over by fire[10]? There is a difference here, because that is the end of their processing[11]. Where has this been said[11]? If one plucks out kernels from ears destined for dough, if it is to eat them rolled[13] they are *ṭevel*, but to make a dough they are not *ṭevel*[14].

8 Does it become *ṭevel* only if the pickling is completed, or at least if the brine is strong enough that the vegetables would be completely cured if left in the brine for a sufficient time?

9 A similar statement in Tosephta 3:1, in the name of R. Simeon.

10 Since grain is rarely eaten raw.

10 Since the ears are lightly roasted as ears, it is clear that the grains should be eaten unmilled.

12 That the intent counts.

13 Rolled between the fingers to make them edible raw.

14 The language here is unclear since if the ears are destined for dough they are not for eating raw. The parallel in Babli *Beẓah* 13a reads: If somebody brought ears from the field,

if it is to make them into dough [and the ears must be threshed and milled] he may eat a snack from them, if to roll them [and eat them raw], Rebbi declares obligated but Rebbi Yose ben Jehudah declares them to be free [since they are called "grain", subject to tithes, only after threshing.] The *baraita* here follows R. Yose ben R. Jehudah.

All the argument here proves is that it is possible that pickling and preserving by cooking makes *ṭevel* only if the intent was to do a thorough job.

כָּבַשׁ וְשָׁלַק שֶׁלֹּא מִדַּעַת הַבְּעָלִים תַּפְלוּגְתָא דְּרִבִּי יוֹחָנָן וְרִבִּי שִׁמְעוֹן בֶּן לָקִישׁ. דְּאִיתְפַּלְּגוּן הַמְמָרֵחַ כְּרִיוֹ שֶׁל חֲבֵירוֹ שֶׁלֹּא מִדַּעְתּוֹ רִבִּי יוֹחָנָן אָמַר נִטְבַּל וְרִבִּי שִׁמְעוֹן בֶּן לָקִישׁ אָמַר לֹא נִטְבַּל. אָמַר רִבִּי יוּדָן תַּמָּן (fol. 51b) אֵיפְשַׁר לוֹ [שֶׁלֹּא לְמָרֵחַ בְּרַם הָכָא אֶפְשַׁר לוֹ][15] שֶׁלֹּא לִכְבּוֹשׁ.

If he pickled or cooked without the owners' knowledge, there is a difference between Rebbi Joḥanan and Rebbi Simeon ben Laqish since these differ: If somebody made a heap [of somebody's grain] without the latter's knowledge, Rebbi Joḥanan said, it is *ṭevel*, Rebbi Simeon ben Laqish said, it is not *ṭevel*. Rebbi Yudan said, there it is impossible for him not to make a heap[16], here it is possible for him not to pickle.

15 Reading of the Rome ms., missing in the Leyden ms. and Venice print.

16 After threshing, the grain must be raked together to be used. Therefore, R. Joḥanan may hold that the heap was made with the implied consent of the owner. This is not the case for pickling olives. R. Joḥanan may hold that pickling without consent of the owner does not create *ṭevel*. Fragments of this discussion are in Chapter 1, cf. Notes 22, 138.

שְׁלָקוֹ בִּרְשׁוּת הַהֶקְדֵּשׁ פְּדָאוֹ וְהִכְנִיסוֹ לַחֲצַר בֵּית שְׁמִירָה מַהוּ. עַל דַּעְתֵּיהּ דְּרִבִּי שִׁמְעוֹן בֶּן לָקִישׁ נִטְבָּל זוֹ תוֹרָה וְזוֹ אֵינָהּ תּוֹרָה. הִכְנִיסוֹ לַחֲצַר בֵּית שְׁמִירָה פְּדָיוֹ וּשְׁלָקוֹ מָהוּ. דִּבְרֵי הַכֹּל נִטְבָּל. וְכִי מַה עָשָׂה מַעֲשֶׂה בִּרְשׁוּת הַהֶקְדֵּשׁ. הִקְדִּישׁוֹ וּשְׁלָקוֹ הִכְנִיסוֹ לַחֲצַר בֵּית שְׁמִירָה פְּדָיוֹ וּשְׁלָקוֹ מָהוּ. דִּבְרֵי הַכֹּל נִטְבָּל.

פְּדָייו וְצִימְקוֹ מַהוּ. אִין תֵּימַר הָאוֹר טוֹבֵל הָאוֹר פּוֹטֵר וְאִין תֵּימַר אֵין הָאוֹר טוֹבֵל אֵין הָאוֹר פּוֹטֵר.

If he cooked it while it was property of the Temple[17], redeemed it, and brought it into a secure courtyard, what is its status? In the opinion of Rebbi Simeon ben Laqish[18] it became *ṭevel*; this is biblical, that is not biblical. If he brought it into a secure courtyard, redeemed and then cooked it, everybody agrees that it became *ṭevel*; what did he process while it was property of the Temple[19]? If he dedicated it, cooked it, brought it into a secure courtyard, redeemed it, and cooked it again, everybody agrees that it became *ṭevel*[20]. If he redeemed it[21]and put it out to dry, what is its status? If you say that fire creates *ṭevel*, fire frees from *ṭevel*; if you say that fire does not create *ṭevel*, fire does not free from *ṭevel*[22].

17 Temple property is exempt from heave and tithes; cf. Chapter 1, Note 19.

18 Cf. Note 7. While it was the intent of the person who had dedicated the produce to free it from heave and tithes by processing while it was property of the Temple, R. Simeon ben Laqish will disregard rabbinic processing when dedicated if it is followed by an action which induces *ṭevel* by biblical law after redemption when the preserve is now fully profane.

19 In the exempt state, transporting to a secure courtyard is not an act of processing.

20 By the second cooking.

21 After a first cooking while Temple property.

22 For R. Joḥanan, the first cooking was the processing and anything done later does not count. For R. Simeon ben Laqish, the first cooking outside courtyard or house would not induce *ṭevel*; therefore, being cooked while Temple property does not count and the later drying is the final processing of profane food.

רִבִּי יִרְמְיָה בָּעֵי טִיגְנוֹ בַשָּׂדֶה מַהוּ בְּלֹא כָּךְ אֵין הָאוֹר טוֹבֵל. אִילּוּ אֵיפְשַׁר דְּלֹא מִיתַּן גַּבֵּיהּ מְשַׁח.

Rebbi Jeremiah asked: If he fried in the field, what is its status[23]? Does not the fire create *ṭevel* anyhow[24]? Is it impossible not to use oil[25]?

23 May it be eaten as a snack without tithing?

24 Since we hold that fire always induces *ṭevel*, the answer seems obvious.

25 That would be the singeing indicated in Note 11. Since singeing creates *ṭevel*, the question of R. Jeremiah is already answered.

בָּעֵי הֲוָה רִבִּי יוֹסֵי בְּשֵׁם כַּהֲנָא אָמַר רִבִּי יוֹנָה תַּנֵּי רִבִּי חֲלַפְתָּא בֶּן שָׁאוּל עָשָׂה הֵסֵב בַּשָּׂדֶה טוֹבֵל. אִם לֹא הֵיסֵב אֵינוֹ טוֹבֵל. אֵין הוּא הֵיסֵב שֶׁהוּא טוֹבֵל כָּל־הֵיסֵב שֶׁיֵּשׁ בּוֹ יַיִן. קָצַב לְהֵיסֵב וְלֹא הֵיסֵב.

Rebbi Yose used to asked in the name of Cahana: Rebbi Jonah said, Rebbi Ḥalaphta ben Shaul stated: If someone organized a meal in a circle[26] in the field he created *ṭevel*. If one did not organize a meal a circle he did not create *ṭevel*. What organizing in a circle creates *ṭevel*? Any meal in a circle with wine. If people prepared to eat in a circle but then did not[27]?

26 To eat together. Snacks are eaten alone.

27 This is Cahana's question; it remains unanswered.

תַּנֵּי הַשּׁוּם וְהַשִּׁחֲלַיִים וְהַחַרְדָּל שֶׁשְּׁחָקוֹ בַּשָּׂדֶה נִטְבְּלוּ עַד כְּדוֹן בְּשׁוּם שֶׁל טֶבֶל שֶׁשְּׁחָקוֹ בְּשֶׁמֶן שֶׁל חוּלִין. שׁוּם שֶׁל חוּלִין שֶׁשְּׁחָקוֹ בְּשֶׁמֶן שֶׁל טֶבֶל.

It was stated[28]: "Garlic, garden cress[29], and mustard seed which were prepared in the field became *ṭevel*." That means, *ṭevel* garlic with profane oil. Profane garlic with *ṭevel* oil[30]?

28 A similar text Tosephta 3:2.

29 A kind of *Lepidium*; Rashi קרש״ון French *cresson*; Maimonides Arabic رشاد *Lepidium sativum*, garden peppergrass.

30 This question should not have

been asked since oil used to prepare condiments is certainly forbidden when *ṭevel.*

רִבִּי זְעִירָא רִבִּי חִיָּא בַּר אַשִׁי בְּשֵׁם רַב אֶשְׁכּוֹל שֶׁסְּחָטוֹ לַכּוֹס נִטְבָּל. לְתַמְחוּי לֹא נִטְבָּל.

Rebbi Zeïra, Rebbi Ḥiyya bar Ashi in the name of Rav: A bunch of grapes which he squeezed into a cup[31] became *ṭevel*; into a *tamḥui*[32] it did not become *ṭevel.*

31 This becomes a formal drink, not a snack.

32 Cf. *Peah* 8, Note 83.

בְּלֹא כָּךְ אֵין הָאוֹר טוֹבֵל. תִּיפְתָּר בְּתַבְשִׁיל צוֹנֵין. לִקְדֵירָה חַיָּיב. אָמַר רִבִּי לָעְזָר לִקְדֵירָה רֵיקָנִית הִיא. מַתְנִיתִין לֹא אָמַר כֵּן אֶלָּא הַמְקַפֶּה לְתַבְשִׁיל פָּטוּר וְלִקְדֵירָה חַיָּיב מִפְּנֵי שֶׁהוּא כְבוֹר קָטָן.

Does not the fire induce *ṭevel* anyhow[33]? Explain it if the dish was cold. "In a pot it is obligated;" Rebbi Eleazar said, that refers to an empty pot[34]. The Mishnah does not say so, but "he who prepares wine sauce for a dish is free but in a pot it is obligated for it is like a small cistern[35]."

33 This refers to the last sentence in the Mishnah, quoted in this paragraph. If one puts *ṭevel* sauce on any hot dish, the entire dish becomes *ṭevel.*

34 Otherwise the statement of the Mishnah were superfluous, Note 6.

35 Which usually is not empty.

(fol. 51a) **משנה ב:** תִּינוֹקוֹת שֶׁטָּמְנוּ תְאֵינִים לַשַּׁבָּת וְשָׁכַח לְעַשְּׂרָן לֹא יֵאָכְלוּ מוֹצָאֵי שַׁבָּת עַד שֶׁיְּעַשְּׂרוּ. כַּלְכָּלַת שַׁבָּת בֵּית שַׁמַּאי פּוֹטְרִין וּבֵית הִלֵּל מְחַיְּיבִין. רִבִּי יְהוּדָה אוֹמֵר אַף הַלּוֹקֵט כַּלְכָּלָה לְשַׁלֵּחַ לַחֲבֵירוֹ לֹא יֹאכַל עַד שֶׁיְּעַשֵּׂר.

Mishnah 2: If children hid figs for the Sabbath[36] and he forgot to tithe them they may not be eaten after the Sabbath[37] until they are tithed. A Sabbath basket[38] the House of Shammai free but the House of Hillel obligate. Rebbi Jehudah says, also one who fills a harvesting basket to send to a friend[39] may not eat from it unless he tithed.

36 They hid it in the field since otherwise the house would have induced *ṭevel*. While children have no legal standing, their actions can show their intent which then is determining.

37 But one may eat from these figs on Friday afternoon between the hiding and the start of the Sabbath. Since children do not legally have a mind, their figs can become subject to heave and/or tithes only through the Sabbath itself.

38 Either from a tree whose fruits are only used for the Sabbath (Maimonides) or any arbitrary harvesting basket filled exclusively for eating on the Sabbath (R. Simson); since the person making the collection is an adult, his intent induces *ṭevel* even before the Sabbath.

39 For the Sabbath (R. Simson) or any day (Maimonides). In any case, the collection in that particular basket is the end of processing by the farmer.

(fol. 51b) **הלכה ב:** רַב הַמְנוּנָא אָמַר תִּינוֹק שֶׁחִיפָּה כַלְכָּלָה לַשּׁוּק נִטְבְּלָה. מְקוֹם שֶׁמַּחֲשַׁבְתּוֹ שֶׁל גָּדוֹל מִתְקַיֶּימֶת שָׁם. מַעֲשָׂיו שֶׁל קָטָן מִתְקַיְּימִין. רִבִּי זְעִירָא בָּעֵי כְּלוּם מַחֲשַׁבְתּוֹ שֶׁל גָּדוֹל מִתְקַיֶּימֶת עַד שֶׁיִּפְתַּח לַשּׁוּק. וְדִכְוָותָהּ אֵין מַעֲשָׂיו שֶׁל קָטָן מִתְקַיְּימִין עַד שֶׁיִּפְתַּח לַשּׁוּק. מַתְנִיתָא פְלִיגָא עַל רַב הַמְנוּנָא תִּינוֹקוֹת שֶׁטָּמְנוּ תְאֵינִים לַשַּׁבָּת וְשָׁכַח לְעַשְּׂרָן לֹא יֵאָכְלוּ מוֹצָאֵי שַׁבָּת עַד שֶׁיִּתְעַשְּׂרוּ. רִבִּי זְעִירָא בְשֵׁם רַב הַמְנוּנָא תִּיפְתָּר בְּשֶׁלִּקְּטוּם עִם דִּמְדוּמֵי חַמָּה וְהוֹכִיחַ מַעֲשֶׂה שֶׁלָּהֶן עַל מַחֲשַׁבְתָּם.

Rav Hamnuna said, if a child covered a harvesting basket for transport to the market, it became *ṭevel*; in any situation in which the intent of an adult has an effect, the action of a minor has an effect. Rebbi Zeïra asked: Since the intent of an adult does not have an effect until he opens on the market, the action of a minor should not have an effect until he opens on the market[40]! The Mishnah disagrees with Rav Hamnuna: "If children hid figs for the Sabbath and he forgot to tithe them they may not be eaten after the Sabbath until they are tithed.[41]" Rebbi Zeïra in the name of Rav Hamnuna: Explain if it they collected close to sundown when their action was proof of their intent[42]!

40 Mishnah 1:5 states that processing of figs for sale is completed when the basket is covered for transport to the market and the basket is actually transported to the market; while for making fig cakes and domestic uses the processing is never completed in the field. It is not really required that the basket be opened on the market for sale but that the transport should have started; cf. Chapter 1, Note 115. In any case, the action of a minor cannot be more powerful than the intent of an adult; the statement of Rav Hamnuna cannot be accepted without due modification.

41 Here there is no action which proves intent and nevertheless *ṭevel* is induced. Maybe the children collected the figs for consumption on Sunday.

42 Children do not plan ahead; they collected for immediate consumption which by necessity must be on the Sabbath.

לֵית הָדָא פְלִיגָא עַל רִבִּי יוֹחָנָן דְּרִבִּי יוֹחָנָן אָמַר הַשַּׁבָּת טוֹבֶלֶת מִפְּנֵי שֶׁלִּקְטוּם לַשַּׁבָּת. הָא אִם לִקְטוּם שֶׁלֹּא לַשַּׁבָּת לֹא. רִבִּי יוֹנָה בְשֵׁם רַב הַמְנוּנָא אֲפִילוּ לִקְטוּם לַשַּׁבָּת אוֹכֵל מֵהֶן עֲרַאי לְעֶרֶב שַׁבָּת. אֲפִילוּ עַל דְּרִבִּי שִׁמְעוֹן בֶּן לָקִישׁ לֵית הוּא פְלִיגָא. וְלֹא תִינוֹקוֹת אִינּוּן. וַאֲפִילוּ לִקְטוּם לַשַּׁבָּת כְּמִי שֶׁלִּקְטוּם שֶׁלֹּא לַשַּׁבָּת. רִבִּי יוֹסֵי בְשֵׁם רִבִּי אִילָא תִּיפְתָּר שֶׁלִּקְטוּם עִם דִּמְדוּמֵי חַמָּה וְהוֹכִיחַ מַעֲשֶׂה שֶׁלָּהֶן עַל מַחֲשַׁבְתָּם.

Does this not disagree with Rebbi Joḥanan since Rebbi Joḥanan said, the Sabbath induces *ṭevel*? Because they collected for the Sabbath; therefore, not if they did not collect for the Sabbath[43]! Rebbi Jonah in the name of Rav Hamnuna[44]: Even if they collected for the Sabbath one may eat a snack from them on Sabbath eve. It does not even disagree with Rebbi Simeon ben Laqish[45]. Are they not children and even if they collected for the Sabbath it is as if they had not collected for the Sabbath[46]! Rebbi Yose in the name of Rebbi Hila[44]: Explain if it they collected close to sundown when their action was proof of their intent[42]!

43 This now refers to the Mishnah: "If children hid figs for the Sabbath". According to R. Joḥanan, any untithed fruit completely processed becomes *ṭevel* at the start of the next Sabbath irrespective of its place. The fact that the figs were collected for the Sabbath should be irrelevant.

44 The names of the authors are switched in the Rome ms., the first answer being by Rebbi Yose in the name of Rebbi Hila, the second by Rebbi Jonah in the name of Rav Hamnuna. The correct chain of transmission cannot be ascertained. Since the speakers in this paragraph are Amoraïm a full generation after R. Zeïra, "in the name of Rav Hamnuna" must mean: giving the answer Rav Hamnuna would have given according to R. Zeïra.

45 In the Rome ms: R. Joḥanan. This certainly is a scribal error.

46 Since for R. Simeon ben Laqish the Sabbath does not induce *ṭevel* by biblical law, there must be clear intent to use the fruits on the Sabbath to make them *ṭevel* but children have no legal intent.

רִבִּי לָֽעְזָר בְּשֵׁם רִבִּי הוֹשַׁעְיָא בְּכַלְכָּלָה שֶׁל תְּאֵינִים הִיא מַתְנִיתָא. דְּבֵי רִבִּי יַנַּאי אָֽמְרֵי אֲפִילוּ נִצְרָה. רִבִּי לָֽעְזָר בֶּן אַנְטִיגְנוֹס בְּשֵׁם רִבִּי לָֽעְזָר בֵּי רִבִּי יַנַּאי תִּיפְתָּר בִּתְאֵינָה הַמְיוּחֶדֶת לַשַּׁבָּת. דְּלֹמָה רִבִּי חִייָה רִבִּי אִימִּי רִבִּי אִיסִּי הֲווֹן יָֽתְבִין. עֲבַר חַד טְעוּן כַּלְכָּלָה דִתְאֵינְיָה אֲמַר לֵיהּ לִיזְבוֹן אֲמַר לֵיהּ כַּלְכָּלַת שַׁבָּת אֵינָהּ מִזַּבְּנָה.

Rebbi Eleazar in the name of Rebbi Hoshaia: The Mishnah[47] speaks of a harvesting basket of figs. In the House of Rebbi Yannai they said, even a branch. Rebbi Eleazar ben Antigonos in the name of Rebbi Eleazar ben Rebbi Yannai: Explain it for a fig tree reserved for the Sabbath.

Example: Rebbi Ḥiyya, Rebbi Assi and Rebbi Ammi were sitting together when somebody passed by with a harvesting basket of figs. He said to him, [we want] to buy! He answered, the Sabbath basket is not for sale[48].

47 The difference between the Houses of Shammai and Hillel regarding the Sabbath basket.

48 Therefore, its processing is completed as soon as the basket is filled.

רִבִּי חִיָּה בְשֵׁם רִבִּי יוֹחָנָן לֹא אָמַר רִבִּי יְהוּדָה אֶלָּא בְּכַלְכָּלַת שַׁבָּת. אִי אָמַר רִבִּי יְהוּדָה בְּלִיקֵּט כַּלְכָּלָה לְשַׁלְּחָהּ לַחֲבֵירוֹ שֶׁהוּא מַקְפִּיד עָלֶיהָ כְּכַלְכָּלַת שַׁבָּת.

Rebbi Ḥiyya in the name of Rebbi Joḥanan: Rebbi Jehudah spoke only about a Sabbath basket. Maybe Rebbi Jehudah spoke about someone who collected a harvesting basket full to send to his friend, that he cared for it as if it were a Sabbath basket[49]?

49 The second sentence questions the meaning of R. Ḥiyya's statement: Does R. Joḥanan imply that only a Sabbath basket induces immediate *ṭevel* or any basket treated with the same care as a Sabbath basket? The question is not answered since practice does not follow R. Jehudah.

(fol. 51a) **משנה ג**: הַנּוֹטֵל זֵיתִין מִן הַמַּעֲטָן טוֹבֵל אֶחָד אֶחָד בְּמֶלַח וְאוֹכֵל. אִם מָלַח וְנָתַן לְפָנָיו חַיָּיב. רִבִּי לִיעֶזֶר אוֹמֵר מִן הַמַּעֲטָן הַטָּהוֹר חַיָּיב וּמִן הַטָּמֵא פָּטוּר מִפְּנֵי שֶׁהוּא מַחֲזִיר אֶת הַמּוֹתָר.

Mishnah 3: He who takes olives from the vat[50] may dip them singly into salt and eat them, but if he salted them as a dish he is obligated[51]. Rebbi Eliezer says, from a pure vat he is obligated[52] but from an impure one he is free because he might put the leftovers back [into the vat].

50 Into which the olives are collected before being transported to the oil press.

51 Since there are many together. The quote in Babli *Bezah* 35a reads (in most mss.) "if he salted ten together"; this is against the Yerushalmi which forbids even two together.

52 The Babli (*Bezah* 35a) explains that the person taking the olives is presumed to be impure. This is understood also in the Halakhah here.

משנה ד: שׁוֹתִין עַל הַגַּת בֵּין עַל הַחַמִּין בֵּין עַל הַצּוֹנְנִין וּפָטוּר דִּבְרֵי רַבִּי מֵאִיר. רַבִּי אֶלְעָזָר בֵּי רַבִּי צָדוֹק מְחַייֵב. וַחֲכָמִים אוֹמְרִים עַל הַחַמִּין חַיָּב וְעַל הַצּוֹנְנִין פָּטוּר.

Mishnah 4: One may drink from the winepress both warm or cold and is free, the words of Rebbi Meïr. Rebbi Eleazar ben Rebbi Ẓadoq declares him obligated. But the Sages say, for warm drink he is obligated, cold he is free[53].

53 In the Babli (*Šabbat* 11b, *Eruvin* 99b) and one Mishnah ms. the reading is: "he is free because he may return it." In that version, Mishnah 4 is parallel Mishnah 3 and cider, cooked or mixed with warm water, is considered completely processed because returning it would spoil the wine. Maimonides, both in his Commentary and his Code (*Ma'serot* 5:15) holds that heating induces *ṭevel* in all cases.

(fol. 51b) **הלכה ג:** לֵית הָדָא פְלִיגָא עַל רַב. דְּרַב אָמַר הוּא אָסוּר לוֹכַל. פָּתַר לָהּ בְּעוֹשֶׂה מַעְטָן בַּשָּׂדֶה וְקַשְׁיָא אִם מֶלַח טוֹבֶלֶת לָמָּה לִי צֵירוּף אִם צֵירוּף לָמָּה לִי מֶלַח. אֶלָּא עַל יְדֵי זֶה וְעַל יְדֵי זֶה.

Halakhah 3: Does this not disagree with Rav? Since Rav said, it is forbidden to eat[54]. Explain it if he makes his vat in the field. It is still difficult: If salting induces *ṭevel*[55], why do we need taking together, if taking together induces, why do we need salting? It must be both.

54 Salted olives from the vat.

55 Mishnah 1. While this salting is not for long-term preservation, it is needed to give the green olives an edible taste.

מַה נָן קַייָמִין אִם בְּשֶׁיֵּשׁ שְׁנֵי מַעֲטִינִין דִּבְרֵי הַכֹּל אָסוּר. אִם בְּשֶׁאֵין לוֹ אֶלָּא מַעֲטָן אֶחָד דִּבְרֵי הַכֹּל מוּתָּר. אֶלָּא כִּי נָן קַייָמִין בְּשֶׁיֵּשׁ לוֹ מַעֲטָן טָהוֹר וְלַחֲבֵירוֹ מַעֲטָן טָמֵא. אָמַר רִבִּי לִיעֶזֶר אָדָם מַחֲזִיר עַל מַעֲטִין חֲבֵרוֹ וְרַבָּנִין אָמְרִין אֵין אָדָם מְחַזֵּר לְמַעֲטִינוֹ שֶׁל חֲבֵירוֹ.

Where do we hold[56]? If there are two vats[57], everybody agrees that it is forbidden. If there is only one vat[58], everybody agrees that it is permitted. Where do we hold? If he has a pure vat and his friend an impure one. Rebbi Eliezer says, a person may return to his friend's vat but the rabbis say, a person does not return to his friend's vat[59].

56 The disagreement between R. Eliezer and the anonymous majority who do not accept the distinction he makes.

57 One pure, the other one impure. Even if he takes from the impure, we do not permit him to return the uneaten olives; maybe he would put them into the wrong vat.

58 Which is impure.

59 An echo of this discussion is in Tosephta 3:7; there, the text tradition is confusing.

אָמַר רִבִּי יוֹחָנָן עַל הַחַמִּין חַייָב שֶׁהוּא קֶבַע עַל הַצּוֹנִין פָּטוּר שֶׁהוּא עֲרַאי יָכוֹל הוּא מַחֲזִירָתָהּ. דְּאָמַר רִבִּי יוֹסֵי בְּשֵׁם רִבִּי זְעִירָא רִבִּי יוֹנָה רִבִּי זְעִירָא בְּשֵׁם רִבִּי לָעְזָר אִם בְּמַה שֶׁבְּלָגִין לֹא נִטְבָּל מִפְּנֵי שֶׁהוּא עָתִיד לְהַחֲזִירוֹ בְּדָבָר שֶׁלֹּא נִגְמְרָה מְלַאכְתּוֹ.

[60]Rebbi Joḥanan said, for warm [cider] he is obligated because that is not a snack; cold is free because it is a snack and he may put it back. Following[61] what Rebbi Yose said in the name of Rebbi Zeïra, Rebbi Jonah, Rebbi Zeïra in the name of Rebbi Eleazar, even what is in a flask

did not become *tevel,* in case it was not fully processed, since he woul put it back in the end.

60 Discussion of Mishnah 4.

61 Halakhah 1:6, Note 151.

(fol. 51a) **משנה ה:** הַמְקַלֵּף בִּשְׂעוֹרִים מְקַלֵּף אַחַת אַחַת וְאוֹכֵל. וְאִים קִילֵּף וְנָתַן לְתוֹךְ יָדוֹ חַייָב. הַמּוֹלֵל מְלִילוֹת שֶׁל חִיטִּים מְנַפֵּיחַ עַל יָד עַל יָד וְאוֹכֵל. וְאִם נִיפַּח וְנָתַן לְתוֹךְ חֵיקוֹ חַייָב. כּוּסְבָּר שֶׁזְּרָעָהּ לְזֶרַע יַרְקָהּ פָּטוּר. זְרָעָהּ לְיָרָק מִתְעַשֵּׂר זֶרַע וְיָרָק. רִבִּי לִיעֶזֶר אוֹמֵר הַשֶּׁבֶת מִתְעַשֶּׂרֶת זֶרַע וְיָרָק וְזֵירִים. וַחֲכָמִים אוֹמְרִים אֵינוֹ מִתְעַשֵּׂר זֶרַע וְיָרָק אֶלָּא הַשַּׁחֲלַיִים וְהַגַּרְגִּר בִּלְבָד.

Mishnah 5: If somebody peels barley, he may peel one by one and eat but if he peeled and collected in his hand he is obligated. If somebody rolls wheat grains he may blow away[62] the chaff from his hand and eat but if he blew away and stored in the fold of his toga, he is obligated. If coriander is sown for its seed, its greenery is free. If it was sown as vegetable, seeds and greenery are obligated. Rebbi Eliezer said, dill is tithed seeds, vegetable, and perianths[63]. But the Sages say, only cress[29] and wild rocket[64] are tithed[65] seeds and vegetable.

62 The majority of Mishnah mss. read: נפה "sifted [from hand to hand]".

63 Concurrent definition of Rashi (Babli *Avodah Zarah* 7b) and Maimonides (Commentary to the Mishnah).

64 *Ševi'it* 7-2, Note 7.

65 For separate tithes.

(fol. 51b) **הלכה ד:** אָמַר רִבִּי זְעִירָא יְכִיל אֲנָא מְקַלֵּף תַּרְתֵּיי תַּרְתֵּיי. וְתַנֵּי כֵן בִּשְׂעוֹרִין שְׁנַיִם פָּטוּר שָׁלֹשׁ חַייָב. בְּחִיטִּין שָׁלֹשׁ פָּטוּר אַרְבַּע חַייָב. הוּנָא בַּר חִינְנָא וְרַב תַּחְלִיפָא בַּר אִימִּי הֲווֹן יְתִיבִין קוֹמֵי רִבִּי לָעְזָר. אָמַר רִבִּי יוֹנָה אִין

כּוּלְהוֹן בַּר אִימִּי הָהֵן בַּר רַב אִימִּי אִין כּוּלְהוֹן בַּר רַב אִימִּי וַהֲוָייָן לֵיהּ עַד קִשְׁרֵי אֶצְבְּעָתֵיהּ וַהֲווֹן סַבִּין מִינֵּיהּ וְהָפַךְ אַפּוֹי לְכוֹתְלָא וַחֲוִי לוֹן מָלֵא שִׁיעָלוֹן. וְתַנֵּי כֵן וּבִלְבַד שֶׁלֹּא יְנַפֶּה לֹא בְקָנוֹן וְלֹא בְתַמְחוּי. וּלְעִנְיַן שַׁבָּת עַד כַּגְּרוֹגֶרֶת. רִבִּי חִייָה בַּר אָדָא בָּעוֹן קוֹמֵי רִבִּי מָנָא הָכָא אָמַר בִּשְׂעוֹרִים שְׁתַּיִם פָּטוּר שָׁלֹשׁ חַיָּיב. וְכָא אַתְּ אָמַר הָכֵין. אָמַר לֵיהּ שַׁנְיָיא הִיא. הָכָא אַתְּ אָמַר שֶׁהוּא מַחֲזִיר אֶת הַמּוֹתָר. וְתַנֵּי כֵן בַּמֶּה דְבָרִים אֲמוּרִים בִּזְמַן שֶׁאֵינוֹ סָמוּךְ לַגּוֹרֶן. אֲבָל אִם הָיָה סָמוּךְ לַגּוֹרֶן אֲפִילוּ יוֹתֵר מִכֵּן מוּתָּר מִפְּנֵי שֶׁהוּא מַחֲזִיר אֶת הַמּוֹתָר.

Halakhah 4: Rebbi Zeïra said, I may peel two by two. It is stated so[66]: "Barley, two are free, three obligated; wheat, three are free, four obligated." Huna bar Ḥinena[67] and Rav Taḥlifa bar Immi were sitting before Rebbi Eleazar. {Rebbi Jonah said, either all are "bar Immi" but this one "bar Rav Immi" or all are "bar Rav Immi"[68].} He[69] had [grains] up to the knuckles of his fingers. They were taking from him. He turned his face to the wall and showed them his hand full[70]. It is stated so: Only he should not sift into a reed-basket or into a wide basket. For the Sabbath, up to the volume of a dried fig[71]. Rebbi Ḥiyya bar Ada asked before Rebbi Mana: Here, they said for barley, two are free, three obligated; there, you say so[72]? He said to him, there is a difference; here you say that he may put the remainder back. It was stated so: When has this been said[73], when he is not close to the threshing floor. But when he was close to the threshing floor [he can have] even more since he may put the remainder back.

66 Tosephta 3:6. R. Zeïra states that practice follows the Tosephta, rather than the Mishnah.

67 He cannot be the Rav Huna bar Ḥinena mentioned in the Babli who was a student of Rav Ḥisda and, it seems, never left Babylonia.

68 In this text, R. Jonah, two generations later, was unsure whether there were one or two Rav Taḥlifa bar (Rav) Immi or only one. In the Rome ms., the text reads: "R. Jonah said,

either all are 'bar Ammi' but this one 'bar Rav Ammi' or all are 'bar Rav Ammi' and this one 'bar Ammi'." Since this version uses the Babylonian 'Ammi' instead of the Galilean 'Immi', it seems to be preferable. In this version, it is clear that there were several traditions ascribed to Rav Taḥlifa bar (Rav) Ammi. None of these have come down to us.

69 R. Eleazar.

70 A handfull of unpeeled grains does not induce *ṭevel* as long as they will be peeled one by one according to the rules.

71 If from private to public domain one carries grains less than the volume of a dried fig, one is not guilty.

72 The *baraita* which allows stripping of barlay grains as long as the stripped grains are eaten directly and not stored in any basket.

73 Two barley grains but not three.

הלכה ה: חִזְקִיָּה אָמַר כֵּיוָן שֶׁלָּקַט מִמֶּנּוּ שְׁתַּיִם שָׁלֹשׁ מוֹדִייוֹת בָּאָה בְּמַחֲשֶׁבֶת יָרָק. אַף לְעִנְייַן הַזֶּרַע כֵּן כֵּיוָן שֶׁמָּנַע מִמֶּנּוּ שְׁתַּיִם שָׁלֹשׁ מוֹדִייוֹת בָּאָה לְמַחֲשֶׁבֶת הַזֶּרַע. זְרָעוֹ לְזֶרַע מִתְעַשֶּׂרֶת לְשֶׁעָבַר. זְרָעָהּ לְיָרָק מִתְעַשֶּׂרֶת לָבֹא. זָרַע לְזֶרַע וּלְיָרָק אוֹ שֶׁזְּרָעָהּ לְזֶרַע וְאַחַר כָּךְ חִישֵּׁב עָלֶיהָ לְיָרָק מְעַשֵּׂר מִיזַּרְעָהּ עַל יַרְקָא וּמִיַּרְקָא עַל זַרְעָא. וְשֶׁלָּקַט מִמֶּנָּהּ לִפְנֵי רֹאשׁ הַשָּׁנָה אֲבָל אִם לָקַט מִמֶּנָּהּ לְאַחַר רֹאשׁ הַשָּׁנָה זַרְעָהּ מִתְעַשֵּׂר לְשֶׁעָבַר. וְיַרְקָא מִתְעַשֵּׂר בִּשְׁעַת לְקִיטָתוֹ עִישּׂוּרוֹ. וּכְשֶׁהֵבִיא שְׁלִישׁ לִפְנֵי רֹאשׁ הַשָּׁנָה. אֲבָל אִם הֵבִיא שְׁלִישׁ לְאַחַר רֹאשׁ הַשָּׁנָה בֵּין זַרְעָהּ בֵּין יַרְקָהּ מִתְעַשֵּׂר לָבֹא.

Halakhah 5: [74]Ḥizqiah said, if he collected two or three *modii*[75] from it, it comes under the category of vegetable. Also for seeds it is so: If he withheld from it two or three *morbiot*[75], it comes under the category of seeds.

If one sowed it for seeds it is tithed for the past; if he sowed it as vegetable it is tithed for the future. If he sowed it for both seeds and vegetable, or if he sowed for seeds and then wanted it as vegetable, one may tithe from its seed on vegetable and from vegetable on seeds, on condition that it was collected before the New Year; but if some of it was collected after the New Year, its seed is tithed for the past and its vegetable is tithed at the moment of its being harvested if it was one-third ripe before the New Year. But if it was only ripe one-third after the New Year, both seed and vegetable are tithed for the future.

74 Here starts the discussion of the second part of the Mishnah, about the tithing of coriander. The two paragraphs refer to *Ševiït* 2:8. The second paragraph is practically identical (except for the order of subjects) with a paragraph there; Notes 80-81.

75 This is the reading here in both mss. and the Venice print. A Roman *modius* is a dry measure, corresponding to the *seah*. Because of the parallel with *Ševiït*, the commentators change מודייות into מורביות *morbiot*, a word that seems to indicate watering periods, cf. *Ševiït* 2:8, Note 83. This must be the intended meaning in the next sentence: If the farmer stops watering in order to hasten the ripening of the seeds, he cannot be interested in the vegetable. Also, one cannot withhold bushels from vegetables. But it does not make much sense to change the reading in the first sentence which speaks of harvesting vegetables. In the second sentence, the expression "two or three" must have slipped in as parallel to the first sentence since the discussion in *Ševiït* 2:8 shows clearly that only the withholding of three waterings determines the crop as seeds.

תַּנֵּי שֶׁבֶת שֶׁזְּרָעָהּ לְזֶרַע מִתְעַשֶּׂרֶת זֶרַע וְאֵינָהּ מִתְעַשֶּׂרֶת יָרָק. זֶרַע לְיָרָק מִתְעַשֶּׂרֶת זֶרַע וְיָרָק וְאֵינָהּ מִתְעַשֶּׂרֶת זֵירִין. זְרָעָהּ לְזֵירִין מִתְעַשֶּׂרֶת זֶרַע וְיָרָק וְזֵירִין. וְתַנִּינָן אֵין לָךְ מִתְעַשֵּׂר זֶרַע וְיָרָק אֶלָּא שִׁחֲלַיִים וְגַרְגִּר בִּלְבָד. כֵּינִי מַתְנִיתָא אֵין לָךְ דָּבָר שֶׁזְּרָעוֹ לְזֶרַע מִתְעַשֵּׂר זֶרַע וְיָרָק אֶלָּא שִׁחֲלַיִים וְגַרְגִּר בִּלְבָד.

It was stated[76]: "Dill sown for its seeds is tithed for seeds but not vegetable. If sown as vegetable, it is tithed for seeds and vegetable but not perianths. If sown it for periants, it is tithed for seeds, vegetable, and perianths." But we have stated: "Only cress and wild rocket are tithed for seeds and vegetable!" So is the Mishnah: The only things sown for seeds which are tithed for seeds and vegetable are cress and wild rocket.

76 A similar text in Tosephta *Ševiït* 2:7. There, the text reads: "If he sowed it for perianths, it is tithed for seeds and perianths but the vegetable is free."

(fol. 51a) **משנה ו:** רַבָּן גַּמְלִיאֵל אוֹמֵר תְּמְרוֹת שֶׁל תִּלְתָּן וְשֶׁל חַרְדָּל וְשֶׁל פּוֹל הַלָּבָן חַייָבוֹת בְּמַעֲשֵׂר. רִבִּי לִיעֶזֶר אוֹמֵר הַצְּלָף מִתְאַשֵּׂר תְּמְרוֹת וְקַפָּרס. רִבִּי עֲקִיבָה אוֹמֵר אֵינוֹ מִתְעַשֵּׂר אֶלָּא אֲבִיּוֹנוֹת מִפְּנֵי שֶׁהֵן פֶּרִי.

Mishnah 6: Rabban Gamliel says, the budding fruits[77] of fenugreek, mustard, and white beans are subject to tithes. Rebbi Eliezer says, the caper tree is subject to tithes for its budding fruits and capers[78]. Rebbi Aqiba says, only the berries[79] are subject because they are fruit.

77 In *Ševiït* and *Ma'serot* Arukh and Maimonides define תמרות as budding fruits; this is accepted by I. Löw. In his Commentary to *Parah* 11:7, Maimonides explains as pods.

78 Flower buds of the caper bush.

79 They contain seeds which can be substituted for mustard seeds.

(fol. 51c) **הלכה ו:** מַה פְלִיגִין בְּשֶׁזְּרָעוֹ לְזֶרַע אֲבָל אִם זְרָעוֹ לְיָרָק אַף רַבָּנִין מוֹדֵיי. וְתַנֵּי כֵן נְהִיגִין בְּבֵיתַנִּייָן בְּיַרְקוֹ בְּהֵיתֵר דִּבְרֵי רִבִּי לִיעֶזֶר. לֹא אָמַר אֶלָּא דִּבְרֵי רִבִּי לִיעֶזֶר הָא דִּבְרֵי הַכֹּל חַייָב.

Halakhah 6: Where do they disagree[80]? When he sowed it for its seeds. But if he sowed it as vegetable, even the rabbis agree. It was stated so[81]: "In Bethany[82] they used to permit its vegetable, the words of Rebbi Eliezer." He said only "the words of Rebbi Eliezer;" therefore, everybody else says it is obligated.

80 The majority who cannot agree with Rabban Gamliel; if they agreed, his statement would have been stated as anonymous. Since he obligates the

pods of mustard seed for tithes, they must free them.

81 Tosephta 3:7: They used to permit the vegetables, the words of Rebbi Eliezer.

82 In the Erfurt ms. of the Tosephta, כמותכם "like you", which S. Klein reads as במותנם "in Batanaia", a name of the Bashan region; cf. *Tosefta ki-Fshutah* p. 698.

תַּנֵּי הַפּוֹל וְהַשְּׂעוֹרִין וְהַתִּלְתָּן שֶׁזְּרָעָן לְיָרָק בָּטְלָה דַעְתּוֹ זַרְעָן חַיָּיב וְיַרְקָן פָּטוּר. אָמַר רִבִּי יִרְמְיָה עוֹד הִיא דְרִבִּי לִיעֶזֶר.

It was stated[83]: "If one sowed Lima beans, barley, or fenugreek as vegetables[84], his intention is disregarded; the seeds are obligated but the greenery is free." Rebbi Jeremiah said, that also is from the words of Rebbi Eliezer[85].

83 Tosephta *Ševiït* 2:8.

84 To eat the green stalks.

85 We could understand that Lima beans and barley are excluded as vegetables, but fenugreek was stated in the preceding paragraph to be freed only by R. Eliezer. Therefore, the entire statement must be attributed to R. Eliezer. The Babli, *Eruvin* 28a, accepts the statement as majority opinion.

שְׁמוּאֵל אָמַר קַפְּרֵס אָסוּר מִשּׁוּם קְלִיפִּין. וְתַנֵּי כֵן וַעֲרַלְתֶּם עָרְלָתוֹ אֶת פִּרְיוֹ דָּבָר שֶׁהוּא עוֹרֵל אֶת פִּרְיוֹ. רַב מְפַקֵּד לְאִילֵּין דְּבֵי [86]אָתִי. רַב [87]הַמְנוּנָא מְפַקֵּד לַחֲבֵרַייָא הֲווֹן מְפַקְּדִין לִנְשֵׁיכוֹן כַּד הִינּוּן כְּבָשִׁין קַפְרִיס דִיהֲווֹן מְרִימִין אִילֵּין בִּיטִיתָא. אָמַר רִבִּי בָּא אַסְבְּרֵי רִבִּי זְעִירָא כָּל־הַקְּלִיפִּין גְּדֵילוֹת עִם הַפְּרִי וְזֶה פְּרִי מִלְמַעְלָן וּקְלִיפִּין מִלְּמַטָּן.

Samuel said, capers are forbidden because of skins[88]. It was stated so: (*Lev.* 19:23) "You shall treat as foreskin the foreskin of its fruit;" anything which envelopes the fruit. Rav commanded those of the House of Ati, Rav Hamnuna commanded the colleagues: Tell your wives that when they come to preserve capers to throw away the calix. Rebbi Abba said,

Rebbi Zeïra explained to me that all skins grow with the fruit but there, the fruit is on top and the skins below[89].

86 Reading of the Rome ms. Leyden and Venice: דבי רב אחי.

87 Reading of the Rome ms. Leyden and Venice: רב הונא המנונא.

88 If the caper bush is not yet in its fourth year, the fruits are forbidden for any use. Samuel and Rav hold that the calix which remains attached to the fruit will become forbidden with the fruit.

89 The opinion of the Galilean academies is that the atrophied remainder of the calix is not a shell in the legal sense, or a part of the fruit, and therefore not forbidden the first three years. In the Babli, *Berakhot* 37b, the same conclusion is reached.

הַקַּפְּרִס וְהַתְּמָרוֹת מִין אֶחָד הֵן. מְעַשֵּׂר מִקַּפְּרִס עַל הַתְּמָרוֹת וּמִן הַתְּמָרוֹת עַל הַקַּפְּרִס. אֲבָל לֹא מֵהֶן עַל הָאֲבִיּוֹנוֹת וּמִן הָאֲבִיּוֹנוֹת עֲלֵיהֶן. אֲבִיּוֹנוֹת נוֹתְנִין עֲלֵיהֶן חוּמְרֵי אִילָּן וְחוּמְרֵי זְרָעִין. וּלְיֵידֶה מִילָּה שֶׁאִים הָיְתָה שְׁנִיָּה נִכְנֶסֶת לִשְׁלִישִׁית שֶׁהוּא מַפְרִישׁ וּפוֹדֵהוּ וְנוֹתְנוֹ לֶעָנִי.

Capers and budding fruits are one kind; one tithes from capers for budding fruit and from budding fruit for capers but not from both for ripe fruits or from ripe fruits for them. On the ripe fruits one applies the stringencies of both trees and vegetables. In which respect? If it is after the second year going into the third[90], he separates, redeems, and gives it to the poor.

90 Or the fifth year of the Sabbatical cycle going into the sixth. Trees are tithed according to the rules valid at the time of fertilization. This would be the 2nd or 5th year in which second tithe is due which has to be redeemed in the absence of a Temple. Vegetables are tithed by the rules of the day of harvest. In the 3rd and 6th years, tithe of the poor is due. Therefore, caper seeds are tithed as second tithe; the tithe is redeemed and then given to the poor as tithe of the poor.

הַצְּלָף בֵּית שַׁמַּאי אוֹמְרִים כִּלְאַיִם בַּכֶּרֶם וְאֵינוֹ כִלְאַיִם בִּזְרָעִים. בֵּית הִלֵּל אוֹמְרִים אֵינוֹ כִלְאַיִם לֹא בְכֶרֶם וְלֹא בִזְרָעִים. הַכֹּל מוֹדִים שֶׁהוּא חַיָּיב בְּעָרְלָה.[91] תַּנֵּי רִבִּי חֲנִינָא בַּר פַּפָּא אֶת שֶׁהוּא עוֹלֶה מִגִּזְעוֹ מִין אִילָן מִשָּׁרָשָׁיו מִן יָרָק. הָתִיבוּן הֲרֵי הַכְּרוּב הֲרֵי הוּא עוֹלֶה מִגִּזְעוֹ. כָּאן בְּוַדַּאי כָּאן בְּסָפֵק.

The caper bush[92]. The House of Shammai say, it is *kilaim* in a vineyard[93] but not with grains. The House of Hillel say, it is never *kilaim*, neither in a vineyard nor with grains. Both agree that it is subject to *orlah*. Rebbi Ḥanina bar Papa[93] stated: Any plant that branches out from its stem is a tree; from its roots it is a vegetable. They objected: But cabbage forms its leaves from its stem! Here[94] when it is sure, there when it is doubtful.

91 This sentence is only in the Rome ms. and the parallel in *Kilaim*.

92 This paragraph is also in *Kilaim* 5:8. A shortened version, not mentioning grains, is in Tosephta *Kilaim* 3:17 and Babli *Berakhot* 36a.

93 The House of Shammai are unsure whether caper bushes are trees or vegetables and therefore apply the stringency of vegetables for *kilaim* and those of fruit trees for *orlah*, so that its fruit is forbidden the first three years after planting (*Lev*. 19:23).

94 He is R. Ḥanina bar Pappai. His statement appears in another version (another redaction) in *Baba Batra* 5:5: "R. Ḥama bar 'Uqba in the name of R. Yose. Anything that grows from both root and stem is a root (a vegetable); from its stem but not from its root it is a tree." In that formulation, cabbage presents no problem since there is no piece of stem free of leaves.

95 The caper bush. Since for cabbage, the lower end of the stem is the lower end of the leaves, it is questionable whether the lowest leaves come from stem or root.

העוקר פרק חמישי

(fol. 51c) **משנה א:** הָעוֹקֵר שְׁתָלִים מִתּוֹךְ שֶׁלּוֹ וְנוֹטֵעַ מִתּוֹךְ שֶׁלּוֹ פָּטוּר. לָקַח בִּמְחוּבָּר לְקַרְקַע פָּטוּר. לָקַט לְשַׁלַּח לַחֲבֵירוֹ פָּטוּר. רִבִּי לָעְזָר בֶּן עֲזַרְיָה אוֹמֵר אִם יֵשׁ כְּיוֹצֵא מֵהֶן נִמְכָּרִין בַּשּׁוּק הֲרֵי אֵלּוּ חַיָּבִין.

Mishnah 1: If somebody lifts out plants from his own property and replants them in his own property, it is free[1]. If somebody bought standing produce, it is free[2]. If somebody collected in order to send to a friend, it is free[3]. Rebbi Eleazar ben Azariah says, if similar [produce] is sold on the market, he is obligated[4].

1 This is neither harvesting nor selling; no obligation of tithe is created. שתלים means "saplings" but this is not the meaning here since it is implied that the young trees transplanted already carry usable fruits and, therefore, are more than three years old. The word שתלים denotes any plant planted, not produced directly from seeds.

2 While a sale creates *ṭevel* (Halakhah 4:1), this holds only for produce already harvested.

3 Since this is not a sale.

4 In that case, the produce could be considered fully processed as far as the original farmer is concerned and is *ṭevel*.

הלכה א: הָעוֹקֵר שְׁתָלִים מִתּוֹךְ שֶׁלּוֹ כו׳. רִבִּי אַבָּהוּ בְשֵׁם רִבִּי שִׁמְעוֹן בֶּן לָקִישׁ רִבִּי עֲקִיבָה הִיא. דְּתַנִּינָן תַּמָּן נוֹטֵל מִן הַגּוֹרֶן וְזוֹרֵעַ וּפָטוּר מִן הַמַּעְשְׂרוֹת עַד שֶׁיִּמְרַח דִּבְרֵי רִבִּי עֲקִיבָה. רִבִּי חִיָּיה בְשֵׁם רִבִּי יוֹחָנָן דִּבְרֵי הַכֹּל הִיא. מוֹדִין חֲכָמִים לְרִבִּי עֲקִיבָה בִּשְׁתָלִים. מַה בֵּין חִטִּים מַה בֵּין שְׁתָלִים. חִטִּין גְּמַר מְלָאכָה שְׁתָלִים אֵינָן גְּמַר מְלָאכָה. מוֹדֵי רִבִּי עֲקִיבָה לַחֲכָמִים בְּלֶפֶת וּצְנוֹנוֹת

שֶׁהֵן פְּסֵידִין. וְחִטִּין אֵינָן פְּסֵידִין. חִטִּין יֵשׁ לָהֶן גּוֹרֶן אֲחֶרֶת. אֵילּוּ[5] אֵין לוֹ גּוֹרֶן אֲחֶרֶת.

Halakhah 1: "If somebody lifts out plants from his own property", etc. Rebbi Abbahu in the name of Rebbi Simeon ben Laqish: This is Rebbi Aqiba's. As we have stated there[6], "He may take from the threshing floor and sow and it is free from tithes until he smoothes, the words of Rebbi Aqiba." Rebbi Ḥiyya in the name of Rebbi Joḥanan, it is the opinion of everybody. The Sages agree with Rebbi Aqiba in the matter of young plants[7]. What is the difference between wheat and young plants? For wheat, it was the end of processing[8]; for plants it is not the end of processing[9]. Rebbi Aqiba agrees with the Sages in the matter of turnips and radishes because they spoil[10]. Does wheat not also spoil? Wheat admits another threshing floor[11], these have no other threshing floor.

5 Reading of the Rome ms. Leyden and Venice: אילן "a tree". The earlier commentators all correct the text to אילין "these" (Aramaic).

6 Mishnah *Peah* 1:6; Notes 275-276.

7 In no way can taking young plants be compared to taking grains from the threshing floor.

8 Threshing is really the end of processing for wheat. Smoothing the heap helps the farmer to know how much grain he has; it is not processing the food.

9 It is not even the beginning since no fruits have been plucked.

10 Taking them out of the ground is the end of processing since in the absence of refrigeration they have to be consumed immediately.

11 The smoothing of the heaps.

לָקַט לְשַׁלַּח לַחֲבֵירוֹ פָּטוּר. רַב אָמַר הוּא אָסוּר לוֹכַל. רִבִּי שַׁמַּי אָמַר קוֹמֵי רִבִּי יוֹסֵי בְּשֵׁם רִבִּי אָחָא מַה דְאָמַר רַב בְּשֶׁהִכְנִיסוֹ לַחֲצַר בֵּית שְׁמִירָה כְּרִבִּי מֵאִיר. אָמַר רִבִּי מָנָא מַתְנִיתָא אָמְרָה כֵן לָקַח בִּמְחוּבָּר לְקַרְקַע פָּטוּר. הָא בְּתָלוּשׁ חַייָב. מָאן אִית לֵיהּ מִקַּח טוֹבֵל בְּפֵירוֹת שֶׁלֹּא נִגְמְרָה מְלַאכְתָּן לֹא רִבִּי מֵאִיר.

רִבִּי חִיָּה בְּשֵׁם רִבִּי יוֹחָנָן דְּרִבִּי יוּדָה הִיא. וְתַנֵּי כֵן רִבִּי יוּדָה אוֹמֵר בְּשֵׁם רִבִּי לְעָזָר בֶּן עֲזַרְיָה אַף הַשּׁוֹלֵחַ לַחֲבֵירוֹ עֲטָנִין וּשְׁתָלִין וַחֲבִילֵי תִּלְתָּן לֹא יֹאכַל עַד שֶׁיְּעַשֵּׂר. שֶׁכֵּן דֶּרֶךְ בְּנֵי אָדָם מְשַׁלְּחֵי לַחֲבֵירֵיהֶן טְבָלִים בִּדְבָרִין הַלָּלוּ. רִבִּי שִׁמְעוֹן בֶּן לָקִישׁ אָמַר אֲפִילוּ חָבֵר שֶׁשִּׁילַּח לְחָבֵר צָרִיךְ לְעַשֵּׂר. חֲבֵרַיָּא בָּעֵי נִיחָא עַם הָאָרֶץ חָשׁוּד. חָבֵר חָשׁוּד. אָמַר רִבִּי יוֹסֵי וְכִי עַם הָאָרֶץ גַּבֵּי תְרוּמָה לָאו כְּחָבֵר הוּא. אֶלָּא כֵינִי נָהֲגוּ בְּנֵי אָדָם לִהְיוֹת מְשַׁלְּחִין לַחֲבֵירֵיהֶן טְבָלִים בִּדְבָרִים הַלָּלוּ.

"If somebody collected in order to send to a friend, it is free." Rav said, he[12] is forbidden to eat. Rebbi Shammai said before Rebbi Yose in the name of Rav Aḥa: Rav said this in case he brought it into a secure courtyard, following Rebbi Meïr[13]. Rebbi Mana said, our Mishnah implies this: "If somebody bought standing produce, it is free." Therefore, after it was cut it is obligated. Who is the person who holds that a sale induces *ṭevel* for produce not fully processed? Is this not Rebbi Meïr[14]? Rebbi Ḥiyya in the name of Rebbi Joḥanan, it is from Rebbi Jehudah. It was stated so[15]: "Rebbi Jehudah says in the name of Rebbi Eleazar ben Azariah, also he who sends to his friend olives from the press, young plants, and bundles of fenugreek, should not eat before he tithed since people usually send these things to their friends as *ṭevel*." Rebbi Simeon ben Laqish said, even if a Fellow sent to a Fellow[16], he has to tithe. The colleagues asked, we can understand a vulgar who is suspect; is a Fellow suspect? Rebbi Yose said, is the vulgar not like a Fellow in matters of heave? It really is so: People usually send these things as *ṭevel* to their friends.

12 The sender.

13 Chapter 2, Halakhah 5.

14 Chapter 2, last paragraph.

15 Tosephta 3:8. There, instead of "bundles of fenugreek" it speaks of "bundles of untreated flax." The Sages hold that people usually tithe these before they send them.

16 See Introduction to Tractate Demay; even a vulgar will always give heave; cf. *Demay* 1:3, Note 130.

משנה ב: הָעוֹקֵר לֶפֶת וּצְנוֹנוֹת מִתּוֹךְ שֶׁלּוֹ וְנוֹטֵעַ לְתוֹךְ שֶׁלּוֹ לְזֶרַע חַיָּיב מִפְּנֵי שֶׁהוּא גּוֹרְנָן. בְּצָלִים שֶׁהִשְׁרִישׁוּ בָּעֲלִיָּה טִהֲרוּ מִלְּטַמֵּא. נָפְלָה עֲלֵיהֶן מַפּוֹלֶת וְהֵן מְגוּלִּין הֲרֵי אֵילּוּ כִּנְטוּעִין בַּשָּׂדֶה.

Mishnah 2: Someone who uproots turnips or radishes in his own property and replants them in his own property for seeds is obligated because that was their threshing floor[17]. Onions which developed roots in storage[18] became pure[19] and cannot become impure again. If a mudslide fell on them and they are uncovered they are as if planted in the field[20].

17 These vegetables are not processed since they are grown for seeds. Therefore, they are considered harvested. If grown for consumption or sale, they cannot become subject to tithes by being transplanted since that would free the later growth from heave and tithes.

18 בעליה "when stored on the upper floor of the farmhouse."

19 They became new plants which in their growing phase are immune to any kind of impurity.

20 Subject to the laws of heave, tithes, *kilaim*, and the Sabbatical year.

הלכה ב: לֹא שַׁנְייָא בֵּין לְזֶרַע בֵּין לְהֶבְקֵר בֵּין לְחוּצָה לָאָרֶץ. תַּמָּן תַּנִּינָן לְעוֹלָם הוּא נוֹתֵן מִשּׁוּם פֵּיאָה (fol. 51d) וּפָטוּר מִן הַמַּעְשְׂרוֹת עַד שֶׁיִּמְרַח. וְכָא אַתְּ אָמַר הָכֵין. תַּמָּן הוּא מַבְקִיר עַל הַכֹּל בְּרַם הָכָא הוּא מַבְקִיר עַל הַגִּידּוּלִין. וְהָא תַנִּינָן חוּץ לָאָרֶץ. שַׁנְיָיה הִיא חוּץ לָאָרֶץ בֵּין לְעִיקָּר בֵּין לְגִידּוּלִין. כָּה לֹא שַׁנְיָיא בֵּין לְעִיקָּר בֵּין לְגִידּוּלִין.

Halakhah 2: There is no difference, whether for sowing seeds, to abandon property, or [to plant] outside the Land[21]. There[22], we have stated: "Forever he gives as *peah* and it is free from tithes until he smoothes." And here you say so? There, he abandons everything, here he abandons only the future growth[23]. But did we not state "outside the Land?" There is a difference, outside the Land both for the stem and future growth[24]; is here not a difference between the stem and future growth?

21 Tosephta 3:8: "If somebody lifts out plants on his own property to replant them outside the Land, either to produce seeds, or to abandon the produce, or to sell it to a Gentile, he is obligated because he intends to remove them from tithes."

22 Mishnah *Peah* 1:6, Note 275. The main objection is from the next clause in the Mishnah: "If he takes seeds from the threshing floor he is free from tithes until he smoothes."

23 This implies that "to abandon the produce" in the Tosephta (and here in the Halakhah) means that he retains ownership of the plant (in the Tosephta) and the core of the turnip (in the Halakhah) and intends only to free the future growth. This is illegal. But irrevocable abandoning a plant to public use frees the plant from all heave and tithes legally and, since the poor profit from it, cannot be subject to rabbinic sanctions.

The Rome ms. has here an addition: תדע לך שהוא כן דתנינן לזרע וזרע לא כגידולין הוא "You should know that is so since we have stated 'for seeds'. Are seeds not equal to later growth?"

24 Since the stem of a plant outside the Land is also outside the Land, he takes produce subject to heave and tithes by the act of taking them out of the ground and removes them completely from obligations of heave and tithes for private gain; this is subject to sanction.

עַל דַּעְתֵּיהּ דְּרִבִּי שִׁמְעוֹן בֶּן לָקִישׁ דּוּ אָמַר טֵבֶל בָּטֵל בְּרוֹב נִיחָא. עַל דַּעְתֵּיהּ דְּרִבִּי יוֹחָנָן דּוּ אָמַר אֵין הַטֵּבֶל בָּטֵל בְּרוֹב יַמְתִּין עַד שֶׁיַּגְדִּיל וִיעַשֵּׂר לְפִי כוּלּוֹ. אוֹ נֵימַר מַה פְלִיגֵי רִבִּי יוֹחָנָן וְרִבִּי שִׁמְעוֹן בֶּן לָקִישׁ בְּטֵבֶל שֶׁנִּטְבָּל דְּבַר תּוֹרָה. אֲבָל בְּטֵבֶל שֶׁנִּטְבָּל מִדִּבְרֵיהֶן כָּל־עַמָּא מוֹדֵיי שֶׁהַטֵּבֶל בָּטֵל בְּרוֹב. הָתִיב רִבִּי

בָּא בַּר כֹּהֵן קוֹמֵי רִבִּי יוֹסֵי וְהָא תַנִּינָן כְּיוֹצֵא בוֹ זֵיתֵי מֵסִיק שֶׁנִּתְעָרְבוּ עִם זֵיתֵי נִיקוּף. עִינְּבֵי בָּצִיר עִם עִינְּבֵי עוֹלֵלוֹת. וְלֹא טֵבֵל שֶׁנִּטְבָּל מִדִּבְרֵיהֶן הִיא. אָמַר רִבִּי מָנָא קִייַּמְתֵּיהָ בְּשֶׁמֶן זֵיתֵי מֵסִיק שֶׁנִּתְעָרֵב עִם שֶׁמֶן זֵיתֵי נִיקוּף.

According to Rebbi Simeon ben Laqish who said[25], *ṭevel* becomes voided by plurality, it is intelligible[26]. According to Rebbi Joḥanan who said, *ṭevel* does not become voided by plurality, he should wait until it is fully grown and tithe for everything[27]. Or might we say that Rebbi Joḥanan and Rebbi Simeon ben Laqish disagree about *ṭevel* which has this status by a word of the Torah[28] but for *ṭevel* which has this status by their word[29] everybody agrees that *ṭevel* becomes voided by plurality. Rebbi Abba bar Cohen objected: Did we not state[30]: "Similarly, olives for pressing which were mixed with picked olives, harvest grapes with grapes of gleanings"? Is that not *ṭevel* by their words[31]? Rebbi Mana[32] said, I upheld this: Oil from olives for pressing[33] which was mixed with oil from picked olives.

25 The disagreement between R. Simeon ben Laqish and R. Joḥanan is in *Terumot* 4:1, Note 10.

26 If he replants in a way which will eliminate the duty of tithing from the ripe fruits, it is intelligible that we require him to tithe now since otherwise also the part which grew under a potential obligation will be free if the new growth is more than what is already grown.

27 Since the original *ṭevel* will not disappear, replanting will never free the current crop and no tithing now should be necessary, in obvious disagreement with the Mishnah!

28 Wine, olive oil, and threshed grain brought to storage.

29 By rabbinical tradition.

30 Mishnah *Ḥallah* 3:7: "Similarly, olives for pressing {harvested by the owner by shaking the tree} which were mixed with picked olives {gleaned by the poor and exempt from tithes}, harvest grapes {subject to tithes} which were mixed with grapes of gleanings {of the poor and exempt from tithes}, if he can provide for {the obligated} from

another place, he should do so; otherwise, he takes heave and Heave of the Tithe for everything but the tithes only in proportion."

31 The obligation for heave and Heave of the Tithe even for the portion gleaned by the poor cannot be biblical; if the exempt amount is more than the obligated, the entire obligation is rabbinical.

32 R. Mana II.

33 Obligated by biblical decree.

אָמַר רִבִּי מָנָא לֹא שָׁנוּ אֶלָּא לְזֶרַע הָא לוֹכַל פָּטוּר. רִבִּי חִייָה בְּשֵׁם רִבִּי יוֹחָנָן לֹא שַׁנְייָה בֵּין לְזֶרַע בֵּין[34] לוֹכַל חַייָב מִפְּנֵי שֶׁהוּא גוֹרְנָן. אָמַר רִבִּי חֲנִינָה מִפְּנֵי שֶׁהוּא מַכְנִיסָן מִן הַשֵּׁנִי לֶעָנִי וּמִן הֶעָנִי לַשֵּׁנִי.

Rebbi Mana[35] said, they taught only "for seeds"; therefore, for eating he is free. Rebbi Ḥiyya said in the name of Rebbi Joḥanan: There is no difference; he is obligated for seeds or for consumption because this is their threshing floor[36]. Rebbi Ḥanina[37] said, because he would transfer it from second to the poor or from the poor to second[38].

34 Reading of the Rome ms. The Leyden ms. has only בין in place of the last three words.

35 R. Mana I. In the Rome ms., the statement is attributed to R. Ammi (Immi). The reference is to the first sentence of the Mishnah, turnips and radishes grown for seeds.

36 Since a vegetable is always tithed when harvested.

37 He is R. Ḥinena.

38 If the vegetable is replanted in one of the years 2,3,5 of the Sabbatical cycle and finally harvested the next year, second tithe of the already grown part would be changed into tithe of the poor or vice-versa.

רִבִּי יוֹחָנָן בְּשֵׁם רִבִּי יַנַּאי עֲרֵימָה שֶׁל בְּצָלִים שֶׁהִשְׁרִישָׁה הַתּוֹלֵשׁ מֵהֶן בַּשַּׁבָּת פָּטוּר וְאֵינוֹ רוֹצֶה בְּהַשְׁרָשָׁתָן. אָמַר לֵיהּ רִבִּי שִׁמְעוֹן בֶּן לָקִישׁ מַאי אִיכְפְּלָה שַׁבָּת גַּבֵּי מַעְשְׂרוֹת. לֹא תַנִּינָן אֶלָּא אֵינוֹ חוֹשֵׁשׁ לֹא מִשּׁוּם כִּלְאַיִם וְלֹא מִשּׁוּם שְׁבִיעִית וְלֹא מִשּׁוּם מַעְשְׂרוֹת וְנִיטָּלִין בַּשַּׁבָּת. אָמַר רִבִּי זְעִירָא לְרִבִּי אַבָּהוּ חֲמִי

מָה אָמַר. לֹא אָמַר אֶלָּא מַאי אִיכְפְּלָה שַׁבָּת גַּבֵּי מַעְשְׂרוֹת. הָא שְׁבִיעִית אִיכְפְּלָה שֶׁאִם הָיָה רוֹצֶה בְּהַשְׁרָשָׁתָן שֶׁהֵן אֲסוּרִין מִשּׁוּם סְפִיחִין. וְאִם לָאו מוּתָּרִין מִשּׁוּם סְפִיחִין. אָמַר רִבִּי מַיישָׁא לְרִבִּי זְעִירָא וְדָא הִיא דְרוֹבָא אִילּוּ תַּנָּא בָּצָל יָד יְחִידִי יָאוּת.

Rebbi Johanan in the name of Rebbi Yannai: If a heap of onions produced roots, if one takes from them on the Sabbath he is free[39] since he does not want their growing roots. Rebbi Simeon ben Laqish said to him: What is the worry[40] of Sabbath compared to tithes? Did we not state[41]: "He does not have to worry either because of *kilaim*, or because of the Sabbatical year, or because of tithes, and they may be removed on the Sabbath." Rebbi Zeïra said to Rebbi Abbahu: Look, what did he say! He said only, what is the worry of Sabbath compared to tithes? So he would worry about the Sabbatical for if he would like them to grow roots they would be forbidden[42] because of aftergrowth; otherwise they are permitted because of aftergrowth. Rebbi Maisha said to Rebbi Zeïra, is that the strongest? If he had stated about a single onion in the hand[43] it would be fine[44].

39 While the onions are growing, taking them is not harvesting.

40 About the verb אכפל see H. L. Fleischer's article in Levy's Dictionary, vol. 2, p. 454.

41 Mishnah *Kilaim* 1:9, Notes 161-162; speaking of harvested vegetables stored in a pit and covered with loose earth.

42 The next year if that happened to be a Sabbatical year. Cf. *Kilaim* 1:9, Note 166, that the Mishnah is accepted only for vegetables which did not grow new roots after being harvested. Therefore, the Mishnah there contradicts R. Johanan's statement here.

43 The word יד "in the hand" is missing in the Rome ms.

44 He certainly does not want to lose a whole heap but a single onion which grew new roots he might replant. If the statement had been

about a single onion we could have inferred that there is a presumption that nobody wants harvested onions to start growing again (and wasting their bulbs) unless there is a clear indication to the contrary.

הִשְׁרִישׁוּ בְּקוּפָּה הֲרֵי הֵן בְּחֶזְקָתָן לְמַעְשְׂרוֹת וְלִשְׁבִיעִית וְאִם הָיוּ טְמֵאִין לֹא עָלוּ מִידֵי טוּמְאָתָן. הִשְׁרִישׁוּ בַּעֲלִיָּה הֲרֵי הֵן בְּחֶזְקָתָן לְמַעְשְׂרוֹת וְלִשְׁבִיעִית וְאִם הָיוּ טְמֵאִין עָלוּ מִטּוּמְאָתָן. בְּחֶזְקָתָן וְאַתְּ אָמַר עָלוּ. רִבִּי יוֹסֵי בְשֵׁם רִבִּי לָא הַתּוֹרָה רִיבָּת בְּטָהֳרַת זְרָעִין מַה טַעֲמָא כִּי יִפּוֹל מִנִּבְלָתָם עַל כָּל־זֶרַע זֵרוּעַ אֲשֶׁר יִזָּרֵעַ טָהוֹר הוּא.

[45]"If they grew roots in a box they are in their previous state for tithes and Sabbatical and if they were impure they did not lose their impurity. If they grew roots in storage[18] they are in their previous state for tithes and Sabbatical and if they were impure they lost their impurity." They are in their previous state and you say they lost? Rebbi Yose in the name of Rebbi La: The Torah emphasized the purity of growing plants (*Lev.* 11:37): "If from their carcass anything fell on any sown seed which may be sown[46], it is pure."

45 Tosephta 3:9. The Tosephta reads: "If they grew one on top of the other, growing roots in a box;" the roots are feeding on other onions. Even so, they are not considered planted if in a box.

46 The multiple expression shows that anything remotely similar to sown plants is covered by the purity of growing plants.

וְתַנֵּי לֹא יִתְלוֹשׁ. עָבַר וְתָלַשׁ. אִית תַּנָּיֵי תַנֵּי חַייָב. אִית תַּנָּיֵי תַנֵּי מוּתָּר. מָאן דְּאָמַר אָסוּר מַתִּיר. מָאן דְּאָמַר חַייָב פָּטוּר. נִיחָא דְּלָא צוֹרְכָה דְלָא מוּתָּר. רִבִּי שִׁמְעוֹן בֶּן לָקִישׁ אָמַר חַייָב.

In addition, it was stated[46]: "He should not take out." If he transgressed and took out? There are Tannaïm who state "he is guilty" and there are Tannaïm who state "he is permitted." Could he who says "it is forbidden" permit?[47] Could he who says "guilty", declare free from punishment? It is clear that it should not be: "permitted". Rebbi Simeon ben Laqish holds that he is guilty[48].

46 Tosephta 3:9. The Tosephta continues (about onions growing roots in storage): "It is forbidden to take out from them on the Sabbath, but if he did he is free from punishment." The language of the Tosephta is consistent.

47 This is the language of the Tosephta; it obviously was not the language of the *baraitot* before the compilers of the Yerushalmi. A *baraita* which reads: "It is forbidden to take out from them on the Sabbath, and if he did he is permitted," is inconsistent.

48 Since above (Note 40) he questions the dependence of the status regarding the Sabbath from the status in matters of tithes.

(fol. 51c) **משנה ג**: לֹא יִמְכּוֹר אָדָם אֶת פֵּירוֹתָיו מִשֶּׁבָּאוּ לְעוֹנַת הַמַּעְשְׂרוֹת לְמִי שֶׁאֵינוֹ נֶאֱמָן עַל הַמַּעְשְׂרוֹת וְלֹא בַשְּׁבִיעִית לְמִי שֶׁהוּא חָשׁוּד עַל הַשְּׁבִיעִית. וְאִם בִּיכְּרוּ נוֹטֵל אֶת הַבִּכּוּרוֹת וּמוֹכֵר אֶת הַשְּׁאָר.

Mishnah 3: A person should not sell his produce after it reached the period of tithing[49] to anybody not trustworthy in matters of tithe, or in the Sabbatical year to anybody suspect in matters of the Sabbatical[50]. If some were ripened early he takes the early ripe fruit[51] and sells the remainder.

49 As explained in Chapter 1:2-9.

50 That he would not eat the fruits in the sanctity of the Sabbatical but use them as objects of trade.

51 For himself to tithe. The remainder which is not ripe enough to be tithed may be sold to anybody.

משנה ד: לֹא יִמְכּוֹר אָדָם אֶת תִּבְנוֹ וְאֶת גִּפְתּוֹ וְאֶת זוֹגָיו לְמִי שֶׁאֵינוֹ נֶאֱמָן עַל הַמַּעְשְׂרוֹת לְהוֹצִיא מֵהֶן מַשְׁקִין וְאִם הוֹצִיא חַיָּיב בְּמַעְשְׂרוֹת וּפָטוּר מִן הַתְּרוּמָה. שֶׁהַתּוֹרֵם בְּלִבּוֹ עַל הַקּוֹטָעִים וְעַל הַצְּדָדִין וְעַל מַה שֶּׁבְּתוֹךְ הַתֶּבֶן.

Mishnah 4: A person should not sell his chaff or his oil cakes or his grape husks to somebody not trustworthy in matters of tithe if the latter wants to extract fluids from it. If he extracted, he is obligated for tithes[52] but free from heave since everybody giving heave also thinks of broken grain[53], what is left on the sides, and what remains in the chaff.

52 Since tithes are fixed percentages but heave should not be measured. "Extracting fluids" refers to oil cakes and grape husks but a similar rule applies to chaff and the single grains that still can be plucked from it after threshing.

53 The parts of grain that cannot be removed from the straw in threshing.

(fol. 51d) **הלכה ג**: כֵּינִי מַתְנִיתָא לֹא יִמְכּוֹר אָדָם אֶת שָׂדֵהוּ רִבִּי שִׁמְעוֹן מַתִּיר מִפְּנֵי שֶׁהוּא אוֹמֵר לוֹ הֲרֵי מָכַרְתִּי אֶת שֶׁלִּי צֵא וּתְבַע אֶת שֶׁלָּךְ. עָבַר וּמָכַר מְעַשֵּׂר וְאוֹכֵל וְאֵינוֹ מְעַשֵּׂר מַה שֶּׁהוּא מוֹכֵר וְאֵין אָנוּ אַחֲרָיִין לָרַמָּיִין.

Halakhah 3: So is the Mishnah: A person should not sell his field[54]. Rebbi Simeon permits since he[55] may say to him, I sold mine, go and demand what is yours. If he transgressed and sold, he tithes what he eats but he does not have to tithe for what he sold since we are not responsible for the dishonest[56].

54 With the produce standing potentially subject to tithes.

55 He, the seller, may say to him, the Levite, go and collect your tithe if you can.

56 Cf. Mishnah *Demay* 3:5, Note 134.

תַּנֵּי לֹא יִתְרוֹם. עָבַר וְתָרַם רִבִּי בֶּרֶכְיָה אָמַר יָפֶה כֹּחוֹ. רִבִּי מָנָא אָמַר לֹא יָפֶה כֹּחוֹ. אוֹתָהּ הַתְּרוּמָה שֶׁהוּא מַפְרִישׁ טוֹבֶלֶת לְמַעֲשֵׂר.

It was stated: He should not give heave. If he transgressed and gave heave, Rebbi Berekhia said, he is empowered. Rebbi Mana said, he is not empowered; that heave he gave creates *ṭevel* for tithe[57].

57 Since the Mishnah stated that heave given for all grain threshed includes heave for what is left in the chaff, giving about .5% for heave does not free from giving 10% for tithes even from what was designated as heave.

רִבִּי חֲנִינָה חֲבֵרוֹן דְּרַבָּנִין בָּעֵי תָּרַם אֶחָד בְּשִׁשִּׁים שֶׁהוּא אֶחָד מִשִּׁשִּׁים וְאֶחָד עַל הַקִּיטָּעִין וְעַל הַצְּדָדִין וְעַל מַה שֶּׁבְּתוֹךְ הַתֶּבֶן. אָמַר רִבִּי יוֹסֵי וְלֹא מַתְנִיתִין הִיא. שֶׁהַתּוֹרֵם בְּלִבּוֹ עַל הַקִּיטָּעִים וְעַל הַצְּדָדִין וְעַל מַה שֶּׁבְּתוֹךְ הַתֶּבֶן. כְּלוּם צְרִיכָה אֶלָּא בְיֶתֶר.

Rebbi Ḥanina, the colleague of the rabbis, asked: If he gave heave one in sixty, which is one in sixty-one including broken grain[58], what is left on the sides, and what remains in the chaff? Rebbi Yose said, is that not the Mishnah: "Since everybody giving heave also thinks of broken grain, what is left on the sides, and what remains in the chaff." Is that not needed only for the excess[59]?

58 Then the heave would be invalid by rabbinical standards, Mishnah *Terumot* 4:3.

59 If everybody gave in excess of the minimum the question addressed in the Mishnah would be no problem. If the Mishnah states categorically that heave given for threshed grain includes all the remainder, it is clear that the rabbinic invalidation of heave which is less than $^1/_{60}$ does not extend to the case here.

(fol. 51c) **משנה ה**: הַלּוֹקֵחַ שְׂדֵה יָרָק בְּסוּרְיָא אִם עַד שֶׁלֹּא בָאוּ לְעוֹנַת הַמַּעְשְׂרוֹת חַיָּיב. וּמִשֶּׁבָּאוּ לְעוֹנַת הַמַּעְשְׂרוֹת פָּטוּר וְלוֹקֵט כְּדַרְכּוֹ וְהוֹלֵךְ. רִבִּי יְהוּדָה אוֹמֵר אַף יִשְׂכּוֹר פּוֹעֲלִים וִילַקֵּט. אָמַר רִבִּי שִׁמְעוֹן בֶּן גַּמְלִיאֵל בַּמֶּה דְבָרִים אֲמוּרִים בִּזְמַן שֶׁקָּנָה קַרְקַע. אֲבָל בִּזְמַן שֶׁלֹּא קָנָה קַרְקַע אַף עַל פִּי שֶׁלֹּא בָא לְעוֹנַת הַמַּעְשְׂרוֹת פָּטוּר. רִבִּי אוֹמֵר אַף לְפִי חֶשְׁבּוֹן.

Mishnah 5: If somebody bought a vegetable field in Syria[60] before it reached the time of tithes[49] he is obligated[61], after it reached the time of tithes he is free and he[62] can harvest continuously. Rebbi Jehudah says, he may even hire workers and harvest. Rabban Simeon ben Gamliel said, where has this been said? When he bought the field. But if he did not buy the field he is free[63] even after it reached the time of tithes. Rebbi said, all according to computation[64].

60 For the definition of "Syria", cf. *Peah* 7:6, Note 119. Produce of Syria is exempt from tithes unless it grew on the property of a Jew, *Demay* 6:11, Note 172.

61 Then the produce became obligated on the field of a Jew.

62 Himself, for his personal use. The reason one does not allow him commercial harvest is only because of the bad impression; it would look as if a Jew would disregard the obligation to tithe his fields in Syria. R. Jehudah disagrees with this restriction.

63 If he only bought the crop there is no difference whether he bought it standing or harvested.

64 Rebbi disagrees with the anonymous Tanna and holds that in any case he has to tithe the percentage of the crop added in the Jew's possession.

In the Tosephta (3:14), the anonymous opinion is attributed to R. Aqiba and that of Rebbi to the anonymous Sages.

(fol. 51d) **הלכה ד**: תַּנֵּי שָׂדֶה שֶׁהֵבִיאָה שְׁלִישׁ לִפְנֵי גוֹי וּלְקָחָהּ מִמֶּנּוּ יִשְׂרָאֵל רִבִּי עֲקִיבָה אוֹמֵר הַתּוֹסֶפֶת פָּטוּר. וַחֲכָמִים אוֹמְרִים הַתּוֹסֶפֶת חַיָּיב. רִבִּי אֲבִינָא עוּלָּא בְּרִבִּי יִשְׁמָעֵאל בְּשֵׁם רִבִּי לָעְזָר אַף חֲכָמִים לֹא חִייְבוּ בְתוֹסֶפֶת אֶלָּא לְשֶׁעָבַר שֶׁאִם הָיָה שְׁנֵי שְׁנֵי עָנִי עָנִי. תַּנֵּי רִבִּי יוֹנָתָן בֵּי רִבִּי יוֹסֵי אוֹמֵר מְנַיִן

לִתְבוּאָה שֶׁהֵבִיאָה שְׁלִישׁ לִפְנֵי רֹאשׁ הַשָּׁנָה כּוֹנְסָהּ אוֹתָהּ בַּשְּׁבִיעִית. תַּלְמוּד לוֹמַר וְאָסַפְתָּ אֶת תְּבוּאָתָהּ בַּשְּׁבִיעִית. רִבִּי אֲבִינָא עוּלָּא בְּרִבִּי יִשְׁמָעֵאל בְּשֵׁם רִבִּי לָעְזָר אַתְיָא דְּרִבִּי יוֹנָתָן בֵּי רִבִּי יוֹסֵי בְּשִׁיטַּת רִבִּי עֲקִיבָה רַבּוֹ. כְּמָה דְּרִבִּי עֲקִיבָה אוֹמֵר אַחַר שְׁלִישׁ הָרִאשׁוֹן אַתְּ מְהַלֵּךְ. כֵּן רִבִּי יוֹנָתָן בֶּן רִבִּי יוֹסֵי אוֹמֵר אַחַר שְׁלִישׁ הָרִאשׁוֹן אַתְּ מְהַלֵּךְ. אָמַר רִבִּי זְעִירָא לְרִבִּי אֲבוּנָא תַּרְתֵּין מִילִּין אַתּוּן אָמְרִין וְאִינּוּן פְּלִיגוֹן הָדָא עַל הָדָא. הָכָא אַתּוּן מָרִין אַף חֲכָמִים לֹא חִייְבוּ בְתוֹסֶפֶת אֶלָּא לְשֶׁעָבַר שֶׁאִם הָיָה שֵׁנִי שֵׁנִי עָנִי עָנִי. וְהָכָא אַתּוּן מָרִין אַתְיָא דְּרִבִּי יוֹנָתָן בֵּי רִבִּי יוֹסֵי בְּשִׁיטַּת רִבִּי עֲקִיבָה רַבּוֹ. אִי דְּאַתְיָיא דְּרִבִּי יוֹנָתָן בֵּי רִבִּי יוֹסֵי בְּשִׁיטַּת רִבִּי עֲקִיבָה רַבּוֹ. כְּמָה דְּרִבִּי עֲקִיבָה אוֹמֵר אִיסּוּר סְפִיחִים תּוֹרָה. כֵּן רִבִּי יוֹנָתָן בֵּי רִבִּי יוֹסֵי אָמַר אִיסּוּר סְפִיחִים תּוֹרָה. הֵבִיאָה פָּחוֹת מִשְּׁלִישׁ לִפְנֵי שְׁבִיעִית נִכְנְסָה שְׁבִיעִית אֲסוּרָה מִשּׁוּם סְפִיחִין וְלֹא חָלָה עָלֶיהָ קְדוּשַּׁת שְׁבִיעִית. שֶׁכְּבָר הָיוּ עֲשָׂבִים וְלֹא חָלָה עָלֶיהָ קְדוּשַּׁת שְׁבִיעִית. הֵבִיאָה פָּחוֹת מִשְּׁלִישׁ לִפְנֵי שְׁמִינִית וְנִכְנְסָה שְׁמִינִית מוּתֶּרֶת מִשּׁוּם סְפִיחִין וְחָלָה עֲלֵיהֶן קְדוּשַּׁת שְׁבִיעִית. רִבִּי יוֹחָנָן וְרִבִּי שִׁמְעוֹן בֶּן לָקִישׁ תְּרֵיהוֹן מָרִין מוֹדִין חֲכָמִים לְרִבִּי עֲקִיבָה בְּסִדְרָן שֶׁל שָׁנִים שֶׁאִם הָיוּ שֵׁנִי שֵׁנִי עָנִי עָנִי.

Halakhah 4: It was stated[65]: If a field[66] became one-third ripe in the possession of a Gentile and a Jew bought it from him, Rebbi Aqiba says the addition is free. But the Sages say, the addition is obligated. Rebbi Abina, Ulla ben Rebbi Israel in the name of Rebbi Eleazar: Also the Sages did obligate only for the past; if it was second it remains second, for the poor it remains for the poor[67]. It was stated[68]: Rebbi Jonathan ben Rebbi Yose says, from where that grain one-third ripe before New Year's day may be brought in during the Sabbatical? The verse says (*Lev.* 25:3): "You shall gather its[69] yield," [even] in the Sabbatical year. Rebbi Abina, Ulla ben Rebbi Israel in the name of Rebbi Eleazar: Rebbi Jonathan ben Rebbi Yose follows the argument of his teacher Rebbi Aqiba. Just as Rebbi Aqiba said, you follow the first third, so Rebbi Jonathan ben Rebbi Yose said, you follow the first third. Rebbi Zeïra said to Rebbi Abina, you say two things which contradict one another. Here you teach that the Sages also did obligate only for the past; if it was second it remains second, for the poor it remains for the poor[70]. There, you teach that Rebbi Jonathan ben Rebbi Yose follows the argument of his teacher Rebbi Aqiba. If Rebbi Jonathan ben Rebbi Yose follows the argument of his teacher Rebbi Aqiba then just as Rebbi Aqiba says the prohibition of aftergrowth is from the Torah[71], so Rebbi Jonathan ben Rebbi Yose must say, the prohibition of aftergrowth is from the Torah. If it grew less than one-third ripe before the Sabbatical, in the Sabbatical it is forbidden[72] as aftergrowth but the sanctity of the Sabbatical did not fall on it since it was grass on which the sanctity of the Sabbatical cannot fall[73]. If it grew less than one-third ripe before the eighth year, in the eighth year it is permitted as aftergrowth but the sanctity of the Sabbatical falls on it[74]. Rebbi Joḥanan and Rebbi Simeon ben Laqish both teach that the Sages agree with Rebbi Aqiba in the order of years; if it was second it remains second, for the poor it remains for the poor[75].

65 Cf. *Peah* 4:5, Notes 90-92.

66 A grain field in the Land of Israel. "One-third ripe" means that the grains are fully formed and one-third ripe; not that one third of the growing period has passed. For grain, "one-third ripe" is the Biblical standard for grain that might be harvested, cf. *Ma'serot* Chapter 1, Note 78, *Ševi'it* Chapter 2, Notes 63,77.

67 The status of grain as far as second tithe or tithe of the poor is concerned is determined by the time it is one-third ripe, rather than by the time of harvest. In this respect, the rules of tithing follow the rules of the Sabbatical.

68 *Sifra Behar* (9). There, the name is R. Jonathan ben Joseph, a Tanna of the fourth generation who also is quoted as R. Natan ben Joseph.

69 The sixth year's.

70 If the Sages determine the rules of tithes by the time the grains were one-third ripe, there is no proof that R. Jonathan ben R. Yose follows R. Aqiba where the latter disagrees with the Sages. Therefore, R. Eleazar should

hold that for the Sages, only the time of the actual harvest and threshing is relevant.

71 *Sifra Behar Pereq* 4(5); Babli *Pesaḥim* 51b.

72 Following R. Aqiba and R. Jonathan ben R. Yose.

73 If the grain was collected as fodder before it was fully ripe for human consumption. It would be forbidden to use the unripe grain as *Grünkern*; cf. *Peah* 4:6, Note 86.

74 It should be eaten following the rules of the Sabbatical.

75 They disagree that grain one-third ripened in the possession of the Gentile should be exempt but they admit that the kind of second tithe to be given depends on the year in which the grain was edible as *Grünkern*.

אָמַר רִבִּי יוֹחָנָן הֶבְקֵר וְהֶקְדֵּשׁ בְּסוּרְיָה[76] מַחֲלוֹקֶת רִבִּי עֲקִיבָה וַחֲכָמִים. אָמַר רִבִּי שִׁמְעוֹן בֶּן לָקִישׁ מוֹדֵי רִבִּי עֲקִיבָא לַחֲכָמִים בְּחָנָט וְהִשְׁרָשָׁה. זָרַע בְּחוֹרֵבָה וְהֵבִיאָה שְׁלִישׁ וְסִיכֵךְ עַל גַּבָּיו. עַל דַּעְתֵּיהּ דְּרִבִּי עֲקִיבָה הַתּוֹסֶפֶת חַיָּיב. עַל דַּעְתִּין דְּרַבָּנִין הַתּוֹסֶפֶת פָּטוּר. זָרַע בַּבַּיִת וְהֶעֱבִיר הַסְּכָךְ וְסִיכֵךְ עַל גַּבָּיו. עַל דַּעְתֵּיהּ דְּרִבִּי עֲקִיבָה הַתּוֹסֶפֶת פָּטוּר. עַל דַּעְתִּין דְּרַבָּנִין הַתּוֹסֶפֶת חַיָּיב.

Rebbi Joḥanan said, abandonment[77], dedication[78], and Syria are in dispute between Rebbi Aqiba and the Sages. Rebbi Simeon ben Laqish said, Rebbi Aqiba agrees with the Sages about budding[79] and growing roots[80]. If somebody sowed a dry spot, it grew one-third ripe, and he made a roof over it: according to Rebbi Aqiba any later growth is obligated[81]; according to the Sages any later growth is free[82]. If he sowed in a house, removed the roof, and then made a roof over it: according to Rebbi Aqiba any later growth is free; according to the Sages any later growth is obligated.

76 The Rome ms. does not have בסוריה. In the Venice text, one should read וסוריה "and Syria", referring to the case of the Mishnah.

77 If somebody took possession of an abandoned field after the grain on it was one-third ripe, R. Aqiba will free the entire harvest from heave and tithes since it was exempt at the time the grain became edible.

78 If somebody dedicated a field to the Temple and redeemed it after the grain on it was one-third ripe, R. Aqiba again will free the entire harvest from heave and tithes. In both cases, the Sages require heave and tithes since at harvest and threshing time the field was obligated.

79 Fruits of trees are tithed according to the rules valid at the time the fruit started to form; cf. *Ševi'it* 5:1, Note 6.

80 Rice, millet, poppies, and sesame are tithed according to the rules of the time they formed roots, *Ševi'it* 2:7.

81 Since it is judged by the rules valid at the time it became edible when it was "produce of the field" as required by *Deut.* 14:22. Whether there is a rabbinic obligation to tithe produce grown in a house is a matter of dispute between Maimonides and R. Abraham ben David (*Ma'serot* 1:10). The position of Maimonides, that the discussion here is only about the biblical obligations, not the rabbinic ones, is supported by the next paragraph, cf. Note 83.

82 Since at harvest time it is produce of a house, not of a field.

וְאַף בְּחַלָּה כֵּן מַחֲלוֹקֶת רִבִּי עֲקִיבָה וַחֲכָמִים. מַה אַתְּ בָּעֵי מֵרִבִּי עֲקִיבָה דְּרִבִּי עֲקִיבָה אָמַר פֵּירוֹת חוּצָה לָאָרֶץ שֶׁנִּכְנְסוּ לָאָרֶץ חַיָּבִין בְּחַלָּה. אִין יִסְבּוֹר רִבִּי עֲקִיבָה כְּרִבִּי לִיעֶזֶר יְאוֹת אַתְּ מַקְשֵׁי.

Is there a dispute between Rebbi Aqiba and the Sages even for *ḥallah*[83]? What do you want from Rebbi Aqiba, since Rebbi Aqiba said, produce from outside the Land which was imported into the Land is obligated for *ḥallah*? If Rebbi Aqiba would hold like Rebbi Eliezer, your question would be correct.

83 This cannot refer to the problem of one-third ripe grain since *ḥallah* is the heave from dough. The problem is Mishnah *Ḥallah* 2:1: "Produce from outside the Land imported into the Land is subject to *ḥallah*. Produce exported from here to there, R. Eliezer makes it obligated, R. Aqiba frees it." The problem is the interpretation of *Num.* 15:18-19: "Speak to the sons of Israel and tell them: When you come to *the Land into which I am bringing you*, when you will eat *from the bread of the Land* you shall lift a heave to the Eternal." There is a clear biblical obligation if both conditions are

satisfied. There is a rabbinic obligation to give *ḥallah* from any dough anywhere. If only one of the two conditions is satisfied, is the obligation biblical or rabbinical?

רִבִּי בּוּן בַּר חִיָּיה בָּעֵי קוֹמֵי רִבִּי זְעִירָא זָרַע בְּעָצִיץ שֶׁאֵינוֹ נָקוּב וְנָקַב. אָמַר לוֹ עַכְשָׁיו נָקֵב.

Rebbi Abun bar Ḥiyya asked before Rebbi Zeïra: He sowed in a flower pot without a hole and made a hole? He said to him, now it has a hole[84].

84 A flower pot with a hole standing on the ground is part of the earth and its produce is "produce of the field"; cf. Mishnah *Demay* 5:10, Halakhah *Kilaim* 7:8. A flower pot without a hole is not subject to the laws governing agriculture in the Land. Since practice follows the Sages, only the status at the time of harvest counts even if the produce grown in the pot is grain.

אָמַר רִבִּי אָבִין אַתְיָא דְּרַבָּן שִׁמְעוֹן בֶּן גַּמְלִיאֵל בְּשִׁיטָּה רַבָּן גַּמְלִיאֵל זְקֵינוֹ. דְּתַנִּינָן תַּמָּן יִשְׂרָאֵל שֶׁהָיוּ אֲרִיסִין לְגוֹיִם בְּסוּרְיָה. רִבִּי לִיעֶזֶר מְחַייֵב פֵּירוֹתֵיהֶן לְמַעְשְׂרוֹת וְלִשְׁבִיעִית. וְרַבָּן גַּמְלִיאֵל פּוֹטֵר.

Rebbi Abun said, Rabban Simeon ben Gamliel goes with the argument of his ancestor[85] Rabban Gamliel. As we stated there[86]: "Jews who were sharecroppers for Gentiles in Syria, Rebbi Eliezer obligates their produce for tithes and the Sabbatical but Rabban Gamliel frees."

85 Why is he not called his father?

86 Mishnah *Ḥallah* 4:7. For Rabban Gamliel, produce grown on the Gentile's property is Gentile produce.

רִבִּי אוֹמֵר לְפִי חֶשְׁבּוֹן עַל רֹאשָׁהּ.

Rebbi said, all according to computation; this refers to the first part [of the Mishnah][64].

(fol. 51c) **משנה ו**: הַמְתַמֵּד וְנָתַן מַיִם בְּמִידָּה וּמָצָא כְדֵי מִידָּתוֹ פָּטוּר. רִבִּי יְהוּדָה מְחַיֵּיב. מָצָא יוֹתֵר עַל מִידָּתוֹ מוֹצִיא עָלָיו מִמָּקוֹם אַחֵר לְפִי חֶשְׁבּוֹן.

Mishnah 6: He who makes after-wine and pours in a measured amount of water, if he found the same amount he is free[87]. Rebbi Jehudah declares him obligated. If he found more than his measure he gives proportionally from another place[88].

87 The Sages hold that the wine he takes out is the water he poured in which only received taste from the pomace, and taste is not taxable. R. Jehudah holds that there was an exchange of fluid between the water and the pomace and now part of the fluid is genuinely subject to heave and tithes.

88 This again is the opinion of the anonymous Sages. Even though the additional amount of fluid certainly came from the pomace, it is not wine in the biblical sense.

(fol. 51d) **הלכה ה**: אָמַר רִבִּי אַבָּהוּ זִימְנִין אָמַר לָהּ בְּשֵׁם רִבִּי לָעְזָר. זִימְנִין אָמַר לָהּ בְּשֵׁם רִבִּי יוֹסֵי בֵּי רִבִּי חֲנִינָא. וְהוּא (fol. 52a) שֶׁהֶחֱמִיץ. תַּמָּן תַּנִּינָן הַתֶּמֶד עַד שֶׁלֹּא הֶחֱמִיץ אֵינוֹ נִיקַּח בְּכֶסֶף מַעֲשֵׂר וּפוֹסֵל אֶת הַמִּקְוֶה. מִשֶּׁהֶחֱמִיץ נִיקַּח בְּכֶסֶף מַעֲשֵׂר וְאֵינוֹ פוֹסֵל אֶת הַמִּקְוֶה. מַתְנִיתִין דְּרִבִּי יוּדָה דְּתַנִינָן תַּמָּן הַמְתַמֵּד וְנָתַן מַיִם בְּמִידָּה וּמָצָא כְדֵי מִידָּתוֹ פָּטוּר. רִבִּי יְהוּדָה מְחַיֵּיב. אָמַר רִבִּי אַבָּהוּ זִימְנִין אָמַר לָהּ בְּשֵׁם רִבִּי לָעְזָר. זִימְנִין אָמַר לָהּ בְּשֵׁם רִבִּי יוֹסֵי בֵּי רִבִּי חֲנִינָה. וְהוּא שֶׁהֶחֱמִיץ. אָמַר רִבִּי יוֹסֵי דִּבְרֵי הַכֹּל הִיא שֶׁכֵּן אֲפִילוּ מֵי מֶלַח נִיקָּחִין בְּכֶסֶף מַעֲשֵׂר.

Halakhah 5: Rebbi Abbahu said, sometimes in the name of Rebbi Eleazar, sometimes in the name of Rebbi Yose ben Ḥanina: Only if it fermented[89]. There[90], we have stated: "After-wine before it fermented cannot be bought with money of [Second] Tithe[91] or make a *miqweh* invalid[92]; after it fermented it may be bought with money of [Second] Tithe and does not make a *miqweh* invalid." That Mishnah is Rebbi Jehudah's since we stated: "He who makes after-wine and pours in a measured amount of water, if he found the same amount he is free. Rebbi Jehudah declares him obligated." Rebbi Abbahu said, sometimes in the name of Rebbi Eleazar, sometimes in the name of Rebbi Yose ben Ḥanina: Only if it fermented. Rebbi Yose said, it is the opinion of everybody since even salt water may be bought with money of [Second] Tithe[93].

89 Unfermented after-wine is simply water. In the Babli, *Ḥulin* 25b/26a, this is the opinion of R. Yose ben Ḥanina. R. Eleazar is reported to hold that the anonymous Sages and R. Jehudah disagree about all kinds of after-wine but that tithing from a different batch is possible only for fermented wine since otherwise the tithe might be invalid, being from one kind for another.

90 Mishnah *Ḥulin* 1:7.

91 Second Tithe which was redeemed and the money taken to Jerusalem. (*Deut.* 14:26) "You may spend the money *for all your heart's desire*, cattle, sheep, wine, or liquor, *or anything you want*, eat it there and be merry you and your house." This has the structure of two general statements divided by a detailed list. Both for R. Ismael and for R. Aqiba, the general statements have to be interpreted in the light of the list; the money may only be spent on food. This excludes water and salt which are not food. Cf. *Ma'aser Šeni* 1:4, Notes 144-151.

92 As water, cf. *Terumot* 10, Note 139.

93 In the Babli, *Eruvin* 27a, this is the opinion of both R. Eleazar and R. Yose ben Ḥanina; in the Yerushalmi, *Eruvin* 3:1, fol. 20d, this is the opinion of R. Eleazar alone. The Yerushalmi there disagrees with the argument here since R. Aḥa qualifies the statement of R. Eleazar and permits salt water only if some oil is added, turning it into food. In the opinion of the Babli, the Mishnah in *Ḥulin* cannot be squared with the one in *Ma'serot* but represents a third opinion ascribed to R. Joḥanan ben Nuri.

מַהוּ מוֹצִיא מַעְשְׂרוֹת. הָא תְרוּמָה לֹא. שֶׁהַתּוֹרֵם בְּלִבּוֹ עַל הַקּוֹטָעִים וְעַל הַצְּדָדִין וְעַל מַה שֶׁבְּתוֹךְ הַתֶּבֶן.

What does he give? Tithes! That means, not heave since everybody giving heave also thinks of broken grain[53], what is left on the sides, and what remains in the chaff.

(fol. 51c) **משנה ז**: חוֹרְרֵי הַנְּמָלִים שֶׁלָּנוּ בְּצַד הָעֲרֵימָה מְחַייֶבֶת הֲרֵי אֵילּוּ חַייָבִין שֶׁיָּדוּעַ שֶׁמִּדָּבָר גָּמוּר הָיוּ גוֹרְרִים כָּל־הַלַּיְלָה.

Mishnah 7: The holes of ants which were near an obligated heap overnight are obligated since it is obvious that they were dragging from what was processed all night[94].

94 Grains found in antholes the day after a heap of grain was smoothed but not yet tithed have to be tithed since they were taken from grain completely processed but not tithed.

(fol. 52a) **הלכה ו**: הַמְמָרֵחַ כְּרָיו שֶׁל חֲבֵירוֹ שֶׁלֹּא מִדַּעְתּוֹ. רִבִּי יוֹחָנָן וְרִבִּי שִׁמְעוֹן בֶּן לָקִישׁ. רִבִּי יוֹחָנָן אָמַר נִטְבַּל. וְרִבִּי שִׁמְעוֹן בֶּן לָקִישׁ אָמַר לֹא נִטְבַּל. מָתִיב רִבִּי יוֹחָנָן לְרִבִּי שִׁמְעוֹן בֶּן לָקִישׁ וְהָא תַנִּינָן וְכֵן נָשִׁים שֶׁנָּתְנוּ לְנַחְתּוֹם לַעֲשׂוֹת לָהֶן שְׂאוֹר אִם אֵין בְּשֶׁל אַחַת מֵהֶן כְּשִׁיעוּר פְּטוּרָה מִן הַחַלָּה. וְאִם בְּשֶׁל כּוּלְהֶן כְּשִׁיעוּר. אָמַר לוֹ שֶׁכֵּן הָעוֹשֶׂה עִיסָּה עַל מְנָת לְחַלְּקָהּ עִיסָּה פְּטוּרָה מִן הַחַלָּה. וְהָתַנִּינָן נַחְתּוֹם שֶׁעָשָׂה שְׂאוֹר לְחַלֵּק חַייָב בְּחַלָּה. אָמַר לוֹ לֹא תְתִיבֵינִי נַחְתּוֹם. נַחְתּוֹם לֹא בְדַעְתּוֹ הַדָּבָר תָּלוּי בְּדַעַת הַלְּקוּחוֹת הַדָּבָר תָּלוּי שֶׁמָּא יִמְצָא לְקוּחוֹת וְיִטְבּוֹל מִיָּד. אָמַר לוֹ וְהָא תַנֵּי חוֹרְרֵי נְמָלִים שֶׁלָּנוּ בְּצַד הָעֲרֵימָה הַחַייֶבֶת הֲרֵי אֵילּוּ חַייָבִין. הָא בְצַד עֲרֵימָה פְטוּרָה פְּטוּרִין. אָמַר רִבִּי יוֹנָה אָמַר רִבִּי אַבָּהוּ בְּשֵׁם רִבִּי יוֹחָנָן מִשּׁוּם יֵאוּשׁ. שְׁמוּאֵל בַּר אַבָּא אָמַר וְהֵן שֶׁגִּירְרוּ רָאשֵׁי שִׁיבֳּלִין.

Halakhah 6: [95]If somebody made a heap [of somebody's grain] without the latter's knowledge: Rebbi Johanan and Rebbi Simeon ben

Laqish. Rebbi Joḥanan said, it is *ṭevel*, Rebbi Simeon ben Laqish said, it is not *ṭevel*. Rebbi Joḥanan objected to Rebbi Simeon ben Laqish, did we not state[96]: "And similarly women who gave[97] to a baker to make sour dough for them, if not one of them had the required amount[98] it is free from *ḥallah*." (But all of them had the required amount[99]?) He said to him, because if somebody makes dough in order to distribute it[100], the dough is free from *ḥallah*. But we have stated[101]: "A baker who made sour dough for distribution is obligated for *ḥallah*." He said to him, do not answer back about a baker. For a baker, it does not depend on his opinion but on the opinions of his customers; maybe he will find a customer and it will become *ṭevel* immediately[102]. He said to him, but was it not stated[103]: "The holes of ants which were overnight near an obligated heap are obligated,[94]" therefore, near an exempt heap they are exempt. Rebbi Jonah, Rebbi Abbahu in the name of Rebbi Joḥanan: Because of resignation[104]. Samuel ben Abba[105] said, only if they dragged tips of ears.

95 This paragraph and the next two are also in *Ḥallah* 1:8. The text in *Ḥallah* is somewhat better; it is the original since the second paragraph following belongs only to *Ḥallah*. The initial statement is also quoted in *Ma'serot* Halakhah 4:1.

96 *Ḥallah* Mishnah 1:7.

97 Flour.

98 The minimum amount of flour to produce dough subject to *ḥallah* is $^5/_4$ standard *qab*. Even if the total amount of flour the baker turns into sour dough is greater than that amount, there is no obligation of *ḥallah* since the flour never became his property. This argument is appropriate for questioning R. Joḥanan's position, not R. Simeon ben Laqish's.

99 This sentence is missing in *Ḥallah*. It introduces an extraneous argument; if the baker makes one big batch of sour dough from the flour and the obligated amount is not recognizable, it is clear that all is obligated.

100 To different people to bake their own bread.

101 First part of *Ḥallah* Mishnah 1:7.

102 This argument can only be understood by a combination with the text in *Ḥallah* 1:8: שֶׁמָּא יִמְצָא לְקוּחוֹת וְהוּא חוֹזֵר וְעוֹשֶׂה אוֹתָהּ עִיסָּה. "maybe he will find customers and he uses it immediately for dough". Maybe the customer buys the sour dough not for making bread at home but for bread the baker will make for him. Then the sour dough is immediate *ṭevel* by the sale in the baker's hands.

The commentators change the text to: "maybe he will *not* find a customer and he uses it immediately for dough *himself*". This is unnecessary and false since his own sour dough in his own bread dough can be put in order by one *ḥallah* given when the bread dough is completely kneaded.

103 In *Ḥallah* 1:8, והא תנינן "did we not state", formula appropriate for a Mishnah. But it seems that the formula (for a *baraita*) used here is correct since מחייבת in the Mishnah is replaced by החייבת. (In *Ḥallah*, one reads only חייבת.) One has to conclude that the reading of the manuscripts, מחייבת, is not a scribal error but a stand-in for מחויבת.

104 יאוש "resignation" is a technical term for the automatic turning of lost property into ownerless property once the original owners have given up hope for recovery. No declaration of abandonment is needed in that case. Since grains taken by ants have to be considered as abandoned, even if recovered by the original owner they can be subject to heave and tithes only if the tithing of the heap by the original owner also extends to grains not in his possession now. Tithing those grains is tantamount to tithing of another's property without the latter's knowledge.

105 He is Samuel, the head of the Academy of Nahardea. He explains "exempt" not as "already tithed" but "not yet threshed", so that the ants took not grains but parts of ears. In that case, the grains taken by the ants do not fall under our rules. He also must hold that ערימה in contrast to כרי denotes an unsmoothed heap which is obligated if the owner does not intend to process further.

מָתִיב רִבִּי שִׁמְעוֹן בֶּן לָקִישׁ לְרִבִּי יוֹחָנָן וְהָתַנִּינָן הִקְדִּישָׁן עַד שֶׁלֹּא נִגְמְרוּ וּגְמָרָן הַגִּזְבָּר וְאַחַר כָּךְ פְּדָיָן פְּטוּרִין. הֲרֵי גִּזְבָּר כְּאַחֵר הוּא וְאַתְּ אָמַר מַה שֶׁעָשָׂה עָשׂוּי. אָמַר לוֹ תִּיפְתָּר כְּמָאן דְּאָמַר גִּזְבָּר כְּבַעֲלִין וּדְלֹא כְּרִבִּי יוֹסֵי דְּרִבִּי יוֹסֵי אָמַר הוּא גִּזְבָּר הוּא אַחֵר.

Rebbi Simeon ben Laqish objected to Rebbi Joḥanan[106]: Did we not state[107]: "But if he dedicated it before it was finished, the treasurer finished it, and then the owner redeemed it, it is free." Is not the treasurer a different person and you say what he did is valid? He said to him, this follows him who says the treasurer has the status of owner and against Rebbi Yose since Rebbi Yose said, the treasurer is a different person.

106 The argument makes sense only as objection from R. Joḥanan to R. Simeon ben Laqish. It seems that Maimonides read in the first paragraph "Rebbi Simeon ben Laqish objected to Rebbi Joḥanan" and in the second "Rebbi Joḥanan objected to Rebbi Simeon ben Laqish" since in his Code (*Ma'serot* 3:7) he follows R. Joḥanan which probably he would not have done if R. Joḥanan disagreed with R. Yose, the preeminent Tanna.

107 Mishnah *Peah* 4:5 (Note 81), about a field dedicated to the Temple and then redeemed.

רִבִּי חֲנַנְיָה חֲבֵרוֹן דְּרַבָּנִין בָּעֵי וַאֲפִילוּ יֵשׁ בְּכוּלְּהוֹן כְּשִׁיעוּר יֵעָשֶׂה כְּדָבָר שֶׁלֹּא נִגְמְרָה מְלַאכְתּוֹ וִיהֵא פָּטוּר דְּאָמַר רִבִּי יוֹסֵי בְּשֵׁם רִבִּי זְעִירָא [רִבִּי יוֹנָה רִבִּי זְעִירָא][108] בְּשֵׁם רִבִּי לָעְזָר אַף בְּמַה שֶׁבִּלָּגִין לֹא נִטְבַּל מִפְּנֵי שֶׁהוּא עָתִיד לְהַחֲזִירוֹ בְּדָבָר שֶׁלֹּא נִגְמְרָה מְלַאכְתּוֹ.

[109]Rebbi Ḥananiah the colleague of the rabbis asked: And even if all were of full measure it should be like something not completely processed, since [110]Rebbi Yose said in the name of Rebbi Zeïra, Rebbi Jonah, Rebbi Zeïra in the name of Rebbi Eleazar, even what is in a flask did not become *ṭevel*, in case it was not fully processed, since he would in the end return it.

108 The words in brackets are in all occurrences of this quote except the Leyden ms. and Venice print here.

109 This paragraph refers to Mishnah *Ḥallah* 1:7. Since nobody makes bread out of sour dough without the addition of plain flour, sour dough is not bread dough ready to be baked,

is not fully processed, and should not be subject to *ḥallah*.

110 The original statement is in Halakhah 1:6 (Note 151) and Halakhah 4:3 (Note 61) and is explained there.

(fol. 51c) **משנה ח**: שׁוּם בַּעַל בֶּכִּי וּבָצָל שֶׁל רִכְפָּא וּגְרִיסִין הַקִּלִיקִים וַעֲדָשִׁים הַמִּצְרִיּוֹת. רִבִּי מֵאִיר אוֹמֵר אַף הַקֳּרִיקָס. רִבִּי יוֹסֵי אוֹמֵר אַף הַקרטנים פְּטוּרִין מִן הַמַּעְשְׂרוֹת וְנִלְקָחִים מִכָּל־אָדָם בַּשְּׁבִיעִית. זֶרַע לוּף הָעֶלְיוֹן זֶרַע כְּרֵישִׁין זֶרַע בְּצָלִים זֶרַע לֶפֶת וּצְנוֹנוֹת וּשְׁאַר זֵירְעוֹנֵי גִינָּה שֶׁאֵינָן נֶאֱכָלִין פְּטוּרִין מִן הַמַּעְשְׂרוֹת וְנִלְקָחִין מִכָּל־אָדָם בַּשְּׁבִיעִית שֶׁאַף עַל פִּי שֶׁאֲבִיהֶן תְּרוּמָה הֲרֵי אֵילּוּ יֵאָכֵלוּ.

Mishnah 8: Baalbek garlic, Rikhpa onion, Cilician grits[111], and Egyptian lentils, Rebbi Meïr says also colocasia[112], Rebbi Yose says also *qrṭnym*[113] are free from tithes and may be bought from everybody during the Sabbatical[114]. The seed of the upper part of arum[115], the seeds of leeks, seeds of onions, seeds of turnips and radishes, and other garden seeds which are not eaten are free from tithes and may be bought from everybody during the Sabbatical[116] and these may be eaten if their father was heave[117].

111 Broken beans.

112 The Rome ms. and the Maimonides autograph of the Mishnah read קרקס. One Genizah ms. and most Tosephta sources (3:15) read קלקס and this seems to be the basis of Maimonides's identification of the plant as אלקלקאס "colocasia, Egyptian bean".

113 This reading has no correspondence in the variant readings of the Mishnah and generally is considered a scribal error of the Leyden ms. The Maimonides autograph reads קוטנין, most other mss. קוטנים, Arabic קֻטְנִיָּה "legumes, flour-containing seeds other than grain". The Arabic is the Gaonic definition (*Ahilut* 18:2) for

Hebrew קטניות "legumes". Maimonides describes the fruit as "a kind of pea". According to *Arukh*, it is called in Arabic צגיר אלאדנאב "small of tail"; I. Löw identifies as *nelumbo nucifera.*

114 These are not cultivated in the Land.

115 The seeds, in contrast to the bulb.

116 Since they are not food, they are not titheable even by rabbinic standards and not covered by the Sabbatical restrictions on "its (the Land's) yield to eat" (*Lev.* 25:7).

117 The principle that "growth from heave is heave" (*Terumot* 9:4) applies only to food. Therefore, the growth from inedible seeds from heave of vegetables is profane since it is not growth from heave.

(fol. 52a) **הלכה ז**: אֵי זֶהוּ שׁוּם בַּעַל בֵּיכִי כָּל־שֶׁאֵין לוֹ אֶלָּא חוֹר אֶחָד מַקִּיף אֶת הֶעָמוּד. אָמַר רַבָּן שִׁמְעוֹן בֶּן גַּמְלִיאֵל כָּל־שֶׁאֵין לוֹ אֶלָּא קְלִיפָּה אַחַת. אֵי זֶהוּ בָּצָל שֶׁל רִכְפָּא כָּל־שֶׁעוּקָצוֹ נִמְעָךְ לְתוֹכוֹ. רַבָּן שִׁמְעוֹן בֶּן גַּמְלִיאֵל אוֹמֵר כָּל־שֶׁאֵין לוֹ אֵירֶס.

Halakhah 7: "[118]What is Baalbek garlic? Any with only one hole[119] surrounding the stem. Rabban Simeon ben Gamliel says, any with only one skin[120]. What is Rikhpa onion? Any whose prick is dissolved in it[121]. Rabban Simeon ben Gamliel says, any that has no poison."

118 A similar text in Tosephta 3:15.

119 In the Tosephta: "One row". Garlic not split into several cloves.

120 In the Tosephta, this is Rabban Simeon's definition of Rikhpa onions.

121 Reading of both mss. of the Yerushalmi. The Erfurt ms. of the Tosephta reads: "Any whose curvature (עוקמו) is dissolved in it."

אֵילוּ הֵן גְּרִיסִין הַקִּילְקִין אֵילוּ הַמְרוּבָּעִין. תַּנֵּי רַבָּן שִׁמְעוֹן בֶּן גַּמְלִיאֵל אוֹמֵר אֵין מְרוּבָּע מִשֵּׁשֶׁת יְמֵי בְרֵאשִׁית. הָתִיב רִבִּי בֶּרֶכְיָה וְהָתַנִּינָן גּוּפָהּ שֶׁל בַּהֶרֶת כִּגְרִיס הַקִּילְקִי מְרוּבָּע. אָמַר רִבִּי בִּיסִינָה כָּל־גַּרְמָא אָמְרָה לֵית לֵיהּ מְרוּבָּע. וְלָמָּה תַנִּינָן. דִּירִבְעֶנָּה הִיא. וְהִיא נִגְעָה מָלֵא קִטְרִין. וְהִיא אֲבִיבָה דְּפִילָא

עָגוֹל הוּא מִלְּמַטָּן. אִית דְּבָעֵי מֵימַר לֹא אָמַר רַבָּן שִׁמְעוֹן בֶּן גַּמְלִיאֵל אֶלָּא בַבְּרִיּוֹת. וְתַנֵּי כֵן מְרוּבָּע בְּאוֹכְלִין אֵין מְרוּבָּע בַּבְּרִיּוֹת.

[122]These are Cilician grits, these are square[123]. It was stated[124]: "Rabban Gamliel says, there is nothing square from the six days of Creation." Rebbi Berekhiah objected: Did we not state[125]: "The body of *baheret* is like a square Cilician grit." Rebbi Bisna[126] said, that[127] in itself says that there is no square. Why did we state that? That he should square it. But there are noxious insects[128]! They are full of knots. But there is the bunch of *pila*[129]! It is round below. Some want to say, Rabban Simeon ben Gamliel spoke only about animals. It was stated so: There is square in foods, there is no square in animals.

122 Essentially the same text is in *Nedarim* 3:2 (fol. 37d) and *Ševuot* 3:9 (fol. 34d). Both Yerushalmi mss. agree here on the text. Therefore, the other texts may be used to instruct the text here but not to correct it.

123 In Tosephta 3:15: "These are Cilician grits: square *algosin*." The last word is otherwise unknown. Lieberman prefers the reading of the quote from the Yerushalmi in *Arukh*, *s. v.* קלקי: אילו גסין המרובעים "these are the fat square ones."

124 Tosephta 3:15.

125 Mishnah *Nega'im* 6:1. In *Ševuot* 3:9, the Mishnah is quoted in its entirety. This is necessary to understand R. Bisna's statement: "The body of a *baheret* {a form of skin disease, *Lev.* 13:18-23} is like a Cilician grit square. The width of a grit is nine lentils, the width of each lentil is four hair-widths; this makes 36 hair-widths."

126 A fourth generation Amora, student of R. Ila.

127 The text of the Mishnah, Note 125. R. Bisna takes the expression "square" in the classical mathematical sense, "determination of the surface area". The Mishnah requires the minimal surface area of a lesion to be $(36)^2$ $(\text{hairwidth})^2$. If the expression did not have its mathematical sense, the numerical indication would be superfluous. "That" in this sentence is the second sentence of the Mishnah.

128 In *Nedarim* הכנעה "lice".

129 In *Nedarim* ארכובא דיעלה "the

knee of the mountain goat." In *Ševuot* עניבה דפילא. This probably is the correct form of the unintelligible word אביבא "springtime" written here; it has been translated. פילא is פילא III in Levy's Dictionary, a spice, not פילא II "elephant" nor פילא I "cleft". Since in general the deviations of the two mss. of the Yerushalmi *Zeraïm* are not very frequent, it seems that both are derived from the same *Vorlage*.

אֵילוּ הֵן עֲדָשִׁים הַמִּצְרִיּוֹת כָּל־שֶׁגַּלְגְּלֵיהֶן חַדִּין. רַבָּן שִׁמְעוֹן בֶּן גַּמְלִיאֵל אוֹמֵר כָּל־שֶׁאֵין לָהֶן צְרוֹרוֹת. אֵילוּ הֵן הַקֶּרִיקָם. כָּל־שֶׁעוּקְצֵיהֶן מוּעָטִין וְהִלְקֵטֵיהֶן מְרוּבִּין. מַה דָּמִי לָהּ אָמַר רִבִּי יוֹסֵי כְּגוֹן אִילֵּין קוֹנִייָתָה.

[124]"These are Egyptian lentils: All whose spheres are sharp-edged[125]. Rabban Simeon ben Gamliel says, any that have no pebbles[126]. What are colocasia? All whose pricks are short and their extensions[127] are many." What compares to it? Rebbi Yose said, like these *qonyata*[128].

124 Tosephta 3:15.

125 They are not formed as spheres but are round and flat with sharp edges.

126 No spots harder than their surroundings (explanation of S. Lieberman.)

127 The capillary roots (explanation of S. Lieberman.)

128 No reasonable conjecture has been offered for the interpretation of this word.

רִבִּי יִרְמְיָה בָּעֵי כַּרְכְּמִין מַהוּ שֶׁיְּהוּ מוּתָּרִין מִשּׁוּם סְפִיחִין. הָתִיב רִבִּי תַנְחוּם בַּר יִרְמְיָה וְהָתַנִּינָן וְהֶחָשׁוּד עַל הַשְּׁבִיעִית אֵין לוֹקְחִין מֵהֶן פִּשְׁתָּן אֲפִילוּ סָרוּק. וּפִשְׁתָּן לָאו קִיסְמִין הוּא. אָמַר רִבִּי חִינְנָא מִפְּנֵי זַרְעָהּ. רִבִּי מָנָא אָמַר אִם מִפְּנֵי זַרְעָהּ וְהָתַנִּינָן הֶחָשׁוּד לִהְיוֹת מוֹכֵר תְּרוּמָה לְחוּלִין אֵין לוֹקְחִין מִמֶּנּוּ מַיִם וּמֶלַח. אִית לָךְ מֵימַר מַיִם וּמֶלַח מִפְּנֵי זַרְעָהּ לֹא מִפְּנֵי קְנָס. אַף הָכָא מִפְּנֵי קְנָס.

Rebbi Jeremiah asked: Is crocus[129] permitted as aftergrowth? Rebbi Tanḥum bar Jeremiah asked, did we not state[130]: "One does not buy flax from anybody suspect in matters of the Sabbatical, not even combed?" Is flax not like wood chips[131]? Rebbi Ḥinena said, because of its seed[132]. Rebbi Mana said, if it were because of its seed, did we not state: "[133]One does not buy water or salt from anybody suspect of selling heave as profane?" Can you say, water or salt because of their seeds? No, as a fine. Here also as a fine[134].

129 Used as dye, not as food. As industrial crop it is subject to the rules of the Sabbatical (*Ševi'it* 7:1) but it should not come under the prohibition of aftergrowth since it is not food.

130 Mishnah *Bekhorot* 4:8. This shows that industrial products which fall under the rules of the Sabbatical fall under all restrictions as if they were food.

131 It is inedible.

132 A source of edible oil.

133 Mishnah *Bekhorot* 4:9.

134 An *ad hoc* decree from which no general conclusion can be drawn. Crocus might be permitted as aftergrowth.

מְנַחֵם בֶּן מַכְסִימָא אָחוֹי דְיוֹנָתָן קַיְפָא בְּשֵׁם רִבִּי אַמִּי פִּשְׁתָּן נִלְקַחַת מִכָּל־אָדָם בַּשְּׁבִיעִית. הָדָא דְתֵימָא בְּשֶׁאֵינוֹ יוֹדֵעַ אִם חָשׁוּד הוּא אִם אֵינוֹ חָשׁוּד. הָא דָבָר בָּרִיא שֶׁהוּא חָשׁוּד אָסוּר. זוּגָא קְרִיבֵיהּ דְּרִבִּי בָּא בַּר זַבְדָּא בְּשֵׁם רִבִּי אַבָּהוּ. בִּיקִיָּא נִלְקַחַת מִכָּל־אָדָם בַּשְּׁבִיעִית. אָמַר רִבִּי יוֹסֵי מַתְנִיתִין אָמְרָה כֵן זֶרַע לוּף הָעֶלְיוֹן זֶרַע כְּרֵישִׁין זֶרַע חֲצָלִין זֶרַע לֶפֶת וּצְנוֹנוֹת וּשְׁאַר זֵירְעוֹנֵי גִינָּה שֶׁאֵינָן נֶאֱכָלִין. וְתַנֵּי עֲלָהּ זֶרַע אִסְטִיס וְזֶרַע קוֹצָה וְזֶרַע בִּיקִיָּא הָא בִיקִיָּא עַצְמָהּ לֹא. דִּילְמָא דְלָא אִתְאֲמָרַת אֶלָּא בְּשֶׁאֵינוֹ יוֹדֵעַ אִם חָשׁוּד הוּא אִם אֵינוֹ חָשׁוּד. הָא דָבָר בָּרִיא שֶׁהוּא חָשׁוּד אָסוּר.

Menaḥem ben Maximus the brother of Jonathan Caiphas in the name of Rebbi Ammi: Flax may be bought from everybody during the Sabbatical. That is, if you do not know whether he is suspect or not. Therefore, if it is clear that he is suspect, it is forbidden[135]. Zeugos, the relative of Rebbi Abba bar Zavda, in the name of Rebbi Abbahu: Vetch may be bought from anybody during the Sabbatical. Rebbi Yose said:

Does our Mishnah say so? "The upper seed of arum, the seeds of leeks, seeds of egg plants, seeds of turnips and radishes, and other garden seeds which are not eaten." We have stated on this: Seeds of indigo, seeds of madder, and seeds of vetch[136]. That implies, not vetch itself. Maybe if you do not know whether he is suspect or not. Therefore, if it is clear that he is suspect, it is forbidden[137].

135 The statement of R. Ammi does not contradict Mishnah *Bekhorot* 4:8.

136 Follow the same rules.

137 To buy vetch as animal feed but vetch seed may be bought even from people known to deal in Sabbatical produce.

כֵּינִי מַתְנִיתָא זֶרַע הַסִּילְיוֹן שֶׁל לוּף. חָדָא אִיתָא הֲוָה לָהּ יַרְבּוּזִין דִּתְרוּמָה גּוֹ כִּפְתָּהּ נָפְלוּ לְגִינְתָא וְצָמְחוּן. אָתָא עוֹבְדָא קוֹמֵי רִבִּי יוֹחָנָן וְשָׁרָא. אָמַר לוֹ רִבִּי חִיָּיה בַּר וָוא וְלֹא מַתְנִיתָא הִיא שֶׁאַף עַל פִּי שֶׁאֲבִיהֶן תְּרוּמָה הֲרֵי אֵילוּ יֵאָכֵלוּ. אָמַר לוֹ בַּבְלַיָא מִן דְּגָלִיית לָךְ חַסְפָּא אַשְׁכַּחַת מַרְגָּנִיתָא אַתְּ אָמַר וְלֹא מַתְנִיתָא הִיא.

So is the Mishnah: The seeds on the stem of arum[138]. Some woman had heave purslain on a block. They fell into a garden and sprouted. The case came before Rebbi Johanan who permitted. Rebbi Ḥiyya bar Abba said to him, is this not the Mishnah: "And these may be eaten if their father was heave?" He said to him, Babylonian, when you cleared a potsherd for yourself, you found a pearl! You said, is that not the Mishnah!

138 This is the reading and interpretation of Maimonides. The other interpretations (R. Isaac Simponti, R. Simson) have to rearrange the sentence except for R. Isaac Simponti's second explanation, "the seeds of the thorns of arum," which does not fit reality since arum, an aracea, has no thorns.

Indices

Index of Biographical Notes

Abba Palaemon 119
Ada bar Gershon 365
Ashian 60

Elopisa 26

Rebbi Ayvo bar Naggari 183
Rebbi Birai 365
Rebbi Hillel 42
Rebbi Ilaï 72
Rebbi Joḥanan ben Gudgada 15
Rebbi Joḥanan the Alexandrian 81
Rebbi Levi ben Ḥina 135
Rebbi Mana bar Tanḥum 189
Rebbi Simeon bar Ḥiyya 357
Rebbi Simeon ben Karsana 82, 421
Rebbi Ẓadoq 355

Index of Biblical Quotations

Gen. 1:10 381

Ex. 20:16 227
22:30 278
23:19 383
25:2-3 5
34:26 383
35:5 121

Lev. 4:23,28 254
5:4 121
10:9 327
11:3 265,267
11:26-28 267
11:34 378,379
11:37 558
19:23 547
21:9 239
Lev. 22:14 197,204,216, 227,228
22:21 308
25:3 563
25:30 527,528
27:30 411

Num. 15:21 14
18:12 86
18:27 6,32,59,62,67
18:28 20,23,35,63,64, 170
18:29 63,147
18:32 32,59
22:10 227
31:30 133

Deut. 11:15 28
Deut. 12:24 308
14:22 410,411,416, 428
14:27 45
14:29 413,414
18:4 138,144,414
19:19 227
22:18-19 221
23:15 48
23:24 121
23:25 486
23:26 481
24:15 486
24:19 521
24:21 223
25:2 220,222,224
25:4 327,482
25:7-9 29

Deut. 26:13	507, 512	Ez. 44:30	133	Ps. 116:6	288,294
		45:11	135		
33:11	257	45:13	133,134	Prov. 4:5	68
				16:6	295
Is. 30:24	440	Zach. 11:8	419		
38:16	18			Job 21:10	367
		Ps. 76:11	526	36:33	345
Ez. 23:37	277				

Index of Greek and Latin Words

ἀλεύω 347
ἄποψις 314
ἀψίνθιον 274

ἐξέδρα 514

ἥμισυς 424

κάροινον 275
κέρασος 383
κιβώτιον 347
κολοβός 334
κολυμβάς 58
κόρδαξ 17
κυάνθροπος νόσος 17

λάγυνος, λάγηνος 331

μελίμηλον 431

οἰνόμελι 370
ὄρυζα 446

Παλαίμων 119
πάγκρεας 83
παρήγορος 378
πίναξ 446
πολιτικός 91
πύργος 514

σάλαξ 289

τύπος 433

χολικός 17
χρυστουμῖνος 387

cordax 17

galearii 317

ludi 281

rego 317

Index of Hebrew and Arabic Words

איפשר 441

בטא 121
ביחילו 419

גלגל 467
גרב 354

טויה 350

יתוש 265

לגלג 273

מסם 424
סולד 446
פקס 435
תבואה 412
תרד 381
اترجّ، اترنج 429

بطو 121
حبّ 352
سحط 179
سلق 381
صحن 339
طوى 352
عضّ 84

قطنية 574
كوارة 157
لجّ 278
نتش 266
نشا 215
همّ 17

General Index

Abraham ben David. 126,131,184, 335,355, 359,375,379,389,525
Adani, S. 53,190
Agency, criminal 230
  termination 106,139
Aggadah 526
Appraisal 396
Arukh 575
As 474
Asher ben Ieḥiel 70,178,493,510
Avery-Peck, A. J. 2

Baer, S. 475
Bastard 236
Ben Adrat, S. 93,356,357
Ben-Ḥayyim, Z. vi, 295
Bēt Happĕrās 311
Blood, prohibition 36
Bóber, S. 527

Caphtor waPherah 525
Caro, Y. 146,188,525
Cirillo, S. 169,525
Clay pot, cleansing 393
Crimes, multiple 229

Deaf-mute 5,12,27
Diocletian 316
Donkey-camel driver 97
Double doubt 246
Drunk, legally 48

Eliezer ben Joel Halevi 190
Eliezer ben Nathan 190
Epstein, J. N. 93
Etrog, Citrus medica 429

Fetus, slaughter of 265
Fifth, as fine 23,196
Fill, *miqweh* 369
Fish, S. 482
Fleischer, H. L. 418,467
Fowl 54
Frankel, Z. 364
Fulda, E. 2,215,408,475,489,518

Gentile, gifts of 32
  sacrifices of 125

Ḥananel ben Ḥušiel 435,460,510
Hermaphrodite 10
Hoffmann, D. 482
Homicide, return of 259
Impurity, preparation 7
  degrees of 61
Insane 5,16
Insanity, intermittent 18

Jaffee, M. S. 2,408

Kanievski, H. 2,41,176,408
Kramer, E., of Wilna 53,408,518
Kutscher, Y. vi

Larceny 141
Levy, J. 412,436,467,577
Lieberman, S. 3,53,88,118,190,283,355, 357,394,408,422,423,436,441,576,577
Lifting heave 146
Löw, I. 383,425,427,431

Maimonides 2,70,73,105,125,126,131 147,162,178,184,190,268,327,335,339 375,379,382,407,412,429,435,436,449, 454,493,510,514,518,525,534,574,579
Margalit, M.. 2,53,203,394,408,436,518
Marriage ceremonies 252
Milgrom, J. 447
Minor 5
  vows of 31
  sacrifices of 36-38
Modius 177,545

Na'arah 225
Neusner, J. 408

Obligation, rabbinic 152
Oil, to burn 398

Passover, on Sabbath 256
Payne-Smith 425
Peruṭah 213,494
Plinius 283
Puberty 32
Punishment, multiple 234
Purification water 52

Qafeḥ, Y. 3

Rashi 174,233,237,309,373,383,432,435, 534
Resignation 572

Sefer Ha'iṭṭur 510
Sefer Nir 203,519
Sexless 10
Simponti, I. 131,579
Simson of Sens. 126,178,333,339,407,514, 579
Sin, by speech 117
  atonement 197
Slave girls, sex 312

Taste 364
Ṭevul Yom 74
Tithe, animal 37
Tithes, rabbinic 410
Ṭur 510

Water, of Tabernacles 337

Yallon, H. vi,436

Zenobia 315
Zuz 356

www.ingramcontent.com/pod-product-compliance
Lightning Source LLC
Chambersburg PA
CBHW031842220426
43663CB00006B/468
9783110681284